SUNLIGHT

The Shadowed Days Trilogy

GARRY KINNANE

*

Shadowed Days

Fare Thee Well, Hoddle Grid

Time of Arrival

Clouds of Magellan | Melbourne

Shadowed Days first published 2008 by Clouds of Magellan Press
Fare Thee Well, Hoddle Grid first published 2012 by Clouds of Magellan Press
Time of Arrival 2016 by Clouds of Magellan Press

Issued as one volume under the title *Sunlight: The Shadowed Days Trilogy* in 2020

ISBN: 978-0-6487469-6-6

Clouds of Magellan Press
http://cloudsofmagellanpress.net

The title 'Shadowed Days' and epigraph are taken from 'Fish in the Unruffled Lakes' from *Selected Poems* by WH Auden, reproduced with kind permission of Faber and Faber Ltd.

Shadowed Days

Garry Kinnane's haunting evocation of his boyhood in Melbourne in the 40s
and 50s brings to life a struggling family. Frank and Thelma and their two boys,
Garry and Ray, are always on the move—from Richmond to Mount Macedon,
to North Melbourne, among the homeless in 'Larundel', and finally to an uneasy
life in Valentine Street.

Fare Thee Well, Hoddle Grid

Mid-50s to mid-60s Melbourne - a Wowserland of 6 o'clock closing, censorship,
endless suburbia ... 'We could settle down. But that was the farthest thing from
our minds. We didn't want security, we wanted adventure, risk, experience, we
wanted to see and grasp the world ...' In *Fare Thee Well, Hoddle Grid*, Garry
Kinnane continues the story of a young man looking for his direction in life.
Having left school early, Garry finds himself at twenty-one in danger of working
forever as an insurance clerk in the city. But gradually he finds an escape route—
through night classes in literature, the folk-revival, The Push, the attractions of a
Bohemian life ...

Time of Arrival

'Greece had changed me ... now I had a greater sense of what was possible, what
potential the world offered to those willing to plunge in ...' In *Time of Arrival*
Garry Kinnane tells of a decade of living abroad—Greece, a war-affected Europe,
London in the 60s and 70s, his involvement in the student movement, a
scholarship to Oxford. His search for direction is aided by friends and the faith
of his wife Jo, through the struggle to raise a family in times of hardship, and the
ultimate desire to return home to Australia.

Garry Kinnane was raised in a working class family in Melbourne during the1940s and 50s, worked at a variety of jobs in his teens, and gained recognition as a folk musician in the early1960s. In 1964 he married and travelled abroad, living first in Greece, then in England for ten years. There he undertook a degree in literary studies at the University of Warwick, from where he won a postgraduate scholarship to the University of Oxford. He returned to teach literary studies at Monash, the University of Ballarat, and Melbourne University, from where he retired in 2004. Garry is the author of two biographies – *George Johnston; a Biography*, which won *The Age* Book-of-the-year in 1986 and *Colin Colahan; a Portrait* (1996).

FOREWORD

When I began *Shadowed Days* in 2007 I had no plan to continue beyond a depiction of my childhood. But I found the memories soon came so readily that by the time that book was finished they were still flooding in, and it felt completely natural to go on with the story. I chose to stop after the third volume, mainly because I had more or less caught up with many people, such as my children and colleagues, who were part of my present rather than my past. And it was really my past that was demanding to be written, not the present. I suppose recalling that is the main impulse behind memoir.

The three volumes, now called *The Shadowed Days Trilogy,* deal with three distinct stages of my past: childhood in *Shadowed Days*, youth in *Fare Thee Well, Hoddle Grid*, and the adult concerns of family and career in *Time of Arrival.* In each of these volumes I tried to use a narrative approach that was appropriate to the nature of the material, so that, for instance, there are passages in the first volume that read like a child's stream-of-consciousness, particularly in the early years when even the smallest experiences make indelible impressions. In volume two I've tried to use distancing effects that catch some of the comedy and self-conscious hubris of youth, and in volume three I have attempted to mix travel description and detailed cultural discussions with personal matters, for instance my relationship with my wife Jo.

Having established three different 'voices' in those books, I am happy that this new edition of the trilogy, *Sunlight*, provides a reminder that the story is also a continuous one, a single journey taken and told from one point of view – my own. My hope is that this combination of difference and continuity has produced a work sufficiently unified to enable cross-connections which might not otherwise have been noticed, locate new strengths and flaws in my behavior and in the writing, and by doing this enhance the reader's enjoyment.

Why *Sunlight*? I think it clear that the trajectory of the trilogy moves from darkness to light, from a childhood of pain through a search for self to an adulthood of love and learning. I feel I've been in the sunlight ever since, warm, growing, and able to see. Mostly.

I want to thank Gordon Thompson, my publisher at Clouds of Magellan Press, for his initiative on this undertaking, and for the faith in my work he has shown in all our projects.

Garry Kinnane
July, 2020

Shadowed Days

To Ron and Yvonne Bowden; honour to the valiant

We, till shadowed days are done,
We must weep and sing

W. H. Auden

NOTHING COMES BEFORE THIS. Emerging from a haze of grey twilight behind points of weak evening street light, my first memories assemble from fragments. I am looking up, there are urgent voices, faces bending over me in concern, but I have only a little pain as I am lifted over our back fence into the solicitous hands of my father. Only on the way to the doctor do I learn what has happened.

'You put your head in the way of a bottle,' he tells me. 'Bobby Lane threw it. He says he yelled look out, and you stood up to see.' I move in closer against him as he holds something soft on the top of my head.

'We were playing soldiers, in the trenches.'

'They're not trenches, it's a building site.' The tram is gently rocking along Bridge Road, and I wonder what is going to happen to me.

'The doctor will put in some stitches. It won't hurt – it'll be just like having a haircut, you'll see.'

Afterward, safe in my father's arms, it seems to my child's mind that it is exactly like this, and I experience no pain either then or on the sunny day when he holds my head to remove the stitches skilfully with the tweezers. A lifetime later, I can run an exploratory finger over that old scar and instantly rekindle the memory of my father's benign insight into the truth. For that is the faith in which I grow up: that my father is right about everything, and that he is a wise and gentle guiding hand. I am sorry for Bobby Lane when his father comes around to our house that night and, apologising for the reckless action of his son, assures us that he has thoroughly thrashed him with a razor strop and sent him to bed without any dinner. The only comfort I feel is that this man is not my father.

That faith is reinforced soon afterwards by a more distressing event. My father's best friend, a man I know only as Uncle Bill, has joined the army. In full khaki uniform, he comes to our house in Dickens Street, Richmond and brings with him an array of service patches, colours and medals of some sort. My mother pins them onto my pullover and I strut around with them on my chest. My father draws me aside and says, 'Now be careful if you go out in the street wearing those, because some boy or other could come along and slip his fingers under them like this,' and here he slides two fingers under a medal and lifts it so that it strains against my pullover, 'and steal them away.'

Days later, having in my pride and incaution forgotten his warning, I play up and down our street showcasing my wares, when two older boys I don't know come up to me on the pretext 'Well, what have you got there? Can we have a look?' And sure enough they do exactly what my father has foretold: strip me of every medal and colour, and run off never to be seen again. I cry bitter tears, as much because of my failure to heed my father's advice as for my victimisation. But it stays with me always how right my father is about the world, that he has a special insight into the way it works, indeed into the way it is destined to work. He doesn't raise the matter with me afterwards, either to commiserate with me or to vaunt his wisdom.

Not many weeks later I find him at the kitchen table resting his forehead in the palm of his hand, a study of deep sadness or despair. I hear him say, 'He was an AIF man, the second twenty-ninth.'

'What is it dad?' I pull at his sleeve.

'It's Uncle Bill. He's been killed in action in Malaya.' He has a copy of the morning newspaper in front of him.

I can guess that it wasn't just the tragic loss of a friend that had so moved him. He was also, like many others who didn't actively participate, gnawed with guilt. He was not in the services; he was not in the War. There was no danger of him being shot down in a plane, or blown up in a trench, or killed by a bullet. And why? Because he had been rejected for the army on medical grounds: accepted on the strength of his physical examination, but subsequently rejected when his x-rays came through.

Instead, he spends the early years of the War as a drink waiter at the Hotel Australia in Melbourne. Despite the menial nature of the work it is associated with a certain glamour, and he will bring home mementoes and small gifts he's received as tips from the rich and famous – a propelling pencil from Noel Coward, an English sovereign from Gracie Fields – during their wartime tours of Australasia. He will leave the house handsome and important in his dinner suit and starched vest, and will tell my mother and me about serving wines to American top brass, and the visiting stars of stage or screen that he's attended. He is very taken with American servicemen, thinks of them as heroes. 'They don't wear singlets,' he tells me, 'just bare under their shirts, with big muscles and hairy chests.' On one occasion, he optimistically brings home a considerably drunk American officer he has befriended, and asks my mother to feed him.

Sitting at the kitchen table the officer astonishes my parents when he turns his head and spits directly onto the floor. My father remonstrates and throws him out of the house without allowing him another mouthful. The incident is eventually turned into family legend by my paternal grandmother who hates Americans, especially American servicemen. But my father, whilst he would go to any lengths in defence of my mother's honour, believes completely that the country that produced Bing Crosby and General Macarthur is beyond reproach, and that the offending behaviour was caused essentially by drink.

*

When I was born my parents had almost nothing in the world but their love for each other. It wasn't especially the Depression that had made them poor, but it didn't help. Both came from working class families that struggled through unemployment and lack of money, and they had nothing to pass on to their children. But my parents were a resourceful and intelligent pair who, by a certain adaptability, managed to hold off the worst ravages of the era. My mother, Thelma, had been dux of her class in her final year at Flemington Girl's School. I know because the prize she received, a large, beautifully illustrated copy of *Lands and peoples*, with its elaborate bookplate on the flyleaf, was one of the very few books in our household during the early years of my life, and on special occasions, if I had behaved well, it would be taken down from its shelf of safekeeping and placed on the kitchen table for me to browse. Its pictures transported me to worlds of strange scenes and people I could never have imagined: bare-bodied men and women of New Guinea and Africa; fabulous forts and palaces in India; boys from Brittany carrying huge tuna fish ashore in their arms; Asian girls dancing in shimmering colours; and a full length colour photograph of the Maharaja of Rewah's bearded executioner, a fearful giant in spike-covered armour holding a long scimitar and shield. This book was an education in itself, exerting a latent power over my developing mind, engendering a life-long fascination for other worlds and cultures.

Thelma was a slight, pretty and smart girl from North Melbourne who dreamed of going on at school and eventually becoming a teacher. But in these Depression years the family needed her to bring in an income as soon as she was old enough to leave school. Her father, Fred, was a labourer for a Jewish baker, and though he liked the work stacking and distributing motzo bread, it was not well paid; every year he would be dismissed just prior to the Christmas holidays and re-employed in mid-January, so he would not receive holiday pay. Thelma started a dressmaking apprenticeship in a sweat-shop in the city. Then Fred suddenly died of a heart attack, leaving his wife, Daisy, and my mother and her younger brother Ron, to fend for themselves. There was no pension available to them. Daisy found a part-time job cleaning the Victorian Racing Club offices in the city, work that was, again, low paid and that had to be done overnight. At 3 o'clock every working morning she walked from North Melbourne through the cold, dark streets to the city, leaving the children to get their own breakfasts and to get themselves off to school and work. For her part, my mother found she was good at dressmaking and despite the long hours and low wages she enjoyed the creativity of it; she especially enjoyed the company of the other women, who were full of humour and high spirits. She became close and life-long friends with some of them. Further, whatever circumstances life threw at her in subsequent years, she was always able to pay her way from behind a sewing machine.

During her teens she met and fell for my father, Frank. He was a skinny, blue-eyed blond from the same suburb, mercurial and street-wise, with a touch of the dandy that sat comfortably within a natural Irish sensitivity. His mother, my grandmother, who as a source of family history could be less than reliable, frequently told how he had been raised by his father Ernest after they separated, while she took care of my father's sister Eileen. According to her story, Ernest pulled Frank out of school at the age of twelve and put him on the streets of North Melbourne selling papers and working as a bookie's runner. He would demand all Frank's earnings, which he then spent on grog, tobacco and horses. So Frank was not properly fed and clothed, was always skinny and undernourished, and developed chronic chest problems that went untreated year after year.

Thelma and Frank went everywhere together. There are photographs of them on country jaunts with groups of young people, happy and apparently carefree, sitting on logs and swimming in creeks, arm in arm and self-consciously posing for the camera. She would wear Garbo slacks and hand-knitted pullovers, and my father liked baggy newsboy caps and white golf shoes. Someone snapped them strolling through Royal Park at their most stylish, he in a full length herringbone tweed overcoat and sporting a pale grey Chicago-style hat, she wearing a fur stole over a dark dress and a small feathered hat tipped down at one eye. They certainly don't look poor, despite the Depression. But then they didn't own a house or a car, so what money they had after paying for the basics they spent on looking good. At least that way they could hold their heads up and match it with the better-off; no cringing or self pity, nor even an admission that they might be struggling. They went to the football together, both North Melbourne supporters. They loved the pictures, and were huge fans of the Hollywood stars of the day –Carole Lombard, Joan Crawford, Cooper, Gable, Cagney, Cary Grant. At the Henley-on-Yarra Regatta, my father, defying the social clique that commandeered the event, sneaked off and put my mother's name forward for the beauty contest; she had no idea he had done it. She came second.

Such were the shared experiences they could afford, and that provided a romantic gloss for the close personal pleasure they took in each other. They knew they would marry. Soon my mother fell pregnant. I look at their wedding photograph now and applaud her insistence on a white wedding: she looking delicately lovely in her long dress and train, and he a little shell-shocked but stylish as ever. Its sepia tones and crisp outlines have withstood the passing of time, and I get a buzz of comfort from knowing the bride's small secret; no one can see me, but I'm in there in my first stirrings, behind the luxuriant bouquet she so nonchalantly balances against the bodice of her dress.

For all his intelligence and skill with his hands, my father never had a settled line of work. He had been a tinsmith, but was sacked when he refused to remove a green St Patrick's Day ribbon from his shirt. This was odd, because my father was not especially interested in Irish matters, and though he was a Catholic, not especially religious. But he hated to be pushed around, and would meet any threat to his pride with hot defiance. For a time he drove delivery vans, first for a dry cleaning firm, then for a grocer. Next, he and my mother started a fruiterer's in Queensberry Street, North Melbourne and he would drive to the market at five in the morning in his old Ford van to buy boxes of fruit and vegetables, but the business failed in a year or so. Then the Ford broke an axle, and my father, without the money to have it fixed, left it to rust in the street. He had other jobs, but none lasted long, and then he picked up the drink waiter's job at the hotel, where he was working when I was born.

It is in the tiny single-fronted house we rented in Dickens Street in the inner suburb of Richmond that my memories really begin. The boy next door is Jimmy Glover, and we are good friends and playmates. There are other children in the street we play with, but ours is a special understanding. My first experience of eating garfish is when I have lunch in Jimmy's house; Mrs Glover teaches me to prise the delicate white flesh away from the fine bones with extra care, and chew it with fresh bread and butter. It is delicious.

All our games are war games; our minds are forming within the strange, ubiquitous absence that is the War. It is talked about by the adults, it is dressed for in uniforms all around us, it is in the cut-out model ships and planes on the breakfast cereal packets, it is in the dimming of our kitchen light-bulb with brown paper as search lights probe the night sky over the city, just as it is in the songs played on the wireless:

Ven de Fuhrer says, ve is de master race
Ve Heil (blurt), Heil (blurt) right in de Fuhrer's face.

But it isn't there before us. The thing itself is far away in another world, though it might one day come to us, people say.

I lie between my parents in bed, snuggling up warm and cosy. My father has a particular smell, not like anything else I know, but hot and pungent and only his. It is in the sheets, in the pillow; I lie close to him and breathe it in. 'How would you like a baby sister?' he says. 'It might be a brother,' my mother says. 'You'd have to look after her. Stick up for her if anyone tried to hurt her,' says my father. 'You'd be the oldest.' 'Eldest,' says my mother. My father farts in the bed, and my mother screams and leaps out and runs into the kitchen in her nightdress. I stay.

He brings home a figure in shining armour one night when he's had too much to drink. He must have seen it in some shop still open after the six o'clock exodus from the pubs, and decided, as a gesture of affection (if not appeasement) to my mother, that it would look good beside our fireplace. It is about three feet high, supports several fire tools on a hook at the back, and its battleaxe, held upright along its left arm, can be slid out from its tubular sheath to be used as a poker. It must have been a taxing labour for him carrying it all the way home from the tram stop; it is solid cast iron, chrome-plated and fixed to a metal stand.

'What is it?' my mother asks.

'It's a knight. It's got implements,' and he demonstrates the use of the brush, shovel and tongs, removing them from the back.

'Yes, but who?'

'Dunno. Richard the Lionheart I suppose.'

'Oh. We'll call him Sir Richard then.'

And Sir Richard he always stayed. Until, that is, he was handed down to me fifty years later as a family heirloom. I put him beside my fireplace and had a good look at him – very kitschy, very unconvincing as a knight from any period, and oddly effeminate in his stance, with the left knee slightly crooked across the other. Was this a gay knight perhaps? And then it dawned on me: our small sentry had never been a cast of the noble English monarch at all, but his opposite in important respects – French and female – for this was surely Joan of Arc, the maid of Lyon, whose soft flesh was meant to be implicit in that hard metal finish. I wish my parents had lived long enough for me to see their faces when I broke the news.

Being a cul-de-sac our street is quiet. At the closed end a factory chimney looms in the sky overhead, and at the open end of the street the huge red brick warehouse of Bryant and May the match manufacturers stares us down.

Between these massive industrial book-ends the street feels small and snug, and I play there happily on my tricycle or making drawings in chalk on the footpath with the other children. Only a couple of hundred yards away, in Bridge Road, it is busy and noisy with trams and cars. Its shops stay open late, and its footpaths are crowded with people. My father takes me to the scene of an accident in Burnley Street at the end of our street one evening, when he is looking after me while my mother is in hospital. Although there is talk of a man being hit by a taxi as it drove out of the taxi station, there is nothing to be seen when we arrive. My mother is in hospital a few days, and then we go to pick her up in a car belonging to a friend of my father. It is raining. She emerges looking pale and thin, and carrying a baby wrapped in white – my brother Ray. My father says he will do as a new playmate for me.

I have the sense that things are being kept from me. There is a tension in the house, and my mother will suddenly start crying for no apparent reason. My grandparents visit us occasionally, and my paternal grandmother, who by this time I have named 'Nair' due to a mispronunciation of 'Nanna', is rough and funny and drinks a lot. 'See you with no clothes on,' she says as they leave, and dutifully, 'See you with no clothes on,' I reply. My grandfather works at the paper mills, and brings rolls of clean white paper for me to draw on. I sit at the table with a pencil and paper and sketch for hours, so I am very easy to keep quiet while the adults talk. My grandmother complains that we have a better house than she does, and that we really should give it to her and my grandfather. My father tells her, however, that we are not to be in it for much longer. He had gone in to join the army, and his x-rays revealed tuberculosis of the lung. The doctor advised him to move from our house, which is too damp, and to find somewhere healthier to live, preferably in some place high above sea level, such as a mountain region. 'The air is cleaner and purer there,' he says.

'It was bloody Ernie did that to you,' Nair says, 'sending you out on the streets in all weather.'

'It's going to be difficult to find a house,' my mother says, 'because there's a shortage. There's no building going on.'

For weeks they look in the newspapers and contact estate agents. They see a possibility on a sheep station at Rokewood, near Ballarat, where the owner wants a cook and a general handyman as a couple to live in. My parents give it a two-week trial. My mother has to be up at 5 am to cook breakfast for eight men, then do the housework in between preparing the lunch and dinner. And of course she has us to look after as well. My father mends fences. I have the dimmest of memories of someone teaching me to milk a cow, and of people moving about in a panic as a huge red bushfire approaches from behind a wall of high gum trees. The experiment lasts only a week; the work is far too demanding on both of them, and we all return to Richmond.

Then an offer appears in the newspaper from two spinster sisters to exchange the tenancy of their house at Mount Macedon for a house in the city. My parents jump at the chance, and the swap is somehow successfully arranged. We are to live in the country, up on a high mountain. I recall well the day our furniture is packed into a large van, with the sofa at the back facing outwards, and me sitting there beside my father and his half-brother Dickie as we drive off, seeing the world rock and turn and pass before us. As we move along backwards I see my house drift away, my street drift away, then Bridge Road gradually unwind its busy length away from us, then unfamiliar streets come and go, and then finally the city itself retreat into the blurring distance. The greys and reds, the walls and hard edges, are replaced by a curtain of green rolling past our peripheral vision and into focus as vivid fresh images of trees and fields. It is exciting, and as the van drops gears to whine up the mountain, the gum trees meet across the road and form a veil that eventually hides everything we have left behind. Aroma of eucalypt fills our nostrils. Soon all we can see is our new quiet place of living.

2

AT THE TURN OF a gravel drive, as the van swings around to reveal the front of the house, an old woman in a dark dress comes into view from our seat at the back. She wears glasses and is unsmiling. She hands my mother a key and says, 'The electricity won't be on until tomorrow, but there's gas. There's no phone.'

The gravel drive disappears through beds of shrubs and roses bordered with rocks and overgrown with weeds. It passes between two islands of holly trees with lavender hedging gone shaggy. There is neglect everywhere. To my parents it promises little but hard work.

Inside, the house is a bewildering series of empty, gloomy rooms leading off a central passageway that opens into a large, step-down kitchen at the end. At the front, the lounge, with its deep bow window, is huge. Above the mantelpiece in one of the middle rooms, a spider sits splayed the size of a handprint on the wall. My father stares at it for a moment and says, 'Ah, another friend to greet our arrival!' Every room has a fireplace, dead and cold, in what proves to be a house that never gets warm.

As my father and uncle and the driver unpack the van, the old woman watches, carefully noting every item of furniture. Then she disappears into a small cottage next to our house with no fence between them. When we are unpacked and sitting on the wide verandah eating the sandwiches my mother has made, my father explains to my uncle who she is. Her name is Miss Goss. She owns the land and both houses, but she doesn't want to live in the large one now. As events turn out, we hardly ever see her. Yet we are all a little afraid of her, and I've been told not to make a noise around the cottage or bother her in any way.

It is Spring, and the garden is my place to run wild. I learn to climb trees and sway in the branches with the wind, and wade waist-high in the paddock of daffodils and jonquils adjoining the front garden. I will see that moment in that paddock in future whenever I place a jonquil under my nose. On each side of the double front gate is a tree called an Irish strawberry, whose inedible fruit I squash in my fingers into a yellow pulp to inhale the pungent odour. In the garden I can do whatever I like – roll in the grass, scream at the wind at the top of my voice (did Miss Goss hear?), find lizards under rocks. But you have to be careful of jumping jack ants; they have a terrible sting, and you have to rub a bag of Reckitt's 'blue' on it or go to the doctor.

I am always alone. I have no friends, Ray is too little to play with me; he trails around behind, howling for something. The neighbours' houses are shut away behind high hedges, and no children seem to live in them. I miss my playmates. I build a 'car' in the middle of the back paddock, made of boxes, cushions, sticks for a gear lever and an old pram wheel on an axle to steer with, and I drive for hours with invisible passengers to unvisitible destinations I create as we go along. 'Fares please! Next stop, Bridge Road. That'll be threepence Mrs Glover.' If I sit Ray in the back seat, he stays for only a few minutes, then wanders off looking for mum. There is a sad forgottenness to everything here, as if we are a long way from things that matter. Most movement is from the wind blowing across the paddocks; you can see its shadow on the grass. This is a different world from the city, and I have to become different too.

Things get slightly better when I start school. The Mount Macedon Primary School, grade one. There are ten of us learning to write a, b, c, and listen to stories. In the playground a group of children call a boy names and punch him on the arms; he is fat and soft, girlish and maybe slightly Chinese, and his face crumples up as he cries pathetically. I am sorry for him, but I don't say anything. I just tell myself not to let it happen to me.

I walk to school every morning, schoolbag over my right shoulder, in my raincoat and sou'wester if it's wet. And if it's sunny, even at this time of year the grass is frosted and crisp underfoot, and the puddles have a coating of ice that I break with my shoe. The mountain stands over me, deep green and huge, and the morning sun glints on the memorial cross just visible at the top. School is not interesting, but it is something to do.

The War is still there, on the wireless, in the paper and in letters my parents read out at the table. 'Tommy Weatherhead was killed,' my mother says, holding a letter from my grandmother, Nair.

'Where did it happen?' my father asks.

'Puckapunyal; he drowned swimming in the Goulburn.'

'What a waste.'

On the breakfast cereal packet there is a cut-out of a Lancaster bomber. 'Can I have it mum?' 'Only when it's empty,' she says. It doesn't matter too much, because those bombers are about England against the Germans. Australia against the Japs is more important.

My father has a trick he likes us to play on him. When I finish eating a boiled egg my mother places the shell back in the eggcup, turned up so that the unbroken bottom is now facing up and the broken part is underneath, invisible. It is important that this has been done without my father seeing. I then have to push the 'intact' egg over to my father and say, 'There you are daddy, a nice boiled egg for you.' He then, going along with the trick, sits down and with elaborate anticipation addresses the egg, buttering some bread, gathering the pepper and salt shakers, tucking a napkin into his shirt, and raising his knife to open the top. With this done, he maintains the pretence, looking up and saying to everyone, 'I'm really going to enjoy this egg!' and plunges his spoon into the open top. His face then has to register utter devastation as the spoon comes up with the empty shell around it, and he groans, 'Ohhh, dear, there's nothing in this one!' At which my mother and I fall into hysterical laughter.

My father likes to listen to the radio, and so do I. Comedy shows like *It's That Man Again*, Tommy Handley and Mo McCackey. My mother likes the songs, and so do I: 'It might as well be spring', 'Paper doll' and 'Let the rest of the world go by'. A particular favourite is 'The Trolley Song sung' by Judy Garland, which they play over and over, and it always reminds me of the trams in Bridge Road. The radio is the way we know about what is happening out there, beyond what we can see.

I do make one friend, a boy called David. He is American, and he and his parents speak in American accents, like they do in the pictures. David has dark hair and spotless creamy skin, and his father has a small black moustache across his top lip. His mother comes to our house in her car and asks if I can go to their house and play. They live on the Main Road, too, closer to the school on the opposite side. David's house is a wonderland; he has a whole room for a play room, warm and carpeted, full of every toy and game you could possibly think of. His mother carefully manages our playing; first we sit on a little bench at a little table and paint with thick poster colours on large white sheets of paper. Then we are told to wash our hands and are allowed to take down a huge box of toy soldiers: old-fashioned redcoats and beautifully painted blue and silver guards, standing, kneeling, lying down to fire. We play for an hour or more and then his mother puts on a Punch and Judy show, with puppets and a curtained stall that she is hidden behind. I have never seen Punch and Judy before, and am shocked by Punch's violence. Why is he so angry? Then we sit and David's mother reads to us. It is a poem about another angry man, called Sir Brian:

I am Sir Brian, as bold as a lion

Take that, and that, and that!

But they punish him by the finish:

They took him by the britches
And they threw him into ditches.

At the end of the afternoon I am deeply envious of David, and exhausted by the time his mother drops me back home. I am struck by how dismal our rooms are, how little I have to play with, how worn and cold our linoleum floors are. I make for the kitchen, where it is warm and my mother is cooking the dinner. I try to tell her what I've been doing all afternoon, try to convey the incredible riches that David is surrounded by. She doesn't seem interested.

'Oh yes,' she says, in that withering way that indicates indifference. Or perhaps irritation. 'Go and wash your hands, we'll be eating soon.'

*

It seems I am not seeing much of my father, and again I have that feeling of important matters being kept from me. To look at he is bony and pale, but never weak or girly. He has clear skin and blonde hair, not like me; I have mousy hair, my mother says, and freckles. Frank, his name is. It is a good name: Francis Charles. My mother's name, we all agree, is a stupid name: Thelma. I like her other name better: Amelia. But my father, I like everything about; he is clever and funny, and can do almost anything well – draw, write, make things with his hands, tell jokes. Yet there is an ache in me when I think about him, an absence of some indefinable thing that I need but cannot get from him. He keeps himself apart most of the time, especially from me.

But he does socialise a little, and appears to have made friends at the local pub. One day he takes me out rabbiting with a .22 rifle lent to him by one of his friends, and we walk for miles, through brown paddocks and deep gullies. My mother has put some biscuits in a paper bag in my pocket. We don't even see a rabbit, but I am happy just to be spending time with him. He stops and takes a few potshots at tin cans, a galah on a fence post, which he misses. He lets me carry the rifle some of the way.

We come to a flat area with a wooden house set back from the dirt road and with nothing around it but bare paddock. My father knocks on the door, and a man in a waistcoat and hat comes and invites us in. There are several children in an untidy sitting room with a single old armchair. There is also a peculiar smell. I come to know that smell very well in subsequent years; it is the smell of clothes worn too long without washing, of food scraps in corners, of floors and walls not cleaned. The smell of poverty and the lethargy that goes with it. We children are told to go out and play while the men drink a bottle of beer.

A girl a little bigger than me takes my hand and pulls me round to the back of the house. I think I've seen her in the school playground.

'Have you got anything?' she demands.

'What do you mean?'

'Have you got anything? There, in your pocket. Money?'

'No.'

I take the bag of biscuits out of my pocket and show it to her, thinking I might offer her one or two. She tells the other children to go away. 'Buzz off, go and play round the front.'

'Give them to me,' she says, 'and I'll let you do anything you like to me.'

I'm frozen with ignorance. What does she mean? What can I do to her? She means something that I don't know about, knows what I don't know. She puts her hands under her light dress and slips off her pants. 'Here,' she says, lifting her dress, 'do what you want,' and she takes the biscuits out of my hand.

Obediently, I examine her. I am surprised: she doesn't have a penis, like me. There is nothing there but a slit. I put out my hand and touch it where it protrudes a little, with her legs together. She is looking impassively into the distance, eating the biscuits. Her slit is soft but firm, and mysterious. I take it between my thumb and forefinger and gently squeeze the two halves together, closing the slit tighter. Suddenly, she opens her legs, offering to give me more access. I pull away as if I've been bitten. 'Okay,' I say.

'Is that all you want to do?' she asks. 'Don't you want to put it up?'

'No,' I say quickly, 'up where? What?'

'Your finger, up properly?'

'No, it's okay. That's all I want to do.'

She puts her pants back on and laughs at me. 'You're stupid,' she says, and runs to the back door.

'Are there any biscuits left?' I call.

'There you are,' she laughs, and throws the crushed-up empty bag at me.

When we go, my father leaves the rifle with the man in the hat. It is apparently his.

Walking back a different way, along the road this time, my father says, 'Brian Smith is a sad feller.'

I know he means something more, but I choose to take him literally.

'Is he sad because he doesn't have a garden?' I say. He puts his arm round my shoulder. 'Mate,' he says, 'that man doesn't have anything except his kids.'

*

We haven't been here long when my mother gets a job. The hotel needs someone to serve behind the bar and to do some cleaning, and my father hears about it and suggests she goes up and talks to the publican.

'He'll give it to you straight away, with your looks,' he tells her. 'He'll think you're Vivien Leigh.'

'Oh yes, smarty pants,' she says, standing with one hand on her hip. 'It's a shame then that I haven't got Clark Gable to come home to, isn't it?'

'Who's Clark Gable?' I ask.

'The man in the moon,' says my mother.

My mother doesn't like pubs and bars; she doesn't even like drinking much. Growing up in North Melbourne she has seen too much of what it does to people. But we need the money, and knowing my mother she will enjoy the chance to talk to people. So every afternoon around three o'clock she goes up to the hotel to work, and comes home around six thirty. She isn't there when I come from school. On her way home she has to pass Greenbaum's store, and she sometimes drops in and buys us some chocolate or a comic book. You can buy everything at Greenbaum's – food, magazines, hammers and nails, billies.

Mount Macedon has a particular history, now fading, already being transformed by the War. It has been a retreat for the rich, who built great mansions with acres of manicured gardens, as a cool haven away from the hot city summer. Here they could enjoy their money in peace, entertain their important friends, and pretend they were Europeans. Now that has all gone. Cameron Lodge seems deserted, no parties of guests from the city arrive for the weekend, no dark limousines speed up the mountain road and enter the property between the huge pair of Grecian urns that straddle the gateway. Several feet wide each of them must be. Farther along the road, the fifty rooms and twelve acres of lawns, oaks, poplars and elms of Sefton stand unvisited, shelter no picnics. Matlock, built by the founder of Woolworths, has a different guest from the flappers and tennis-players of two decades earlier: interned in death-quiet luxury, the Japanese consul practices one-man billiards, alone with his shame and anxiety over the events of Pearl Harbour.

I know nothing about all this, of course, but even as a small boy I am able to feel the past in looking at what's left of it. It is strange to be surrounded by all this apparently abandoned luxury. It is the War, I know; people are saying all the time that Mount Macedon will never be the same. It is as if I've come across Paradise, empty after the inhabitants have sinned and left. In a funny sort of way, wandering around it alone, I am able to lay some sort of a claim on it as my own.

One day the unusual does happen, and there is in fact a gathering, some kind of garden party at Cameron Lodge, organised by people who frequent the hotel. Along with everyone else in the village, we are invited. Most of the house is closed to us, but you can sense an elegant, gracious purpose in the architecture; the wide balustraded verandah, the spacious rooms and feeling of solidity. It is beautiful summer weather and we spend the day in the garden, eating, talking, running about. The massive lawn rolls down from the house between tall trees to a little creek, which runs into a pond with stepping stones across it. I pick my way across the stones, and halfway across I stop because something catches my eye. Lying on the bottom of the pond is an orange canoe. I can see every line of it through the clear water. It is strange.

Why would anyone leave a canoe down there? What happened, was it an accident, or did it get too old and just sink? It is mesmerising, as if it is part of an underwater world, but an unnatural one where things are a distorted version of the right world, but oddly coloured and beautiful. What kind of people leave a perfect canoe lying at the bottom of a pond?

As things get more familiar, I grow more adventurous. At the bottom of our land is a track that one day I decide to follow. It leads down to a small creek, the same one I suppose that flows through Cameron Lodge, fast-flowing and so clear that you can see every pebble on the bottom. I can't resist cupping my hand and taking a drink of the cold, sweetish water.

Then I begin to walk up the rising mountain side, under a canopy of tall trees. There are no tracks, so I have to find a way of my own. It gets steeper as I go higher, and the vegetation gets thicker; I have to pick a more roundabout route between trees and bushes, ferns and tangles of vine, around rocks and rotting stumps. After maybe half an hour of climbing it gets darker and colder, and the ground takes on a damp sponginess that occasionally causes me to slip and slide.

Breaking through a clump of bushes I come to a place that feels special, inviting, and I seem to have no choice but to pause there. The ground has levelled out, and there is a cleared area of moss and grass, with a patch of sun lighting it up like a bright green carpet. The effort has made me hot and sweaty by this time anyway, so I sit on a dry rock next to the grass and rest. I am in the centre of a circle of tree ferns, and some of the fronds reach out long and gentle above my head. The light is dappled over the ground and over me. The quiet makes my head ring. An occasional whip-bird breaks in, but this only adds power to the silences between calls. This is a magical place, I sense. Overhead, the tree-tops and fern-trees seem to be slowly spinning, making me giddy. I am almost fainting with joy. I tell myself, I am the only person who knows this place, this is mine only, my hideaway, my retreat. I will be able to come here whenever I like, and no one will be able to find me. I stay, sitting there, until the sweat on my forehead has dried and I begin to get cold. Then I resume my push on up the mountain.

After a long haul and with aching legs I come to an area where the bush begins to thin out again, and the trees let in more light. It levels, and suddenly I am on a road. There is no one around – not a person, not a car, just me and this world. Along the road ahead I can see objects and a footpath leading somewhere. I pass a big round concrete container, with a ladder attached to its side. I climb it and look in. Floating on its black water are dozens of bluish-white dead frogs on their backs. Tadpoles too. I think the cold has killed them. I nudge a frog with my finger; it sinks and surfaces again, and drifts away. Death, I tell myself, feels icy and empty.

The objects ahead turn out to be concrete vases and urns in classical style. In fact the whole area has been made as a formal classical garden, with marble chip paths and moulded borders. There are urns and statues on pedestals of various sizes – some quite large – everywhere, and neat Cypress shrubs lining a virtual maze of walkways and steps. A statue with no arms and no penis at first looks like a maimed soldier, but then I recognise it as female, like the Smith girl. I follow the paths, puzzled and entranced at the same time, because I have never seen anything like this in my life. It is another world again, strange, man-made this time, but equally magical in its oddness, its contrariety to the surrounding bush.

At the end of the main path is a giant cross made of creamy smooth slabs of stone, mounted on a massive base at the top of a dozen steps. It has a sword forming a smaller cross inside the larger one, and written on a plaque it says:

TO THE GLORY OF GOD
AND IN
MEMORY OF AUSTRALIA'S SONS
1914 – 1918

Standing beside it, I can see the world for miles, stretching away to the horizon on one side, and becoming green mountains on the other, lower than me. There is no wind, just warm sunshine and a cloudless blue sky. I feel I am on the roof of Australia. Looking at the farthest horizon, I try to discern the War. Somewhere in the distance people are flying aeroplanes, sinking ships, firing guns, killing each other. But all I can see from here is a calm, motionless expanse of soft colours and flat indistinguishable shapes. No people.

*

It doesn't take me many visits to get bored with playing in David's toy room, and one day I coax him to go exploring with me in the paddocks over behind his house. We don't say anything to his mother as we slip out of the back door. David is a softie when you get him outside. I lead him on a long escapade through knee-high grass, under barbed wire fences, down steep gullies, and he complains most of the time about getting burrs in his socks, or that his mother will be worried. We play soldiers for a while, but he has no idea how to stay hidden behind cover or to make convincing firing noises. 'Bang,' he goes, 'bang!' That's silly, and isn't the sound that guns make. I try to set him an example by making the right noises for rifles, hand grenades, the sound of dying victims, but he doesn't get it.

On the way home we come to a nice soft area of sloping ground, which I accidentally slip down on my backside, onto a boggy part at the bottom. It is good fun, so I do it again. At first David doesn't want to do it, afraid of getting his pants muddy. But when he sees how much I am enjoying it, he gives in and does it too. By the time we've had enough our pants are muddy and completely soaked through.

David's mother is angry with us. We shouldn't have even left the house, she says. David tells her it was my idea to slide in the mud; I confirm it.

'I can't send you home like that,' she says to me. 'Let's get those trousers off and washed.' She takes down my trousers, and looks at me in shocked disbelief.

'Don't you wear any underpants?' she says. 'David always wears underpants.' And indeed, when David takes off his short trousers, he is wearing dazzling white briefs. He laughs at my bare loins. That, and his mother's obvious distaste, make me blush. I didn't know about underpants. My mother has never put them on me. I don't understand it – my father said Americans don't wear singlets, as Australians do. Yet they wear underpants. It must be because I'm Australian that I don't wear them, I think. Obviously both David's mother and my father think Australians are not as good as Americans. I'm not as good as them.

*

My parents' bedroom feels important. It is where special things are kept, like money, a metal box with papers in it, and my mother's book with the pictures in that she occasionally lets me look at. I wander in to feel the quiet gravity; the dark furniture, a suite with rounded corners, hides all its adult secrets –the large bed, the wardrobe, the dressing table. The mirror on the dressing table is the only one in the house that is low enough for me to see into. I stand looking at the boy in front of me; he moves when I move. It is self. Self has freckles, is scrawny and tousle-haired, mousy and wary-looking eyes that stare back at me. He wears a checked shirt and short trousers held up by braces.

Christmas is the best time of the year. My mother helps me place a pillowcase at the end of the bed, and I'm so excited I can't sleep. I lie in the dark thinking if I stay awake all night I'll catch Father Christmas and then I'll find out if he's real or not. I think he probably is, but unfortunately I eventually fall asleep and my suspicions can't be confirmed when I wake up in the morning and find the pillowcase full with presents. There is a large tip truck that my father says is made of bakelite, and a red net stocking full of lollies and whistles and games like Snakes and Ladders and Ludo. My favourite is a big thick book with a dark red cover called The children's golden treasure book, which has stories and pictures and poems that I read over and over. 'Rikki Tikki Tavi', and 'Lost, a very good temper' and 'Horatius at the bridge' by Lord Macaulay. I get into bed with my father and he reads this long poem to me right through, and though I don't understand a lot of the words, the story catches me up completely:

> *...I will stand at thy right hand*
> *and keep the bridge with thee ...*
> *..........*
> *To every man upon this earth*
> *Death cometh soon or late.*

18

And how can man die better
Than facing fearful odds,
For the ashes of his fathers,
And the temples of his Gods,
………
Through teeth, and skull, and helmet,
So fierce a thrust he sped,
The good sword stood a hand-breadth out
Behind the Tuscan's head.

By the end of the poem my father's voice is breaking and he wipes tears from his eyes. My mother comes into the room carrying Ray and says, 'Come on you two, time to get up and have your breakfast. It's a beautiful day.' But my father grabs her arm and pulls them both into bed. She shrieks and we have a family wrestle, Ray as well. We roll about, laughing, tickling each other. These are good times, but they do not happen often.

It is also a good time of the year because of the holidays, which means that people come and stay with us. My Uncle Ron, my mother's brother, brings his pretty girlfriend, Dot, who hardly speaks she is so shy. Ron had wanted to be a jockey, and loves horses. He hires one and rides it up and down the road in front of our house at full gallop, flicking a small whip behind him. He is a good rider. I like Ron so much that when he says he would like to walk up the mountain to see the Cross, I take him on my own special route – down over the creek and up through the tree-ferns; he likes it a lot. He agrees not to tell anyone else about it.

Some of my father's family come to stay too – his twin half-brothers, my grandmother, Nair. After spending two days mostly drinking up at the pub, they go back to North Melbourne. Nair says the publican insulted her, so she wouldn't drink in there again. The truth is they are bored here, don't understand the country. They have made my mother so angry that my father has virtually ordered them to go. Still, I am disappointed because there is always a lot of interesting talk when Nair is around.

Brown paper parcels come in the post from friends and relatives in Melbourne. Biscuits, chocolate, clothing. It is always exciting undoing the string and opening them to see what has been sent. The fact is, we are poor and people feel sorry for us, try to help us. There is no prospect of my father working, this much has dawned on me. There is only what little my mother can earn here to supplement the invalid pension he gets. It is important that my father gets well again. But he coughs badly every morning and every evening.

One of the best things we do is go to the pictures in the evenings at the Church hall just past the hotel. Once a week there is a picture show, when everyone gathers on bench seats and a screen on a stand is put up, and they show one of the latest pictures, usually from America. You have to put up with the film stopping when they turn on the lights and change the reel, and with the occasional breakdown, when everyone starts cheering and hand-clapping till they get it going again, but the films are good. We see *National Velvet*, with Elizabeth Taylor, and one that is a favourite of my father's called *The Fighting Sullivans*, in which a family of boys grows up on a farm and the smallest is always trailing behind yelling, 'Hey, wait for me!' Then when the War breaks out they all join the Navy and are torpedoed and killed. The final scene has them all climbing a staircase to Heaven, and still the smallest is trailing behind calling, 'Hey, wait for me!' It is very sad, and about dying for your country, which I think is why my father likes it. My own favourite is called *Reap the Wild Wind*, because in it two men, played by John Wayne and Ray Milland, go down under the sea in diving suits with big steel helmets and fight a huge octopus; its tentacles are as big as giant pythons, and sneak up behind and wrap themselves around the struggling men. I could see it every week if it was on.

And then something new happens: three housepainters turn up, wearing white overalls and carrying ladders on the top of their car. There is not enough room for them at the hotel, and my mother hit upon the idea of offering them accommodation in our house. She cooks for them, does their washing, makes their beds. It means I have to sleep on a camp stretcher in the huge lounge room with the bay window and no furniture, but I don't mind.

They are good company to have around, joking and telling stories. One of them is called Bill, and he owns the car – a dark red Terraplane. Bill lets me sit in it and pretend to drive when it is standing in front of the house. Unfortunately my little brother Ray decides to replenish the fuel tank one day, so he gets the cap off and tips a milk bottle full of water down the fuel pipe. It takes a lot of work and many days to get the car going again.

They are with us for a number of months, painting Cameron Lodge; it's a big job. Sometimes they go down to Melbourne for the weekend, but sometimes they stay. One night Bill asks my father if he would like to go out with him catching eels. My father would love to go, but he is not well enough, his temperature is up. He spends days in bed with the door shut, and I rarely see him. But Bill goes out alone, and in the morning there is a big black eel in a tin bucket in the kitchen. Later, Bill skins it and my mother fries it for breakfast. Everyone (except Ray) has some, even my father. It tastes strong and fishy, and I am happy to get back to a bowl of Weeties. The Weeties packet has a picture of a man like a bug holding up a packet of Weeties with a picture of a man like a bug – and so on, getting smaller and smaller, so when you think about it, it will never have an end, because each packet has to have a picture on it that makes it Weeties.

Playing in our garden, whether I'm climbing trees or driving my pretend car, or any of the other activities I can usually find to do, I am always aware of the mountain standing above us, huge and unchanging, except that sometimes you can see the cross glinting in the sun and sometimes you can't. The mountain is calm and peaceful, full of secrets – some of which are now mine – and ever-present in its massive greenness. It can be good and friendly, as it is when I climb it along my special route and enjoy the wonderful view from the top, or it can be dark and cold in bad weather, and freeze the lives that dwell on it. It can also be dangerous, as I am reminded by the fire that blazed and smoked on Mount Toorong, which is a smaller mountain in the opposite direction from our house, when we first arrived. That fire lasted for weeks; I would see the flames suspended in the black sky from my bedroom window at night, and hear the concern in my father's voice about the direction of the wind. If such a fire ever roared through Macedon, it would bring a whole world to an end.

Not for the first time, we all have to make a trip down to Melbourne on the train, while my father has a check-up. My mother dresses Ray and me in the colourful pullovers she has knitted for us, and which we call our 'town jumpers'. The Macedon taxi comes up our drive and takes us to the station, fitting our cases into a huge boot. It is a black Oldsmobile, and is rounded and modern and has a distinctive smell of leather and something indefinable and comforting inside.

The train is crowded and noisy with soldiers – in the compartments, in the narrow corridors running along the windows. Some of them stand up and let us have their seats, with my mother nursing Ray on her lap. They all seem to smoke, and their khaki clothes give off a smoky, musty odour. My father likes them, jokes with them. And though they are young, at twenty-seven my father is not much older than them, and certainly wishes he were with them – you can see it in the way his eyes ravish them. But then one of them says something that changes the look on my father's face. To his mate he says the word 'pissed' loud

21

enough for everyone to hear. My father stands up and says something in his ear; the soldier blushes and bends down to my mother. 'I'm sorry missus, I forgot meself.' My mother just smiles. 'Oh don't worry,' she says.

Looking out of the train window, I watch the empty paddocks pass and count the advertising signs for Robur Tea, Creamota porridge, Beck's Powders, Dunlop Tyres. When we get to Digger's Rest, we are closer to the city and houses become more frequent. It begins to rain; it always begins to rain when we approach Melbourne. Two soldiers carry our cases off the train and out onto Spencer Street. 'Good luck,' my father calls to them as they head for the trucks their mates are climbing into.

My father stays with Nair in North Melbourne, while my mother, Ray and I stay in West Melbourne with my grandmother, Daisy, whom I now call 'Ninny'. She has a new husband and a new family. He, too, is a soldier, or at least is in the army and wears a uniform and officer's cap, though he is an older man than the troops on the train. His name is MacDonald, but everyone just calls him 'Mac', and he talks with a Scotch accent. The thing about Mac that you can't forget is that he has only one good hand and arm, and on the other he wears either a hook or a false hand depending on what he is doing. I am very scared of Mac. He has a fierce, angry manner and everyone has to do what he says in the house. I know he doesn't like me.

Mac has several children, mostly grown up and living elsewhere, but I get to know three of them while we stay with them – Heather, Angus and Kelso. Heather is mostly out with her boyfriend Bill, who can blow smoke out of his ears. Angus is in the navy, and Kelso just a few years older than me. I play with Kelso most of the time, and he knows a lot about things: the names of all the weapons they use in the War, that the Jap leader is called Tojo, and what Japs do to their prisoners – cut their cocks and balls off and give them to their pigs. He knows, too, that Japanese soldiers all wear glasses because they can't see properly.

Kelso also takes me to a football match to watch his team – Essendon –play; we sit right on the fence, and I can see the players up close. The red and black colours of Essendon look dramatic and beautiful, and a player called Dickie Reynolds is their star, and leads them to a win. From that moment on, Essendon is my team too.

I sleep in the same bed as Kelso, and Angus is in the other bed. When we have our pyjamas on Angus comes over and makes me suck his cock. It is big and tastes salty. Nothing like that has happened to me before. I don't mind it, but I don't like it. Angus and Kelso think it's a great joke. I turn and face the wall to go to sleep; the wallpaper has an orange pattern that spreads through the whole room, a strange, curling pattern that, as I lie facing the wall, I trace with my eye and finger, over and over, the same shapes, leading to other shapes and joined up on and on over the whole wall. I will be glad to go home to Mount Macedon and my own bed and my own house.

3

THE PAINTERS STAY UNTIL the end of the summer, and then it is time for them to pack up and leave. They have become good friends to my parents in this time, and their money has been a real help to us. If they get another job here, they say they will board with us again. My mother says she is going to stop working at the hotel and try to get more house guests, because she can then look after my father better. But it is going to mean less money to live on.

As the winter approaches, the trees around Mount Macedon change to bright colours, and our own trees change with them. Red and orange and brown and gold leaves, and the wind whips them up and blows them away. Miss Goss's cottage looks bare and exposed, and I note for the first time that it is painted green. Walking to school is colder than ever, and in the classroom the teacher sets a big, warm blaze going in the fireplace.

Several problems with our house become more evident: when it rains the wide hall echoes with the tinny drips that leak from the roof into the pots and pans my mother carefully positions. Our electricity is dangerous, and on one frightening occasion my little brother Ray touches a plug on the kitchen skirting board and is thrown with a thud against the opposite wall. 'We are so lucky we didn't lose him,' my mother says. And the house is cold all the time. My father tries to chop wood and put fires in the several fireplaces, but with little success; the wood is green and just sends up a lot of smoke and a few flickers of flame with little warmth. Also, he no longer has the strength to wield an axe with any power. It is impossible to buy seasoned wood, which is easier to cut, even if you have the money.

We all seem to spend a lot of time in bed, trying to keep warm. I especially like it when my mother puts me to bed early and brings me my tea. After I've eaten it I snuggle down in the warm blankets, and read a comic: Captain and the bosun; Felix the cat; Boofhead; Donald Duck, especially the one where everything takes place at the North Pole, with deep soft snow over everything. My mind is there, thinking freezing coldness while my body under the blankets is feeling warm.

My mother is a wonderful cook, and most of the time feeds us well; she can come up with a good meal from the most basic ingredients, and over the summer has drawn on a vegetable patch in the back paddock that my father has tended. But the vegetables have finished now, and on more than one occasion all there is on the table are toast and scrambled eggs, from a neighbour's chooks, or spaghetti with grated cheese on top. Fortunately, I love spaghetti and grated cheese, and could eat it anytime. But I know my mother worries now about money, about our health, about whether or not we'll be able to manage on just my father's pension.

Luckily, we get another guest staying, and for an extended period. A young man, Tom, who has come here to be the local baker, moves into my bedroom. So I am back in the huge front room. Tom is good-looking, quietly spoken and wears a navy blue roll-neck sweater most of the time. My mother fusses over him a little. He likes to put a whole slice of bread and butter into his soup. I ask Tom, 'Why aren't you in the War?'

'Don't ask questions,' says my mother.

'Too young,' says Tom. 'I won't be eighteen till next year.'

'Are you going to the War then?'

'Mind your business,' says my mother.

'Probably,' says Tom.

'Give him some more soup,' says my father, 'he's too skinny.'

'Can I have some more, too?' I ask. And when it comes, I think of putting a slice of bread and butter in it as well; but it would be too difficult.

Tom neatly breaks off pieces of the soggy bread with his spoon and swallows them. I don't think I could do it properly.

On the radio there is a song I like:

Clang, clang, clang went the trolley.

Ding, ding, ding went the bell…

It is a memory of the city, especially Bridge Road, and being at Nair's.

Over the course of this year, I begin to be troublesome. I start to sense something about myself, which is that I have a capacity to be unlikeable. I'm not sure what the reason is, but without really intending to I keep causing mischief. First there is David. Usually we play in his games room. But on this day, since he has a cricket bat and ball amongst his possessions, I persuade him to come outside and have a game. I pick up the bat enthusiastically and play a shot at an imaginary ball, unaware that he is coming up behind me, and hit him with the blade of the bat right over his eyebrow. He yells and reels about, clutching his face, and I am very scared. His mother rushes out.

'What's happened, what have you done to him, oh my God you've blinded him!' After a few minutes she manages to pull his hands away from his face, and his eyes are full of angry tears, but there is no blood. There is a swelling about the size of a penny coming up, and his mother places a cold wet flannel over it. Then she turns on me.

'Go home, boy, and stay there. I don't want you coming here ever again.'

Later, she drives her car up to our house and tells my mother what has happened. I never play with David again.

Some time after that I am walking home from school and a couple of girls from a bigger grade are making fun of me for some reason. They live farther up the Main Road from us, but we don't really know them. They call me names, threaten to bash me, but I keep twenty or so yards ahead of them as we approach our front gate. Just at that moment my little brother Ray comes through the gate to greet me, and he isn't wearing any pants. The girls shriek with mocking laughter, and I feel so embarrassed and humiliated that I pick up a piece of quartz from the edge of our driveway and hurl it at them. I see it curve high through the air, slowly like in a dream, its destiny already decided by an invisible thread, and smash into the girl's face. Straight away I know that this is major drama. I run into the house, trailing a grizzling Raymond behind me. I go straight into my parents' bedroom, throw myself on the bed and start crying as if my beating has already begun.

The girls come to our front door and show my mother what I've done. One has a cut somewhere on her face, and sobs quietly while the other does the talking. 'He just threw a rock at us for nothing. Her father will be down when he hears about it,' I can hear her say.

When they go, my father comes into the bedroom. I am in terror, knowing I am due for some dire punishment. And yet I can't remember what happens. Does he beat me? I don't believe so. What does he do? I know he is severely displeased with me, and reprimands me in a way that makes me feel deeply ashamed and afraid. He delivers, I suspect, a serious warning about what happens to boys who throw stones, who get into fights. But what makes it hurt so much is not the punishment, or even the threat of it, but the knowledge that he –he, of anyone in the world – is angry with me. Just his disapproval of me knocks the bottom out of my world. Might he stop loving me? The thought is dark, stealthy, like some monster coming up behind, too terrible to look directly in the face. I resolve with all my heart to be a better person.

And yet before long I am in trouble again. This time it is about Ray. There is an old shed at the back of Miss Goss's house, also painted green. Inside is a massive old washing mangle, its iron stand rusted, its rollers fat and heavy. I try to wind its handle, and to my surprise it moves. Ray stands beside me and just as I try another wind, he places his fingers between the rollers, and the tips are pinned. He yells and, panicking, I quickly try to release them but wind the handle in the wrong direction, and the tips disappear in between the rollers. Ray's screams bring my mother flying across the yard. She clutches him and looks at his hand.

Then there are urgent decisions, the Macedon taxi is called and we all head to the doctor's surgery in Woodend. My mother nurses a whimpering Ray beside me in the back, my father is silent in the front. The atmosphere in the taxi is heavy with fear, especially mine. I know my father is displeased with me again, but again I can't recall if I received any punishment, or what it might have been. I think I would remember if I did. But Ray has a bad hand for a long time, and some fingers that remain damaged for many years. And it is my fault.

Ray is a likeable little boy, yet I tease him a lot, and make him cry. I am probably jealous of him, resentful that he takes attention away from me. He has different looks from me; I have sharper, more rat-like features, with a thin freckled face and large front teeth. He is chubbier, wider-faced, blonde-haired and unfreckled. Everyone likes him. Nair calls him 'Wookie', after the little elephant that is the companion of the Space hero Buck Rogers. People praise me, say I'm clever; but it is Wookie who they take up and cuddle.

Why am I so bad? Why do I keep doing wrong things? I know my parents love me, but still I make them angry. I know that somewhere inside me is a knot of badness. At the same time I am growing a sort of scar tissue that is less sensitive, less vulnerable to further pain. I am learning to detach myself from the possibility of joy. It is not that I am living in pain – not yet. It is more a state of deferred expectation: something that should happen is not about to happen. I am forming the anticipation of disappointment. I have a sense of something ominous haunting our life.

The cold and gloom of the house is not just the winter and lack of heating. Something is absent, something that none of us is getting. It can't be spoken about, at least not by me or to me; it can't be seen, but it can be felt. A sadness that is in my mother's silences, that has something to do with being here, with the food parcels that come, and the respectful visits by relatives. They are sorry for us. We are out on the margins of life. And my father is getting sicker.

I stand at the front gate and watch the occasional cars going up and down Main Road. Most of them have big bins on the back called gas producers, again because of the War. The only ones who don't have them are the Macedon taxi and the milkman. The milkman has a ute with great silver cans on the back. What he does, he drives up to the very top of the mountain road, Main Road, then he switches off the engine and silently coasts down, stopping at each house to do the milk. Like us, people leave their billies on a tray at the front gate, and into these the milkman ladles the fresh, white milk with a small metal cup. I watch him, already looking forward to my breakfast. Sometimes as I carry the billy full of milk into the house I do an overarm swing with it, never spilling a drop. Maybe some time I will, though.

Tom, removing his rollneck sweater, energetically tackles the pile of wood delivered by a friend of the publican's. He makes a loud hissing noise as he brings down each blow, invariably embedding the axe in the knotty log. He is strong, accurate, but the wood is green and gnarled, and won't chop readily. Just as it won't burn readily.

'We might have to burn the furniture,' says my father, watching Tom from nearby. I don't always know when my father is joking; something about him suggests he could easily take to burning the furniture if he chose to, and my mother would probably laugh along with him. Adults are not easy to understand.

One day it is so bitter cold that it snows all the way to school. The fire is lit in our classroom, and everyone keeps their coats on, but it is still impossible to keep warm. Some ladies give us cups of cocoa at lunch time, and by the afternoon we have all thawed a little. When I get home there is still white everywhere – over the garden, on the roof, in the tree branches. My mother says, 'Did you see the snowman we made you?'

My parents take me outside and point him out. He is standing on the edge of the gravel driveway – I missed him because he is white like everything else. He is a bit pathetic compared to the ones in the comics I read, but I like him. He is small – about the size of Ray – and is wearing one of my father's hats and has coat buttons that my mother has stuck into his front.

Because the falling snow has now become mixed with rain, he has already begun to melt. He is leaning over to one side and one arm has fallen off completely, and both the buttons that were his eyes have disappeared into his watery head. He stands, silent and icy, his hours already numbered; by morning he will be nothing but a puddle of water on the gravel. But I am so happy that my parents did this together, and for me, as an attempt to give me something new, some fantasy thing that they thought might cheer me up. The fact that he doesn't last long of course is disappointing, but that is, I realise, just the way things are with snowmen.

Two nights later our whole life is changed. I am reading a comic in bed, when from way down the hall I hear my mother yell, 'Frank! Frank!' There is something in her voice that I have never heard before – not just panic, which is the first thing that strikes me, but a deeper note of fear, and not just immediate fear but a fear that expresses what has been building up in her now for our whole time here, in her worry over money, in her frustrations over the state of the house, in her prolonged anxiety over my father's worsening health, in the very state of living that we have been delivered into – and it tears something inside me and drags me in a rush down the hall and into the kitchen. My father is on the floor, unconscious. My mother is standing over him, her arms covered in soap-suds, turned up and out in helplessness. Her eyes are wild and frightened. My appearance seems to trigger her into action.

'I'm going into Miss Goss's – stay with daddy till I get back. I won't be long…'

She must have gone to phone the doctor. I sit down on the floor next to my father; his face is burning hot, and he is very still. I sit there and wait, reaching out with my hand to give his shoulder the occasional stroke.

There is an unpredictability to tuberculosis that makes it difficult to judge. In some victims it is spectacularly obvious – the blood-spitting, the drawn, emaciated look, the burning fevers that turn eyes into points of fire, these are the features loved by the culture-spinners. In my father's case, such signs are minimal. It is as if he is trying to keep his illness a secret. He seems to be making a huge effort to remain calm, quiet, to prevent the familiar symptoms from showing out, especially, it seems, to his family. I never see his blood, I never witness the racking fits of coughing that he suffers behind the closed door of the bedroom. It is only later that I see him glowing with fever. Some of this secrecy is purely medical: he knows how infectious he is, and is doing everything he can to prevent the three of us from catching it. But some of it draws, however strangely, on a sense of decorum; he does not think it decent to make suffering and illness a public event. Nor does he want us exposed to horrors that would leave a legacy of nightmares. In his mind, that would be an intolerable education to foist on children.

The doctor must eventually have come, and the trauma calmed down. My father has regained consciousness, and I am sent back to bed. But decisions, serious decisions, flow from the event. The end of our time at Mount Macedon is now in view. The idea that this would be the place of his cure has proved to be wrong. In fact, it has made him worse. For most of the following months of that year he stays in bed, propped up by pillows. Standing in the doorway, forbidden to go any farther in, I watch him listening to the radio, or spreadeagled with his head back in a febrile sleep. 'Frank,' my lips whisper, and 'Frank,' the word echoes in my head down through the rest of my days.

*

I know that winter is coming to an end because the vacant paddock next to us is once again covered in jonquils and daffodils. Snow-drops, too, their little white heads bowed in a way that I interpret as sadness. All this yellow and green and white is gleaming in the morning sun with a dew so heavy you could wash your hands in it. The mountain stands reassuringly tranquil above us. The milkman waves to me as his ute coasts silent as an apparition down the Main Road, betrayed by the odd rattle of a milk can.

I get to school this day and everything is normal until just before lunchtime. Suddenly, there is a commotion all around us, and an older boy starts ringing the school bell, a melon-sized brass bell that hangs over the timber balustrading on the back verandah. On and on it clangs, its tongue hammered by the dangling cord against its brass sides.

'It's over! It's over! The War is over!' our teacher is calling.

We are all crowded onto the verandah. Teacher and child hug each other. Still the bell rings on. Eventually someone announces that it is a half-holiday, and we all start thinking of going home. But first we are told to eat our sandwiches, and our teacher produces jugs of bright red drink that she calls raspberry vinegar, which is good and tastes nothing like vinegar. Then, with a sense of anti-climax, we slope off to our homes. My mother is sewing at her machine when I walk in.

'We got a half-holiday. The War is over,' I say.

'I know,' my mother says, 'the Japs have surrendered. The Americans dropped the atomic bomb on them.'

'Must have been some bomb,' I think to myself, 'to make them surrender just like that.' Not long after this my father makes a special effort to get out of bed for a reason that is particular to him. He wants to go to Mass. It is a strange thing that I learn about my parents: he is a Catholic, and so are Ray and I, but my mother is not. And now, for the first time in my experience, he is doing a

Catholic thing. Some acquaintance has agreed to pick him up in his car and take him to the church down in Macedon. 'Would you like to come?' he asks me. I'm not sure. My mother is not going. This is something my father is doing for himself, that doesn't involve my mother. What do I do? I have to choose between what each is choosing to do for themselves. There is no pressure from either side, and no feeling of resentment by either of them towards the other or towards me. I can go, or stay.

I go with my father. We are rugged up in our overcoats, and, entering the small church, we remove our hats. Inside, it is crowded with people and the service has already begun. People move up so that we get a seat in the pews about halfway down, and I look about me the whole time, following my father's lead about when to sit and when to kneel. The priest, in flowing robes of purple and white, chants a strange language, and a boy and he perform mysterious actions as they move about their fenced-in area. Like others about him, my father withdraws into a kind of private world, bowing his head, casting his eyes down, not giving any sign that he is with me. I copy him, but don't know what it is I should be thinking. Around the church walls are pictures of a man being punished; he is dragging a huge cross over his shoulder, just like the one on Mount Macedon. In some of the pictures soldiers are whipping him, in others people in long robes fall down on their knees in front of him. He has a circle of thorny branches around his head that is causing blood to flow down his face. It is horrible; what has the man done wrong? Then, at the end of the line of pictures, the man is pinned to the cross and it is stood upright, against a stormy sky. He hangs there, apparently dead, blood on his bony and pale body, soldiers looking at him, women holding out their hands in distress. It is a sight that puzzles and distresses me: why are they torturing and killing a pleasant-looking man? It seems unfair.

The church fills with a strong, sweet smell at one point, and bells are rung. People go up to receive something in their mouth. I whisper to my father, 'Are we going to get some of the food, too?'

'No, mate,' he whispers back, 'we can't; we're not in a state of grace.'

I have no idea what he means, but I don't press it. I'm getting pretty bored by this time, and can't wait for it to be over. Eventually everyone stands and sings a song, and the priest and boy leave. We file outside, and my father talks to a couple of people for a time. I can sense that it has been an important event for him, but have no idea why. And I can't think of how to ask. Going home in the car, he says, 'We'll have to get you to a decent Catholic School when we move back to the city.' I'm hoping its more interesting than Mass.

The day arrives when it is time for us to leave. It is a hot summer day, the holidays have begun and my uncle – the same one who helped us move up here – has come from Melbourne in a large furniture removal van. They spend all morning loading our belongings into the van, while my mother helps with the packing and cleaning. At lunch time everyone stops work and sits around our dining room table for the last time. I finish eating before anyone else, and go out for a last play in my favourite parts of the garden. At the corner of the front verandah, with its head down the storm water gully and its body trailing motionless across the gravel driveway, is a long, dark snake. I watch it for a few minutes, then through the open front doorway I call to my father.

'Dad, there's a snake out here!'

There is no answer from inside the house, so I call again.

'Dad! A snake. Hurry up, before it gets away,' though in fact it still hasn't moved. Then a voice echoes along the hall.

'Well son, there'd better be...'

In fact it is my mother who turns up first, and let's out a cry. My father and uncle join us, and I am proud of being proved right.

'A copperhead,' says my father.

The snake changes position slightly, lifting its head out of the gully and placing it on the gravel. My father disappears for a moment and returns with a pitchfork, and without hesitation or forewarning he spears the snake to the gravel by two of its forks, just behind its head. He then uses his foot to sink the fork in even deeper, while the snake writhes about furiously, twisting and doubling back on itself – first the whitish belly shows, then the black back, over and over.

'He's not going anywhere,' says my father, and walks away leaving the fork where it is. Then they all go back inside to finish their lunch. I keep playing in the garden, keeping a look out for any more snakes, and every now and then cast a look over to the verandah to see the pinned snake still writhing, but with slower, smaller movements now.

Suddenly, Miss Goss appears from the front door of her cottage. She makes her way over to the snake, an axe dangling in one hand. Stooping, not uttering a word, she begins to chop at it. On and on she goes as I watch her, the axe coming down in little forward movements, not with much force or accuracy, but still with enough weight to keep separating the snake into smaller bits. And each bit keeps moving, as if it is a smaller, new snake and is full of life. But these get chopped in half again, as Miss Goss works determinedly on, chopping every last possibility of danger, every last twitch of wickedness, out of the snake.

'I think you've got him Miss Goss,' calls a voice. I look across from where I stand amongst the yellow-flowering Broome beside the driveway. The glare of the hot sun off the gravel wounds my eyes, but I can make out, through the shaded depth of the front verandah, my father leaning against the front door jamb with his arms folded, laughing with his head tossed back, as if nothing in the world is more amusing nor more worth watching than the scene out on the drive in front of him. He laughs again, then he disappears.

4

ALTHOUGH WE ARE RETURNING to the city, we have no place of our own to move into. Accommodation of any kind is still hard to find through the War years, and for a long time afterwards. Our only choice is to crowd in with relatives, who in every case are already pressed for space to meet their own needs. As a family we are going to be split up anyway, with the doctors isolating my father in Gresswell sanatorium in the outer northern region of Melbourne. Now, my mother, Ray and I have to move in with Ninny and Mac in his house at Roden Street, West Melbourne. I wonder, now, whatever happened to the furniture we brought down in the van from Mount Macedon. There is no room for it at West Melbourne. I can only think that my mother has placed it into storage somewhere.

This arrangement is an unhappy one for my mother. Consider: under duress, she has to give up her home and be parted from her husband, and she has no space of her own or for her children; and she has to find a life in the interstices of an already tacked-together family. She sleeps with her three-year-old son in a single bed in Heather's small bedroom, Heather who likes to take her boyfriend Bill into the bedroom for some necking whenever the opportunity arises. My mother has to find whatever privacy she can in this room, to dress herself, dress and care for Ray, get some sleep and get her head together, because she still has to get out there and look for someplace for us to live.

Once again I find myself sleeping with Kelso, in the room he shares with Angus. I don't mind this too much, as Kelso interests me and to some extent leads me into new experiences, a kind of Huck Finn companion. Angus, I fear, would be a more dangerous presence if he were not in the navy and away for extended periods. I don't recall any more fellatio or such, but then there was so much going on in this house that my memory is swamped with information, most of it again fragmentary, and much of it hazy. But I believe around this time Angus's ship sails for northern waters, and I see little of him. In fact I am able to move into the relative comfort of his empty bed for the rest of our short time here.

It is something to do with the times, and something to do with the way Mac's family lives, that the house has a rural feel about it, even though West Melbourne is an inner city suburb by anyone's definition. The streets are wide and lined by tall terraced houses adorned with iron lace verandahs and ornamental tops, yet the house has a chook pen at the end of the long back yard, not uncommon in those times of food shortages and rationing. It stinks and is noisy, especially since Mac insists on keeping a rooster, which of course crows every morning, no doubt waking the whole neighbourhood. On the good side, there are fresh eggs every day, which Kelso shows me how to collect, and on a couple of occasions little yellow chickens scrambling around the pen after their mothers. He shows me, too, how to mix the pollard with warm water and feed them. Not five hundred yards away the city traffic roars past.

At Christmas Ninny seizes a chook from the pen and, while Kelso holds it on the block, cuts off its head with the axe. 'Watch this,' Kelso says to me, and releases the headless chook from his grasp; it runs aimlessly around the yard while we all shriek with laughter. Afterwards, I can't resist looking at the separated head lying on the ground beside the block, its eyes staring at nothing and its beak faintly moving. Then there is a strong, revolting stink though the house as Ninny dips the dead chook in hot water in a tin bath, and its soggy grey-white feathers are spread all over the table as she plucks and guts it ready to roast for the family dinner.

The fact, too, that they keep a cockatoo chained to the dead stump of an old fig tree just outside the back door, is an urban anomaly common to the times. This excitable bird has a strained relationship with Ninny, who takes out some of her frustrations on it, only to hear them regurgitated later on. 'Oh you swine, look at your chain,' it says as you pass it, perched on its branch. 'You're a bad, bad boy,' and 'Kel-soo, get off that bloody roof.' We often see the cocky angrily storming up and down its fig branch, repeating these sayings over and over, and shrieking loudly in protest, no doubt at the gnawing injustices of its own life around humans.

I wonder if the cockatoo's repetitions have developed in Ninny a kind of confidence in her own ability to produce memorable one-liners. And she does produce them, always with a degree of mock-anger, always on the cusp of laughing at her own raffishness.

I'll kick you so far you'll starve walking back.
I'll foot you in the backside so hard your nose will bleed.
If you do that again I'll cut your water off.
Don't put that penny in your mouth – a Chinaman's had it in his ear.

His ear? I ask myself; how on earth could anyone fit a penny in their ear? Ninny is a woman full of character: she is kind and generous to her children and grandchildren, with a hair-trigger laugh so infectious that it is easy to forget how tough a spirit inhabits that slight, stringy body. She has done much, seen much, within the limited scope of her life in Victoria; she has travelled to no other state or country, but she knows both the country and city life from her struggle as a housekeeper, cleaner, wife, child-bearer, child-rearer and widow, always on the edge of poverty. Yet she remains energetic and optimistic in outlook; whenever she is angry or depressed she deals with it by sweeping or mopping the floor with intense concentration, at the same time humming popular melodies to herself in a high-pitched continuo: 'Sally, Sally', 'We'll meet again', 'Beautiful Dreamer'. There is a dam of emotions walled up inside her, released only in this little trickle of music that she chants through her compressed lips.

Just as I found the first time I met him, Mac is a very frightening man. He never smiles or laughs, but scowls and orders everyone around in the house. He talks in a Scotch accent that I can't understand half the time. You have to be quiet if he is speaking, or on the phone, or just reading the paper, and you have to obey whatever command he issues. His own children hate him, and Kelso tells me that he has often beaten him and Angus by tying them to the bed and lashing them with his army belt. I can't take my eyes off his missing arm. Occasionally, I see him put on the prosthesis: it comprises an enamelled, flesh-coloured 'forearm' made of either metal or wood, which in turn is strapped onto his stump and over his shoulder. Into this he can insert an attachment. When it is the hand – which is usually when he is dressed up in his best uniform with his cap on – what shows from out of his sleeve is a dark brown leather glove, the thumb of which can be somehow moved in opposition to the row of fingers, so that he can hold things in a way that looks real. But around the house, if he wants to lift or pull something along, he attaches the hook. This is a fearful object to me, cruel looking and, to my combat-conscious imagination, capable of inflicting serious injury. I wonder might he hit me with it?

He sits at the head of the table in the dining room, and everyone waits on him, defers to him. There is a particular command he issues during meal-time, which is that we are all to eat mashed potatoes in a bowl with milk and salt, like porridge. I guess it is a Scottish delicacy. I don't mind it at all, but my mother hates it, and after the first time chooses to go without potatoes rather than eat it. Mac is very displeased with her, and gives clear indication that he thinks she is picky and ungrateful.

Despite my father's expressed hopes, I am not placed in a Catholic school at this time. Instead, I go to King Street State, just up the hill from where we are living. Still, there is a lot of religious instruction. We learn to sing 'Jesus loves me', and 'My cup is flowing over', and others. I don't learn much else. The kids in the schoolyard are a sight more intimidating than at Mount Macedon. One boy – Dennis – astonishes me. He is about the smallest child in the class, is thin and has pale skin and white hair, with reddened eyes peering through white-bleached lashes. Yet he is the toughest, most feared fighting machine in the class – and beyond. He mercilessly and skilfully thrashes a bigger boy behind the shelter-sheds, punching accurately, purposefully, like grown men in the pictures, while the other boy just flails and gropes wildly, mostly missing. Everyone treats Dennis with respect, yet he seems to have no actual friends. But then neither do I, and I don't think I could beat anybody.

Much of my playtime is spent in the surrounding streets – Roden and Spencer Streets mainly. Kelso promises to take me down to Dudley Flats, but my mother hears about it. 'Don't you dare take Garry down there, Kelso,' she says. 'If you do I'll tell your father and he'll give you his belt.' But even so I see many unforgettable things in the streets during those months of 1946. A massive rumble of tanks and army trucks file along Spencer Street as I watch, deeply impressed by the grandeur. This is almost like being in the War itself. On the back of a truck is a mini Japanese submarine, captured in Sydney Harbour. It is so small it looks as if it has been designed for children to play in.

Playing in Spencer Street one afternoon, Kelso and I witness a fight between two men. It happens outside a pub a couple of streets down from Roden Street, and we take our places amongst a dozen or so onlookers, most of whom are quiet and content to just watch, but a few others are urging the fighters on or supporting one or the other of them. The atmosphere is tense with drunkenness and violence, and it seems that everybody there is touched by it, smeared by it like a dirty substance that for the moment you don't care about. Both men are covered in blood – the blood and snot from their noses wiped across their faces like paint, the white shirt of one man a wet red all down the front. This man is younger and bigger than the other, but the other, with bushy dark eyebrows and an intent, older face, is beating him easily. When the younger man falls to the footpath, the other begins kicking him, one of the kicks landing in his face. This goes on, mercilessly, horribly wild and relentless, for some time until the younger man lies still. I feel desperately sorry for him. The older man leans up against the pub wall exhausted and panting with his blood-stained tongue out like a dog, a show of thick dark blood oozing from his nose unwiped. Two of the onlookers say aloud, 'You've done him, Bert, you've done him.' Eventually the crowd breaks up and the younger man is left to struggle alone into a sitting position on the footpath. His face is a bloody mess, and his eyes indicate he is either so drunk or so dazed that he doesn't know where he is.

Walking home, Kelso says, 'Did see that? When he kicked him? Did you see his teeth on the ground? When he spat, he spat out teeth?'

I hadn't seen the teeth. It was the blood that I saw and can't stop thinking about. Its redness, its proof of the shameful exposure of what should remain hidden; blood is for inside, for containing within yourself; bleeding is making your private, your personal self a matter of public ogling. It means you are no longer intact, and the world knows your injuries, your weaknesses. That's why the sight of blood is so alarming, and why I hate the thought of it.

The atmosphere of violence that marks that day is not uncommon around these times. Something makes people edgy, angry, ready to let their hatred off the leash. It shows not just in the physical violence, but in the way men in particular talk. If I am with my mother in the city, and she sees a drunk ahead, she will grab my hand and keep as far as possible from him; I can hear her little groans of fear as she hears him say 'fucken cunts' or some such, as if this is personally directed at her; she will flinch as if struck a bodily blow. People can get into arguments on buses, trams, shout their abuse at each other down corridors and at their departing backs. In my understanding this, too, has something to do with the War and its immediate aftermath, with a sense of danger that is even more intense now that 'it' is over. In later years it becomes the common belief, especially in the light of newsreel pictures of people dancing in the streamer-filled streets, that the end of the War opens the way to a time of unqualified personal joy and domestic bliss. But in truth such moments are brief and occasional. There are many matters to be angry about, and many people primed to give way to that anger. Soldiers have returned damaged, physically or psychologically, by what they have been through, and are ready to blame someone and demand reparation. They can be deeply resentful of those who did not enlist, believing them to have enjoyed a cushy time of it at their expense. 'I fought for you,' is a common post-War reminder, said in anger. Again, many of them feel either they were or might have been betrayed by wives who might have tried to relieve their wartime loneliness socially or sexually. The uncertainty could be worse than the certainty.

On the other hand, many service personnel had never had such a good time; the War had enabled them to travel, to experience exciting new places, to mix with a range of people like never before, and in an unprecedented context. In wartime, the rules of behaviour are relaxed, and people make friendships and do things that in peacetime they would never do. Such intensity is no longer there when they come home, and many of them quickly grow bored and impatient with the domestic routines of peacetime. Food is rationed, jobs are slow to be made available, houses are nearly impossible to find, life is lean and bland. Is it any wonder the streets are full of men looking for mischief or even just excitement?

Although the War is over, there are still simulated incendiary bombs lit in the middle of the road, and extinguished by helmeted firemen with hoses. We still stand on the front verandah at night and watch the long beams of searchlight criss-crossing each other as they probe the sky for aircraft. Occasionally something shows up, glinting and disappearing and glinting again, but it is never an enemy plane. In the daytime you can see our own warplanes flying low overhead. 'Wirraways,' Kelso points out, as a bunch passes right above with a thrilling combined roar of engines. 'Mustang,' he says of a lone fighter banking against the blue air, 'made in Canada.'

I am playing with Kelso in the street one day – playing marbles in the cobble-stoned gutter – when Ninny calls us in from the front doorway.

'Why?' Kelso asks.

'Just come in when you're told.'

'We're playing chasers.'

'I don't care if you're playing the piano, come inside straight away.'

When we don't show any sign of obeying, she says, 'The pair of you, right this minute: Black Elsie is on her way up the street, and she'll cut your throat as soon as look at you.'

This moves us, not because we know who Black Elsie is – at least I don't – but because Ninny's voice has sufficient urgency and particularity in it for us to sense serious danger in what she is saying. We hurry in and shut the front door, then Kelso and I press our faces up to the lounge room window and scrutinise the street. Eventually, sure enough, she appears. A small, pale-skinned woman with black curly hair straggling down her cheeks and a noticeable black moustache on her upper lip, she strides purposefully along the footpath and into our view. She has a thin dark dress over her skinny body, and is waving her arms about and railing angrily at nobody in sight. Someone in her crazed head, obviously, is the object of her tirade. Kelso and I think it a bit funny until I notice what she carries in one hand: a white handled, wide open cut-throat razor. She stops suddenly, sees us at the window and peers enquiringly at us. I don't feel like laughing now; I have a sudden fear that she might somehow break in through the front door. Then she steps through the gate and onto our path, approaching. Her look in our direction is murderous, and I grab Kelso's arm. 'Let's go,' I say, wanting to fly down the hall to Ninny in the kitchen. But then Black Elsie stops; she seems to actually see us for the first time, and stands looking and pursing and working her wide mouth, not saying anything now. I wonder if she could break the window. Then, almost heartbreakingly, she grins at us, and turns back. Stopping at the front gate, she turns around again and looks at us, still grinning. Like a soldier departing the presence of an officer, she raises her empty hand and salutes us, then stumps off up the street. Though I never see her again, I am to hear many a reference to her; it is said she is part-aboriginal, is a metho-drinker, and lives on Dudley Flats. I understand why my mother won't let me go there.

*

I have not seen my father now for many months; again that constant absence aches in me, and I dwell on the reports of his life in the sanatorium whenever my mother returns from visiting him. She brings home items of craftwork he has made for us – slippers for my mother made of felt and macrame, a toy green elephant called Elly for his beloved Wookie. I, too, would have liked a soft toy. A rabbit, maybe, but my mother says I am too old for one.

'Can we go and visit him,' I ask.

'We'll see,' says my mother.

'Why can't we?'

'Because why's a crooked letter that can't be made straight.'

My mother searches constantly, but it is impossible to find rental accommodation on the private market. She goes to the Housing Commission office and asks for help. The man there takes all our details and concludes that, officially, we are homeless. He says he will consider the possibilities, and let us know.

My parents have a friend called Les Kitson, who I call Uncle Les. He has been a mate of my father's since they worked together as tinsmiths. Uncle Les will turn up at unexpected moments, like recently when he wanted to show us a new sports car he had just bought – an old silver Bugatti with chrome exhausts flaring out from under the cowling. He insisted on sitting my mother beside him while he drove noisily up and down Roden Street. He has a strange, almost idiot-like voice and is always baring his teeth in a deep manic laugh. But he is funny and good-hearted, especially towards my mother. He takes us to the beach one day; we take the train to Brighton Beach station and turn into a street that has a glowing blue ribbon at the end of it: it is my first glimpse of the sea. Magical. As we get closer to its brilliance my excitement mounts until I am bursting with desire to embrace it, to plunge into it. While my mother spreads the towels I sprint through the soft pale sand down to the water and fling myself at it, but I am hit by an appalling shock; confused, deceived by the cold and the brine entering my mouth and nose, I gasp, I tip, I fall, I sink into a sprawling panic and am under. Then it is all right, and I am sitting up to my waist in water as the wave recedes. It is not quite what it looks, the sea. I spend most of the day playing in the sand with Ray, making castles with the bucket and spade my mother bought near the station. My mother covers all of us in sun lotion, and she and Uncle Les sit on the towels in their dry bathers talking and eating the picnic they brought along. Despite the lotion, my freckly skin is sunburnt when we get home that evening, and my mother dabs it with calamine lotion; it feels cold on my hot back.

*

I am just beginning to settle into some kind of routine at Roden Street. I am getting used to King Street school, Kelso is becoming something of a big brother to me, I am learning how to keep out of Mac's way, and Ninny is always around to keep a caring eye on me when my mother is out. I miss the freedom and the countryside of Mount Macedon, especially my secret places on the mountain, but I find some consolation in the hard asphalt of the footpaths and roads that I play on; I can kick a football with Kelso, bowl a tennis ball to him while he clobbers it with a lump of wood miles away down the Roden Street hill for me to fetch. The cars and trucks around give a kind of comfort, are a kind of company, as if we are back in an important world. The rural feel of the back yard doesn't diminish that sense of importance here.

And then it happens again: everything is thrown upside down, and all this steadily building stability is smashed into irreparable pieces. I never do get to the bottom of what causes it all, probably because it involves those matters that people always find difficult to speak about, especially to children. My family does not, at that time, have a language to make such things clear without feeling soiled or shamed by their own words. Fragments of memory have stayed with me, but these are frustratingly few. I am playing in the back yard with a ball, and it lands on the tin roof of the chook house and onto the factory roof behind. Kelso bunks me up and I clamber over to retrieve the ball, clattering across the corrugated tin as I go. The noise must have alerted Mac, and he sees me on the factory roof. Then there is angry shouting from all directions, my mother ushers me down off the roof and into the bedroom, and violent scuffling takes place in the hallway, with crashing noises and groans. Ninny is screaming, 'You dirty, dirty wicked man,' and young Heather seems to be yelling at Mac, 'Leave her alone, leave her alone! You bastard dad, leave her alone!' Finally Mac's booming voice in all its Scottish stringency yells, 'Out! The lot of ye! Out! I'll have nay more o'this from any of ye! Out!' followed by a violent slam of the front door. Then quiet. My mother, Ninny and Heather are comforting each other in the dining room as I emerge from the bedroom. The hall mirror lies broken on the carpet, and the telephone, a black wall-mounted type with a separate hand-held receiver, is hanging uselessly from the wall, wrenched off by a feat of considerable strength. But it is not the details of that day that I remember most vividly; it is the atmosphere, the smell almost, of fear and violence in the house. Something, some appalling secret, has burst in that hallway with catastrophic force. As it would be with a bomb, you remember the effects in a daze, without any clear idea of why it happened. And what has been left behind is a family in ruins, of decisions of finality and hatred that will last for lifetimes.

Even now, my fragmented memories are not properly connected by the few scraps of information that have since been relayed to me second-hand. It seems that the clash had been coming for some time. First, Mac, Ninny discovered, was an insatiable womaniser. His actual job in the army was as an entertainment officer, putting on plays and shows of various kinds for the troops stationed in Melbourne. When I learned this, only recently, I marvelled at my childhood impressionability. All that terror of his dummy arm and forbidding voice was based not just on his demeanour, but on some imagined sense of him elevated above us by bitterness, by his impatience with our failure to measure up to ideals hard-won by suffering: the maimed war-hero's disdain for feckless civilians. Now I see he was nothing more than a side-showman. But it was a role that gave him plenty of access to pretty girls and a certain power to wield over them. Apparently Ninny had known for some time that she was well down his list of preferred sexual partners, and that he had married her essentially to do the housework and finish raising his children, work that she did with an unswerving sense of duty. The way she kept the house spotless and treated Angus, Heather and Kelso had always given my child's mind the clear impression that she had spent a lifetime in this house, cleaning, feeding, caring as if the whole menagerie belonged to her; in fact she had been there, I now realise, little over four years. She was already unhappy with this marriage, and possibly even thinking of leaving, though for the time being, and for the sake of my mother and us two boys, it was convenient for her to let us go on living there and say nothing.

But then, the night before the incident with me climbing on the chook-shed roof to fetch the ball, Mac had, in the middle of the night, crept into the bedroom where Heather and my mother slept – Ray was now in a cot – and tried to get into bed beside my mother. I imagine he thought her to be in no position to deny him, an assumption he was no doubt used to making. My mother did not react hysterically, or make a scene, but simply turned him away and told him to go back to his own bed. Next morning, she said nothing, until Mac performed his outburst against me. Then, she returned fire for all to hear. When Ninny heard it she believed it immediately, and joined in the battle against a rampaging Mac. When things quietened down, Ninny would have added it to her reasons for winding up this absurd charade of marriage and family, and discussed with my mother how we could all get out. My adventure on the roof, therefore, is the mere pretext, the spark that lights the fuse that blows the whole Pandora's box open. Mac orders us out of his house, but it is an action we are already preparing to make.

The suddenness means of course a further disintegration of the family. I am taken to North Melbourne to stay with Nair for the time being, a prospect I have not the slightest objection to; my mother takes Ray and moves in with a cousin over the other side of the city. Ninny goes to stay with one of her own cousins, Aunty Myrtle. I never see Mac, or Kelso or any of the Macdonalds ever again, though I gather that Ninny kept in touch with Heather who, not long after all this, fell pregnant to Bill, married him and moved away from Mac. They drop out of my life, and the shroud of secrecy is gradually redrawn over the whole life-turning event. There is a momentary prospect of the violence all flaring again when my father's twin half-brothers, Johnny and Dickie, who are no more than seventeen and still living at home threaten to go down to Roden Street and exact some retribution on Mac. But my mother intervenes and forbids it.

*

I sleep in Johnny's room, because he has joined the army. This would seem a strange thing to do given that the War has just finished, but he has only just become old enough. Besides, they are recruiting to take a clean-up force to Japan, to do whatever has to be done to tidy up after the bombing. Soon Johnny will be going with them. Nair says living in Japan will make him go yellow, like the Japs.

Johnny and Dickie don't look much like each other, despite being twins. Johnny is bigger, heavy-faced, dark-haired, and quite handsome. Dickie is fair and slight, like my father. In fact he looks remarkably like my father, which is why I've always had a special liking for him. Dickie is too old for me to play with; he comes in to sleep and have dinner, and the rest of the time he is working at a job somewhere or mixing with his friends. Johnnie is away with his army unit. The only others in the house are Nair and Uncle Alec, who is my step-grandfather. He is not my father's father, but he is Johnnie and Dickie's father.

Uncle Alec doesn't talk much, but when he does he has a deep, gentle voice, and when he comes in from work he always says, 'Where's that Wookie?' even though he knows Ray is away living with my mother. At times in the night I can hear Uncle Alec coughing, long terrible coughs that come from deep inside him and end up in a hacking spit. Nair says he was gassed in the War, and not to let it worry me or keep me awake. She doesn't.

As a grandmother, Nair is quite different from Ninny. They are both comical in their own ways, or they try to be, but where Ninny is gentle, hard-working and doesn't drink, Nair is tough, hard-mouthed and what my father once called 'a practised drinker'. They do not like each other at all, and rarely meet. Nair insists that Ninny tried to stop my mother marrying Frank, because she thought he wasn't good enough for her. I suspect it was my father's family, especially Nair herself, who gave Ninny cause for concern, once she knew how much time Nair spent in the pub. But as for stopping the marriage, there was no way anyone was going to get between my parents: their love was absolute. Ninny and Nair are just two oldish ladies who happen to be opposed in almost every conceivable way. With Ninny in West Melbourne and Nair in North Melbourne, my father calls them 'the wicked witch of the west and the wicked witch of the north' after we saw The Wizard of Oz up at Mount Macedon. Trouble is, I love them both, and hate to hear them criticising each other.

Sometimes Uncle Alec takes me with him on his waste paper round. He has a horse-drawn cart with a big wooden frame at the back that holds a large hessian bag, and the horse pulls us around to the places in North Melbourne that give him their waste paper to put in it. His horse is called Dolly, and he occasionally hands me the reins and lets me drive it. Funny thing is, Dolly goes where she wants to regardless of what I do; Uncle Alec says pull on the left rein to go left and on the right rein to go right and on both to stop her, but Dolly always beats me to it, because she knows which way to go by heart. She will also pull over whenever it suits her to one of those steel horse troughs that are placed on the side of some of the streets around here, and will have a good long drink of water while we patiently wait for her to finish. Uncle Alec teaches me a song to sing while we are clomping along:

Horsey, keep your tail up, keep your tail up, keep your tail up.

Horsey, keep your tail up, and keep the sun out of my eyes.

It's meant to be rude.

Nair sits at the kitchen table most of the time, always in the same place. Her table has an emerald green velveteen cloth with fringing, and the light shade above has fringing, too. She sits at the end of one side facing the back window, and beside her is an ash tray, a box of Redhead matches, and several small packets of Turf cigarettes. From here, Nair holds court on the events of the day, or places SP bets through her friend Bob Campbell. People drop in for a chat, or else she reads *The Sun* newspaper through the glasses she bought second hand at the Victoria Market, and provides a voluble commentary on the contents. Bob Campbell comes every day, places the notes and coins of any winnings Nair has due to her, and has a cup of tea. He has a huge, booming voice and a bulbous red nose, and always wears exactly the same clothes – a ragged, filthy navy blue suit with a waistcoat displaying a watch chain, a grubby striped shirt buttoned up at the collar but no tie, and a dusty bowler hat. He looks like a clown, or a character out of Dickens, but there is a whiff of danger about him. My mother tells me to keep away from him, and never to go to his place in Abbotsford Street unless I am with someone. Bob Campbell is another one who is always asking where Wookie is. I do go to his house with Dickie one day, and peering through the front door that opens straight onto the street, all I can see are piles of clothes and old newspapers strewn all over the floor and iron-framed bed, and empty beer bottles lined up along the wall. And that particular smell again – poverty, but not just poverty: stale tobacco, sour alcohol, rotting food. 'Not home,' says Dickie, and slams the old front door shut as we leave.

Nair's house is behind a boot repairer's shop, which is why there are only two domestic rooms downstairs: the front room is actually the shop. The doorway through to it has a curtain across it and a sideboard in front of it, so you can't go through. The only way into the shop is through its front door, off the street. Nair's front door is beside this, and opens to a passageway that leads alongside the shop and into her lounge room, which has no windows in it, and is therefore always dark unless the light is on. The shop is run by her brother-in-law, Uncle Garn Woolcock, who actually owns the whole building and lets her and Uncle Alec live there at a modest rent. Uncle Garn has a built-up boot on one leg, and limps noticeably. He sits me up on his counter and chats to me while he goes about his work.

'Did you know North Melbourne have got a new champion in the making down there?' 'No. Who?'

'Young fella called Eyelet. Mick Eyelet.'

'I don't barrack for North Melbourne.'

'Yep, sixteen he is. They reckon he's already a good'n. They can use a few more champions down there, that's for sure.'

They certainly could, I think to myself. North Melbourne is one of the worst teams in the League. A chopping block for the competition, rarely winning a game. The shinboners, they call them, because of their blue and white stripes, like a butcher's apron. Tough, emotional, but always failing, always disappointing. They sum up almost everything about this area in these years – the drunks, the rats in the lanes, the Bob Campbells, the fights, the sense of hopelessness. Despite the fact that everyone I love barracks for North Melbourne –Nair, Uncle Alec, my mother, even my father – I do not. Essendon is my team. They are dramatic, glamorous, slick, and they win often. Just thinking about them makes me feel good. Yet I do go down to Arden Street often and watch North play. Nair says to me, 'Just go up to a man – any man – outside the members entrance, and ask him to take you in for free on his season ticket.' So I do. And maybe three or four games I see in this way. And North always lose.

I watch Uncle Garn mend shoes. First he fits one upside down over an iron last, and with a large pair of pincers rips the old leather sole off. The old tacks all around the rim of the inner sole stick up and have to be removed one by one. Then he takes a sheet of brand new leather, light brown coloured, holds it firmly on the shoe and with a small, very sharp knife, cuts a new sole by tracing around the edge of the shoe. He then takes the new sole, brushes one side with a delicious-smelling glue, presses it firmly in place, and starts tacking it down. His tacking technique is wonderful. He fills his mouth with little black tacks, and almost faster than you can see, takes one from his mouth, places in on the rim of the new sole, and with one stroke of his little fat tack hammer knocks it completely in, all in one movement. So all you hear as he goes around the shoe is bang, bang, bang, in rapid succession, till the sole is firmly on.

'Who do you barrack for then?' he says.

'Essendon.'

'I had a mate played for them years ago. Half back flank.'

'Does he still play for them?'

'Nah, nah, that was years ago, before the First War. Before North entered the competition.'

Now he takes the shoe off the last and sands the edges down on an electric sanding wheel, and then uses the buff at the other end to polish it up nice and smooth. Then he paints the sole with black paint and puts the shoe upside down on a rack alongside other shoes to dry. I love watching him do all this over and over, never varying. He is quick, skilful, and friendly to me at the same time. I spend a lot of my daytime here; I seem to have stopped going to the King Street school, which is quite okay by me.

When my mother visits, we sit around the table with our arms on the green cloth while Nair and my mother gossip. Ray is there too, and gets fussed over by Nair. They are talking about finding us a place to live.

'I went into the Housing Commission again…'

'What they say?'

'Said now that we're classified as homeless, we're eligible for public housing. Said should put us in Camp Pell, but he isn't going to.'

'Why not?'

'Looked me up and down, said a young woman like you, with your looks and no husband, I'm not putting you in Camp Pell. No fear, he said.'

'That's all reffos. Terrible place, Camp Pell. Balts.'

'Anyway, he won't put us in there, he said.'

'Give you a Commission House, will he?'

'Don't think so. They haven't got any.'

'So, what then?'

'Larundel. Said he'd try to find us a place in Larundel.'

'Hmmm, fancy.'

'It's not far from Frank's sanatorium, either.'

'When will you go?'

'Well, it isn't definite yet – he's going to see what he can do. It depends on someone moving out.'

'What is Larundel? Where is it?'

Nair often tells people she has 'gone on the wagon', which at first I think means she might have gone out to collect waste paper with Uncle Alec and Dolly, but which I eventually work out means she has stopped drinking beer. But this doesn't alter the fact that whenever she goes shopping up to Errol Street, she ends up in what she calls the dog-box, and Uncle Alec sends me up to fetch her home. The dog-box is a tiny room at the pub that you can enter straight off the street, with space for one person only to sit on a stool at the small bar. Nair regards this as her own room, because she isn't allowed in the Public Bar, and refuses to drink in the Ladies' Lounge. 'I'm a Kelly,' she says, 'and Kellys don't drink with the ladies.' It's true: her maiden name was Kelly, which is supposed to have some special glamour around the pubs she frequents. I go up to the dog-box to fetch her, and there is usually someone squeezed in beside her as well as the publican behind the bar, all in a huddle of smoke and beery talk. When I turn up they envelop me in an effusive welcome.

'This is Frank's boy. You know Frank, my eldest.'

'Frank's boy? How old are you son?'

'Frank's in the sanatorium.'

'Would you like a lemonade young fella?'

'Give him a shandy.'

'Don't you give him any beer – his mother'll kill me.'

'What are you going to be when you grow up, son?'

'A jockey.' I don't believe this for one moment, but I know it's the answer they will all love to hear. Jockeys are smart, almost heroic in a sport that they all have an interest in, and usually wealthy. Footballers, for instance, have the disadvantage of playing mostly for despised teams, and make little money.

'A jockey? We better keep sweet with ya then.'

'Did Uncle Alec send you up love? You run home and tell him I'll be along soon to get his tea. Tell him I'll get a taxi home.'

My mother says Nair is the most amazing cook. Her house has only two rooms downstairs, the lounge and kitchen, and the bedrooms upstairs. The kitchen is where she cooks and where we eat. There is no sink or bench, only a small basin on the landing at the top of the steps outside. She prepares all the food sitting up at the table with the green velveteen cloth while she is talking, and smoking her Turf cigarettes, so you hardly notice what she is doing. You get so engrossed in what she is saying that you find it hard to believe at dinner time when she goes over to the green and white gas stove in the far corner and takes out a sizzling pan of roast lamb, potatoes and carrots, spoons fresh peas from a saucepan onto the plates she has taken out of the dresser with the glass doors behind her, quickly makes gravy in the roasting pan that she tips into a jug, and we all hoe in to the best roast dinner you could dream up. My mother says she can never make a roast that would compare, no matter how hard she tries. 'It's that oven,' she says in excuse for herself. 'I've never had one as good.'

But I don't think Nair can cook much else. For dinner Dickie often goes up the street and brings home a great newspaper parcel of fish and chips: a piece of flake, which is actually shark, for everyone and enough chips each to cover a large plate, piled high. Dickie and Johnnie always smother theirs in tomato sauce, but Nair squeezes lemon juice over hers, and so do I. She never makes me lunch, and she doesn't seem to eat any herself. Instead she gives me two shillings to go up to Errol Street and by a Rath's pie and a malted milk. There is nothing as good as a Rath's pie – it has peppery, good quality meat, flaky pastry that melts in your mouth. I am never to taste a pie that measures up to it in all the remaining years of my pie-eating life. It costs a shilling, and the milk shake is tenpence, which leaves me with tuppence for a chocolate frog. I buy the milk shake at the corner shop, where the man pours the creamy froth into a large fluted glass for you, then he leaves you the metal container out of which you get a second full glass. I arrive back at Nair's bursting. 'Full as a goog, are you?' she says.

There is a man who owns the paper shop just up Queensberry Street a little from Nair's, before you get to the corner. His name is Mr Lowe. Mr Lowe has no arms, just two small stumps that protrude an inch or two below his short-sleeved shirt. No one seems to know what happened. Nair says he was probably run over by a train, but I think it would have cut his head off as well, if he was lying down with his arms extended; the imaginary line between the two stump-ends goes right through his neck. The stump ends are smooth and rounded, with one made into a little point at the tip. The thing about Mr Lowe's stumps is that he can do the most amazing things with them. When Nair sends me up on Saturday nights to get the Sporting Globe, the shop is very busy and I watch Mr Lowe at work. He can flip through a stack of newspapers to find someone's order as quickly and accurately as someone using their fingers. He picks up ten-shilling notes deftly by bringing the stumps together, and he can count out coins on the counter one at a time, even singling out the threepenny bits, stacking them on one stump and dropping them into the cash register. I've seen him at other times roll a cigarette with them, taking a wad of tobacco out of the pouch with the stumps, placing it on one stump and spreading it evenly with the other, then wetting the paper so that it sticks on one stump while he puts in the tobacco from the other stump, then he rolls it expertly between the stumps, licks the finished cigarette and lights it, all by himself. He is a bald, no-nonsense man with little good humour in him, but he is famous in Queensberry Street and everyone buys their papers from him.

At night I lie awake in the dark listening to the trams rattle past. My bedroom is at the front upstairs, and Queensberry Street runs practically underneath me; the reflections from the tram lights travel across my wall, and the noise the trams make is beautiful. I hear them coming from some distance away, and their wheels squeal as they turn the corner at Abbotsford Street. Something about them is comforting, something suggesting a world getting on with its busy routines, a normality. The trams have always run along here, and I feel they always will, even when, like late at night, there is practically nobody on them. I sometimes get out of bed and watch one from the window, lit up like an empty loungeroom going somewhere: CITY; MARIBYRONG Rvr; ESSENDON, written on the front, and I try to imagine what these destinations might be like when the tram arrives there.

Much as I like living with Nair, as I did with Ninny until things went wrong, it has all been an unsatisfactory time since we left Mount Macedon. We are disintegrating and directionless, like a wrecked ship with people and pieces floating off in all directions. We badly need the centred feeling, the light, that my father gives. Even when he is sick and can't work we are better off with him than without him. He binds us together, makes us into a family. As we are, we are just people drifting apart. The first thing we need is a place of our own to live in, but there is no indication of that happening yet. If we get that, maybe my father will join us. I want this more than anything.

It is a Saturday night, and Nair and Uncle Alec go to a party around in Abbotsford Street. Because they can't leave me home on my own, they take me along. It is a small house, crammed full of people drinking, talking, shouting at one another. The noisier it gets the louder they have to shout to be heard. There are no other children there, so it is very boring for me. Fortunately, Nair has given me the money to buy a new Captain Marvel comic from Mr Lowe's, and I go through into the kitchen and read it sitting up at the table. Even in the kitchen there are people crowded in, bumping me with their backsides, arguing loudly over the top of me. A man is pressing himself into the front of a woman, backing her against the wall and kneading her breast with his hand on her white pullover as if he were making dough. When he tries to lick the side of her neck he shifts suddenly and knocks over a bottle of beer, and it floods across the table onto my comic and into my lap. This is awful; I wish I were somewhere quiet by myself.

Then there is a commotion from the lounge room and someone screams, 'Fucken bitch!' I can hear Uncle Alec saying, 'Lize! Lize! Come out of it. Come out of it Lize!' I push my way through into the lounge room and see Nair holding a woman by the front of her blouse, pulling her close into her. Uncle Alec is trying to get past several bodies to reach Nair, but suddenly it is too late. Placing her cigarette between her lips, Nair delivers a short, almost unnoticeable right fist into the woman's face, and her nose makes a strange smacking sound. Then there are people pulling Nair away, the woman is screaming in strange ape-like whoops, the blood dribbles through the fingers she holds to her face, and Nair is saying, with calm intent, 'I'm a Kelly, don't you forget that. A Kelly. Don't forget it.'

The room has gone dead quiet and Uncle Alec pulls both Nair and myself out through the open front door and hurries us away. From the front step the woman's daughter is yelling abuse at us: 'We'll remember this, Woolcock. My father will make you pay. Just don't drink up at the Town Hall in future, that's all.'

Uncle Alec, too, is berating Nair for fighting. 'That's the last time; back on the wagon for you.'

'Don't you start.'

'What was it about anyway?'

'Damn! I just remembered. I've left two good cold bottles of beer back there in her ice chest.'

'Do you want me to go back and get them Nair?' I say.

'Listen to him, he's an angel. Do anything for his grandmother, wouldn't ya love?'

'He's not going back there,' says Uncle Alec.

'Whaddya think I am? I know he's not.'

'And remember, you're on the wagon from now on.'

We make our way up Queensberry Street, the three of us. Nair holds my hand as we cross the road. Suddenly she laughs that wheezy exhalation peculiar to smokers, but there is no humour in it.

'Anyway, she's been looking for that for ages. She tells lies. About me, about you; thinks she's better than us because she owns that house. Goes around telling people we're not married.'

'But we're not married.'

'That's not the point.'

*

My mother takes Ray and me into the city; walking past Myers window in Lonsdale Street, we spot Uncle Les in the grocery section. He is wearing a white coat, and waves to us to come in. He is smiling with his big teeth and talking in that slow, deep voice while he slips two tins of peas into my mother's handbag. She protests, but he puts his finger to his lips and makes her take them. Then mum and I have lunch in the cafeteria of Coles in Bourke Street, sitting on a stool up at the long bench. This is absolute luxury to me. I have a plate of mixed sandwiches cut into little triangles, and each one is something of a surprise –egg and lettuce, corn beef and pickle, cheese and gherkin; my mother has to tell me what each one is. There is a delicious smell of coffee in the air, so I have a cup of that, too, for the first time. It needs lots of sugar, then it's okay. Afterwards, we go down an arcade off Collins Street to the factory where she used to work. She wheels Ray's pusher into a dark, rattly old lift with diamond shaped folding steel doors. Upstairs is a whole big room of women sitting at benches and working at sewing machines, with clothing materials and garments all over the place. When we arrive a number of the women give my mother a friendly greeting; obviously they are old girlfriends, and she is very much at home amongst them. When she takes Ray in with her to talk with the manager about her getting some part-time work, they joke with me:

Have you got a girlfriend yet?

He's going to be one for the ladies, I can see that.

Break a few hearts.

Takes after his father.

Let's feel your muscles.

Afterwards, we go to the Housing Commission office, where the man confirms that he has found a place for us at Larundel, and that we can move in soon. My mother is very pleased at this news. When we come out she is so happy that she says, 'Let's go to an hour show; they'll have lots of cartoons.' So we head back along Bourke Street and go downstairs to a tiny basement picture theatre that runs all the time; after an hour you've seen all the newsreels, shorts and cartoons and they begin over again. You could stay all day if you could stand the repetition. The newsreels are grainy black and white, full of fire and explosions and people milling about, with the dramatically urgent tones of Ed Herlihy filling the little auditorium. I can just glean that they are about places where the War was, but the images of skeletal people and piled-up bodies are compelling. In contrast, the cartoons are well-meaning but boring – chickens dancing and singing to Mexican music, and Pluto the dog getting himself into unlikely mischief. Outside, we all have an ice-cream and catch the tram back to Queensberry Street; on the way, a drunk insists on singing 'Moonlight Becomes You' to my mother as she sits holding onto Ray's pusher and I look out the window. When I check her response she is trying to ignore him and looking tight-lipped at nothing-in-particular. In all it is a great day out for me, teaching me a lot about the city – how to catch trams, what kind of food and entertainment you can get, where some of our friends can be found. The city, I decide, is even better than Mount Macedon.

There is one more memory I have of the time just before we leave North Melbourne: we visit my father at Greswell sanatorium. It takes a long time and several buses for us to get to the outlying northern suburbs and beyond, and when we do it consists of a number of wooden huts standing in broad park-like grounds with a few small trees around. A narrow road winds through the grounds. My father is sitting on the end-porch of his hut. He is not in his pyjamas and checked dressing gown, but in a shirt and trousers, and he looks quite well. He shows us his macrame materials and some of the slippers and soft toys he is making, mostly to send to children in hospitals. It is wonderful to see him, but also very sad, because he isn't allowed out. It is just like a prison. I have to keep a distance between him and myself, and once again this brings on the ache. Would it matter if I just sat in his lap, lay my head against his chest? Would I get tuberculosis from just doing that? I don't think so. Yet we all stick strictly to the rules. He is so gentle, so pleasant, so clever, and yet what is his life? He must go mad here all day by himself. He is so happy to be with my mother and us; I know it will hurt him to the very quick when we leave to go home.

5

I AM NOW A PRACTISING Catholic. I am preparing for my first Holy Communion, which will take place later in the year. The nuns are teaching us all the things we need to know, and to keep our souls in a fit state to receive the Lord. So we must learn to make our first confessions, which means recalling all our sins to date and telling them to the priest in the Confessional. I have a hard time trying to remember the sins in my life to this point, especially since it is not clear to me just what is a sin and what isn't. Is hitting David with the cricket bat a sin? Is throwing the stone at the girl a sin? Was it a sin to look upon the Smith girl under her dress? I know I feel shame about these things, so I can't ask anyone whether they are sins or not. I have also learned that I am in a state of Original Sin, which means that even if I hadn't personally done anything wrong, I'd still be a sinner.

I have started at a new school now that we live at Larundel. Every day I catch an orange-coloured bus to the West Preston terminus, then walk down the hill to school, St Bernadette's in West Preston; it is small, and converts into a church for Sunday Mass when the dividing doors between the two rooms are opened. I am in grade three, but what we learn is not interesting. We spend a lot of time learning the catechism:

Who made you?

God made me.

Why did God make you?

God made me to know Him, love Him and serve Him in this world, and to be happy with Him forever in the next.

The nuns are both old, with flowing black habits and white wimples. One of them is particularly severe, and beats the children on the backs of their legs with a long ruler if they do anything wrong. She seems to be constantly hawking in her throat and discharging the snot through her mouth into a white handkerchief. She never smiles. On either side of her nose a long disappointment crease runs down her cheek.

West Preston is different from North or West Melbourne; it is one of the outlying northern suburbs, where there is a mixture of country and city. The streets are bitumen, but there are grassy vacant blocks between houses. Larundel is a half-hour bus ride farther out in an area called Bundoora, which is almost a country town. Straw-coloured paddocks stretch away to the horizon. My father's sanatorium is somewhere around here, as in fact is a place called Mont Park, which is where they keep mentally retarded people. 'Loonies', all the kids at Larundel call them. So together with Larundel, which is a series of brick buildings to house the homeless, this seems to be a broad remote area set aside for people of misfortune of one kind or another. We are among them.

Our flat is upstairs on the first floor; you go straight off a long public corridor into the kitchen, which opens to a bedroom on each side, one for my mother and one for Ray and me. There is no bathroom; you have to go down to the communal toilets and showers at the end of the corridor – women at one end, men at the other. Everything smells of disinfectant and cooking, and there is never any hot water in the showers in the afternoons.

There is a certain frenetic quality to our time here. People are in a state of deep unhappiness, and it occasionally bursts through the surface. Just on our floor there are two women who have frequent fits, though they are not actually sick in the way, for instance, that my father is. Mrs Davies and Mrs Waghorn will unexpectedly explode into screams, or go running along the corridor shouting at no one. The last time, Mrs Waghorn had to be held down on the corridor floor by Barney Lee and Mr Waghorn, and she had foam and spit coming out of her mouth. It is as if she is possessed, but you know that the demons are not so much inside her as all around her in the form of terrible forces that drag her spirits down: dirt and squalor, that smell of poverty always in their flat, the unemployment of the men, the lack of anything enjoyable to do. Mrs Davies, who has a large purple stain across her face, is quieter and furtive looking, and positively dangerous, my mother says, so we keep our distance from her and her two daughters. Things are just too much for them – the poverty, the crowdedness (the Waghorns have four children in the same size flat as ours), the humiliation that sits over all of us like a black cloud. We are society's outcasts, so we think like it, behave like it.

I, too, have some of this unhappiness in me, and it emerges one day in a capacity for violence that takes me completely by surprise. I am downstairs playing on the covered concrete walkway that runs between the red brick buildings of Larundel, as you see in hospitals; Larundel is more like a hospital than anything else. A group of children that includes three of the Waghorn children, Arthur, Marjorie, and Deirdre who is a couple of years older than me, plus a number of boys about my age from one of the buildings farther away, start picking on me for some reason. I say 'some reason', when really I know that their lives are as full of unhappiness and frustration as mine, and that they look upon every unfamiliar face, such as mine, as just one more threat that must be confronted. I am not an aggressive child, I do not look for fights. But as they gang up on me, first calling me names and then Marjorie slaps my face quite hard, I realise that it is me against all of them; they are united and are moving in on me just as they did on the fat boy at school in Mount Macedon, who just stood there crying and taking it all. I do not take it. I hit back. They have me almost trapped in a corner where the brick walls meet, but I start fighting my way out. I punch, wildly. I kick Arthur Waghorn in the balls. I seize Marjorie Waghorn by the hair and swing her around several times and then let her go so that her head hits the wall with a hollow thud. I get one of the other boys in a headlock and wrestle him to the ground, sit on him, punch at his face. I want to do this until I kill him. I am soon up and so unstoppably wild, so frenzied in my determination to beat them all off, that they back away. The fear has left me and entered them now. I am still hitting out at them when a man I've never seen before intervenes and puts a stop to it. 'Come on now, break it up, break it up. Go home all of you, go home and find something better to do. Go on. Home.'

With them all gone, the man wants to speak to me, kneels at my side and wipes the tears and dirt from my face with a handkerchief.

'Now young feller, that was some fight you put up there. That's a lot of spirit you've got. But you know, you could use that spirit a little bit better, a little bit more skilfully. Now over at the sports centre we have a gymnasium, and we have a boxing competition; I think you'd make a great little Golden Gloves candidate after a bit of training, a bit of teaching how to handle yourself. Whaddya say you come over Thursday night and we'll see how you go? Are you prepared to give it a shot?'

I did go, and I did take up regular boxing lessons. The thing that I found surprising was how easy it was to beat people in the ring. I can't say I liked it much, but not because I ever got hurt. The punches in the face with the gloves made my eyes water and gave me that stunned, burning sensation behind the nose, but that didn't particularly worry me, and it didn't last long. No, the reason I didn't like it was because I liked it. I could feel myself enjoying landing good punches on another boy's face, and the more he was hurt and backed away, the more I went after him and contrived to land that one terrific effective punch that would destroy him. Yet while I was doing this I was conscious of how wrong it was to want it and do it. Once you knew you could beat another boy, there was nothing to be gained from going ahead and doing it but a kind of shameful sadism. But I did keep going to the gym and boxing for some months, without it ever being important to me. It taught me a few techniques and to not mind being hit, but that's about all. What mattered about the day I fought off that attack was what I learned about myself: that if pushed far enough, and I would have to be pushed very far to reach the extremities I had then discovered, I was capable of terrible violence. There is a pool of anger lying deep within me that, if released, could be murderous. And, thankfully, it has rarely been released.

At school, the less unpleasant of the old nuns tells us the story of Christ. How they victimised him, contrived to find him guilty of something so they could bring him down. He was a good man, who went around healing the sick, helping the poor, imparting a gentle grace wherever he went. All he wanted was for people to love each other. But the world of power and politics was against him, and they treated him brutally and finally crucified and killed him. This is what was happening in the pictures around the walls I saw with my father at Mass that day – the beatings, the driving of the nails, the image of the cross against the sky, just like I would often see on Mount Macedon. As the nun talks it all comes back again, and her detailed, emotionally indulgent account has a similarly moving effect on me:

'Imagine the pain, children, imagine having nails driven through your hands and feet –big nails as thick as pencils – and a ring of thorns hammered into your head. Imagine a spear piercing your side and being left hanging almost naked up on a hill for days. The pain alone would kill you. But this is what Jesus suffered for us, to save every one of us.'

I can feel the tears welling up in me at the sheer unfairness of it all, at the brutal indifference of the world to a man's goodness. Show any sign of gentleness, and they will punish you for it. Show any sign of weakness, and they will take advantage of it.

But the Romans had made a big mistake, says the nun: 'What they didn't realise until it was too late was that he was the son of God, and therefore a version of God himself. So he had the power to rise from the dead, and appeared in person to his disciples, who could hardly believe their eyes. He asked one of the doubters to feel his wounds, place his fingers inside the hole in his side. Then he ascended bodily into heaven, and the Romans, for their wickedness, were cast into Hell.'

The part that makes the deepest impression on me is her description of the disciple placing his fingers in the wound; this is the proof of Christ's humanness, and of his capacity to inspire love. This is the test of love. I, too, would do this, willingly, I tell myself, willingly touch his pale, ravaged body because it would enable me to know what love feels like to the skin, what power the source of his pain, the wound, might have to connect with my own pain and perhaps even assuage it. This is what I find so thrilling, finally, in the story of Christ: that he has the power to transcend the world's pain and injustice, that he can transform his victimhood into a triumph. It is what I want to happen to me, to my father: to let the touch of skin cure the pain inside. If I could only cuddle him, throw my arms around him and hold him close.

After that terrible fight, relations settle down between me and the other children. They never try to pick on me again, and in fact most of my time out of school is spent playing contentedly with them. They are not Catholics, which I am perfectly happy about; the only other Catholic I know at Larundel is a boy called Robert Delaney, who goes to my school. Robert lives in one of the blocks on the other side of the complex, but he is also a bit delicate, a bit of a sissy, so on both these counts I don't have much motivation to play with him.

The Waghorns go to a State school somewhere – when they go to school, that is. True to their name, they constantly wag school. When I feel bold enough, I join them, deliberately missing the orange bus and heading off to the incinerators a few blocks over from ours. We spend a lot of time at the incinerators, mucking about with the fire and smoking 'cigarettes' made of rolled up waste paper. We inhale pure paper smoke. A couple of times during the hot weather we head off over the distant paddocks to a dam full of gravy-coloured water, take off all our clothes, and spend the day lazing in the sun. There is Arthur and the two girls Marjorie and Deirdre, and a boy called Geoff Parnell, who is pretty smart. Arthur is well built and has clear, olive skin, but the rest of us are pale and freckled. Arthur shows us his rupture, which means basically he has only one ball. I ask him if it was caused when I kicked him. 'No, I've always had it. You made it hurt, but.'

We find some bits of wood and other stuff in an old farm shed and make a raft, which we then float on the dam and jump from into the water, over and over. Deirdre constantly sings a song, 'Sailing down the river, on a Sunday afternoon' as she lies on her back in only her cotton pants on the raft. We boys are naked, so we don't have to go home with wet clothes. I try to put my guilt out of my mind and enjoy it as much as the others seem to, but all the time I have a nagging fear that when you do something wrong like this, like wagging school and taking off your clothes, there is some way you are going to be found out. I guess it will be something to confess. When the time comes.

Sure enough, that night at home, I am found out. My mother sees me dressing for bed, and before I get my pyjamas on she says, 'What have you been doing today?'

'Nothing. Just school.'

'You're telling me lies.'

'No.'

'I'll ask you again. What did you do today?'

'Nothing. I told you.'

'Well, I know you're not telling the truth. Do you know how?'

'How?'

'You're sunburned from your neck to your feet.'

'Am I?' And as she says it, I feel the hot tingle over my back. I hadn't really noticed it before.

'And your face,' she says. 'Where did you go?'

'We went to a dam over in the back paddocks.'

'Who with?'

'The Waghorns and Geoff Parnell.'

'Without your swimsuit.'

'Yes.'

'Never, never do it again. Do you hear? What would daddy say if he knew you were wagging school, taking off your clothes? What would he say?'

I didn't really have a clear idea of what he would say, but I had to concede to my mother's greater knowledge of what he would say, which I guessed would have been intense disapproval. But at least, under the circumstances of the moment, he was unlikely to find out.

There is a boy in grade four named Kevin Green who is famous in the school for singing cowboy songs and yodelling brilliantly. If there is a concert, or if the nuns just ask him to perform for us all at lunchtime, he stands up on a chair and sings unaccompanied while the whole school sits very impressed and applauds enthusiastically. Then, without any apparent reason he stops coming to school, and after a few weeks one of the nuns addresses us at lunchtime, and says very solemnly:

'Kevin Green has died...'

Can anyone so young just die? I ask myself. This means we won't see him or hear him sing ever again. A shadow of sadness passes through me. The nun goes on:

'Yes, little Kevin Green has died. And let this be a lesson to all of you.'

Kevin Green bought his lunch down the street at the milk bar every day. And almost every day he bought a pastie and ate it. And now he has died. So tell your parents, all of you, that it is not healthy to buy your lunch and eat pies and pasties every day. Tell them to send you to school with a healthy lunch. Salad sandwiches.'

I am shocked at her assertion. Even at eight years old I have enough sense to know she is talking rubbish. Pies and Pasties can't kill you, or everyone would know about it. I've eaten pies at Nair's many times, and my mother has eaten pasties. Admittedly they were Rath's, but the nun isn't saying don't eat just one brand of pie or pastie, but any. The nuns like to make things up, I realise. Storytelling is their way, and not always very convincing.

*

I am in the kitchen with the late morning sunlight streaming through the window when there is a knock at the door. I open it and standing there, hatless, an apparition drained pale by the effect of the sun on his hair and face, wrapped in a dark wool overcoat, is my father. He carries a Gladstone bag in his hand, and smiles beautifully as his eyes light on me. 'Hello son,' he says. 'Where's your mother?'

It is the first of several unannounced, magical appearances. I say magical, but his presence is real, without any question. He has, in effect, escaped from the sanatorium. Unable to bear the loneliness any longer, desperate to be with us, his family, he has thrown a few things into a bag, pulled on his overcoat over his pyjamas, put on some shoes, and walked out of the place. Somehow he has evaded the authorities, somehow he has negotiated the few miles between Greswell and here, and found us. It is he, in the flesh. He looks wonderful to me, though when he strips off his coat and sits down breathing hard at the kitchen table in his pyjamas it is clear that he is exhausted from the effort. His face is thinner, his eyes bluer than I remember; it is, after all, almost a year since I last saw him, but it feels like a lifetime. My heart burns from joy, and I have him to myself for a short time until my mother comes up from doing the washing down in the communal laundry. I try to think of something to say that will please him.

'I am making my first Communion next week.'

'I know it, and look what I've brought you.'

He takes from his bag a glossy white hard-covered Missal. Inside the front cover is a delicate relief moulding of the Virgin Mary in cream bakelite. There are coloured pictures throughout, illustrating the Mass and scenes from the life of Christ, and its pages are fine and elegantly printed. It feels a great treasure to me, as much for where it comes from as for what it is.

He sits up in my mother's double bed and listens to the wireless. He tells me, 'Essendon and Carlton are playing in the Grand Final; who do you think will win?'

'Essendon, of course.'

'Well, I'll tell you what: I'll give you sixpence if they win.'

He listens to the game on the wireless while I am out playing. When I come inside he says Essendon has lost by a single point. It is the tone of disappointment in his voice as much as the news of so narrow a failure that prompts me to tears. He is a little shocked by my collapse.

'Hey, hey come on. It's not that bad, only a game. I tell you what, I'll give you the sixpence anyway. Okay? C'mon, cheer up now, here you are.'

Once again the power of his love elevates me to a place of happiness. Once again he is my saviour and my guiding hand. I know I've been stupid and soft in giving way to tears, and that I should have taken the disappointment in a more manly way, but I was responding to a note of dejection in him, and in that I have no choice but to go down with him. But it has provided an occasion for him to be generous to me, and for this I have nothing but gratitude.

He stays for a couple of days and then leaves, returning to the sanatorium. But in the meantime he has cheered us up. He watched from the bedroom window as, down below, I demonstrated to him my football-kicking ability. Unfortunately it was still in the early stages of its development, and I couldn't bring myself to actually put foot to ball until I had run half the length of a field first. I think I was almost out of his line of vision by the time I completed the kick. According to my mother, my father said, 'Give him a letter to post, it'll save us the walk.'

Magical because of its suddenness, its unexpectedness; I am left with the impression that he is capable of coming and going, that if he chooses he can simply appear. And that is something I didn't know before, and it fills me with a kind of hope for the future.

The time passes at Larundel as a kind of squalid quarantine before a better life to come. That will happen when we get the Commission house we have applied for. We are in the queue, and the government is building them now as fast as it can. Some families have already moved out and into theirs. The place names become familiar to us all as signifiers of utopian dreams: West Heidelberg; Preston; Reservoir; Coburg. Where will our house come up? What kind of place will we get? Will it have a garden? You took whatever one was available when it was your turn.

Ted the Looney wanders around the blocks in the daytime, hanging around the kids when they are playing, leaning against the brick buildings talking to himself. The kids all like him because he carries a bag of boiled sweets in his pocket, bought with his weekly allowance. He breaks into their games to hand them out, carefully, as if each sweet is purposefully selected for that child. I hesitate to take it sometimes because the bag is so crumpled and soiled from his pocket, I wonder what might end up in my mouth. He is also unshaven and his clothes are old, which makes him a little scary. Every night he finds his way back to Mont Park, where he sleeps and gets fed. Some of us kids venture over there one Sunday afternoon and discover an orchard of apple trees in full fruit. But when we start picking them a couple of the loonies, including Ted, come running towards us shouting at us to clear off. At least, I suppose they are all loonies.

*

My mother has been working at the dressmakers' in the city a couple of days a week; we need the money, especially since uniforms, my First Communion, bus fares, make it more expensive to send me to Catholic school. She leaves Ray with Mrs Parnell, whose flat is up near the Larundel entrance; she is one of the longest residents here, and has two sons, Geoff and James, who are nearly grown up. Mrs Parnell likes looking after Ray.

It means that, for a couple of days during the week at least, I am completely free to do what I want. Naturally, rather than going to school, I spend my time mucking about with the other kids who don't go to school, exploring across the paddocks, more swimming in the dam (I learn to keep my shirt on when I'm not actually in the water now), long treks through fields of farm produce – sweet corn towering two feet above my head, crops of broad beans that stretch on and on. This is still a country area, even though the tramline is only half an hour away by bus, and the red brick buildings of Larundel stand up in the paddocks like city buildings out of place. It is on one of these free days that I have what could be termed my first experience of sex, the Smith girl at Mount Macedon notwithstanding. It is Deirdre Waghorn's idea, on an occasion when we are mucking about at the incinerators, smoking, lighting small fires in the rubbish piles, singing and telling war stories, mostly about fictional Jap atrocities.

'Let's do some fucks,' she says.

Geoff Parnell agrees. 'I'll fuck on you,' he says to Deirdre, 'and Garry can fuck on Marjorie. Arthur can keep a look out for anyone coming.' There seems to be a tacit recognition that Arthur is disqualified from fucking his sisters.

'Where can we go?' Marjorie asks. Geoff knows a good spot at one of the unused residential blocks. We all traipse over to it, a cold and silent ghost block, with broken windows and the smell of urine in every corner. Deirdre and Geoff go out of sight at the far end of the building, and Marjorie and I seclude ourselves in a dark place under the concrete stairs. It stinks, but I am too nervous to care. I am not sure what to do, having only the vaguest notion what fucking means, apart from being a good swear word. I ask Marjorie for advice: 'Do we lie down?'

'I lie down and you lie on top of me,' she says. 'I've done it with Geoff before, and that's what we did.' She takes off her dress and pants, spreads them on the concrete floor, and lies down on them. I am aware that my penis has somehow to be brought into play, so I take down my trousers and lie on top of her. It's a bit uncomfortable, but her slightly fat body is a nice warm shield against the cold floor. We stay like this for a time, with her grunting now and then from my weight. I can hear Arthur out there throwing stones at the building, managing to shatter one or two more windows against the silence. I begin to envy him. After a while Marjorie says, 'You're not doing it properly.'

'Why not?'

'Well Geoff sort of … moves it up and down, in and out. You're just lying still.' Since I have no idea what she is referring to, and indeed have no instrument with which up and down or in and out are meaningful or indeed possible actions, I give up and roll off her.

'It's no good,' I say, a little ashamed of my failure to measure up to Geoff's standards, but otherwise not really aware of how farcically abject my attempt has been. The full embarrassment doesn't hit me for another decade, when I at least have some understanding of what qualifications fucking actually requires. But at eight years old I had not even had my first erection, and was merely trying to enact in the callow flesh what had been nothing more substantial than a rumour passed from child to child, inspired perhaps by the word adultery in the sixth Commandment. Adultery. This was a word full of intrigue and obfuscation that always tantalised the imagination into a desire to know, to experience what is exclusive to the realm of adulthood and so important to them that it must be controlled by law. But children read adults against the grain, and always want what they are told they should not want.

Deirdre and Geoff Parnell return from their end of the building quiet and flushed in the face. Despite the casualness with which we all went into these actions, I have the sense that they, at least, have attained some state of knowledge, some contact with the secrets of adultery, adultery even if it can't be grasped or talked about. I regard them both with a degree of awe, as one looks at people who have achieved some impressive feat, come through some difficult ordeal and are the stronger for it. As we leave the decrepit building behind and go back to playing with the incinerator fires, I wished I had been able to do what they did.

But eventually I learn that what they did, and what I tried to do, was in fact a serious sin, which it was necessary to confess. It wasn't adultery, I learn during a religious instruction class, it was impurity. The nuns tells us there are three kinds of sins of impurity: thought, word and deed, and I conclude that what we did was all three. Of course the others, not being Catholics, won't have to confess it, but I do when I make my First Confession. This is another event in my life that leaves a deep impression, but for an odd reason. From behind the grille in the Confessional, the priest questions me in a soft voice: 'What do you want to tell me, my child?'

'I have told lies.'

'How many times?'

'Forty.' (This is nothing but a wild guess and probably an overestimation, but it seemed wiser to allow for some credit rather than underestimate and leave some lies unabsolved.)

'Anything else?'

'I have committed sins of impurity.'

'What kinds of impurity?'

'Impure thoughts – about twenty times.'

'Yes.'

'Impure words, about thirty times.'

'Yes.'

'Impure deeds, twice.'

'These impure deeds, child. Were they alone or with others?'

'With others.'

'And these others, were they persons or animals?'

My mind goes numb. Animals? Can you commit impure deeds with animals? What? How?

'Child?'

'Oh, others, children …'

'Is there anything else?'

'No Father.'

He gives me my penance – a string of Hail Marys and Our Fathers and tells me to make a sincere Act of Contrition, then mutters absolution in Latin while I wait for him to finish and send me off. As I emerge from the Confessional I feel light and cleansed, just as the nuns told me I would feel, with the image planted by them in my head of my soul white and spotless as a freshly laundered tea towel. Theoretically, at least, I could walk in front of a bus now and be killed and go straight to Heaven. But animals? That is a strange thought to ponder; I resolve to keep my eyes and ears open in case anyone else knows something about it.

The next day I make my First Holy Communion, which goes off pretty much as we rehearsed it. My mother was there, proud of me dressed in my best short-trousered suit and carrying my Missal carefully in my hand. A certain fear enters my mind as the priest places the wafer on my tongue; we had been warned so solemnly by the nuns to make sure we didn't bite it or chew it or let it fall that my mouth has become dry from nervousness and the wafer clings to the roof of my mouth like a limpet until I can work up enough saliva to disintegrate it.

'Remember, it is the precious body of Our Lord, and you don't want to inflict suffering on it like the Jews did,' said the nun.

Outside the church we line up for the group photograph, the girls all wearing their white veils and carrying bouquets, and the boys with white rayon sashes over their suits. Afterwards, we retire into the already reconverted schoolrooms and are let loose upon tables of sandwiches, sausage rolls, cakes and orange cordial by way of breakfast after our long night's fasting. I gorge myself so much that I don't want any lunch.

*

Christmas arrives, and my father appears again. This time he has permission to be with us over the holidays, and sits himself up in the double bed bolstered by pillows and surrounded by things he wants to do – books, newspapers, writing materials, his macrame work, and continues to listen to the wireless. We are visited by Nair, Uncle Alec, Dickie and Johnny who has come home on leave from Japan. It is a hot day, and we sit in the bedroom around my father. Nair complains about the distance we live from North Melbourne, but Uncle Alec shushes her up. My father says, 'What difference does it make to you? You just do what you do every Christmas – give the taxi driver ten quid for the day to take you round to all your relatives. It's not costing you any more.'

'It's too far,' she says. 'I get uncomfortable sitting in the taxi for so long.'

'You get thirsty you mean.'

Johnny takes some large photographs out of a buff-coloured envelope and hands them round. They are black and white and at first seem to be just blotches that don't make any sense. Johnny explains: 'Hiroshima. This is what the atom bomb did.'

The blotches resolve into a grid of streets that separate blocks of blackened, unidentifiable rubble and twisted matter. Only the odd post or partial wall is standing out of the morass.

'I bought these when I was there; we had to clean up a lot of the mess. There was nothing left of the city, and that was from just one bomb.'

Another photograph is of a woman showing her back, which has large areas of skin burnt off and charred pieces hanging off at the edges.

'Look at this one,' says Johnny. 'You can see the person's shadow on the step where they were standing when the blast hit them.'

Indeed, you could see the outline of a human form on a stone step. Can this be true? Could a blast be so quick, so powerful, that it blows away the person and leaves their shadow behind? The feeling we all have, I can sense, is that this is a new enormity in the world, that there is something grave and frightening, even shameful, in what has been done at Hiroshima. It isn't something any of us have the words to express. Suddenly, our side in the War has fought without the fairness and decency we claimed for ourselves, and in putting an abrupt stop to the fighting we have also put a stop to our righteousness and our heroism. These photographs are to stay in my mind for decades afterward.

'It's hot,' says Nair, waving a piece of paper in her face. 'You should have a fan. Frank needs a fan, Thelma.' And she takes some notes out of her purse and presses them into my mother's hand.

After we have tea and scones, they all get up to leave. My father stays in bed as we walk with them to where the taxi stands waiting for them near the entrance gate. Nair makes derisory comments about Larundel all the way: 'No bathroom and lavatory of your own? They've got a bloody cheek.'

'All those steps. It's criminal expecting an invalid to climb all those steps.'

'The sooner you get out of this place the better.'

The taxi driver sits reading the paper and listening to his car radio. He looks pleased to be going at last. Nair winds down her window and blows us a kiss. 'See you with no clothes on,' she calls as the taxi pulls away. 'See you with no clothes on,' we call back, waving.

Not very long after that visit at Larundel, we received the news that a Commission House was now available for us. It meant, to my mother especially, that the lowest point in our social dignity had been negotiated and could begin to be put behind us. And because my father was allowed to stay with us for the time being at least, it also meant that we were back together as a family again, albeit in a somewhat fragile state.

It was never explained to me why my father was allowed to come home to be with us. I assumed, if I thought about it at all, that his condition had improved. He could occasionally, during this time, be relatively active – he would put on his checked dressing gown and walk about the flat, and certainly he was fully alert talking, reading, listening to his favourite radio programs. It was almost back to some sort of normality, except that he was – it was the word always used to describe him now – an invalid. This word came to have a special resonance for me, always suggesting a special state of being for which allowances had to be made. Invalids don't work, don't leave the house, don't wear everyday clothes, don't drink, don't smoke, don't fully participate in the usual routines of life, like shopping, driving cars, going to the football, playing games, walking in the park. So allowing for the fact that he was an invalid, he nevertheless seemed to be very much alive and with us, and that is as much as I cared to ask for; just being in the same room with him was enough for me. I was happy if he were going to stay like this. But I now wonder if there was a more sinister reason for letting him come home: that his condition had deteriorated to a point from which there would be no recovery, that there was nothing more they could do for him, and that he might as well be happily amongst his family in his decline as unhappily alone with the same inevitable outcome. But I did not sense this at the time.

For me, Larundel was a time of vivid, almost hallucinatory experience. The blend of religious instruction, delinquency and deceit that characterised my daily life at that time threw me out of balance morally and psychologically; almost no evidence of my true abilities, my intelligence, my verbal and physical skill, was allowed to show forth in that tense and unhappy limbo. What did emerge, almost by necessity, was a boy intensely combative and confused, utterly directionless, and subject to chaotic imaginative impressions. With my father absent, my mother struggling under the weight of effort to keep us going on what little we had, and therefore too busy and too depressed to give me the parental focus I needed, I fell under the unqualified influence of ignorant nuns and a derelict environment. My mother, remember, was still hardly more than a girl, twenty seven years old, and with the prospect of widowhood already staring her in the face. Little wonder she was not up to reining in the smart-arsed, lying boy I had become. In my defence I can only plead my tender years, and the circumstances that would have distorted the life of almost anyone. Thankfully we were there only eighteen months.

6

120 VALENTINE STREET, WEST IVANHOE was the first house we felt able to call our own. Even though it was rented, at a manageable rate, from the Housing Commission, the fact that it was brand new and ours for as long as we wanted, made it feel like our property. It was modest-sized, had five rooms and stood on a quarter of an acre of uncultivated land. And while Housing Commission residences, and the people in them, were regarded as socially inferior, we nevertheless felt fortunate to have the chance of a new start that government policy provided.

The great bonus for us in this move was that my father was allowed to come with us, in fact living with us again. He could not manage any physical work, but he nevertheless was able to act as something of an overseer in his pyjamas and dressing gown while the furniture removalists took our belongings into the house. He stood on the verandah surveying the scene like some recuperating lord in exile, quiet, observant, as happy as I'd seen him in ages.

Gathered around our arrival was a group of frecklefaced look-alikes from across the road, who all turned out to be called Cloney. There was Bernie, who willingly pitched in to help carry in our belongings, and a spray of smaller boys and girls – Frankie, Josie, Patricia and Catherine. Bernie was maybe two years older than me, and I immediately gravitated to his open-mannered energy and good-heartedness. He laughed out loud when my father commented that with the long grass growing on all our front yards, they were 'going to need a haircut.'

Our house had certain experimental features. Its external cladding was roughcast cement rendered over nothing more substantial than a chicken wire base; if it cracked, pieces could fall off. There were not many of these houses – most were brick veneer or weatherboard – so we were unlucky to get one. Its internal walls were made of a new material called Canite – a processed sugar cane product, thickish but soft enough for the surface to break if you fell against it. None of these shortcomings bothered us, because the advantages were too evident; the house was light and airy inside, with big modern windows, a functional family-sized kitchen, and a bathroom with a shower heated by a gas water system. My mother soon had the good hardwood floor-boards beautifully polished. There was a back porch leading to a laundry and a separate WC, so we had a lavatory we could go to without getting wet. Compared with the way we had lived since I was born, we were happily steeped in modern comfort.

The large front and back yards were tough grass and thistles, and it was clear that only a great deal of time and hard work could turn it into a garden. The soil was of the poorest type – heavy yellow or black clay that was rock hard when it was dry and a quagmire when it rained. In fact the very streets themselves were simply this – unmade beds of dark clay running between rows of houses. In winter your feet could sink out of sight in the bog as you crossed the road, and we watched car after car fail to get through to the bitumen sections and become stranded like beached whales on a sea of black mud that was supposed to be a thoroughfare. For many months we had forty feet of planks leading from our front porch out to a spot where a car might have a chance of stopping to take you on board, and we found great amusement watching my mother or grandmothers wearing shoes with heels stagger like tightrope walkers over the boards, with disaster threatening on either side.

The utopian expectations we fashioned in Larundel proved to be no more than that, and we were quickly educated into a more realistic grasp of what we had come to. This was a chance to make a fresh start, that was all, and you could seize it and make the best of what was on offer, as some families quickly did, or you could tread water and simply drift along doing the bare minimum, not bothering to make improvements to the property. Many residents did this. The Housing Commission seemed to place no requirements on its tenants other than to keep up the rent payments and not do any damage. There was a small temporary rent office standing in the next street from us, where every fortnight I was sent with notes and coins to pay the collector and bring home the receipt.

In our case, we had a limited ability to improve the place, obviously, with my father struggling to stay on his feet for more than a couple of hours, my mother still doing part-time dressmaking in the city, and Ray and I too young to tackle the garden. Johnnie and Dickie gave us some help, digging over the front yard one weekend, and coming back later to break up the clods of clay and level it enough to throw down some lawn seed. And they erected a low front fence of hardwood posts connected by two strands of wire all the way round, though it soon slackened, the bottom strand dragged on the ground, and it served none of the functions of a fence for the rest of its life; people just stepped over it.

*

The nearest Catholic school was about a two-and-a-half kilometre walk from our house. Every morning about half a dozen of us from the neighbourhood trudged up to Ivanhoe village, to the Immaculate Conception Primary school. There was Jim Thornycroft and Alan McHugh and Margaret McLaughlin from a couple of streets away, and several of the Cloneys – Bernie, Josie, Frankie – from across the road, all of the Faith. We had our favourite route through minor streets and lanes, along and over a small creek, up the long hill that led into Rockbeare Park, a semi-wild reserve bearing several ancient mulberry trees. In summer those trees could delay our progress for an hour or more, as we ate fat berries and swung in the branches, and would arrive home with fingers and lips, shirts and jumpers stained an indelible purple. Even as we wound our way through the thoroughfares and streets – Green Street, Ford Street, Darebin Road, Kenilworth Parade – we could make ourselves sick on damsens and cherry plums, loquats, apples and quinces during the season, all reaching down to us from branches overhanging the back fences. This part of the journey took us through an area recognisably different from the Housing Commission streets where we lived; here the houses were older, cared-for, privately owned and dignified by established gardens and tall shade-giving trees. I suspect we felt a certain entitlement in pinching their fruit, as though a skerrick of social justice had been clawed back, but it was a very subdued revolt; no one would ever know about it but ourselves.

The small creek we followed for part of the way to school was another favourite resource for adventure; we referred to it always as the 'little creek' to distinguish it from the larger Darebin creek, which lay in the other direction from the route to school. The 'little creek' was fed largely by storm water drains from houses, and could occasionally look a bit polluted, but it was by today's standards relatively clean. Certainly it was clean enough to support a healthy population of yabbies all along its length. On weekends and holidays we would spend hours with a lump of meat on a string patiently luring these small freshwater lobsters into nets fashioned from wire and old nylon stockings, or if you were really clever, flipping them out of the water because their ecstatic feasting had made them so careless they could be brought close enough to the surface for their long feelers to protrude and be grabbed. A good afternoon's catch might include a dozen or more six-inch blue-claws, which would boil up into a worthy mud-flavoured feed for those interested; for most of us boys it was the catching that we valued, not the eating. Another feature of the little creek was an area known as the 'ups and downs', which was a series of small dirt hills and valleys that ran through a shady grove of giant willow trees, their green curtains dangling over the paths that we followed on our bicycles, climbing and descending, climbing and descending, in an endless pursuit of joy. It became a meeting ground for children from a variety of local families, not always a harmonious one, as different groups jockeyed for the rights and privileges that the 'ups and downs' offered. I recall the odd scuffle taking place.

The school itself was a small brick rectangle on about two or three houseblocks of land, and it had an established and friendly communal feel about it. The Sisters of Mercy who ran it were gentle and good-humoured; the favourite with the children was a young, stunningly beautiful girl called Sister Mary Veronica. Bernie Cloney wasn't the only child who would have given an eye for a smile and a touch of her hand; the smile was always on offer, but a kind word was as much else as one could hope for. I don't recall any beatings taking place in this school. During breaks we played a game of toothpaste 'taws', in which we took a folded square and flattened portion of a lead toothpaste tube and skidded it up against a wall; several players competed, and the nearest to the wall in each throw won the round and pocketed the other 'taws'; unusual brands, like 'Ipana' (used by few households) were highly prized. There were concerts, and once a good-looking senior girl called Pat Benson stood out front and sang 'Oh, no John' accompanied on the piano by Sister Mary Veronica who played well. Pat Benson brought her black Labrador, 'Nigger' (in those racially unconscious days) to school every day; he would sleep patiently in the sun on the front step of the school, and then join in the break-time games, chasing balls, sticks and children all over the playground, apparently in the delusion that he was one of them. No one even suggested he was a problem.

I spent the year in grade four, which was taught by a cheerful lay teacher, Mrs Malone. For the first time school began to have some semblance of meaning and stability for me; up until then it had been nothing but a series of temporary daytime incarcerations where, under threat, we performed largely empty tasks. But Mrs Malone was a good teacher, and she helped me discover that I had some ability in arithmetic, spelling and art. There did not seem to be a great deal of religious instruction, and we rarely experienced a visit from the local priest, an old firebrand called Father Geoghegan; on the few occasions he did turn up the nuns fussed over him like lackeys.

Despite the long walk to school and its many distractions along the way, I wagged it on only one occasion, together with Bernie Cloney. We spent most of the morning up in the Ivanhoe Village, pinched a couple of trivial things from

Coles and Woolworth's, bought pies at the local bakery and then got so bored that we made our way on to school at lunchtime. Unfortunately we had been seen and reported by a local busybody and got into trouble from the Mother Superior that afternoon, were kept behind and made to recite a whole Rosary for our penance.

We and our immediate neighbours lived in an offset junction of three streets, into which our houses – about eight of them – faced, like a committee seated round an irregular table.

Directly across the road from us was a pale brick veneer lived in by the Willams family: Mr and Mrs Willams, a small daughter Venita and her older twin brothers, Lennie and Keith. I could never tell the twins apart; they were younger than I, and were to become playmates with my young brother Ray and his age-group. Mr and Mrs Williams kept much to themselves, and seemed chronically bad-tempered and anti-social. I got the impression they did a fair amount of drinking, and though their house and garden were neat, this was only in the most basic way; like us, they were not especially energetic improvers of the property.

Next to them on the right was a couple who were rarely seen; the curtains remained forever drawn, and they had no children. Their red brick house had no garden save a patch of cut grass, and no front fence: a depressive's house. On the left side of the Williams were the Bowdens, the youngest of whom was my good mate Ron. We were the same age, had similar intelligence and imagination, and spent many hours together catching and executing the thousands of black crickets that lived in the cracks in our clay backyards. Mrs Bowden was a kindly woman with a nervy manner and prone to talking too much; on weekends, Mr Bowden, a slow, vague man who worked at the Alphington Paper Mills, retreated into his never-completed garage, where he listened to the horse-race broadcasts and quietly sipped himself into oblivion on seven-ounce glassfulls of port: 'fourpenny dark', my father called it. There was an older brother, John, a loner, and a good-looking older sister, June, whose social life centred around her work in the city.

On the corner beside them were the Cloneys, an old-fashioned Australian-Irish Catholic family who had moved from the Murchison area in northern Victoria. When we first arrived there were five Cloney children; over the next nine years there were eight more added, plus a boy John, almost my age, who was a cousin from Murchison. This family existed on Con Cloney's modest wage at the local Council, plus whatever child support was available. They had the barest minimum of furniture in the house – a kitchen table and a few chairs, enough shared beds for them all, and an old sofa in the front room. The older boys – Bernie and Frankie – slept in a separate bungalow in the back yard, and this was where they entertained their friends when it was too cold or wet to play in the open. The Cloneys' house was a hub of activity for several generations of children, which is odd considering how little by way of comforts or food or equipment they possessed. Their house certainly had the smell of poverty about it, but what mattered more to us children was the freedom with which everyone could come and go there, and the fact that there was nothing of value to be damaged or interfered with. There was always something going on – talk, story-telling, especially by Mr Cloney who was full of swagger and blarney – games dreamt up by the girls for the girls, and the boys always onto some new venture. If people were hungry, somehow a doorstep of bread and jam or a plate of cornflakes was produced. No one was made to feel unwelcome there. Agnes Cloney, a dark-haired, straight-backed Irish beauty, glided through the house calmly and quietly, often with the latest child at her breast. Even when she looked tired she never raised her voice, and would often make a considered, intelligent contribution to the talk going on in the kitchen. She rarely went out, except to hang the washing on the line in the back yard.

On the opposite corner to the Cloneys was a family that kept to itself; the two boys seemed decent enough, but they didn't join in our activities. I believe their parents had an attitude not uncommon in Housing Commission areas, which passed as self-containedness but was in reality a kind of snobbery. They gave every indication of believing that through no fault of their own life had given them a bad deal, that they really should be buying their own home in a more respectable suburb, but something had happened – unemployment through illness or incapacitation, or debt or some such – to prevent this. So at a time when there was a desperate shortage of housing, a Commission house was their only option. Which was fine so far as it went, and one could understand their frustrations, but then they went that one step farther and assumed that all their neighbours were not only different from them, but were beneath them, and deserved nothing better than a Commission house. So they kept their distance from their neighbours, and kept their children apart from their neighbours' children, to the point of virtually imprisoning them. In this way there was a somewhat pathetic attempt to invent class superiority on the part of a few people, even though they hadn't the money for the symbols of class superiority – expensive cars or lavish parties, and their houses were no bigger or better than anyone else's. Insularity was their only weapon, and they applied this rigidly and, one felt, mostly to their own and their children's detriment.

Our house was on a corner, and our immediate neighbours were the Grants at the rear, and the Pinchbecks on our right. The Grants had a small daughter, Sandra, who sometimes slept overnight in my mother's double bed when her parents went out late; Mr Grant would carry her back through the cold night to her own bed. Mrs Grant had a speech peculiarity: she would use aitch incorrectly, as in 'would you like an horrange dear?' My father joked that she 'dropped her aitches at 'eidelberg and picked them up at Hivanhoe.'

In these first months Bob and Roma Pinchbeck were my parents' closest neighbours, so much so that Bob had a gate cut in our adjoining fence for easy access; we frequently darted through to each other's houses, and I'm sure this helped to cement the friendship. They had two small boys, too young for my interest. Bob and Roma had been hurt in a serious accident with their motor cycle and sidecar. Roma was thrown clear and had a broken arm; Bob's leg had been badly smashed, and he was to spend years having major operations to save it. He had a keen interest in cricket – had played at a respectable level – and I often sat and listened intently as he discussed the technical aspects of batting or bowling while he sat on his back steps doing some job with his hands, his leg in a huge plaster cast stuck out in front of him. He was a handsome, athletic, sun-tanned fellow, who often said in his crisp, unemotional way that his playing days were over.

This was the profile of immediate neighbours around us, and who meant something to me in these early days of our new start. There were others in the surrounding streets who soon came to be part of my life also, as the whole district was virtually teeming with children of all ages in these post-War years – the beginning of the baby boom – and we came and went in each others' houses, connected through school or sport or family friendships. Despite the rawness and inconvenience of muddy streets and treeless, unmade gardens, and the lack of transport and shopping facilities (it was two kilometres to the nearest shops at Ivanhoe village, and the only means of getting there was on foot), and despite a certain fragility and lack of purpose on the part of many of the adult tenants – we seemed all to be damaged in some respect, which I suppose is how we qualified to get a Commission House – there was nevertheless a degree of optimism and even camaraderie between most of the families. Tragedies and deep problems were common: we knew of suicides, family break-ups, marital betrayals, incest – a girl with a deaf and dumb older brother from a few streets away openly boasted that they had regular sex together. Such matters seemed to be accepted as part of the fabric of Commission House life, an indication of the tenor of our social standing, which was never in our own estimation high. But either despite or because of this, the contact between the children forced the adults to practise an at least occasional communality, even solidarity, and open rows and hatreds were quite rare. Everyone's basics – income, assets, work prospects – were probably so similar, and so limited, that the divisions were not apparent enough, nor the stakes high enough, to fight over.

This was also a possible consequence of having all moved into the area at about the same time; with the single exception of the King's pre-War Californian Bungalow farther east along our street, all the houses had been built and occupied within two years of each other. It had been raw open grasslands and unmade roads going back forever, and now suddenly it was a new massive housing development. Even in a country as young as Australia, this is unusual; normally towns and suburbs are settled gradually, are grown, and there is testimony to their historical development in the range of housing styles along each street. But Housing Commission areas, and this was one of the biggest in Melbourne, simply mushroom overnight as it were, and the houses are all of the same era and style, notwithstanding variations of design and materials. I'm not sure how this ultimately affects the people living in them, but I felt it gave us a degree of group identity, for better or for worse, not unlike refugees must feel. This didn't erase all differences of opinion or status-seeking in us, but it did create in us a sense that we had all been given an equal opportunity to make a new start, that we were all in the same boat, and it was what we did from here on that counted, not what mistakes or misfortunes haunted our pasts.

*

My father walks about the house still in his pyjamas and dressing gown; this gives me a sense of hope. He switches on our big cabinet wireless, and a deep voice singing 'The Road to Mandalay' comes out. I am struck by the line 'and the dawn comes up like thunder'; it doesn't quite make sense to say that something you see is like something you hear, but it is still striking enough to stick in my mind. My father enjoys listening to it. He sits in the lounge chair reading the newspaper, the morning sun streaming through the window behind him, bathing his blond head in a golden glow, as if the richness of his presence requires an especially lit environ. I don't even think about whether he will get over his sickness any more; all that matters is that he is here, now, with us, centring us, making us a family again, the source and conduit of our love for each other. I know the sickness is there, lurking, awaiting its chance to strike again, waiting to destroy us all, but at this moment, in this place, we can shut it out and stay together, alive, functioning.

He sleeps in a room by himself, the front bedroom, from where on the days he stays in bed he can look out across the junction of streets, still a mud flat. Like us children, he is entertained by watching the cars struggling to get through, some of them failing. He says they don't know how to avoid getting bogged. 'What you do, you keep your foot on the accelerator the whole time and your forward movement will usually carry you through. The mistake many people make is to lift their foot when they hit a deep spot; this is fatal. It guarantees that you'll get bogged, because the car loses momentum and its weight comes into play.' These ideas stay with me a lifetime, and they have proved to be absolutely right; I've driven through lots of deep mud and sand over the years, always remembering my father's advice, and always getting through successfully. It's a matter of learning to hold your nerve.

He asks Uncle Les to buy us a dog, and a few days later there is a straggly, nervous, not quite full-grown black and grey Cocker Spaniel running about the yard. We decide to call her Misty. My father tries to get her to obey commands, but all the dog wants to do is lick and sidle up gratefully. My mother is tolerant but not enthusiastic; she doesn't like dogs. If she is walking along the street and a dog of any size comes into view, she will cross the road or turn up a side street to avoid it; she is scared of them. Uncle Les says Misty has a pedigree, and could be trained up as a show dog. But a few days after her arrival, my father says she is a dog that has had a serious illness. 'Look at her back legs when she tries to stand still,' he tells my mother. And sure enough the dog's legs are constantly shaking; she can't keep them still. She has a nervous condition. 'Distemper,' says my father. The dog only lasts a few weeks, and has to be taken away to be put down. They gas them, Uncle Les tells us. Fortunately, I never become especially attached to it.

He comes out and stands on the back porch in the sun, his face slightly turned to cut down the glare. He is in his checked dressing gown and striped pyjamas, clean shaven and hair neatly combed, looking characteristically dapper. In his hand is a mug of tea, black as always. Never with milk.

I am cleaning my school shoes, as requested by my mother. He watches me put the finishing touches to polishing the toecaps.

'Is that it?' he asks.

'I reckon.'

'What about the rest?'

'The rest?'

'The backs.'

'Oh. Yeah.'

I turn a shoe round and see that the back is all scuffed and spotted with dried mud; I forgot those bits.

'Good soldiers,' he says, 'always look behind.'

It goes in, pungent and unforgettable, like a whiff of eucalyptus oil.

In the kitchen my parents are sitting holding hands across the table. As I enter from the back door I see my mother is quietly crying. 'I'm sorry darling,' she whispers. 'I do love you so much.' Both their heads are bowed. It is clear they have had a row, but have just this moment made it up. They seem unaware of my presence, enveloped as they are in the intensity of feeling between them. I can feel it too. I see them as through a greyish mist that drains the colour from their faces, their hands, their clothing, the Laminex table that should be red, and they all become like faded pictures. The mist has a viscosity that slows their movements, muffles their voices, sets them apart from me to the extent that I cannot penetrate it, cannot move inside it and be part of their world. I am an outsider, an intruder, except they ignore me. I cannot stand it, fear the sudden loneliness of it, as though I am on a rock in the middle of a lake, with no way of getting to shore. I must act.

'Your washing is dragging on the ground outside,' I say.

'Oh, is it? Thank you dear, I'd better see to it,' says my mother, pulls her hands away and goes out to the yard. The intensity is broken, the mist dissipates. My father turns to me again, and I am happy to have him to myself.

'What have you been up to this morning?' he asks.

'Nothing much. The Cloney's have got a new pup.'

He begins to sing:

When I was a lad and Old Shep was a pup,

Over hills and meadows we'd roam …

'Don't,' I say.

'I thought you liked *Old Shep*?'

'Don't sing.' I never liked that song; he used to sing it to me at Mount Macedon, and it would make me sad, sometimes even cry. It is about a man and his dog, from the time they were young and used to play together. They grow up together, loving each other. Then the time comes when Old Shep grows old and is going blind, and the man has to shoot him to put him out of his misery, and finally Shep goes to dog's heaven, which is rubbish because according to Sister Mary Veronica dogs aren't allowed into Heaven.

My mother comes in from the yard, crashing the screen door behind her.

'What game are you playing?' she says to me.

'What.'

'The washing.'

'What?'

'Dragging on the ground my eye; it's perfectly okay.'

'Oh, is it? It looked like it was going to drag on the ground to me. You must've caught it in time.'

'You little bugger,' she says. I am, too, but sometimes I can't help it.

Suddenly there is a rap at the back door.

'Ice!' a voice calls.

The ice man is making his weekly delivery. He is short, heavily built, with tight-curled sandy hair. My mother skips across the kitchen and opens the flywire door for him. He grunts his way in, holding a large block of ice part-wrapped in a hessian bag, and staggers bandy-legged with its glittering weight across to the ice-chest. The block is as usual too large to fit in the compartment at the top, so he places it on one knee and with his ice-pick deftly chips one side away, catching the shards in the hessian bag, until it fits neatly in the compartment. He packs the shards in at the top, and hands me a leftover the size of a glass, which I proceed to suck.

'Do you have time for a cup of tea?' says my mother. She goes a little girlie when she talks to him, treats him as someone special.

'I won't say no,' says the ice man.

This exchange is always the same, with the outcome always the same. He then sits at the Laminex table and passes the time of day with my father or whoever is in the room, until his tea comes, which he drinks quickly and then says,

'Well, this will butter no parsnips. I thank you for the tea missus, and we'll see you next time.'

Next week he will do the same things, my mother will ask him if he wants a cup of tea, and he will say the same things back. Strange.

It is Christmas again and Bob Pinchbeck proposes to take us to the Melbourne Cricket Ground to see the Test Match between Australia and India, starting on New Year's Day. The great Don Bradman is batting and is 127 not out; if we get there early enough we will see him continue his innings. My father is immensely excited at the prospect, because Bradman was one of his great boyhood heroes, yet he has never seen him play. I, for my part, have never seen so much as a game of cricket, so I am just as excited. My mother laughs out loud at us getting into the taxi-van; it pulls up as close as it can get to our houses in the road, which consists of deep channels of black water and drying mud, so the three of us carefully tread the planks. First my father, barely able to walk without running out of breath, shuffles unsteadily across in his slippers and clean, freshly pressed slacks, his hair and cardigan whipped by a hot wind threatening to blow his frail body off the planks at any moment. Behind him, the taxi driver pushes Bob Pinchbeck in his wheelchair, his white plastered leg extending before him like a strange divining instrument, and the wheels on one side of the chair constantly sinking through the dry crust into the mud. He is followed by myself, small and careful on the planks, carrying our lunch in a Gladstone bag almost too heavy for me to lift. One behind the other we trail over the planks, and my mother laughs, 'Talk about the blind leading the blind!' Is there a disabled version of this idea?

My first sight of the Melbourne Cricket Ground is almost overwhelming. The vast grandstands, the tiers of descending seats full of people, their talk rising expectantly as the starting time approaches, the field broad and flat like a green table cloth, are impossible to take in all at once. The excitement is almost unbearable. We sit in front of a low single-level grandstand out in the open with the sun behind us; these are good seats, Bob Pinchbeck tells us, which he was able to get through some contact of his. On the other side of the ground, bathed in sunshine, is the huge semi-circle called the Outer; it has many empty seats.

'Oh damn!' says my father, looking up at the scoreboard; his disappointment is palpable. 'Bradman's declared overnight; we'll be watching the Indians bat, I'm sorry to tell you mate.'

Since I don't understand the rules of the game, I don't quite know how his disappointment has been brought about, but I learn eventually that Bradman, who is captain, thinks Australia has made enough runs and so has declared its innings closed, which means that India now has its turn to bat.

'At least we'll see Miller and Lindwall bowl,' says Bob.

In a moment of magic, the players file onto the ground in their whites. They are like beings apart, immaculate ghosts tossing an invisible ball around in the centre, as the Indian batsmen walk to the wicket, dark-skinned and delicate-looking. I am mesmerised by the grace and skill of the bowlers and fielders, the way they can handle a cricket ball. My attention is drawn to Keith Miller, who is tall and handsome, with dark hair flopping over his eyes. He is always doing something interesting, such as flicking the ball up into his hand with his foot, or suddenly turning to bowl when he is only halfway to his marker. Sid Barnes is another character in the field; he takes a catch in the slips and, in an action so fast nobody sees it, pockets the ball and suddenly looks behind him as if the ball has broken through his hands. For a moment the crowd thinks it's a dropped chance, until they realise there is no ball to be seen. At this point Barnes takes the ball out of his pocket like a conjuror would do, holds it up and the batsman is out; all the players, except maybe the batsman himself, know what has happened and go along with the trick. But Bob Pinchbeck disapproves: 'He is a lout, that one; you shouldn't do things like that in a Test Match. What if the umpire hadn't seen it?'

My father points out Don Bradman to me, who is fielding near the fence close to where we are sitting. He seems surprisingly ordinary for a man with such a huge reputation. I expected him to have something of a superman about him – his phenomenal abilities clearly visible in his appearance – but he looks like a grocer or a bus driver, not an athlete. It strikes me at that moment that there is a difference between truth and appearance; a person may not appear to be what they are. What we see at the pictures, for instance, can deceive us, for there the actors almost always contrive to look like what they are: certain colours, tone of voice, state of clothing and so on are meant to make us believe that this is a good person or a bad person, and whether what they say is likely to be true or not. But in real life, you can't tell by those things; you have to know the person better.

When a player fields the ball, a green light flashes beside his name on the scoreboard. This is very modern, says my father; no other ground in the world has it. The morning is eventful as the Indian wickets tumble; the batsmen trudge on and off the field in a dejected procession, one of them wearing a dark red turban. They have no chance against this powerful Australian team. The match is over by lunchtime, and when the last wicket is taken the players scramble to souvenir the stumps and bails, running off the ground with them like thieves. It has been a memorable day for me, not least because it has been such a tonic for my father. He talks about it for days afterwards, and as he does I realise that I, too, have been bitten by the cricketing bug, and would like nothing better than to get out somewhere and have a bowl or a bat with some kids. I wish now I had asked for a cricket bat for Christmas.

*

I wake in the night with terrible pains in my legs. No matter how I stretch and writhe, or how I position my legs, nothing I do makes it better. I moan helplessly in the dark, and Ray in the opposite bed stirs a little but stays asleep. My mother comes and pulls back the blankets, takes down my pyjama trousers and rubs my legs. 'There, there,' she croons, as I whimper pathetically, 'it's only growing pains, it will pass, it will pass.' She persists, gently stroking, kneading the muscles. 'You'll probably keep getting them for a few years, but then they'll stop. I used to get them when I was young, too; it just means you're getting bigger.' Eventually, under the warm pressure of her hands, the pain fades. She pulls up my trousers, kisses my brow. 'Back to sleep,' she says. 'Would you like some water?' I nod. She brings a glass of water, and kisses me again, tucks me in and turns out the light as she leaves. Comforted, at ease again, staring into the dark, I soon begin to sink away …

*

I have begun to tell lies. Not just lies about something trivial – everyday kinds of lies – but big lies, extravagant lies that no one believes. I boast to the children in the school playground that I have my own gun, which I keep locked in a box under my bed. 'Show it to us, then,' they say mockingly. 'Can't,' I reply. 'I've left the key at my grandmother's in North Melbourne.' I spread the story that my father owns a cricket bat that used to belong to Don Bradman, but that no one can see it because he won't let it out of the house. My father, I tell them, is sick because he was wounded fighting the Japs; he has medals, including a Victoria Cross.

This lying takes a bizarre turn when kids at school start insisting that I have made claims that I know very well I haven't. 'You told us last week you swam the English Channel,' they say. I've never heard of the English Channel. So it's they who are lying this time, but because of the lies I know I have told I can't challenge them over it. Once you start telling lies, I realise, you can become trapped by them. Still I do it. I tell Bernie Cloney that at Larundel I won the Golden Gloves championship in my division. I don't think he believes me, but then again he doesn't seem to have heard of the Golden Gloves competition, so he lets it go with a shrug.

*

Along with the children in the immediate vicinity, I formed part of a gang of
about eight whose time was spent increasingly on the banks of the Darebin
Creek, sometimes referred to as 'the big creek.' This was a large wilderness to the
west of our house, basically where Valentine Street ends. The creek lay at the
bottom of a long, steep gully running maybe two miles between Bell Street and
Darebin Road. At the end of a steeply descending dirt path, there was a
widening of the creek into a pool called The Devil's Hole, which had been
formed by the damming effect of rocks a little downstream. The Devil's Hole is
where we fished, swam, sat and talked, and generally made our focal point for
adventures; we kept alive the legend that it was bottomless. Along the banks we
could hide and chase and muck around on the tracks that passed beside the
creek, up between thickets of hawthorn and cotoneaster, through slopes of native
grasses punctuated with blue-crowned Scotch thistles and weed locally called
Irish liquorice. We could cross where the strewn rocks made the water shallow
and fast-flowing. It was a creek with good volume, clean and varied enough to
support fish – Perch, Redfin, the odd Mountain-trout – and eels, yabbies, frogs,
leeches, water-fowls, dragonflies, water-boatmen, as well as bulrushes, reeds,
freshwater algae and water-lilies. A boy called Mickey Poge so hated his home
life that he became a virtual hermit in this wilderness, spending full days killing
lizards and snakes with his shanghai, constantly wagging school, never going
home for lunch or dinner, and staying out until it was too dark to see any more.
For Mickey, as for the rest of us, the whole place was a school and an adventure
playground in one, teeming with living things to be discovered and chased,
caught, killed, stroked or simply observed. Now, sixty years later, a proliferation
of factories has replaced the wilderness on the western bank, turning the Darebin
Creek into a murky trickle of toxic waste, in which all that is generated is
chemical scud. Nothing could live in it.

How came this whole area to be so devoid of the native shrubs of the type we
now grow? I can't recall seeing a grevillea, a melaleuca, even a eucalypt apart
from the odd old gumtree, in all my time spent in this uncultivated and
undeveloped area. How did these exotics get there? Self-sown probably, seeds
blown from older gardens in the established inner suburbs. On the western side,
where the slope up is more gradual, the bank was covered by a tangle of rich
green ivy that grew for some seventy metres along and twenty metres wide. How

did this get there? It was all like a leftover garden from the colonial era that had gone rampant, and now formed a non-native jungle. Probably the grasses were native, and had been there for hundreds of years, but there were no native trees or shrubs to speak of, and certainly nothing like the feel of Australian bush that we associate with wilderness.

In summer the days were hot and dry, with north winds ripping across the brown grass that as I pushed through it snapped and crunched underfoot. Socks full of grass seeds and burrs, legs pricked by thistles as I passed, hair bleached, skin burnt, dried, freckled, eyes narrowed to reduce the cruel glare, forming crow's feet even in a child. The winter skies were grey and cold breezes whipped about my ears, my nose ran and dripped. I spent long hours exposed to such conditions, active, going without food and drink, pissing into shrubbery when the need arose, totally absorbed in this vast outdoor theatre. It formed my skinny body just as it formed my mind, at ease and at home in open, unprotected spaces.

We passed through phases, obsessions almost, lasting only a few weeks until they were replaced by another. First we started fishing in the Devil's Hole, catching mostly redfin and the odd eel. Suddenly everyone was making a fishing rod, getting flour and water from their mothers to make dough for bait, spending hours patiently casting into the pool. I brought home two small, uneatable specimens and put them into the laundry trough until I could think of what to do with them. Unfortunately, we got a visit from Nair that weekend and she dropped her cigarette butt straight into the trough. In the morning, both my fish were dead. 'That's Nair for you,' said my father, 'the Wicked Witch of the North.' After a while we all got a bit bored with fishing, and were ready for something more active.

The idea of making wooden rifles was started by a peculiar boy, an only child called Rex King. For a brief time Rex was, in a sense, our leader, but it was hard to see why. Well, I knew why, but it was strange all the same. Despite his name, he was not powerful looking. In fact, his nickname was 'mousey', which he clearly did not like. But it was an apt term for his thin, small-boned, pasty features. What gave Mousey King his authority was the fact that his house, which was only a few hundreds yards east along Valentine Street from us, was not a Housing Commission residence. It was older, a Californian Bungalow with a wide, deep verandah and mature trees and shrubs almost hiding it from view. The point was they owned it, or at least his widowed mother, a recluse, did, and this made all the difference to the way we regarded Rex. At the rear, where I went only once, was a large shed and workshop full of high quality tools and equipment – several long benches, vices, fixed electric grinding wheels, drills and a circular saw, racks on the wall holding ranges of screwdrivers, chisels, saws and hammers of every imaginable size, all well used and in good condition. I'd never seen such beautiful tools. They belonged to Rex's father who had died a couple of years earlier, and Rex knew quite a bit about how to use them. No one in a Commission House had anything like them. It was these possessions, and what they seemed to symbolise for the rest of us, and the fact that he was able to use them, that gave Rex his power and authority. Despite being merely children, we had unconsciously absorbed, and were influenced sufficiently to act upon, a particular truth about suburban living: material possessions and knowledge are the most successful sources of power, not physical strength or personal likeability. If you owned your house, and had the adornments of stability that were implicit in that, you were more important.

So when Rex made himself a relatively convincing looking rifle, constructed in his workshop from a length of timber and metal tubing, we all wanted one. If Rex liked you, he would take you in and make you one. Some of us – myself, Ronnie Bowden – were not among the privileged, and so had to fashion our own crudely inauthentic attempts as best we could. Kilby and Geoff Groves, however, had sufficient kudos to sport beautifully finished, glossily lacquered weapons made by Rex himself. With these 'rifles' we would hunt each other for hours on end down at the Darebin creek, hiding in the tangle of ivy and rocks on the western bank, or being ambushed from behind trees and shrubbery along the pathways. No girls ever played with us; the creek was strictly a male preserve, and any girl found in the area would immediately be suspected of being up to no good.

It was the same story of leadership some time afterwards when Rex presented himself in the nearby paddock flying an impressive kite, on a length of good, strong cord so long it flew almost out of sight. Again, it was his idea, and again it dictated a fashion. Everyone was getting brown paper, making paste with flour and water, finding thin sticks for the frame, and having difficulty getting hold of a ball of string sufficiently long and strong; surveyor's cord proved to be the best option, if you could get it. Ordinary string could break, and your kite could end up several streets away on someone's roof. We sent up into the sky ever-larger, ever-better diamond-shaped creations that we taught ourselves to make dip and swerve, dart horizontal left or right, and sometimes crash to the ground and need repairing, until, again, after a few weeks, we got bored and started looking for a new diversion.

Our prime stimulant for new ideas was the Saturday matinee picture-show at the Ivanhoe Hoyts theatre. Groups of us would happily trudge the mile or so up the hill to be there in time to buy sweets or ice-creams to take into the auditorium, and not miss the cartoon features that came on first: *Tom and Jerry*, *Mighty Mouse*, *Heckle and Jeckle*. We would hope the feature film would be a war film with plenty of action and not a dreary grey-toned talk-fest before a backdrop of venetian blinds. After that would come the serials, which were what we really wanted: *Batman*, *The Phantom*, *Tom Mix*, *Rin Tin Tin*, and my favourite, *The Last of the Mohicans*, featuring the magnificent Uncas and the fearful Magua. It was this latter serial that triggered off another of our obsessions – bows and arrows. This time, however, Rex King went far over the top and bought himself a genuine archery set that was well outside the budget of any of our parents. It was a large, powerful, beautifully polished longbow that took some strength to pull back, and its heavy gut string cut into your fingers. The arrows had brass points and evenly cut feathers. None of us even tried to compete with this; instead, we found strips of inch-and-a-half hardwood and fine dowelling for arrows, firing them harmlessly at each other as we scampered through the undergrowth, preferring always to be Indians rather than cowboys. I think in this particular fashion Rex had outsmarted himself, because he stopped participating when he lost one of his precious arrows in the thicket. Superiority came at a price, sometimes too much to pay.

A relatively long-standing obsession was the one of go-carts and mud-sleds. Go-carts came first, made of a strip of six-by-one-inch timber for a chassis, something broader attached for the seat, and four pram wheels on axles, the front one fastened at the centre so that it could be steered with a pair of rope 'reins'. In these contraptions we would ride down the gentler slopes of the gully, which were slightly towards the Bell Street end, but still steep enough to develop a hair-raising speed halfway down. Sleds followed, involving smoothly sanded runners instead of wheels, and pouring water down the slope to make slippery mud, on which, again, a good speed could be worked up. The crashes at the bottom were, of course, part of the danger that was part of the fun. On and off we ran go-carts and sleds for a year or so, until the next diversion came along, and the go-carts and sleds were abandoned to rust and rot in a distant corner of the yard. Yesterday's treasures.

*

Saturday, and it is grey and wintry outside. I am stuck in my bedroom reading my latest Dick Tracy comic for the second time. I collect them, have every one so far. Sitting on my bed, I gaze through the window and see two men fighting on our nature strip. They completely ignore the cold wind and rain, and are standing up to each other punching. Both are covered in blood. One of them is wearing only trousers, shoes and a white shirt, torn open down his chest and bloody all over the front and collar. The other has blood streaming over one eye from a cut on his forehead. At least he has a pullover on. It is frightening, yet strangely remote and unreal because I can't hear them; only the wind.

As I watch them I realise that they are actually trying to make progress along Valentine Street towards Liberty Parade. One of them will be knocked down, and the other will stalk off along the nature strip until he is caught up with and the punching will start over again. It occurs to me that they have probably come from Ryan's pub up in Ivanhoe village, and have been having this drunken fight the whole way. Then I recognise them; it is the Lee brothers, Barney and the other one whose name I never remember. I knew them at Larundel, and liked them both. They had a flat in our block where they lived with their little bow-legged mother. I would see them in the men's washroom, showering, shaving, in front of the mirror carefully combing their long fair hair, 1940s style. We would joke, splash water at each other, and I would wave to them if I saw them waiting for the bus. I recall now that they live somewhere up in Liberty Parade, so they must be on their way home.

How awful, I think, that they have come to this. Something is destroying them. It is a reminder of Larundel, which is only just behind us, those who were there. We, my family, have gotten away from that squalor, that filth. The Lees have not, at least not yet. Will they? I shiver as I watch the brothers stumbling, falling, clutching at each other in a silent struggle that could at times be mistaken for embraces, gestures of support, passionate demands, if it were not for the blood. Their havoc takes them gradually out of the line of vision available from my window. A memory comes to me of the Larundel incinerators surrounded by the piles of stinking rubbish waiting to be burned in them, and charred paper rolled into cigarettes, lit from the smouldering bins and drawn into our lungs in imitation of our elders.

7

BECAUSE I SPEND SO much time with my friends now, I see less and less of
my father. But this is also because he is less visible; he has stopped going outside,
and the last time I saw him on the back porch was when I implored him to
watch me ride Ronnie Bowden's bike in the back yard; it was my first ride, and I
wanted him to witness it. But now he hardly gets out of bed at all, shut away in
the front bedroom by himself. My mother sleeps in the double bed in the main
bedroom. His infectiousness is the problem, and also he often lies awake at night
coughing and struggling for breath.

One night I hear him cough and groan, and I get out of bed and go to take a
look at him. It is eerie in his bedroom: there is a blue glow coming from a little
candle-lit shrine to the Virgin Mary on the table beside his bed. He lies on his
back, propped up on several pillows, his head back and his eyes closed. The blue
light gleams on one side of his face, highlighting the raw cheekbone, the sweat
on his forehead. He is fighting for breath, his chest heaving, his head turned first
to one side, then the other. I stand in the doorway watching, the fear mounting
in me; he is bad again, obviously, and it will last a long time, just as it has before.
I can see the fever growing hot on his skin, hear the strange rasp of his breath
passing through his bubbling lungs, his suppurating, open-wounded lungs. Why
is this happening? Why to him? He is the best man alive; if he were well he
would do good to people.

He does not deserve such torture. I find no fault in this man. When will it
end, how will it end? I ask myself, feeling my own agony to be worse than his; it
is not fair, comes the voice, it is not fair.

Suddenly he opens his eyes and sees me standing in the doorway; his face
hardens. 'Out,' he waves a hand at me, 'out, now!' I have not realised I had
moved so far forward into the room. I am paralysed for a moment, rooted to the
spot halfway across the floor.

'Dad,' I murmur.

'Get out!' he shouts this time, his face distorted, his voice straining for power.
He reaches down the side of the bed, leaning far over and coughing weakly in
the act, and comes up suddenly with a boot in his hand. I watch mesmerised as
he turns the boot round in the fingers of his right hand – his throwing hand –
and flings it end-over-end straight at my head. I duck and the boot flies past me

and crashes into the wall. I make for the door as he yells again words that strike terror in my heart, 'Don't you know… don't you know: I'm dying!'

My mother emerges from her bedroom in time to grab me and usher me back to my bed. 'You shouldn't be out of bed, now go on, or you'll catch your death.' I lie in bed shaking, unable to sleep for hours, convinced that he hates me and that his anger is about punishing me for the things I have done wrong. And I can't stop thinking about his final word: is dying what he is now doing? He will stay there in the bed until he dies? How will he die, will he fall unconscious again and not wake up, will he have a terrible, explosive coughing fit that will rip him apart, will he bleed inside and drown in his own blood, will he not get enough breath and suffocate? What is dying exactly? Doesn't it mean being emptied, becoming a shell? Like a dead frog, or a cricket?

In the morning I can see through to his bedroom that he is pale and tired, but talking calmly. My mother explains that he didn't mean to be angry with me last night, that his fever and the sulphur drugs he is taking make him delusional, and he probably didn't know who I was. I'm not so sure; the pain I feel is still sharp.

Dr Downing comes in his green Chevrolet car; my mother has phoned him using Pinchbeck's telephone. He spends some time in the bedroom with my father, talking in low serious tones with him and with my mother. I can tell something ominous is happening.

Later in the morning Father Chauder comes; my father wants him to hear his Confession. Father Chauder is the new priest at the Immaculate Conception, younger than Father Geoghegan, and much more popular with the kids. After he has been in there a good while, Father Chauder leaves with some kind words of support to my mother. Then my father calls me.

'Come in here, son.'

I hesitate at the door. He is sitting up in the bed, looking much better than he had in the night. He eyes me evenly, gestures for me to come into the room. 'Come here while I hit you,' he says.

'No. Why?'

'Because I say so. Come on, come here while I hit you. You know I can't chase you, so you'll have to come here.'

'Why do you want to hit me?'

'Don't ask questions, just do as you're told. Come here while I hit you.'

I can't resist him. I move toward him, obedient but scared, and ready to receive it when he strikes. I have no idea what I have done to deserve it, but I accept that I have done wrong things that I have gotten away with. I am within arm's length of him, the closest I've been for some time, and suddenly he raises his hand above his head and, as I flinch in anticipation of the blow, he turns his hand and nonchalantly scratches the back of his head. He laughs out loud.

'Gotcha mate!'

I laugh with him, though of course with great relief. I should have realised, because he has done that trick before.

'I'm sorry about last night,' he says.

'Okay. It's okay. Mum said it's your sickness.'

'And these bloody pills.'

'Dad?'

I want to ask if it is true. If what he said in the night is really true, that he is dying, but it is a thing too big, too frightening for me to ask or to want to know. Instead I say, 'Do you like Father Chauder?'

'He's alright. Do you?'

I think about it for a while. He is a foreigner, and speaks with an accent that sounds a bit German. I like that.

'He's alright.'

'I need to sleep now, so you hop out and play.'

As I leave he starts to sing 'Who threw the overalls in Father Chauder's Murphy' … I get the joke; it's a take-off of a song that has been around for years, which I've heard Nair and others sing. 'Who threw the overalls in Mrs Murphy's chowder …' Still, it's a bit bold of my father to sing that about Father Chauder; I wonder if he'll have to confess it next time?

*

On some quiet day at the end of that summer, when the world was at work and I was at school, an ambulance arrived to move him almost unnoticed up the hill to the Heidelberg Repatriation Hospital. Perhaps my mother had prepared me for it, told me he had to 'go back into hospital for a while', leaving me with the impression that this was nothing of any great significance, nothing that hadn't happened before, and would happen again. It was the condition of life for our family, and he would eventually be home again. So when I got home from school and heard no sound of the wireless coming from his room and saw his empty bed, I felt only the old familiar absence that had come and gone every year of my life. There was nothing new or different in it.

It might seem strange that he was placed in the Repatriation Hospital, designated as it was to the care of war victims. He had wanted to join the army and participate in the adventure of soldiering, and one of his greatest regrets was that this had been frustrated. So how did he qualify to take his place among the sick and maimed brought back from the war? The answer is that technically he had been accepted into the army – for a week or so, until his x-rays came through and revealed his tuberculosis. Only then was his application denied. It was on this ground that Dr Downing fought the reluctant authorities to have him admitted to Heidelberg, where he believed my father would receive the best treatment at the time. Downing was a good man; he would come out day and night in his green Chevrolet to do house calls in the Housing Commission area, where many of his patients must have been at best slow to pay, and even though the man himself had a quietly patrician air and lived in an expensive house in a better part of Ivanhoe, he had a genuine dedication to his patients. He tended me many times, and I don't recall his ever refusing to come even when I was suffering from nothing more than a bout of flu. When he saw that my father needed to be hospitalised, Downing confronted the administration and would not take no for an answer, so that was where my father was admitted. Whether or not he did in fact receive the best available treatment is a question open to some argument.

I would stand on our front porch and gaze up the hill at the ship-like decks of that modern cream brick hospital. There was something grand about it, swank hotel-like. Now it contained one special patient, whose progress, demeanour, activities were hidden from me; I was not allowed to visit him, so even my imagination had precious little to launch itself from. All I knew, whenever my thoughts turned to my father, was again that familiar pain, but the scar was old now and feeling had become duller with time. For days, weeks on end, I forgot to think about him, caught up as I was in the hectic neighbourhood of boys.

The changes in my mother at this time became more marked; she had always been, and remained, the steady, dependable but seemingly unfeeling engine that kept our lives going. Now, for her own reasons, she also became difficult to get close to – cold, remote, edgy and sharp-tongued – and had formed a hard shell around herself that I sensed held together an unhappy mess of feelings within. There was a disturbing conflict between her tough exterior and her deeply sentimental taste in songs and films. She had always loved popular music, film, Hollywood stars, radio shows, but in the early days her taste seemed to be fixed equally on humour and glamour, the oddball as much as the sexy. Now she preferred songs like 'You'll never know just how much I love you', 'These foolish things', 'Embraceable you', songs that, after her own mother, she would sing to herself in reverie while doing the housework, transporting her to some dream-world. Similarly, she loved American musicals with gushy love songs and idiotically happy endings. I couldn't stand them, and I resented her dragging me along to the cinema to see them as much as I resented the hypnotic effect they had on her. Yet at other times she would nag, smack, lose her temper or get a particularly tense look on her face if I did the slightest thing to annoy her: *Put your clothes away. Don't bite your nails. Don't pick your nose. Why are you walking like that? Why are you breathing so noisily? Pick up your feet when you walk. Take your hands out of your pockets. Elbows off the table. Close your mouth when you chew. Don't sniff. Use your hanky. Put your clothes away. Clean your shoes. You're not getting any pudding until you eat up all your pumpkin. Did you wash behind your ears? Clean your teeth? Put your clothes away.* Her one aim in life seemed to be to make me miserable, and I could feel her intense dislike of me. More than once she threatened to 'place me in a home', which indicated that some such thought had crossed her mind, whatever the practical possibilities of that would have been; I've no doubt she would never have gone through with it. But I was astute enough to detect the desperation behind it.

Not that I went out of my way to be more helpful; I did not, and I take no pride in admitting it. But then, I had never been trained or encouraged to take the initiative in pitching in around the house. My mother found it quicker and more convenient to do everything herself, even to the point of bringing breakfast in bed to me and Ray on her work mornings rather than have us dither around in the kitchen while she was trying to get herself organised. Typically in working class families, and certainly most of the ones around us at the time, boys were not taught to do domestic chores. On the contrary, they were waited on by the women – mothers, sisters, grandmothers if they were around. The Cloneys were like this; only the girls did housework, and this encouraged a domestic laziness in the boys that might last their lifetime, but which had been assigned to them by tradition. At this time, when my mother needed all the help she could get from me, I largely failed her, and this only added to her frustration and unhappiness. We long for the wisdom of hindsight. I wish I had been a better eldest son to her, had been one of those selfless, willing, helpful children who anticipate all of their parents' needs. But I was not; I was one more chore, one more cross for her to bear, and her anger and growing bitterness owed a great deal to my personal failings.

*

Driving out to the Austin Hospital was an exercise in negotiating an almost but not quite lost past. Bell Street, Oriel Road, Waterdale Road, the area of the 1956 Olympic Village – the geography of my boyhood, or much of it, now almost unrecognisable. Almost, but not quite: the bridge over the Darebin Creek remains, but it is all squalidly industrial, the wilderness gone, the creek ruined. The cream brick remnants of the Heidelberg Repatriation Hospital are recognisably the same bricks, but the grand ship-like building has disappeared and been replaced by small administrative offices. Not enough injured soldiers these days, I guess. As I drove past I saw in the streets fleeting ghosts of children playing cricket or football, houses transformed by age, the harshness softened by gardens, the rawness gone. Fifty-nine years had passed, after all.

Evelyn's voice on the phone made the situation clear without her spelling out the details. 'Dickie doesn't seem to be the best after the operation; the doctors are worried about his breathing. If you want to see him, you'd better go soon.'

A week earlier she'd told me about the decision to operate. I hadn't spoken to either of them for two or three years, when they were still in Pambula. It had been a dream of Dickie's after a lifetime of hard work as a metal polisher. I understood it perfectly, that Melbournian desire to spend one's last years in a stable, comfortable climate. I had it myself, and one reason Jo and I went to stay with them was to investigate the possibilities of buying something of our own to retire to – land or a house – in nearby Merimbula. It was great to catch up with them both, and Evelyn reminded me of the last time – the only time –we had met. It was way back when I was about eleven years old, and I had gone to visit Nair – I often went there as a boy out of sheer need to see her and return to my North Melbourne roots –and Dickie, who was at that time in the army but still living there, said he was going into town to meet his new girlfriend Evelyn. When we got to the city he gave me her photograph and sent me to find her while he went to the pub.

'Are you the lady in this photo?' I asked.

'Looks a bit like me,' she said, 'so I guess it must be.'

How attractive I found her open good looks, her humour. How lucky was Dickie. I was not surprised to learn of their marriage. That was over fifty years ago, yet in all that time our paths never crossed, until my brother Ray brought us together again. He had found himself living near them in Reservoir, and Dickie asked after me. I rang him a couple of times, and he told me about his imminent retirement, gave me the Pambula address and phone number, and a year or so later, heading over to that coast, we arranged to stay with them. I realised as soon as I saw him again that he was the sibling who looked most like my father – same sized body, same colouring, same lean face, though Dickie's ears were a bit more prominent. Anyone would have spotted them as brothers straight away. I realised also, with mild shock, that how he looked now, in his seventies, is very much like my father would have looked at the same age. For that reason I have always had a soft spot for Dickie, the great survivor of the family. Roy had died young, tearing open his heart muscle, it was said, trying to lift a car. Johnny, Dickie's twin, had been dead some years due to cancer – not from smoking; the memory of that Hiroshima visit, those horrific photographs, his wandering nonchalantly through that radioactive bombsite, springs immediately to mind. Nair and Alec had been long gone; lung problems – the family blight – mainly through smoking, though not in my father's case.

I regret that I lost touch with all this side of my father's family, especially Nair, Uncle Alec and Dickie. After my father's death, and especially once Richard came on the scene, my mother no longer visited them. She sent Christmas cards without fail, as she always did to everyone, but once her main emotional link to the North Melbourne crew was gone, she could see nothing but the painful past in them, and she was determined to put all that behind her. Only the future now mattered for her and her boys. In fact, I discovered recently that she never placed a headstone on my father's grave at Fawkner cemetery, never tended or even visited it. It was a shocking neglect, which I plan to put right, but I nevertheless can understand her attitude; some suffering is so great and so prolonged that any reminder puts you through terror, as indeed returned soldiers often point out. You don't go there. But Ray and I paid the price for this fear in forfeiting loving family members who'd been part of our growing up. Nair, Alec, Roy, Dickie, even Johnnie, were significant characters in our childhood world, and for them simply to evaporate from our lives like that must I'm sure have added to that feeling of entropy that haunted our early years. Who knows, its effect may be continuing.

Dickie was the only one of those characters to come through, thanks hugely to the stability Evelyn provided, had lovely daughters, grandchildren, stayed in work until retirement age. But now fate had caught up with him.

When the doctors opened him up they found more cancer than they'd anticipated, and so had to resect more lung. That was the day after he was admitted; since then his recovery had stalled. 'They still don't know,' said Evelyn on the phone. 'They're talking about fluid in his chest restricting his breathing; once they clear that they think he should be okay.'

I went about my week not giving the situation much thought, presuming as you do that the doctors would sort it out, that the technology would be applied, and he'd be out in a week or two as chipper as ever. Then Evelyn's last call: '…If you want to see him, you'd better go soon.' There was no mistaking the implication of this, nor the weariness in the voice.

I went on my own; there was a tacit understanding that Jo had no emotional investment in this part of my family, though she had enjoyed staying at Pambula with Dickie and Evelyn. No, this was my seed-bed, my blood, my memories, all formed long before she came into my life, and any serious impact that might come would be on me alone.

I parked in the new underground car park in a section of the Mercy hospital still unfinished; there were massive renovations and extensions going on, restricted areas yellow-taped off and lifts not yet working. So I got a bit lost finding my way through the maze of empty passageways and stairs until I finally found a functioning reception area and was directed to the lift that took me up to the Thoracic Ward. Evelyn was already in the waiting room, looking tired but calm, as was her way. Her two daughters, attractive young women, were with her, and after we did the introductions they said they were familiar with my best-known book, and we chatted in subdued tones about nothing very much. It was the old part of the hospital, with narrow corridors and weak lighting, and the waiting room was small and grubby and not at all capable of bolstering morale. Green scuffed walls, and not a flower in sight.

'We can't go in yet,' said Evelyn. 'They're hoping to clear some of the fluid away so he can breathe better. Hopefully he'll be able to talk.'

I looked at my watch; it was about ten forty-five in the morning. A man of about my age wearing a grey suit came in and greeted the women. Again introductions, and it turned out he was my cousin – Roy's youngest son, Brian. We did our best to pass the time in that dismal place, feeling for common memories and family stories.

'Have you been in touch with Wookie?' Evelyn asked.

'He's in Japan of course; I phoned him, so he knows what's happening. I imagine he'll be in contact soon.'

Eventually, after perhaps half an hour, a nurse came and said we could go in, but only one at a time. The girls went first, and were not more than a few minutes each; they, like Evelyn, were staying the whole day and said they could go back later. Evelyn suggested I go in next as I had a long way to travel.

I pushed through the green door into the Thoracic Ward and was confronted by a scene I was completely unprepared for; a largish room, some fifty feet long and twenty feet wide, no internal walls, and a complete shambles of equipment, trolleys, gurneys, drip-trees, tubes, occupying every available space. White masked-and-gowned bodies busily talked or tended beds facing in all directions containing mostly patients with so little of their persons visible, what with their oxygen masks and gowns, that it was impossible to identify Dickie. A nurse asked me who I wanted, and took me to him. He was sitting up on a gurney parallel to the central thoroughfare, and hooked up to an oxygen mask. I may have gasped audibly at what I was seeing; if the term 'fighting for breath' had become a meaningless cliché, it now acquired for me a renewed aptness. Dickie was locked in a struggle of terrible violence, convulsing like a choking dog, as his rapid gasps sucked desperately at the air around him. Forward back, forward back, forward back, forward back the spasms wrenched his whole frame, at a rate of thirty every ten seconds, as his debilitated lungs strove for oxygen. A brief flicker of his blue eyes was as much as he could afford to give in recognition of my presence, and then his concentration returned to the sole task, the only task that mattered, and which every fibre of his body was committed to, which was to keep breathing. I spoke to him, something hollow like 'How are you, matey?', reached out and touched him on the shoulder. But he was too busy. He was working, my god he was working, at the task of getting breath: nothing left for anything else.

I stood there for a few minutes, gradually accepting that communication was not possible. How long could he keep doing this? The energy he was spending was enormous. He must get more lung capacity, or inevitably tire. I felt helpless, ridiculous. I looked around, hoping for something – advice, comfort, someone who would explain what strategies for recovery were planned. Nothing. Everyone preoccupied with someone else. Eventually a nurse did come, and placed his oxygen mask back on, but it didn't change his agony. I stood watching him until I became desperate to get out of there. Finally, with a wave and a stupidly cheerful utterance of 'good luck' I left, feeling an abject failure.

In the waiting room, too stunned for graceful goodbyes with the others, I gave my mobile phone number and wandered out to the lift. In the gloom of the underground car park, I sat behind the wheel with my head resting on the backs of my hands. Death by slow suffocation, in the full knowledge of what was happening to you, given enough energy to wage a fight, but not enough to recover. Is this what it was like for my father? Is this what my mother witnessed, maybe more than once, when she visited him in the Repat? Was it the passion of his struggle that she was determined to keep hidden from me? Of course, it was tuberculosis then and cancer now, but is the process any different? Both eat the lungs away, reduce the capacity to breathe, kill by slow drowning in productions of fluid. The thought of my father reduced to this animality, of his end being not the pale saintly fade that I had always imagined but the ferocity of an execution, took hold of me and I broke. The tears welled up, and a huge sob shook my chest. It was some ten, fifteen minutes before I could bring myself to start the engine. Emerging from the darkness of the car park out into the grey, cloud-streaked midday light, my wet eyes stung a little. They didn't feel better until I had driven all the way home.

About dinner time a text message rang through on my mobile phone. 'Dear Garry. I'm sorry to tell you that dad died at 2.40 this afternoon. Mum will be in touch about the funeral. All the best, Jenny.'

*

I place my fingers inside the hole in the wall in the front bedroom, about a foot above the floor. Canite is soft, cheap. The hole is horseshoe-shaped, where the heel of the boot has broken through first, depressing the canite back into the hole. I feel around, but it can't be fixed; it will stay here forever, as long as the wall remains in place, no matter who lives here. His throw was excellent, the whip-like throw of a man who has lived outdoors, thrown rocks, aimed at targets with care and pride. Lucky I ducked.

The room is empty, the bed made all neat, the pillow clean and smooth, waiting for someone to sleep on it. The shrine to the Virgin Mary has gone, the bottles of tablets, the bucket for spitting, all gone. I am there in the house with Ray, who is playing with the cushions in the lounge room. Mrs Grant is there also, reading the *Women's Weekly* at the kitchen table, minding us while our mother is at the hospital. She has been summoned, and relatives have arrived to go with her – Nair and Uncle Alec in a taxi, Ninny on the bus yesterday. They all go in Nair's taxi. We wait all morning and then, just as Mrs Grant is making banana sandwiches for our lunch, they arrive home, doors slamming, voices low and confidential, coming up the path. They all assemble in the lounge room drinking cups of tea while we have our lunch, and then my mother calls to me.

'Garry, come in here; I want to talk to you.'

The whole event is so unusually formal that, of course, I know that something important, ominous even, is coming. My mother looks grave, pale, has been crying, clutches a handkerchief in her lap. She sits on the lounge chair by the door, holds out her hands to me and I take them.

'Your father – daddy – has died. He died peacefully in the hospital this morning. He wanted you to know he loved you and Ray very much.'

My only feeling at that instant is pity for her, she looks so distraught, so weary. All I want to do is respect everyone's gravity and fit in with it, as if what matters on this day is a certain way of behaving. But about the information itself I feel nothing very much, except numbness and a kind of ... responsibility to conform to the requirements of the occasion. What I have received is a report, not an experience of his death. As far as I am concerned he might still be alive in the hospital bed, might even still come home when he gets better. This won't happen of course, because I believe the truth of the report, believe my mother's grief. But it is not my knowledge, not my grief, not yet. All there is is this cold, empty bedroom, these mournful faces around me in the lounge room, these bewildered, searching confidentialities taking place between my relatives. Their released words fly round the room, voices with no owners:

It was a mercy.

He'd suffered long enough.

Only thirty-three years of age.

He had no more than a quarter of a lung left.

He was a saint.

Remember we're always here if you need us.

But for me, death is not here. Death is in another place, and the pain of it reserved for another time.

*

I was not allowed to attend the funeral. Ray and I were left out of the proceedings altogether, not I think from any repressive motive, but simply because it was another one of those strange ideas of decorum that characterised the early post-World War Two period. It was somehow not good for children to be put in contact with the darker side of life, or to witness adult grief or anything connected with death, horror or the macabre. No funerals. There was an American film in the early fifties called *The Three Faces of Eve* that used a popularised version of psychoanalysis as a way of getting to the cause of the main character's multiple personality disorder. The origin, the story discovers, lay in a crucial moment back in childhood when the character was forced to kiss her dead grandmother lying in the coffin, an old tradition in some parts of America; the sheer horror of the experience leaves the child with deep psychological problems that show up in adulthood. Even at the time I saw the film, which was just a few years after my father's death, I was sceptical about this 'single origin' explanation of a long-standing and complex illness. Later, reflecting on my own grief at the loss of my father, I came to a total rejection of the idea that the knowledge and experience of death should be hidden from children; on the contrary, if they do not have the opportunity to see for themselves that their loved one has died, and perhaps 'say goodbye' to them as is now a popular idea, then their grief can be distorted by delusions and extended for years.

My mother came home from the cemetery with a small crowd of relatives and friends. They had been somewhere for drinks and a buffet lunch, and they now sat around in our lounge room in their sober clothes and various expressions of sadness. She looked strikingly beautiful in a black suit and no lipstick, her face lightly powdered to hide her bruised eye-sockets and flushed cheeks. All looks, wherever they searched about the room, inevitably were drawn to her, and came to rest on her slight, elegant brilliance. Uncle Les was being attentive to her, as was Mr Dewar from down the road, the first time he had ever been in our house. The mood was sombre and dignified, and despite her beauty and the attentions given her, my mother never looked so alone as on that day. I stood up next to her and she put her arm around me, one of the few memories I have of affectionate contact between us. I kept projecting into the future with questions: What would this mean? How will we exist as a family now? What are children, what am I, without a father? Will my mother marry someone else?

The next day a large black sedan pulled up in front of the house driven by the director of the firm that had conducted the funeral service. He was tall, lean, with dark hair balding at the front and an easy, reassuring manner. He sat with my mother, again in the lounge room, just the two of them, and, as he handed her the account for the different expenses of yesterday's service, he put this to her: that he wanted her to understand him right, that he knew she lived in modest circumstances, didn't have a lot of money to throw around, that funerals are expensive items by anyone's measure but that if you had only a limited income they could be a terribly crippling burden on a family, that with two young boys to support and rent to pay she had plenty of other demands to meet, and that he had nothing but sympathy for a woman in her position and that he hated to see unnecessary expense added to an already painful time of her life, but that she was a young woman – indeed a lovely young woman – who more than anything at this moment needed a helping hand from someone in a position to give it. Like himself. That she knows, doesn't she, that she does not have to pay that account if she chooses not to; that he could see his way to waiving payment if she were willing to, well shall we say settle matters in some other way. He would like to. He would be happy to. It's up to her; she can make him tear up the account there and then. He simply wants to help her. Funerals don't come cheap. She is an attractive woman, who should not feel alone at this time. The offer is there.

My uncle Ron told me about this many years afterwards, for of course it was not known to me at the time. He, in turn, got it from my mother. I'm sure she would never have told him if she'd had anything to be ashamed of over the matter, which was unimaginable to anyone who knew her; my mother was a romantic at heart, and selling herself was simply outside her idea of life.

Nor was that the final act of pressure placed on her in this, the most immediate moment of her grief; Mr Dewar, for the second time in two days, came to talk to her. Vulturine Mr Dewar, a man himself of funereal bearing, was a respected member of the Catholic Sodality which, amongst other undertakings, had lobbied for the construction of a new church and school, St Bernadette's, being built in the local area. The Sodality kept a sharp eye out for Catholic interests, political or personal. Having discovered that my mother was not a Catholic, Mr Dewar perceived in my father's passing a potential for a lapse in commitment to their sons' education, and had come round to press some advice upon her, just in case she was thinking of some other schooling option for the future. Did she realise, he pointed out, that it had been a condition of her marriage to Frank that she had accepted a sacred duty to raise the boys as good Catholics, which meant of course, Catholic schooling? 'In any case, it was what Frank would have wanted,' said he, who knew as much about my father as he knew about me, which was next to nothing (though in this case, preaching good Catholic doctrine, he was probably right about my father).

What she should do, he suggested, was send Ray to the new St Bernadette's when it opened next year, and as for me, whose adventurous nature could easily turn into delinquency in a couple of years without a father's hand to exercise control, I should be sent to the Christian Brothers, who know how to keep boys on the right path. Mr Dewar was of the view that the best option for me was St

Thomas Aquinas' in Clifton Hill, a small secondary school that ran classes to Leaving Certificate (year ten) level, and charged modest fees. But I would need to apply and could be accepted only if there was a place available, and attend an interview. It is interesting that Mr Dewar did not send his own son, David, to this school; he chose the larger, more prestigious, more academically inclined and more expensive Marist Brothers College in East Melbourne, though clearly he was not well-off. The economy model, especially since it came with the firm hand of the Christian Brothers, was right for an unruly monkey like me.

My mother was in no state to quarrel with these suggestions; in her grief she was not able to think carefully about my education, and in any case, she probably agreed with much of Mr Dewar's argument. But it was not a good choice for her or for me: State education would have cost her nothing, as compared with the fees she had to find every year to keep me at St Thomas's. And the Christian Brothers had no academic reputation, a failing she should have made herself aware of and concluded would not be suitable for an intelligent child like myself. I would have received no worse an education in the State system. But she agreed to Mr Dewar's suggestions and the matter was settled.

So it was that these few days in June 1948, the time of the death of my father and the decision over my schooling, proved to be the crucial turning point in my life. I was nine and a half years old, small and unprepossessing, with no obvious gifts except an ability to learn quickly from experience, and keener to be outdoors than in the house. In some respects a blank sheet, I was ready to be written-on by whatever controlling hand took up the task.

Inside, knowable only to me, was a seething brew of emotions and imaginings, longings and frustrations that were eager for expression, desperate at times to latch themselves onto something bigger and more effective than myself. That something was about to inscribe itself upon me.

Questions have always dogged me about my father's death, or more particularly about his illness. What were the circumstances of his last weeks? How bad was he when he was admitted to hospital, and how quickly did he deteriorate? More to the point, what treatment did he receive? Were antibiotics ever considered? I know I've looked to lay blame somewhere – that he was denied the best and latest treatment for some reason of neglect or conspiracy or low priority (was there a hierarchy of patients?) – in my difficulty in accepting the silence surrounding the subject. The hospital records have been destroyed; no family documents exist to provide any clues.

Of course, what I have wanted to do, in the search for the origins of my grief, is change the course of medical history. I have wanted to turn back the clock, to push the moment when drug research succeeded in defeating tuberculosis back to an earlier time – only a tiny bit earlier in the scheme of things, in the long history of this most successful of all killers. Two, three years at the most, and the drugs would be available. That is the terrible irony of my father's illness – it was badly timed; by the 1950s treatments were rapidly curing it, but by then he had gone.

Small wonder that my childhood feeling about my father was that there was something deeply unjust about his suffering and death. I look back now and see that what was against him was nothing more nor less conspiratorial than that huge, uncontrollable historical lottery called Luck. But to a small child, brought up to believe that the world is in the control of adults, of a system of government, of an all-powerful God, it felt overwhelmingly like a conspiracy. It felt exactly as it did in the case of Christ, that he was going to an unjust death at the hands of an unfair world, and the worst of it was it had been preordained; this was what was meant to happen, so all the strategies for survival, the raised hopes followed by the disappointments, the belief that somehow justice would eventually win out, were all the mad delusions of the innocent and powerless. The big decisions had been made elsewhere, at a remote chief executive level, and your minor administrators, your doctors and priests, your Jewish elders and Pontius Pilates, are unwitting players in the charade devised just to keep everyone frightened and guessing.

I may turn these questions over in my mind now, but the truth is that at the time all I felt was the presence of this unknowable, unfeeling but irresistible power that lay behind the events. A world goes to war, mates are killed, a family is homeless, a father dies, a mother weeps, a child longs for comfort, friends mourn, people are poor and struggle to fashion a home in the starkest surroundings, and no one has the power to prevent it. We are creatures who are done to; we are not in control of very much at all, it all happens to us, at us, upon us, with us. Who does it? What does it? What is this force that opposes our happiness? It is huge and amorphous, but it is also awesome and demanding of our respect. When we love each other, as I did my family, I felt that we did so in spite of this force, that it did not want our contentment, that we bonded together small and vulnerable in the teeth of this malevolence, threatening always to deprive us, to disappoint us, to defeat us. I might have been an outgoing and unruly child, but I was also a fearful and less than happy one, trying to make sense of a world dominated, as ours seemed to be, by pain.

My Catholic education stepped into the gap here and purported to supply the image and the mythology for this force: God and Christendom. It is, I came to believe, what was meant when the nuns, the priests, the brothers and the Faithful spoke of God. God is the one with the power, and the thing to do, as the message of the Faithful clearly implies, is get on His side. You'd be crazy not to. Opposition is pointless. These were the feelings behind my increasing willingness to take the religious messages of my teachers more seriously.

*

It was felt that we should spend the weeks following my father's death in some mode of mourning. I was taken out of school, given some money and sent to stay with my cousin Jack in Footscray, while my mother took Ray to stay with relatives somewhere on the other side of the city. This period with cousin Jack was an eye-opener; he was even more of a street kid than I was, though in his case Footscray was an urban working class area, more like North Melbourne, with no wilderness like the Darebin Creek to roam about in.

I found my own way to the house, catching buses into the city and then the train to Footscray. They lived in a small two-storey terrace in Buckley Street, and when I arrived only my Aunty Eily was there; Jack was off somewhere and Uncle Akey, as everyone called him, was at work at the meat factory. The house was dark and gloomy downstairs, with a ramshackle kitchen and bathroom added out the back, cold and smelly, with an uninvitingly stained tin bath. The toilet was right down the bottom of the yard. My auntie Eily – my father's sister Eileen that is – was welcoming, though it was noticeable to me that she didn't smile much. She talked about Jack in his absence in oddly glowing terms. 'He's always at the Footscray baths. He's a wonderful swimmer, stays out in the sun day after day. Gets blisters on his back as big as saucers, and at night he peels big sheets of skin off till he's red raw.' I resented a vague implication in this that I should admire Jack's devil-may-care heroics, or that I wouldn't have been up to them myself. She took me upstairs and showed me the double bed in Jack's room where the pair of us were to sleep. Then she said she was going down the pub to meet Uncle Akey, and that I could wait here until Jack got home, which wouldn't be long. In the meantime, I could play with the litter of kittens that were running around in the washhouse and out onto the back pathway.

Jack eventually came home; he was quite a bit bigger than me, being a couple of years older, and he had set routines that he introduced me to. He turned on the radio so we could listen to a very funny program called *Yes what?* that he never missed. It was about a school where the kids were either cheeky or stupid, and confused the teacher so much that by the end of every program he was reduced to babbling despair. For breakfast every morning, which Aunty Eily brought up to him in bed, Jack had a mug of tea and four thick slices of buttered toast, which he proceeded to dunk in the tea. With his encouragement, I did exactly the same. The toast became a deliciously soggy dripping mess which left the tea with streaks of melted butter on the top and detached lumps of bread floating in it. It tasted quite good, and was certainly a change from cereal every morning.

There was a freedom and knowingness in Jack's life that I admired, but was also a little afraid of; essentially he did what he liked. But he didn't have a lot of time for me, and frequently went off to his friends. I met some of them one day when he took me to Footscray Park, down near the Flemington racecourse. They were tough and older, and talked mostly about things they would like to do to girls. One of them said they'd had a great time the night before putting stones on the railway line near Footscray station, but to their disappointment they didn't succeed in derailing the train. Jack said to me that we might go up later that afternoon and see if we could do it. If he did, he didn't take me or tell me about it afterwards.

Uncle Akey hardly looked at me whenever he came in. He always smelled of beer, and spoke in a threatening tone the whole time. 'Your mother never comes to see us,' he said one night. 'Too good for us is she?'

'Arthur,' said my aunt, 'he's only just lost his father. Go easy on 'im.'

It was not a comfortable time for me there; Jack either ignored me or did rash, delinquent things, things of no imaginative value. Uncle Johnny had given him a Samurai sword that he'd brought back from Japan, and when we were playing about on the bed after breakfast one morning he aimed a thrust at my head and ran the sword right through the pillow only inches from my face. In that moment I saw that Jack, indeed the whole household, had a fundamental instability that did not appeal to me. The ultimate confirmation of this came one late afternoon when we were playing near the back door with the kittens. Uncle Akey had brought a friend home, both of them loudmouthed and the worse for drink. The friend, on his way through to the toilet down the yard, stepped square on one of the kittens with a huge black workboot. 'Fuck,' he said, and without a second thought, the man picked up the mewling kitten, took a few steps into the back yard, and hurled its flailing body so high, so far that it must have dropped several houses away in someone's yard or on a roof. For days I kept thinking about it, wondering if it was dead before it hit, or if it wasn't really that badly hurt in the first place and could have survived, or whether it was still alive and full of feeling when it landed on whatever it landed on. It made me feel sick, and hate that man's brutal, unnecessary act.

I spent the rest of my time there pretty much on my own. I walked down Buckley Street to a busy junction of trams and shops and came upon a cinema covered in strange posters written in a foreign language. 'La Scala,' they said, 'Risorgimento' and 'Vittorio de Sica' plastered over the columns beside the entrance. I worked out that there was a picture showing later that afternoon called *Ladri di Biciclette*, so after I'd gone down to the Park to look for Jack and not finding him, I went back to the picture theatre and watched the film. There weren't many people in the theatre. It was difficult to tell what was going on in the film because they were speaking in a foreign language, and the words at the bottom of the screen came and went too fast for me to read them all, but I could work out that a man's bicycle was stolen and a little boy was helping him look for it. Two things made a deep impression on me: the town where they were was the most desolate place on earth – ruined buildings, bare streets with no shops, slums and waste ground everywhere; and the little boy, wearing oddly short trousers and a dowdy coat, but with the face of a sad old man, aged well beyond his years. He haunted me for ages, that boy, and that town, though I never did work out what happened in the story. I sensed it had a lot to do with the War, that it was what it was now like in the places bombed by the Germans and the Americans and where all the fighting had been. So different from Australia, Australia the normal.

I was glad to be back home in West Ivanhoe, and didn't really want to visit my cousin ever again. Just how it was meant to be a period of mourning I never discovered. I guess it was some kind of gesture to appearances; if we weren't seen by the usual people for a while, they would think we were secluding ourselves away in some dismal corner, recovering from our loss. The only comment from the children at school was to ask if I'd been off sick, and when I said no they lost interest.

The day I got back to school a boy walked up to me at playtime howling in panic and holding an upturned hand out at me to look at; a piece of fence paling a foot-and-a-half long, had gone right through his palm and out the other side, as if he'd been shot with an arrow.

At some point before the end of that year my mother took me for an interview at my proposed new school, St Thomas's. It was night time and a good hour away on two buses. The moon-faced, smiling headmaster, called Brother Williams, wearing a full-length black frock, took us into his office. He seemed to discourage us for quite a long time, saying that the classrooms were full to bursting as it was, and that they had a very small playground and no room for any more buildings. In a serious tone he insisted that it would be a great trouble to find room for me, that I would have to justify him squeezing me in somehow by bringing credit to the school once I got there. My mother mouthed a whole lot of assurances, saying I was good at spelling, had very nice handwriting and got good marks at arithmetic.

'Sport?' he asked.

My mother and I answered at the same time, saying opposite things: 'No,' I said, and 'He likes playing games,' she said.

'Well, he'll find lots of opportunities to develop his sporting prowess here,' he said. He talked about the fees and my mother explained that she'd just been widowed and was on a pension. 'We can be a little flexible on the figures,' he said, 'but I think you'll find they're reasonable anyhow.' So we came away knowing that I had been accepted, which we both took to represent some kind of triumph, an admittance to the halls of privilege. At some point my mother had to contact the school to purchase the school cap and uniform, which were navy and bore a mid blue and gold coat of arms and a Latin motto, the meaning of which I have long forgotten.

*

On a hot summer night I have a dream so clear that I remember every detail. We are in a dark house that is supposed to be our house but is not really like it. It is more like Nair's house in North Melbourne, but with differences. There is my mother, and Ray, my grandmother Ninny and one or two other people in the background, all moving about to no special purpose. We are all quiet under a heavy cloud of sadness in the place, so much sadness that no one can speak. Then, without warning, he comes; the door opens and let's in a dazzling light that silhouettes him in the doorway of a room that is now Nair's lounge room. His outline is sharp, unmistakeable, but I can't quite see his face or make out the colours or type of clothing he wears. The light behind him forms a ring behind his head, his hands turned out in a gesture of welcome as he comes through the room, and from her chair in the dark, unable to be seen, Nair's voice says, 'Jesus Christ, it is Frank!' and I know in my heart that my father has come back, that in fact he never died, it was all a mistake, they gave out the wrong information and now here he is, back with us, with me, and I can be happy with him again forever. I am bursting with joy, such that I am almost choking, yet my delirium is so total that I care about nothing but this transformation in my life from misery to ecstasy, and it is with this intense happiness that I wake up, open my eyes and expect to find my father alive, awake somewhere in the house; I can go to him. Then the truth dawns. It is a dream. He hasn't come back after all, he is dead forever. The cruel, melancholy truth creeps back like a dank fog, sits heavy inside me, and I am back in the real world again, the one that aches, the one that always has something missing that should be there.

8

NO PREVIOUS SCHOOL HAD prepared me for my first day at St Thomas's. The playground was totally concreted, not a tree or blade of grass in sight, and hemmed in by buildings and high fences. At break times the yard was a seething crowd of navy blue, with boys jostling, yelling, playing in every claimable space. Every wall and the area in front of it was used as a handball court, but with no lines to mark it out, so as I stumbled around trying to orient myself or simply find somewhere to stand I was shoved or pummelled aside and off the court! was barked at me by some irate boy. The noise and confusion simply made me want to go home, or back to my shady little schoolyard at the Immaculate Conception.

Every Monday morning the whole school stood to attention in rows, pledged allegiance to the King, said a prayer and listened to announcements and warnings from Brother Williams, standing high on the second story balcony of the newest building. The Brothers on duty roster would keep an ear out for any wisecrackers in the ranks who would be promptly made an example of. The atmosphere was busy and strict, with routines that were rigidly applied. I was in grade five, which was taught mainly by a teacher called Mr Carroll, a bald man with a wart on his head that won him the nickname 'Conker' Carroll. He turned out to be a colourless man, however, and left little for me to remember him by.

These early days were full of confusion and fear of failure, of getting things wrong. In the scramble to make friends I seemed either to miss out or to connect only with the sillier boys, the ones with no sporting kudos or no personal sophistication. This was perfectly just, I should have conceded, because I had neither quality myself. I was undersized and relatively innocent, and yet there was a fierce desire in me to attach myself to some greater force or person than myself.

I continued to dream the same dream at night, that my father came back to us, that his death had all been a terrible mistake, and I was filled with joy, until I awoke and returned to the painful truth. There was no one I could tell this to, no one to whom I could turn for understanding. My mother, for all her strength and goodness, was not such a person, at least not in my mind. Her role was keeping us going; what I needed was someone who fed my imagination, someone who would put the tumult inside into some kind of sense. It would have to be a man.

My uncle Ron, my mother's younger brother, was not such a one, at least not to me. Nevertheless, I was delighted when my mother announced early that year that he was coming to live with us. He moved into my father's old room, and I liked his jokey manner and stylish looks, which he carefully groomed in front of the bathroom mirror. He was a help to my mother and would occasionally put in a word of reprimand to bring Ray and me to heel. I never resented him. He was almost an older brother.

Horseracing was still a strong interest of his, though mostly at the betting level now; he was also keen on playing football. He kept up with all the sports news, read the *Sun-News Pictorial Turf Guide* and *The Sporting Globe*. One morning he said to me, 'I see Essendon have got a new full-forward, young Jack Coleman.' It was the first time he'd shared a piece of sporting information with me, and I took it as a recognition that I was now a member of the male world, mature enough to talk seriously about sport. What he said stuck in my mind.

At school, they had recently introduced a somewhat forced scheme to create a collegiate spirit by splitting the school into four different 'houses', uninspiringly named after the colours blue, red, green and gold; we were supposed to identify with our colour, yell frenzied support to our swimming or athletic teams, chant such concoctions as 'Yah, yah, rooting-jar, gold, gold, rah, rah, rah', and 'get behind' our house captains. Somehow this aping of English-style private school culture didn't work, and after a year or so seemed to transmute into something much more hierarchical, based on individual achievement. Importance was granted increasingly to the school sporting heroes, especially footballers, who were proudly paraded before us as exemplars of life's highest ideals. I was beginning to see that maleness and sport were deeply connected, and that the connection mattered.

From the start, the school had for me a heavy atmosphere of fear within which any achievements or moments of pleasure took place. One will hear from Old Boys that it was something one 'got used to', which is true enough; we usually adjust to our circumstances, however uncomfortable, but this doesn't mean that we aren't affected by them, unconsciously or physically. Certainly we found fun and pleasure, we had moments of excellence and pride, some fair proportion of which we owed to the spirit and teaching of the Brothers. But what was never far away, ugly and frightening, the sanction that would be resorted to at the merest opportunity was official, systematic and merciless violence upon the boys.

Each Brother carried in the inside breast pocket of his black frock a stiff strap, consisting of stitched-together layers of leather, perhaps three-quarters-of-an-inch thick and around ten or eleven inches long. When, at the moment he felt a need to impose himself on a situation, he reached into that pocket for that strap, all eyes followed the action, and all hearts pounded with the fear of what might be coming their way. School legend had it that no more than six 'cuts' could be administered at any one time, but on one occasion I saw a boy receive six on each hand and walk back to his seat with both hands locked under his armpits, fighting back tears of pain and humiliation before the class. The cuts across the palm of the hand were painful enough, and on a cold morning those fingers could be useless for an hour or so, which was why the brothers usually selected your non-writing hand; I often wonder, decades later, whether the osteoarthritis that has wrecked my right hand but not my left hand – my writing hand – is a direct legacy of the discipline meted out to me at St Thomas's. But what was in its way worse than the pain of being strapped was the psychological fear in which it took place. To small boys, that action of reaching to the inside pocket for the strap was the punitive equivalent of a flogger taking up the cat-o-nine-tails, and immediately induced a panicked search for guilt; what have I done wrong? On days when the Brother felt particularly challenged for control, and driven to displays of power, your mind could be in a state of near constant terror. An especially fearful tactic was to send you to the Waiting Room, which was a kind of rarely used hallway, to ponder your fate until the Brother found the time to administer your punishment in private. Here you could wait for twenty minutes or half an hour, enduring the frowns of school elders and noteworthies in the old photographic portraits that lined the green walls of the room, undergoing the agonies of punishment over and over in your mind before the first blow on your body was even struck. So between the strapping and the fear of strapping, an inordinate amount of a pupil's time was concerned with punishment and being punished.

It was made worse by a sense of injustice that often followed the punishment. Boys were frequently strapped for trivial and often unintentional transgressions. For instance, being late for school. In my case, I was often late for reasons outside my control. The journey from West Ivanhoe to Clifton Hill would be a good twelve miles, which at the time I travelled by taking two buses – the 'yellow bus' that ran along Darebin Road and stopped at High Street, Northcote, and the 'green bus', usually a double-decker, that ran along High street to Queen's Parade, Clifton Hill, where my school was. Both services were highly inadequate for the population they served, especially at peak hours, resulting in overcrowding, breakdowns, missing buses and buses too full to pick up any more passengers. Often I would stand at the stop and watch an overcrowded bus sail past, only for the next one to do the same, with the result that I could be anything up to fifteen minutes late for school; many a time, however, it was no more than a couple of minutes. Depending on the whim of the Brother, I would either be strapped or given lines to write:

I must get to school on time

I must get to school on time

I must get to school on time

Fifty or a hundred times. As if I wasn't trying to. As if I missed the bus on purpose. Similarly, boys were strapped for not doing their homework, for talking in class, for failing to wear their school cap going home, and other minor blemishes that happened to give annoyance to the Brother on that day; at other times he might decide to be generous and make a joke about it. Inconsistency and mercurial emotions were common in the Brothers, which, allied with almost unfettered power in the classroom, was a frightening mix.

Their performance as teachers, it has to be said in their defence, was made all the more difficult by the sheer numbers in each class. None of my classes had fewer than fifty in them, and in year eight there were seventy-seven, all in the one room. Keeping us disciplined was a major task, undoubtedly. But the problem was of the school's own making: Brother Williams could hardly have been serious during that first interview when he lingered doubtfully over admitting me, because clearly the policy of the school, driven by money, was to cram as many bodies into the rooms as they would take. He was never going to pass up an opportunity for more fees, just as he was never going to be too bothered about the educational disadvantages to the boys of overcrowded classes. The Church liked to blame the government for not giving financial subsidies to Catholic schools, thus forcing them either to charge much higher fees or inflate their class sizes; overcrowding was a useful political tool in the Church's agitation for subsidy, so they had an interest in its continuance. Pedagogically, the school's concerns lay more in fostering loyalty to the Catholic Church than in preparing minds for the tasks of life, and so long as the boys were firmly embedded in the Faith and brought credit on the school, matters of educational achievement or academic integrity, which always carried certain dangers for Catholics anyway, were well down the list of the school's goals.

I can illustrate this by recalling the teaching of European History in year eight: a Catholic History text published in Australia, I think by Pellegrini, was used, and in its pages somewhere it showed pictures of Karl Marx and Voltaire – and possibly others I can't recall – under which it clearly stated that these writers were, under pain of mortal sin, never to be read. In other words, even opening their works, quite apart from agreeing with them, could bring you eternal damnation. No matter the encouragement of enquiring young minds, or the acknowledged significance of the prohibited writers; it was anti-education, like so many of the practices at the school. These were not Jesuits, it should be remembered, they were Christian Brothers, and there would not have been three university degrees among the lot of them at St Thomas's. Ideas, and how to deal with them, were not their strong point, and intellectual integrity was of no interest to them.

On the other hand, the school authorities continued their attempt to give the place a private school veneer; they hired an elocution teacher, a stout lady with a fake English accent, who put us through hours of parroting mindless phrases that were meant to instill correct pronunciation in us:

Ah - eh - ee - ouw - oo - aye – yoo.

How now brown cow.

Harry hit him on the head with the hard, hard hammer. The rain in Spain stays mainly on the plain.

Don't put your feet on that wet seat.

We were exhorted to sound our vowels round and full or to grin them through bared teeth, to puff our aitches from our chests with unnatural emphasis (perhaps creating the Catholic 'haitch'), to roll our double 'r's like stage Scotchmen, and to make our final 't's as audible as snapped sticks. Few of us, I think, had heard anyone talk like this in our lives, nor would until Professor Higgins in the musical came on the scene.

The statuesque lady also taught us a subject called 'Christian politeness', for which there was a slim, unimaginatively illustrated text. No doubt it contained many genuinely useful points designed to improve the typical rudeness of teenage schoolboys, but unfortunately the ones that have stuck in my mind have mostly proved useless or bizarre in adult life. A well-known one is to walk always on the side nearest the road when accompanying females in the street, which is a vestige of times when streets were unmade and muddy, and carriages passed close to the kerb; the gentleman took the splash in order to protect the woman's clothing. Without thinking, I still do it, though I've never seen anything especially Christian about it. Perhaps one that did have our Christian morals in view was the one about accompanying ladies on staircases: always walk in front of her on the way up (so that there is no possibility of temptation to impure thoughts from glimpsing any part of the lady's leg). However, when accompanying her down the staircase, one should also walk in front of her, lest the fragile creature should trip, in which case your presence would mercifully break her fall. The clear implication is, of course, that when there is a choice between sin and injury, injury is always to be preferred. The 'politeness' that has most puzzled those I've eaten at table with over the years, is the one of always leaving a small portion of food on the plate, rather than completely cleaning it up. The idea is not to give any indication to your feeders (parent, cook, host or waiter) that you might be still hungry. The problem is, some might take it otherwise, and think you didn't like the food. Nevertheless, the authorities responsible for these exercises in idiotic etiquette have deemed that the little mound of potato or pumpkin, or the untried mouthful of meat, left on the plate's edge, will comfort the feeder in the knowledge that they have filled you to satisfaction, and don't need to offer you any more. But it still leaves you with a problem: how do you then justify saying 'yes' to the dessert that is to follow? Do you, in order to be consistent, lie and say, 'No, I've had plenty thank you,' even though you'd love to hoe into the rhubarb pie just brought to the table? Do you say 'yes' to it, thus implying that you'd had about as much as you could take of the Irish Stew, and need something decent to wipe away the taste, thus risking giving offence? At moments like these it would seem that 'Christian politeness' is something of an oxymoron, and that sometimes the requirement to be polite, assuming that others can even recognise your action as such, is at dangerous odds with the Christian imperative to be honest. But I'm sure our socially informed teacher had not the slightest inkling of the paradox.

*

My mother seems sad much of the time now, though she never cries. She sings to herself quietly in the evenings while working at her dressmaking in the lounge room, or at the machine in my bedroom. She sometimes listens to plays on the radio. But she is tense, too. Often on cold nights she puts me to bed in her big bed, where I read a comic while she busies herself in the kitchen before joining me. Sometimes she makes me go back to my own bed, and sometimes she lets me stay the night with her. We are never comfortable together. 'Don't fidget,' she'll say, or 'Stop sniffing.' She'll read for a time while I lie there next to her, frightened to move, but I know she is aware of me and I'm aware of her. I think of her body next to mine, and I wonder what it is like under her thick nightdress. But I make sure that no part of me touches her; I don't know what would happen if it did, and this thought creates a kind of electric tension between us. One time when I have slept right through the night with her, I feel her stir and get out to pee in the pot she slides out from under the bed. I pretend to be still asleep, watching her through my near-closed eyes. She is oblivious to me. She hitches up her nightdress and holds it up clear of her body, and in that brief moment I see between her thighs a thick, black bush of hair, so rich and dark that it almost glows in the grey half-light of the morning. This is the part of her that is not mother, not for me to see and know. But I have seen it and I am secretly thrilled, and have to fight to stop myself from twitching in my new knowledge. She squats over the pot; her stream of pee is loud, affirmative, mysterious – how does it come out, I wonder, and from where exactly? When she is finished she stands up and drops her nightdress, and I see nothing more. She gets back into bed and it is all I can do to keep myself still and to keep up the facade of sleep, terrified that she will sense I have been awake and have seen her. I have seen her, and she must never know. Never. And it was not a sin, because I thought nothing.

*

One particular Friday night a group of us from the neighbourhood was walking up to the Ivanhoe cinema to see a much anticipated film called *Spitfire Parade*. We had seen the trailer the week before, and had talked about it all week. On the way up we took the route along Waterdale Road, where the houses were privately owned though modest, and several of us were joshing, as you do. Geoff Groves, always inclined to be over-boisterous, pushed me in the chest and I fell backwards into a two-foot high privet hedge forming a front fence. Amid the laughter they pulled me out, and we continued on our way. The brightly lit cinema with the people milling outside and the advertising posters in their glass cases in the foyer augmented our already high spirits; we stood noisily chatting in the ticket queue eager to catch the cartoons before the main film. Suddenly a hand grabbed me by the shoulder and wrenched me out of the queue. At first I thought it was one of the boys, but in fact none of them had even seen it happen. A strong male arm around my neck from behind dragged me forcibly backwards out of the cinema onto the footpath. There I was presented to a woman and another man. 'That's him,' said the woman. 'Yes, that's the little bugger,' said the man beside her. 'C'mon son, you're coming with us.' I still couldn't see who was frogmarching me along the street. When our positions became too awkward to keep up he released his hold and walked alongside holding my upper arm; I then saw he was an oldish man, tall, with dark bushy eyebrows. I still had no idea what it was all about.

'Where are you taking me?'

'You'll see.'

The march continued along Waterdale Road until we came to the house with the privet hedge. 'Recognise this?' the woman said. I was too terrified to reply. They pushed me down the path and into the house, where they sat me on a chair in the hallway. 'Wait there,' said the big man, and the three of them disappeared into a room leading off, leaving me sitting there anxious and confused. As the time passed I thought about my friends and what they would think, and realised I was going to miss the cartoons and maybe even the start of the film. It was not unlike waiting in the school waiting room for Brother Hickey to come and hand out the inevitable belting; gradually it dawned that I was being punished for the business with the hedge, though it was hardly my fault. I thought about sneaking out of the front door, but was too scared to try it in case they caught me and made things even worse. So I sat there, getting increasingly frightened about what these people were planning to do to me, and dejected about missing a film I so much wanted to see. After what could have been forty-five minutes, the woman and the older man emerged from the room and asked me where I lived.

'Valentine Street. One twenty.'

'Up near Liberty Parade?'

'Yes.'

The woman turned to the man and threw a look to the ceiling.

'Housing Commission,' she said.

'I might have known,' said the man.

'Do you know why we've got you here?' said the woman.

'Is it because of the hedge?'

'It's because you have to learn respect for people's property.'

'It wasn't my fault; I was pushed.'

'You were laughing. We heard you.'

'Can I go now?'

'No you can't. You need to learn a lesson; if you damage people's property you have to pay for it. I'll bet your father wouldn't be too pleased with you if we asked him to pay for the repairs to the hedge. Would he?'

'He couldn't anyway.'

'Out of work is he? On the dole?'

'Anyway,' said the woman, 'it isn't the money. You have to learn to respect people's property. We could take you up to the police station and have you charged. How would you like that?'

This went on until their interest in the interrogation gradually waned. They must have realised they had succeeded in ruining the evening for me, and I'm sure this was part of the point. When they had had enough the big man felt in his pocket and handed me a sixpence, opened the front door and told me to be on my way and not to do it again.

I walked fast, occasionally ran, back towards the cinema, happy to be free from their hold on me, hoping I could still catch the main feature. I hurried round the corner and up the cinema steps. It was all quiet. The foyer was empty of people, apart from the woman in the ticket office who was busily engaged with her back to me. I thought of going up and asking her if the interval had passed, but something made it seem pointless. I couldn't get any indication from the deserted foyer whether or not the main picture had already started. All I had to do was ask, or go up to the theatre door and take a quick look. But I couldn't bring myself to, or perhaps didn't want to know. A mounting humiliation and anger rose in me, and I fought back hot tears of frustration; what did it matter now, how could I enjoy myself now? They had ruined everything. I hated the unfairness and their contempt and my powerlessness in the whole business. I told myself I knew what kind of people they were: they belonged to the force that did whatever it liked to people like us, like my father, my mother, Commission House people. They did, we were done to. It was part of the unfairness of things.

I turned and left the cinema, shoved my hands deep into my jacket pockets as I liked to do, and walked all the way home on my own. I deliberately avoided Waterdale Road, took the route along Darebin Road and the Little Creek – my old school route – along the unlit walkway that wound through the big willows, nursing my wounded pride and whistling to myself to help ward off my fear of the dark. Only after I had walked half the distance home, still burning with disappointment, did I realise that in my pocket my unthinking fingers had been turning over and over the sixpence that the big man gave me, very likely hoping that it would make me keep my mouth shut.

*

My uncle Ron says to me, 'Did you see the news? That new Essendon full forward kicked twelve goals in his first game today. Coleman.'

This grabs my attention. I am still relatively ignorant about football, but I know enough to understand that twelve goals is an extraordinary number for a single player to kick in any game, let alone his first. Uncle Ron has brought home the newspapers, *The Herald* and *The Sporting Globe* which is printed on pink paper. *The Herald* has an article profiling Coleman, which I read avidly. He is called John, is only twenty years old and is doing university studies. The photograph shows a good-looking, thoughtful young man reading at a desk, an unlikely looking football hero. He comes from Hastings in country Victoria. And he plays for Essendon. Already I am captivated by the romantic image he presents, sense that there is something different about him from the general run of footballers, none of whom have made claims on me of this intensity.

The Sporting Globe gives racy, breathless descriptions of his feats during the match:

Coleman split open a pack to mark in the goal square.

Coleman was too fast for his opponent, and goaled on the run from the forward pocket.

Coleman was doing as he liked as he marked over an opposing ruck-man and kicked truly.

The writing feels rushed and repetitive, but it has a vividness and an energy that I find compelling. Its short paragraphs in their narrow columns conjure images of action that are the nearest thing to being at the game itself.

On that day I vow to get to as many Essendon matches as I can; Kilby Groves from Stortford Avenue, who is also an Essendon supporter, says we can go together, which is good because he is older than I and knows how to get to the football grounds.

*

Bernie Cloney has started helping a man called Jack Purdy on his night time milk round. Bernie is always finding ways of doing jobs, helping out not because

117

he is being generous to them, though he is a basically generous person, but because he loves the adventure of working, the world of men. I catch a little of this liking from him, and when he suggests I might like to come with him one night, I jump at the chance. Since I am going to have to be up at four in the morning, I ask my mother for the alarm clock. She says the whole thing is a stupid idea, and Uncle Ron bets me sixpence I won't be able to get myself out of bed when the time comes, but I do. I am so excited that I wake before the alarm, unset it, dress quietly in the chill morning so as not to wake Ray, and run across to Bernie's house. He is already up and waiting, eating a bowl of cereal. I have one too, and we leave for the dairy, a mile or so away. In the cold night, with only a weak outside bulb to see by, we have to hitch up the horse, a white draught mare called Lofty, and load the cart with crates of bottled milk from the dairy refrigerator room. Jack Purdy is a quiet man who smokes non-stop; I get the impression he hates the job. Bernie, on the other hand, clearly loves it, and does most of the loading. We set off around the streets, Lofty clopping along pretty much under her own slow-paced steam, so well does she know the route. I discover that most of the time we aren't actually riding on the cart, but are running back and forth from the cart to the houses, delivering the ice-cold bottles of milk and bringing back the empties. This keeps our bodies warm, but my hands are freezing; I didn't think about gloves, but then neither did Bernie or Jack, so this must be the norm. Lofty keeps the cart going at a steady pace while we run to keep up with her, sometimes falling behind when someone has left a note with their empties asking for an extra pint or a bottle of cream, which of course we have to try to read in the dark. After nearly an hour I am exhausted, and my fingers are so cold I could weep. I tell Jack I need a break. He tells me to sit up on the cart and they will do the rest. Bernie keeps going as if unaffected. Now that I have stopped running it isn't just my hands that are feeling the cold – I am shivering all over as I sit huddled against the crates, praying for it all to finish soon. It seems to go on for ages, street after street, delivery after delivery. The sky over Ivanhoe village grows gradually lighter, and the dark begins to bleach into grey. On the way home I put my arms around Lofty's neck and walk pressed up against her side to get some of her warmth. Finally back at the dairy, Jack gives Bernie five shillings and me a shilling; I want to tell them both it was the most miserable night of my life, but I keep it to myself.

It is not, however, the end of my relationship with Lofty. A week or so after that I run into Georgie Spain, whose family runs the dairy. Georgie says if I like I can ride any of the dairy horses during the daytime, that they need the exercise.

So the following Sunday I go round to the dairy and choose Lofty to take out. I've never ridden a horse before, but can't believe it's difficult. There is no saddle, so I have to go bareback, but there is a bridle, which George puts on for me. I have to stand on the fence rail to mount her, and when I do it's like sitting on a house roof, she is so high. My legs are pushed so wide apart by her huge girth that I'm virtually doing the splits. We set off, but Lofty won't move at any pace faster than her milk-round clomp, one massive hoof placed lazily after the other. It is also hard to get her to go in any direction that is not her usual route. I try to kick her in the flanks to make her run, like they do in the films, but my legs hardly touch her ribs, and she ignores me. Eventually we turn along Valentine Street and I get the idea of showing off my riding skills to my mother, so I head for our house. As we get near I try to kick Lofty into a canter in the hope of getting up enough momentum to make her jump the fence, which is only some eighteen inches high. But Lofty's pace is beyond anyone's power to change, and she merely lopes up to the fence and instead of jumping it tramples it down with her giant hoofs. I'm thinking about what I'm going to say to my mother if she sees it, when suddenly Lofty stops, halfway across the fence, her front half in our lawn, her back half on the footpath. She has caught her foot in the fence wire, and is trying to wrench it free. I have to dismount and get her out. I slide down her flank like a kid in a playground, and begin untangling the wire around her fetlock. Luckily, she is co-operative or I would never have managed to get her free. I decide to take her into our yard through the back gate, so I lead her across the lawn. The gate is only normal sized, and Lofty is huge in width, and unluckily this time, she becomes wedged halfway through. I didn't imagine I could get myself into so much strife just by taking a horse out for a ride. I am trying to talk Lofty through the gate, to get her to use her strength to squeeze herself through, but she isn't keen to go forward. I'm cursing and swearing, and then I look up and staring at me through the lounge room window is my mother, her eyes popped, and making wild gestures to me to take Lofty back out. Finally she comes out through the back door yelling at me to stop.

'I have stopped.'

'Whose horse is this?'

'The dairy's.'

'Take it back straight away.'

'I wanted to show you how well I can ride.'

'You can't ride.'

'She's stuck in the gate.'

'Get her out. And not in the yard. Take her back to the dairy, before she runs away or something.'

'She won't run away. She won't even run.'

Looking over my shoulder, my mother suddenly gestures towards Lofty, and I turn to see her back herself sensibly out of her predicament and turn, trampling my mother's garden bed in the act, and trot, actually trot, back across the lawn and out across the broken down section of fence and into the street. She is now moving quite fast. I have visions of chasing her for miles down Valentine Street, but she turns right at Stortford Avenue and disappears from view. I run after her, my mother's angry groans over her daisies fading behind me, fully expecting to see the back of Lofty disappearing out of sight. But to my relief I can see her as I turn the corner, standing absolutely stock-still in Groves's front garden, her head up, her ears pricked, like some gigantic white garden ornament, staring absently into the distance. She had expended as much energy as she cared to for the day, and as I approach her she starts grazing on Groves's lawn. Somehow I am able to scramble back up onto her, and together we placidly walk back to the dairy. Those two occasions were my only experiences with Spain's dairy; I kept away from the place from then on, regardless of the generosity of Bernie Cloney or Georgie Spain.

I notice Uncle Les visiting us a lot more often these days. He came for Christmas dinner and gave us all presents, including a book for me: Huckleberry Finn by Mark Twain. He was funny as usual; when he carved the roast lamb he said, in that deep, slow voice, 'What have we got – the jaw bone of an ass or the arse bone of a jew?' Everyone laughed, which was noticeable because the house has been pretty quiet in recent times.

It is obvious that Uncle Les is sweet on my mother. But she doesn't seem interested in him, not in that way. She laughs at his jokes and she likes him to come for meals, but at the same time she doesn't take him seriously. There is always a suggestion of mockery in her attitude to him, and when she speaks about him in his absence, it is always to disparage him. At present he owns a motor cycle, a Triumph Four-Square, like the police use. He has always liked fast cars, and has something of a risk-taking personality. A bit dotty. At the table one time she says to Uncle Ron, 'He can be relied upon to choose the stupidest way to get about. Frank used to say, "If Les's brains were dynamite they wouldn't blow his hat off." He won't be getting me on that thing, that's for certain.'

He is not the only man to pay my mother an increased amount of attention now; Bob Pinchbeck, from next door, frequently limps into the house on weekends, his leg in plaster, wanting to see her on some pretext or other. They sit in the kitchen and talk over cups of tea. Roma Pinchbeck, his wife, has developed a serious illness, and hardly comes out of her bedroom now. I realise he needs someone to talk to.

One night, totally without warning, Johnny, my father's half-brother, and twin to Dickie, turns up. He seems lost and a little drunk. He comes into the bedroom where Ray and I sleep and makes desultory, unconvincing conversation, although I am pleased to see him, as I always am pleased to see anyone from my father's family. He turns our light out for us and I hear him and my mother talking in muffled tones in the lounge room, and realise it was really her he came to see.

Ninny comes to visit us more often these days, too. Nearly every Sunday she sits and gossips with my mother for hours in the kitchen over tea and scones, and fossicks in her bag for presents she has brought for me and Ray, usually chocolate bars. There is a whole mythology of aunts, uncles, cousins and acquaintances on that side of the family that I know almost nothing about. But Ninny and my mother do, and from the bedroom I hear them swapping dramatic tales of 'she said' and 'I said', spoken sotto voce. Often one of them will be knitting, and when I enter the room the talk and the knitting stops and cheerful questions are directed at me:

How's school?

Why don't you go for a ride on your bike?

Where's Ronnie Bowden today?

My mother makes dresses for some of the women in the neighbourhood. Mrs Grant is having one made, and another woman from the next block as well; people are getting to know her reputation for high quality work, and she makes extra money this way. She is always measuring some woman in the lounge room, and more than once I have walked in on a neighbour in her underwear while my mother fusses around her. I linger to get a decent look until I'm ordered out, but they are good humoured about it. On days when she isn't at work, she busies herself at her sewing machine, which she keeps under the window in my bedroom. There isn't much space there, but the light is good and she works away surrounded by swathes of material, happily humming to the comforting tuck, tuck, tuck, of her treadle machine, a Singer with open decorative metal sides and footplate. I love the sound of this machine; comforting, quiet, orderly, it reminds me of some classical music. Also, she has bought herself a dressmaker's dummy, which stands naked on its pedestal behind our bedroom door. I look at the outline of its womanly shape and on one or two occasions, when my mother isn't in the room, I run my hands over its cloth breasts, feeling the bulge and then the inward dip of the waist. What would it be like, I wonder, what will it be like, when I feel a real woman's breasts for the first time? What will she say? Will she like it, do they like it? Or do they just let boys do it to please them? Somehow I know that when I'm older I can expect to want to do this sort of thing. I'm already curious about how it will feel.

The second week of that football season, Kilby Groves and I start going to the games together. I like him a lot, much more than his brother Geoff, and though he is at least five years older than me he talks respectfully to me, is open-minded, good-looking, smiles directly at me when he talks. He has left school and works in a factory somewhere.

We go to the Essendon ground mostly, but also when they are playing away – Fitzroy, the St Kilda junction, Victoria Park, the MCG. Gradually I pick up the finer points of the game, and gradually I come to appreciate John Coleman's genius. He is dazzling, as if there is a spotlight shining on him, and I can't take my eyes off him. For a footballer he isn't all that big – just over six feet and slim in the upper body, though his legs are strong and beautifully built. This physique gives him great speed and ability to leap high into the air; he soars above packs to grab marks in fingers like steel claws. But the secret to his marking ability is his timing; he has an unerring sense of where the highest point of his leap will be in relation to the ball's trajectory, and he will usually take off slightly earlier than his opponents, somehow hang in the air and take the ball inches before they can reach it, even if they are taller than he. I am of course becoming obsessed with him, because he succeeds over all attempts by his opponents to stop him.

*

The whole business of girls is something of a puzzle to me. I've had little to do with them so far, though I can see that friendships between boys, girls, men and women are part of growing up. I actually like girls, like their company, find that they can have a certain energy and intelligence that many boys lack. Uncle Ron brings home girls he has met at dances; they are grown women really yet my mother refers to them as 'his girls', and they sometimes stay for Sunday tea. Their presence in the house is fragrant, colourful, they wear bright frocks that spread out around them and push up in front when they sit, and I want to hang around and talk with them. One is a blonde with tight, curly hair and freckles just visible beneath her heavy face powder, who seems tense and preoccupied when I try to talk to her; she smokes cigarettes the whole time. Another is a short, solid and very pretty girl with dark hair and clear skin, who is friendly and likes to chat. Her name is June, and Ron begins to bring her home regularly, and she gets on well with my mother. The thing about girls is they like boys but they have to pretend they don't, or people will think badly of them. Sometimes they don't pretend, and people do think badly of them.

This is exactly what happens to Kathy Butler, who lives up the road. Kathy is very popular with a number of us boys; several of us – Jim Thornycroft, Alan McHugh, Eddie Weaver who is related to the Pinchbecks next door and now lives there – hang around Kathy's house and she flirts with us, or tells us about things she likes. She particularly likes the film *Annie Get Your Gun*, which she has seen at least three times and can't stop praising, and she likes jeans because they are American. No other girl I know wears jeans; Kathy's are tight and blue and folded up at the bottoms, and my mother says they make her look like a tomboy. She is strong-looking, but she isn't big and all the boys regard her as pretty. Now and then she suggests we play 'spin-the-bottle' on her front porch, which means she gets to kiss whichever one of us the bottle points to. After a time we've all had a fair number of kisses, though it is clear that Kathy contrives the spin to come round to Alan McHugh as often as she can. At the same time, she tries to avoid it pointing to me without hurting my feelings. She is a kind and lively girl, open to having fun whenever she can. But the neighbours disapprove of her, especially the mothers: Mrs Key, whose husband has the unfortunate name of Don, won't let her son Bruce go near Kathy; Mrs Taylor told my mother she was a slut; and my mother says that her parents are too easy with her.

My mother works most days now, travelling by bus into the city every day. She leaves even earlier than I, getting breakfast and packing lunches for me and Ray before she goes. Ray walks to St Bernadette's a few streets away, and is looked after by a neighbour until my mother gets home. I always get home before her, and she leaves the key under the back doormat. Sometimes – too often – she forgets, and I am unable to get into the house until she gets home, which might be as late as six o'clock. I hate this. I am able to use the lavatory, because it is accessible from the back porch, and I can get into the laundry beside it. But I can't get into the house to change out of my school uniform and read my comics or listen to the radio or any of the other things I like to do. I am stuck there, disappointed in my mother's forgetfulness, and getting angry with frustration. On one occasion I am so angry at being locked out that I take hold of the oddball cat that strayed years ago into our household and shut myself in the laundry with it. It looks suspiciously at me. I spot the boxing gloves I received last Christmas, and put them on. I then go after the cat, who can't get out and can only retreat into corners and try to hide from me. But I am too persistent, and manage to land punches on it as it scrambles over laundry baskets, piles of clothes. It hisses at me, but I only laugh with a sense of my own power, and land another punch, this time on its head. My pursuit continues, cunning with controlled anger, and I talk out loud to myself as I do it: 'You think you can get away do you? Oh you do do you? Well, I'll show you something – there, how do you like that? Eh? Eh? Your turn for punishment, eh?' Eventually the cat finds a corner under the copper boiler where I can't reach it; I grab the mop and poke it at the cat to make it move. But it won't. It knows I can't get in there, and is prepared to put up with my poking it rather than my punches. I give up, take off the gloves, sit on the porch step. After a short time I begin to cry. My body shakes with sobs dredged up from deep within me, sobs that take the old ache of absence that I have always felt and bring it up into my chest and throat and expel it out of me in bursts of fiery tears. Why, Why, Why, I say at myself. I don't even know what question I am putting to myself – am I asking myself Why do I do such bad things, Why does it give me such pleasure to hurt a defenceless cat? Or was I asking Why does my mother do this to me, Why was my happiness so unimportant to her that she just forgets to leave me the key, or even Why does life conspire to make me so unhappy, Why is there so little joy or satisfaction in the way I am made to live? I don't know the answers to these questions, or why I feel so tormented. Sometimes I wonder if I am a little mad. More than a little.

*

I get growing pains in my legs quite often now – maybe once or twice a month. They hurt just as much as they ever did, but I refuse to moan or cry out now. I don't want my mother to come, it would feel babyish. I rub them myself, long and hard, I stand up beside the bed and flex my muscles, until eventually the pain subsides. It helps knowing what the cause is, and that it will eventually stop happening.

After I'd been at St Thomas's a couple of years I began to feel an increased pressure to take my Catholicism more seriously. As the religious instruction sessions from the Brothers and the visiting priests constructed an ever-growing, complex edifice of principles and practices around me, that edifice seemed to produce within me little else but psychological conflict. On the one hand, everything seemed to be dark or negative: the images of Hell and Purgatory, formed in the many icons and illustrations on the walls and in the books around me, or inside St John's church opposite the school, or in the language of the sermons and prayers, were gothic and dismal. Goodness was all about what you couldn't do, what you would be punished for, what desires and appetites you should reject in your life. When, on the other hand, they spoke of love, it was a principled sort of love, a love of forces above one, a love of Jesus, or a love of God. Abstractions. How could you love Jesus? He was dead, he had no presence, save in morbid crucifixions hung everywhere around the walls, or sentimental illustrations. How could you love God, when he had no face, no body save for the unconvincing depictions of him peeping though clouds in children's books? And as for the Holy Ghost, what can this conjure in a young mind but fear or mystery? Certainly not love. And the clear images, those that felt real, were designed to frighten, to cow one into submission, like the well-known metaphor for eternal damnation:

Imagine a rock, the size of a house. Now imagine a bird (or an angel) lightly brushing its wing on the rock as it flies past. Imagine the time it would take for the wing to completely wear the rock away to nothing. Well, in eternity this would be a mere split second. Your agony in the flames of Hell would go on for all eternity; that is what damnation means.

There was a power in this edifice that had its effect. It would cross my mind that maybe the teachings were right, maybe you were a sinner by nature, maybe you would go to Hell if you did not obey God, and maybe it made sense to conform just in case; why take the risk if you are not sure?

And in many of the anecdotes that humanised the edifice there was an undoubted attraction. There was something comforting to me in the idea of Mary, girlish and motherly at the same time, of Jesus growing up in an ordinary family, just as there was in the tales of saints and martyrs, sacrificing themselves for their Faith in a world that opposed them, hated them. There were child heroes and girls who saw visions, there were converts who turned away from lives of depravity to lives of caring for others, and there were great achievers who turned around whole nations – St Patrick, St Augustine. All this was a wonderland for one to inhabit, to be enclosed within a protective culture of the select, providing you obeyed the rules and stayed loyal to the community. Pagans, heathens, protestants, were excluded and condemned: better to be among the chosen. Without understanding it, I could feel the power of all this, and I could see it working effectively on many of my schoolmates. Moreover, with a certain degree of inconsistency, I participated in it. I went to Mass, taking Ray along with me, I took Communion, went to Confession, sang the Latin hymns with some pleasure in their otherworldly beauty, found some elemental satisfaction in the rituals, the incense, the poetry; even the gloomy shadows of St John's pseudo-gothic arches had an aesthetic appeal that I responded to.

And yet, I never did believe. Not in my early days of preparation for first Communion, nor under the nasty and the pleasant nuns, nor the sport-mad Brothers nor the more intelligent priests, was I ever fully convinced that the teachings were true or valuable. I remember a discussion I had with Jim Thornycroft and Alan McHugh on the way home from school one afternoon. As we dawdled along from the bus stop they were arguing about how children were produced. Jim insisted that sex was involved, and that it meant men and women getting their organs in contact with each other. Alan totally rejected the proposition, disgusted at the notion that any of the decent adults around us, like our parents, could resort to this sort of behaviour. With Jim's argument sounding stronger by the sentence, Alan got angry and desperate, and finally burst out, 'You don't think the Virgin Mary would have done anything like that do you? She would never have done a filthy thing like that!'

In that very moment, as I listened to them, I knew I didn't accept the idea of an immaculate conception. Alan clearly did not even grasp what it meant. I did. I thought to myself, if babies don't come from adults having sex, then what is so special about Mary's conception being 'immaculate'? Everyone else's is too. And if babies do come from sex, the fact that the Church insists on Mary's conception being immaculate suggests that sex is, as practised by the rest of the world, a dirty and undesirable practice. But how can something that is necessary for existence, something that our parents (whom we are meant to love and honour) have done to bring us into the world, be undesirable? It's like believing that breathing is undesirable. I was astute enough to sense that the virgin birth story was another attempt by the Church, if not to cow us into credulity, then certainly to spin us into an elaborate web of tricks, bent on making us feel that to be human is to be a lowly creature.

Some of the boys felt a similar degree of scepticism, judging by their behaviour in class. Coming from Catholic families, they ought to have been in awe of the doctrinal mysteries. But instead they were bumptious, irreverant and mock-ignorant. One of my favourites in class was Norman MacPhee, who always sat among the smart-mouths at the back of the room. His sense of the absurd was impressive. During a religious instruction session on differences between mortal and venial sins, another classroom wag, my mate John O'Brien, asked the priest,

'Excuse me Father, is a sin of impurity a mortal or a venial sin?'

'Well now, that would depend on the precise circumstances of the impurity,' said the priest.

'Well, say, having sex with a girl.'

'Are we talking about outside of marriage here? Outside of marriage is a mortal sin, no doubt about it,' said the priest. 'And further,' he went on, 'you don't need to be actually doing it to commit a mortal sin; wanting to do it, and giving way to thoughts about it, are equally as bad. Because, as you know, sins of impurity may be committed in thought, word and deed.'

'So, if I think about having sex with a girl, that is a mortal sin?'

'Providing you dwell on it so that you … become aroused by the thought, yes.'

'And what about kissing a girl,' said the boy. 'If I walk a girl home from the pictures and kiss her on the way, what kind of sin is that?'

'Well now, generally speaking, that would be a venial sin, because it would be only brief and would not arouse seriously impure thoughts.'

At this point MacPhee jumped in, as he often did after a situation had formed itself enough for him to spot an opportunity. 'Father,' he said in a tone of weighty philosophical doubt, 'how long would you be able to kiss a girl before it became a mortal sin? I mean, before that moment of crossover from venial to mortal, how long have we got – twenty seconds?' A huge laugh burst from the class.

'Oh well, of course that would depend on the individuals involved,' said the priest, trying to maintain dignity by echoing MacPhee's tone. 'But as a general rule, let's say a few seconds. Anything more, and you would be putting yourself in moral danger. Of course,' his eyes twinkled, 'I wouldn't want you to be looking at your watch at the time.'

'You stop if you get a fat, right?' More laughter followed this.

'Don't be crude MacPhee.'

'No, but the line between going to Purgatory and going to Hell here would be – say –five seconds? I can kiss a girl for five seconds and be okay, but if I go on longer than that, I'm damned?'

The priest hesitated, sensing the weak prestige of the example he'd been led into. 'Look, MacPhee, and the rest of you boys, it isn't as simple as that; I don't want you thinking in such categorical terms about these moral questions. It's the spirit of the thing that matters.' But it was too late; by engaging the priest on such literal terms, MacPhee had exposed the childishness of the teaching.

Similarly, at a session when we were discussing the question of the Real Presence in Mass, the priest was offering advice as to the treatment of the wafer while taking Communion.

'Remember,' he said, 'that it is no longer a wafer of unleavened bread; when the priest blesses the chalice, that is the moment of transubstantiation, and it is now the body of Our Lord Jesus Christ, just as the wine becomes His blood. From that moment on the wafer is to be treated with the same reverence as if it were Christ himself; when you receive it in your mouth you do not bite or chew it, but let it dissolve gently on your tongue, and if you were to have the misfortune of letting it fall to the floor, you must pick it up carefully and consume it without unnecessary handling, in the proper way: place it on your tongue and let it dissolve.'

'What if someone stands on it and it gets dirty?' asked MacPhee.

Unfazed by this facetiousness, the priest replied, 'Pick it up and gently brush off as much of the dirt as you can, and consume it. Remember boys,' he addressed the whole class, 'this is no longer merely bread, but is the precious body of our Saviour, and therefore cannot be let out of our sight, or be brutalised or wasted in any way.'

'What if there's a dog in the church,' interjected MacPhee, 'and he gets to the wafer before you, and swallows it? Has the dog received Communion?' Howls of laughter rang through the classroom.

'MacPhee, see me after this class in the Waiting Room, will you? I've had just about enough of your profanity.'

'But Father, it could happen. Shouldn't we kill the dog and cut it open so that we can save the body of Jesus? Otherwise...'

'MacPhee, leave this room immediately! You disgust me! Out, go on!' He left, and the priest warned the rest of us: 'I don't want to hear any more if this nonsense. Mass and Communion is a serious business, and you would all do well to realise how important they are to the saving of your immortal souls!'

To me, MacPhee's refusal to take any of it seriously was admirable, not because he had a penetrating point – he didn't, although when the Church becomes so insistent on the physical reality of its symbolism, it is looking for trouble. What MacPhee's ridiculous inventions indicated was his underlying refusal to believe, despite all the pressure tactics of Church and school, that such extravagances had any relevance to his life. I admired his guts in indicating this. It accorded with my own scepticism towards what we were being taught. From somewhere in our make-up we both had enough common sense, and mental courage, to resist the control of our lives by the tactics of fantasy and fear.

*

Though I am only eleven years old, I often go by myself into the city. I take myself to the pictures, or to a football match if Kilby Groves isn't able to take me that day. I love the city cinemas, such as the Esquire in Bourke Street, and the Regent in Collins Street, with their elaborate classical style arches and columns, their statues and deep plush carpets. At the State Theatre in Flinders Street, the ceiling has been made into a night sky with stars glinting down, giving a very convincing sense of sitting in a cosy outdoor setting.

During the interval a massive Wurlitzer arises from the orchestra pit, and a girl with a tray at the end of the aisle sells ice-creams and chocolate bars; I rarely go out at the interval, but gorge myself and listen to the popular tunes resounding through the auditorium.

Some days I go to Arden Street if North Melbourne are playing there, and lend the Shinboners my temporary support for the day, out of recognition of their importance to my family. Naturally when I do this, I will drop in to see Nair, either before or after the game. Again she tells me how to get in for nothing: 'If you walk in backwards, they'll think you're coming out.' I love her humour.

If it is lunchtime, Nair will, as usual, send me up to Erroll Street with the money to buy a Rath's pie, and if it is teatime she'll send me out to get fish and chips. If Dickie is there he will unwrap them and smother the lot in tomato sauce; I don't like tomato sauce on fish and chips, or eggs for that matter. If any visitors come while I am there she will be sitting up at the green-clothed table smoking her Turf cigarettes, and will introduce me with great pride: 'Frank's boy; he goes to the Christian Brothers, you know. Wears a uniform and all. It's a college.'

One time when Dickie, my father's half-brother, is still living there, he suggests I go to the pictures in the city with him and his new girlfriend, Evelyn. He has joined the army, like Uncle Johnny, and there is some talk that he might even be sent to Korea. Getting off the tram at the corner of Swanston and Flinders Streets, he pulls a photograph from his tunic pocket and says to me, 'This is Evelyn; you wait on the corner here in front of the Cathedral and spot her for me when she gets there. I'll be in the pub, so the pair of you come and get me and we'll go to the pictures.'

I wait there for some time, checking various women against the photograph as they walk past. It isn't easy to tell how much they resemble the girl in the photograph, because in it she is looking down. Eventually I realise that a woman in a coat has been standing on the other street with her back to me, so I decide to approach her.

'Excuse me,' I say. 'Are you the lady in this photo?'

'Looks a bit like me', she says cheerfully, 'so I guess it must be'.

Straight away I like her ironical, good-humoured tone. We cross the road and find Dickie in Young and Jackson's pub, and then head off to the pictures. I like the way Evelyn and Dickie get along together – matey and full of jokes, though the affection between them is obvious and tender. There is something basically likeable about Dickie that makes him different from his twin brother, Johnny.

*

Uncle Ron has helped to start a local football team in West Ivanhoe, which they are going to call Bellfield. They have adopted the colours of an old football jumper he brought with him from West Melbourne, chocolate brown with a red 'V'. Not great colours, but unusual I guess. They have entered the Victorian Amateur competition, the bottom classification. I go to watch him play a couple of times. He is small and light, and plays as a rover. He doesn't figure in the play a great deal, mainly hangs around the goals, but he is quite clever and usually gets at least one goal each game, sometimes several. But Bellfield don't win any games. In fact they get slaughtered by twenty or so goals sometimes. But it has broadened Uncle Ron's social life in the area.

The dream of my father being alive happens again. This time I am the only one who knows about it; there is no one else in the dream, and my father has no special aura about him, just sitting at the table reading the paper. But he is there in the kitchen, so real that when I wake up in the morning I go to check if he's still there. I would like him to see John Coleman play, just once.

9

A PATTERN WAS SET for the remaining few years of childhood: school at St Thomas's, a dutiful rather than enthusiastic compliance with Catholic teachings, the weekends and holidays spent mostly outdoors with mates, either in the street or, less often now, on the banks of the Darebin Creek. Sport was of growing importance too, especially football, which meant the Essendon Football team, which meant John Coleman. Plastered all over the wall above my bed were premiership flags bought at the 1949, 1950 and 1951 grand finals at the MCG, photographs, picture cards, newspaper and magazine profiles of Coleman. It was this JC who became the real miracle worker in my life, every Saturday providing ample justification for my faith in him.

The Cloney family across the road mattered to me too. I looked up to Bernie as an older brother, admired his instinctive practical skills and his responsible attitude to his parents and siblings. He announced that he was leaving school when he turned fourteen and was going to work with his uncle in his furniture making business in Brunswick; this made perfect sense for Bernie, for whom school was nothing better than time-serving before he could get out in the world that mattered to him – the world of manual work, of learning how things were put together and functioned, the culture of the male workplace with its endless anecdotes and adolescent jokes. Already he was going over to Brunswick during school holidays and weekends to help his uncle out, and on a couple of occasions he took me with him. All we did was sandpaper wardrobes by hand ready for veneering, but like Bernie I enjoyed it immensely. It felt to be serious work, the making of something handsome and useful; you could see the wardrobes being made from start to finish, the dovetailing of drawers, the cutting and assembling of the frame, the fitting of the doors, the application of veneer, the French polishing and finishing with keyholes, escutcheons, handles, mirrors. What you then had made was something that would go directly into people's bedrooms, be part of their lives. I had been entranced by the making of everyday things ever since I watched Uncle Garn in his boot making shop in North Melbourne, and I longed to do something practical like this myself. Bernie was always a great example of how to tackle such tasks, and I always carefully noted how he went about it, whether it was tying knots in rope, 'walking' a wardrobe across a room singlehanded, or using a hammer in a way that won't mark the timber underneath (that is, using a punch to finish off).

It was Christmas 1950 when Bernie told me that his whole family, together with his grandmother, uncle and aunts from Brunswick, were to spend the summer holidays camping at Bright in Northern Victoria. I was deeply envious and made it obvious I longed to be included. He said he'd ask his mother, but Mrs Cloney said no, they were already overcrowded in the tents that they had. She must have noticed the look of disappointment on my face, and remembered the rough time my family had had lately, because she went quiet for a moment and then changed her mind. 'He'll have to bring his own bedding and make sure he's got all the clothes he needs,' she said to Bernie. 'And bring a camp stretcher, too. I don't know how we're going to squeeze him into the boys' tent, but we'll see.'

We went by steam train. At Spencer Street Station its huge black engine steadily soughed as we hurried past it on the platform. The adults arranged for the many boxes, trunks and bags to be placed in the baggage van, and the women and children – ten of us, including Mrs Cloney's mother and sister Bridget – packed into a saloon compartment. Underway, we excitedly pointed out the obvious to each other through the train window, and I felt a private pang of recognition from our Mount Macedon days of the kind of countryside we passed through. We made up jokes about the town names that flew past: Kilmore, Seymour, Benalla, Euroa ('Euroa da boat, I catcha da fish,' said young Frankie Cloney, prefiguring the smart mouth he was to later become). We branched off at Wangaratta, and took the line east that ended at Bright, passing a bare-topped Mount Buffalo along the way.

Carrying what we could of our gear from the station through the little town to the camping ground, I thought I had never seen a more beautiful place. The town is tucked in a small valley walled in by high hills, leafy and tree-thick, with the Ovens river flowing through, fed by a crystal clear creek that bisects the camping ground, called 'The Wattles' on one side, and 'The Willows' on the other. It was all small-scale and snug, peopled with holiday makers but not crowded. When we got to our camp site Bernie's Uncle Pat and his mates – all in their early twenties – had already arrived on their motorcycles, had claimed a site for us all to use, and had thrown up a couple of small tents to make it secure. The banks were flat and grassy, close to the fast flowing creek, which provided handy drinking water. Soon the bigger tents were up, the beds all set out, a fire lit and good-smelling bacon and eggs and billy tea on the way under the matriarchal watch of Bernie's grandmother, Nanna Pelly.

I had the time of my life. I was up at six every morning with Bernie, Josie and Frankie and straight into the river, a hundred yards down the creek from where we were. The flow had been dammed with rocks, making a wide, deep natural swimming pool where it was joined by the creek. At that time of the morning the Ovens was cold and clear, its movement gentle enough to create a glassy surface reflecting the green shrubbery along the banks and the dark glades overhung with branches farther upstream. It was such an idyllic summer that even at that time of the morning the cold water didn't discourage us, and we stayed in for a good couple of hours until we were so ravenously hungry that we gave it up for the more urgent pleasures of breakfast. I couldn't swim when we arrived; at the end of our few weeks there I had mastered freestyle, breaststroke and short bursts of backstroke, and could stay under water for twenty yards, though always with my eyes closed.

It was wonderful to have the women in charge of the daily routines; they cooked stews and fry-ups, made sandwiches and tea, and generally made life for the children both easy and organised. You had to be careful with your tea, which if you left standing too long would end up with little black flies floating in it. At night, joined by the men after their motorcycling adventures during the day, we sat around the fire talking, or else Bridget, in her lovely Irish voice, would lead us in singing songs from the Hit Parade, hemmed into cosy togetherness by the dark all around us. We stared at the fire and sang 'A you're adorable' and 'Goodnight Irene', or 'On top of Old Smokey', which Frankie Cloney dubbed 'the tomcat's theme-song.'

I felt distinctly part of the family, and once Bridget, having noticed my choirboy's voice, asked me to sing a solo while the others listened. I knew 'Londonderry Air' and 'Goodbye from The White Horse Inn', and Mrs Cloney afterwards came up to me and said she was glad she had let me come along.

During the day we walked through the bush or the pine forests, or climbed the steep hills or were taken for a fast ride on the pillion by Pat and his mates; they talked incessantly about 'Hird Black Lightnings' and 'Trumf Tigers' and other motorbike lore, and then disappeared out onto the hot roads for the rest of the day. Bernie had a fishing rod and we went up river after trout, and caught two. The men went out after rabbits and came back with enough for Nanna Pelly to make a big stew in her black iron pot, which we sat around that night and gorged ourselves on.

It was a rare and memorable time, and when I got home I couldn't stop talking about it; it hit me hard that this was the very spirit that had never flourished, never been allowed to flourish, in our ill-fated family and its disintegrating extensions. How my father, and my mother, would have enjoyed such a close family gathering, if it had ever been possible. At least I had tasted it once, and it was a great joy.

*

My love of singing had developed in the school choir, and came about like this. In year eight the curriculum called for an increased allocation of time to mathematics and science, and our home room teacher, Brother Dillon, was the nominated and very able science teacher in the school. Certainly his teaching was clear and well organised. Yet there was a problem, resulting in the whole teaching of maths, science and algebra being done badly, for Brother Dillon also had an interest in music, and had taken on the task of leading the school choir. He auditioned the whole class early in the year and selected the best singers, myself among them. It turned out to be a particularly gifted group, and Dillon became more and more enthused by them, and gave them more and more of his time. He exhorted us to 'tuck in your chin and send the voice to the top of your head, not down through your throat'; he taught us to listen to the whole sound of the choir so that we kept together, to articulate with snap precision so that every word was crystal clear, and he taught us to handle two- and three-part harmonies to great effect. We learned a wide range of musical forms, and made great progress under him.

Then he did an extraordinary thing: he took the choir out of the year eight science and mathematics classes, and set them up in the only room available to him, which was the science laboratory. Thus was science teaching, as such, abandoned for this class, in favour of the choir. As for the rest – the ones with poor voices – they were sentenced to work unsupervised at their desks in their home room for hours, tediously beavering their way through dozens and dozens of algebra and maths problems set out in a huge task book. I imagine half of them went to sleep, though they were tested afterwards on the number of problems they got right. Again, this showed the cavalier attitude the school took towards academic achievement and the teaching of knowledge-based subjects: the science lab used for the choir and the teaching of maths pretty much left to languish on its own.

What in effect Dillon taught us was that singing was more important than hard thinking, and this bias stayed with me for the next decade or so. I don't completely regret it, as it happens, because music, singing, and the arts generally proved important sources of happiness and direction to me. But did some of those other choirboys think otherwise about being deprived of science teaching, and some of those non-singers grow up hating the thought of maths and science as pursuits in adult life? I've heard of no distinguished academic or professional careers, nor even of other university graduates, to come out of St Thomas's. There must be a few, and if so, I believe their achievement, like mine, was in spite of, rather than because of, the teaching practices of that school.

Yes, it was a good choir, which sang from a broad program at a number of different venues including the annual school concert, of course, which surprisingly, given the other failings of the school, was always a huge success. Apart from sport, more time and effort went into preparation for this than any other activity; it was always held in the Collingwood Town Hall, always packed with family and friends, and the orgy of prizes and speeches, and of self-congratulation by the school authorities, was punctuated happily with entertaining items such as solo performances of poetry or songs, scenes from Gilbert and Sullivan and such, backed by the choir, and comedy routines with girls always played by the tougher boys and frequent references made to famous footballers and politicians.

The choir went beyond this, however. It sang Gregorian plainsong on Church occasions, Latin hymns for Benediction, and it travelled to compete in festivals and competitions, where it accounted for itself well, performing music from light opera – *The White Horse Inn* is one that springs to mind – and arrangements by Brother Dillon of Irish folk songs. It was the most enjoyable activity I undertook at the school, and awoke in me the pleasures of teamwork and performing for an audience. And the very act of singing in itself proved to be a kind of solace, and an exercise in emotional development of a kind that no other activity could have given me.

*

Despite the rule of the strap, several boys in my class possessed an open defiance; they were mostly from poor, unhappy or broken homes in the struggling suburbs of Collingwood or Fitzroy, and had seen some rough times. I recall a boy – I will just call him Teddy – who used almost every means he could to challenge the teachers to take him on: refused to do his homework, talked in class, smoked in the toilets, came to school with his uniform incomplete, fought with other boys, and produced an impertinent, though sometimes quite witty, commentary on the teachers' efforts. Again and again Teddy was brought up to the front and beaten, and for a long time he would walk back to his seat with a smirk on his face and a stoic refusal to show his pain or embarrassment. And then one day I noticed a different look on his face. It was Brother Hickey who brought it about, lean, bespectacled and unpredictably ill-tempered Brother Hickey, who had few gifts, and the typical bigotry of the Christian Brotherhood; he once, unprompted and bewilderingly, slaking some private rancour, barked at the class 'suicide is a mortal sin!' as if we had somehow given the impression that we were all about to slash our wrists as soon as the recess bell rang. On the day in question, Brother Hickey was in an unsettled state the whole history lesson, and when Teddy uttered yet one more cheeky comment for all to hear, Hickey called him out. One could tell by the look on Hickey's face that he had reached a point of unusually cold fury, even for him. Teddy stumped up, truculence in every movement of his body, and a smirk on his face. 'Hand out,' demanded Hickey, and with his thick leather cosh (for that is what it was) delivered six cuts with as much power in his arm as he could muster. We all presumed that was it, for it was always our belief that some regulation or other prohibited the delivery of more than six blows on any one occasion, and I had never known it to be transgressed. So we were shocked to hear Hickey snap, 'Other one; keep it high,' and see Teddy push out a visibly shaking other hand. I stopped my breath as the cuts came down, and I wanted it to finish at every blow. But unmoved, Hickey completed the second six. The room went dead quiet, listening for something – a cry of pain or protest from the boy, self-justification from Hickey, but there was nothing.

Awful silence. Hickey, too, paused for a moment, as if to weigh the pros and cons of the situation, and then, in a slightly less mechanical voice than before, said, 'Now get back to your seat, and not another word.' Teddy turned, and it was then I saw the change in him. It was not just pain and the welling tears, it was total shock and humiliation; he was pale, his mouth dropping at the corners, his demeanour struggling against utter collapse, and his eyes for the first time signalled defeat. For the rest of the year he was quiet, distant, occasionally even helpful to the teacher. There was never again a sign of that defiance, or a word of cheek, from him. He had been broken. As far as I know there was no protest from his parents about the beating, but he did leave the school at the end of that year.

I saw him seven or eight years later, long after we had both gone out to work. He was playing basketball in a YCW team that I was briefly involved with. In the dressing room after the game there was, as usual, a degree of mindless bad language flying about, and one of my friends, who happened to be a non-Catholic, said 'Jesus Christ', to no special purpose. Teddy, smug and righteous, demanded he apologise. 'Who to?' said my friend. 'To me; I don't approve of anyone taking the Lord's name in vain.' 'Tough,' said my friend, 'it doesn't bother me in the slightest.' But Teddy insisted, wanted to take it further, wanted to fight to defend the Lord's name. He had become a self-appointed crusader, at war with the world's disregard of Christian morals and conventions. Also a bigot in the making, I thought, and completely changed from the tough larrikin I so admired. I don't know if it all sprang from that beating he took, but that had certainly marked the moment of his first humiliation.

*

If anything, I miss my father now more than ever. As life begins to get more interesting, as I grow more adventurous and able to do things, I wish he was around to see me, encourage me, advise me. He would want to see me play cricket, fly for marks against the other boys, swim and dive. He would have ideas on how I might improve. He would go with me to the football, even to see Essendon. I would certainly go with him to see North Melbourne.

When I go to bed at night I say my prayers, that is whenever I remember to; when I do, I always pray for the same thing, that my father will come back. Then I sometimes have the dream again, that he is still alive, and will walk in through the back door any moment and we will all go to him and be united into a family again.

Then I wake up to a feeling of desolation that seems to be more acute each time.

*

My experiences at school were by no means all bad. I made good friends, and it indirectly put me in touch with a different suburban world than the one I was living in. Nearly all the boys in the school came from the immediate area – Collingwood, Fitzroy, Clifton Hill, Northcote, and certainly lived closer to the school, and for that matter closer to the city, than I did. Occasionally I would be invited to a boy's house after school, and would find there a world much more like the one I had known in West and North Melbourne. Their houses were dark and small, their back yards and sideways cramped and cluttered. The narrow streets and public parks were the only spaces to play in. I liked these areas, despite their restricted feel. They were less free, less wild, less innocent, than I had become accustomed to along the Darebin creek. It seemed to me always that boys in these suburbs were tougher and older, grew up faster and had more advanced experiences, than we did in the outer northern suburbs.

As I moved up through the grades, the academic offerings became marginally more interesting. *Treasure Island* was set for study, and I became totally absorbed in it. Although I had owned *Huckleberry Finn* since a couple of Christmases earlier, I was too young to appreciate its quality, and had not been able to get far into it. But Stephenson's great storytelling ability, his line-up of strange characters, and his romantic otherworld of 18th century pirates, gave me my first experience of the imaginative power of a novel.

Of course I identified with Jim Hawkins, and was impressed by Long John Silver, but they were less gripping to me than the revelations of the plot – the black spot, the discovery of the map, the search for the treasure, Jim in the apple barrel, Ben Gunn's cunning 'madness' in relocating the treasure –which, better than any story I had so far known, gave me the sense of getting to the heart of a mystery, deeply satisfying in its completion. Studying that novel had awoken in me a lifelong love of imaginative writing.

At the beginning of every year we would be given a list of books set for study in all subjects during the course of the year, and these were to be purchased usually at McGill's or Hall's bookshops in the city, unless you happened to come by a second-hand copy somewhere. But I never particularly liked acquiring a book second-hand; in the fact of another name on the flyleaf and the sense of it having already been read, there was something less exciting than a new one. The year's books all had to be purchased at once, because the shops were reluctant to reorder once their initial stocks ran out. My mother would give me a ten-pound note to go on a spree of acquisition that felt like total luxury. I would wander through the alleyways of book stacks, browsing, inhaling the fresh gluey smell and handling the immaculate pages and jackets of newly printed texts. It would take an hour to do what should have been completed in ten minutes. At home I would unwrap my treasure and carefully paw through it, treating it not so much as the basis for work through the year, some of which I would come to loathe, but more as the promise of a journey I could hardly wait to enjoy. There is nothing as promising as a new book.

Brother Dowd, who took us in year seven, was a red-faced volatile man with an understanding of how to keep boys interested in their schoolwork. He created a competitive system in which each of the four rows of desks in the classroom was a team that could win points, or marks, for quick accurate answers to questions, writing tasks achieved promptly and well and the odd moment of inspiration from an individual; I had one such moment in a geometry lesson, when he promised threepence and ten points to his row to any boy who could locate the halfway point of a straight line without resorting to geometrical measuring. I offered, strode to the blackboard, and using my pretty good eye for proportion, put a mark on the line that proved to be exactly right. Dowd kept his promise, and on the way back to my seat I heard him say, 'There's no doubt about Kinnane; set him a challenge, and he will do it.' It was one of my proudest moments.

Dowd's system worked such that, at the end of each week, the row with the most marks was let out fifteen minutes early. Further, if the performance of the whole class was sufficiently good, Dowd would devote the last period every Friday to reading to us either a humorous book, such as *Tom Sawyer*, or items from a special 'jokebook' he had compiled, containing a ragbag of schoolboy howlers, nonsense poems, ancient comic routines, and a few bluish, or racist (lots of 'nigger') jokes, and even the odd laugh at the expense of the Church. He clearly enjoyed these readings, which he did using theatrical voices and funny faces. He was not an especially clever or well-qualified teacher, but he certainly knew how to make school enjoyable for many of us.

Equally enthusiastic but better academically qualified was a lay teacher we had in year eight, Mr Borrack. His area was geography, but he took us for some basic science subjects as well. I have guilty memories of Mr Borrack, because of the way we treated him, and I include myself among the villains. His problem was an easily detectable softness of heart. In the case of Brother Dowd, his enthusiasm could be seen to have a reverse side, which was a very volatile temper; he was powerfully built, and occasionally, when his temper broke, he could lay into a boy with frightening, red-faced fury. But Mr Borrack, small, stooped and nervous in his grey three-piece suit, absently carrying his morning teapot across the playground to the tuckshop for hot water, had no such other side; his softness was deep-centred and simple, and although he often lost his temper, his anger revealed only impotence in the face of our defiance, and he was prone to crumble and panic rather than find a way to control us. It is not a good idea to give a classroom of seventy-seven boys clear indication that they can undermine you simply by mockery. But Mr Borrack, nicknamed 'Percy', was the class's victim from the moment he walked into the room.

Which was a pity, because he was the most knowledgeable teacher in the school, and the only one committed to ideas. In a geography charade which he knew himself was comic, he would place a boy out in front and nominate him as 'the Sun'; he would then dance around the boy with objects in his hands – an apple, a tennis ball, an ink bottle –representing the nine planets, and even try to indicate the orbit of the moon by passing one hand over and under the other, all the while circling the 'Sun', who would be grinning daftly at his momentary importance. In this way Borrack tried to make real a universe that the Brothers and the Church typically represented to us as of purely metaphysical interest.

Moreover, precisely because of his devotion to ideas, I have the distinct sense that the school itself failed to take Mr Borrack seriously; they threw him to the wolves and failed to give him the support he needed to survive it. He was already a broken man when he retired not long after I left, and within a couple of years he died.

Handsome, athletic young Brother Shepherd who taught me in grade five stood in front of the class one day and made an extraordinary political speech. Mr Menzies the Prime Minister, he said, wants to ban Communists from Australia. A referendum will shortly be held allowing the whole country to vote on whether or not he should have that power. What you must do, he told us, is to go home and advise your parents to vote against Mr Menzies' proposal. Otherwise, insisted Shepherd, Menzies will be able to go up to anyone, tap them on the shoulder and call them a Communist, which would result in them being thrown out of the country. I took in what he said and believed it completely, and when I got home I passed his advice on to my mother. 'I don't need to be told that,' she replied. 'I wouldn't vote for Menzies in a fit. I'm only sorry Mr Chifley isn't still there.' It was the first time I realised that we were against Mr Menzies, which took me by surprise after hearing his distinctive and authoritative voice on the radio. After all, I noticed that his elocution was perfect.

*

My mother began at last to give herself some semblance of a social life. Every Friday night she went to the pictures with a group of women neighbours – Roma from next door, if she was well enough, Mrs Jolley from farther up and one or two others. After getting their families an early evening meal they would walk together chattering buoyantly on their way to catch the yellow bus that would take them along Darebin Road to the relative sophistication of High Street Northcote, where they could take a green bus to a choice of some five different cinemas, showing the latest films. I would often end up on their bus home after I'd also gone to a film with my mates – never the same one as my mother went to – and with a parcel of chips or potato cakes in my hand, lurching about with the boys down the back of the bus, I would studiously ignore my mother and her friends as if I didn't know them; it would have been far too embarrassing for both of us to acknowledge each other openly, so we kept up the pretence until we got home not more than minutes apart. Then she would turn serious again, hustle me into bed. I was pleased that she'd been able to have herself a bit of fun and find some relief from her endless grind of keeping the household going; I liked hearing her girlish laugh and seeing her enjoy herself, for which, when she allowed it, she had a fine talent.

She loved dancing, a pleasure that had been denied her since before the War. Again, at the prompting of some of her women friends, she began to go dancing of a Saturday night at one of the many venues that were hugely popular during the nineteen fifties. Heidelberg Town Hall, Hawthorn, Caulfield, Collingwood Town Halls, The Trocadero in the City; they all had live dance bands, some had singers, all under the influence of the Dorseys, Duke Ellington, Paul Whiteman and Sinatra, Ella Fitzgerald. My mother had a friend, Madge, with whom she had worked in the city dressmaker's for years, and who was determined to get my mother 'out of herself' by taking her dancing. We would all go to Madge's home in Oakleigh, sometimes stay the night, and her husband Gordon would look after me and Ray while the women went off to the dance. At other times, Uncle Ron would stay home with us while my mother went over to Oakleigh for the weekend.

Around this time I began to get a series of illnesses, and the fact that my mother was now working full time meant that if I was bad enough to stay home from school, I was often left all day in the house on my own. Sore throats and flu dogged me through the winter, and a severe dose of chicken pox kept me home in bed for over a week. The situation distressed my mother, who felt bad about abandoning me at such times, but her job could have been at risk if she took more than her entitled leave. She couldn't call on Pinchbecks next door, who had their own problems with Bob's immobility and Roma undergoing a worrying relapse. There was no one else she could ask who was free to look in on me in the daytime. I remember a particular illness I had – tonsillitis I think – that brought on a high fever, causing me riotous dreams and heavy sweats as I woke and slept throughout the day. When she got home she heard me screaming as she came in the back door, and found me standing at the foot of my bed in my pyjamas wild-eyed with delirium, yelling that I was being attacked by someone with an axe. Doctor Downing came and settled me down with something, and advised my mother that I shouldn't be left alone until I had fully recovered.

I developed stomach pains later that year, and was taken to the Children's Hospital in Rathdowne Street, Carlton for an appendectomy. 'I won't go under,' I told the anaesthetist, ignoring his reassuring efforts to talk to me about football, secretly determined not to let the operation proceed. In the aftercare ward at St Vincents, an English boy called Lester, slightly older than me, taught me a couple of dirty songs, and managed to get one of the nurses to come to his bed during the nights and 'snog' him, as he put it. I was very impressed by his sophistication and daring, compared to which I felt an absolute baby.

When I got home from the hospital, with a fortnight off before I had to resume school, I felt strangely strong and energetic; looking back on it, I believe I had been getting thinner and more stress-prone since the death of my father, and also because of the tension of getting to school on time and fearing the consequences of failure in that strict and punitive atmosphere I was essentially melancholy and lacking in confidence. I needed the break and the rest and good food that the hospital provided, and I came back much healthier and full of new vigour. It showed in my energetic interest in street football and cricket.

On one of her weekends at Madge's my mother met a man at a local dance venue, and a relationship started up between them. She and Richard had been seeing each other for some weeks before she invited him home to meet us; he came for tea one Sunday on his old Indian motorcycle. Instead of a sidecar, it had a large delivery box, because Richard was a butcher who ran a shop in Oakleigh and used the motorcycle to make deliveries. My mother turned on one of her special Sunday teas in his honour – Ninny had come over with her new 'friend', an Anglo-Indian we called Uncle Chris, and we had a roast lamb lunch. They stayed for tea, which was the usual cold cuts off the lamb, salad, potato salad made with my mother's own dressing. She had baked a cream sponge and a lemon-meringue pie, so the kitchen table was laden with food. Richard said practically nothing the whole time. He was some years older than my mother, with dark, tightly curled hair, a large nose, and dressed in a navy-blue suit. He showed no enthusiasm for anything, and almost completely ignored Ray and me. On our side, we thought him totally uninteresting. Chris, on the other hand, wouldn't stop talking, producing endless stories about his past, and made the running on every topic that came up. He was what my father would have called a 'know-all', and his presence at the table was tiresome and combative, especially with me who was becoming an increasingly opinionated child eager to argue with adults. I once spent a whole morning debating with Uncle Ron the odds of entering a raffle with just one or with several tickets. He insisted that you did not improve your chances of winning by buying more than one ticket, because the draw was random and could select one from anywhere. I disagreed, insisting that the more tickets you had the better your chance of winning. I think what made him dig his heels in was my cocky, schoolboy insistence, and my lack of respect for my elders. Boys without fathers can be irritatingly pushy.

Richard continued to court my mother, who spent increasing amounts of time over on his side of the city, including, she told me, meeting his mother who lived in Ormond. 'Near the beach,' she said, as if this would elicit my approval of whatever it was that she was being drawn into over there. Personally, Richard seemed to offer me no prospect whatever; he seemed not to be interested in football, cricket, music, religion or me. Why would I get interested in him?

*

Around about twelve years of age I began to acquire a more active interest in sport, meaning football and cricket, which was an inevitable consequence of my adoration of John Coleman and the influence of Bob Pinchbeck next door.

I was never good enough to make the school teams, which were of exceptionally high standard, producing numerous players that in a few short years were Victorian Football League stars. St Thomas's punched well above its weight in competition with other, larger Melbourne schools such as Xavier and St Patrick's.

Nevertheless a few mates and I got together regularly to play 'end to end' in the street in front of our house. Often not having a real football, we made one from tightly rolled up paper bound fast with a few turns of string. This we would kick twenty or thirty metres, practice our marking and goal kicking through any handy front gate, until the 'football' disintegrated into a soft and tattered mess. If someone could get hold of a real football, it would often crash through the neighbours' front gardens or even break a window, and we'd be banished to some boggy distant paddock.

Cricket was a different matter because it is a game where physical size is not so important, though this will usually influence the kinds of skill one will choose to develop. My mother gave me a full-sized 'Don Bradman' bat for Christmas, and Bob showed me how to 'play it in', oil it, keep it in good condition. Of course, I had nowhere I could use it seriously, though we did set up a rubbish bin and marked out a pitch on the road outside my house, where using a tennis ball we played many an intense and noisy game. I had a taste for batting and was very hard to get out once I got my eye in; at that time, however, there was nowhere I knew where I could actually join a team and play a proper match.

*

In our back yard, beside the concrete path and just near the back gate, is a lemon tree my mother planted in the first months of our living here. She dug into the hard clay with a fork, bending its prongs out of alignment, firmed the tree into place and gives water to it regularly. But it struggles. In over two years it has grown no more than six inches, is sparse-leaved, and never produces any fruit. It is the only tree in the whole of our garden. Because of its nearness to the back gate, I always notice it, and always think of its pathetic lack of progress. It doesn't die, but it doesn't thrive.

10

ONE EVENING MY MOTHER took us into the lounge room to make a more or less formal announcement; the lounge room was where all events of any such significance took place, and my mother kept it spotlessly clean and orderly, placed her best glasses and dinner ware – a wedding present – in a round-fronted leaded glass cabinet there, alongside the new radiogram she had bought on lay-by from Myers.

'How would you feel if Richard came to live with us?'

'Where would he sleep?' I asked. Of course I knew the answer, but since Uncle Ron was still in the front bedroom and there was no space where Ray and I slept, this was my way of drawing her out into the open.

'Well,' she said, pausing for balance over it, 'we thought we'd get married. He doesn't have a house of his own, so I think it best if he comes here.'

I said nothing, Ray said nothing.

'He doesn't want to try to be your father,' she said, looking at me. 'He knows you don't think of him like that.'

The thought flashed *just as well, because there is no way I'm ever going to call him my father.*

'What would he be?'

'He'd just be my husband. But he has his butcher shop over in Oakleigh, and he would keep running that, and would look after us and be here with us the rest of the time.'

'What will Ray and I call him?'

'Call him what you do now – Uncle Dick; he doesn't mind that.'

It wasn't as important a matter to us as it was to my mother; clearly she was anxious about broaching the subject with us, and relieved now that she got no fuss from either of us. For myself, I didn't care one way or the other; it was my mother's business, and nothing much to do with me. I had my world, and Richard had no part in it. I was a little concerned that she was going to marry someone so boring, but she no doubt had her reasons. That she was going to take Richard's name and be called Spencer irritated me; I couldn't believe she would drop Kinnane, and certainly neither Ray nor I would.

They married in a civil ceremony which Ray and I did not attend, and have never seen photographs of; I don't believe there were any. He came to live with us, bringing his Indian motorcycle with him, which he continued to ride over to Oakleigh to his butcher shop, leaving in the dark hours of the morning. He remained as taciturn as on that first day, and apart from inconveniently occupying the bathroom for mysterious lengths of time on weekends, hardly seemed to impinge on my life at all.

He had a mother and a sister and two brothers with families living in Melbourne, and a half-brother, called Jim, who lived at home with their mother, whom I was instructed to call 'Grandma'. Jim had a regular routine of bringing Grandma to our home on Sundays for tea and gossip, which my mother prepared with her usual skill and enthusiasm. Jim was a younger and more interesting man than Richard; my mother had a particular affection for him, and my interest in him hugely blossomed when he started bringing his guitar and singing songs as we sat in the lounge room after tea. From the moment I heard the mellow sound of his acoustic 'f' hole Maton, accompanying his twangy renderings of country and western songs fashionable at the time, I was mesmerised. You didn't need anything else: the guitar and your own voice did it all, and you could sound as authentic as the radio.

As a consequence, I asked my mother to pay for lessons to go to the Victorian Banjo Club in the city and learn guitar accompaniment. I was able to buy a suitable instrument from the Club, and pay it off together with my weekly fees. A handsome young man who wore a cowboy-style fringed shirt taught a group of us to make chords and to use our thumb to stroke the strings, adapting it to a song such as 'Red Sails in the Sunset' or other Country and Western songs. I kept going for many months until I had paid off the guitar, and the effort of travelling all the way into the city every week became too much. But I kept playing my guitar in my bedroom, and occasionally taking it over to the Cloney's sleepout to show off some of my new-found achievements. I noted to myself how singing and playing for people gained you popularity, gave you a certain status, that you otherwise might not enjoy.

*

On the way home from school I have to buy a pair of football shorts at the Sports Store in High Street, Northcote. The shop seems empty when I go in, so I wander around in the dimness, looking at footballs, boots and other stuff untidily strewn about. Eventually a man emerges from a back room, still chewing something he has been eating there. He is a heavy, sad-eyed man with black hair combed straight back, without a part. He looks a little like Lon Chaney, the actor who plays the wolf man. He asks if he can help me, and I tell him I'm after football shorts. He produces a black and white heap, dropping them on the glass case in front of me.

'What colour?'

'Black.'

'What size?'

'Not sure.'

He gives me a couple of pair of different sizes. 'Try these on,' he says. 'You can go through there to the fitting room.'

I follow his direction through a curtain into a back room. I always feel awkward dressing and undressing in strange situations, as if I have to hurry and get it over with, when in fact I am a slow dresser and like to take my time.

I have to remove my cap, blazer and pullover because my short trousers are held up by braces, which I slip down my arms, and stand there in my shirt and school tie and shoes and socks. There is a hook to hang my bag and clothes on. I am just about to put my legs into the shorts when the man joins me in the fitting room. 'How're you going in here?' he says in a too matter-of-fact way. 'Let's see how they fit.' I haven't had time to get the shorts properly on, and I feel he has deliberately come in too soon, maybe to hurry me along, to take charge of the whole process so that he can enforce the sale.

He squats beside me as if to get a better idea of the fit of the shorts, tests the elastic for snugness at my waist, and says, 'I think these will be okay.'

'Maybe a bit loose?'

'Let's just slip them off,' he says, and tugs both the shorts and my underpants down to my knees. There is an awkward moment when we both treat it as an accident, and then he reaches under my shirt and gently but firmly cups my genitals in his hand. I freeze. It is not an unpleasant sensation, but it catches me by surprise and I don't know what to say or do.

'That's a decent sized package you've got here for a little bloke,' he says, jiggling my genitals as if weighing them. I look down and see his large heavy head, his swept-back greasy black hair with flecks of dandruff in it, and I am moved to act. I push away his hand, pull up my underpants, and kick the shorts off past my shoes.

'These will do,' I say a little too loudly and quickly, and grab for my trousers. For a moment I am afraid that he could do something to prevent me leaving, he appears so strong and there is no one else in the shop, but he doesn't. He just snaps out of it and takes the shorts back to the counter while I finish getting dressed. The wrapping, the paying, the leaving are all done in a pretence of normality on both sides, though I am fearful the whole time, and I emerge from the shop relieved and eager to get home as uneventfully as possible, burdened with a secret that has left me feeling not so much soiled as strangely matured, experienced even, and almost comically impressed that my genitals should suddenly be a matter of interest to anyone.

About a week later I happen to be glancing through the local paper when I see his photograph in it. There is that heavy face, that slicked-back hair smiling out engagingly, and underneath it a small article headlined Local businessman to stand for Council. I wonder what would happen to his prospects if they knew what he liked to get up to at the back of his store.

At what point did he decide I was a suitable prospect? Was it impulsive, as he directed me through to the fitting room? Or was it more calculated than that, acting to a plan that would go into action when the right type turned up. And what is the right type? Was I chosen because I was relatively small and unlikely to challenge him, or oppose him physically if things got to that stage? Or was it something more total than that, something about my appearance, or manner, that suggested I was likely to respond well – gratefully? Did he sense I needed intimacy, would welcome any gesture of warmth? Could he spot a lonely boy just by his looks?

I look back now with a certain sense of amusement and relief on the several moments of genital contact that occurred in my childhood. I cannot speak generally about child abuse, because I have never felt that these were in fact occasions of abuse, though certainly this last incident might have ended up in the courts if it had ever come out, and the man's reputation at least would have been finished. But I have never felt particularly violated by such sexual explorations. I hurried out of the sports store because the man was sleazy and insincere, not because he was interested in my body. I could well imagine a different man taking a different approach and my reaction being quite different, possibly cooperative. Violence itself is another matter; sexual exploration done violently is in fact violence, and this is abhorrent, and I thank my luck in never experiencing it. But sexual exploration done gently, or probingly, seeking co-operation, which has been my experience, has not produced the trauma in me that it seems to have produced in others, and I also seem to have escaped the deeper feelings of guilt that a Catholic education might be expected to induce. By calling it a sin of impurity, the Church sets us up to feel guilt about wanting to know the mysteries of these oddly pleasurable parts of our bodies. Sex fascinates us, even at an early age; it has never felt wrong or disgusting to me that I and others want to exercise that fascination in moments when the possibility presents itself. Of far more concern to me, again looking back through my childhood experiences, was that one occasion after I was pushed into the hedge on the way to the cinema, when I was virtually abducted by those three adults and held captive for over an hour in their house, terrified and bewildered about what was happening and what they might do to me. That was violation. That was the exercise of raw unprincipled power by adults over a child. It still makes me angry just to think about it. Nor is it any consolation to realise that had things happened a little differently, and there had been someone to call the police to find out what had happened to me, those three adults might well have been charged with abduction or some other serious offence; the fact that they had the power and will to do it still burns inside me, far worse than anything sexual that ever happened to me. It wasn't fair, and if any one thing haunted my childhood, triggered my sense of outrage time and again, it was the terrible effects, the frustrations, the hurt, the arbitrary resort to power, of unfairness.

*

I noticed my mother being sick in the mornings. I could hear her out in the lavatory, vomiting; she was one of those people who make a lot of noise when they vomit, as if it is tearing the lining off their stomach. She also was much fussier about her food, and certain food smells sent her rushing out to the lavatory again, as she did when I had a boiled egg for lunch one day. She never ate eggs anyway, but now just the thought of them turned her green.

I knew enough to have my suspicions about the cause, and sure enough she grew steadily bigger month by month, belatedly announcing that she was having a baby. In March she went into the Ivanhoe maternity hospital near my old school and gave birth to a daughter, who is called Susan. The baby came home chubby and cute, and Ray and I were encouraged by everyone to regard her as our full sister. We went along with it, and in fact grew to become very fond of her. She looked more like Richard than my mother, which was bad luck for her. Having a baby to look after meant more work for my mother, of course, but as always she coped. Richard said little, as usual, and did even less to help. I can't recall him giving cuddles or changing Susan's nappy, or giving any outward shows of affection to her, nor for that matter to my mother. Or anyone.

*

Later in that year an event took place that affected me deeply. My obsession with John Coleman and Essendon was central to my morale; Coleman had topped the goalkicking in both years since he began, and Essendon had been premiers in both years. I had gone to the Grand Finals of 1949 and 1950, squeezing myself between adult legs in the Outer section so I could see, witnessing the dream of Coleman kicking his hundredth goal in the Final against Carlton, and a year later the team's subsequent crushing of a valiant North Melbourne.

In 1951, there were forces mustered to put a stop to Coleman's dominance. At Princes Park, during the last home and away match of the year, Carlton sent out an untalented big-man called Harry Caspar to rough him up. On this day I had actually seen Coleman park his pastel green Holden sedan on the grass outside the ground, and make his way, looking strangely ordinary in his fawn gabardine overcoat, to the players' entrance. During the game, the adults all around me suddenly exploded into howls of outrage. All I could see when I finally got a clear space was a Carlton player down on the ground holding his face, and Coleman being turned around by the umpire to record his number in his notebook; he was being booked for striking. Then the angry Essendon supporters explained: 'Caspar punched Coleman right in the face to stop him going for the ball! Twice he hit him!'

'Yes, but Coleman's been reported,' said another.

'But Caspar hit him first, with no provocation; just king-hit him. All Johnnie did was hit him back. He's been done for retaliation.'

The papers were full of sensational headlines, and the whole of the football world was caught up in speculation at what lay behind it and what the outcome would be. The tribunal heard the case on the following Monday night, and to everyone's shock and amazement, Coleman was suspended for four weeks, the same as Caspar, despite evidence from a boundary umpire that Caspar had initiated the fight with two punches, and that Coleman was only defending himself. Many people wondered about the role of the Vice President of the VFL, Sir Kenneth Luke, who also happened to be the president of the Carlton Football Club, surely placing him in a conflict of interest. The suspension meant that Coleman missed the finals series, and Essendon lost the premiership to Geelong.

Once again, the event raised in me that deep feeling of unfairness at the way the world works. Like Coleman himself, who bitterly confided to his friends that he had no wish ever to play again, I wept angry tears, convinced that there are forces at work opposing the gifted individual: Christ, my father, John Coleman. Life presented these figures to me as victims with some obscure link to the magical, instruments of extraordinary feats that can neither be learned nor manufactured by whoever runs the power structures, but can be destroyed by them. I could articulate none of this disappointment and rage, being both too young and too emotionally confused, but I could feel its depth and irresistibility as I howled to myself that life, whatever else it was, was not fair.

*

New things begin to happen. During the Easter break I notice a girl playing in Cook Street in front of the house opposite our side fence. The family in there are friendly but, since the children are all girls younger than me, I've never had much to do with them. This girl is unknown to me, but as she plays ball with the others I can't tear my eyes away from her. She has on a navy school tunic and pullover, but since it is school holidays I know she isn't from a local school; there is a laughing vitality about her that attracts me. Lithe, well-proportioned, fleet-footed, she seems to float above the ground. I want to go up to her and ask questions – Who is she? Where is she from? Equally strong is some inner resistance preventing me doing this. I go out in the street and watch her, and she looks at me and laughs again, and speaks to me. 'Hello,' she says. 'Want to play French cricket?'

Foolishly, I say 'Nope', when there is nothing in the world I would like more. I deny my attraction to her, approaching her only in the most indirect, undeclared way. I stay out there, being and not being part of their game; I field the ball if it comes in my direction, but nothing more.

All day I keep a look out for her, but she doesn't show again. Next morning I peer out of our lounge room window and there she is, this time riding a bicycle in small circles in the road. I wander out again. She smiles and says hello, and then rides off towards Hawker Street and turns out of sight while I stand watching.

'She likes you,' says a voice. It is the girl from the house – I guess she is about eight – standing in her driveway eating a slice of bread and jam.

'Who is she?'

'Her name's Lorna. Lorna Keene. She's my cousin. She lives in Clifton Hill, but she's staying with us for the holidays. Do you like her?'

'Where's she gone?'

'Just round the block. It's my bike. She likes you; you could be her boyfriend if you wanted.'

Without knowing exactly what a boyfriend is supposed to do, I feel that this is exactly what I want, if it means spending more time in her company. A few moments later she appears on the bike from the opposite direction along Valentine Street, and rides right up to where I am standing beside the road and stops.

'You go to St Thomas's,' she says, looking at her front tyre.

'Yes.'

'I go to St John's, just opposite.'

'Mmm. Maybe I could come and see you sometime: lunchtime?'

'I always play behind the Church.'

For the next few days we meet in the street like this, play different games, talk, but never look each other directly in the eyes. She doesn't call me by my name, though I call her 'Lorna'; the name has a romantic ring to it, and I am enchanted by her laughing energy. I can't tell whether she really likes me or not, but I am not discouraged. Eventually she leaves to go back to Clifton Hill, with nothing ever actually said about boyfriend/girlfriend matters, but I think about her all the time. I want to find where she lives, and so I ask the girl across the road for her address. Her mother hears me and amusedly tells me the number in Fenwick Street, Clifton Hill. Several times I ride all the way there – miles – on my bike just to look at her house, to nonchalantly ride past it and back and do pointless circles, and hope she will emerge. Eventually she comes out and speaks to me.

'Don't hang around here,' she says. 'My father will see you and be angry. Come and see me at school.'

We are not supposed to go out of the schoolyard at St Thomas's unless we live nearby and have to go home for lunch, or else are going across Queens Parade to St John's Church for lunchtime Confession; school prefects patrol Queens Parade all the time, watching for transgressors. Notwithstanding, the very next schoolday I slip across to St John's, tell the prefect in front of the school that I am going across to Confession, and look for Lorna. The element of danger and intrigue makes it all the more compelling. She is there just as she said, behind the Church. But instead of just her, I find I am surrounded by about five of her friends, all giggling and using a slightly mocking tone to me.

'Are you the boyfriend then?'

'Are you Garry?'

'Lorna says you're too young for her.'

'If you wanna kiss each other we won't say anything.'

Lorna is in the middle of them, obviously embarrassed and torn between loyalties; she looks at me with an apologetic expression and doesn't join in the banter, but at the same time she has her arms around two of them and seems to be implying that she is one of them and is not free to prefer me. She laughs still, but the laughter is too much like that of her friends' to be of any comfort to me; in fact, it hurts me a little. I stand around for a few more minutes, hoping for an exit line, and finally say, 'Well, I'll see you sometime – maybe if you come over to Ivanhoe again.' She never does, and though I never see her again, she stays in my thoughts for months afterwards, and occasionally I dream about her.

An unhappy little coda to the excursion over to St John's occurred when I got back to school; I had been spotted by the prefect on duty, and reported to Brother Hickey. Immediately class resumed Hickey sent me to the Waiting Room, and came along minutes later.

When he asked me what I had been doing behind the Church, rather than in it, I said, not without a degree of pride, that I had been meeting a girl. I can still hear his shrill voice, and smell his halitosis, as he bawled into my face, 'Kinnane, you're girl mad!'

In a sense, he was right. My attraction to Lorna had made me a little mad for a time. The tumult racing through my blood made me behave and feel in ways I never had before. But I was not without a certain pride in what Hickey was accusing me of, and a certain sense that I had shown a degree of boldness that Hickey himself had probably always lacked. When he finally delivered the cuts to my hands the pain was somewhat mitigated by my private satisfaction that I was not in the slightest like him, and that I had things to look forward to in life that he was denied.

The other important development was the decision to leave school at the end of the year, when I would turn fourteen and be legally able to go out to work. I was eager to put the regime of fear and constriction at St Thomas's behind me, which apart from anything else had taken a toll on my health and spirits. Underneath the educational disappointments, which were as much my own fault as they were the school's, I sensed a link between the school and the death of my father. The Catholicism, the moralistic intentions behind the decision to send me there, the daily travel strain, the feeling of being an outsider, all these discomforts sprang from the overarching catastrophe of his loss, and weighed heavily on my heart. Rightly or wrongly I believed that getting away from the school would get me out of my despondency, would start a new, fresh phase in my life, or at least I hoped it would.

The very thought of being out in the world, free of the school uniform, free of rules and dictates, mixing with adults on a footing somewhere above childhood if not quite on their level, of earning my own money, was irresistible. Like Bernie Cloney, I believed the working world of men to be interesting, dignified and valued, where the life of a schoolboy had nothing to recommend it. I could hardly wait to get out and be part of it.

Deciding what work to embark upon was not so straightforward; I had no clear idea of being anything or doing anything, except for the few models that had drifted into my life. My father was not one of these, unless being an invalid could set me an example, and fortunately it did not. Christ and Bernie Cloney were the nearest I could think of, and both were trained in carpentry. So I decided I would become a carpenter, or at least a cabinet maker. I would find out how I could start an apprenticeship, and look for a job. This, I imagined, would bring me power, self-possession and freedom.

Notwithstanding the fact that this was my choice and probably nobody could have talked me out of it, it was in effect an appalling act of irresponsibility on the part of the adults in my life to do nothing to discourage me from this course. For my mother, Richard, my teachers, the school authorities, to allow an academically gifted boy of fourteen in their charge, who was always in the top three of a massive class, to decide his future without counselling or talking through the implications was a dismal abrogation of their responsibilities. Given what they knew, or should have known, of my abilities, they should have helped me to see the long term value of an education. But I was left completely alone with my fanciful, ignorant ideas about the world of everyday work, out in the factories, and no one lifted a finger to disabuse me of them. I say this in hindsight, of course, but not with bitterness. Their neglect reflects on them, not on my own feelings about the course my life took. That was, is, will continue to be, largely in my own hands, and other people's mistakes or wisdom have not been as important as my own in determining my successes and failures.

*

Progress came to West Ivanhoe when two local neighbours started a general store in Stortford Avenue, only a few hundred yards from our house. Mr Britten and Mr Foreman pooled their resources and equity, built a shop on a spare block of land and served groceries, dairy products, hardware, sweets and smallgoods, admittedly at inflated prices, but to a neighbourhood grateful to be spared the tiring walk up to Ivanhoe village. By this time all the roads in the area had been levelled and sealed and concrete gutters and driveways completed, 'nature strips' created bearing young prunus or ash trees, and many houses had established promising gardens and neat lawns. Sunday morning became a symphony of motor mowers and automatic sprinklers, and in the driveways stood new or recent Holdens and Vanguards, Fords and Vauxhalls, proudly washed until their pastel shades were spotless and their chrome bumpers and trims gleamed in the morning sun. The differences between the Housing Commission and the older areas were fast becoming less glaring, as suburbia spread its levelling blueprint all through Melbourne of the mid-1950s. When it was announced that the City was to host the next Olympic Games and that the Olympic Village housing the athletes was to be in the neighbouring suburb of West Heidelberg, everyone felt a small glow of pride that we had been noticed, and that maybe we weren't as socially inferior as we had always thought. A new green bus service running along a re-made Oriel Road directly to and from the City was started, meaning it was no longer necessary to suffer the unreliabilities of the yellow bus in Darebin Road. Gradually the post-War stringencies gave way to a new spirit of acquisition and purpose, and there seemed to be noticeably more money about.

My brother Ray was growing up fast: better built and better looking than I, he was already showing promise at football and cricket at school. He had developed a waggish sense of humour and often had us in stitches with some funny story over the dinner table.

Being that much younger he had nothing of the sense of loss over our father that I had gone through, and thus seemed to have escaped my kind of melancholy and pessimistic outlook. We began to get along as friends as the four-year age gap between began to feel less and less important.

In the course of this year Uncle Ron and his girlfriend June got married. My mother made June's dress; she stood plumply pretty on a chair in her petticoat in our lounge room while my mother fussed around her with a mouthful of pins. Her family turned on a big wedding. Ron's football club mates were there, and our family including Ninny of course. It would mean that Ron would be moving out of our house to a place of his own with June. I knew I would miss his presence in the house, his talk of football and racing – he was no cricket fan – and his jokey banter generally. But he wasn't going far away, and I would continue to see him whenever I took it into my head to watch Bellfield get thrashed yet again.

*

Secretly, helpless against the urge despite knowing full well that it is impure, in fact that it is a sin of deed if nothing else, I masturbate in the lavatory or into a hanky in bed, and afterwards sink into shame and guilt. It is a passion that overtakes me when I am least expecting it; I try not to look forward to it, or even think about it at all, but it remains there, waiting to call me to it again, to promise a joy that always turns out to be disappointing. This is what growing up is all about, I tell myself, but I am worried in case I am doing myself some damage that might later on come back to haunt me. It does leave my penis swollen and sore. I don't believe I will go blind or such, but why does everybody say it is wrong? It must have some detrimental effect on me, but what?

Whom do I ask about this? Whom can I turn to in total honesty, who will be wise, and not judge or punish or laugh at me? Not the priest in Confession, because he will only berate and give me penance; that will not help me understand or control or accept it. Not my teachers: certainly no brother or priest I knew. Richard? I can't even ask him if he likes football, let alone anything this private. My mother? She is the very one I am hiding my shame from, so how can I tell her? Uncle Ron? We never talk about anything but sport, so I wouldn't know how to begin. There is no one, so I have to wrestle with my guilt and anxiety in my own way, which is to just let things happen and hope for the best.

I do get around to asking Kilby Groves something about sex, though not about jerking off. Kilby recently got Pat Benson pregnant, Pat Benson the nun's favourite girl at the Immaculate Conception school, whose dog 'Nigger' came to school with her every day. Pat is from the older, non-Commission area of West Ivanhoe, and everyone is gossiping about their having to get married – the Cloneys, kids in the street. Pat now lives with Kilby and his family in Stortford Avenue, and I see her and her big stomach when I pick up Kilby to go to the football. She looks beautiful and unashamed.

'How many times can you do it when you're married?' I ask him as we walk to the bus. He laughs out loud.

'As often as you like,' he says. Pondering this, I think I can see why people are so keen to get married. I wonder if there is any other reason. Girls are certainly on my mind more and more these days, and my thoughts turn again to Lorna and whether or not she has a boyfriend now. But I never get around to finding out.

*

When the results came out at the end of the year I had come third overall in the class, having been beaten by Joe Mastrioanni and Jim Thornycroft, both of whom were excellent at Maths, Algebra and Geometry, and were not in the school choir, so they spent more time on these subjects. I came first in English, and received a prize at the school concert at the Collingwood Town Hall. It was a busy, exciting night, and I was on stage a lot of the time with the choir and during the prize-giving. My mother and Richard were in the audience. Brother Williams presented me with an inscribed copy of *The Gorilla Hunters* by R M Ballantyne. It turned out to be a dreary novel with no interesting characters and a superficial story, which I read about halfway through and lost interest. Nevertheless, I gave it a proud place on our very small bookshelves.

My good friend John O'Brien, who sat next to me in class, never won a thing, but he didn't care. It was all just a laugh to him anyway, since he was always a little mad. He once roller-skated all the way from his house in Preston to see me in West Ivanhoe, a feat which impressed my brother even more deeply than it did me. It would have been around five miles, mostly along Bell Street, a busy and difficult road. We spent the day playing in the street in front of our house before 'Obsy' said it was time he went, and he roller-skated all the way back again. We always caught the bus home together from in front of the school in Queens Parade, and I got out at Darebin Road while he went on to Preston. Obsy didn't barrack for any football team, couldn't sing well enough to be in the choir, was no good at sport or at schoolwork, but he was the funniest and most unpredictable boy I've known. I never liked any boy more, or felt more appreciated by any boy, than him. I would miss him when I stopped going to school. He wasn't leaving, because his parents had insisted that he stay on to obtain his Intermediate certificate.

On Tuesday the 9th December, 1952, I turned fourteen. Three days later, Friday, I went to Brother Dillon at the end of lessons and told him, 'I'm not coming back next week or next year. I'm going to become a carpenter.'

'Good for you,' was all he said. My unexpressed feeling was relief: I was happy not to be challenged, not to have to defend or justify my decision to anyone in that place.

*

I lie on my bed and think about the world, about myself. Through the window the clouds skim over the sky and my mother's struggling camellia beats against the wall as the house is buffeted by a hot north wind. I am becoming aware of certain things about this life. For instance, that there is something called an energy shape. Things can begin full of promise and even success for a time, but then, inevitably, they will wind down, run out of energy, or simply fail. Time and again I see this happen – in myself certainly. I will start well, will impress people with my abilities, and then it will all start to fall away and failure takes over. I seem to lack stamina. That is why I develop the habit of starting new ventures, because in new ventures I sparkle, until I get to the consolidation stage. I will have to learn either how to continue on right to the end, and thus achieve success, or else get out before things go completely sour.

The problem is not just in me but also in the world in which I have grown up. It has all been about beginnings, never achievements.

Richmond, Mount Macedon, West Melbourne, Larundel, West Ivanhoe, my parents' marriage, my father's life, my mother's good temper, the promise of my schooling. The truth is I have come to believe that promise is always followed by failure. So sad.

My father understood this even in his youth, and yet it did not make him cynical or self-pitying. Except in the moments when his illness overwhelmed him enough to trigger his anger, he remained optimistic, thoughtful and above all, a gentle and loving man. His suffering, his knowledge of his impending death, were always put second to his love for my mother and his two boys. My childhood frustration at not being able to make physical contact with him – that 'ache' of something missing in my life – was undoubtedly an ache that he felt as well, though my childish egotism prevented me from seeing it at the time. Now, as I reflect, I can see the irony of the situation. That imposed distance that was causing our pain was the very expression of his love for me; he could only show

159

his love by keeping himself hidden, like Robin Hood, maybe like God. I daresay he did something similar with my mother, for whom he had an even fiercer desire for contact. The much over-looked torture of tuberculosis is the loneliness of sequestration.

'Your trouble,' a wise woman once said to me, 'is that you just close off doors in your life, one after the other.' I've somehow managed to construct a principle around this self-negation. It's a good thing, I tell myself, to reject people, to reject opportunities, to deny chances for enrichment. You don't need them, you're better off without them. Meaning, I'm less likely to be hurt without them. It is a kind of cowardice, produced by too much early unhappiness.

At the same time, I developed independence, a willingness to trust myself. My lack of confidence was not an inner conviction; in fact I have always secretly believed in my own strength and ability. A number of times in later life this has given me the power to seize my opportunities with both hands. Those moments have brought success and happiness. But I've learned not to make these the paradigm for living: the success has to be accompanied by failure.

*

When I arrived home from school on that Friday I threw off my uniform for the last time, buried my cap at the bottom of the wardrobe, together with my school bag, and began to anticipate life as an adult. Summer was already here, and the holidays stretched before me, but I would have to start looking for a job that would start some time soon after Christmas. The next morning, Saturday, I combed through the employment pages of *The Sun News Pictorial*. There were several possibilities, but the one that caught my eye was an advertisement under 'Vacancies' that read:

Lad wanted: factory hand and learn furniture trade; possible apprenticeship to cabinet making. £2/5/0 p.w. Ring the Manager, Alrob Furniture Pty Ltd, North Coburg.

I could hardly wait to follow it up.

To this day I have no real idea what my mother thought about my leaving school. She might have sounded some warning tones in questions such as 'What will you do?' but since I had my answer ready, she had nothing to argue me down with. The fact is, her attention was drifting away from me, and there were new demands on her time and energy with her new marriage, her baby and Richard's family. None of it interested me. I had no bitterness towards her; on the contrary, I was pleased she now had the chance for a life she had been so cruelly denied in the years of my father's illness and death. But I had my own course to run now.

I have always known that it was her strength that kept us going in those bleak days, and I have always known what a huge struggle it was for her and how much courage and intelligence she needed to keep us fed and clothed and decent in the face of every misfortune that was thrown at her. She is the unacknowledged hero of my childhood, and hers was the heroism of stoic self-sacrifice, the will to keep going when many would have collapsed under the strain. The fact that I survived, that I came through it with my health and my capacity to love and work and pursue goals, was in no small measure due to her. It all took its toll, there's no doubt; she never fully recovered from the years of tension, daily grind, hopeless future prospects. It was always hard for her to laugh and relax, and she took medication for high blood pressure most of her life. The toughening left her with a cool indifference to intimacy. I know she had a sensuous, warm, loving nature underneath, and that she had once, in her romance with my father, freely lived it. But she changed. I saw it happen, I was on the receiving end of it, and I can reflect on the sadness of it.

I see her now through this haze of memory and mixed emotions. She sits at her Singer sewing machine, the smooth tuck, tuck, tuck tuck of the shuttle accompanying her low humming of popular tunes of the 1930s, the occasional curse breaking from her lips. She is surrounded by dress material, and her diligence is some kind of compensation for a pleasure she might otherwise enjoy. She is still beautiful in my mind, but dressed dowdily, and is tense with concentration. She rarely laughs, though she enjoys her gossip sessions when Ninny visits. They sit at the red Laminex kitchen table having tea and scones, and occasionally Ninny will laugh, a high-pitched, hearty laugh that is her signature. Somehow, for all the tough times she has gone through, Ninny has never lost her sense of fun the way my mother has. Mother and daughter both lost husbands relatively early. Both knew poverty, homelessness, the struggle to raise children on their own. But they have been affected differently by it.

I stand in the kitchen waiting to hear something of interest in their talk. They go quiet at my presence. 'Would you like a scone?' says Ninny. I take one, spread with raspberry jam.

'Go on, out you go,' says my mother. 'There's nothing in here to interest you.'

She's wrong about that. Adult talk always interests me. That's the one thing I'm longing to be: an adult.

Fare Thee Well, Hoddle Grid

BREATHING IS DIFFICULT IN THE HOPPER. The entrance recedes as I back farther in, as far as the first bend, where it is dark and narrow and the air tastes thick with sawdust, so the nostrils block, the eyes smart. The tube is dark and tight and the metal surface slippery. I fear the smoothness will prevent my edging my way out, that I will die in there, before I can be pulled out. This is what being born must be like, but if you jam. At the bend I feel the blockage with my boot, kick at it till it crumbles like cake. Thank god. Now I can work my way out, inching forward on cramped elbows, a child imitating a chicken. As I get closer to the light my efforts grow more frantic, until finally my head emerges into the cool, clear air, and I have made it yet again, safe until the next time. The foreman, John Bounty, offers his hand to help me down, a lady alighting from a carriage.

'Good lad, let's hope it's the last time. Get yourself cleaned up, take yourself down to the shop and get a Coke,' he says. He doesn't offer to pay.

My job, mostly, is to sweep up piles of sawdust and shavings from the factory floor and feed them into the vacuum duct that leads to the hopper. The hopper is like a big, upturned metal bottle that stands on a frame above the factory roof. I hate it, going up there, but I have no choice; I am the lad. I do all the shit jobs.

This is my first workplace, the Alrob Furniture Company, Coburg. Gone are the frustrations of school. I am fourteen, presuming to feel superior to all my school mates who have stayed on to get their Intermediate or Leaving certificates. How small and deluded I am, standing there covered in little question-marks of hardwood shavings. Among the men at last, the workers, the comrades. How would I fare? How would I end up?

My mother insists that I pay something towards my keep, now that I am earning an income. Out of £2/5/0 weekly I have to pay tax and then ten shillings to her, which leaves a little over £1.0.0 a week for lunches, clothes and entertainment, mostly the pictures and the football. At least I am young enough, and small enough, to qualify for child entry to these, despite being a full-time factory worker; the irony is lost on me at the time.

I go often to the Essendon ground, which had not yet acquired the name Windy Hill. Kilby Groves from the next street, or sometimes my brother Ray, who is now ten years old, go with me. John Coleman is our hero, the flying genius who does the impossible every week, or so it seems. He will kick a goal with his wrong foot, over his shoulder from forty metres out on the boundary, without even being able to see where it is going. He will take a mark over five or more players, after the defenders have blocked him at the back of the pack, just by somehow rising in the air above them as if being hoisted on wires. His outrageous flair brings thousands of people to the grounds every week to watch. The recollections will stay in my mind, little filmic events to be played and replayed, often at unexpected moments.

On the way home from work I stop to explore the shops. At the hairdresser's I take a seat alongside several others, while the two barbers talk in matter-of-fact tones to the customers in the chairs. I love the barbershop - the male smells, men's magazines - *Lilliput, Man, Photoplay, The Sporting Globe*, the talk of sport and politics. I am sure that within the often cryptic exchanges of men's talk there is some secret code, some access to a world of male meaning and importance, if only I can find it out. The walls of the shop bear little glass-fronted cabinets, labelled 'sterilizer' under a red cross, and contain scissors, combs, clippers, creams and rubber syringes, most of which I've never seen I used. When it is my turn to take the chair the barber will ask, with a touch of mockery, how I want it styled. I've been thinking about a change for some time; ever since primary school, when my mother designed it, my hair had a left parting and a front wave, and cut short at the back and sides. But some of the sharper boys in the last year of school, such as Norman MacPhee, went in for new fashions, such as the 'Cornel Wilde', where the sides were grown long and swept straight back into a 'duck's arse' at the back, and a carefully untidy curl hung down at the front. I say to the barber, 'Can you give me a 'Cornel Wilde'?

'Well, I can start it off for you, but it's still a bit short to train back'.

'Okay, do it.'

When it is finished the general effect doesn't look much different, but the barber has plastered the hair back with 'Californian Poppy' oil, in the hope that it will encourage growth in the new direction. When I leave the shop I catch a few people looking at me, and wonder if their looks are approving or otherwise. I think maybe I should have stayed the way I've always been. Maybe this explains the hint of mockery in the barber's tone.

There is music shop a few doors along the street, where I buy my first ever music recording, called 'Do Not Forsake Me', from the film *High Noon*. Westerns are my favourite kind of film, and this one haunts me for months. In the film the song, sung by Tex Ritter, is calm and melancholy, suggesting the terrible loneliness of the sheriff in the story. As I listen to the recording the steady drumming of the music is reminiscent of the ticking clock in the film, counting down the moments before the sheriff has to face three killers. These two elements, the sad voice and the regular beat underneath, continue on into infinity as the song fades away without actually coming to an end, and the fade-out suggests it is not just the sheriff's loneliness, but also my own loneliness that the song empties into. I play the record over and over, re-experiencing this sense again and again. On the radio Hit Parade they play a version by Frankie Lane, who tries to inject desperation and heightened emotion into it; the result is terrible, almost comic, missing every nuance of the story.

Every afternoon just before knock-off time I took a huge brown paper bag of khaki coloured glue pellets out of the storeroom, tipped them into a ten gallon drum, added water and mixed it up with a length of timber. It had to be well mixed, which meant stirring for at least twenty minutes, and it gave off a nauseating stink, like dead animal. And every night for the first week I thought I was going to vomit before I'd finished. But I didn't. Somehow, I fought it down. The only other job I did, which took up most of the day, was 'pulling through' behind the machines. This I didn't mind too much, because it felt important. This was because I had to work with one of the proper workmen who was operating the machine. If it was a circular saw, say ripping lengths of timber, which meant cutting them lengthways along the grain, I stood behind the machine and took the pieces of timber as they came through; without me standing there the timber could fall awkwardly and cause a problem. At other times I pulled behind a planing machine, which again meant ensuring that the piece of timber emerged safely from the machine, and more importantly didn't 'buck' as it came through due to the planer chewing on skew-grained or knotted planks. Both jobs were deafeningly noisy, and boring in that you couldn't hear yourself, let alone anyone else, speak, so all you could do was think to yourself the whole time, and even that was made difficult by the noise. The man I worked with was called 'Chips' something; he was tall and lean, in his forties perhaps, with dark hair, dark eyes and always days-old dark stubble. He never said much at any time, came over as surly, and gave the impression that there was no love lost between him and just about everyone else in the place. As I watched Chips feeding the timber into the circular saw I noticed that he had very few fingers left – three on one hand and two on the other, with the thumb missing on that hand as well. It took a while for it to dawn on me that this was why he was called 'Chips'.

These were the only jobs I was permitted to do. I was not allowed to pick up a tool of any kind, or to make any part of a piece of furniture, until my apprenticeship began, which was not to be until I was fifteen. And that was another year away.

North Coburg was a difficult place for me to get to every day from West Ivanhoe. I would have caught the Bell Street bus, only Bell Street was about a half-hour walk from our house; there was no transport going along that route yet, though there was one planned, along Oriel Road, to cater for the Olympic Village to be built in a few years. So my only option, unless I wanted to get up at five-thirty instead of six, was to ride my bike. It was about sixteen kilometres, mostly along Bell Street, which had several steep hills, heavy traffic, and both the north and the west winds seemed always to blow straight into my face. It was hard work, with no gears on the bike, a heavy old third-hand banger prone to losing its chain however much it was tightened, and it had lousy brakes. I had to leave about six-thirty in the morning to get there to clock-on by seven-thirty. But though I was small and skinny, I was tough and determined, so was rarely late. Perhaps I had the Christian Brothers to thank for 'instilling' this habit in me, though of course it was by means of the leather cosh, so I am not inclined to make the gesture.

The Alrob factory was small, employing only about a dozen tradesmen, including three apprentices. Two of these, Alan and Glenn had almost finished their five-year term. Both were stockily built fellows, always in shorts displaying legs and buttocks capable of brutal power. In comparison I was puny. They talked non-stop through morning smoko, sitting on palettes with their brown army-booted legs stretched before them, eating pies with sauce and drinking pint bottles of milk, though it was only nine-thirty in the morning. Their talk was almost exclusively of sex, and every second word, it seemed, was an obscenity. They exchanged competitive anecdotes, while the other men, older, probably married and more interested in sport or the price of wall-to-wall carpet, sat only half listening. I, in contrast, hung on their every word:

'Fucken mate and me picked up these three fucken sheilas last night'.

'Yeah? Whereabouts?'

'Fucken Footscray.'

'Lotta fucken spag cunt down there mate, wanna watch yourself.'

'Nah, fuck not these. Aussies, for sure. Mate's got this truck, see. Down the Footscray Park, near the river, plenty of fucken tree-cover down there. In the back of the truck and into 'em, one of 'em keepen a look out while she's waiten 'er turn. She's sayen, come on, come on, hurry up for fuck sake, *someone might come*, and me mate Dunnie – he's got a bottle of C.O.R. Ten in the front seat and is already a bit pissed and can't get it up and can't stop laughen so *he* won't *come* I said through the window and the crow he's supposed to be rooten starts laughen too and sayen 'what's ya name? What's ya name? Dunny? Dunny? No wonder ya pissed. Ha!' So he gives her a belt round the ear and they start arguen. But me, I'm goen fucken great guns.'

'What are ya doen?'

'Having – you know, whaddya think – given it to 'er in the truck tray. An then, when I finished her, the other bitch says 'do me too, can't ya, do me too', so she swaps places with the girlfriend and I give it to her too.'

'Two of 'em in one night?' His envy is palpable.

'Bullshit,' says John Bounty, the foreman, sitting on the floor on the opposite side of the room.

'How would you know, ya cunt?' comes the reply, with just enough zest for the good humour to register.

'I get more than you do, mate, that's for sure,' says Bounty.

'Yeah, only because ya married, ya weak bastard.'

As I listened to this I wondered whether there really were girls like that. Would any of them really allow that to be done to them, I wondered. And talk like that. Surely Bounty was right, I thought, and they're just lying or exaggerating. Of course I never said so; very rarely did I speak, so intimidated was I by their confidence, their command of the situation. And rarely did they speak to me, so insignificant was I in their eyes. Later on, when I asked one of the other workmen, I learned that 'C.O.R. Ten' was a jokey name for CORIO whisky, a local product; C.O.R. stood for Commonwealth Oil Refineries, and their well-known brand of petrol.

Cricket was becoming a major interest in my life around this time. Occasionally I went to a Sheffield Shield match or even a Test Match with Ronnie Bowden, or my brother. I saw Australia play South Africa at the MCG, and became a passionate admirer of some of the players – Neil Harvey especially, who performed with silky grace whether batting or fielding. And Hugh Tayfield, the South African off-spinner, captivated me with his Gregory Peck looks and crafty bowling. For some time I had been playing in the nearby paddock with some of my friends. We had fashioned a pitch of sorts in the clay ground, digging out weeds and levelling the ground with a mattock, then rolling it with Bob Pinchbeck's roller. We all used my 'Don Bradman' bat from a couple of

Christmases ago, made stumps out of boxwood, and Eddie Weaver, the brother of Shirley Weaver who now boarded with us, bought a couple of four-piece leather balls. Eddie lived next door with the Pinchbecks; Shirley and Eddie had lost their mother to cancer and their father was a travelling house painter, so they had no home of their own. We now had all the equipment we needed to play an authentic kind of cricket in the paddock, much better than using a box and a tennis ball in the street. In the first week of using the pitch I was injured; Eddie Weaver threw the ball to me from some distance away while my back was turned. Eddie saw that the ball was going to hit me in the head, so yelled 'look out'. I turned to see and was stunned by an explosion like a punch on the mouth that sent me reeling. When I saw the blood running onto the palm of my hand, I knew it was serious. 'I can see your teeth through your split lip,' said Jim Thornycroft, as they walked me home. When my mother saw it she shrieked, 'Oh my god, you're going to have a harelip! We must get you to the doctor.' Bob Pinchbeck ran us in his car to Doctor Downing's surgery in Ivanhoe village, where I was attended to straight away.

'I'll stitch it up here,' said Downing. My mother sat on a chair in the surgery, looking anxiously on.

'Will he be scarred?' she asked.

'There is less likelihood of scarring if I do it without anaesthetic,' he said, and proceeded quietly. It didn't hurt as much as I expected, but at one stage I could feel the needle coming out through the external skin of the upper lip, and I gave a little cry of surprise more than pain. Suddenly there was a crash on the other side of the room: my mother had hit the floor. Fainted. Downing dashed across to pick her up and place her back on the chair, leaving the needle dangling by its cotton thread from my mouth. When it was over I had a bright plaster across my upper lip, and difficulty eating for a few days, until the stitches were removed. And Downing was right: the scar disappeared after a few months.

At work there was another apprentice, Brian, only two years older than me. Brian had large ears and wore a Coburg football jumper every day, with number eleven on the back, and he was allowed to do certain small cabinet-making jobs, like hand sanding and glueing the dovetailed ends of drawers. Brian also liked to make me look foolish, which was not hard; on my second day I was told to go to the man in charge of stores and pick up two skyhooks and a left-handed screwdriver for John Bounty. Of course, without thinking twice, I did it, much to the amusement of everyone in the factory; for the next week Brian would sing out loudly when he passed 'Have you picked up those skyhooks yet?' and those around would laugh.

In my first week John Bounty had said to me to me 'We might put you on the lunches soon', but when Brian heard about this he complained. 'That's my job,' he said, 'I'm all right with it. They know me down at the shops now – always keep the prices down for us.'

'Well, okay,' said Bounty, 'we'll leave it the way it is for now. But I'll be wanting you for other things soon, and young Garry can do the lunches.'

Afterwards Chips told me, 'Brian doesn't want to lose the lunches because it's a good lurk; he works it so he makes money. He does deals with the shopkeepers as a regular customer, and he pockets the discount. He told me once he makes about two quid a week extra, plus they give him a free sandwich or cream bun from time to time.'

I noticed, too, that Brian gave extra little touches of attention to John Bounty on the days that he bought his lunch, like pointing out that a couple of potato cakes had been thrown in to his order of fish and chips, or a sausage roll had been popped into the bag with his pie and pasties. A smart lad, Brian.

But as the weeks passed, I grew less and less happy at the Alrob. I couldn't talk to many of my workmates, and the bike ride to get there and home was becoming more and more exhausting. What with the chain coming off – the bike's whole frame was basically twisted – and then the back tyre getting punctures, eventually requiring a new tube, causing me to be late one morning, and having to walk the bike home from Coburg one afternoon, I was finding it too hard. Finally, one morning in June, after pushing most of the way into a freezing west wind, and the rain pelting into my face, so that I arrived at work completely soaked – even my socks were wringing wet – I'd had enough: I would get out of this. I looked in the paper the next Saturday morning, and found a vacancy with another furniture maker, C.J. Baragwanath, in Arthurton Road, Northcote. Monday morning I skipped work, and rang Baragwanath's from the telephone box on the corner near our house. They told me to come along straightaway for an interview. The following week, I began the new job. It was closer and easier to ride to, through territory that was much more familiar – almost the same route that had taken me to school – High Street, Northcote, where it was civilised and had lots of shops.

There were several points of difference between the Alrob and Baragwanath factories. The new place was bigger, making a greater range of furniture. They had their own mirror-making section, their own veneer press, and they employed more people – around fifty. There was a full-time manager, Mr Schilling, who wore suits and talked only to the several foremen when he walked around the factory floor. It was Schilling who had interviewed me, very briefly, during which he had said that my situation would be reviewed at the end of the year when I turned fifteen, and that an apprenticeship might be possible. I was also paid more – the princely sum of £3/15/0 per week, before tax.

There were other differences. Sweeping the floor was still fundamental, but it was confined to only one area – the drawer-making section; apprentices in the different areas swept their respective floors. I continued to make cold-water glue, again, specifically for the drawer makers, but also I made small pots of hot-water glue for individual carpenters, placing them carefully on their workbenches. A roster existed among the apprentices and myself to clean the lavatories. These were in a large rectangular area in the middle of the factory sealed off by great sheet metal walls that reached up to the roof. Inside, the corrugated iron roof was left open to the sky, reducing the smell, but making a visit to the toilet a cold and windy event. Along one wall was a long concrete urinal, into which were put little orange cakes of disinfectant; they seemed to augment rather than reduce the stink. A row of booths containing the usually filthy toilet bowls, which had to be kept clean by brushing and flushing, had stable-type doors that stopped a foot above the floor, so that the inhabitant's boots, trousers, underpants and shins were on public display. The brick floor had to be hosed each Friday just before knock-off time. Every one of the sheet metal walls, including the booths, was covered in chalked graffiti, which was being constantly updated by the scribes, erasing old ones to make space for the new. Many were about someone called 'Abo', whose sexual and general bodily functions were the topic of obscene and witless postulations. 'Abo fucks his mother', 'Abo sucks Schilling's arse', and so on. I eventually discovered that 'Abo' was not, as I had supposed, an indigenous Australian but 'one of the lads' in his mid-twenties, of Italian extraction, with heavy dark eyebrows and hair, swarthy skin and dark stubble, and an adolescent sense of humour, which inspired his popularity in the toilet block. As well as crude poems and epithets, the graffiti ran to stereotypical scrawls of disembodied genitals and of women on their backs, legs up, vagina facing the world. It was not part of my job to clean any of this off, since it was held to be of general value to the workers, giving them something to read if they didn't have a copy of *The Sun* or *The Truth* as they ruminated over their morning discharges.

Another first was getting the lunches. As Brian had discovered at Alrob, it was possible to make a little money on this. It was also possible to come to grief. At Baragwanath's, there was a huge number of lunches to be ordered and picked up every day, and the number made it easy to get things, such as calculations, wrong. The method was this: I would go around to everyone on the factory floor at around nine in the morning, writing down their lunch order and taking their money. Often they would not have change, and would give me a ten shilling or one pound or even a five pound note, expecting me to give them the change later when I brought them their lunch. I would then ride off on my bike, placing the orders with the various shops – the sandwich shop, the fish and chip shop, the cake-shop, the newspaper shop, to be picked up around eleven thirty. I would pay while placing the orders, and put all the change into my bicycle bag. For pick up, I carried a large wooden box made to fit the handlebars. Here's where grief might strike. On more than one occasion I came off the bike, tipping the lunches onto the road, so that pies and pasties were broken, sandwiches deconstructed, cakes squashed, fish and chips unravelled. It might rain, and though I had a plastic Mac that went over the box, rain inevitably got in and the food arrived back at the factory soggy and cold. This made some of the men angry, and they made their feelings about me only too plain.

More grief could occur over money. By some mysterious set of miscalculations the finances rarely balanced out correctly; mostly I had change left over, occasionally finding myself short. Then there were the embarrassing times when I thought I'd made a handsome 'profit', only to be approached by an irate workman in mid-afternoon demanding the change out of the pound he'd paid. I took to keeping a tin in which I put any leftover money, not pocketing it until the end of the week in case I had to make up any losses. As welcome as the few shillings I might make were the free handouts the shop staff gave me – a couple of free potato cakes from the fishmonger, a cream bun from the baker, a Coke from the sandwich shop. The goodwill generated by these gestures injected a degree of pleasure into the whole exercise, and made getting the lunches the best part of my day.

Much of the time I worked in the vicinity of Alby, a large man who uttered a constant stream of unfunny jokes or tacky remarks. Alby was married with five children and had worked at Baragwanath's for eleven years, doing the same job. He would ask, 'What number do you live at in your street?'

'One-twenty.'

'Do you know Dick Withers at sixty?'

I would often wonder, through the years of my youth, whether that dismal prospect was true or not.

Alby would also say disturbing things like 'I've got a cock like a baby's arm', and would tell me things about his wife, such as when she was having her period and they were unable to have sex. I noticed that few of the other workers gave Alby any of their time.

As matters turned out, I didn't stay long at Baragwanath's either. In fact, by the end of that year I had given up my dream of being a carpenter altogether. It wasn't entirely of my own accord. The week after I turned fifteen I became concerned that no one had said anything to me about an apprenticeship. I had a bad feeling about it, and plucked up the courage to go to Mr Schilling's office and ask if I could start an apprenticeship in carpentry or cabinet making at the start of the next year. With his mouth pulled down at the corners, which was his natural expression anyway, Schilling shook his head. 'No son, we don't need any more cabinet makers. We'll apprentice you to wood machining.'

'Wood machining?' I asked, 'but I want to be a carpenter or a cabinetmaker. That's what I came here to do. You said you'd apprentice me to that when I turned fifteen.'

'No, son, I said I'd consider the possibilities. There isn't much of a future in cabinet making, you know; we need people who can operate the machines well – that's where it is all heading. Take it from me, you'll be better off.'

I talked to my mother about it, but she didn't know what to say. I told her, 'None of the wood machinists have all their fingers. It's a dangerous job.'

'Why don't you talk to Uncle Dick about it?'

I wasn't keen to do this. Uncle Dick was only my stepfather, my mother's new husband after the death of my father, and though he was my half-sister Susan's father, he showed no personal interest in me or my brother. He was a butcher, and perhaps my mother thought he might know something about apprenticeships. But so far, in the two years I'd known him, we hadn't said more than three words at one time to each other. I knew it would be useless to go to him with my problems.

In fact, though I had sought my mother's advice, I had already made up my mind. I didn't think about it in a rational or informed way – informed that is by finding out about apprenticeships or employment opportunities from the relevant authorities; I had no idea how to do anything like that. I simply went by my own observation, and what this told me was that I had spent a year experiencing life in furniture factories, and apart from my own activities being dreary, repetitive and at times dangerous, I couldn't see that the qualified tradesmen enjoyed their work any more than I did. There was nothing creative or even interesting going on – just routine tasks day after day, and there was nothing about their work that I envied except in an immediate and shallow sense, and certainly nothing that suggested I should be like them and do their jobs for the rest of my life. Carpentry, cabinet making, furniture making, in the way that I was witnessing it – in factories – had proved to be a disappointment, and I had no desire to continue it. As it turned out, the year had been a good opportunity to learn all this before I committed myself to an apprenticeship that would have been difficult to get out of.

What I did wonder about, and what seemed an attractive proposition, was working in an office. Where this notion came from is unclear. There was a fellow I knew, a little older, who lived a couple of streets away, who worked as a clerk in some sort of office, and he seemed to like it, so maybe it was he who started me thinking about it. There were many ads in the paper for different kinds of clerks, many of them not requiring experience or qualifications, so I started telephoning for interviews. Employment was easy to get in those years; there were staff shortages on many fronts, and I soon picked up an interview, which led straightforwardly to a job. And it changed my life. It opened up an entirely new idea of what constituted work and the workplace, and revealed to me just how enjoyable a job could be.

2

THE FIRST TIME I SAW HER, I felt a change in my body. For a few moments I couldn't breathe, and then I felt a pit in my stomach; yet I was not able to grasp, not as one would from experience, what this condition was meant to resolve into, since I was still sexually undeveloped, a kind of amphibian. And here was the source of my condition, this luminously beautiful creature who had appeared seated at the receptionist's desk in the Managing Director's suite. Like myself, she was fifteen, and her name was Margaret Kendrick. I wanted nothing other than to walk past her desk every five minutes just to look at her. For weeks I was too overawed to speak to her. And after I finally managed it – a poor 'hello' – her smile and reply stayed with me for the rest of the day and half the night.

The presence of females marked the biggest difference between this job and the two previous ones. There were other differences of course – yes, the offices were cosy and clean, and the sounds were the diligent tappings of typewriters, purposeful footsteps in the wide, polished corridors, the almost intellectual and certainly elevated social tone of a kind of talk entirely missing from the factory floor, and the clothes possessed a variety that was a welcome change from khaki overalls. And then there were the subtleties of hierarchy and pecking order that had quickly to be learned. But over and above all the situational and structural differences, there was that one ingredient that women brought to this kind of workplace and that was the raw, biological reality of sex. The office was made colourful, fragrant, romantic, frustrating, dramatic, melancholy, bitter, and full of all those imaginary triumphs that it so decorously and crushingly denies, by the sexual presence of women. Why, I might have asked myself, would I ever want to work anywhere else?

The firm was The British United Shoe Machinery Company of Australia, in Smith Street, Fitzroy, a mere five-minute walk from my old school in Queen's Parade. I had applied for and gained a junior clerk's job in the Purchasing Section, a small department with the elderly boss, R.T. Carter, in one room, and four others, comprising one typist, Mrs Kneale, two men and myself as clerks, in the only other room. The situation created a certain level of intimacy, particularly between the four of us in the one room.

In the first week I achieved a wonderful moment of unlooked-for success that won me Mr Carter's respect. One of my more important responsibilities, remembering how junior I was in this huge and imposing corporation, was that of supplying coffee, tea, sugar, gallon cans of soup and a few other foodstuffs from a small storeroom to Mrs Wilson, the lady in charge of the staff cafeteria. Mrs Wilson placed her daily takings in a large screw-top jar, and after lunch every day dutifully took it round to the accounts section for banking. Before tidying up and going home in mid-afternoon she would hand me the jar to lock away in the storeroom for safekeeping. On the very first occasion I was placing the jar on an eye-level shelf in the storeroom when something protruding below the lid inside the jar caught my eye, and when I unscrewed the lid I found it was a pound note that had become lodged and therefore missed by the accounts clerk. Without giving it a moment's thought I took the jar and the money straight back to Mrs Wilson, and showed her. By her reaction you'd have thought it was a hundred pounds. 'Oh, how wonderful!' she said, 'What an honest young fellow you are! What a good fine boy you are …'

The following morning Mr Carter called me into his office, and gave me a long inscrutable look over the lenses of his horn-rimmed glasses, which lay comically perched on the tip of his nose. Mr Carter was a storybook boss, shortish, solid but not fat, gracefully aged, bald-domed, with a deep but soft voice that never registered emotion. He prided himself on being an ambidextrous scribe. Every day after lunch he fell asleep in his chair in the cafeteria, chin on tie, glasses pushed back on his pate like an airman, snoring faintly to himself until, on the dot of two o'clock he would wake with a start, stretch and return to his office. A man of immense common sense and honesty himself, he always sounded surprised and gratified when he came across either in others.

'Mrs Wilson has told me about your act of decency; you might easily have taken that money without anybody knowing, and it says a great deal about your character that you resisted the temptation. Be assured young fellow that it is much appreciated, and won't be forgotten on into the future.'

It had never even occurred to me that I might pocket the money; if it had, and I thought I could get away with it, chances are I would have done so.

The Purchasing Section was regarded as the least important area of the company's activities, a matter that showed in the allocation of space in the building. The four of us, plus the filing cabinets, desks and a small service counter, and an adjoining small office for Mr Carter, occupied half the space that Mr Conabere in the office directly across the wide corridor had entirely to himself. Mr Conabere was an important executive with links to the Collingwood Football Club, and presented a gruff and unfriendly manner on the few occasions I went in to his uncluttered, unbusy office. Heavy, navy-suited, horn-rim-spectacled, baritone-voiced, self-important, Conabere was terrifying.

My priority work lay in keeping the Kalamazoo filing system up to date. Thanks to Mr Carter's diligence it was a model of good, accessible record keeping, requiring written or typed entries on removable overlapping cards in trays that slid into a metal cabinet. As well as this I looked after the storeroom, wrote out purchasing orders, took phone calls and ran errands to all parts of the multiple-sited company. I was busy and, for the first year or so, happy.

The most interesting aspect of it was my colleagues. In some respects Mrs Kneale's job was the most important in the section, since she had to type weekly orders of literally hundreds of machine parts to be sent to Head Office in England, parts with strange names and complex identification numbers, and any mistakes in the list would have been expensive and time-wasting to re-order. She typed furiously with Mr Carter at her shoulder reading out the descriptions of machine parts, parts for interlockers and overlappers, toe-cap moulders, eyelet riveters and so on, for page after page, rarely making an error. Compared with this, the work the rest of us did was unexacting, casual. Yet Mrs Kneale was always able to join in the lively, jokey, personal, at times quarrelsome banter that took place between the four of us in the one room.

Fred Clarke, deputy to Mr Carter, was a difficult man to work with. Tall, wavy-haired, he was something like the actor Ray Milland in appearance, intelligent and sensitive. But he was unhappy most of the time; some important aspect of his life had gone wrong. He had the typical deputy's craving for authority, but Mr Carter kept all the important decisions, such as they were, for himself, and Fred would either complain bitterly about not being consulted, or would overcompensate whenever he found himself in charge, putting everyone's backs up. At other times he indulged in self-pitying confessions, mostly about the difficulties he was having with his wife. She had left him on more than one occasion, taking their small child to her mother's for several weeks. He had served in the war – Air Force ground staff – and occasionally when his opinion was challenged he would resentfully drag out the cliché, 'I fought for you', to which I could only respond with laughter. I should not have done this, but I had a keen nose for emotional blackmail, especially on the matter of war service. Underneath my mockery was the memory of my father's thwarted desire to enlist in the army: he would have given anything to have had Fred's opportunity to fight for us.

Jim Skinner, well-built, twenty-something, with a large, oddly back-sloping head, blonde hair combed Bing Crosby style and the dress sense of a man twice his age – he wore a navy reefer jacket almost every day – was a different presence altogether. He possessed one ability, and one ability only, that fitted him for clerical duties: he had beautiful copperplate handwriting, and for hours he would sit at his desk writing out purchasing orders in a carbon-copied octavo book to his heart's content. He was a strange amalgam of the predictable and the unreliable, not very bright and not well-educated. Pleasant enough, he liked to join in any jokey banter in the office, his humour based on repetition of something, like a saying he had heard at the pub, over and over for months, even years, on end. 'Look at 'em,' he'd say, 'heads on 'em like mice,' the meaning of which I could never fathom. The confirmed bachelor type, he lived at home with his parents, didn't seem to have any interest in women, though there was not the slightest suggestion of homosexuality about him; on the contrary, he was culturally a product of old working-class Fitzroy and Collingwood, with a social life dominated by sport, betting on the horses and drinking in the pub bar. Despite living within walking distance from work, he often drifted in late in the mornings looking the worse for last night's binge with his mates, and before he did anything else, lit up a cigarette, the first of many throughout the day, and immediately indulged in a long, loud, chest-clearing cough followed by a spit into his waste basket. Jim ignored all cultural pursuits such as art, music and theatre, had never read a book, and rarely seen a film. He was always promising to do something about his several missing bicuspids.

Though I would not have chosen these people as my friends, the fact is they were a dominant presence in my daily routines, and I inevitably got caught up in their lives. For instance, Jim invited me to take part in a social cricket match one Sunday; and Mrs Kneale, on learning that my mother was a dressmaker, asked if she might make her a dress for a particular occasion. Fred regularly asked me on lunchtime walks along Smith Street, ostensibly to buy some household item at the hardware store, but really to complain to me about his wife, or the behaviour of teenagers at the suburban cinema where he worked as a part-time usher. I of course must have done something the same with them, otherwise they would not have known of my cricketing ability, my mother's work, or my mildly prurient interest in personal matters.

Running errands, I soon got to know the different working areas – accounts, sales, the stores section, the other building sites. Jim would take me on his many travels around the Company, introducing me to all and sundry. He seemed to know everyone - the section managers, the workers, the office girls – and had a joke and a laugh with them all. We went to the Tack Factory in Alexandra Parade, where you entered the office directly from the street, and found yourself in a building of constant low thunder, the office separated from the factory floor by double-glazed partitions. Out through the glass I could see the hyperactivity of the massive machines, twenty feet high some of them, and all the time I was being introduced to the manager and office staff the deep rumble continued around us and up through the floor. When someone entered from the factory area, the blast of machine din crashing through the opening door obliterated all other sounds, and all possibility of thought. Leaving the building, Jim told me, 'The tack machines never close down; all the workers on the factory floor stop hearing it after a while. Anyone who's worked there for any length of time is stone deaf.' After that, whenever I had to run errands to the Tack Factory I dived in and out of the place as quickly as I could, anxious to be out of range before my ears suffered any damage.

In the stores section the men were set apart by their long grey dust coats, and went in for a prickly, faintly malevolent kind of talk. I didn't like going down there, always felt unwelcome. The foreman, Bob Bond, did not offer to shake hands when Jim introduced me, and made a sardonic joke that I quickly forgot. Jim said later that Bob was an important member of his union, and 'never to mess him around'. I saw a reason for this on one lunchtime occasion. The cafeteria was a sectioned-off area upstairs, with trestle tables and chairs, where you could buy hot and cold food and drinks from Mrs Wilson, or take your own lunch and eat it at the tables. I always sat on the window side of the aisle, with a group of clerical staff that shared roughly the same status – clerks from accounts, marketing, purchasing. Fred Clarke and Mr Carter would often be there, and two Englishmen always enjoyable listening to, a short, wire-haired accountant who ate a strictly healthy diet, and a tall, urbane economist who completed his lunch every day with cheese-spread slowly and fastidiously applied to a bread roll. At least once a week this man produced an argument in favour of Australia being economically self-subsistent, even though no-one ever disagreed with him – the country had the oil, the food products, mining, its own car industry now, everything it needed to live independent of the world. Listening, I wanted to ask how Australia could possibly manufacture the kind of machines and parts that this very firm traded in, imported from England, though I was too unsure of myself to come out with it.

On the other side of the aisle a group of Storemen/Packers always sat together in their dustcoats at the same table, a closed circle, talking and laughing among themselves. Bob Bond used to bring his sandwiches and a thermos of tea, and, sitting always in the same place, finished his lunch every day with a whole white onion, eating it in chunks sliced and delivered raw to his mouth with a sharp knife. On this particular day it happened that before the group arrived, a youngish executive from the sales area – one of the favoured in the Company – who did not normally eat in the cafeteria and therefore was ignorant of the customary arrangements, had bought a hot meal from Mrs Wilson and sat himself, alone, in Bob Bond's usual seat. He was nonchalantly eating and reading a document when the dust-coated group arrived and headed to the table they used every day. Bob Bond stood adjacent to the interloper and bluntly said, 'Move mate – you're in my seat.'

The man looked up puzzled and said, 'How is this your seat? There was no-one here when I came.'

'It just is; I sit here every day with my mates. This is our table.'

The man pointed about them with his fork, 'There are plenty of other tables – look. I don't see why I should move now that I'm eating. You can't reserve tables here.'

The other clerical staff at our table, just opposite all this, went on talking oblivious to what was happening. But I could see that the situation had quickly developed into an impasse, with neither man prepared to back down – if Bond went to another table he would have failed to exert the authority he was claiming, and if the other gave up his seat he would look weak and foolish, surrendering his rights. Suddenly, Bond yanked the executive's chair away from the table and tried to tip him off it; the man stood up, his cutlery clattering to the floor, and tried to push Bond back. Next thing, they were grappling wordlessly with each other, like schoolboys, only their adultness made it more shocking. Bond had the man around the throat now, mercilessly digging his thumb and fingers into the flesh, and the face above going purple with either anger or strangulation. Bond's workmates started pulling them apart, and chairs were crashing over, the table pushed awry, and noisy protests began to break out. Suddenly Mrs Wilson came flying down the aisle holding a tea towel, and with it she leapt at Bond and began to thrash at him, lashing it angrily across his eyes and head. Between them, they managed to prise Bond's fingers away from their hold and separate the two men. Then Mrs Wilson's voice took charge in a display of surprising unflustered eloquence:

'Who the hell do you think you are, Bob Bond? You get the hell out of this cafeteria, and don't eat in here again until you can behave like a civilised human being! And you can take your crew with you – go on, all of you, clear out until you behave yourselves! I've never seen anything like it!'

The whole cafeteria was now staring at Bond, whose look was defiant and full of anger, but he stood frozen to the spot. Mrs Wilson began helping the executive to straighten his clothes and tie, and then pick up his chair and cutlery. Bond retrieved his dropped lunch from the floor, and truculently taking his time, left the cafeteria muttering 'Pack of jumped up arseholes.' His mates, however, chose not to follow, but sat in a huddle at an empty table farther along the aisle. None of them engaged with the diners around them. The scene had all the ugly reality of class warfare, and though I could understand from the inside, so to speak, given my own background, the reasons behind Bond's constantly simmering resentment, nevertheless my instinctive response was one of personal sympathy for the executive.

He, his face slowly returning to normal, gathered his lunch, his reading matter, what he could of his poise, resumed his place at the table, and finished eating. But no one was in any doubt that he was badly shaken by the ordeal. The odd thing was that, as far as anyone knew, nothing further came of it – Bond was neither sacked nor apparently even reprimanded, and within a week or so was back eating with his workmates in his usual spot. The executive went about his work in the building, occasionally eating in the cafeteria again, and the whole matter seemed to go away and leave no residue, as if it had never happened. Except, of course, in the minds of the witnesses, especially myself.

Who could I talk to about my fierce desire for her? What could be done with it? Just looking at her made my head spin. I couldn't imagine what it must be like to touch her. I had the sense that she knew all this, the way she looked back at me. She sometimes walked down the wide corridor past the Purchasing Section office, and I knew instinctively that the clack of high heels on the polished floor was hers, though I couldn't see her through the frosted glass partitions and doors. Occasionally, all too rarely, she came into our office for something, sat on the corner of my desk looking self-conscious and vibrant. Her eyes were a lachrymal blue, her lips full and soft, her breasts definite beneath the dark green uniform. Fred Clarke was besotted also, and found jokey reasons to handle her, tickle her about the waist. She giggled and revelled in the attention. How, how, I asked myself, could I ever win her attention, small, skinny, freckled type that I was?

The Company always gave its employees a half-holiday on Melbourne Show Day. I had been taken to the Show once by my mother when I was a child, but usually it held no interest for me. On this particular day, however, a golden opportunity presented itself. Margaret came into our office to chat, and asked if anyone was going. She'd never been, and since the weather was so fine outside, she rather fancied going but had no one to accompany her. Without hesitation, I leapt in, 'I'll take you,' I said. 'Will you?' she said, in that particularly English way of inflecting a question. 'Oh, that would be grand. Let's go as soon as we knock-off for lunch!'

And so I had at last managed to get my wish – to take out Margaret Kendrick, and to have her all to myself for the rest of the day. It happened that Show Day was also pay-day, and the Company was good enough to ensure that the pay came round during the morning instead of the usual late afternoon; the paymaster, Ormond Wilkins, a short, slow, fat man, did the rounds of the building with his tray full of small brown envelopes, and handed them to people with the solemnity of a priest delivering the communion wafer. It meant that I could escort Margaret with my pocket as full of cash as it could ever be, and as we caught the bus into the city I was flushed with pride and power, secure in the belief that at this moment I was the luckiest, most enviable fellow in the whole of Melbourne. And even better, as we flopped into our double seat on the near empty bus, Margaret slipped her hand, cool and pale, the fingernails chewed ragged, into mine. My throat constricted with joy, and for the rest of the journey into town I was blind to whatever was going on in the world out through the bus window.

We went to just about everything at the Show. We saw sheep dog trials and equestrian events, the judging of cows and dogs, of cakes and bottled fruits, we walked through every hall and along every avenue, we watched performing animals and clowns, listened to music and singing performed in the central arena. I bought her show bags containing samples of liquorice and peanut butter, and tiny replicas of tomato sauce bottles and jars of jam, of potato chips and fruit cordial and baked beans. I presented her with wads of sticky fairy floss and paper cups of terrible takeaway coffee, a hot dog and a box of Koolmints, and we walked and consumed on and on until we grew almost sick and certainly tired and sat down on the grass under a tree in a quiet spot near the cafeteria and talked. Then it was late afternoon and the crowds began to leave, so we sat on the steps of the grandstand of the central arena and watched the sun decline in a red western sky. We talked about nothing and yet it felt to be everything. She had, I learned, only recently migrated along with her father, mother and small brother, from Bristol in England. This was why, I realised, she seemed so apart from the general teenage crowd. She had no school friends, no neighbourhood history to draw upon. Family and work were her only social life. I didn't get around to talking about myself; I just loved to listen to her clear, crisply turned phrases, the classy tones of her voice. Occasionally I would say something that would prompt a little spat of temper from her, and in this I perceived a troubling limit in her make-up. There was an instability, either in her character or her experience that made me uncertain about how to connect with her, or just where I could at times take the conversation without suffering rebuke. Also, it was clear that she was holding back from me to a degree, as if not convinced that I was the right match for her. She seemed to tolerate me more than really like me. None of this mattered to me in the moment, so grateful was I just to be with her like this. I was never going to make a move to go home.

As night closed in the lights on the arena switched into full blaze, we stayed to watch a musical march-past by Scots guards followed by an exhibition of trotting on the sandy Showground track. The fast pacing horses flew in tight packs against each other and stirred the swelling night-time crowd to enthusiastic cheering. When it was all finished, and the lights were extinguished one by one, and the patrons drifted away, and the September breeze stirred up the day's strewn litter, I resisted as long as I could the admission that it was time to go. Finally, it was Margaret who said, 'We'd better leave I guess, or they'll end up locking us in for the night.'

We caught the train back to the city, and another out to her home in Reservoir, not far from the station. Tired and happy, hands full of show bags, we walked slowly to her house on the corner of High and Southernhay Streets, and stopped in the dark near the gate in the back fence. I insisted she take all the bags in with her. 'My brother will love the samples,' she said. She thanked me gracefully for the day, and for my generosity, and drew herself into me and rewarded me with a gentle, earnest, soft and head-spinning kiss full and long on my mouth. Then she disappeared through the back gate.

All the way home my heart sang like an ecstatic magpie. It didn't matter that it was past midnight and I'd missed the last bus along Bell Street, and had to walk the whole way, several miles, in the moonless, windy night. It didn't matter that I was flat broke because I'd spent every penny of my two weeks' wages on her. I'd have spent a year's wages on her if I'd had it in my pocket. I didn't care that my mother would almost certainly tear strips off me when she learned I'd spent my whole pay, including her board money, on a girl – a girl she'd never even heard of, and she didn't know I was taking to the Show. All that mattered was that I'd achieved my dream, and I was no longer a boy; I was a man, who could escort, pay for, touch and kiss the most beautiful girl I'd ever laid eyes on.

The Darebin Road bus is a problem to catch in the mornings, unreliable and overcrowded, and now and then I am late for work, drawing some terse comments from Mr Carter. One morning I watch it go right past my stop, people dangerously hanging on the step, the old yellow International leaning precariously to the left as it strains to make headway under its load. As it disappears up the road I stand at the stop groaning with the others, fearful of another reprimand from my boss, when I realise a car horn has been tooting just in front of them. No one else moves to the little maroon Singer sports car, so I go to investigate.

'Hop in,' calls a middle-aged man whom I do not recognise. Inside it is cosy and low, the first time I have been in a sports car. We take off with a light, pleasant burble from the muffler, and I feel quite honoured to be so generously treated.

'You don't know me?' says the man.

'Douglas Plant. From Sales. I've seen you getting around the building. You obviously haven't noticed me.'

I hadn't, but I certainly would from now on, I say. Plant is an oddly flat-faced man, who wears an old raincoat over his suit and tie, which makes him seem uncomfortably squashed in behind the wheel of the Singer. The passenger's seat has a little more room, and behind us is a narrow half-seat, on which he keeps his briefcase. The road-hugging ride is somewhat at the expense of comfort, and I feel every bump and cavity in the road, but I like the smart, direct handling under Plant's experienced control.

We travel together in virtual silence, with the gap in age and interests evident to us both from the first day. Plant picks me up at the bus stop on most mornings. There is no formal arrangement – he seems not to want this, as if it might undermine the spontaneity of his gesture. I am always slightly puzzled by it, nevertheless: why should he bother to give a lift to a boy of no consequence, with no conversation of interest to an older man, who just happened to work for the same firm? But it certainly is an improvement over the bus.

Elaborate changes are taking place along the route to the city, which passes my place of work. They are putting in tram tracks from the end of High Street Northcote to join up at Nicholson Street Fitzroy, almost in the city. The centres of High Street, Queens Parade, Smith Street and Gertrude Street, a distance of many kilometres, are to be dug up at huge inconvenience to everyone who uses them. It is because of the impending visit of Queen Elizabeth, who is to be driven along that route when she visits Melbourne early next year, 1954.

I had begun playing cricket for a local team in the district amateur competition. The idea came from Bob Pinchbeck, next door. Bob was trying to revive his own game, after years of inactivity with a badly smashed leg, and had made contact with the club, who welcomed his experience and ability. Bob could bat, but only with a runner, which reduced his effectiveness considerably, and he couldn't field or bowl. Occasionally he made runs in his very stylish manner, but never big scores, and he was more useful to the team as a coach than a player. Anyway, he took me along to evening practice sessions, where I immediately made an impression. I bowled left arm, still unsure whether to try to be a fast-medium or a spin bowler, so I did either, switching from one to the other whenever I chose, and was generally accurate at both. I had modelled my action on Australian and Victorian bowlers I had seen at the MCG, and had managed to develop fluency and balance. I could also bat well, benefiting from the lessons in technique Bob had given me – using my feet to go forward or back depending on the length of the ball, keeping the bat straight and close to my pads. I was never easy to get out. The club was made up of mostly grown men, some of them in their twenties, many of them in their thirties and forties. Few of them had any real ability, but there was always something I could learn from any one of them.

After just a couple of practice sessions I was given a place in the team, which played two-day matches on Saturday afternoons. I spent the whole day in the field without being asked to bowl, dropped a difficult catch at fine leg, and when it was my turn to bat the following week, was sent in last wicket and ended the game not out on two after facing just four balls. Given such a disheartening start I might easily have given up, but I had already developed a passion for the game, and was determined to get closer to the action in future. By the middle of that summer I was opening the bowling with my medium pacers, and doing my best to change the captain's view that I couldn't hold catches. Even better, I had been promoted to number eight in the batting order.

I spent less and less time at home. What with cricket practice and going out several nights a week, home had become merely a place to eat and sleep. My stepfather, Richard, was, I have already made clear, a strange man – quiet and uncommunicative, though he did often laugh in response to the humorous banter at the dinner table between me and my brother Ray, who was now a good-looking and bright-humoured twelve-year-old. We were growing closer in interests and pursuits, mostly sport, although he was still at school, and was planning to go to the local Technical Secondary School next year. I was glad my mother had decided to keep him away from the Christian Brothers; I suspect she took note of how much I had disliked them, and didn't want him leaving school as early as I had. We were both keen to start playing cricket and, in the winter, football in one of the local junior competitions. But we each had our own, separate circle of friends, and didn't spend a great deal of weekend time together.

I have a vivid memory of a warm Saturday morning, and wearing only a pair of shorts I sit on the back porch step in the sun cleaning and whitening my cricket boots. The tortoiseshell cat rolls and stretches happily in front of me on the concrete path. Ray is there, tinkering with the Victa motor mower, preparing to cut the lawn. My mother takes a break from doing the washing and sits beside me on the step, and the three of us talk about nothing very much for a while, soaking up the warmth in the quiet suburban start to the weekend. My mother surprises me by reaching out her hand and running it sensuously down the length of my back, saying 'You're brown; you're growing bigger and stronger now.' In her voice I hear mixed emotions: admiration, a woman's instinctive interest in the male body, a mother's regretful recognition that I am changing into a man more quickly than she had realised. She has never touched me like that before. Her pride engenders a certain amount of my own.

My cricketing ability was rapidly improving. For some weeks I had been taking wickets with my medium pacers, and then unexpectedly I was given the new ball to open the bowling. It was a great experience; its spotless red surface, gold lettering, clean white stitching, filled me with a sense of importance. Confident that I would achieve some prominence on the field, I asked Margaret to come to watch the game, which was at the Rosanna ground. She agreed, and caught the bus all the way out from Reservoir. When I met her at the bus stop she was wearing a cornflower blue and white dress that set her blonde hair off wonderfully. We walked hand in hand to the pavilion, where I introduced her to my teammates. I watched the looks on their faces as they eyed her over, enviously I fancied. I was a little worried that she would be bored sitting in the stand on her own while we spent the afternoon in the field, but my pride in knowing that she would be watching me bowl overshadowed that. I performed well, bowling two long spells and taking a wicket. When the team came off for tea, she smiled happily at me. I put my arm around her and kissed her on the lips, and some of my teammates joshed. 'Can we have some too?' they called out, and, 'Steady on, we'll never get you back on the field.'

'Did you see me bowl?' I asked her.

'Yes, and I thought you were very graceful,' she said.

At the end of the day's play I didn't want to part from her, and suggested we go to the pictures that night. She said yes, but suddenly I was in a quandary: by the time I got home (via a lift in a team-mate's car) and changed my clothes and ate dinner, I would need to leave immediately to catch the bus to Reservoir to pick her up. This meant I wouldn't have time to escort her home first. The logical thing for me to do was to take her home with me and have her stay for dinner, and then catch the bus together to the pictures in Northcote, and take her home afterwards. But this hadn't been pre-arranged, and I was reluctant to just turn up with her and expect my mother to feed her. Still, I suggested it to Margaret, but she didn't want to. 'My parents will be expecting me home for dinner,' she said. 'Look, I'm perfectly happy to go home on the bus alone now, and I can meet you at the pictures later; besides, I need to change my dress before I go out again.'

So this is what happened, but I felt nevertheless that I had failed, that I was guilty of shoddy conduct, sending her home on the bus by herself, and arranging to meet her at the cinema like that. If I'd been older, of course, and had a car, none of these problems would have arisen. But as it was, with the distances between us so great, and depending on public transport, I couldn't treat her, look after her, in the way I felt I should. It occurred to me that I really was too young to be trying to do these things, to be a proper boyfriend to her. And I wondered what my mother would have said if I'd suddenly turned up at home with her, unannounced.

Mrs Kneale asks me to go with her to buy her ten-year-old son a cricket bat for Christmas. At lunchtime we go to a local sports store in Smith Street, and choose a full size 'Don Bradman' model, quite expensive, more than I could ever have afforded. The Kneales are well off, live in the posh suburb of East Ivanhoe, and believe in always buying good quality things. But they don't know anything about cricket, and I have to inform them about caring for a bat, oiling it and 'facing' it ready for use. Bob Pinchbeck taught me that the willow on a new bat is still a little soft and green, and needs a good beating with a flat stick to give it a hardened face. It then needs several good rubdowns with linseed oil, so it won't dry out. I take the bat home and do all this, then the following Sunday I ride my bike with the bat on the handlebars over to the Kneales' house to give it to them. Mr Kneale answers the door, peers out from a gloomy background in the barely foot-wide opening, takes the bat and thanks me curtly, but doesn't invite me in. I leave feeling something of that old shiver of unworthiness. This, despite the fact that Mrs Kneale came to our house to be fitted for the dress my mother made for her, stayed and chatted in the kitchen over a cup of tea while they talked over the details of the dress.

The Queen's visit turns out to be something of a disappointment. For weeks I have been helping Mr Carter do the decorations for the Smith Street drive-past. Together we drape the massive two-storey brick building in red, white and blue bunting, with large bows at each join carefully tied by Mr Carter. Since her arrival in the country we have been flying the two flags at each end of the building every day, the Union Jack at one end, the Australian flag at the other. Everyone is very conscious that this is a British firm, with a number of English executives and decidedly English allegiances. Every morning and every night I go up on the roof with Mr Carter to hoist the flags up and later take them down. Expectation rises throughout the office all through the morning, as everyone talks about nothing else, and where they will position themselves to get the best view. We in our office look down into Smith Street from our office window, so we will be able to see easily. Eventually, around mid-afternoon, with the street lined two or three deep – somewhat fewer than expected – with people waving occasional small flags and cheering in a half-hearted, faintly embarrassed manner, the Queen and Prince Philip are driven past in an open Rolls Royce, waving without enthusiasm to the onlookers. Then it is all over. Everyone stands wondering what to do next, drifting away feeling a distinct sense of anticlimax. All that preparation for all those weeks, all that newspaper talk, all these decorations; somehow, you felt that there ought to be an afternoon of festivities, entertainments, people enjoying themselves in the streets, but there is nothing except a sense that you had glimpsed the royal presence for a fleeting moment, and were meant to feel privileged. I didn't.

One day I push through the door into Mr Carter's office and find my mother there, talking with Mr Carter. I almost reel from the shock. She looks up at me, and gives a brief, self-conscious smile, and Mr Carter stops what he is saying. I back out, apologising for the intrusion. That night, I ask her what it was about. 'I just dropped in to ask Mr Carter what your prospects were at that place,' she says, 'and Mr Carter was very nice about you.'

'You didn't tell me you were coming in.'

'I had to go into the city, and when I saw your building I suddenly thought I'd get off the tram and talk to your boss. I just wanted to know what kind of a future you might have there.'

'And?'

'As I said, he was very nice. He said if you stayed there and kept working at the standard you've shown so far, there were no limits to where you could go – sales, administration. There were plenty of opportunities for promotion, over time.'

This sets me thinking. I consider Fred, and how frustrated he is in his position; Fred might wait another five, ten years for Mr Carter to retire, and even then would he become Head of Purchasing? Someone else might get it. Fred has no special qualifications, just experience; not really the kind of person who the company considers for its top positions. There is a fellow in Sales, a rep, as they call them, Dennis Lemke, young, good looking, private school and university educated, a prominent tennis player whose name and photograph has been in the papers. He is the kind of person who the company looks to promote – glamorous, well connected, well qualified. That is what you need if you are to have 'good prospects' in a company like this one, and I can see that I, like Fred, will never be that kind of person, could never attain those sorts of heights. So what is my future here, I wonder.

I was about to experience my first broken heart. A warning sign appeared when Jim Skinner came into the office and casually said, 'You better watch out – someone's trying to pinch your girlfriend'. I leapt up and peered along the wide corridor to where Margaret sat at her desk. Standing in front and above her, laughing with her, was a tall slim youth who I had seen before, in the office of the Tack Factory in Alexandra Parade. He looked about eighteen. Something in the pit of my gut dropped as I watched Margaret push back coyly in her chair in response to his talk. I wanted to fly up there and break in, put a stop to it, but of course I didn't. You can't do things like that. But I worried about it for the rest of the afternoon, waiting for a chance to go and talk to her. When the youth had finally gone, I made my move.

'Hi. Who was that you were talking to?'

'Chris Beale from the Tack Factory.'

'So, what's he doing over here?'

I noticed a change come over her features. Her mouth tightened, her eyes avoided mine, focussed on her typewriter. I was making her angry, but I couldn't help myself.

'He comes over here sometimes to get documents signed,' she said with mock weariness.

'So what was he talking to you about?'

'None of your damn business!' she hissed, this time looking me square in the face with those huge blue eyes, full of withering fire. I slunk off, crushed. But I was not finished yet.

At five o'clock, after we all departed the building, I caught her up at the tram stop in Smith Street so that I could ride part of the way home with her as we usually did. At first she was cool, but when I didn't say anything more about Chris Beale, things settled into normality between us; that is, in so far as what passed between us could be described as normal. There was something uncomfortably private and undeclared about our relationship. It was odd that she had never invited me in to meet her parents, though I did catch a glimpse of her father once in the front garden, a stocky, pleasant looking man with very English features – clear skin, greying fair hair. But then again, I had never invited her to my house either, so there was the sense in both of us that we had been playing a game of pretend romance, and were reluctant to declare it to the world. Our feeling for each other was uncertain, yet high in emotional affect. In that tram, together on the slatted wood double seat in the breezy centre section, we uttered strange things to each other, clichés from bad movies. 'Do you love me?' I asked, pressing into her shoulder. 'More than you will ever know,' she crooned, gazing through the window into the distance. But I took no comfort from her words, wincing inside at their crude insincerity. I asked her to go to the pictures with me on Saturday night, and diffidently she said okay. We were to meet at the cinema, in High Street, Preston.

When I arrived in the foyer I was delighted to find her waiting, bright and cheerful, and looking ravishing in a sleeveless floral summer frock with a low cut neckline. It had been a hot day, and I told her about the cricket match I had been playing, fielding all day in the sun.

'Well I,' she said perkily, 'have been to the beach this afternoon, and got myself sunburned. Look.' Her arms and shoulders had a bronze burnish, but her noticeable make-up hid any redness on her cheeks or nose. Then, as we took our seats in the cinema, she lowered her voice and laughed to me, 'And do you want to know something? My back is so sunburned that I'm not wearing any bra. So, there.'

'You're a terrible girl,' I said back.

'I am, aren't I?' she said.

But I couldn't get the thought out of my head. Whatever the picture we were watching, I was not taking it in. Time and again my mind went to her declaration, and what it could mean. Just the fact of her breasts, naked right there under her frock, overwhelmed me, played on my mind until I could think of nothing else. Eventually I calmed down, tried to think more clearly. Why did she tell me that? I asked myself. What does she expect me to do? Is she extending an invitation? Is she trying to tease me? She certainly had a teasing note in her voice. All through the film the tumult boiled in me, a mixture of desire and guilt, boldness and fear, until my trembling heart knew that something would happen but not when or where or why, just that it would happen, something somewhere. And then it did. In the dark, I had had my left arm comfortably around her back and resting lightly on her shoulder. Almost involuntarily, as if in the control of another, my hand suddenly plunged down inside the low-cut bib of her frock and held, as one palms an apple, the shockingly firm nakedness of her breast, with its little nipple of hardness lodged between my first and second fingers. For a moment she did nothing, except draw in a small breath of surprise. Then she tersely whispered, 'No. Take it away.' And I was humiliated, crushed. We sat an ocean apart for the rest of the film, counterfeiting strangers. The walk home was an agony of cold silence. I apologised, but she seemed not to be listening. At the gate there was no kiss, no embrace, no words of affection. 'Good night,' she said, and hurried in. All the long way home to my house I was torn between elation and regret, my thoughts haunted by that moment of joy, the sheer electric current that shot up my arm from her crackling flesh, to the withering abjectness of my recoil and rebuke. But I was certain that I had done a terrible thing, and that it had brought things between us to a shameful and tragic finish.

As indeed it had. Plead as I might in the following weeks, with growing impatience she refused to listen or to go out with me again. She avoided going home with me on the tram, and then, the final ignominy came when I saw her emerging from the building after work and get into a car driven by Chris Beale. The next day, when I asked her to walk along Smith Street with me at lunch time, hoping that I might talk with her and bring her round, she said, with a new brutality I could hardly credit, that she was now 'going steady' with Chris Beale, and that she never wanted to talk to me again. Not only was I shattered by all this, but I realised I would have to go on seeing her at her desk when I walked past, catching glimpses of her in all parts of the building or going home on the tram, while all the time aching to win her back, to hold her again, knowing I had ruined everything by my own reckless act. I didn't know how I would bear it; I thought I would die from shame and self-hatred. I thought I should kill myself.

My mother is forming a solid friendship with Richard's mother, who everyone calls grandma. She is a stout, forbidding woman with set routines, and has outlived two husbands. My mother has found she can talk to grandma in ways she could never, for instance, talk with Nair. She never quite trusts Nair, who is not above peddling poisonous gossip about anyone. In fact, since my father died, and Richard has come into our lives, we see very little of Nair. She has not paid her Christmas visit in recent years, and my mother has gone over to North Melbourne only once or twice. But I miss Nair, miss her funny ways, miss her talk.

Grandma, on the other hand, visits us regularly on Sundays, brought over by her youngest son Jim in his little Austin A30. Jim often brings his guitar, and sings songs before tea, allowing me to practice chords and strums afterwards. My mother and grandma talk constantly, and my mother seems to like grandma's kindly but always authoritarian advice, seems to need the solid, secure sense of established routine that she brings with her. When we go on occasional summer picnics, crammed into Jim's car, grandma reveals her genius at providing picnic lunches. Where my family's experience is limited to sandwiches and biscuits, she lays out bacon and egg pies, cold meat salads, breaded chicken drumsticks, dishes of jellied fruit and lemon sago, hot tea and coffee, lemonade, whole sponge and fruit cakes, food I never imagined could be eaten outdoors.

Richard has two full brothers and a sister, who have all made some effort to welcome us into their family circle, possibly at the express request of grandma. They all show a real soft spot for my mother, less so for Ray and myself. Of course they dote over five-year-old Susan. One brother, Doug, who owns his own butcher shop, invites us all to lunch one Sunday, with his wife Flo and their daughter Lorraine. They are pleasant enough, but I feel an outsider among them. There is a whiff of charity about their attitude to me and Ray. Doug promises to take me to the football, which means a match at the Collingwood football ground, where Doug is a member, and we do go, in Doug's brand new Ford Consul, but I have to put up with Collingwood supporters all around me; the opposition is not Essendon, so I have little interest in the match. A number of the players in the Collingwood Reserves team played as a curtain raiser to the main match are from my old school – Brian Beers, Ray Murnane, Barry Patmore, Micky Bone – but I keep this knowledge to myself as we watch the game.

I had stopped going to Mass. In fact I had lost interest in religious matters completely. This disconcerted my brother, who one morning in the small bedroom we shared reprimanded me. 'You shouldn't be missing Mass,' he said, without explanation. He meant well, had only my interests at heart, which I understood, but still I resented the presumptuousness of the comment, and responded with 'Mind your own business', sharply but careful not to say anything more that might dissuade Ray from his own religious duties. Because I knew that Ray was influenced by me, looked up to me in most things, and was likely to copy anything I did. But it also impressed me that he had developed to a stage that he had his own opinions on things, and could come out so strongly with them.

The fact was, religion had never had an unshakeable grip on me. It seemed important to me when my father was alive, because it was important to my father, at least when he knew he was dying. I could sense my father's desperation to save his own soul. But I could now see that there was a kind of indignity in it too, that my father was being coerced into belief by his emotional and physical fragility, his fear of death. And under the pressure applied to me in my school years, I found it impossible to challenge the power of the edifice that rose around me on all sides; religion was an almost total *milieu*, full of threats and promises, stories of warnings or of miracles and magic designed to seduce a young mind, masquerading as something spiritual but in fact a broad social party that provided for its faithful the rewards of friendship, marital and educational benefits, and secure employment contacts for a lifetime. The Catholic 'club' was a network of admitted and unadmitted biases, log-rolling, back-scratching its way through life, and felt to me to be more a kind of weight around the neck. Now that I was old enough, strong enough to reject it, I wanted no part of it.

And beside all that, the simple fact was I did not find Catholicism interesting. My impulses were to be free of constraints, for life to be open-ended. I felt I must be free to choose my own commitments or to reject them, and suffer the consequences. This was what seemed to me to be exciting – to test life to see what it could yield, not to have it all parcelled up and predictable beforehand. I would wander, I would search, I would make mistakes, I would enjoy the sense of power that comes from rejecting – not just religion, but employers, friends, family and anything along the way that seemed no longer interesting enough for me to give my time and energy to. There would be things I would gladly embrace, people I would readily give myself to, but only by using my own powers of discrimination. Only in this way, I instinctively knew, could I grow.

One day it occurred to me that I no longer wanted to work at the British United Shoe Machinery Company. Something more interesting had crossed my path, and I decided, simply and unhesitatingly, to have a try for it. I gave my notice to Mr Carter, who said he was very sorry to lose me, but that I must do what I thought best. Fred Clarke treated the whole matter sourly, clearly envious that it was not he who was heading off to new prospects. Jim seemed indifferent, and Mrs Kneale gave a hint that she approved, as if she was of the view that anyone with any ambition would be crazy to stay in such a dull place. The one who most surprised me was Mr Conabere, who clearly knew of my resignation and mentioned it when next I entered his great spartan office. 'I'm sorry to hear you're leaving us,' he said in his booming tones, 'You had a bright future here, young fella.' I went away amazed that Mr Conabere had ever entertained a single thought about my abilities or future. What did he have in mind? I wondered.

My one regret was Margaret. I continued to look up the wide corridor in her direction, hoping she might return my gaze, but she studiously ignored me now. We hadn't spoken a word to each other for many weeks, and my hopelessness was so entrenched that the pain actually began to subside. She regularly got into Chris Beale's car after work, and the typists in the accounts section gossiped about their affair and passed some of it on to me – that they had been seen together at the races, at the cinema, and that she talked constantly about Beale at morning tea. I was sad that it has ended like it did, and remained full of guilt and self-loathing at my idiotic, destructive behaviour, and was sorry that we were parting under this cloud of hostility. Yet the mere fact of moving on to a new job, to a new workplace and friendships, to new discoveries and experiences, and in the big city furthermore, was some compensation, and helped me not to wallow in all that regret. I had my life, I had my freedom; I had plenty.

3

WHEN I WAS A CHILD MY VISITS TO THE CITY were exciting but brief, and I always felt what in fact I was – a visitor, a spectator, an amusement-seeker. Now it was my place of work, where my daily presence was official and purposeful, so I felt the satisfaction – deluded as it was – of the insider, the possessor and possession of the serious culture of city business. The morning rush to work by nine, the lunchtime stroll through the arcades and department stores, the sandwich-shop queues, the smells of coffee and cosmetics, the smart clothes in the store windows, the spilling of workers out onto the streets at five, and always the din of traffic, entranced me from the first day. My confidence rose with the sense that I was at the centre of something. And I was happy to put behind me the odd mixture of boredom and frustration that had marked my time at the British United Shoe Machinery Company in the fringe suburb of Fitzroy.

My new job was, I told myself, a profession: I was to be an insurance clerk. It had a definite, recognisable ring to it. John Cloney, who lived on the opposite corner of Valentine Street, had told me of the job for a junior in the Claims department of his office in the city, and my application had been successful. I went to Myer's menswear department and bought myself an oatmeal tweed jacket, a pair of grey slacks, a blending tie and some white shirts, all carefully considered for their effect, having acquired something of my father's liking for dressing well. He always looked stylish and well groomed, even as an invalid in his dressing gown and slippers, and when he went out in public he was dapper from the top of his well-chosen hat to the toes of his highly polished shoes. Undoubtedly, this had left its mark, for it was an image of elegance I always aspired to, though never quite reached.

On that first day I was introduced to the staff of the Claims department, who all seemed formidably intelligent, sophisticated, professional. Arnold Winton, my supervisor, a tall, studious looking man with rimless glasses and a slight stoop, seemed more like a professor than an insurance man. In his friendly manner he explained the nature of the work in Claims, and that my starting point would be to help Mrs Bosselman in getting the details of the claimants from their Policy files. One look at Mrs Bosselman and my heart sank: in her sixties and fragile enough to break in half if she made a sudden movement, there was a taut-mouthed look of life-long disappointment about her, and a determination in her eye to make somebody pay. I had been hoping to work closer to one of the younger women in accounts or in the typing pool.

As I got to know the place better, I found it less harmonious than I'd first thought. At the rear of the ground floor office were two desks side-by-side, occupied by two ancient men, Ralph Edwards and Mister Harrington (no one used his first name). Edwards, small and wizened, crackle-voiced on the rare occasions he spoke, endlessly entered arcane records in handwritten ink in huge journals that he would show only to management. Harrington, a tall, white-haired, huge-girthed, pompous chatterbox, was an official Commissionaire, which meant that he wore a navy uniform with silver decorations and collected the mail. These two men, not six feet apart, had not spoken to each other for ten years. Apparently they formed their mutual detestation the first week of Harrington's arrival, when they discovered they were on opposite sides of every conceivable fence, from political to religious to family. Since then, if either could not avoid making communication with the other, he would do it through a third party, as in 'Tell Edwards if he has any mail to go to have it on my desk by four'. No other connection between them was practiced or expected.

Interesting stuff could be found in the Claims department. Junior as I was, I could access an absorbing human drama in the files that passed through my hands every day. Accompanying the claim form would be crude sketches of vehicle pathways, collision spots, photographs of damaged or wrecked cars, and details of passenger injuries and positions of bodies. I would reconstruct the scenes in my head, soaking up the atmosphere of tragedy: a young woman killed when she was thrown out into a tree; an ambulance driver speared with a metal pole when he ran off the road near a bridge; a collision at an intersection causing the two cars to catch fire, killing both drivers. There was an attraction in all this violence that held me in its grip while I read, oblivious to the human misery it must have caused. I gradually learned, mostly from our team of assessors (dandified panel beaters), about costing repairs to damaged cars, which repairers to trust, how to discern contradictions in accident reports. All this was new and enjoyably real to me.

I need not have worried about not working among the younger women, because they were all around me, smiling, chatting, putting themselves close. Their made-up and perfumed presence, their body shapes, their sing-song voices, their moody shifts from eagerness to please to prickly defensiveness was a source of constant pleasure. The younger men, Charlie Mason, Russell Symonds, Barry Mumford, flirted with them, or smart-mouthed behind their backs, and occasionally took one out to a show or the pictures. 'She come across?' one would ask. 'Wouldn't tell you if she did,' was the common reply. Tough-looking Scot Chrissie McPhee, in her forties, with a wide, sensual mouth and grapefruit-sized breasts ('You don't get many of those to the pound,' said Charlie, repeatedly), fancied herself as the office babe, and loved to drop *double entendres* around the men. Her favourite, as she squeezed in next to some man in the tiny Company lift, was to look cheeky and say 'Ah hope ahm nought makin' it harrd for you dearrr'.

And there was a tall, freckled redhead called Naine Fallu, who was calm and intelligent, who wore a winning smile and no make-up. I would imagine her naked as she moved around the office. Would she have red pubic hair? What would her small breasts look like, how would they feel to touch? I was, obviously, well into teenage preoccupations. It was of course the Age of the Breast. The clothing industry strove to make this the central focus of male desire, and size and shape decided the degree of sexual attraction, and even, in the view of some men, registers of a woman's libido; if she had big tits, she was a 'goer'. I learned lots of terms for them: tits, norks, knockers, boobies, brace-and-bits, bristols, melons, jugs, headlights, and undoubtedly more. When my mother was young there had been little interest in this part of a woman's body. Now, films, magazines and whole careers were built around breasts. Girls wore bras to lift them high and make them stick out, and low-cut tops to show them off; men would happily strap-hang on buses or dictate letters standing over secretaries in order to take furtive glimpses at cleavages and near-nipple fringes on the more daring presentations. Like others, I believed that breasts were purely sexual objects, and that paradise lay in the discovery of their nakedness. It was the first thing I looked for when a young woman passed.

Eventually I 'took out' ('dating' was a term used only in American pictures) several of the girls in the office. There was an annual office Ball usually held at the Dorchester in the Alexandra Gardens. This year's Ball would be my first ever. I wondered who I could take, and a week before the event I was still without a partner. It happened that a popular but rather plain girl called Judy was also without a partner, so when she asked me if I would accompany her, I reluctantly agreed. I asked my mother's advice about a corsage. 'A gardenia,' she said, 'it will go with whatever she wears, and has a nice perfume.' In the event I had only a moderately good time; despite my going to some expense for the corsage, and the taxi, and a smart-looking hired tuxedo, she danced with me only once, and sat the rest of the time at another table gossiping with one of her girlfriends. Half my night was spent sitting alone watching the dancing couples and hungrily waiting for the supper to start.

By far the most important relationship I formed in this job was with my supervisor, Arnold Winton. Arnold was a senior clerk in the Claims department during that first year, and we became friends, despite the difference in our ages. I liked his quiet, formal manner, keenly ironic sense of humour, his air of integrity. All this first showed itself one afternoon when Arnold drew my attention to a situation that developed around the Claims Manager, an overweight, scrannell-voiced bully called Frank Darcy. 'Watch this,' Arnold said to me one day after a man with blond hair and a badly pockmarked face had come to the counter with a rejection letter and asked to see the signer, Mr Darcy.

'That,' whispered Arnold to me at his desk at the back of the room, 'is Snowy Diamond, the gangster; rumour is that he carries a gun. Last week Darcy turned down his claim for damage to his car, probably not recognising him from the name 'George Diamond' on the form. Listen to what Darcy does.'

When Darcy emerged from the privacy of his office, looked at the letter and went to the filing cabinet to take out the file, his mouth was working with the remains of his lunch, indicative of not only his bad manners, but also of his total indifference to the man waiting at the counter. And it wasn't just myself and Arnold who were straining to listen in to what was about to take place; half the office was interested.

'No,' Darcy was saying carelessly, 'no case here Mr Diamond; the damage to your car is clearly not consistent with the speed you say you were doing on the form.'

The man leaned forward and lowered his voice, so that he could barely be heard. But we were able to make out 'Are you calling me a liar?', which he said directly into Darcy's stuffed face. He stopped chewing but didn't answer. Diamond spoke again.

'In case you don't know who I am, I think you should take a gander at last week's *Truth* and read all about me.'

Truth was a notorious newspaper full of lurid stories from the courts and the back streets of Melbourne's crime scene.

'Never bother to read that garbage,' said Darcy, 'I don't care who you are, I don't see any case for us to pay it.' He snapped the manila file shut as if to finalise the matter.

But Diamond moved in even closer to Darcy and was heard clearly throughout the office to say, 'If you don't pay it, I'll be waiting out in Lonsdale Street for you at five o'clock ...' There was no special drama in the nasally voice, just an everyday matter-of-factness, like a friend arranging a meeting, making a promise more than a threat. But that in itself produced a disturbing sense that this was how actual violence is prefaced, this and the near certainty, which afterward we all swore to having noticed, that Diamond seemed to be patting the left side of his double-breasted navy suit with his open hand as he spoke.

It was wonderful to see the change in Darcy's behaviour. It was as if a light had been switched on inside his head, and his little pig's eyes glowed with confusion. He reopened the file in his hand and turned to lean on the counter with it, so close to Diamond that their shoulders were almost touching; the body language was that of an Aussie mate leaning on a bar over a beer. This time their voices couldn't be heard, but Darcy was reading the file as if every word was a revelation of sacred lore, and muttering for Diamond's exclusive benefit. When, after several minutes of this faux confidentiality the two men broke apart and shook hands, and Diamond said 'thank you' and left while Darcy disappeared back into his office with the file, it was as if we all had just witnessed the conclusion of a one-act play. Chrissie MacPhee actually produced a round of light applause and grinned wickedly at everyone in the room, once she was sure Darcy was out of earshot. Arnold Winton said, 'I knew something like that would happen; typical Frank Darcy.' And this was believable; it was clear all along that Arnold had anticipated the whole thing. It was this, and his refusal, despite his being technically a member of the senior administrative staff, to give his loyalty to a coward like Darcy, who had done plenty of bullying himself whenever he got the chance, that so impressed me. On repeated occasions I saw Arnold stand up to Darcy, and to the Manager, Mr Crosby, who was another self-styled 'hard man' with an acid tongue. Yes, Arnold Winton was his own man, and at the same time decent and friendly, and I was honoured by the special relationship that seemed to be forming between us: it was an unspoken accord, but real and respectfully felt on both sides.

I moved through my sixteenth and seventeenth years dimly conscious of my growing manhood. Sex still caught me off-guard, with masturbation my only recourse in a world of coy, uncooperative young women and my own increasing obsession with them. But sex was not yet at the centre of my life, which during this time was mainly taken up with family, work and sport.

Yet without being especially aware of it, I was gradually growing emotionally distant from the family base. I had never been truly comfortable at home since my father's death some six years earlier. My mother did not seem especially happy either in these years. The marriage to Richard did not realise the hopes she seemed to have had, apart from giving birth to Susan, who was now a cute little tot running around happily, with a devoted mother and two attentive big brothers to amuse her. But Richard paid little attention to his daughter or anyone else; he seemed emotionally moribund, uninterested and unresponsive to the family living around him. He moved about the house in silent preoccupation with the contents of his own mind, which seemed to me when I tried to fathom it, to consist of nothing but the banalities of horse-race betting and his interminable bathroom ablutions.

Reflecting on the marriage, I could see a certain sense in my mother's decision. On first acquaintance Richard seemed a reliable, well-mannered man, with a family background of middle-class pretensions and business acumen. He appeared to have a thriving butcher shop in Oakleigh, his brother Doug owned a butcher shop and his sister Daphne was married to a wealthy Ford dealer in country Mansfield, while his young half-brother Jim was a well-qualified technician at the GPO. The prospects she had when my father died she knew to be unpromising; she had no money, owned nothing, had two half-grown boys still to be educated, and few opportunities for fun in her life. When her friend Madge pressed her into joining her at the Saturday night Oakleigh Town Hall dances, she eventually met Richard, a bachelor in his forties who was no doubt on the prowl himself for some female company. Given my mother's good looks and brightness it is not surprising that Richard made a strong pitch for her, and given her vulnerability, not surprising that he succeeded. She wanted the security of marriage, and he could provide it. But she very likely misunderstood his financial position. Living as he was with grandma and Jim in the respectable suburb of Ormond, a bachelor with no history of marital mess-ups, running a business in a well-heeled eastern suburban area, he seemed to promise a secure future and a decent family life for us all. And though he was twelve years older, she would have seen this positively, sensing he might be a surrogate for the two lost men in her life – her beloved father, who died in her teens, and her young husband who had never been able to share his prime years with her. So in Richard she might have seen the prospect of an amalgamation of father and lover, and the chance of a happy, secure, even affluent, future.

How wrong she was. After the marriage, if she had hoped to be quickly housed over in the eastern suburbs, she would have been deeply disappointed with his choice to move into the West Ivanhoe Commission house with the three of us. Perhaps they both saw this as the only way to save money for a house of their own, but it gave him the absurdly onerous task of riding his old Indian motor cycle, with its coffin-like delivery box instead of a sidecar, right across Melbourne to Oakleigh every day to be in the shop by 8.30 am; on Fridays he had to leave at a wearisome 4 am to prepare the meat for the weekend shoppers. More important, this decision denied her the chance to promptly move out of the detested Commission house into something better. The reason, too, must have come as a blow: he had no money – nothing at all. His middle-class pretensions were a fraud; he did not own the butcher shop in Oakleigh – he merely managed it. Nor was it doing well enough to pay for a rented house for them in that area. This man had been working since he was a teenager, over twenty years not counting his war service; what had he done with his money? The bookies might well have bagged it, I guess. Whatever he did with it, there was nothing now but his weekly wage to contribute to the upkeep of his new family. Like many Australian men of his class and era, he had no idea how to handle money, whether in savings, investments or enterprises. He gambled on the racehorses, he drank at the pub, he probably paid board to his mother while he lived with her. If there was money in the bank he would spend it, if there was none he went without. His mother had cooked and washed for him all his life, and perhaps even bought his clothes. Now that he was married, he would expect my mother to do the same. Contrary to her expectations, he was not to be her saviour; he just increased her workload, like another child. The disappointment became even sharper in the years after Susan was born. He gave up the Oakleigh shop, sold the Indian motorcycle, and found jobs in more local butchers. For a long period he was out of work, earning nothing. My mother had to increase her part-time hours dressmaking, even going full-time, to keep the money coming in. Fortunately, she didn't mind this, because she enjoyed work. Richard's excuse was a recurrence of his dermatitis, which he had picked up in the War in New Guinea, but he did not even try another sort of work in those years. He still went to the pub of an evening, still bet on the horses, and continued to indulge his habit of drunkenly bringing home mates from the pub, expecting my mother to feed them. Not only that, but he would cheapen her, giving her rough squeezes and pinches on the backside while she was busy in the kitchen, all for the amusement of his mate, at times encouraging the mate to share sexual innuendos at her expense; it was his way of showing off his wonderful piece of sexual success. 'Look what I've got,' he was implying, 'isn't she a humdinger? Bet you haven't got one of these at home. And she cooks too!'

As this painful charade played out, I would watch and burn with shame and resentment. Of course there were times when Richard was sensible, quiet, inoffensive. He did have a sense of humour, albeit a passive one (he rarely told a joke himself) and continued to laugh heartily at some of the funny things Ray and I would say at the dinner table. Together we brothers were comradely and full of wit and mischief, and Richard appreciated this. But he didn't contribute anything of his own, locked as he was into some kind of mute anguish, which might have had something to do with his war service in New Guinea. His habit, whenever visitors came, was to disappear into the bathroom for most of the afternoon, ostensibly making himself presentable, but in fact he was retreating from any form of engagement with people. Sometimes he might emerge as they were leaving. 'Oh, are you off?' he would say, a disingenuousness that fooled nobody. There was never any prospect that he could take over the role of father to me and Ray. We didn't want it from him, and to give him his due Richard never tried to do so, though this was more from indifference than tact. So our mother still had the job of decision-making, discipline, advice, setting an example and generally taking responsibility for us boys; in effect we were still utterly fatherless, and our mother was still in this respect no better off than a widow. In a way her situation was now worse, especially in the times Richard was out of work; she was living in the same place on little more income, but with two more mouths to feed. Except for having someone to sleep with, re-marriage had solved none of her problems.

Sport has become increasingly important to me. Now that I am growing stronger, I am able to make my presence felt on the football field. I watch my team, Essendon, and the great John Coleman, as I have for six years now, and learn something of how to play the game. Naturally, I long to play as a full-forward, but my slight frame and lack of height are against me. I show up to train with the Bellfield football team, the team my uncle Ron has helped get started, who play in the Victorian amateur competition. Despite my lack of muscle, I show speed and skill, and am placed on the wing. In only my second game I take a mark near the boundary that draws applause from the group of supporters nearby, applause that rings through my head for many nights afterwards. This is an unexpected bonus to the pleasures of the game itself.

In that year a disaster occurs that throws me back to some of the pain of earlier years. John Coleman sustains a serious knee injury whilst taking a pack-mark over North Melbourne opponents at the Essendon ground. He will be out for the rest of the season. At the time this news is bad enough to cause me depression, but I do not realise that it will get worse as time goes on. Not even the distracting music on the radio can console me – Frank Sinatra, Buddy Holly and the Crickets, Elvis Presley. If anything, they make it worse by rekindling my melancholy associations with Coleman's accident. The first time I hear 'Heartbreak Hotel', it's gothic imagery reinforced by the strange echo and quaver in Presley's voice, I am reminded only of the tawdry North Melbourne hotels of my childhood; and the glitzy romantic flights of the Hit Parade ballads offer only a temporary, and unbelievable, escape from the ugly reality that my one true hero has been brought to earth a cripple, which over the next couple of years will never go away because he will never recover.

These preoccupations, work and sport, are increasingly taking me away from the family. Home now is little more than a place to eat and sleep and change into clean clothes. Still, because I am still living there, there is a feeling of being trapped, of being kept apart from a broader world beyond, one I cannot know unless I change my circumstances. I mix with my football and cricket friends with a sense that they are part of the same world as my family. But when I go to work, there is a whiff of this larger world that will occasionally drift my way. But how you get to know it, or become part of it, I have no idea. I sense, however, that of all the people I am friendly with, Arnold Winton is the one person who knows something about that world, and is therefore an important figure in the fabric of a life that is steadily forming in my imagination.

Norman Pickering, married to Richard's sister Daphne, was tacitly acknowledged as the family aristocrat. He had served as an officer in the air force during the war, and returned to build a hugely successful motor repair business and Ford dealership in Mansfield in country Victoria. He was a town VIP, on the committees of the important organisations, including the golf club, in which both he and Daphne were noted players. Not only did he have more money and power than anyone else in the family, but he maintained an air of dominance in every situation, family and beyond. He would never let you forget that when you entered his world, it was he who called the tune, because it was he who paid the piper.

Within these acknowledged terms, 'Uncle Norm', as he was called by everyone in the family, behaved with generosity to everyone alike. Not 'blessed' with children, as grandma would have put it, Norm and Daph were hospitable hosts for extended holidays to parents, children, grandchildren and pets over several decades. All stayed in the Pickerings' stolid country house, and in the summer holidays trekked into the bush under his leadership to enjoy the spartan comforts of 'the hut', a remote cabin deep in the wilds along the Howqua River, where you could swim, fish, cook on open fires and laze away the time to your heart's content. All this of course made Uncle Norm a popular figure in the family, though few had any illusions about the tenor of his affection; he would never tolerate a challenge to any of his opinions, and could without warning round on anyone with frightening vehemence if you said or did something he did not like. And a frequent and tired-eyed recipient of this anger was his wife.

My first visit to the Pickerings was Easter 1955, when I was seventeen. I went with Richard's niece Lorraine and her boyfriend Vin. We left in the very early hours of a Saturday morning, hurtling through the dark country roads and hills in Vin's new Rover, driven at breakneck speed the whole way. Vin and Lorraine were to stay the weekend and return to Melbourne Sunday night, leaving me another week with Norm and Daph. The first night, sitting around the fire in the lounge room after tea, a huge row broke out between Vin and Uncle Norm. Vin had said something about cars – possibly about the Ford brand. In a short time Norman grew abusive and red-faced, and his anger, I sensed, was as much about defending his family authority on all motor car matters as about the particular issue Vin raised.

And yet a few days later Norman did an extraordinary thing. With Norman having to be at the office during the week, and Daphne committed to golf this particular day, they were concerned that I might be bored on my own. 'Can you drive a jeep?' Norman asked, 'Because if you can, you're welcome to take my old army jeep out and enjoy yourself with it for the day.' Norman obviously had forgotten that I was still too young to have a driver's licence, but in my excitement I was not about to remind him of this. 'Of course,' I said in my best matter-of-fact, I've-been-driving-so-long-I'm-all-but-bored-with-it, voice. 'No problem; just take me through the gear-shifts, and she'll be fine.' I could in fact drive a car, having picked it up from older friends in the neighbourhood, like

Bernie Cloney, and in any case I seemed to have always known how to drive a car, as if it came as naturally as combing my hair.

Norman pointed me towards an area where there were quiet dirt roads and few people living, and told me to keep the speed under 40 mph. That afternoon was one of the most joyous of my life. The jeep was an authentic WW2 American Willys, left-hand drive, and in mint condition. Lively, open to the elements (happily it was a beautiful April day), it could, as they say, spin about on a sixpence, and sent every bump, pothole and corrugation in the road jolting through my bones like a jackhammer. Its driver's seat was virtually a metal box with a thin leather cushion under my bum, and my teeth rattled in my head such that I had to make sure to keep my tongue out of the way in case I bit it. But the big, thin steering wheel, the feisty acceleration and handling, the heroic reputation, and the fact that it was just me and the jeep out together, free to go where we liked, boys on the open road in a lonely landscape, made me feel like the central character in one of those movies without women, blokey, stylish, rugged, independent. I drove well over the 40mph much of the time, along gravel side roads, up steep gradients, off-road along ravines, up to a hill-top where I stopped, got out, put my foot up with masculine poise on the deep-lugged tyre while I self-consciously smoked a cigarette, and gazed out to the horizon like a millionaire grazier pondering the future. I might have imagined myself in a Marlboro ad.

It didn't last long. After maybe an hour and a half I became bored with my own company and imaginings and took the jeep back to Norman's garage. Then I walked home, and actually found walking through the town of Mansfield, looking at the houses and their nice gardens, quite stimulating. I would have liked to come across someone my own age – preferably a girl – to provide a bit of interest other than my own thoughts, but Mansfield was a quiet town, and any young people living there were definitely not out on the streets.

I returned to Melbourne on the train the following Saturday, accompanying Daphne, who wanted to spend a few days with grandma. We travelled first class (she paid), in a compartment to ourselves, and we chain-smoked cigarettes the whole way. I blush to recall that the cigarettes we smoked were all Daphne's; I was too low on cash to buy any. She would always offer, with that generosity between smokers based on an unspoken recognition that they are doing something unhealthy ('if I go down I'll take you with me'), and I never refused. I saw her cast her eyes to heavens at one point, after about my fifth acceptance from her packet, and knew I should, out of sheer self-respect, say no for once at least, but something drove me to ignore it. I guess it was nothing less than the desire to play the adult; I was with a grown (smoking) woman who was not my mother or sister. A man and a woman, travelling together. Naturally I would behave like a man. Naturally I would smoke. It's just that, in my state of current penury, they would have to be hers.

I did spend one more holiday with them on my own, a couple of years later, during Easter. I was getting over a broken heart at the time, looking to get away from all reminders of my lost girl. Daphne must have said something to Norman about the unwisdom of my driving about unlicenced, because I was not offered the jeep, or any other car, this time. Ironically, I had by then acquired a licence. Perhaps Norman changed his mind about trusting me. You could never be sure about Norman's generosity. He could offer you something spontaneously, and at other times be tight-fisted, mean-spirited, wouldn't give you a brass farthing. It depended on his mood, and in any case it was always about him; if it suited him to give you something, fine, if not, forget it. Not getting the jeep again was disappointing, and added to the reasons piling up for my never being very keen to holiday with them in future. But I did go this one more time, several years later. I had by that time begun to be interested in painting, influenced and advised by an artist friend, and one glorious afternoon I sat in the Pickerings' back yard and did a passable impressionistic likeness of Daphne's Liquidambar tree. It was no Monet, but it was in-the-style-of, a bit *pointilliste*, Monet-ish, maybe too hectically coloured (it was autumn after all), but Daphne loved it, and kept it hanging on the wall of whatever house they lived in for the rest of her days. After that she, if not Norman, looked kindly upon me, and always remembered me with affection as the artistic one in the family, and probably readily forgave me for that boorish botting of her fags in the train at the end of my last visit years earlier.

I began taking evening classes in Insurance Principles and Practice. Without admitting it, I knew in my heart that it had been wrong to leave school when I did, at fourteen years of age. Sure, I hated the Christian Brothers, and couldn't have borne staying on there. But there were other schools, and it didn't occur to me or my mother and certainly not Richard to suggest them – a State school even. So there remained the vague sense that I was missing out on something, that I was in the margins of the world, and that even though I was working in the city and could indulge a certain pride in this, I was not, and never would be, near the centre of what was most valued – whatever that was; I was too green, too ignorant and ill-advised to grasp even that. My only way of feeling for the path, which might, I sensed, lead me towards such a centre, if it existed, were qualifications. To acquire knowledge and the pieces of paper that attested to it. If I took the insurance exams, I could apply for promotion, better positions, even have letters after my name, which some in the profession actually put on display. So I went to classes organised by the Insurance Institute, and began learning about Contract Law and Underwriting Principles and such. It was all very simple stuff really, and the only idea that has stayed with me on into maturity was what was described as the justifying purpose of insurance, started in the 17th century with Lloyd's of London as a means of addressing the growing shipwreck problem: to spread the individual's losses over the whole community. What a neat, decent principle, I thought: to spread the individual's losses over the whole community. It didn't occur to me, nor was anything said in classes, that another purpose was to make a profit for the underwriters.

I liked those evenings in the city before classes began at seven o'clock. Instead of going home at five, I would work on for maybe an hour, for which I would be paid overtime rates, and then, at six o'clock I would wander down to Elizabeth, Collins, Bourke Streets, explore whatever stores might be still open, stroll through the lovely arcades, feel the gradual slowing of the city's mighty engine after its day's work. It was that twilight hour between the businesses closing and the entertainment venues opening, and there were only scatterings of people on the streets. The restaurants were open, and I had a couple of favourites where I would grab a cheap meal – usually Italian, or Aussie-Italian as most of them were then. There was a basement place in Little Collins Street near the corner of Elizabeth that I particularly liked, and which as I descended the stairs recalled a far distant memory of being taken to a similar downstairs restaurant as a small child by my mother and father, where a delicious seafood aroma – no doubt oysters – filled my nostrils, and the waiters wore spotless white aprons, and the bentwood chairs were of dark polished walnut, the ambience of an earlier era. Seated alone in this cosy basement I would try to look relaxed and urbane, though I was actually tense with fear of making a fool of myself in some way, and would order ravioli or spaghetti with meat sauce and parmesan cheese – a dish my mother would never have cooked or known anything about – accompanied with fresh white Italian bread and butter, and would follow it with an ice-cream sundae and a cup of the new coffee that some places in the city – the smarter ones – were serving. Espresso, it was called, though I always had a cappuccino, froth-topped and sprinkled with powdered chocolate that joyfully coated my upper lip. One time, in another café, in The Causeway, I was eating ravioli when a cocksure young fellow came in and, with that confidence only youth can maintain, ordered a 'cappuc*iano*'. I was delighted to have found an even less sophisticated version of myself. Sometimes I would order sausages and mash or steak and onions, but Italian was my favourite.

Afterwards I would sit for a while on the steps of the Post Office, or more particularly on the ledge of the base of one of those gigantic Victorian Classic columns looking out onto Bourke or Elizabeth Street. I would simply enjoy looking – thinking of very little, dimly aware of the directionless, unexamined nature of the life I was living. A few other time-spenders, and maybe the odd derelict, would hang around there too; its elevated position was a good one from which to look down on the passing world as the sun went down behind McCall's book shop. One particular derelict I had seen often – the first time when he actually came into the office one day and stumped up to my desk in his tattered, stinking overcoat. 'Would you have a shilling for me bed?' he growled through a brown-stained, face-concealing beard. His eyes were aggressive, wetly red, and stared right through me, frightening. This fear, I blench to recall, became instant loathing: yeah, right, bed, I thought. I'll bet. Metho more likely. Much more vehemently than I needed to I barked back at the man, 'Get out of here, go on! There's nothing in here for you. And don't come back!' He had turned away without hesitation, yet also with no sign of appeasement, or fear, but as one who was getting only what he was perfectly used to and had long since accepted as his lot, and silently left. Immediately I regretted my response. Yet I still hated the man, and looking at him here now on the Post Office steps my hatred was revived. I had seen him scrounging though the rubbish bin on the edge of the footpath, and continued watching him unwrapping a half-eaten sandwich he had salvaged. 'Filthy bastard!' I said to myself, and wondered how he could eat such refuse. Whenever I saw him wandering the city streets, I would feel exactly the same way. But this, I see now, was more fear than anger. What was it I was really afraid of, I wonder? The squalor of my own childhood returning to haunt me? That this might be myself at some point in the future? The feeling that all our constructions of security and progress are built over a huge abyss, which could open up and swallow us at any time? Who knows why we behave with unnecessary cruelty towards those less fortunate than ourselves.

SUNLIGHT

4

NOT MUCH HAS CHANGED IN MY LIFE until I reach my eighteenth year. Then things begin to happen. First, I acquire a car, a cream 1934 Hillman Minx sedan, which I buy from my uncle Johnnie for thirty pounds. It has a few problems, such as overheating on hills and some broken wire spokes on a front wheel that I can never fix properly, which makes it hard to keep the car running straight. But I love driving it, love the sense of freedom and power, modest though it is, of taking it out onto the open road. For years afterwards, in dreams and fleeting memories, even when I am grown up with a family and have had many other cars since, I will recall the joy of driving along in that Hillman, like others might recall their first experience of sex. For a time I drive it to work, parking it near the Victoria Market, but when the wheel gets worse I take the car off the road for many months, parking it on the nature strip beside the house.

Arnold Winton's influence on me has deepened. I admire everything about Arnold: his shabby hopsack suits ('I never wear anything else to work,' he tells me, as if all other materials are inferior); that he will smoke only unfiltered cigarettes, preferably *Temple Bar;* that he is totally free of bullshit; that he has definite tastes in all kinds of things. Humour, for instance: every man in the office tells dirty jokes, but Arnold tells ones that are witty in such a way that they send up the whole idea of telling jokes. Such as:

There was this huge cinema in a Basque town in the centre of Spain, which was packed to capacity one night when it caught fire. In the panic to get out through the only doorway, most of the cinemagoers were killed. And the moral of the story is 'Don't put all your Basques in one exit.'

Another joke is of the same order:

In a village in the Congo there lived a great chief who was very proud of his elaborate and very desirable throne. On hearing one day that he was to be paid a visit by a powerful neighbouring chief, he became fearful that this visitor might covet his throne and subsequently launch an attack to steal it away. So he had his subjects hoist it with ropes up to the rafters of his hut, and fasten it there out of sight. In place of the throne, he had a large mat set down with generous provisions of food and drink laid out, and there the two chiefs sat and held their discussions. But in the course of the meeting the throne suddenly broke from its ties, and crashed down heavily onto the two chiefs, killing them both instantly. And the moral, quite obviously is, that 'People who live in grass houses shouldn't stow thrones.

I now copy Arnold's unique handwriting – for instance doing a large small 'a' for a capital instead of the daggy copperplate I was taught at school – and to copy his preference for dark-coloured shirts with lighter ties, rather than the dark tie and white shirt that is the boring standard; it looks sharp, American, gangsterish. Arnold becomes the measure of all things that comprise style, what is then called 'taste'. 'It doesn't matter if you have bad taste,' he tells me, 'it's better than what most people have, which is no taste at all.' I have not liked any man so much since my father died.

I notice that Arnold himself has acquired a mentor of sorts in a Mr Singer, a retired accountant who has been employed part-time to audit the company books over a period of several years. Arnold spends Monday and Wednesday lunchtimes taking slow walks around the city streets, arm in arm in intimate conversation with Mr Singer, who always dresses in an impeccable navy three-piece suit and black Homberg, and carries a black umbrella. Arnold has great respect for him, will always refer to him as 'Mister Singer', never anything more familiar. Eventually, after having been several years with the Company, Mr Singer decides it is time to retire, and some weeks after he ceases coming to work, Arnold informs me that his good friend, Mr Singer, sadly, has died quietly at home. He was with him at the time.

'And you know what he told me, just before he went?' Arnold says, 'He said he had experienced a momentary insight into the truth of death, and that there is nothing beyond this world; all the talk of life after death is nonsense.' So earnest is Arnold, he seems to really believe that Mr Singer had in fact been taken somehow to the border between life and death, and had experienced an actual sighting of oblivion. Further, I detect a hint of approval in Arnold's retelling of it, as if he believes that Mr Singer could in fact bear truthful witness to a sighting of the abyss beyond life. I am touched by Arnold's confidence in me. No one has ever said anything like that to me before. It makes me feel proudly and unexpectedly adult.

When, months later, Arnold moves from the Claims department to become Head of the Underwriting section, he asks if I would like go with him to take charge of motor vehicle business. I jump at the chance. The job is more interesting, more positive than the Claims department, where you are constantly expected to work against the clients to save money for the Company; but in underwriting, you are trying to keep them happy if they are good clients, or make tactful decisions about them if they are not. I write letters, talk on the phone and in person with the sales representatives on important accounts, keep agents and car dealers happy whenever possible in order to keep business flowing to the company. I make contacts and friends in the car industry, and occasionally see them socially. The Italian owner of a large crash repair company in Werribee takes me to lunch on one occasion, picking me up in a gleaming white Mark VII Jaguar and driving across the city to the restaurant of an Italian friend, where we eat huge tender steaks and where, for the first time in my life, I drink sparkling Burgundy. Generous and attentive, the small brown-faced Italian flashes a gold-toothed smile at me while he talks nothing but football and family (three sons, all in the business), and his love of cars. There is no mention of work, nothing as crude as 'special treatment' or 'reciprocity' or such, but all the time he knows damn well that this is a tried and true method of doing business and having one's name remembered with gratitude. And the flattery works; I do remember their name and I do always attend to their requests promptly. I am a friend to Werribee Motors.

I perceive, too, that Arnold recognises my intelligence and communicative abilities with clients. He trusts me. Often at lunchtime we chat together in his office as we eat our sandwiches. It is on one of these occasions that I learn that Arnold plays the piano in a jazz group. He talks knowledgeably about modern jazz and in particular Errol Garner, who, it emerges, is something of a model, and I realise then how little I know about the world of music, or art, or culture generally, apart from the popular offerings on the radio. There, the only inkling of modern jazz is Ella Fitzgerald, who Arnold says is good, but the best jazz singer alive is Anita O'Day. I am intrigued to know what Arnold's playing would be like.

'Why don't you come down and listen to us one Saturday night – we play at the Mentone Hotel, which is set up as a kind of nightclub,' says Arnold.

And so a few weeks later I do just that – motor on my own down to Sandringham in the Hillman. I had announced my intention on the Friday before, and Arnold said, 'Come to us for dinner first, and we can go together.' I pull the Hillman up in front of a modest single-fronted weatherboard, its neat garden washed in a pink glow by the setting sun; Arnold comes to the door and ushers me into a house deep in gloom, with every blind pulled down to within an inch or two of its length. We sit and talk for a few minutes until his wife emerges unsteadily from a dark bedroom. She is tall and slim, attractive in a languid, very English kind of way, but pale and tired looking. The talk is desultory, directionless. There is an uncomfortable sense that the marriage has somehow lost its way, that some disappointment haunts their lives. It might have something to do with their decision to leave England for Australia not very many years earlier. 'I hope you don't mind cold meat and salad,' she says without enthusiasm, 'I haven't had time to go to the shops today.' Their small daughter Ella sits shy and subdued opposite me at the table, staring with enormous blue eyes over her bowl of mashed vegetables. After coffee Arnold hurries into his blue tuxedo and red bow tie, which looks incongruous on him, grabs the satchel holding his music, kisses his wife and daughter at the front door and says, 'Let's go; I won't be late darling, but don't wait up.' There is an excitement in his voice that I haven't noticed before, and I note that this – playing his music – is what makes Arnold happiest; there is a sense that she and Arnold are at odds over this and over his departure. 'Nice to have met you young man,' she calls wearily as we head to Arnold's car in the driveway.

I am pleased to find that he drives a Riley, navy blue and a little shabby, but nevertheless a car I have always admired. Inside it has a distinctive leather smell and a cool, dark feeling of quality, though its maroon upholstery has a few tears and scuffing at the edges. It runs a little roughly too, but this doesn't spoil the pleasure I get from the ride, sitting beside a careful, competent Arnold as he drives us quietly along the Beach Road. When we get there I am surprised by the popularity and sophistication of the venue. This bayside pub is the nearest thing Melbourne has to offer by way of a nightclub – the Embers had not yet opened – and good musicians play to a knowledgeable crowd of modern jazz enthusiasts sitting at tables or dancing in casual dress under atmospheric lighting. I find myself an out-of-the-way spot against the wall next to the bandstand, where the musicians leave their gear, and despite being still underage, order a beer so I won't look like a bag handler. Not long after Arnold's group begins to play I realise I am out of my depth; my ignorance of jazz, especially modern jazz of this kind, makes me bewildered and self-conscious. Some of the pieces they play, such as 'Take the A Train' or 'Moonlight in Vermont' are vaguely familiar as they lay down the tune, but when they quickly head way out into unchartered territory I am lost. Arnold has a particular thing going with the sax player, and time after time they chase each other way off shore where the waters are deep blue, dark and wild, and you feel the risk at every new distorted scale, every strange chord, every outreaching phrase. Yet I am not bored. Even my sugar-pop educated brain, raised on Johnny Ray and Patti Page, can appreciate serious engagement, even if it is on a level I couldn't hope to grasp.

At the piano, Arnold seems a different person. His scholarly stoop becomes an intense crouch over the keys, and his usual diffidence becomes the wariness of a stalker looking for the moment to strike. 'There,' his hands will say, 'There, there, there,' as he firmly lays down the chords, and he will steal a brief glance and nod at the sax player to encourage him to connect the chords with a thread of notes. Here Arnold is not so much the professor as Charles Lindberg, or Neil Armstrong, taking that bold step. I watch him grow in stature, see the blend of mastery and exploration in his playing, and then, out of the blue the thought comes to me, *apropos* of nothing at all, that Arnold is Jewish. That this, in some vague way unfathomable to me, explains Arnold's apartness from the crowd, and his inscrutability. He is a Jew. And so was Mr Singer. And that is why Arnold was able to be so close to him, to admire him, to respect him as a wise elder; he was one of the tribe. When Mr Singer said 'There is nothing beyond' it was for Arnold the utterance of a truth to be respected, if not agreed with. Though I believe that Arnold did agree with it. I think Arnold, heroically, is a man without religious faith. Also, he is a Jew who doesn't want to be thought of as one.

Baffled by the unforgiving, unaccommodating music, I at the same time know I am experiencing something I will have to bring myself to grasp at least in the way that these other people around me seem to grasp. As an introduction to modern jazz, it is more pain than pleasure, but this first shot has found the target and it is in my veins now just as surely as if I'd injected a virus.

During a break, I wander outside to get away from the hot, smoky atmosphere. Against the wall, near the doorway of the pub, a young couple is enthusiastically kissing, oblivious to anything going on around them. Embarrassed, I turn away and pace off in the other direction. This, and the realisation that I don't know Arnold as well as I thought, and that really he is not in the slightest like my father, who was a devout Catholic and never listened to anything but popular music – a huge Bing Crosby fan – leaves me unsettled and feeling out of my depth. I can't wait for the evening to be over and to get off home. When he is finished Arnold introduces me to the band and they stand around chatting for a few minutes while packing up their gear. I am surprised, after all that heady musical adventuring, how 'everyday' they suddenly seem – just blokes with a plain line of talk and families to go home to. They joke and chat in their Aussie voices, all of them seeming ordinary. Except Arnold – he never seems ordinary or everyday.

Driving back with him I go into one of my tongue-tied states; can't think of anything to say. My mind feels strangely overcrowded and empty at the same time – packed with more than it can handle, and empty of anything I can articulate. Eventually Arnold breaks the silence. 'What did you think? Did you enjoy it?'

'Oh, yeah, great, fantastic; what a night, what a place – incredible music …'

'I thought we got somewhere with 'Georgia on my Mind' tonight.'

'Sure, you certainly did … Not that I've heard you play it before, of course, so I wouldn't be able to compare, but I mean … wow, that was definitely getting somewhere'.

Once again, how ignorant I am, not just of the music, but of any *language* with which to talk about it. The aficionados, of which I am certainly not one, have the terminology down pat – 'way out'; 'a gasser'; 'dig this'; 'cool cat'; 'split', among other phrases that came to define hipsters – but I am struggling to find any words that can connect with the experience I've undergone that evening.

I don't go in when we get back to Arnold's house, but say I'll go straight on home. The interior of the Hillman is cold and smells of engine oil, pleasant, as old cars always are back then, and she starts straight off and gets me home without the radiator boiling. It is well after midnight when I tiptoe through the sleeping household, and undress in the dark so as not to wake Ray in the other bed. I climb in shivering from the cold, doubling myself up to get warm quick, and when finally I am able to relax and stretch out under the tingling sheets I think back over the events of the night, and the one thing that keeps recurring over and over is how wonderful it would be to be able to play music at that level of ability, to be listened to by people, to be able to call yourself a *musician*. Wonderful.

In that year a very pretty girl joined the typing pool. Her name was Betty Theodorou. She was bubbly and a bit rough round the edges, and constantly flirted with the younger men in the office. Small and shapely, with a tiny waist emphasised by a tight wide belt, she wore flaring skirts with stiffened petticoats, and above the belt her tight pink or turquoise tops stretched smooth over apple-firm breasts. I took her out a few times, including partnering her to my second of the annual company Balls. But Betty, unfortunately, was uncooperative, would hardly let me touch her. There was a whiff of trouble beneath this defence, reinforced on the first night I drove her home in the Hillman. We parked in front of the house where she rented a room, but she had no intention of inviting me in. 'Who lives here?' I asked.

'No one you know,' she said, 'just some Greek friends of mine.'

'What about your parents?'

'My mum died. Don't know where me dad is, and I don't care.'

Her tone didn't encourage me to ask more questions, so I moved to kiss her, and she let me do so briefly before pushing me away.

'Don't try anything,' she said, looking me directly in the eyes. As if to reinforce her warning, she opened the car door a little, so that the overhead light came on.

'I won't,' I said, wishing I could get my hands on those shapely breasts, high on her chest under her pink top. I looked down to where her petticoat showed under the folds of her skirt, and was struck by how filthy it was. Supposed to be white, it was a dirty grey with darker mottled streaks; it hadn't been washed for ages, and then I realised that Betty herself smelled a bit, which she tried to hide with heavy perfume. I understood in that moment that she was struggling with living alone, probably ignorant of even the basics of laundering, how to cook properly for herself – her beautiful olive skin was dotted with pimples – and that her typist's wage left her little spare money after paying the rent. There was something more, too, behind the unwillingness to talk about her family. Something had thrown her out into the world long before time – she was no more than sixteen – and whatever it was lurking beneath that bubbly surface, it was messy and haunted her; I was not keen to explore it any further. It would be too complicated. But all this defensiveness and distancing puzzled me; why would she want to go out with me then? Then one day as we chatted, when she brought some letters she had typed for me, I got something of an answer. She had been standing beside where I was seated, looking over my shoulder, when she remarked, 'Garry: you are so lovely and *clean.*' To her, my cleanliness was an achievement not to be treated lightly; to me, her observation was one more indication that girls did not find me especially sexy. Clean! When they would gossip incessantly in the typing pool about how handsome, gorgeous, fantastic, this or that film star was! They never praised Elvis for being *clean.*

How long would I remain a virgin? I hadn't even touched one girl under her underpants.

Apart from the occasional event generated from my workplace, my social life remained anchored in the Housing Commission area of West Ivanhoe. The suburb had been spruced up in the last decade, and many houses were well cared for and were developing attractive gardens. Organised community activity was slow to form, but the gradual emergence of football and cricket teams, and the occasional visit to the area of Verfurth's carnival and the odd circus, and the creation of a local Progress Committee that organised things like the mobile library, added to the suburban life around us. Then there was the Church, St Bernadette's, where I still occasionally attended Mass, though this was more of a social routine in conformity with other Catholics, including my brother, than from religious commitment; that had grown very weak. There was also a scout troop, which some of my friends joined, though I chose not to for some reason. But this was all a strangely self-contained culture of sorts, an enrichment of the lives of the growing families certainly, but unengaged with the larger world outside it. While becoming dimly aware of that world, I was not yet quite dissatisfied enough with the dullness and narrowness of this one to want to abandon it.

My neighbourhood friends were now in their late teens, and they were on the whole a directionless and unambitious lot. Most, like myself, had received little secondary education, few had learned a trade, and the only person I knew who had plans to go to university was the asocial David, son of the staunchly Catholic busybody Mr Dewar. All the rest were clerks, semi-skilled workers of various kinds, factory hands, the odd butcher, storemen packers, typists or shop girls. We didn't engage in any kind of studies in the evenings, or reading or family activities, and no homes had television yet. Consequently there was a lot of mischief making, particularly under cover of darkness, between sundown and midnight. In our early teens we had confined ourselves to 'Knick Knock', a silly game of knocking on the door of a house and running away to hide, so that when the door was answered there was nobody to be seen. We particularly enjoyed knocking on the doors of the less popular neighbours, such as Mr Dewar and Mr Wood. Later, we discovered in Valentine Street a truck regularly parked in the driveway carrying a full load of watermelons under its tarpaulin, and we got into stealing, eating and finally throwing the fruit at each other as we ran laughing through the streets. When we were old enough for cars to figure in our lives, I joined a group of boys who played more dangerous games. Teddy Walker, from a couple of streets away, had bought his first car – a 1928 Graham Page, not in great condition, but large and very stylish, with wire wheels, two spares mounted behind the front mudguards, a chrome luggage carrier on the back, and an interior of hotel-lounge plushness. Together with Alan Craig, Geoff Conley and Bernie Cloney, I would hurtle round the streets at night in Teddy's car, mounting the footpath and circling whole blocks driving on the 'nature strips', or dare-devilling by crouching in the mudguard curves, or standing on the running board or even lying on the bonnet peering windswept into the night as Teddy raced the car at high-speed along Oriel Road; one slip, and I'd have been thrown off into oblivion. We were all after excitement, challenge, danger, and this was the only way we could think of finding it.

Geoff Conley was perhaps the most interesting of these young men. Bernie Cloney had met him during National Service training in the army a year or so earlier – they were a couple of years older. Geoff lived in the neighbouring suburb of Fairfield, not in a Commission house, and he began coming over to see Bernie in his smart little Morris Minor convertible. It was a fine little car, with great handling and cornering ability, even if its performance was somewhat sedate. Eventually it was myself Geoff came to see and take around in his car, sharing his intelligent interest in motoring and travel. Geoff worked in the office of the Goodyear Tyre Company in the city; he liked to talk, was tall, handsomish, sensitive and good natured, but also openly unsure of himself, which made him a good companion. When the new Olympic Games village in West Heidelberg was completed that year Geoff drove me over to see it, and later, when the Games were starting, we visited it again to see his workmate, the champion swimmer John Marshall. Driving in the city one night we picked up a black American athlete who wanted to be shown a little of Melbourne, which Geoff was eager and happy to do. We drove him around for hours. At Easter 1957 we motored to Adelaide together – my first venture out of Victoria – simply to see what the place was like. We'd not arranged accommodation, and ended up sleeping in the Morris in Memorial Drive gardens, and being woken at dawn by a policeman who eyed us suspiciously – we might have been gays – and told us to move off. We went to Glenelg beach for the day, talked and lay in the sun, and dutifully drove the 700 kilometres back to Melbourne that night. Yet while we remained friends, Geoff was eventually drawn to favour yet another of the group, the forceful and somewhat self-regarding Alan Craig.

Alan's mother had migrated with her three sons and a daughter from northern England after the War, which took her sailor husband's life and left her lonely and bitter with grief for the rest of her days. An obdurate and emotional woman, she would complain openly about her life in front of Alan's friends, and insist desperately on being informed about and even included in his social life. The daughter had married and kept her family mostly away from her mother and brothers. The two older brothers were even more forceful than Alan, and never found a happy or settled life in Australia; they got into violent rows and dodgy situations, hurt people and got hurt themselves. Eventually I heard that the oldest, Ronnie, was killed and Norman had gone to prison; Alan had become not just the caring youngest son, but the star of hope in his mother's future. The two of them lived in a Commission house in Hawker Street, one street north of Valentine; neither of them bothered to do the garden or any but the most basic maintenance on the house, nor even bothered to furnish it beyond stringent basics. She always hoped that Alan would make good at his butcher's trade, and move them into a better place of their own.

Alan and I were not entirely trusting friends. In some ways we were too alike – Alan took an interest in music, had boxed as a boy, was good at drawing, all things for which I had myself been long recognised in the neighbourhood, so there was a certain amount of jealousy between us. We were also both argumentative, which put together, could make for a volatile mix. We went once on a rabbiting trip to Murchison with the Cloney males, and camped at a disused abbatoirs on the outskirts of the town. It was early in our relationship, and Alan, clearly threatened by my particular personality, made persistent attempts to bully me in long, mocking tirades in the tent where we were all supposed to be sleeping. At one point I left the tent, and was so angry that it crossed my mind to seize one of the .22 rifles in the back of the Cloney car, return and simply put a bullet in Alan. There was, I knew, a point beyond which I should never be pushed, having given in just once to the terrible violence I was capable of. I cooled down and resisted the idea; but for a moment it was a close thing. Back in Melbourne soon after, I mentioned this incident to Frankie Cloney, who'd been along on the trip, and Frankie, always looking for mischief, had in turn passed it on to Alan. Alan wanted to make something of it, to take this opportunity to bring the enmity between us to a head, to put me in my place once and for all. I was out in the street working yet again on the front wheel of the Hillman, when Alan approached walking his bull terrier 'Jeep' down Cook Street. 'I want to talk to you,' he said in a threatening voice. I was a little scared, considered slipping off into my house to avoid a fight, but pride wouldn't let me do this. Alan grabbed me by the shirt front.

'I hear you were going to shoot me; I ought to knock your bloody head off.'

Nothing came of it. I stood my ground, but knowing Alan would beat me in a fight, I took to placating him. The fact was, there was no real cause for Alan's aggression, beyond looking for an excuse to master me in some way. He would be in the wrong, and further, a reasoning voice at the back of Alan's mind just might have been whispering that he had more to gain by friendship than by enmity. And this is in fact what happened. We became quite close in time, and Alan confided to me in his typically condescending way, 'I used to think you were a pain in the arse, but I can see that you're really quite a good bloke now that I've got to know you.' But I never had any illusions about Alan; there was a family instability there that you could never completely forget, and I could never put all my trust in him.

One boy who did not mix with this group was my childhood friend, Ron Bowden, from across the street. Ron had stayed on at school to get his Intermediate Certificate, and had found a job in the State bank in Eltham. Already a lot more mature in outlook than most of his contemporaries, Ron had no time for teenage hubris. He was looking to give his life direction, was saving for a car, and keen to do well in his work. Indeed, he was the only true professional amongst us all, with John Cloney perhaps a close second, and though Ron played cricket well and took a keen interest in sport and in girls, you felt that to a significant degree he had a private plan that he was determined to make work, a future he was not about to threaten with stupid behaviour. Consequently, Ron and I did not see a great deal of each other between the ages of fifteen and eighteen, because I was quite happy to be stupid.

We longed, all of us, for contact with the opposite sex, but not in any committed kind of relationship. The fantasy was that you would somehow pick up a willing girl, or even a group of willing girls, who would know how to give you a good time, though not of course prostitutes, who belonged in a separate and forbidden adult world. This good time undoubtedly meant sex, which never happened of course, and if it had, none of us would have known how to go about it, being not only virgins, but inept communicators, the lot of us. We were vigorous, physical, argumentative about unimportant matters; we had absolutely no interest or knowledge of such things as politics, art, ideas of any sophisticated kind. In summer we would go to the beach together in our various cars, or to drive-in cinemas, or parties in nearby suburbs; the car-driving provided most of the enjoyment. And it was at one of these parties that I had my first tangible encounter with an aroused vagina. A girl called Leila had taken a fancy to me, which she was making embarrassingly obvious, and I suggested we go outside and 'snog' in Teddy Walker's Graham Page. There she immediately removed her knickers and sprawled all over me. I was both thrilled and terrified at the same time: thrilled at my sexual success, sinking my middle finger deep into her wet opening, which gave off a head-spinning aroma, and terrified lest we should actually 'do it'. I told myself I could only do it if I had a condom, so asking her to wait without moving, I dashed back into the house to ask whether any of my mates had one on them. They didn't, of course, a fact which I knew all along;

what I was indirectly doing was telling them that I had made a sexual conquest, a male triumph whose main value lay in the advertising. I did feel keen disappointment when I got back to the car to find that Leila had been joined by one of her girlfriends, who was bent on protecting her from me, and so the opportunity for my first fuck was thwarted, though I was pleased with my little trophy all the way home, sniffing my middle finger and consoling myself with the thought that Leila would be there for the taking if I ever found myself alone with her again.

Really, we were a pathetic crowd of callow mates, knowing nothing very much, skilled at nothing very much, suspended in chaos as we waited for the chance that life might, by some miracle, throw something or someone our way that mattered. It was, perhaps like all teenage years, a strangely closed, repetitive, desperate life that had little connection with all the interesting, beautiful, purposeful things taking place in the world outside. I had a fleeting sense of its inadequacy, but did not really understand how or why or what, if anything, I could do about it. Power was something I had no idea how to obtain.

Songs on the radio are an important accompaniment to life in these years. Almost everything we do seems to bear some relation to them: one Spanish-Mexican piece, 'Vaya Con Dios' by Les Paul and Mary Ford, featuring an echoing slide-guitar, runs through my head for weeks. Others, by Perry Como and Nat King Cole, seem to express something about the constrained, limited possibilities of the world about me in a way that, for instance, modern jazz does not. Listening to a song like 'No Other Love' or 'Rags to Riches' by Tony Bennett, reminds me strangely of what is actually there around us, of the banality and greyness of our everyday routines. But the kind of music I experienced a while back with Arnold Winton does not have this effect. It does not, on the whole, comment upon life around me. This is not just because it is instrumental and not using words and emotions, but also because there is something self-contained about it: jazz *is* a world, a complete, uncompromised field of sounds and rhythms suggesting that anything is possible, that we can feel and imagine things beyond our daily lives. That, I think, is why it is so difficult to listen to: it is unsettling, requires an effort on our part, an effort which at this time in my life seems beyond me.

So I let the pop songs do their work, express my feelings for me, remind me of the things I am merely able to do – go to work, drive the car, go to the beach, take out a girl for whom I have no strong feelings, or she for me, hang out with my mates. Pop music seems designed both to colour and crystallize these banal activities.

From time to time I work on after five o'clock with a few of my fellow office workers. Usually we stay an extra hour, being paid overtime rates. When this happens I catch a later bus home – a green bus from the city to Heidelberg – that everyone calls 'the six o'clock special'. This is because it catches the spill of patrons from the pubs, which close at six o'clock. There are always a few drunks, some of them entertaining, though most of the other passengers, especially women, don't find them so. Often they will sit at the back singing or letting loose with some incoherent diatribe, usually against the government. A short, red-faced man in a stained reefer jacket is a regular performer, often singling out some quietly sitting middle-aged woman as his target audience, to her great discomfort. On one occasion he chooses to treat the whole bus to his own version of the song 'I Get a Kick Out of You', stumbling about the moving bus, falling across passengers in their seats, bumping against others, reeking of alcohol. Not only is the song completely off-key, but he has the words wrong, interestingly wrong. He keeps singing the final line of each verse as 'But I get *no* kick out of you', a complete reversal of the original. Does it say something about this man's life? I imagine a fading wife at home, an angry, a bitter, a disappointed wife keeping her husband's dinner hot in the oven, who presents a disapproving face as he walks in. I foresee a marriage gone sour on both sides over the years because of his drinking, which itself is prompted by failures elsewhere, brought about by personal weaknesses, the inability to cope with life's demands. Is she sexually repugnant to him now, just as he is sexually repugnant to her? The words of the song have been accommodated to his own bitterness, twisted into an expression of his private despair at ever finding the love and glamour implicit, indeed promised, in the melody and lyrics of the song.

As the bus turns a corner the man lurches heavily across the aisle and his shoulder hits a chrome steadying pole with a deep thump, causing the man to cry out. 'Hey, hey! Easy, easy! This driver's erratic, you know. Erratic. He's a danger to the Travelling Public,' he slurs, desperately clutching the pole. And then, the crowning moment to the whole mad display, a middle-aged woman in the seat nearest the man, suddenly stands up and says, 'Here: sit down before you hurt yourself,' and half pushes the shambles of a man into her vacated seat. Five minutes later he is snoring loudly, with his head on the shoulder of the attractive young woman next to him.

Occasionally I spend time with Ron Bowden. We share an interest in cars, often go round the used car lots dreaming and tyre-kicking. One evening we come upon a handsome red Singer sports, in apparently excellent condition. We sit in it, feel the steering, the brakes, let the canopy down; the Singer sports was designed to take on the MG market, with more fluent lines, a small back seat, and lower cost. I have already had some experience with them when Douglas Plant gave me a lift to work in his little maroon job, and have a soft spot for them. Ron starts the motor, and apart from a puff of blue smoke, it runs well and makes a nice throaty burble as it ticks over. The salesman suggests we take it out for a spin; together we drive down the main shopping street of Ivanhoe, hoping to turn heads, feeling on top of the world. When we get back the salesman gives us a pitch, offers to lower the price. By this time we are both hooked, and Ron is determined to buy it, though he can't quite afford it, even on hire purchase. I would love to have a stake in owning such a sweet car, so I suggest we share it. All I can offer is ten percent, but it is enough. It is understood that it is essentially Ron's car, but that I am allowed occasional driving rights.

With the Easter break coming up, we decide to drive to Bright in northern Victoria for the holiday weekend. Bright has happy memories for me of a Christmas with the Cloney family five or so years earlier. We pack our gear into the Singer and set off, taking turns at the wheel. Everything is going wonderfully, with the car purring along at a steady speed, until we are on a stretch of road between Euroa and Benalla.Suddenly the engine emits a loud bang, and the power drops alarmingly. We stop to examine it, and eventually work out that two of the four cylinders are out of action; the car will only struggle along at less than 50 percent power. It kills our fun, and our holiday too, and we limp back to Melbourne in bitter disappointment.

The Singer sits in Ron's driveway for months, until he can save enough money to have it repaired.

Another girl arrived to work in the accounts department around this time, a type utterly different from anyone else in the office. She was short, slightly solid, but small-waisted and nicely curved, and her long blonde hair, Dorothy Malone style, swept her shoulders as she tossed her elegant head. Her eyes were deep blue, almost violet, her teeth were small and slightly tobacco stained, in a carmine-lipped mouth that was generous and a little mocking. The moment she spoke in her educated, husky contralto I knew I was in the company of someone from that other world, that place of culture and experience, and I wanted to know about it, about her; I wanted her to take me into it. Her name was Beris Sullivan, and she began to find reasons to come down from the accounts department and sit beside my desk for long, absorbing discussions about anything vaguely philosophical. This was noticed by Mr Crosby, the ill-tempered, acid-tongued General Manager, who from his office perched high in the centre of the ground floor like a prison watchtower saw everything, and would occasionally come down and break us up. 'Garry's got work to do,' he would say to her with unnecessary and rude force, 'even if you haven't.' You could feel something else itching him when he said these things, and it was probably jealousy. In the toilet he once said of her, 'I'd be careful of that one if I were you: you might catch something.'

Though she was more than a year older, somehow I found the courage to ask Beris out. Would she like to see *The Pajama Game*, showing at Her Majesty's Theatre? To my delight, she agreed. I didn't go home – worked on and ate in a café, having arranged to meet her in the theatre foyer. When she arrived she had changed her tight-fitting leopard skin skirt and black top for an emerald green dress, high heels, and a short navy topcoat with a white fur collar that wrapped high around her cheeks, caught up her blonde hair and framed her face in a coquettish, wonderfully good-looking way. It was an evening I would never forget, and floats back into my memory every time I hear one of the many songs from that show: 'Hernando's Hideaway', 'Hey There', 'Steam Heat', 'Seven and a Half Cents'. I bought her chocolates and afterwards we had coffee in Pellegrinis in Bourke Street, and then I took her in the Hillman home to her place in Middle Park, where I briefly met her father, who was short and stocky like her, and when I was about to depart she pulled my head down and gave me not only the hottest, most full-blooded kiss I had ever experienced, but in the midst of it I felt her strong, wet tongue push past my teeth and deep into my mouth, which seemed to stretch the top of my head to bursting point and at the same time send an electric current down to my loins. I drove home happy and full of hope.

But not many days after, the situation took an unsettling turn. We had arranged to go for a drink after work, but half an hour or so before finishing time she came down to my desk.

'I have to tell you something,' she said, 'I was going to mention it, but hadn't got around to it. I'm married. Separated. My husband phoned me just now, and is coming to pick me up after work. He wants to meet you. It'll be okay. I hadn't planned this, I thought I'd escaped him, but he's found out where I work. He isn't awful or anything, but I do feel sorry for him. He's had a rough life – out on the streets when he was sixteen, earning a living playing the guitar, bumming around Australia.'

Again there was that sense of a different world about her and her friends. Nobody I knew was like that, like some fantasy idea of a life, where you simply drifted and did what you wanted, had sex with whoever you wanted, didn't work at a normal job, do normal things. The idea of such a life fascinated and troubled me. I was a little scared of how this man might act towards me, what he might be capable of; Beris gave the impression she was, too.

My desk being right next to the front window looking out on Lonsdale Street, I kept looking out to see if anyone was waiting. Eventually someone arrived and stood adjacent to the entrance, on the edge of the footpath. He was huge. At least six feet two, and broad-shouldered, in a navy reefer jacket and grey trousers. He was quite good-looking in fact, and didn't seem to have any sort of menacing air about him. Neither did he look like someone who bummed around with a guitar, more like an insurance clerk, I thought.

At five o'clock Beris came down in her coat, carrying her bag, and led me out into the street to introduce us. He came forward, smiling, offering his hand.

'I just want to thank you,' he said, 'for looking after Beris for me. She's told me how kind you've been to her. But I just have to have a serious talk with her right now, so if it's okay with you, she'll have that drink with you another time …'

It was all very civilised, not a trace of aggression, nor any but the merest hint of possessiveness in his attitude. Indeed, his apologetic tone and water-filled eyes seemed almost abject, and immediately it was clear there was nothing to fear in him, that he was in fact soft, despite his size. This meeting with her, I immediately realised, was not one of male repossession, but of pathetic pleading with her to take him back, and moreover with the unmistakeable whiff of failure about it. The man was fixed to his smile by desperation, and even, it felt, the hope of getting me on side with his cause to win her back.

After that I no longer entertained hopes of making Beris my girlfriend, not because of the husband, who was never seen nor mentioned again. It was because I knew that the gap of experience between us was so wide as to be unbridgeable. She could never be serious about me, could never look up to me in the way she obviously liked to with men who had gone beyond her. This must be the key to sexually attracting women, I thought: you have to be greater than them in some way, or at best they will treat you as a mere friend. Beris found me convenient to play the game of boy-girl with, and she genuinely liked me I was sure, but she would never take me seriously enough to be a lover. We went out together several more times, even after she left the insurance company, sacked by Crosby for latecoming (she did often look the worse for the night before). She got a job teaching dancing at Arthur Murray's in Preston, and I would sometimes pick her up in the Hillman afterwards. One night, heading down Plenty Road, a front wheel – *that* front wheel – got caught in the tram tracks and the car jolted suddenly to one side; it must have broken another spoke or two. From then on the front of the car began to lurch alarmingly from side to side, and Beris called out, 'What's wrong with it? Can't you do something?' as we hurtled along barely in control. I got her home safely, though somehow the silliness of the car and the hopelessness of our situation all came to a head that night, and I gave up on her. It was the last time I took her out, although I was, happily and unpredictably and yet somehow inevitably, to run into her again from time to time in very different circumstances in very different places in the world.

The reports on John Coleman were frustratingly bad. For almost a year now his playing future was in doubt; he'd had numerous operations and said in interviews that he was determined to get back on the field as soon as possible, but so far the doctors had not been able to repair his dislocated knee satisfactorily. A newspaper photograph of him recuperating at home in his pyjamas and checked dressing gown reminded me of my father, who'd had a similar gown. It struck me how these clothes separated him from the rest of the world, almost like a prison suit that marked the way he could not participate in normal, everyday activities, just as prisoners can't. It robbed them of manly power, made them passive, gentle, less consequential. On the rare occasions when my father had put on 'outside' clothes, he looked different, regained some of his missing dignity, looked like a man again; but the pyjamas, when they went back on, turned him into that special type of being, an invalid, which did not allow him to act like a normal man. I longed for the return of Coleman to the field, just as I longed for the return of my father to our house, but in my heart I knew that one longing was as futile as the other.

5

PUCKAPUNYAL, 1957. National Service Training. A certain tension has run through the platoon ever since the sergeant announced hand grenade instruction this afternoon. Everyone is scared, but no one will talk about it. Even the sergeant is edgy, noticeably snappier than usual. 'Shuddup in the ranks! Keep in step!' he barks, when at other times on informal marches he doesn't bother. No doubt his concern is the havoc that might issue if we do something wrong. He is, himself, a flaky kind of man, often showing a silliness that doesn't inspire confidence. So it isn't altogether a surprise that he does make a mistake, and it is partly his fault that things almost turn out badly. He has explained clearly what is to be done:

'We don't *throw* hand grenades in the Australian Army,' he says, 'we *bowl* them, overarm like in cricket. Keep your arms straight and your hands back to back, knuckle to knuckle in front of your groin, and as you pull out the pin, take your arm back keeping it straight while holding the grenade and keeping the lever pressed down. Now, before you bring your arm through for the release, make sure you look back to see that the pin is properly out, and when you've done that, bowl the grenade in the direction of the target. You have four seconds before it detonates.' But a weak link in the procedure is my own fear, which has prevented me from concentrating on the sergeant's words. I'm afraid of the thing itself, its surprising iron heaviness in my hand correcting the innocence of its pineapple looks, a reminder that it is pregnant with explosive, that those little chocolate-like squares are designed to fly off in all directions and rip through the body as if it were paper ('*Through teeth and skull and helmet*' I recall from somewhere in the past). All I want is to be rid of the thing. A second weak link is the sergeant himself. Here's what happens.

I stand behind the low wall of sandbags, the sergeant beside me, the rest of the platoon sitting, standing, smoking, some fifteen or twenty metres behind me waiting their turn to throw. I measure up, fix my eye on the target ahead, as I do so often when bowling my left-arm quickies at West Ivanhoe Cricket Club, but as I bring my shoulder through, the sergeant suddenly throws up his arm and blocks my action. The grenade is jerked loose from my hand and drops about ten feet away, just over the sandbag wall. 'You didn't look back to see the pin was out!' the sergeant bawls. Immediately I fall flat on the ground behind the safety of the wall. The sergeant grabs the collar of my khaki jacket and hauls me to my feet.

'See where it lands!' he barks. In a flash I recall that this was another of the sergeant's instructions earlier: to know where your grenade has fallen in case it has to be retrieved unexploded. I stare over the sandbag wall at the live grenade, almost invisible against a brown-green grass tussock, awaiting the inevitable.

'Right,' says the sergeant, 'Down!'

We both hit the ground just as the very air erupts around and above us. The sergeant has been counting, has stayed calm, known what to do. I have to admire him. Without the sergeant's experience I might have been killed, or badly injured. But he was wrong to block my throw like that: anything could have happened. He should have let me go through with the throw, then reprimanded me. I get up and see my platoon mates all still lying flat on the ground, staring wide-eyed. Some of them start to laugh. 'On ya Gazza,' calls Pottsy Dillon, the blond larrikin who occupies the opposite bed in my hut. But I don't feel like laughing. I feel sick, in fact. The sergeant isn't laughing either, though neither is he conceding any wrongdoing on his part. He simply hands over another grenade, telling me, 'Get it right this time, or you'll be up on a charge for endangering your mates' lives.' This time, I get it right.

Mostly, National Service Training is wearily dull. It is about learning to adjust to primitive conditions: breakfasts of sour milk and cold fried eggs, the fight against sleep through a dreary, freezing night of guard duty, the marching along dirt roads in the heat carrying heavy packs and rifles, dragging yourself out of bed at six in the morning into the shock of a cold shower, the daily grind of childish sameness, and the farce of being told what to do by men with the mentality of parrots. Worst of all, there is not a girl or a woman in sight the whole time – just male company, male talk, male humour, male smells, male bullshit.

I am in the Signal Corps. Just what qualifications or interests fitted me to this sector of the Army, I will never know. It is a technician's outfit – we mostly connect up telephones. We carry out pointless exercises laying cable in the bush (that was in the last War – communications in the next War, in every next War, are always new and need to be anticipated), using outdated and defunct equipment, and we spend most of our days in the bush unsupervised, not knowing what we are supposed to do, or to what purpose, or who is in charge. So weary is everyone of all ranks with the whole charade of Corps training, that one day when I fall a few feet out of a tree in which I was attaching cable, giving myself a scratch across the ribs which hardly breaks the skin, an ambulance is sent for (via crackly telephone line – so this one, at least, did work) and I am taken to the Base hospital, where it is insisted I stay for two days, and am placed on light duties for the week, simply because it is a good opportunity to pretend there is a medical emergency to deal with. My platoon sergeant, my corporal, my officer-in-charge, Lieutenant 'Swampy' Marsh (who, it is breathlessly rumoured round the camp, has a *university degree*), all in turn visit me as solemnly as if I have had both legs shot off in an action that deserves a VC, such is my sudden fame throughout the desperately bored Company. The lieutenant stands at the end of the bed, tall and straight-backed as though he had a tent-pole up his arse, touches his cap with his baton. 'Well done Sig. Kinnane,' he says through tight lips. None of this can be real, I think.

Neverthelesss, it is my own doing that I am even in the army. I had missed being selected in the ballot, so could have simply ignored it and gotten on with my life and work in insurance. But most of my mates had been conscripted in recent times – Alan Craig, Jeff Conley, Bernie Cloney – and their excited accounts of youthful shenanigans and anti-authority escapades made me envious; I wanted my turn at this male rite of passage. When I received the letter from the Department of Defence informing me of my omission, it explained that I had the right to volunteer for the draft if I wished. So I ticked that box and posted it back. In a short time I was nominated for the October 1957 intake, and informed Mr Crosby, the manager at work that I would be taking the three months leave that employers were required to provide. Mr Crosby was not happy, especially when he learned that I had volunteered. But there was nothing he could do to prevent it.

As I might have suspected, a lot of the stories of defiance and punishments at Puckapunyal told by my mates prove to be exaggerations or just plain lies. In fact I find the whole National Service experience absurd. Militarily, it is money totally wasted. This was to be borne out only a few years later when Australia became involved in the Vietnam War. One of the chief justifications for a National Service policy is that it provides the country with a large contingent of young males with some useful training and understanding of military procedures, which the country can call on in time of war. But of course this is precisely what did not happen when the government decided to commit troops to Vietnam. They conscripted by ballot a whole new generation – 20-year-olds – and trained them from scratch, completely ignoring those who'd already been trained. The reasons are obvious and cynical: the younger and less socially enmeshed the recruits are, the easier it is to drag them into the conflict. They don't ask questions, and their unquestioning courage is more readily exploited.

Men with careers and families, not to mention a grasp of politics, are less easy to recruit.

The pointlessness is felt by everyone in the platoon, who indulge in 'taking the piss' as an antidote to boredom. We openly mock the NCOs, parody their speech, mispronounce their names (Corporal Bowles naturally becomes Corporal Bowels) pretend not to understand, and indulge in infantile silliness, such as flinging small stones from our closed fists as we march past a building. 'Who is doing that?' the officer will shout, 'Find that man, sergeant', but he can never be found. In all my three months of faux-soldiering there is only one positive that emerges, and that proves a very special positive. On the very first day we moved into our hut, twenty-two of us, names from A to K, as we unpacked our kit bags onto our beds and began to size up the guys we would be living with, I had noticed a dark-haired young man farther down the room on the opposite side. There was something about him, not just his good looks, but an intensity and self-possession of an exceptional kind. His name is Bob Haberfield, and he is a commercial artist. We gravitate to each other from the first. One day I sit on the bed while he makes a superb pencil portrait of me wearing my beret. The thought occurs that this is the first time I have been close to someone of whom the word 'talent' had real meaning. It isn't just his drawing, it is his whole demeanour, his outlook. He knows what he likes and doesn't like with a conviction that sometimes alarms me. He will dismiss things that are widely popular, enthuse over things that others can't appreciate. For instance, he is the first person I know to walk out on a movie. The movies are among the few entertainments available at Puckapunyal and most people, including myself, will sit through any old rubbish. Not Bob. It is as if something he doesn't like actually offends him, and he won't give it his time or attention. On this occasion we are sitting together, and after about fifteen minutes he says, 'I'm not watching this crap, I'm out of here,' without asking me if I am also prepared to leave. My first thought is that this is an unfriendly act, a placing of his own taste ahead of our friendship. But then I grasp that Bob sees our mutual attendance at the movie as a convenience, not a partnership. Each is free to decide on what experience he wants. It is a strangely individualistic way to practice a friendship, but it has a certain honesty that I can respect. I do feel in that instant an uneasy pressure to choose between my loyalty to him and my interest in the film. I choose to join him. And anyway, it was a lousy film.

On completion of the three months at Puckapunyal just before Christmas, having saved all my army pay, I bought a 1953 Morris Minor four-door saloon for £300, which left me flat broke. I was also soon out of a job. I had known from the first that the management at Transport and General Insurance were annoyed at my volunteering for National Service, and I had a vague notion that it had caused them some inconvenience to find a replacement. They had said nothing about requiring me to resign when I went into the army, so I assumed I would go straight back into my old job when the Christmas holidays were over, but when I got back to work on the first Monday in January, there was another young man sitting at my desk. Arnold Winton called me into his office.

'I'm sorry to have to break it to you,' he said, 'but they're not prepared to take you back.'

I was shocked, completely thrown by this news. It registered that Arnold had said 'they're' and not 'we're', making it clear that he was not in agreement with their decision. Perhaps there was a glimmer of a chance, then.

'Not in any position in the Company?' I asked.

'Well,' said Arnold, moving out from behind his desk, 'Let's go and find out.'

Arnold led me to Mr Crosby's office, but it was empty. 'He's up with Mr Darcy,' said the secretary, so we took the lift up to the first floor together. Arnold was silent, gloomy, all the way. When we knocked and entered Frank Darcy's office, it was clear the two executives had known we were coming, had gathered their poise and prepared their positions in advance.

Arnold pointed out that I had come in on the expectation of going back to my old job, and added that I was of course still an employee, even though receiving no salary during my National Service. Crosby, the senior man in the room, assumed charge of the situation, speaking with his usual brusqueness. 'No,' he said, looking me straight in the eye. 'Why should we take you back? We're not bound to – you volunteered.'

I thought, by sounding reasonable and with Arnold's support, I might have been able to argue them round. 'I've been here three years now, I like the job, and I'm sure Mr Winton would say I do my job well …'

'I know how well you do or don't do your job,' cut in Crosby, voice like a scalpel.

'But it was National Service, surely I'm entitled to some consideration for that,' I replied, hoping that as an ex-Army man himself Crosby might have some sympathy for my actions; I was certain Crosby was one of those who approved of National Service training for the young, whom he categorically detested.

'Why should we? You didn't consider *us* when you volunteered. You gave *us* no choice.'

'We've had to take on someone to replace you,' said Darcy, his first sound since we entered the room, 'it's hardly fair to throw that bloke out now, is it?' Neither I nor Arnold could think of anything more to say. There was a moment more of silence, until Crosby said,

'There's nothing here for you. Miss Emms will make up your outstanding entitlements, and off you go.'

And that was it. Arnold mumbled something apologetic but was powerless to do anything, I went to Miss Emms in Accounts, who said she would post me a cheque, and then, somewhat stunned, I found myself standing outside the building in sunny Lonsdale Street at ten-thirty on a Monday morning, with nothing to do and nowhere to go. The world was getting on with its busy pursuits all around me, but I was adrift, trying to take in this first experience of actually losing a job. I'd been dumped. I didn't know whether to laugh or cry. Or what to tell my mother when I got home.

I am beginning to find the company of Alan Craig, Ted Walker, Jeff Conley, boring. We go to parties, to the beach, to the motor races at Phillip Island, mainly to drive our cars about – we all have one now – and we hook up with the occasional girl or groups of girls, but these guys are all fundamentally creatures of habit who have, like myself, dropped out of the secondary education system and taken uninspiring jobs, and I feel bogged down in the dumb routines of our lives. In fact the whole West Ivanhoe neighbourhood, my home, the streets, the people around me I have known for a decade now, seem stale and predictable. Compared to the life of Bob Haberfield, theirs is a kind of non-existence, and mine is headed the same way.

As it turned out I was unemployed for almost no time at all. I happened to run into an old school chum, Brian Joyce, a few days later, and he knew of a job I could walk straight into. We had not seen much of each other since school, though we lived only streets apart. But I did know of Brian's somewhat chequered career in recent years, having stayed on at school after me, and entering a seminary to train for the priesthood. Then I heard of his having left the seminary and gone into accountancy (he was always good at maths), and then, surprisingly, getting into some sort of trouble that landed him in prison, embezzlement or some such. So when I ran into him again I was somewhat in awe of his exploits, though not inclined to trust him. He was now running the accounts department of Vanguard Insurance Company, in Elizabeth Street, and told me they were looking for an experienced underwriter. So I called the manager and arranged an interview. He was pleasant and gave the impression that by taking the job I would be saving their bacon; I agreed to start work the following Monday.

When I arrived, the place seemed deserted. There was one woman – the receptionist – in the downstairs office, who showed me my desk and told me the manager wanted to see me. I sensed immediately that something was wrong, and it was.

'Have you seen or heard anything of Brian?' the manager asked.

'No'.

'He hasn't arrived for work yet, and I don't think he's going to. Come with me.'

We went into the Accounts section, and in the office that I presumed was Brian's, the safe door was wide open with papers strewn on the floor. We stood in silence as it dawned that the manager was assuming Brian had been responsible.

'It was mostly petty cash; I've called the police.'

'You think it was Brian?'

'It's got to be, hasn't it. Only he and I and my secretary know the combination, and it hasn't been forced in any way. Oh, don't worry – I knew his background when I took him on, but he managed to convince me he had put it all behind him. More fool me.'

I wondered whether in some vague way, because the manager knew Brian and I were friends, perhaps I was implicated. But he assured me this was not the case. 'I was relieved when you turned up this morning, because if you'd had anything to do with this you wouldn't be here.'

Nothing more was said about it for a few days, during which I tried to make a start on my task of sorting out the underwriting. It was a hopeless job. Nobody had kept proper records for the past year, and it was often difficult to know whether a policy was current, renewed, lapsed, or whether the premium had been paid, or any claims logged against it. Hardly any new business seemed to have come in, and some that was waiting to be processed had been sitting in the 'in' tray unattended for months. The system of acquiring new accounts was unfathomable, since there was no information available from the freelance sales representatives. The whole place was in dismal chaos. I battled on every day that week trying to get things sorted out, and then on the Friday the manager told me, 'They've caught Brian; he was shop-lifting in a Sydney store, and was identified.'

That afternoon I got a phone call from John Cloney, back at Transport and General. 'Did you know Vanguard are broke?' he said. 'I told Arnold Winton where you were working and he said, 'Doesn't he know they're virtually bankrupt? They've made three attempts at refinancing, all failed.'

'Shit.'

'Just thought I'd let you know; maybe you should get your salary in cash,' he laughed.

The following Monday I went to the manager and resigned. He was somewhat philosophical – clearly he was getting used to this happening all around him. 'I was hoping you'd stay and help us get the place on its feet. The Company's position is not as hopeless as some make out; we've got plenty of re-insurance backing us,' he said. But I was not convinced and couldn't wait to get out of the place. I saw the week out, and by Friday night was once again unemployed. Over subsequent years I noted that Vanguard Insurance kept struggling along, being bought up by other firms, until they finally went out of business.

But in most areas in the 1950s it was easy to find a job – a buyer's market. I answered an ad for a clerical position at South Pacific Insurance Company in Queen Street and was successful. This was another strange, small-scale company, though very different in atmosphere from either of the other two. It was virtually a one-man show, despite the fifteen staff working in the office, plus several freelance sales reps. The boss was a tall, large-gutted Phil Silvers look-alike, who personally oversaw every decision the company took – settled claims, signed cheques, approved new business and underwriting proposals, appointed staff and kept an eye on the work rate in the office. Norman Stiles, sir, managing director, bottle-washer and chief whip, ably assisted by his fanatically devoted secretary Miss Beryl Charlton, built like a brick dunny, with dark German-helmet-style hair cut around a bullish, unsmiling face unscored by a single emotional experience in all her forty-six years of life in the south-eastern suburbs of Melbourne. Adoring and protective of her boss since she joined the company at the age of fifteen, Miss Charlton had been granted unassailable power in the management of the office, and woebetide anyone who crossed her or failed to attend the Christmas party she insisted on running every year. She was out to prove that the Company was a warm, caring, happy family, and anyone who disagreed was unceremoniously sacked.

At the Christmas party her *pièce de résistance* was a 'revue', performed by participants of her choosing, as self-appointed director of entertainment. I was roped in immediately, along with a couple of the prettier girls, a blokey mate and fellow Essendon supporter Barry Roe, and of course Miss Charlton, to be this year's *artistes*. Every Friday night at the Moorabbin Fire Station, where her widowed father was Fire Chief, we rehearsed, during which Miss Charlton directed exactly as she behaved around the office – like a Stasi *kommandant*. Naturally this included creating singing and dancing roles for herself, fully imagined as Mitzi Gaynor. Sharing a bottle of beer, Barry and I watched her in disbelief. If it weren't for the risk to our very jobs, we would happily have pulled out and been content to be spectators. But Miss Charlton insisted on my coming up with an acceptable solo act, and on Barry accompanying her in a performance of 'Younger Than Springtoime (sic)' from *South Pacific*, including the actions.

After rehearsal we took the two girls home in the Morris, and on our way digressed to a well-known spot off the Boulevarde down near the river. Since the two in the back were enthusiastically snogging, I encouraged the other girl, a pretty brunette called Jan Stirling, to join me in doing likewise. As young and inexperienced as myself, she felt oddly soft and floppy on my arm, so limp she might have been unconscious. I found this a bit off-putting, but continued on. She made it clear she didn't want to go any further than kissing, so after a while we motored off home. It was quite late – after midnight – when we pulled up in front of Jan's house, and suddenly a figure appeared out of the dark, wrenched open the car door and dragged Jan out onto the nature strip, where she overbalanced and fell onto one knee, and was struck a resounding smack across the side of her head, knocking her to the ground. 'Get in there you bitch!' a man's voice screamed. No word was said in my direction, but I nevertheless defiantly called out, 'Hey steady on – leave her alone.' Ignoring me the man was brutally dragging and pushing a terrified Jan into the house. The girl in the back of the car said tensely, 'Her father – he's a real bastard.' As we drove off I again couldn't resist another moment of defiance by winding down my window and calling out, 'Goodnight Jan,' but there was no reply, only silence from the darkened garden in front of the house. Her father hadn't even left a front light on for her see her way in, or had the decency to do his chastising inside in private; he had to stalk her in the dark, attack her in front of her friends, effect a total humiliation. A real bastard.

One morning in the office I am informed that someone is at the counter to see me. To my astonishment it is my old flame Margaret Kendrick, standing blonde and blushing, jiggling a pram with a baby in it. She says she has come to ask me for some advice about insurance. I know we both don't believe this, but I go along with the pretence, advising her briefly about the issue she has raised. 'How did you find me?' I say, impressed at the trouble she must have taken.

'I knew you'd gone to Transport and General Insurance Company, and when I rang there they told me you now worked here, so here I am.' She shrugs and angles her head, her hands open in the language of appeasement.

With half the office looking at us, no doubt noting the presence of the baby, I want to get them out of the place as soon as possible. I suggest we have lunch and she waits for me downstairs. Along with the pram and baby, we go to my favourite Italian café in The Causeway, where I ask what she has been doing since I last saw her, four years ago at the British United Shoe Machinery Company. She has grown rounder in the face and body, has lost much of the self-possession of earlier years. She is married, but separated, and it doesn't take much to see that she is unhappy. 'The last I knew, you were going steady with Chris Beale; what happened there?'

'Oh that didn't last; I dropped him very soon after you left. I had a couple of different boyfriends, and then I met Kevin.'

As she talks I wonder who was the first to take her virginity, to enjoy that perfect body, but of course I can't ask. Undoubtedly she has had plenty of sexual experience by now, unlike myself. I am moved to probe a little.

'How old is the baby?'

'He's nearly two.'

Some quick mental calculation tells me that she must have become pregnant within a year after I last saw her, and that it was her probable reason for marrying. How ironic, I think, that we broke up, ostensibly because I touched her breast, suggesting I moved sexually too quickly, when within months she was giving all of herself up to this Kevin.

'What does Kevin do?' I say.

'He drives a truck.'

An image passes through my mind of a muscular, good-looking tearaway who won't take no for an answer, one of the tribe I knew in my factory days, treating her as something merely to fuck. Whereas I who had adored her as some goddess, would have done anything for her, made any sacrifice, wasn't good enough to touch her. Now I am torn between pity and self-righteous contempt for her, the moralistic wimp's last refuge. In the silence that falls between us I am tempted to dish out some form of punishment. I tell myself that by being unresponsive I can hurt her, maybe even force her into saying what her real reason is for coming to see me, knowing it certainly isn't insurance advice, but to ask for my forgiveness. She might even beg me to take her back. But the fact is there is something else to our silence, something more basic, which I am in this moment not admitting. And that is that we do not – neither of us – know how to speak about our situation or our true feelings. We are made dumb by youth. My only recourse is to wish for her humiliation.

As if reading my mind, she says, 'I am sorry I broke with you the way I did. I know it must have hurt you.'

This seems to leave an opening for some sort of reconciliation. But I am committed to self-defence, and merely say, 'I'm over it now – don't worry about it.'

She looks long at me with those huge, blue glittering eyes; anyone might think she is on the verge of breaking down, and maybe she is, but all I will admit is that she is acting dumb, doing her own kind of hanging back, waiting for me to launch a rescue, to get her out of this misery and bring back the happy confidence she once felt when we spent that day at the Show together. For a moment my ego is tempted, is on the verge of playing the hero, until I remember the fact of the baby. A situation projects itself, of me in a suburban house coming home to her and another man's child every night, trying to pretend we are a happy couple when it is based on a fraud, and maybe suffering constant harassment from a bloody-minded Kevin, and I recoil at the prospect, the squalor of it all. So I do not make the move.

'I must be getting back soon,' I say, 'I'll chase up that insurance matter for you – give me your address and I'll write.' And in that moment the spirit of our meeting has passed. She writes a Preston address down on a scrap of paper, gives it to me; we bring things to a close and go our separate ways. I am sad, feel deep regret and pity for her unhappiness, but I know we will never see each other again. I can't quite shake the sense of failure and cowardice that I know I showed throughout the meeting.

The small-scale, domestic feel of South Pacific Insurance Company was both amusing and suffocating. It was not a job I could take seriously. At the Christmas 'revue' Barry Roe and I tried to ignore the embarrassing fatuousness of it all. Beryl Charlton insisted on performing 'There Was I Waiting at the

Church', in the belief that she was achieving burlesque, when in fact the whole event was nothing short of the Return of the Repressed. I even gave a rendition of 'Stand Up and Fight' from *Carmen Jones*, and forever wished I hadn't. Yet somehow the grotesquerie of all this was a perfect expression of the absurdity my life was becoming; I was desperate for something of consequence to happen; everything was drifting, pointless, directionless, ridiculous.

Happily, I got a call from Bob Haberfield, who suggested we went for a Chinese meal together. He picked me up in his new red Ford 'Zephyr', and we went to a restaurant off Little Bourke Street. Months of not seeing each other had made us talkative, eager companions. He ordered steamed duck in a mould, which was like a pudding of compressed filleted duck and bean shoots turned out of a basin, with gravy running over it, plus steamed vegetables and rice, followed by Chinese pickles, lychees and ice-cream. It was all new and wondrous to me, part of Bob's greater knowledge of the world. He had left the advertising agency and was now working as a freelance commercial artist, with his own office and studio in the city. As well as this, he sang with big bands at several of the suburban town hall Saturday night dances. Frank Sinatra was a big influence on him. I resolved to go along and hear him.

Without intending to, I find myself one day visiting Nair in North Melbourne. I haven't seen her now for some years, and I happen to be driving along Queensberry Street not far from her house, when I get the idea to drop in. Dressed in a light grey suit of which I am particularly proud, and driving my beloved Morris Minor, I want to show off, and who better to appreciate my man-about-town successful look than my impressionable, devoted and utterly impoverished grandmother. I park right in front of the doorway beside 'uncle' Garn's boot repair shop, and approaching I see the shop-front window is covered on the inside with old newspapers. Nair's door is ajar, so I tentatively push it open, put my head in and make the sound 'Ooh-ooh'. 'Come in,' her voice resounds along the dark corridor; it takes a minute or two before my eyes adjust enough to see the doorway into the lounge room. This room is also in total darkness, which is made worse by the light from the window out in the kitchen having a blinding effect as I stand peering into the dark. I can't see Nair anywhere; she is not at the kitchen table, which I can see from where I stand in the lounge. Suddenly I am aware that she is in this room, her presence suggested by a faint stirring in the corner where there is usually a club lounge chair. Then she speaks. 'Who's that? Oh my God, is that you Frank?'

I am alarmed. *Frank? My father?*

'No, it's Garry; thought I'd drop in and see you.'

'Garry? Jesus bloody Christ you gave me a fright. I thought it was your father. Standing there in that grey suit, you look like his spitting image. Oh luvvy, you gave me a turn; don't ever do that to me again.'

Poor Nair, having a momentary delusion, forgetting the dreadful reality that we all found so hard to face those many years ago. Her feelings hadn't entered my mind until that moment, but now I see that my father's death must have been just as hard for her, his mother, as it was for me. Also, I hadn't realised that I had grown so much to resemble my father.

'Sit down love,' she says, 'do you want a cup of tea?'

'No, I'm not stopping; did you know the front door wasn't shut?'

'Bob Campbell left it open; he's gone up to Erroll Street for some cigarettes. He'll be pleased to see you.'

But I don't especially want to see him, I think to myself. Instead of waiting for me to find a seat in the lounge room, she gets up from her chair and shuffles slipper-footed ahead into the kitchen, where she picks up the kettle, fills it at the tap on the outside landing, goes back and puts it back on the stove, turns on the gas and clicks the gas gun repeatedly without effect for what seems an eternity until the hissing gas ignites with a loud 'pop', then she shuffles over to sit in her old place at the kitchen table, still covered in its now threadbare green baize cloth with the fringing. She isn't the only one seeing ghosts. I look around and recall what it was like years ago, feel a tinge of sadness at the vivid absences – no Johnny, no Dickie, no signs of their presence, such as comics on the window seat, football photos pinned up or boys' stuff lying about. The picture of Don Bradman is still on the wall beside the gas stove, though badly faded. This sudden awareness of the past has a feeling of newness about it, the freshness of the unfamiliar; is it the first time I have looked back? The first time I have reflected on a past already slipping from my grasp, bedding down in the archive of memory? Until now, everything seemed to just happen, one thing after another, all continuous as yesterday flowed into today and the day before into yesterday. But now there is a break, a separation into Then and Now, a sense that everyone and everything is different from what it once was.

'Where's Uncle Alec?'

'He's crook. In bed upstairs love.

'What's wrong?'

'It's his bronicals again. I'll go up and see if he's okay soon; better still, do you want go up and see him? You can ask him if he wants anything while you're there.'

I open the four panel door to the stairs. There is no light, and the long, steep staircase is in darkness, with a dim mist of daylight at the top. I feel for the banister and guide myself up. The room on the immediate right of the landing is their bedroom, which has one narrow window, covered now by a heavy curtain, so this is another space in gloom. I can hear Uncle Alec's heavy rasping breaths as I stand in the doorway. His illness is not just bronchitis, of course, despite the vague inclusiveness of the term that they and others have used for many years: it is lung damage from inhaling chlorine gas on the Western Front forty years ago, plus emphysema from a lifetime of smoking. His cough is terrible and incurable.

'Is that you Bob?' says Alec, between breaths.

'No, it's Garry.'

There is a pause while the information sinks in.

'Garry? Thelma's Garry?'

He would say Thelma's Garry because *her* memory is the one that has stuck, *her* fresh-faced smile that lit up those gloomy rooms back then, he would not say Frank's Garry because Frank was not his own, not his family to encroach upon, not his right; he knows Nair likes him to keep out of that part of her life.

'Yes. How're you feeling?'

'Good,' says Alec in a barely audible croak, 'turn on the light.' (Why do we always say good when we're not?)

I reach for the old brass switch, which moves unresisting and loose under my forefinger. A dim, probably 25 watt bulb comes on, revealing crumpled blankets hanging off the foot of the heavy timber bed, various items of clothing strewn about the floor, a shit-brown painted chest of drawers in the corner with a blue and white statue of the Virgin on it, a small bedside table covered in medicine bottles, matches, papers, a half-empty green packet of 'Havelock' ready-rubbed tobacco. The walls are covered in an orangy-pink wallpaper, and the only picture in view is a washed-out, slightly skewed 'Sacred Heart' print of Christ with bright lines radiating from a red stylised heart on his chest. Alec is on his back under nothing but a white sheet, takes an arm out and waves me forward. The room is heavy with human body smell, and I just notice the whiteness of the po beside the bed before my foot kicks it. Nevertheless, I am hit by a powerful stink of stale urine rising from it.

'Nair wants to know if you need anything.'

'Tell her I'll have a cup of tea in a while,' he says after clearing his throat, and his voice takes on that deep, sonorous bass that has been his trademark all his life. 'Anyway, let's look at you. It must be years. You've left school then?' He pushes himself up the bed a little, forcing the pillow to lift his head enough to allow eye contact between us. His is still the stretched, horse-faced, long-nosed, mask I have always known and liked, only older, more than ever ravaged by deep vertical creases in his cheeks from above his eyes all the way down to his chin. He still has a head of thick dark steel-wool hair. His teeth are in a glass on the bedside table.

'Yeah, left a few years ago. I'm working in Insurance.'

'Thought you were going to be a jockey!' and the air splits with a crackle like breaking ice; it is Alec's laughter, released from his throat.

'I got too big.' I want to steer our talk away from our shared past, a distant idyll in my heart that is, under present circumstances, too difficult and too painful to revisit. I say, 'I suppose you're off work now?'

'Retired. On the pension. Do you play any sport?'

'Yeah, I play cricket, a bit of football in the winter.'

'North are still hopeless; maybe you should go down and have a run with them.' He isn't totally unserious. I laugh to myself at his failure to distinguish between fancy and reality – a family trait; I must be good quality because I'm family.

'Anyway Uncle Alec, I'd better get off now; good seeing you. Hope you're better soon ...'

'Oh, I'll be right ... but listen, do us a favour Gazz ...' And here he suddenly explodes into a fearful, phlegm-rattling cough, and I wait in anxious suspense while convulsions rack his chest and lungs and airways until he finally hawks and spits spitefully into a crumpled handkerchief, and finally can draw breath and fix me with eyes brimming liquid from the strain. He extends an arm and points to the floor.

'Take that down and empty it in the lavatory for Nair will you? It's hard for her to get down the stairs with it.'

'Sure,' I say nonchalantly, but am dreading it. As I expected, the po is not only heavy and full with Alec's (and Nair's?) pee, but the smell rises even more pungently as I lift it closer to my nose and move slowly and carefully across the room so as not to spill the deep yellow contents, which are only millimetres from the rim. Then as I near the top of the stairs, Alec calls, 'Can you get the light?' The po is too heavy to hold in one hand, so I place it on the floor of the landing while I switch off the light, then resume my mission, letting myself down each step with careful concentration, down into the dark area of the lower staircase, holding the po as steady as I can, though I think I have already heard one or two splashes onto the stairs, and I can feel one of my thumbs getting wet from curling over the rim. But as I reach the door at the bottom of the stairs I realise I will have to place the po on a step while I free a hand to open the door, and in doing this I again think some of the liquid has spilled out. Once down and in the kitchen I am at least on a level floor, and Nair greets and watches me with a surprised smirk on her face as I cross the room. 'Oooh you're a good boy,' she says, 'you can come here anytime.' I reach the outside landing, where stands the only tap and sink in the house, and consider for a moment emptying the po into the sink, but Nair seems to have read my mind, and calls, 'Out in the lavvy sweetheart; otherwise it stinks out the trap at the bottom.' I see what she means when I negotiate the outside steps now, for at the bottom I can see that the drainpipe empties into an open gully trap, which they have the sense to keep clean and free from collected matter. So I cross the yard with my burden to the small outside dunny, which Uncle Alec has kept spotless and freshly kalsomined inside and out all the years they have lived there, and I empty the pee with a deep 'slosh' into the bowl. I reflect: this is what they have taken for granted all these years; they have no inside toilet, no taps or sink in the kitchen area, and no inside bathroom or laundry. The bathroom and laundry are even farther down the yard than the toilet – a shed, once, when I was a child, burned to the ground by a fire in the wood-fuelled copper, now rebuilt to a quite serviceable standard, but built hard up against the back fence, an inconvenient walk from the house. It contains a bath with a shower over it, and a small laundry with an electric twin-tub washing machine. The whole journey has taken me down the long staircase, across the kitchen, down the outside steps (at least six) right to the end of the completely open yard. I tell myself this is the kind of thing the people around here have had to put up with for many generations.

When I am back in the kitchen Nair says 'Do you want a cuppa?'

'No, I won't stay. I have to be getting off.'

'How's your mother? She never comes to see us any more, now that she's married to Dick. Too good for us, is she?' she laughs.

'She's pretty busy these days – she has to work full time since Dick gave up butchering.'

'What, he's bludgin' off your mum now?'

I can't think what to say. What Nair has said strikes a chord, and I realise it is what has been running through my own mind – that Richard has gutlessly become unemployed and therefore my mother has to bring in the money now.

'He's applying for jobs closer to home,' I say. 'Anyway, come and see my car.'

Nair accompanies me out the front and we look at the Morris.

'Aw, that's very posh,' says Nair, 'that's nearly *new*!' In Nair's frame of reference, the idea of owning a brand-new car is the ultimate success, proof of riches beyond imagining, and which no-one in the family could ever hope to possess. But here, before her very eyes, her grandson has come closer to it than anyone else, and she radiates pride and joy that I have been the first to do it. No matter that she has never owned much more than the clothes on her back, she seems not to possess the slightest trace of envy or self-pity. Desire for more money, for comforts, yes, resentment of the rich, yes, in a defiant, perfectly justifiable way; but not that abject, mean-spirited envy that is so self-destructive. She has always been too proud to lose either her sense of humour or her ability to celebrate others' good fortune.

As I open my car door, Bob Campbell hoves into sight coming down Queensberry Street. He calls to us in his huge baritone, and as he draws near it is noticeable that his navy suit and waistcoat, his bowler hat and boots, are even shabbier and dirtier than ever. Bob hasn't recognised who is standing beside the car at first, and Nair clarifies things: 'Whaddya think of Garry's new car,' she boasts, 'it's fully paid for!'

Bob Campbell cocks his head as he eyes the car circumspectly. 'Where's *wooky*?' he laughs, handing Nair two unopened packets of Turf cigarettes, and dutifully filling her open hand with the change of a pound.

Driving off, I exchange waves with them both, standing there on the footpath in front of Uncle Garn's shop, now dead and blind with its newspaper coverings. I curse to myself that I forgot to ask what had happened to Uncle Garn, and whether or not it has implications for their future security renting his house. Maybe I will call back in the near future to check it out. Maybe.

6

IT IS AROUND THIS TIME that I acquire my first steady girlfriend. Loretta. We had in fact spoken about a year earlier, when she'd walked past as I worked on the wheel of the Hillman in front of my house. I looked up and saw this tall, slim blonde with a fetching smile and friendly manner, who candidly stopped to have a chat. Now she does it again, when I am mowing the front lawn; I like to think she has taken the route past my house in the deliberate hope of finding me there, because it is not on the direct route to her house two streets away. And now that I have a decent car in the Morris, I am emboldened to ask her out; she agrees to go to the drive-in cinema with me. When I arrive at her house, she skips out fresh and sparkling in white matador pants and a matelot top, a pink band holding the blonde hair from her forehead; she might have been the model for today's Barbie dolls. She introduces me to her parents and younger brother, and off we go, my confidence soaring. On the car radio Buddy Holly's 'Not Fade Away' is playing. 'Oh I love this,' she screams, and reaches for the knob to turn it up, making cute little 'Ump dah, ump dah, umpah dah dah' sounds, and shifting her hips sideways in the seat next to me in sexy little movements. I think she looks as edible as a lollypop. At the drive-in we kiss and cuddle and talk; she has a good sense of humour, is bright, open-minded, open-hearted. She works as a laboratory assistant at the Commonwealth Serum Laboratories in Parkville, and tells me funny, risqué stories of the chemists at work. It's late by the time the double feature finishes, so I take her straight home. We part at her front gate, happy in the knowledge that it has all been the start of something, though just exactly what and for how long we aren't certain. And after that first night we spend all our free time together, at the pictures, going to dances, especially the new kind of 'casual dances' at fashionable clubs near the city, or just to the beach or for walks. She takes me completely away from my mates and into a world of smarter, more educated types with the latest taste in music and clothes, although she is from the same background as myself – Catholic and Housing Commission. What this suggests to me is that we are not bound by the choices we have made before, that we can simply walk out on them. This feels liberating.

Loretta's mother, unfortunately, is a nut case, a toothy crone with a spiteful tongue, who spends most of her time watching television. She has made it clear that she doesn't like me. It is hard to credit a beautiful girl having a mother like that; could Loretta turn into her in later years, I wonder? God forbid. We arrived home from a dance late one night ravenously hungry, so Loretta looked in the fridge and found some leftover cold chicken, which we snacked on, with some coffee. I later learned her mother was so furious next morning when she discovered what we'd done that from then on she made sure to take any food, including the milk, out of the fridge before we got home. She kept it, Loretta told me, under her bed where we couldn't get at it. Nuts, for sure. Her father on the other hand is the exact opposite – quiet, laid-back, his head stuck in the newspaper, always makes brief, friendly chat with me. How he copes with a wife like that is an interesting question. My mother seems to like Loretta, calls her 'dear', and treats her as part of our family.

We go out with other couples, including Bob and his girlfriend Varna. Loretta does not take to Bob, seems out of her depth with him, and Varna too for that matter, who she seems to regard as a threat. She is happier with Ron Bowden's recently acquired steady girlfriend – another tall, beautiful creature-called Yvonne. All that summer we make up a regular foursome, go to the beach often, to the Embers night club, to casual dances, to the motor races. Ron and I proudly watch our girls in their new tight 'pedal-pusher' slacks and dazzling tops, with their shoulder length hair puffed and held in place by spray. Or in their two-piece swimsuits and sunglasses, playing, lolling on the sand, their bodies deepening to the colour of biscuit, tempting to caress. They do what women do – make well-planned picnic lunches, feed us, attend to us, talk about us proprietorially within earshot. Sometimes we all talk cars, sport, movies, family; never books or politics. I look back now and reflect on the old black and white photographs we took: how certain we were of our own place in the world, how satisfied with our style, how eager with our appetites, and how oblivious to our limitations we seem. Youth in its peak hour, glowing, captive of its senses, forever hungry, unaware of its ephemerality. I hardly recognise us.

As I leave Loretta's house at night we snog on her front porch in the dark. We have been gradually getting closer to having sex, and eventually one night she slips down her pants and lets me enter her standing up. Because she is tall, we can manage it comfortably without me having to stand awkwardly or bend my knees. But it is fraught, tense, spoiled by our terror of pregnancy. I squirt into my hand, an inefficient receptacle, the drips staining the concrete floor. I guess her mother will see them when she cleans the porch. What we are doing is called *coitus interruptus*, Loretta tells me. On the way home my warm loins remind me that, officially, I am no longer a virgin, but for such a landmark in life it has hardly been a gala event. Yet it is better than masturbating, and certainly better than nothing. '*Coitus interruptus*' I repeat, walking along a moonlit Cook Street, my second form familiarity with Latin giving me a certain delight in the precision and elegance of the phrase.

I was at this point dimly aware that there were such things as university degrees and university education, though so far I had not met anyone, or at least not talked with anyone, who had done this, and there was no idea in my head about attempting it myself. Insurance studies, which were brief and minor, offered no challenge. I knew I had better than average abilities, and felt a growing need to test them. With this in mind, I began attending a coaching class way out in East Malvern, which again I learned of from John Cloney (he was a constant source of information), and we went together in the Morris. The coach was a retired teacher who gave classes in his garage, and who reduced the curriculum for the Leaving Certificate to the bare basics required to pass the examination. I wondered what good it might do me to pass, but I was nevertheless determined to find out.

An advertisement for vocational guidance assessment at the Royal Melbourne Technical College took my eye, so I made an appointment. Walking up Lonsdale Street on the way to the College a strange thing happened. I felt a tug at my sleeve, and it was Arnold Winton, the same-as-ever rimless glasses, the hopsack suit, the professorial stoop, and we started chatting. He asked what I was doing. I considered telling him about the test I had signed up for, but didn't. Instead I started a bitter, depressive and completely gratuitous complaint about my prospects in a world that was closing me out.

'What's the point in trying?' I said.

'What's the problem?' he asked. And here is where I came out with something I had never even thought of before, and had no idea where it came from or why I said it.

'Oh, you know – everything really. There doesn't seem to be much likelihood of my getting anywhere. I mean, let's face it, the Jews control everything in the city now, and if you're not on the inside you haven't got a chance.'

It was as if another mind had taken over and was using my voice. I thought I noticed Arnold give a slight wince, while keeping a steady gaze ahead, and making no reply. We paused for the traffic lights at Swanston Street, and Arnold said, 'I'm going straight ahead here.' I wished he wasn't, I wished I could keep talking with him and find out how to take back what I'd just said, or at least put it in some explanatory context that made it make sense, so that he wouldn't think badly of me. But it was hopeless; I'd said it now, and could've bitten my tongue off, and there was no way to undo the damage.

'I'm heading up to RMIT,' I said, and we nodded our goodbyes. As I walked on I kept thinking what an appalling thing I'd said. My cheeks burned with shame and self-disgust. Why didn't I remember that Arnold is Jewish? That it would be taken as a direct insult? And what the hell did I know about the 'city' and who ran it? The answer is nothing, I knew nothing. I had represented myself as a bigot, a know-all, a fool, and had no doubt hurt a decent man, a man I had real fondness and respect for. What was I trying to do, destroy myself and everything good along with me?

I proceeded on to RMIT, where the psychologist running the program, an odd-looking man of stick thinness, with a bald, skull-like head and jaw, asked, 'What is your present job?'

'Insurance clerk; I want to see if I have the capacity to be something better.'

'Good, well just fill out these forms, and we'll put you through various tests – I've just acquired this new speed-reading machine, so you can start out on that.'

For several evenings I went along and did comprehension, mathematical, cognition tests, most of which were box-ticking or puzzle-solving. Nothing requiring written descriptions or argument. The psychologist said to come back the following week, when he would reveal the results and advise me accordingly. The tests had measured only certain aspects of my abilities, not my strongest ones, but I was looking forward to the report. On the day, I sat across the table tensely waiting for the verdict, and after describing some of the particulars of the results, the psychologist summed me up:

'… So far as vocational advice goes, I can tell you that these results suggest that you are not likely to succeed in getting a university degree, though you could benefit from some kind of further study. The kind of work you are most suited for would be at lower professional level, office work, that kind of thing. Something like, say, an insurance clerk …'

I couldn't believe my ears, and laughed out loud at the irony: after all that testing, I found I was capable only of staying where I was. I had a strong suspicion the psychologist did not even remember that I was already an insurance clerk, but that hardly mattered: if that was what the tests showed, maybe I was not as good as I'd thought. I left the building feeling depressed and trapped; how foolish was my ambition to go beyond what I was, to get out of this prison of dullness, of a working life of predictable routines? How now could I find a future worth pursuing?

New fashions are coming in, and the choices young people make define their social identity. Most of the teenagers in my Housing Commission area have for some years dressed in 'bodgie' or 'rocker' style, with longish hair 'Brylcreemed' down and combed into a 'duck's arse' at the back with a curl hanging over the centre of the forehead, James Dean style. Alan Craig, Teddy Walker, even Jeff Conley, have adopted this style. They wear black stovepipe trousers and zip-up jackets with a thread of glint, and black pointy-toed shoes. These are the preferences of the less-educated, the tradesmen and semi-skilled workers, those with no social ambition. West Ivanhoe, West Heidelberg, the inner-city suburbs of Collingwood, Fitzroy, Richmond, tend to be dominated by these types. They drive FJ Holdens or, if they can afford it, one of the big Fords.

I do not like this style, nor does Ron Bowden nor Bob. We like the new 'ivy league' clothes – striped shirts with button-down collars, casual slacks and bulky fishnet pullovers worn over the shoulders with the sleeves tied round the neck. On our feet are suede desert boots, and we have 'college boy' haircuts, short all over and kept dry and natural. These are signifiers of the superior taste of middle-class, professional or arty types, especially university and private school students. Like them, I would, if I could afford it, own an MG sports car or Volkswagen 'Beetle', but something, not just the money, holds me back. Somehow, even if I could afford it, it would feel pretentious, too assertive a statement of difference, would lay me open to resentment from my Housing Commission friends and their families. Something like class betrayal. So I have my Morris minor, and Ron has traded-in the Singer for a black, second-hand Holden FX.

There is a third group whose style goes back several years, before new fashions began to be big business. The young men, just like their fathers and older brothers, still depend on the suit or the sports coat and slacks as their basic clothing, the latter without a tie and the shirt collar worn outside the coat. If they are too hot they simply take off their coats and roll up their sleeves, showing their braces, or if they are too cold they wear a tight pullover under their suit coat or jacket. They wear polished shoes at all times, and their hair parted on the side with a front wave, Bing Crosby style. The clothing stores still cater for this style, but it is not fashionable, not part of the new movement catching all the attention.

The entertainment the three groups prefer also helps separate them; generally, the first group likes rock music such as Bill Haley and the Comets,

Buddy Holly, Elvis Presley, Little Richard, Patti Page, Teresa Brewer and their kind. They dance 'rock and roll' style at parties, or some local venues, twirling the girls under their arms, leaning back on each others' grip, pumping hands and feet in a high-energy swing. The 'ivy league' crowd prefer the new 'folk' and jazz type groups – The Kingston Trio, Pat Boone, The Four Lads, Jimmy Rodgers, and Duke Ellington, Henry Mancini, and of course 'cool' exponents like George Shearing, Peggy Lee and Dave Brubeck. They frequent the 'casual dance clubs like Keyboard and Powerhouse and the 431 Club in St Kilda Road, and dance in the new 'minimalist' casual style of barely holding onto your partner, or else if it is your girlfriend, in an intimate embrace, shuffling almost unnoticeably together on a darkened dance floor. The less fashion-bound, the third group, still listen to Frank Sinatra, Bing Crosby, Perry Como, Guy Mitchell and Swing groups, and do their dancing to big bands in the suburban Town Halls, which hold regular Saturday night performances. This is traditional 'ballroom' dancing, both modern and old-time. Of course there is a lot of overlapping of these groups, and they are often seen on each other's 'territory', though not many 'college' types would be seen dead at a rocker's dance.

With Loretta's encouragement – she is now training as a laboratory technician – I answer an ad for a position as a trainee chemist at William Angliss the meat processors, a huge conglomeration in Footscray near the Newmarket abattoirs. They have a small laboratory which exercises control of the food processing – canning, margarine, cured meats. I attend an interview with the chief chemist, Mr Bell, a round-faced Englishman with a very precise manner, who does not seem concerned at my lack of scientific background and qualifications.

'We will train you in food chemistry techniques; all we require of you is that you are willing to learn, and to study for a diploma in chemistry part-time, for which we'll give you a half-day study-leave per week.'

The salary is less than I am making currently, but the work seems interesting and provides the kind of intellectual possibilities that I am looking for, and if I eventually became a qualified chemist I would earn very good money indeed. Besides, I know it will impress Loretta. So once again I change jobs – giving Norman Stiles notice is an enjoyable moment – and I believe that I have finally escaped the world of insurance for good. No more suits and ties, no more 'city culture', which has long lost its mystique for me, as it eventually does for many who are not among the small percentage making it to the upper echelons. From now it is casual wear travelling to work and school, and a white chemist's coat during working hours. I will wear it with an absurd and unwarranted pride, and think myself a new type of man: a scientist, a man of knowledge, in a world apart from the manoeuvrings of status and ambition. All that is needed is a change of appearance and type of work, and you can become a completely different person.

Because the route to the new job in Footscray takes me through Parkville, it is convenient to take Loretta with me in the mornings and drop her at the CSL. This is enjoyable and helps bring us closer together. But it all begins to go awry when the Morris begins to give starter trouble. The problem is not just a weak battery – the electric fuel pump and the starter motor are behaving unreliably too, especially on cold mornings, and their failure means milking the battery flat trying to start up. So every few days – far too often for her liking – Loretta has to help me push the car down Valentine Street to turn the motor over. Sometimes it takes hundreds of yards and several attempts, with her pushing on her own while I operate the clutch and accelerator. One rainy morning she falls flat on her face in the road, and when I drive back she is standing covered in wet dirt, her knees bleeding, tears of pain and anger rolling down her cheeks.

'Why don't you get a new battery?' she screams at me.

'It wouldn't make any difference; the battery would still go flat.'

'Well why don't you get it fixed?' she groans.

'Can't afford it,' I shrug.

'I'll pay,' she says. But when I get a quote for the job, it will run into hundreds of pounds. I have lost my faith in the Morris, and besides I am struggling to manage on my lower wage, and with the added expenses of taking her out, I am living beyond my limited means. I think maybe I should sell the Morris and buy something more reliable and economical.

Cricket is still important to me, and I now play a much more mature game. I am the team's opening batsman, a role I enjoy, and I regularly make quick runs and get the team off to a good start. As a bowler I have dropped my medium pacers and am usually called on to bowl spin – left-arm 'chinamen' – which are generally expensive but on occasions, when the ball is coming out right, can take out several good opposition batsmen cheaply. Every Saturday I clean and whiten my cricket boots, oil my bat, put on clean nicely pressed cream trousers and shirt, carry a cream pullover and green cap, and join my teammates at one of the many local playing grounds in the Heidelberg district. Some of the grounds are windswept and brown-grassed, exposed to glare and hot sun that burns the skin and dries the mouth, but others are picturesque green swards in little sheltered valleys, and at these I can think of no better way to spend a sunny afternoon than standing at first slip or even deep in the outfield listening for the sweet 'dock' sound of the ball coming off the middle of the bat, the songs of magpies in the tall gums ringing across the ground. And there is nothing more thrilling than being alone at the crease, taking guard against a fast bowler with the new ball. Occasionally rain and cold wind make me think otherwise, especially when the hard ball strikes ice-cold fingers, or the rain collects on my spectacles (recently I was diagnosed with myopia, and need glasses to see clearly farther away than ten yards). Cricket is something I have stayed faithful to, is a separate interest from either my car-oriented mates or Bob Haberfield. I barely mention it to them, keep my love of it to myself.

Loretta often goes along with me to the matches, helps the 'ladies' serve afternoon tea of cheese and tomato sandwiches, home-made cream sponges, lemon slices and scones washed down with a cup of strong hot tea. She likes the social side of it, and is popular with my teammates, but like my other friends, does not really understand the rituals and culture of cricket; nor do any of them understand the language and specialised knowledge required to play and talk about the game with any authenticity. This is still largely a male preserve, but only for those who caught the bug early enough.

The chemistry idea seemed to work out for a while, and I certainly enjoyed the work in the laboratory, with its line-up of interesting and largely agreeable males. There was Robert, a well-qualified, intelligent, cheerful man in his thirties, who probably had a bright future in Industrial Chemistry administration, and Mark, a student in his early twenties in the final year of his Chemistry diploma, who painted abstract pictures as a hobby. Then there were two recent migrants, Jaroslav Bulka, a fiery Ukrainian of stereotypical Slavic bearing, and a tall, professorial German doctor whose qualifications were not recognised by the medical authorities, and who therefore had to accept the humbler role of food analyst, which Joe did with a certain dignified resentment. Mr Bulka and Joe were at constant loggerheads over just about everything, and yet they maintained an intense relationship that bound them together emotionally, politically, culturally and linguistically in a permanent state of love-hate tension. For instance, they both loved chess, and played each other constantly. The chessboard would be set up on a side bench, and they would play throughout the day, returning to their workbenches between moves, and one game might take the whole day. Mr Bulka liked mischief, and would sing songs of gentle mockery in Russian about his rival: to the tune of 'O Tannenbaum' he would sing,

O Trumbulunka Meester Joe,

He make me schlagen, thet I know.

The recent history of their two countries lay darkly behind their banter, though neither would raise the subject directly, and both were making an effort to be good Australians over and above their differences. But Mr Bulka's persistent baiting sorely tested Joe's patience, and he rarely smiled.

Everyone in the laboratory made allowances for my inexperience in science, though down in the factory areas it was a different matter. Twice a week I would walk through the processing sheds collecting samples for analysis, once through the canning section and once through the bacon section, where I took samples of the brine. Nearly all the canning work was done by women, many of them migrants, large, peasant stock, rough and bawdy. The moment I appeared in my white coat their derisive whistles and catcalls greeted my ears, though some of them seemed to be suggesting I might like to sample an offering of theirs behind the conveying machines, out of sight. Mark joked to me that the going rate was five shillings. I tried to laugh with the women, though I was scared of them and always careful not to get too close, and never hung about longer than I needed to, hurrying back to the laboratory with my fussy little samples.

But after a few months I began to doubt my future in chemistry. For one thing, I was not enjoying the part-time study at the Royal Melbourne Technical College. Bored out of my mind while the maths teacher droned on about equations, writing dozens of them on the blackboard for the class to solve, giving the most dreary and opaque explanations of method, I knew I could never get through the heavy program of maths required over six years in order to get a diploma. Similarly I could not grasp physics, though I liked chemistry. After a couple of months I dropped out of the classes, though I kept up the Leaving coaching, with my gaze set firmly on the exams in December. I resolved to resign from Angliss' at the end of the year and look for something else. Loretta was disappointed in me, and it might have been one more cause of things going badly between us. She had several reasons for becoming disillusioned. I finally decided to sell the Morris, luckily finding a buyer who paid what I'd bought it for, and hit upon the idea of a Vespa motor scooter. For a while it was fun – I certainly enjoyed riding it – but she never liked it. Riding it was cold, blew her hair all over the place, and when it rained we got soaked. I came off it a few times, luckily not when she was with me, and once I was leading a swarm of cars around a bend in South Melbourne when my front wheel got caught in the tramline, and I was spilled onto the road. The traffic parted and went round me as if I were a traffic cop, but I was terrified.

Another thing that upset her was my recent talk about my future. Education had begun to look more and more the answer to my needs, and I was growing more interested in pursuing it. Somewhere, possibly through my coaching class, I got the idea of becoming a teacher, and wrote off for the brochures. This would require me to go to university and teacher's college, but the only way I could do this was to gain a teaching bursary with the Education Department, which if I obtained matriculation would pay my fees and provide an allowance while I studied, and committing me to teaching for at least two years. I thought I might like to do it at the Ballarat Teacher's College. When I mentioned this Loretta burst into tears. 'What about us?' she said, 'When would I see you?' It hadn't occurred to me to put our relationship before anything else; I had assumed she wanted me to find out what sort of work would make me happy, and that we would build our future around that. We had certainly begun talking, in a casual, indefinite way, about marriage.

In retrospect it is clear that my feelings for her were confused. When she accused me of taking her for granted, she was right; that was exactly what I did, selfishly, presumptuously expecting her to fit in with *my* plans. At the same time I was deeply troubled by our relationship, especially the sex. The ease with which we had overcome all that mystique and anxiety about losing our virginity had hardly registered on us. Somehow we had just gradually fallen into it, and now I could think of myself as a sexually active being, whatever the value of that was, I wanted it to have some sort of meaning. Increasingly she wanted our sex to be total; she would encourage me into situations where we could 'let ourselves go', such as on my bed when no-one was home one Sunday, though neither of us raised the question of contraception, and on several occasions we both waited anxiously for her to report on an alarmingly late menstrual period. Some of this anxiety was undoubtedly Catholic guilt, for I had never really liberated myself from that aspect of my Christian Brothers' upbringing, but it was also fear that Loretta and I were flirting dangerously with Chance, and in a classic case of bad faith were simply allowing Chance to determine our future for us. As with so many young people around us in those days before the Pill, pregnancy was allowed to decide the most important choices of our lives. I did not want this. Did she? We couldn't talk about it – rational discussion, or even any discussion, seemed beyond her on this matter. I decided to go to Confession and talk to the local priest about it; if I was lucky enough to strike a sympathetic, intelligent listener, I might reason through with him my doubts and uncertainties. In any case, there was no-one else I could approach.

Through all this, her mother was doing her utmost to drive a wedge between us, and undoubtedly pointing out to her my worthlessness, my selfishness, and my lack of feeling towards her and her family. To survive, we would need me to take over as the strong one in the relationship, to give her belief in my commitment to her. But I was in no state to do this. Essentially I was addicted to our little bouts of lovemaking on the front porch at night, torn between need and fear. Her parents must at least be suspecting, I thought, what with all the little stains on the concrete. On one occasion her father suddenly opened the front door on the pretext of putting out the milk bottles, though he did have the decency to cough as he did so. We froze in mid-coitus, aching to move, she shivering with fear, or was it climax, me rigidly attached to her while she nonchalantly spread her skirt to hide our loins. We smiled innocently at her father as he went back inside, but he probably guessed. There was in fact a lesson in all this tension and guilt, this feverish but unsatisfying pursuit of genital excitement, though it was a lesson I was either unable or unwilling to address, which was that I was uncertain about my true feelings for her. Play as we would at romance and sex and talk of marriage, I was in my heart not facing the fact that I was not committed to her. I wanted more than she offered, not just more out of the relationship, but more out of the life she envisaged we might live together. That, I feared, would suffocate me. Yet I was not ready to give her up; I still wanted what she did have, selfishly, onanistically, because it was convenient and for the moment it stroked my ego. And it was this conflict between desire and dissatisfaction that had me trapped in a state of desperate unhappiness, and in need of help.

The priest, a young man I'd never met, which is unsurprising since it was a good few years since I'd been inside a church, listened to my confession, and to my plea for advice as to how we should work out our future. He then launched into an angry outburst, hardly keeping his voice down enough to maintain our privacy within the walls of the confessional. 'Advice? What advice do you expect? You've insulted this girl! You've defiled her! You've ruined her for any other choice but to marry you! If you loved her, as you no doubt told her, you should have honoured her, you should have put her up on a pedestal. There is only one piece of advice I have for you: marry her straight away, and put an end to this foul behaviour. Now get out of here and say the Rosary twice for your penance, and I expect to hear of arrangements for your marriage in the near future!'

My reaction to this, once I was outside the church, surprised even myself. What a mistake that was, I thought. What a useless, mindless piece of doctrinaire bullshit that was. If I'd hoped for a reasoned response, I had forgotten the very factor that had driven me away from the Church in the first place – its insistence on the supremacy of authority over reason. Instinctively, for I had no intellectual training of my own, I knew that the priest and all he stood for was the enemy, the enemy of understanding, the enemy of creativity, the enemy of complexity, the enemy of independent thought. It had confirmed that the Church offered me nothing, and never would. I was finally finished with it.

When I told her I'd been to Confession, Loretta was aghast. 'You didn't mention my name did you? If my mother finds out, there'll be hell to pay. They know her at that church, they know us. What were you thinking?' Even if I'd been able to explain what I'd been thinking, I doubted she would have approved, or even understood.

As that winter of 1959 gives way to summer, the months ahead seem to promise much. My twenty-first birthday is approaching, I am healthy, slim, strong and athletic, and from some angles and in certain light might even be considered good-looking. I still live at home, and although my brother has his own circle of friends, we do play in the same cricket team. My half-sister Susan is a sweet, sensitive eight-year-old who has had her problems. For a while when I owned the Morris I would give her a lift to school in the mornings to keep her off the school bus, where she was being mercilessly taunted by a group of bullies, including her friend from next door, Carol Pinchbeck. I know Susan looks up to Ray and myself as big brothers who might protect her. While not much else about my family life is important to me, my mother is working hard, saving up with Richard to build a house of their own, a long-held dream. But I have little to do with them now, not in any spirit of conflict or dislike, simply I have my own life to work out, and they can offer me little help on how to do that.

7

FOR MY TWENTY-FIRST BIRTHDAY PARTY my mother and Richard take Susan to Grandma Spencer's for the night, and turn the house over to me and my friends. Loretta has organised the food, and I have bought in plenty of beer and soft drink. Ray and a couple of his mates are there, taking charge of playing the records on the radiogram, as is Bob, Ron and Yvonne, Barry Roe and a few of my friends from over in the Essendon area, with whom I sometimes go to football matches. Some of my cricket teammates are there, too. What emerges on this unhappy night is the realisation that my friends comprise disparate groups who have little in common, have had almost no contact with each other, and in fact as the evening proceeds I discover that they do not even like each other. I have foolishly presumed that the fact of being my friends somehow makes them a unity, and that they would all be drawn together in happy concordance around me. No such luck. The groups entrench themselves in separate parts of the house – some in the lounge, some in the kitchen, some outside – and tend to talk with only those they already know. As I pass from group to group I hear them criticising the others. 'Who is that fucken poser in the dark glasses?' says one of Barry Roe's mates, 'I can't stand *posers!*' He is referring to Bob, who has a bout of conjunctivitis and is wearing shades against light glare. Even though I feel protective towards him, I say nothing for fear of creating a scene.

One of the cricket team has a girlfriend who objects to anyone using bad language, and she complains to her boyfriend about one particular culprit. 'Listen mate, cut out the swearing in front of the girls will ya?' says the boyfriend.

'Who are you to tell anyone how to talk?' comes the reply, 'anyone doesn't like it they can piss off.' Only the intervention of cooler heads prevents a fight. Then the girl demands that she and her boyfriend leave, and I watch them slip out through the backyard without telling anyone. The first of the night's disappointments.

Also, the different groups like different music, and are constantly harassing Ray and his mates to play something else. In the chopping and changing several LPs get damaged, much to my anger and embarrassment, since they have been borrowed for the occasion. I'm probably going to have to replace them. But the worst event is the row between me and Loretta. It seems to come out of nowhere and to have no real cause. She believes I'm showing a too-obvious preference for

Bob, standing talking to him for long periods about things of no interest to others. Then she introduces me to a couple of friends from her workplace, a young woman and her boyfriend, who I believe I've been quite civil to despite talking to them only briefly before I have to rush off to attend to something. Soon after, Loretta confronts me.

'You were so *rude*,' she insists, 'just because they're my friends and not yours.'

Then when people start dancing to Buddy Holly she wants me to get up with her, but I put her off. 'I will later,' I say, turning back to joking with Barry Roe and his mates. I guess I was trying to give her a little payback for criticising me. The next thing I know is that she is standing in front of me with her duffle coat on and her bag in hand. 'I'm going home,' she says, dark fury in her eyes – large, gorgeous blue eyes under that precise, beautifully knitted brow. I try reasoning with her, and she looks like she's going to cry, but she nevertheless storms off.

Soon after, others begin to drift away as well, and though it is not yet midnight, there are only a few people left to eat the food – my brother and his mates, one of the cricketers, Ron and Yvonne if memory serves me right. They sit around munching sandwiches, cold cocktail frankfurts, badly sliced, disintegrated cake. Taking a large brown bottle of beer from the ice pile in the bath, I decide to make a concerted effort to get drunk, and swill the lot in quick time. Sitting on the front porch staring into the dark street I feel miserable and lonely. Twenty-one, I think, so what? What is so great about that? I don't know what I want, or who I want, or what I am. The world spins around me as if I am on a merry-go-round, a shiver through my body tells me I'm going to throw up, and I stagger over to the side fence so as to heave it all onto my mother's sweet-peas. My first real drunken chunder, I tell myself – something I'll always remember. Supporting myself against the fence with an outstretched arm, I am spitting the last foul threads of sick when suddenly, out of nowhere, Loretta is standing beside me in her duffle coat, a wry look on her face. 'I'm sorry,' she says, and helps me back over to the porch step, where we sit together. I put an arm around her and we stare out across the dark empty road to the street light on the corner. A soupy-toned piece called 'Canadian Sunset' wafts over the air from inside the house. 'Happy Birthday,' she says, and kisses me on the lips. I wonder if she can taste my vomit. I really do love her, I think, and hate it when we fight. After a while we hear sounds of tidying up from the kitchen, and we join two of the stay-behinds, washing dishes, putting away the leftover food. As we joke around and Loretta and I are good again, my spirits lift; at least something has happened to reduce the misery of a disastrous night. I'll never give another party, at least not with my present lot of friends.

There was a lesson in it though, one that I didn't see at the time. It actually gave a true indication of my unsettled state, that I was moving between different groups of friends trying to be loyal to them all, which seemed to demand that I adopt a different persona for each group. I was smartly blokey with Barry Roe and his mates, who lived up-market in Essendon, then I was trying not to abandon the innocent gaucherie of the local crowd, who in any case I had drifted away from when I started taking out Loretta, who in turn was taking me more into a kind of aspirational 'college' style of socialising, and finally there was the attraction to Bob and the intriguing possibilities of the world of Art that he promised. I was still a part of each of them, because I still didn't know who I was and what direction I should choose to go in. In fact, at that point in my life, I didn't even fully realise I had a choice.

I was cheered soon after Christmas by the news that I had passed the three Leaving subjects. Success must have spurred me on, because in January I sought out a little coaching college in the city, called Imperial Coaching, where I enrolled for what was then called the Adult Matriculation qualification. That is, if you were over twenty-one you could be admitted to university with a pass in three subjects, one of which had to be English. The college offered a limited range of subjects, mostly the humanities, which were taught by the Principal, a neatly suited and slightly fey man, and a retired girls' schoolteacher, Miss Lillian Scholes. English Expression and English Literature were her subjects, and the moment I sat in her class I was enchanted. There were no blackboards, no dreary equations or exercises to copy down, just her kindly tones and benevolent Segovia-like presence seated at the front row of bench tables, intimately facing the class of about ten students, engaging everyone in a shared, text-focussed discussion. Though she was somewhat hard of hearing and inclined to drool a little when she talked, what she imparted was a gold vein of deep learning – perceptive, fair-minded, sentimental, moralistic and irrepressibly enthusiastic. Under her guidance I discovered the republic of literature, from the eighteenth century artifices of Sheridan and Pope, to the daring, self-advertising glamour of Byron (with whom she was half in love), from Shelley's soaring imagination, and the prodigious openness of Keats' senses, and Emily Bronte's narrative mastery, to Hardy's fascination with female sexual power, and a whole world of dynamic human conflict in Shakespeare. She taught us clear-thinking and how to discern the faults, the rhetoric, the illogicalities, the tired clichés, the solecisms, the deceptions and many other traps in the English language I thought I knew and understood; never again would I take what I read at face value. An appetite for imaginative experience and critical argument had awoken in my mind and heart that would remain for life; if in later years I failed to absorb and practice all these indispensible skills, or to practice them well, it was certainly no fault of Miss Scholes.

With my plans for the future becoming clearer, and with my error of trying to become a chemist put behind me, I was once again casting about for a job. The idea was to get something that would tide me over until I could take the Matriculation exams, which, I decided, I would do over two years. I applied for a relatively junior position in the insurance section of British Petroleum Limited, whose offices were in Queen Street in the City, not far from the building that accommodated my old employers, South Pacific Insurance Company. But BP was a totally different kind of workplace, huge and complex, with a broad range of departments on several floors, employing young and old, male and female, educated and less so, brilliant and plodding, local and British imports, and everywhere riddled by class-consciousness of a rigidity that reminded me of British films, especially the comedies. In the hierarchy of this workplace the insurance section was about the lowest of the low, and my position the most recent and the most junior. In my heart I knew I was going to hate this job, but I told myself that this would spur me on to do those things, like study hard, that would propel me out of it into a career more to my liking.

I had hardly settled in to the work, when two life-changing events occurred – a catastrophe and a rescue. The first caught me completely by surprise, and for years afterwards I still could not fathom exactly what triggered it and what I could have done to prevent it. Loretta and I, I thought, had been getting on well since the party, and everything seemed settled in the weeks after Christmas. We were photographed around that time along with Ron and Yvonne at the Embers night club, and we both looked happy, relaxed, in love. I recall that I had not seen her for a few days, and had walked the two blocks to her house after dinner one evening as I often did, knowing I'd find her in, and we might watch television or chat, or go off to the pictures at the Hoyts cinema in Ivanhoe. But this night when she answered my knock she did not welcome me in. In fact she opened the door only a few inches at first, and looked at me as if I were a stranger. Keeping me out, she put the snib on the door and joined me on the porch. I laid my hand on her arm, tried to draw her to me for a kiss, but she stiffened. I could sense something ominous coming. 'I don't want to see you any more,' she coolly, huskily told me. I couldn't believe it.

'Why not? What have I done?'

'You haven't done anything. I just don't want to see you any more. It's finished.'

Her face was stony, expressionless, her voice low and terse with the effort of maintaining control of what she had set herself to do. I reached out again, tried to pull her towards me into an embrace, putting my faith in the efficacy of touching, of familiar body warmth. She pushed me away. 'Don't,' she said, 'Just go.'

'What, just like that? What have I done, what have I said – surely you can talk about it?'

Now brutally, she said, 'There's nothing to talk about. I just don't want to see you any more.'

She moved away to go back through the doorway, then turned back and looked me straight in the eye. 'Goodbye,' she said quietly as she closed the door. I was numb at first, could not bring myself to go. And I certainly couldn't accept what she had said. Walking home through the shadows along empty streets, across a moonless paddock that led to Valentine Street, my eye fixed for direction on the weakly lit telephone box ahead as on a buoy in a black sea. I was in turmoil, telling myself she was merely angry with me over something, that her anger would pass, and that tomorrow or the next day would see her get over it and we would resume as we were. I couldn't accept she could stop her feelings for me just like that. Me! Her lover, the one she gives herself to, the one who possesses her, who is possessed by her! I would ring her tomorrow and undoubtedly find that she wanted to come back to me. Could there be someone else? Could this be all her mother's doing? She certainly hated me enough, and I knew she had been working on Loretta, chipping away at turning her against me. Perhaps she had succeeded. Tomorrow I would call her, arrange to see her, win her back, talk her round as I had often done in the past. It wasn't over. It couldn't be.

But when I called her from the telephone box next day her voice was as cold as it was the previous night. My persistence finally persuaded her to agree to talk with me again that evening at her place. All day I rehearsed what I would say, tried to anticipate her objections, plot various events designed to change her mind – a skiing weekend that the social club at BP was organising, she would like that, or a musical comedy in the city. Full of hope, I arrived at her front door after dinner earlier than usual, and knocked. But it was not she who answered; it was her mother. She was determined not to let me see Loretta, nor even to get a word in.

'Get it clear,' she told me through the half-open doorway, 'Loretta doesn't want to see you; she's finished with you, and damn good thing I say. She can find someone better than you, don't you worry ...'

'I just want to talk to her for a few minutes ...'

'But she doesn't want to talk to you Garry, now go away.'

I stood my ground. She stared at me, buck teeth sneering in defiance, like a snappy watchdog. I felt ready to scream at her, almost ready to take her by the throat and strangle the life out of her. 'That's you talking, not her. You've turned her against me; let her come and tell me herself ...'

'It's got nothing to do with me. She's not coming out because she doesn't want to see you any more. Now if you don't leave I'm going to call the police.'

I was convinced she was mad, really quite mad, and Loretta, who was undoubtedly inside listening, was letting her do this to me. She had finally surrendered her will to this raving crone. I turned and left. By the time I got home I was beside myself, could not think straight, could not hope nor accept, nor grasp the reasons for her obduracy, was conscious of nothing but my own despair. I made for my room and hurled myself on the bed, and there, for the first time since I was a small child, I released a howl from deep within my guts, so loud it could be heard throughout the house, even by those in the lounge room watching television. I pushed my face into the coverlet, muffling the sobs shaking my body, my despair so profound it astonished even myself; I had no idea such depths of feeling lay within me. My mother came and tried to comfort me; she had guessed what had happened. She sat beside me on the bed, stroked my neck and shoulders, soothed my cries while they quietened to a whimper, until after a good thirty minutes, exhausted, I fell asleep in my clothes. Never, not even when my father died, had I been reduced to devastation of that kind and intensity. It was of course the passionate cry of every rejected lover, every broken heart, right down through the ages. I didn't know this, of course, and even if I had it wouldn't have helped. All I knew was my own devastation.

After that night my behaviour changed, even though the pain did not go away. My outrage at being wronged had dissipated, but in its place there grew an abject refusal to accept the situation, and I could not stop thinking about her or overcome my grief. For months I virtually stalked her, obsessively keeping tabs on everything she did. I phoned her at home until they wouldn't let her come to the phone any more. I called her at work, despite being told to stop, and being hung up on. I kept passing her house in the hope of catching her. I asked her friends about her movements, what new relationships she might be in. It seemed she was making significant changes in her life. On one occasion she answered my phone call at work for a few minutes, during which she told me she had joined a repertory group in Ivanhoe, and was keen to do some acting. Her tone was a little self-satisfied, suggesting she had moved into new, arty circles, beyond my reach and understanding. I thought I would see about that, and track down this repertory group. I hung around one cold night outside the church hall where they were rehearsing, hands in pockets, breath turning to steam in the chill winter night. Finally obsession overcame timidity and I strolled in to the hall and stood in the wings of the stage. She was out in front stage reading a part, dressed in black tights and rollneck pullover, her blonde hair fresh-washed and longer, and she looked ravishing. I waited while she finished, and as she turned and came across in my direction, she suddenly saw me. The shock on her face told me immediately that this had been a mistake. She angrily hissed at me to go away. I said I would wait and take her home. She refused, pointing to a young man on the other side of the stage, a slim, long-haired East Ivanhoe type who, she said, would be giving her a lift 'in his MG' she said, as if the make of car was the final nail in my coffin. I was crushed, slinking off in defeat.

Even months later, settled in my new job at BP, I was still grieving, still trying to get her back. By this time she, too, had changed jobs, working at OPSM in Collins Street. This, I hoped, would make her easier to see. At lunchtimes I occasionally walked past her shop, peering through the window for a glimpse. Once I caught sight of her, but mostly she was out of view. Luck seemed to change for me during one phone call, when she agreed to have lunch with me. We went to a little basement restaurant in Collins Street called 'Le Jardin', and I was so nervous I shivered the whole time, and was so sick with the need to win her back that I couldn't eat my expensive food. She had certainly changed – more mature, more self-possessed, more serious; the smiling blonde girl I had always known was barely in evidence. I asked about the repertory group. She had been doing small roles, nothing too difficult. And the fellow? Came to nothing, she said, not that it's any of your business. I wanted to take this as a signal of hope, but the dark thought passed through me that I was out of my depth now, that she looked upon me in disbelief that she ever felt anything for me. I went back to work struggling against my self-pity, certain that the game was over, but at a loss to know how to move on.

It was during these sad months that the second life-changing event took place, which promised new opportunities at least. Bob had contacted me early in the new year and invited me to dinner at his flat in St Kilda Road. His girlfriend Varna was there, though Bob had done the cooking. The flat struck me as wonderful – furnished in modern deep grey upholstery with orange cushions, the latest trend in indoor plants and pieces of driftwood, snug and stylish, on the ground floor looking out on St Kilda Road. During the evening Bob revealed that he had a reason for the occasion, which was to invite me to share the apartment with him. I was flattered and overwhelmed, but how could I afford it? Bob was quick with his usual generosity. 'There's no-one else I would want to live with,' he explained, 'so whatever you can afford will be better than my living alone and paying the lot. Just contribute what you can.' Of course I couldn't resist, and of course I moved in. Apart from the army, this was my first home away from home. The flat was smaller than I'd realised, with a tiny scullery and a dining area partitioned off from the lounge, and we shared the one bedroom. This clearly did not bother Bob, so of course it did not bother me, despite the thought that privacy might at times be an issue – such as if either of us brought a girl in to take to bed.

Anyone reading this will almost certainly wonder about the question of homosexuality, for in the 21st century the most common assumption about two males sharing a one-bedroom flat would be that they are gay. But this was not the case at the beginning of the 60s. Homosexuality was still a secret world, tolerated by a minority of liberal thinking people, deplored by the majority, and certainly not fashionable as it is today. Few would have leapt to the conclusion that Bob and I were, in the common parlance, 'poofters', and we were not ourselves concerned that we might be seen as such, and never even discussed it. Indeed, what Bob did not bother to mention was that his previous flat mate, an advertising copywriter, had left precisely because an astonished Bob had rejected his advances soon after the man had moved in, a few weeks earlier. I had no idea of this until Bob told me many years later.

Installed in the flat, I was struck by the irony that I was now free from the constraints of my parental home just at a point in my life when I was in no state to take full advantage of that freedom. How fantastic, I thought, it would be to bring Loretta here whenever we felt like it, to impress her with my new sophistication and independence. I grew morose on such thoughts, a frequent feeling in the following months. I must work through it, get myself out of it somehow, I told myself, but there was no instant cure for grief. Time, I would learn, is the only healer.

The job at BP is so boring I am driven to pass the time simply chatting around the huge area of the sixth floor, which accommodates various departments – personnel, public relations, market research and insurance. My boss, Head of the pathetic little insurance department, is a repressed, unimaginative nonentity who chain-smokes and wears the same grubby navy suit every day. He writes in tiny, crabbed handwriting, which when he answers letters he scribbles on the bottom of the page and extends vertically up the margins for his secretary to decipher when typing the reply. To me this gives a clear indication of his strangled personality. There are three others in the department, all low-salaried men with families and mortgages, and we are all seated in a line directly outside the boss's office where he can watch us through a glass panel. If we engage in too much chatter, he will bustle out and intervene on some completely spurious pretext, such as asking if we've 'seen the file on Albany crude oil tanks', which is his oblique, and cowardly, way of telling us to get on with our work.

So rather than risk these embarrassing little charades, I move about the building and chat where I can't be seen. A number of the people are interesting. Rosemary, the woman who types all our work, is a fanatical Pentecostal whose whole life is ruled by her religion. Already plain, she does none of the usual things to enhance her appearance, such as wear attractive clothes, high heels, or styled hair. Yet she makes no secret of her longing to find a husband, and is joshed about it by the other girls in the typing pool. She is not much older than me, but she acts like an ancient aunt. Yet she is intelligent, sensitive, even sexually candid at times. I am not sure whether she would like to convert me or go out with me. Either way, I am well resistant to her; on both counts, religion and sex; I have already been tempered in a hotter forge than she can fire. Across the floor ahead of me is the irrepressible Brian Moll, of the Public Relations department. Brian is a well-known actor outside of work, a loud, stereotypically camp, shaven-headed extrovert, who loves to shock the office with outrageous stories. He is probably homosexual, but 'coming out' as such has not yet been invented, so it remains unspoken of. When a colleague puts on a display of temper one day, Brian calls loudly across the room, 'What's the matter Graeme, hasn't your wife been giving you any fucks?' He loves to mock the trappings of 'straight' life.

Behind me is the Market Research department, the intellectuals of the office, all university educated and self-contained. I talk often with Lucy, an elegant, detached, bored-looking young woman, who listens sympathetically to my self-pitying talk about Loretta. She also talks to me about art, music, education – I try to learn something about university life from her – and I admire her understated judgments on the world. One of her colleagues, Susan, a short, pretty-faced girl, interests me briefly, and when I ask her out to a musical comedy she agrees, though it turns out to be a wasted evening. She hardly says a word to me, and when she does it seems to be for the purpose of making me feel stupid, she won't let me touch her or hold her hand, and certainly not kiss her goodnight. University education, I think, can go to some people's heads. Maybe she went with me just to see the show.

The class element is rife throughout the staff, and the many British employees have toffee accents. A recent arrival, who has been placed temporarily at a desk within earshot of me, spends much of his time on the phone talking about his settling-in problems, which he does in a calculatedly loud, upper class voice. 'Warranwood,' he says with exaggerated precision, as if the word is a solid object in his mouth, 'twenty-seven Highridge Road. My name is Williams. No, that *is* my surname: Williams.' This Williams wears English tweed suits and makes great show of appearing busy, though all his conversations so far seem to be on the phone to tradesmen and utility companies. On one occasion I try to engage Williams in conversation, quoting something in the paper about Australia supposedly having no history.

'Oh, I wouldn't say that,' he intones in a vague, serious way, 'it has a *little* worth mentioning, surely?' It is the only time Williams ever speaks to me.

Many of the Australian executives dress and talk in imitation of these British upper class ways, which I guess is supposed to help them gain promotion. They don't wear bowler hats at least, but they do wear regimental ties and carry umbrellas. I see them in the lift and in the corridors, making sounds consistent with the hollowness of their permanent smiles and hearty manners. They tend to say 'down' and 'around' with tight, circular lips, and 'day' and 'away' with a certain bathetic limpness that travesties British pronunciation. More like bad acting. And acting is all many of them will ever do, I think, because they are not many of them likely to climb very high up the corporate ladder. Wrong nationality, I believe. At least they provide me with an amusing distraction from the mind-numbing work.

The pattern of living I settled into was busy enough, but it did not bring me much happiness. I was up by eight in the mornings, leaving Bob asleep on the other side of the room, snatching a quick breakfast before catching a crowded tram along St Kilda Road into the city. Occasionally I rode the Vespa, but there was a risk of rain wetting my good clothes, and it could be cold. Being freelance, Bob could start and stop work whenever he liked, one of the several advantages he enjoyed, along with the glamour and the better money from artwork and from singing. In comparison, I felt a bit like a plodder and a sponger, given that I contributed less to our living costs. If Bob was aware of this, he either ignored it or tried to counter it by sharing with me every new thing he bought. He would bring home exotic things to eat he'd bought at the South Melbourne market, or an exciting new LP, or we'd go out to some new restaurant he'd discovered. He bought a new car, a smart Simca 'Vedette' in two-tone white and yellow with white wall tyres, and we drove about, the two of us, feeling on top of the town. We once pulled up at traffic lights alongside a car which, to our astonishment, was being driven by one of our jazz idols, Mel Torme, who was in town performing at the Embers night club. We gave him a matey wave, and he returned a nod and a smile, and made our day, our week in fact. Grateful as I was for the things Bob would share with me, they tended to reinforce rather than mollify my sense of diminished self-worth. And though I was absorbed in my evening studies, and seemed to be progressing well, these were not enough to bolster my confidence or soothe my still broken heart. For I missed Loretta, and could not find or even expect to find another girl to take her place. I tried. The 432 Club and Keyboard were both only a few minutes from the flat, and on Saturday nights when Bob was off singing I went along hoping to strike it lucky. If I managed to dance with a girl, I lied about my background and work, told her I was a university student, that I owned an MG that was unfortunately out of action at present, that my parents were wealthy farmers from the Western District and were paying for my flat. Once or twice I made a date with a girl, including one pretty brunette who spent the following Sunday afternoon with me. We went to a concert at the Music Bowl and then back to the flat, which I hoped would impress her and maybe win me some sexual action, or at least a bit of affection. It turned out disastrously: she was suffering as badly as I was from a recent break-up with her boyfriend, and though we held hands and kissed a few times, we knew we were both seeking in each other our missing lover, and there was no genuine connection between us. In desperation, I attempted to force myself on her on the sofa, but after becoming angry, she burst into pathetic tears, at which moment I felt ashamed and began to disburden myself of my lies. 'I don't have an MG,' I told her, 'and I don't go to university, though I'm hoping to.'

'That's okay,' she said, pushing back her hair and wiping her eyes with my handkerchief, 'I just want to go home now.' I walked her to the tram stop, and waited with her in the cold wind, unable to think of anything to say. The sight of a Malvern tram brought blessed relief, and as I watched her mount the step without looking back at me, I hoped I wouldn't run into her again when I next went to the Keyboard.

But one female seemed to have developed a feeling of sorts for me, a feeling I was happy to reciprocate. In evening classes, Miss Scholes increasingly directed her comments and questions to me, and we frequently opened up a dialogue confined to the two of us. The fact was, despite my failing love life, I was finding great consolation in my English studies. I had become a refugee to the worlds of *Far From the Madding Crowd*, *Crime and Punishment*, *Hamlet*, and the *Regency poets*, worlds in which my imagination thrived. For months I was so possessed by Raskolnikov's agony that it was more like having an illness than reading a novel. And I saw in Hamlet's bitter denunciation of his mother's marriage to Claudius an action I thrilled to, and intensely identified with, but didn't grasp its implications for my relationship with my own family until many years later. All this produced an enthusiasm that Miss Scholes was moved to take in hand and direct into good scholarly practice. It turned out to be something she undertook with several of her young male students, though rarely with the females, even the very bright ones. Twin sisters, Frances and Dalene Koops, breezy, friendly girls, with whom I sometimes went for coffee after class, somewhat resented Miss Scholes for this. It came as no surprise when Miss Scholes took me aside one evening after class and asked if I would like to go to a play with her. Of course I could see, when she asked if I had a car, that she liked to have someone take her to night-time events for reasons of safety and convenience, but when I told her I did not, she wasn't at all discouraged. 'We can get a tram,' she smiled.

The play was at the Union Theatre, in the grounds of the university, a place where she was at home and I felt desperately overawed. As it happened, she had arranged for another young man to meet us in the foyer, an ex-pupil now studying at the university, and who would run her home in his car afterwards. He was friendly, confident, clean cut, a strong whiff of the Christian about him. We saw *Juno and the Paycock*, which was on the English syllabus, and which the class had been reading. It was my first experience of 'serious' theatre, enchanting, the staging and acting bringing to life an Irish past in a quite different way from the realism of a film. I learned that some of the actors taught at the university, and wondered at the attainment of this level of sophistication, how they created Irish voices, larger-than-life characters – the strutting Captain Boyle, the sycophantic Joxer Daly, the weary Juno Boyle – the musical rise and fall of the language. Yet in our discussion afterwards it was not these things that Miss Scholes talked about, but the thematic and moral implications behind them, the human failings and virtues, the political despair behind an Ireland made childish by ignorance and superstition. All these ideas excited me, and I thought about them on the way back to the flat, tried to talk to Bob about them when he came in, but I couldn't get him to share my excitement, couldn't find a language to convey the powerful complexities in my head. Besides, he was more an Art person, fired by visual events. So, I pondered, literature was a field where I might command something of my own after all.

Occasionally Miss Scholes would suggest we have lunch together in the city. The first time, she nominated a health food shop that ran a café at the rear, where we had fried brains in breadcrumbs with brown rice and vegetable juice. I didn't mind the food so much as the cold, dismal atmosphere of the place, a mixture of church and hospital, with pale green walls, cream laminex and chrome tables where was seated a sprinkling of oddballs in their fifties wearing tweeds and silently reading library books. She sensed my discomfort, and said, 'Next time we'll go to a place of your choosing.'

In the event I wish we hadn't. Thoughtlessly I chose a modish café in Little Collins Street, busy and fashionable amongst the city lunchtime crowd. We were shown to a table after waiting some considerable time, and sat through another age before a slapdash young waitress turned up to take our orders. We must have looked an odd couple, a callow youth and a doddery septuagenarian in a noisy throng of expense-account types out to impress. The menu was full of things she had never heard of, let alone eaten. Conservatively, I decided on Spaghetti Bolognese, and she, with a shrug, followed suit. I had eaten it enough times to develop some skill twisting it with spoon and fork, but she had no idea. Maybe I should have tried to show her how to do it, but I was too embarrassed in public, and so I left her to her own devices. At first she tried picking up forkfulls by stabbing it, but of course it all fell off back into her bowl. She tried cutting it with the spoon, but this only yielded two or three short pieces of spaghetti on the tip of her fork, and no meat sauce. She tried copying me, but with no dexterity in her fingers, she brought up a huge mound insecurely positioned between the fork and spoon in each hand, drew it trembling towards her lips until, fast losing confidence in her aim, she made a desperate lunge at it with her mouth; some of it went in, but the rest that hadn't fallen off dangled from her lips and she began to poke it in with the fingers of one hand as one stuffs the aperture of a chicken. It was difficult to look her in the face as she nervously beamed across at me with a mouth smeared red from cheek to cheek with Bolognese sauce. I was praying that no-one had noticed, half-dying with shame. With her napkin she wiped her face, though it still bore traces of red, so that the seriousness with which she now spoke became merely lugubrious: 'And how are you getting along with your Chaucer?' she said louder than comfort required. I pushed back in my chair, struggled to focus for a moment (I'd been thinking of escaping to the Men's), and whispered, 'Oh fine, fine ...' I couldn't wait for it all to be over and to get her out of there.

But I always enjoyed our discussions, and her kindly encouragement was the single strongest influence on my growing love of reading. And if I was embarrassed and a little protective towards her at times in public situations, it was only because I feared seeing her stumble into the path of a society I knew only too well could mock or insult her without the slightest hesitation. Under her guidance I passed the English Expression exam at the end of that year, 1960, and looked forward to continuing on with the remaining two subjects of the Adult Matriculation, English Literature and Modern History. Since they didn't teach the History at Miss Scholes' College, I had to enrol at Taylor's Coaching College around the corner. Pleased as I was with myself, I knew I had a long way to go before I could stand on a level with the university graduates at BP. One such young man, John, gaining work experience in the Market Research department over the summer, sat in the desk behind me. He was conscientious, confident, smiled a lot, awaited the results of his exams with a touch of anxiety. When it emerged he had obtained high distinctions in all subjects of his Commerce finals, everyone around him showered him with congratulations, and he was offered a permanent position by the Company, who made it clear they saw him as an executive in the making. But John was canny enough to tell them he'd think about it over the summer break; obviously he knew his value, and was casting about for the best option. Part of me envied him his success. But I wondered, Is this what I want too? And I thought, No, an important part of me rejected it; there was something predetermined about it that I feared, something that closed out the mystery of those undreamt-of possibilities that only the condition of freedom can engender. I didn't know this, I didn't have a plan for it, but negatively I sensed it, like a cat senses danger. I knew I would not be happy to be 'on track' as a future executive of BP, essentially because I feared living my life like a train.

There were changes in Bob, too. He had split up with Varna, and now brought back to the flat a succession of young women, none of whom seemed right for him. There was something about Bob that confused women. He was handsome, had a touch of glamour, but he was also highly original and skilful in the things he did, and the passion with which he pursued these interests seemed to threaten many girls, as if they resented sharing their feelings with it. One affair in particular turned out to be a minor disaster. He began mentioning a girl called Marlene with particular enthusiasm, such that by the time he brought her back to the flat I was expecting someone truly wonderful. She turned out to be short, sexy in a raw, hyperactive way, but, it was obvious to me, totally ill-suited to Bob. It was difficult to tell her age, but she was older than Bob by a few years. He seemed unable to see how dumb and uninteresting she really was, though part of his keenness might have been precisely that she was such a blank page and he saw the possibility of writing her role for her. Within weeks they became engaged, and she smugly showed off the expensive diamond ring he had bought her. 'We're off to a restyouaront to celebrate,' she blurted out. I noticed Bob wince at the mispronunciation.

Then, late one night, he crashed into the flat like a storm, threw himself on the couch, and wailed in terrible despair. Weeping, he told how he had learned that Marlene had in fact been married, to an American sailor on a brief leave from his ship. The image he had built of her as an ingénue had from the first been a complete fiction, and now it had disintegrated in the first light of reality. To me, Bob's wretchedness felt disproportionate to the loss, but nevertheless I put an arm around him, listened sympathetically while he talked his disappointment away through the night. What gradually became apparent was the extent to which his confidence, his self-dependence, masked a loneliness and desperation for love that was similar to my own, and that perhaps the reason we got along so well was that we were not so different as it might at first glance have seemed.

This was somewhat confirmed when his mother paid a brief visit to the flat one day. He had never mentioned her before, in fact neither of us had talked about our family background to this point. She was probably in her early fifties, but looked older, seemed fragile and nervous, a face marked by suffering. After she had gone Bob opened up: his father had been a prisoner-of-war, and had died in Malaya. Like many war widows, his mother had taken the loss hard, struggled valiantly to keep the family going, turned to alcohol. He felt protective of her, but had been distancing himself from his home life for some years. As he recounted this I began to see the similarities in our childhood deprivations. Both fatherless, both sensitive, outsider types, both struggling to find the path that would bring us happiness and satisfaction, with only our wits and abilities to rely on. Maybe we saw this mirrored in each other, and this drew us together.

Restless for experience, Bob now turned to serious painting as a contrast to his commercial art work. On weekends he took lessons with the renowned painter Clifton Pugh at his home in Cottles Bridge, north east of Melbourne. He brought home his work – striking, modern, a little intimidating, though happily I liked it. After a time I thought I, too, might try to paint; I bought canvas board, oil paints, brushes and asked Bob for some tips. The first efforts were absurd, but I persisted. Bob even took me to Cottles Bridge one Sunday, where Pugh was quite happy to include me in the lessons. It was a memorable day, leaving me with a few important ideas to contemplate. His way of teaching was to sit his pupils in the bush around his property and let them get on with a project of their choosing. Pugh himself sat among us, doing likewise. He then came around commenting on what we had done, making a constructive suggestion here and there. While struggling to make something coherent out of my own rendering of a eucalypt and native grass clumps, I had watched Pugh working some fifteen metres away and was struck by the way he refused to be bound by the given arrangement of objects in front of him. Instead, he would take a branch from a tree over to his right, fit it with a trunk from his left, bring a distant shrub up close and place it where he wanted it, put in a bird that wasn't even there: the artist dominating nature, free to remake the world how he wanted it; I'd never thought about it before.

Later in the afternoon, the painting lesson over, Cliff invited everyone inside to talk. The house was a wonder, with massive weathered timber beams and supports, broad flagstones on the floor, windows of leadlight glass in native animal designs, challenging artwork everywhere – huge menacing paintings, primitive sculptures, bits of old machinery, clay pots distributed about among small items of hand-made silver jewellery. Cliff's wife Marlene, a striking woman with long, dark hair, wearing a purple pullover and black tights, brought in wine, cheese and coffee. She put classical guitar music on the record player – Bach – which echoed through the high-ceilinged rooms setting a mood of otherworldliness for the talk that was taking place. I had no idea anyone could live in such a wonderful, self-made way. 'I never used a single ruler or set square when I built this house,' Cliff said to the gathering, 'I judged everything only by eye – the uprights, the door and window frames, everything, because it is the eye that sees them, so that is what you have to please.'

Later, Pugh asked me what I was studying. 'Literature and Modern History,' I told him.

'I don't believe in history,' he said, 'schools shouldn't bother with it. All that matters is now.'

This provoked a lively argument, which, I understood, was exactly what Pugh was after. Clearly, part of his way of life, including these weekend events, was to create a world apart from the usual preoccupations of mainstream Melbourne, with its television, it's sport, it's obedience to convention. I liked it, envied Pugh. But how would one go about creating such a world for oneself?

Bob's work included designing record covers for the World Record Club, which allowed him to bring home the latest LPs. This provided another source of education for me, discovering the great classical composers – Beethoven, Mozart, Tchaikovsky, Bizet, Stravinsky, all were new to me then. And we were both taking in developments in Modern Jazz: Jerry Mulligan, Clifford Brown, Miles Davis, John Coltrane, Bill Evans, Oscar Peterson and many others. Listening intently to all this music was a new experience for me; we'd had so little of it at home in West Ivanhoe, apart from popular tunes on the radio.

Being so much a part of Bob's life like this was both a consuming interest and a reminder of how green I still was. Enriching, it could also demoralise me. My own resources, my work, my other activities, were so banal and uninspiring that my self-confidence was probably at its lowest ebb since I could remember. When I was first within the new working environment of insurance, in the city for those first years, it was a world I had quickly gotten the hang of, and so within that world I could function with confidence, felt myself to be of some consequence. Similarly, living at home, I was never really tested, everything was done by long established routine, nothing needed to be thought through. You do this, you learn to accommodate yourself to an environment and within that you feel safe and recognised, unchallenged at any important level. But now, confronted with new experiences every week, I was constantly being broken open, forced to change my outlook, which was as painful as it was irresistible, even at times exhilarating.

Something similar was happening through my literature class. Here I was developing a passion that I couldn't explain to anyone, except that I had in Miss Scholes one person who could recognise it in me. None of my family and friends from around West Ivanhoe could, although Ron Bowden's girlfriend Yvonne had a family friend I had met once or twice who was studying literature at Melbourne University, and who intrigued me with her talk of Shakespeare's sonnets; she did notice something of my intense interest. Week after week Miss Scholes' class explored a new poet, a new novel or play, and I hungrily took it in. The Modern History class did not excite me as much, mainly because the teacher was dry and less-than-enthusiastic about the subject, taught it to get us through the exam, not because he loved it. I knew I would have to work hard to pass both subjects at the end of the year, but if I did I knew there was a good chance of getting into university on a teaching bursary, which was probably the only way I could afford it.

Almost unnoticed, sport was fading from my interest. I had not played football for some time, and now had lost the desire to continue on in the cricket team. Occasionally I would glance at the football reports to see how the Bombers were doing, or watch Test Cricket on TV for an hour or so, but it no longer had me in its grip. Was it, I wondered, a sign of my maturity, that I began to see sport as essentially childish, and that I had to move onto more adult concerns? Or was it a kind of snobbishness, that I was ashamed of the enthusiasm I once had for it in the face of people more concerned with books, ideas, the Higher Pursuits? I was always inclined, in my determination to change, to reject all the things that once defined me, to favour the new at the expense of the old, rather than attempt the sensible course of hanging on to what was good in my past and balancing it with these new interests. Immaturity licenses many errors, and for some, hard experience is the only teacher.

At Easter I made another trip to Mansfield to stay with Norman and Daphne. This time he did not offer to lend me the jeep, though we do spend a couple of days at their little cabin deep in the bush along the Howqua River, an idyllic retreat, with the river flowing past not twenty feet away full of trout, and not a soul to be seen nor heard for miles around. I enjoyed it, but I didn't enjoy the constant pressure from Norman to sing the praises of his prize possessions. In fact, it was a common element in Norman's relation to the world: the act of generosity in order to secure admiration; if you couldn't like him, it implied, you could at least like his possessions. It sustained Norman's popularity with all that side of the family. Everyone wanted their turn at 'The Hut', their collection of photographs of swimming in the river, fishing upstream, lazing in the hammock, cooking on the open fire. Everyone except myself; something in me recoiled at what really ought to have been seen as simple enjoyment of new family harmony. That legacy of bitterness, of failure within my own immediate family, a childhood watching my father destroyed and my mother suffer, a family who owned almost nothing, a poverty that reduced possession to cheap furniture bought on lay-by, never a new bicycle or even a scooter, had planted a seed of resentment that disabled me from ever celebrating the wealth of others. I was, I now realise, psychologically damaged, but at least I had enough pride to keep my resentment to myself. I didn't confront anyone's claims to superiority based on wealth; I simply turned my back on it. It was different on the question of personal achievements; I never begrudged success earned by skill or hard work.

Daphne was thrilled when I sat through a whole day making a painting of her Liquidambar tree in the back yard of the Mansfield house. She always cherished it, drew the family's attention to it, so that even well into the future, during my long absence abroad, I was an unknowing participant in the family myth, a kind of wandering ghost on the obscure fringes of their world of solid, conventional, paid-up comfort. But we must not get ahead of the story. For the moment I am still an untraveled, inexperienced youth, trying this pursuit and that, in the hope that something would show itself as the one glorious vocation to which I could dedicate myself and at last make my mark. Anyone good at reading the signs would undoubtedly see even at this early stage that it would have something to do with literature.

SUNLIGHT

8

1961 WAS THE WATERSHED. It was not fully apparent to me at the time, but this year marked the culmination of a crisis that had been building since I came out of the army, at the end of 1957. I see now that all the attempts I had been making to build some sort of adult life had, up to this point, come to nothing – work, love life, family, any sense of who I was – all of it successively disintegrated. BP was providing no career answer, my family were unable to understand me, my boyhood friends, with the exception of Ron Bowden, seemed to have ceased developing and so offered me no stimulation of the kind I needed, and an energetic hunger within had no idea of what would satisfy it. This frustration was quite dimly sensed, a subdued ache, more of an absence than a presence of something painful, just as it had been in my childhood when I craved the affection of my quarantined tubercular father. Our deficiencies, the things we yearn for but don't possess, are the least apparent sources of unhappiness. In a way we don't notice we are unhappy until we pause to reflect, or unless we are lucky enough to find the very thing we yearn for. If that happens we might experience the sudden sense of 'yes, yes, this is what I needed all along and didn't quite know it'. But we have to be lucky for that to happen. So far, not much luck had come my way, though I kept striving to make something change, kept outwardly positive and cheerful. I was not a morose youth, save in private moments of loneliness, listening to music or contemplating something beautiful or melancholy, or reflecting on a particular injustice. Mostly, I was a cheerful fellow who looked positively to the future. The two most important things I hung onto in that pivotal year were my friendship with Bob, and my matriculation studies, both of which pointed optimistically to the future.

There was still no replacement for Loretta, and I was still, after more than a year, grieving pathetically over her, though I tried to get interested in other girls. For a time I was infatuated with the lively and attractive Frances Koops from my evening class, who like her sister Dalene, dressed in the latest 'Beatnik' style – duffle coats, desert boots and long straight hair; they represented a new taste among the young, a taste for what may be called the 'authentic', which was anti-glamour, anti-commercial, anti-mainstream, and I was intrigued by it, though not part of it. Unfortunately Frances did not respond to my interest, except to be friends. I went on occasional dates with other girls, but they came to nothing, and have, not surprisingly, disappeared entirely from my memory, lost in the flux of events more vivid at the time.

If I was craving a development in myself that was frustrated, Bob in contrast was showing marked signs of change in his make-up, and our friendship, while never seriously threatened, was feeling the stress of our insecurities. Early in the year, during the Christmas holidays, we had driven to Adelaide in the Simca to stay a few days with his bother, Brian, who had recently returned from England with his new wife Barbara. It was fearfully hot in Adelaide, and their tiny modern flat was like an oven. At one point a discussion arose about race; Brian and Barbara had been to see *South Pacific* and were disagreeing over the song 'You've Got To Be Carefully Taught', which argues that racism is culturally, not biologically acquired. Brian agreed with the song, Barbara did not. In the heat of the moment, Bob and I disagreed too, and though I cannot remember which side I took, I suspect that I, still an entrenched participant in the politically unconscious, plumped for the biological view. My ignorance aside, it was the fact that we argued at all that was troubling, a suggestion of a tiny fissure opening in our friendship; up till then, we had disagreed on very little, and certainly never with any heat.

It happened again a few months later, after a game of chess. We played often, and up until this night I had never beaten him. But something had fired my determination – another of those 'back-to-the-wall' moments when I will refuse to let the odds cause my defeat – and I spent long minutes over every move, until finally, after two or three hours, I manoeuvred him into checkmate. His reaction shocked me. 'It took you long enough,' he muttered, and petulantly struck the board and chess pieces off the coffee table, scattering them to all parts of the room. Then he stalked off to bed, without another word. I had never seen this side of him before.

The feeling of our growing apart coincided with further changes in his interests and friendships. Through his contact with Clifton Pugh he was meeting more serious artists of various kinds, quite different people with different attitudes from the ones he had known for some years in the advertising industry. And his own attitudes were changing: he was becoming a more thoughtful, more creative painter now. His wonderful command of all the technical skills of graphic art gave him a foundation to paint in any style on any subject. He had given up singing with dance bands, had begun to move on the edges of what was known amongst themselves as The Push, a motley underworld of painters, poets, musicians, philosophers, hangers-on, bludgers, petty criminals, and the variety of girlfriends, mistresses and wives that went with them. The younger ones consciously aligned themselves with the American 'Beat' movement, as they were doing in many Western countries then, but the older ones turned their noses up at this or any other designation of a group identity, and saw themselves more as anarchistic individuals. In their relationships, for self-styled Leftist liberals (indeed libertarians), most participants in The Push were remarkably sexist in those pre-feminist years – the women were generally satellites to their males, who made all the running on matters of activity and opinion. It was rare to find a female artist, though the folk music scene was probably better in that regard than writing, painting and sculpting, and it was rare to find a woman holding forth on intellectual issues, which males were doing regularly at parties and other gatherings. Just as in the hated mainstream society, women in The Push were still mainly sex objects, figures of desire and decoration, and of course for doing the housework, on the odd occasions when it was done.

One of Bob's new friendships was with Max Beatty, a Wesley College product turned dropout, who painted *pointilliste* abstracts and lived on the dole in a loft in Prahran with his beautiful, then heavily pregnant partner Beth. Max wanted not so much to be a painter as to make lifestyle into an art – to live in beautiful places surrounded by sensuously beautiful things, without doing soul-destroying jobs to get by. Living freely, cheaply, close to the earth, was his goal. He was a remarkably good-looking man, short and muscular, with long golden locks and beard, and loved to get around in skimpy shorts and open shirts to show his body. When I first met him, when Bob took me to his loft, I began to mouth envious complaints about being chained to a job I hated. He bluntly interrupted me: 'Don't tell me about it, don't tell me about your problems; if you don't like going to work, don't go.' I never forgot this brutal comment, which I took as a piece of advice. I couldn't get the idea out of my head, that if you didn't like working, you could just leave, find some other way of getting money – the dole, anything. Surely, I thought, this is impossible? What would I live on, how would I pay the bills, rent, buy clothes, a car, without a steady income, without financial security? But Max had shown me the answer: find a way of getting the dole, live cheap, don't buy clothes, forget cars. You don't need them.

As Bob's contacts with artists introduced me to more and more Push types, not all with Max's flair or organising ability, I began to see it as less strange and increasingly attractive, though I was not yet ready to try it out myself. Bob, on the other hand, was ready, and indeed doing so with increasing alacrity. Sharing the flat no longer suited him, and he didn't want to keep up his city office; he needed a decent-sized studio, where he could set up his easel permanently, and where he could live and work in a manner and at hours entirely to his own convenience. He continued to earn an income from his commercial work, but he was well enough paid to restrict himself to jobs that gave him some artistic satisfaction. This meant a break with 'business-hour' routines and the freedom to paint all night with music playing loudly if he chose, a lifestyle hardly compatible with my nine-to-five existence, and my need to study in the evenings. So we decided to give up the flat and go our own ways. I went back home to West Ivanhoe, he found himself a great two-roomed apartment in East Melbourne, where I would drop in on him from time to time. He was living more intensely now, alone and immersed in his painting through the nights, accompanied by the music of Stravinsky, or Hindemith, or Rodrigo or Miles Davis; *Kinda Blue* was the talk among the *avante garde* jazz enthusiasts, as was the *Concierto de Aranjuez*, both of which Bob was among the first to acquire. Gone was the neat, well-groomed commercial artist, replaced by an impassioned, carelessly dressed bohemian living in a jumble of dirty dishes and unwashed clothes, the apartment fragrant with the smells of oil paint and joss sticks. His pictures were superbly imitative of Cliff Pugh's, mostly strikingly dramatic bushscapes, handled with at least as much competence and power; the pupil had already caught up with the master. From time to time a new friend, always someone from the Push, usually with long hair and provocative opinions, would be there when I dropped in, and I would listen intently and try, hesitatingly, to respond with something intelligent, usually not very convincingly.

My return home had something of a hint of defeat, but there were still the December exams to focus on, still reasons to think that next year would bring my hopes to fruition. The Modern History classes at Taylor's had not been going well. I never enjoyed Taylor's, which always felt impersonal and business-like, reductive in its aim to get students through the exams rather than to teach them how to read and think and argue for themselves. I respond best when I am interested and involved, get bored quickly when placed in a passive role. So I didn't study properly for History, and consequently struggled. Sitting with hundreds of others at our little tables in the massive hall of the Exhibition building on the day of the exam, I fought with memory and concentration to come up with answers to questions that as soon as I read them had me rattled. The Literature paper was much easier, and I found plenty to say. All the same, when the results came out in the newspaper in January I was disappointed to learn I had failed the History – by a single mark. The fact that I passed the Literature did not help: Adult Matriculation required a pass in three subjects, and I had only two. The failure meant that the Education Department turned me down for a teaching bursary, and so my plans for university study and a teaching career were now in tatters. I was devastated. I'll never forget what my mother said when I told her. 'Oh well, there you are: university is not for people like us.' Could this be true? Was I not the sort of person who goes to university? But Miss Scholes seemed to think I was, and she would know better than my mother. It grated that a past of deprivation and pain was apparently determining my present and future. In any case, what could I do? There was no other way I knew to obtain the education I wanted, needed, than to do it part-time. When I told Miss Scholes of the situation, she was not fazed in the slightest. After making sympathetic noises, she simply said, 'You'd better enrol again, and make sure you pass it next year.' I said I would, and I meant it, but nevertheless my confidence was severely dented, and I knew that with the teaching bursary now out of the question, finding a way to go to university was going to be almost impossible.

In the new year, trapped in the dullness of home and work at BP, I needed to start doing things that would take me out of the house as much as possible. I traded in the Vespa and bought myself a well-used blue Volkswagen Beetle, so I was mobile at least, and feeling very much on the lookout for experience. A new sort of music was beginning to emerge, folk songs to the accompaniment of acoustic guitars. At Cottles Bridge I had heard Peter Laycock strum and sing a couple of Australian bush ballads, and reviving my long-held affection for the guitar, I went out and bought one – an inexpensive but pretty and nicely made Spanish 'Tatay', which came with a few basic finger-style lessons. I relearned chords and bought a couple of books, including a Burl Ives song book, and began teaching myself finger-style accompaniments in my bedroom at night. I have always found in the guitar, simply holding it, close to my body as one does, playing an arpeggio, fingering a few chords, a deep delight. There is a sensuousness that the guitar gives back to you especially when you play well. To this day I love to play the instrument, even just to sit with it, and if I hear the sound of classical guitar even at a remote distance, even in the hands of an amateur, I will stop whatever I am doing and listen transfixed.

Watching television one night, I was struck by a brief interlude on the ABC of two American singers performing in succession. The first was a beautiful, long-black-haired young woman with a glorious untrained contralto, playing the most deft finger-style accompaniment I had ever seen. Her name, given in the end credits, was Joan Baez. I called to my mother to come and look; she drew back and eyed her suspiciously. 'She's *awful*,' my mother said, and I saw straight away that our connection to each other had, some time ago and without my previously noticing it, changed utterly; we belonged to different eras, and had totally different cultural interests. The people and interests I was increasingly drawn to were beyond her understanding.

The second performer was a black man maybe in his fifties, with dark glasses and an impenetrable self-possession, a man who looked like he'd seen plenty of the downside of life, expressing it through powerful but paradoxically delicate blues on the guitar, who sang in a manner that made you come to *him*, made *you* figure out what he was singing, a man not interested in creating easy entertainment for the listener. He had me on the edge of my chair; his name was 'Lightning' Hopkins. Immediately I longed for contact with the kind of world they moved in. I heard about and went along to The Reata coffee lounge in High Street, Malvern, where Martyn Wyndham-Read the English folksinger sang, looking Christ-like in his shoulder length hair and beard, and Brian Brophy, the flamenco guitarist, both played. I longed to be able to do what they did. I dropped in on Max Beatty, who had heard of these singers, and who, when I mentioned I wanted to learn finger-style guitar, suggested I contact a man called Karl Ogdon, who gave classical guitar lessons.

In the meantime, having learned about half a dozen of the Burl Ives songs, I stopped one evening at a coffee lounge in Burwood Road, Camberwell, and had the cheek to walk up to the proprietor and offer my services as a folksinger. To my surprise he took me on straight away for the princely sum of five pounds a night, one night a week.

Coffee lounges were the only viable venues in these early stages of the folk music revival. Pubs were still subject to six o'clock closing, so as soon as the frantic swilling was over, they were socially dead for the night. Coffee lounges were the mainstay hangouts for the young in the evenings, but they were fundamentally dull places to sit in for more than twenty minutes. By adding a guitarist or folk singer, they could at least provide a semblance of background entertainment. Restaurants might occasionally do the same – the *Reata* was in fact a restaurant – but the serving of food complicated the atmosphere somewhat, made for distractions and increased noise, and were of course more expensive. From the singer's viewpoint, neither was satisfactory, because many customers wanted to talk rather than listen, and singing to a crowd of uninterested, even at times hostile, people could be very discouraging. Brian Brophy tells a story of being thrown a scrunched up pound note and told to 'take your banjo up the other end of the room while I talk' by a customer. The best solution all round was the creation of folk clubs, such as Traynors in the city, dedicated to performance and listening, but that was still a couple of years away at the beginning of 1962. In these early days many coffee lounges were willing to give a singer a try, but in most cases they dropped you after a couple of months, a casualty of the effect of a limited repertoire on irritated staff and patrons.

The Burwood Road gig started me off, gave me some experience of playing to an audience, and motivated me to add to my repertoire. To 'Click Go the Shears', 'Jimmy Crack Corn' and 'The Wild Colonial Boy' I added some English songs I picked up from recordings bought from Peter Mann's little outlet in Block Arcade, including a wonderful sea-shanty called 'South Australia', which I believe I was the first person to sing in the Melbourne scene. Peter Mann was a groundbreaker in making available European and American recorded music that other outlets didn't carry – avante garde, little-known modernist composers, medieval and renaissance music, modern jazz and folk music, in particular Folkways records and Library of Congress material. And it was at Peter's that I was able to get hold of my first Joan Baez record, from which I immediately began to learn some wonderful Appalachian ballads, and to work out some of her accompaniment techniques. The audience at my little gig were a bit outer-suburban, out-of-touch, and hardly knew there was a folk revival gathering momentum, but they listened politely, applauded mechanically, and soon grew bored with me. I was surprised when Martyn Wyndham-Read turned up one night to check me and the venue out – he made a few jokey comments, but didn't seem impressed with either me or the place. Within a few weeks I picked up a second gig in High Street, Malvern called The Copper Kettle. This was run by a fellow I knew from evening classes, whose mother put up the money and worked in the kitchen. It was in the vicinity of The Reata, but didn't have a comparable atmosphere, and took some time to establish patrons. One night a fellow from work turned up, after I'd told him I had started singing there. Ian Bannon was his name, a junior executive from the personnel department. Ian had an eye for the latest trends, though he was himself always keen to conform to established mores. One time when I returned from annual leave sporting a beard, he looked at me in the lift with astonishment. 'Why did you do that?' he asked. I kept the beard for about six months, until I decided I didn't like it, and one Monday morning came to work with it shaved off. Again Ian confronted me in the lift, looking just as astonished as before. 'Why did you do that?' he asked. Non-conformity puzzled him. So Ian turned up at The Copper Kettle, eager to keep tabs on my movements. He had with him a pretty, somewhat over-groomed blonde, very eastern suburban in style; they sat close and chatted to me during breaks, and she wouldn't take her big blue eyes off me the whole time. At one point the subject of politics came up, and she revealed, with inexplicable pride, that she was a member of the Young Liberals. Just right for Ian, I thought.

In March my old mate Ron married his beautiful Yvonne, in a church in Fitzroy. Deeply in love since they met back in 1959, they had been engaged for some time, had succeeded in their relationship where Loretta and I had failed. Yvonne's early planning had included me and Loretta in the wedding party as groomsman and bridesmaid, but now that we had split up she had to choose between us. Ron insisted that I was to be in the party, and so Loretta was simply invited to attend. I look back now with little memory of the day, but a photograph shows Loretta entering the church on the arm of my old friend, neighbour and ex-workmate, John Cloney. It was news to me that they were seeing each other, though when I thought about it later I recalled noticing a certain envy in John whenever she turned up to watch me play in the local cricket team, and it was always in the back of my mind that he fancied her. What was interesting about seeing them together on that day was that I felt nothing; I was finally over her, so that if Yvonne had been concerned that there could be a climate of ill-feeling between us, she need not have. Feeling between us had cooled forever, and we were moving in totally opposite spheres. In fact it was not just Loretta and those times that I was putting behind me, it was a whole attitude to the kind of life I had been brought up to lead, to my past, my family, my idea of a future. And this is what I mean by 1961 being a watershed: I was undergoing a fundamental renovation of self. To this point, nothing I had done had proved to be lasting – no kind of work, no relationship, no friendship, no place of living. I had been raised and contained within a working class, Housing Commission, Catholic, poorly educated community, and it did not make me happy, any of it. Simply, though I say this without intentional arrogance, I felt I was better than it, but I did not know how to prove it to myself or anybody else. And that is what I had to do – prove it. I had to go out into the world on my own, take it on, search and find what it was that could satisfy me, and in order to do that I had to abandon the person I'd so far been, including all the trappings that kept that person locked in place – family, friends, work. They all had to go. I had to walk out on my family – even my brother, for whom I always had much affection – because they would not have understood my need for a total change. My friends, with the exception of Bob, who was an important instrument in shaping this new self, they too had to be left behind, even Ron and Yvonne, who in their own way were taking a new direction together; marriage would commit them to a kind of life I wanted no part of. None of my boyhood friends had anything I wanted now. And work – well, no kind of work that I was qualified to do was worth wasting my time on; it simply kept me in a routine of nine-to-five, playing silly games for the good of a corporation that didn't do anything interesting. I wanted something more, something else.

It was in this spirit that I walked into the office of my boss, Norm McGuinness, at BP and announced that I was resigning, in fact giving up work altogether. He looked puzzled, as if I was speaking a foreign language. 'Some illness – you or your family?' he asked.

'No, I'm going to sing folk songs in coffee lounges.'

He gave a grin as if to say I was pulling his leg. But when he realised I was serious, he quickly found a positive in the prospect of my leaving. It had long been obvious to him and everybody else that I didn't like the job, and was not doing it properly. So he nodded and asked me to put my notice in writing, and went back to what he was doing. The personnel manager in his best fake English voice said, 'Where are you going, Shell?' as if that would be the only desirable alternative to working for BP. Brian Moll said, 'Good for you,' and meant it. Lucy Mitchell shrugged carelessly and smiled her approval. 'I don't blame you,' she said, 'no-one in their right mind would want to spend their life here.' My two colleagues in the insurance section wanted the addresses of where I sang, and said they'd come and listen to me, though they never did. And Ian Bannon wanted to know how much money I was going to be making, and whether I could live like that for long.

It was a great moment, a moment of sheer liberation, walking out of the Queen Street building for the last time, knowing that it was not just BP I was free of, but the whole imprisoning world of office work, indeed of any strictly routine employment, and I told myself it was forever: never again would I take a permanent job I didn't like, never again would I pretend that I was embarking on a career when all I was in fact doing was marking time to the tune of others, and being poorly paid for doing it. I was free to make a new start.

By this time I had tracked down Karl Ogdon where he worked at the State Library, and had begun taking guitar lessons. He insisted from the start that I learn strict classical technique, because that would establish the best basis for whatever music I wanted to play, though he was not able to help with any of the more sophisticated American picking techniques that Joan Baez used, and which I longed to imitate. His teaching was based around Matteo Carcassi and Fernando Sor studies, with lots of arpeggios, chords and attention to proper left-hand position. These were very useful for adapting to folk-song accompaniment, and in fact Karl had an interest in folk music, belonged to the Australian Folkore Society, and had been involved in their production of *Reedy River* a few years earlier. His own playing was, I eventually saw, somewhat limited to arpeggios, block and broken chords, base runs and tremolo. He was not strong on scales, certainly had no speed in this technique, and because he did not use his fingernails (he bit them), he could not generate much volume with his right hand. He also knew little about rasgueado or apoyando techniques. Nevertheless, he played sweetly, with few errors, and, more important, composed his own music. When the Emerald Hill theatre in South Melbourne began holding Sunday afternoon concerts, Karl played a beautiful sonata he had written. His friends, including me, had watched with bated breath as his small, nervous, black-bearded figure sat in the stage spotlight; he was very shy and stammered badly at times, and I was worried that his lack of volume would make him difficult to hear, but in fact the audience was so taken with him you could hear a pin drop, and he played flawlessly and rose unsmilingly at the end to rapturous applause.

Gradually, now that I am not working, I get to know more and more people in The Push. My first experience of one of their shared houses is in Collins Street, the top end of the city, when Bob takes me one night to visit people he had first met at Max Beatty's. From the street it is a grand Italianate creation of the 1880's boom, with walled stone steps leading up to a huge entrance, a massive front door with brass furniture, and a fanlight above with a broken pane. The grey stone exterior is markedly shabby, but the ground floor inside is respectable enough – clean, its white paintwork only a little chipped and stained. The floors above – three or four of them possibly – become increasingly derelict as you climb the uncarpeted staircase with its partially broken banister, its damaged arches and holed walls exposing the laths. No doubt, it is headed for demolition, given its prime position. For the moment, however, its shabby grandeur is enjoyed by a tribe of scruffs, renting it cheaply and living like princes in exile. I actually feel a little threatened by them at first. Mike Herron, Mike someone-or-other who is responsible for the rent, his moody girlfriend, the lovely Liliane, Spike Jones and his rotund girlfriend June, all talk in a mixture of intellectual precocity and obscenity. Spike is obsessed with fat women, can't stand skinny ones. He will follow a fat woman through the city, begging for her phone number, simply because of her size. Mike Herron is an angry young man, full of violent opinions, provocative sex talk. 'I masturbated with a carrot stuck halfway up my arse,' he laughs. He is a schoolteacher and talks frankly about his sexual interest in some of the boys. In one of the huge rooms is a girl calling herself Lilith. She has red dyed hair and teeth stained green from neglect, dresses in purple and black, and acts weird, as if on drugs. But this is a time before drugs in Melbourne. Not even these people take them, not even marijuana, which within the span of five years will be easily available throughout the city, throughout the country. But not now. Booze and sex are the chief stimulants, and of course Art, in all its modes. Lilith calls herself a storyteller – she doesn't write or paint, simply talks her fantasies to anyone who'll listen. I wonder what she would be like to have sex with, but she creates the impression that she is untouchable, above that kind of thing, though this, surely, is part of her act. Of all the residents, I prefer Spike. He is funny, self-deprecating and idealistic in a not-very-bright way. June is the same. He tells the story of getting her away from her parents when she was fifteen – that is, under the age of consent. Her father did everything he could to prevent her going with Spike, even locking her in her bedroom at night, though she forced the window open and fled. He followed her after school to Collins Street, and planning to surprise them together, waited a while before searching out their room. Failing to find them *in flagrante*, he yelled abuse at them from the doorway, and, stepping into a pile of sweepings June had not yet taken away, he screamed, 'Look at this! I'm up to my knees in filth!'

Spike always has a funny story to tell, and always has a new complaint against mainstream society. He works as a seaman, goes off on ships for long stretches, preaches socialism to his shipmates, and then lays off at home for months, during which time he says he wants to paint and draw, though he never gets around to it. June models at the National Gallery School, has an ideal body for an artist's model – rounded, smooth-skinned, large breasted, a cherub-face and long auburn hair.

One night after playing at The Copper Kettle I drop in at Collins Street. Often after singing, now that I am not working, I look for something to do, someone to talk to, in the early hours when I am still on a high and unable to sleep. Which means I don't get to bed until three o'clock sometimes, which in turn means I sleep till around lunch time. My mother doesn't like this, nor did she like it when I gave up work. She says I am becoming a Beatnik, and am going to end up on the streets. As soon as I get the chance, I will move back out of home and find somewhere else to live. This particular night, I park the VW in a lane at the back of Collins Street, expecting to go in the back door. But it is closed and locked, so with my guitar in my hand I walk around via Spring Street to the front, which is usually left with the latch snibbed. It is a warm, dark night and the streets are almost deserted, except that, as I approach the front steps, a black Holden is moving slowly along Collins Street towards me, and a voice calls through its window 'Hey, there's a Beatnik. Let's get him!' and the Holden screeches to a stop. My heart races, anticipating trouble. I hurry towards the building, hearing the doors of the car slam and footsteps hurrying toward me. I race up the solid steps to the deeply shadowed front door, only to find that someone has locked it and I can't get in. Always smart in an emergency, I leap the low wall of the steps and drop into the shadows beneath, and freeze, not moving a muscle, not breathing. Their footsteps slow to a walk as they approach the building. One of them goes up a step or two until, seeing the heavy door shut, he stops and says, 'He's gone in – missed him.' Obviously they have not seen me take refuge in the shadows. They leave, return to their car, screech off. I wait until I am sure they are well away, then knock loudly with the brass knocker, until Spike hears me and lets me in. He wants to go out and find the 'rockers', as he calls them, and give them a lecture on the error of their ways, but June, bug-eyed, absolutely forbids it. 'My biggest worry,' I tell them, 'was that they would smash up my guitar.' But I'm not sure that it really was my biggest worry.

Another character I meet is Adrian Rawlins, again through Bob, in another apartment in Park Street, South Yarra. Adrian is everywhere, and it was inevitable that I would come across him sooner or later, so much so that the more difficult tack is avoiding him. A collection of painters, poets, musicians and others hang out at Bob's flat from time to time, including Sid Clayton, a quietly spoken bass player with an off-beat sense of humour, and Adrian is always among them, getting the coffee, answering the phone, busily lubricating the talk with promotional schemes for their respective talents that will bring fame and fortune to each of them. Adrian is a sponger in the best Beat tradition, though most of his acquaintances don't mind too much, because he does try to give something back by way of encouragement. In the same vein, Adrian writes to the American poet Allen Ginzburg around this time, asking the Great Man for some words of wisdom and encouragement. Eventually the reply comes, 'Send money, send money!' Adrian protests at the insult, but it must occur to him at some point that he lives by the same philosophy.

I am, of course, nobody in these gatherings, and am thus treated with scorn by Adrian, who has that tendency of the deprived to compensate by kicking the person below, if they can find one such. A feeble appeal by me one night for a 'tolerant' attitude to the world is met with a furious outburst from Adrian that there is already 'too much tolerance' and that what is needed is more hatred and anger. In front of the others I am chastised and humiliated. He has no qualms about exploiting me, however: I am one of the few with a car, and he frequently gets me to drive him to some out-of-the-way place at some godforsaken hour, not with gratitude but as a right, issuing orders. 'Go down the next street, there's someone I must drop in on', or 'Wait here for me,' until he emerges with some new member of The Push, and insist I take them both somewhere even more out-of-the-way. It does not take me long, however, to learn to say No to Adrian, or at least to always have a reason to keep him at arm's length.

Bob has developed a new direction in his painting through meeting Ian Sime, who does large, very dynamic abstracts with considerable flair and technical wizardry. Sime is also something of a self-educated philosopher, will extemporise unstoppably for hours on Buddhism, Irish history, esoteric beliefs from different cultures, peppered with his own opinions and value judgments, with such passionate fluency that it is difficult for anyone else in the room to get a word in. His painting, moreover, is wonderful, and I can see very easily why Bob is so impressed and wants to learn some of his methods, as well as absorb his approach to art. Sime is worth listening to when he turns up at a party, or at his house, where he lives surrounded by astonishing pictures, and shares with his beautiful, sophisticated wife.

Late in that year I go with Bob, Max and Beth and one or two others to the Arts Ball, held in the Exhibition Buildings. I have never seen anything like it. There are people of all ages and types, shapes and sizes, in any kind of mad dress-up they could conceive – top hats and bathing suits, long old-fashioned dresses and cricket caps, snazzy dark suits with gum boots, girls with almost nothing on, bearded long-haired men in vari-coloured cloaks made from bedspreads. There are strangely made-up faces and exotic masks, and dozens of crazy costumes patched together from bits and pieces found in family attics or second-hand shops. The one thing that this motley array has in common is its wildly abandoned behaviour, both on and off the dance floor. To raucous Dixieland jazz played by a well-known local band the dancers hurl themselves around each other, either drunk or acting so, but certainly self-induced into a state of near hysterical joy. I watch as Adrian Rawlins, writhing in shapeless arabesques alone in the centre of the floor, sheds his casual clothes one-by-one until he is standing in grey, filthy underpants that because of the tired elastic are gradually slipping down his legs, exposing his crotch. Calmly observing this and the seething mass of bodies all around him are Max and Beth, preoccupied in their own personal ecstasy; leaning forward on his chair and facing her, Max has his hand all the way up Beth's skirt, as she sits knees wide apart and smiling beatifically down on Max's equally happy face. The frankness, the defiance, in their private-made-public sexuality, is both shocking and enlightening to a working-class Catholic boy raised to believe that sex should take place in private behind closed doors, but who is nevertheless pleased in this moment to have his ideas challenged. Why is it that sex is only okay at night, in the dark, and that to do it in the daylight, in the open, is indecent? Is this something to do with shame, something to do with our First Sin and the banishment from Eden as the nuns taught us, to live forever in guilt?

Some months after my first visit to Collins Street, it turns out that everyone has to depart, because the building is to be totally renovated. Bob, Spike and June and myself decide to find a share house together. I am eager to get away from home, which is becoming increasingly annoying, not just because of the differences between me and my family, but also because West Ivanhoe is so far from the things that matter to me, which are now, or perhaps I should say once again, centred around the inner city, though to a very different purpose now. Spike and June have a knack of finding good places to live, and soon come up with a great venue – a double-storey stone terrace of grand proportions with Italianate porch arches, a little run-down through its many years as a renter, but comfortable enough for the four of us. I can just manage my share of the rent on my earnings from singing, which I have recently supplemented with a weekly spot at the Café Ad Lib in Toorak Road, South Yarra. That particular gig came to me after I sang at one of the first of the concerts at the Emerald Hill Theatre, which were run by Wal Cherry, who also ran a Repertory company there. Wal, a man of the Left, had a long-standing enthusiasm for folk music, especially the 1950s American movement that went back through Pete Seeger and the Weavers to Woodie Guthrie and Huddie Leadbetter. The concerts were to be a regular event, and along with established ones such as Martin Wyndham–Read, Brian Mooney, Peter Laycock, the Seekers, many emerging performers were given an opportunity there. Fearfully nervous, I sang a couple of American ballads, which seemed to go down okay. Afterwards, Glen Tomasetti, a seasoned performer with good looks and a lovely voice, befriended me and asked if I'd like to take over one of her nights at the Ad Lib, because she had more work than she could handle. It was typical of Glen's comradely spirit, indeed typical of the spirit of the folk movement in those early years, to look out for each other and share songs, stories, singing venues with each other.

Bob does not stay long in the Lygon Street house. He has found himself a new girlfriend, Carol, who is not particularly enamoured of Spike and June. So Bob and Carol take a place of their own together, leaving me with Spike and June. Soon it is only me and June, rattling around in the huge house, when Spike, always in need of money, signs on to a ship that will keep him overseas for some months. June is a little down and neurotic, is afraid to be left in the house alone, and though it occasionally crosses my mind that we could end up in bed together, I am not keen for this to happen. I don't really fancy her, and am not sure how Spike would take it if he knew. So there is a certain tension between me and June which makes living in the house a bit dismal, with the consequence that I stay out a lot. I am of course pursuing my own sexual interests, taking out various girls, mostly from the coffee lounges where I sing. One in particular, Patti, who frequents the Ad Lib, is a strange, attractive girl who takes me back to her shared flat for long, soulful conversations, but won't agree to sex. Several times I give up on her, but then she turns up at the Ad Lib again and revives the relationship, again without sex. She is caught between two worlds – the mainstream respectability of her office job, and her occasional brushes with The Push that brings her into contact with characters such as me. She can't decide where she belongs, though I eventually learn that her real interest lies in a cameraman from the Channel Seven network; that, I conclude is her real milieu: TV, creativity with recognition, a bit of glamour, money. I and my new friends have nothing but disdain for it.

For some time during this year I try to keep attending the Modern History class at Taylor's, but my interest is waning, giving way to music. Miss Scholes insists on keeping in touch, and we meet for lunch or to see a play together from time to time. When she hears I am singing she wants me to visit and sing for her, so I do. Her response surprises me, because I hadn't counted on her having a deep knowledge of and affection for the old English ballads. When I sing 'Mary Hamilton' to her, she is moved to tears, and wants me to sing more. I go through some of my Joan Baez songs, which she listens to intently. But she can see me slipping away academically, and is powerless to stop it.

I am spending more time at The Reata, singing occasionally, but mainly because I have become good friends with Brian Brophy, the flamenco guitarist. I have never seen anyone play the guitar more brilliantly, in fact I have never seen a genuine flamenco guitarist before. Brian was a carpenter in Brisbane until several years ago, when he became seduced by the gypsy folk art. He bought albums by the master Sabicas, and developed a way of slowing down the record and identifying the notes and techniques being used, and applying them. Research into the culture and meeting other guitarists helped him develop, so that he has become an authentic, knowledgeable and highly skilful musician in the field. He is a stocky, blond, taciturn fellow with no interest in copying the Beatnik style of Push people, wears ordinary trousers and shirts, scuffed dress shoes, and plays a custom made flamenco guitar, yellow-blonde with a very thin spruce top, wooden string pegs and a white plastic guard under the sound hole, all looking the worse for wear. He makes a meagre living from his playing, and rents a room above The Reata. When I tell him I want to learn American picking techniques, he works them out for me using his slow-down record-player method, until I am able to master every pick that Joan Baez uses. When I start using these picks in performance, other singers in Melbourne regard me with interest, and some want me to pass it on to them, which I always do.

I have no thought for where my singing might take me. I do not think of it in 'career' terms, am not ambitious to establish myself as a popular performer, getting on television, making recordings, being managed. It is an expression of my present desire to 'find myself', according to the cliché. There is something satisfying in the act of singing to an audience: it makes one the centre of an action, which I like. It gives me physical pleasure just to let the voice flow forth, and it gives me intellectual pleasure to relate the stories that traditional folk songs tell, and to be the vehicle for the point they often make. It also gives me an artistic satisfaction to marry a well-worked out accompaniment to the melody, so that on all fronts my decision to become a folk singer, if decision is what it was, is proving to be a good one, and is certainly turning my life in a new and happy direction. Even my mother is showing a certain pride in my efforts, and when the *Sun* newspaper does a feature on me in their weekend edition, she cuts it out and folds it safely away in a drawer. Instructive, how a little recognition can bring people round to your way of thinking.

9

IT WOULD BE PAINTING A FLATTERING PICTURE of myself to say that at this time I lived very much in the present, when it could just as easily be said that I gave no thought to the future. Glass half full, glass half empty. Either way, I was indulging in this new freedom, especially freedom from the boredom of work. And there was a positive side: I was finding that being the focus of attention and playing a guitar was a great help in the pursuit of the opposite sex. Singing in The Reata one night, I chatted to two attractive girls from Adelaide, from German families, one of whom, Helga, seemed keen, but they were leaving early the following morning, so the best she could do was to give me her address. A week or two later I hitchhiked to Adelaide for the weekend just to see her. I couldn't afford the petrol to drive all that way, and I was sure she would find me a bed for the night, so I figured to do it at the least expense. Unlike a man I got to know around that time, one David Bradbury, I was not the type to make hitchhiking into an art-form. Tall, bearded, slightly but not too dishevelled, an American baseball cap tipped back on his head, carrying a neat and manageable back-pack, David always looked like he would be an interesting travelling companion when merely standing at the side of the road with his thumb cocked. Nor did he disappoint when picked up. He was a lively raconteur, spoke in educated tones, infectiously good-humoured. It was easy to believe his claim that most who gave him a lift were sorry to part from him, and more than once he was taken home for supper and a bed for the night by an enchanted farmer, and heartfelt goodbyes and contact details were exchanged with the family when he left in the morning. David lived half his life on the road, half doing part-time work at anything he could get. He was a prodigious reader, which provided the source of his entertaining yarns to his providers. As a hitchhiker, I unfortunately was no Bradbury, and generally was happy to let the driver do the talking.

This journey to Adelaide took several stages in a variety of vehicles – a travelling salesman-driven Holden from the outskirts of Footscray to Ararat, to Horsham in a ute driven by a youngish farm-hand with the standard brown dog in the back, a short ride in a sleek Jaguar with a tough faced Lady of Property who told me about her plans to breed poodles, and dropped me at a point about half way to Nhill, while she sped off on a side road in a cloud of dust. I sat on my pack for nearly an hour in the breezy afternoon sunlight, my guitar prominent against my leg in the hope it would make me look interesting, imagining myself a wandering loner, like someone out of Kerouac.

When I got to Adelaide, though her mother kindly allowed me to stay the night in the spare room, Helga was less hospitable. It soon became clear that she was an irretrievably conventional and priggish young woman, with no intention of letting me touch her, and as I became more familiar with her way of thinking my desire to do that cooled rapidly. She was deeply absorbed in the office intrigues where she worked, which she rattled on about as she sat on the end of my bed, and precipitately said she couldn't be my girlfriend because I was a musician and didn't have a steady job, and that this was the wrong way round for the two sexes – the man should have the steady job, and the woman involved in the arts and be not working. I got away from her as soon after breakfast as I could. So much for impulsive romances.

But stumping along the roadside back to Melbourne under a huge blue sky and morning sun, I consoled myself with the belief that I had at least taken myself on a bold adventure. Thumbing for a ride with my guitar slung over my shoulder, imagining myself a wandering minstrel, wondering if I could spend my life on the road doing gig spots and moving on, I did feel truly free, unreal as it was. These were the years when freedom was the catch cry of existentialists, Beats, Dharma Bums and drop-outs all over the world, and folk singers were a modest expression of this mood of the times. I didn't know much about the philosophy or even the literature at that stage, but I had caught the sniff of this new liberality all around me: schoolkids were getting into trouble for growing their hair long, teenage girls were giving lease to their sexuality with increasing defiance of convention and parental control. The sixties, albeit from a slow beginning, were gradually getting underway, and I felt it was my time too.

I had visited Bob in his flat early in the new year, and he read to me a letter from Max Beatty, who had finally realised a long-held dream and gone with Beth to live in tropical Queensland, just out of Cairns. The letter was full of funny descriptions of the local way of life, some of the strange characters they knew, and the bizarre, sun-soaked existence Max and Beth and their baby were leading. Bob was so impressed that he and Carol, now his wife, had decided to drive up and join them. My first impulse was to go too, though travelling with them would not be comfortable for any of us, so in the end I didn't ask. Days later, chatting with Brian Brophy in his room above *The Reata*, along with a tall, apparently American folk singer called Larry King, I told them about Max and Bob and Cairns. 'Why don't we go?' they suggested. With the three of us pitching in, we could cover the expenses of driving up in my VW, staying with friends along the way – Brophy knew people in Sydney and Brisbane who would put us up for a night. We had no idea of how long we might stay or what we would do when we got there, but such matters were incidental. All we wanted was change, a new experience. And for Brophy it was a chance to revisit his Brisbane friends. So the three of us, along with our guitars and a few clothes, piled into my little blue VW and headed for the north. In Sydney we ended up in a houseful of Push types whose pet snake slept in the bed with two of them, and who dismissed us as bourgeois Melbourne nobodies. When we got to Brisbane I realised that we were barely half way, that in fact Cairns was as far from there as it was from Melbourne. In Brisbane, a friend of Brophy, Sebastian Jorgensen, then living in Brisbane, took us to Wynnum to visit John Manifold, the renowned folklorist and collector. A descendant of an old Landed family, educated at Cambridge, a veteran of World War Two, and a member of the Communist Party, he lived in a stately Queenslander on a large outlying property. He was at odds with 'progressive' post-War Australia, living a kind of emblematic retreat from the way things were going. Not that I had any grasp of his importance at the time; I blench when I recall how green and ignorant I was, and how little I understood him. He scorned this new folk revival, said the young did not appreciate the beauty and political meaning of Australian folk culture, and that all this complicated guitar playing was totally unsuitable for the songs, which should be sung unaccompanied or with simple arpeggios at most. My unspoken reaction was that he was a pompous, out-of-touch old curmudgeon, but as I reflect now I can sympathise with his disappointment over a nation that was losing its old identity and heading with increasing momentum into capitalist dependency, as I can with his suspicion of the young. That did not, of course, make him right, but I was not wise enough then to see the good that was clearly in him.

It took us five days on the road to reach Cairns. The journey was uncomfortable and tedious, with the inevitable moments of tension between us. Our clothes, our bodies, the car, stank of sweat, dirty socks and tobacco – we all smoked constantly – of farts and stale food dropped between the seats, and I still can't recall where we slept some nights. Larry turned out to be a fake – he was from Tasmania – who finally gave up putting on an American accent, and whose name, which I've forgotten, was not even Larry. Nor had I ever liked his music – his speciality was 'Scarlet Ribbons', a soupy Country and Western piece that got smuggled into the folk repertoire from time to time but didn't belong. 'Larry' departed from us in Brisbane, and Brian and I took turns driving the rest of the way. Notwithstanding the hard work of getting there, Cairns proved a delightful and memorable place. Warm, casual, friendly, it was the most cosmopolitan town I'd seen, full of people of all colours and cultures, from Aborigines and Islanders to Maoris, Indians, Filipinos, Chinese, mixing freely among the various white tribes in the streets. Brophy introduced me to a Queensland delicacy – the pie with peas, sold from the back of a street vendor's van. The meat pie is stuffed with a green mush under the lid, and eaten straight from its paper bag. Delicious.

In the afternoon we drove the twenty minutes to Yorkey's Knob, where the Beattys lived; Bob and Carol had already been staying with them a week or so. The house was essentially a large timber cabin on two-foot stilts, comprising a long rectangular room with a kitchen scullery and dining table at one end, and a double bed where Bob and Carol slept at the other. A doorway led off to Max and Beth's bedroom and bathroom. The floorboards were bare and unpolished, the lining-sheet walls hung with Max's *pointilliste* abstracts, looking surprisingly apt in that setting, the furniture basic but uncommon – kangaroo-back chairs, a battered table with turned legs, mattresses on low pallets, an Indian throw on the bed. Outside, the garden was luxuriant with rich green buffalo grass and fruit trees – guavas, carambolas, custard apples, bananas, paw-paw, and with Max and Beth getting around semi-naked in frayed bits of clothing, the general feel of the place was of Bohemia in the jungle, starring Tarzan and Jane and their small son, Boy Beatty (whose name I can't recall). Yorkey's Knob itself was a beach promontory covered in tropical plants and bush grass, wound through with sandy paths that led to cement-sheet shacks hidden away in the shrubbery. Some of these were residences, others were rarely used holiday huts. Facing the beach was a long, low green painted pub, where people came on weekends to party and enjoy the pop-rock band. The sparse population was white – there was an aboriginal community a mile north at Trinity Beach, and a few living a similar distance south at Holloway's Beach. The Knob itself was raw and exposed to the elements, but back from the beach it was a natural overgrown garden, unfortunately ideal for future development as a resort, though that would be some years off. In the sixties it was a largely forgotten postscript to Cairns.

Within a day or so Brophy and I found a little cement shack to rent, tucked off the main road behind tall shrubbery, with basic cooking and sleeping facilities and an outside dunny. After sitting in the sun, chatting and practicing our guitars, cooking a meal and wondering what to do next, the thought struck me, 'What am I doing here? How am I going to pass the time? There's no place to sing, no one to sing to, no way of earning any money. I'm closer to Nature, but so what? It's Culture I do my living in, and there is precious little of it here.' Thank god I had the car – my little blue VW, my lifeline to the world, my escape route from boredom.

Later that week I went for a solo walk up to Trinity Beach. The sand was immaculate, pure white and unmarked for as far as I could see along the beach, and the palm trees up behind it were tall and shade-giving. Coconuts lay scattered in the tufts of grass underneath, many of them brown and ripe. I saw not a soul for the two hours or so I was there, feeling something of the solitariness a castaway must feel when landing on a desert island. There was something exciting about experiencing such isolation, and being in an environment that had not changed for hundreds, maybe thousands, of years. On the way back I took a different route, through a forest of palms and soft green carpets of sunlit grass, not especially noticing the little black smudges that hovered around my ankles as I walked through it. But later that evening I paid the price of my ignorance; my lower legs and feet began to itch maddeningly. Sand flies, Max laughed; keep away from them. The relief from scratching was wonderful, but addictive: the more I scratched, the more it itched, and on I went till little droplets of blood oozed through my skin, and the mixture of pain and relief was deliciously horrible. I even got hold of a stiff-bristled scrubbing brush from Max's kitchen, and raked my legs and shins till I thought I would go crazy, at which point Beth dabbed some methylated spirits on my skin, and I was able to make the supreme effort to leave myself alone. By morning, the itching had ceased.

Money was an issue, and under Max's expert guidance I decided to apply for the dole; the last thing I wanted was a job. Max pointed out that you have to actually apply for work, but the trick is to nominate a type of employment they can't find for you. Apparently, the CES (Commonwealth Employment Service) was duty bound to make an initial effort to find work that you are qualified to do, and in the meantime to pay you the appropriate social security. So I went along to the office in Cairns, filled out the form, and in the 'Required Employment' box I wrote 'poet'. As he read through the form the officer baulked. 'Poet?' he barked, and without a hint of irony said, 'We can't find you work as a poet up here!' There was a vague implication, however, that he would look into the possibility. A few days later a cheque arrived in the post, so that at least the rent and food were taken care of for the time being.

Before long Brophy had befriended a Maori called Jim, who played electric guitar Friday and Saturday nights at the pub. Impressed by Brophy's guitar prowess, Jim asked for lessons, so this small income gave Brophy something to contribute to the housekeeping; he was not keen to apply for the dole, fearing they would find him work at his old carpentry trade. Jim was a likeable, powerfully built young man with a pretty wife called Lola, who sang and did little sexy 'hula' moves on stage with Jim's band. They had a couple of young children, lived in a ramshackle house surrounded by chickens and old furniture, beside the raw hull of the substantial boat Jim had been building for two years in the front yard. Lola constantly urged him to finish the boat, so they could sell it and pay some bills. Brophy helped occasionally, and was paid with free meals and drink. On one occasion Jim put on a feast for family and friends, the centrepiece of which was a young pig which they slaughtered, wrapped in banana leaves, and packed under rocks that had been heated in a fire for hours. With Lola 's salads, rice, fruits, bread all laid out on a table in front of the house, people heaped their plates, topped it with steaming cuts of baked pork, and took it to eat on their laps in little chatty groups around the lush garden. It was a memorable feast, and afterwards Jim set up his amplifier and his group played and Lola sang and was the star turn, and very watchable she was too.

Bob and Carol did not stay in Queensland for long. They had gotten off to a bad start on the long drive up, when the trailer with all their belongings had disintegrated behind them at seventy miles an hour, strewing the contents along the road for hundreds of yards. Much was broken and lost. Carol, who did nothing with her time but sit around in a morose boredom, wanted badly to go back to Melbourne. Bob may have painted a little, but was himself not properly settled into any kind of routine of work, so he seemed unhappy too. Within a month or so they had gone, and I worried about Bob. Carol seemed to be yet another woman who was not right for him.

None of us, except the Beattys maybe, should have thought of this mad venture as anything but a holiday. But Max and Beth's entrenchment in the place was so rooted that it lured us into thinking of it as a possible way of life. Whilst I never quite moved from possible to definite, I did find the place so beguilingly different from anything I known, and so full of surprises, that I was prepared to hang on indefinitely throughout that year. I recall trips we took, up to the Atherton tableland, where lush tropical rainforests and crystal waterfalls created a magical world apart, the music of birdcalls echoing through the steep gullies, tree-lined into darkly natural cathedrals. At Mareeba in the Tablelands we spent a day picnicking around the lake, enchanted by dozens of small tortoises swimming up to nibble food from our hands. And all of this in the most perfect weather, warm but comfortable, sleepily remote from civilisation, unconcerned with what the rest of the world might be doing. Nothing pressed me to make any plans to return to Melbourne, and as the late summer gave way to winter, and the hot, steamy Cairns days moderated into consistent, mild temperatures, encouraging even more outdoor liveability than was advisable in the full summer, I grew more and more content with the place. Unless something happened to change my mind, it would be difficult to tear myself away.

Michael, a handsome young Thursday Islander, comes around with his guitar, an old 'f' hole with strings set too high for comfortable fretting, and sings 'Moon River', strumming some nice chords with his thumb in the old fashioned Country and Western way. When I play Carter Family licks and fancy on/off-beat finger picking, he wants me to show him how. He is quick to learn the techniques, but the trouble is he doesn't have suitable songs for this kind of accompaniment. Still, he plans to work on it. A number of the Aborigine guys play guitar, sing cowboy songs. I wish they would learn some of the Australian folk songs, but they don't seem interested in that kind of music, it doesn't seem to speak to them as much as Pop and Country and Western music does, which is not so culturally specific, or being American, has nothing to do with the white Australian culture that they feel excluded from. With this non-Australian material they feel free to make the sentiments in them their own.

Max talks about a character called George, who lives at Holloway's Beach, a little community down the coast. He has recently run into George, who wants to meet us new arrivals from the south, so a small party has been organised at George's house. On the way we drop in on another local called Ron Edwards. Ron is interested in Australian folk songs and folklore, is a friend of John Manifold, and we have an interesting chat about versions of songs he knows and collects, is planning a book on the subject. He is a casual friendly fellow, following his interests unconcerned with cultural correctness. As far as he is concerned a folk song is anything that people like to sing – a bush ballad or a song from the hit parade. He is also something of a painter, went to art school when he was young. To help pay his way, he does watercolours targeting possible tourists, though so far there are no signs of such a market taking off at Holloway's Beach. His method is to place a dozen or so sheets of watercolour paper on a long bench, and then go along with his brush and paint in all the skies first, then go back, take a different colour, do all the ground areas next, then go back, put in all the trees, with small variations. Art on the Fordist principle. Ron sees no problem in it – an economical way to maintain production.

George is a large, very fat German, with a tall, gaunt wife called Jenny. He has lived around Cairns for some years, until, having lured Jenny away from her family, getting her pregnant (she lost the baby), and marrying her, he moved out to Holloway's Beach. She seems mentally retarded, is scrag-haired, a skinny counterbalance to George's rotundity, Laurel and Hardy, billiard cue and ball. They live in a large corrugated shed with nothing more than a sink and portable gas stove in one corner, and a double bed with a battered chest of drawers far off in the other corner. It has a dirt floor with chunks of old linoleum scattered inadequately about, and a weak electric bulb failing to improve on the feeble light leeching through the small windows on the shady side of the shed.

The so-called party comprises a stagnant pool of local oddities sitting on the few chairs, or on the dirt floor, or standing in the half-light against the wall. It is stifling hot and airless, the beer is warm and everyone seems to be waiting for some sort of a beginning. Beth sits eating a carambola at the table next to Jenny, who sits dumbly staring into space. A menacing looking character chain smokes in the background, sucking on a large brown bottle of beer in between puffs. An old man called Swampy, bearded and brown as a nut, sits on the floor cackling to himself about some private matter. George is walking around impatiently, doing most of the talking in his caricature German accent. He has a theory, or a scheme rather, a solution to "the aboriginal problem". They would make excellent storm troopers, he is saying, in the National Socialist party he is thinking of starting. It is impossible to tell whether he is joking or serious, but nobody challenges him. He is forceful, erudite and I think mad as a snake. Suddenly Jenny speaks.

'George wants to start a Nasty Party,' she says in her slow, dreamy voice.

'Nazi, Nazi!' George corrects.

'Nazi then,' she mumbles, and goes quiet again.

Max, nursing his child on an upturned fruit box, looks at Beth then at me, and shrugs. But George's talk, and the effect of the beer going around, seems to have prompted several tangential conversations, still in low murmurs at this point. A young couple who seem to live in the next house along the road from George and Jenny begin outlining their plans to move to Green Island, off the coast of Cairns, by means of a boat they have built. 'We want to get away from society: there's too much materialism, too much emphasis on competition. We want to live in a community based on co-operation, and be self-sufficient,' says the young man, wiry, black-bearded, gleaming-eyed. Competitive materialism does not appear, from the look of them, to hold them in its vicious jaws. They have already tried and failed once when the rudimentary boat they built to take them across the strait sank not a hundred yards from shore, and they waded back with embarrassed grins carrying waterlogged bundles of their belongings in their waterlogged clothes. Now, apparently, they are about to try again.

Somehow the bottle opener gets mislaid, and while everyone is searching for it the menacing-looking man promptly comes forward and opens three large beer bottles in a row with his teeth, spitting the metal tops across the room. 'Zat I could never do,' says George, drawing back his lips and showing a mouthful of gold fillings, 'Zey might be pulled outvards, ja,' and he refills his teacup with beer from one of the bottles.

From his sitting position on the floor, old wizened Swampy calls out, 'You know,' he cackles, 'sometimes I bite me toenails till they bleed.'

'Bullshit, you old bugger,' says the bearded young man, 'you haven't got a tooth in your head.'

At no point does George show any interest in me or in the fact that I've come from the south, which is why we've come here in the first place. But when I talk with old Swampy, he is prepared to reflect on the subject. 'I went down south once, years ago,' he says, 'but I didn't like it. Too cold, too many people. Oh, no, no I couldn't live down there in the south,' he mutters.

'Well,' I say, 'we get some hot weather down in Melbourne too you know. Depends on the time of year. When did you go?'

'Where?' he says, scowling.

'Melbourne.'

'Melbourne? Melbourne be buggered, never been there in me life. I'm talken' about Brisbane. Brisbane's too cold, too crowded.'

What does he think Melbourne can be like, I wonder. It might as well be the middle of the Antarctic, or Africa for that matter, for all Swampy knows about the world.

Eventually the menacing looking man sidles over to me. He is still mouthing the brown beer bottle and smoking the butt of a hand-rolled cigarette. 'Wanna hear a good joke?' he says. I nod. 'It's not really a joke – it's a true story for all I know. There's these two blokes working up in the rain forest near Daintree, timber-cutting, and living in a shack in the bush. There's nothing to do up there but work and drink. Every night and on the weekends, these two blokes drink themselves stupid, wipe themselves out till they can't see straight. Anyway, this weekend they've really put it away, so pissed they can hardly stand up. Suddenly one says to the other, 'Have y'ever played rooster?'

'Rooster?' says the other, 'wosthat?'

'Well, iss easy. You go over there and put your head on the choppen block, an' I go and get the axe, and then I chop your head off.'

'Yeah? No, I've never played that game.'

'Ya wanna play it now?'

'Sure, why not?'

'Okay, you go over there and put your head on the choppen block.'

So the other guy goes over and does as he's told, puts his head on the chopping block, and the first guy goes and gets the axe, makes his way over and says 'Y'ready?' and his mate says 'Yeah,' and the first guy chops his head off.'

I wait for a punch line, some ending that will turn it into a joke, but there is none. I've had the punch line, that was it. The menacing guy is giving me a sickly grin, relights his extinguished cigarette with a match, offer me a suck of his beer bottle. 'No, I've got a glass somewhere,' I say, and go in search of someone else to talk to.

On the way home Max, Beth with the child in the back, Brophy, laugh about the 'party'. For all his mad talk, George is harmless, says Max. The police know him, keep constant tabs on him. After I've dropped them at their shack, and Brophy has gone in to do some guitar practice, I go for a walk along the beach to the Knob. A rising moon creates a shining path across the sea, and gentle waves glide up the sand making little slopping sounds. The breeze is so balmy I could be naked and not feel cold. From a vantage point on the Knob I can see several cane fires burning in the distance, bright flames against the dark, where the farmers are clearing up the sugar thresh. I am haunted by the image of that timber-cutter, headless in some bush clearing, for some nightmarish reason seeing his bloody trunk standing up in a violent spasm, like a medieval knight searching for his head. And what his drunken mate would wake up to in the morning, when he saw what he had done, wishing it was he who was dead. Northern Queensland is a weird place, I think to myself, a paradise full of human flotsam. These are people who can't live in the mainstream, which is itself marred by predation of every sort. Here, the world is beautiful but the people are infantile, too naïve to cope with anything but the simple easiness of living that this world provides. What is this relation between wonderful places and deformed people, ugly places and capable people? And where do I fit in, able to accommodate myself to either, but feeling at home in neither? I still don't know where I belong, am still on the path to whatever lies ahead, god knows what it is. I turn and look again at the sea, as if to find the answer there. But of course, there is only the sound of the little waves slopping up to the sand, and the silent moon above it, tracking its course without choice. No answers to be had here.

A letter from the CES is a summons to an interview, and when I attend the officer comes to the counter and says he has found work for me. There is something sly in his manner, the reason for which becomes evident when he says that having failed to find anything of my choice, he is now bound to offer me whatever is available. 'You're a single man?' he says, knowing the answer.

'Yes.'

'There's no reason, then, why you couldn't travel?'

'I suppose not.'

It is clear that he intends to correct a situation that rankles with him, that he has seen a way to bring my smart-arse little ploy to an abrupt end.

'Good. There's a job for you up at Mareeba, working on the railway. A bit of physical labour for a change.'

Mareeba is miles north of Cairns. And me go labouring like a navvy? No thanks.

'No thanks. Not for me.'

His tone is expectant. 'You're refusing to take it?' he says.

'Not suitable for me.'

'Okay, then I'll mark you down as having refused the offer of work, and your social security payment will cease. Is that clear?'

'Perfectly.'

He turns and goes back to his desk. Fair enough, I think. At least I got six weeks' out of them. But I am going to have to find work for myself if I want to stay living at Yorkey's Knob. It turns out to be not too difficult, which tells me something more about the fellow in the CES – he wasn't trying too hard. Max knows that it is coming up planting time for the local cane producers, and that they usually need some help to get the work done. He suggests I try Alec Hale, a farmer along the Cairns highway. I drive up his gravel road through an expanse of bare fields strewn with scattered brown stalks, up to a substantial white Queenslander standing proud in a neatened clearing. 'Yes, sure,' says Alec opening the screen door after I've knocked; he's an impressively rangy man in his mid-forties, a deep, confidently Aussie voice, 'I can use a bit of help with the stripping – thirty bob a day, an hour for lunch.'

The first morning Alec is showing me how to strip the dried brown thresh off the stalks, which have been chopped into pieces about a foot long, which are then planted by tractor, pushing them into the earth to grow into next year's crop. While we are talking, a group of four or five Aborigines wanders across the paddock towards us. One, a short and stocky older man in a white shirt and dark trousers, breaks off from the others and comes smiling up to Alec. 'Hey boss,' he says, 'you got work for us fellas?'

'Nah, sorry Billy – no work, I'm all fixed up now.'

The black man continues to smile, and says, 'I tell you what boss. We don't work. What we do, we stand here along side ayou, tell jokes and stories while you work. Keep you happy while you work. Five quid a week, orright?'

It takes a moment for me to realise he is serious, and not just taking the mickey. Alec says, 'Billy, you and your mates can bugger off right now, ok? I've got enough on me mind without listening to your bullshit all day.'

'Okay boss,' comes the cheerful reply from the black man, 'We go now, us fellas. Bye bye.'

After they've gone Alec gives a snort of a laugh and shakes his head. 'Jokes!' he says, 'can you believe it.' Personally, I wouldn't have minded hearing them, for an hour or so anyway, I think. It would have been interesting to know what their jokes and stories were like.

The job lasts only about three weeks, till all the stalks are stripped and planted. But Alec knows of a pineapple farm a few miles south of Cairns that wants workers to box up the harvest for transport interstate, so I turn up there and am put on case-making work. I have to place pieces of rough sawn pine on a jig – that is, ends, sides and bottom – and nail them by hand (no nail guns then) with one-inch brads. The pay is five shillings per box, and according to Alec you can make fifty or sixty pounds a week once you get the hang of doing it at speed. The first morning, starting at 7 am, I am understandably slow, despite being given a few tips by one or two of the other workers in the shed. I bend nails, or send them flying with botched blows, I hit my thumb or fingers, I split wood by positioning the nails too close to the edge, and have to throw those pieces on a discard heap. By morning smoko I have an aching arm and bleeding fingers, and have made one box. A strong looking young farm hand asks me if I'd like a pineapple for morning tea. I wait while he goes out to the crop, brings back a fresh cut pineapple, and with a machete proceeds expertly to slash off the skin with a few clean strokes, and hands me a whole, golden, dripping pineapple. I have never tasted anything so good. The pineapples we get down south are a travesty of the name, picked green to resist travel damage, never fully ripening because pineapples are low in residual sugar. So the standard pineapple taste I have grown up with is tart. Not the case, though, when they are allowed to ripen in situ, cut from a fully matured plant. Juicy, tender, with a divine sweetness superior to any other fruit, a northern Queensland ripe pineapple is food for the gods.

I struggle on trying to speed up my box-making efforts, but by the end of the day I have made a mere five boxes. I never do get much faster, but I do acquire huge painful blisters on my hammer hand, several black nails from inaccurate blows, sore muscles and fingers, a stiff back from standing all day, and at the end of a painful week, tired and miserable, I have made the grand sum of nine pounds – the wage for 36 boxes. The others, experienced at the game, have made five, six, seven times that number, and no blisters. So I go to the farm manager and quit, hugely relieved to be free of the agony and to savour the prospect of sleeping till a decent hour each morning. But money is going to be a problem again, when my meagre savings run out.

By June, Brophy has had enough of roughing it, and needs to get back to earning some money with the guitar, and to find some decent social life. Our goodbyes are not particularly felt ones, since Brophy is the most undemonstrative of friends, and in any case we know we'll be seeing each other back in Melbourne in the not-too-distant future. He gets himself a lift back south with one of the several drop-ins who appear from time to time. In typical Push fashion, word has gotten around Melbourne and Sydney of our little sojourn here, has been exaggerated into an 'alternative' community (the word 'commune' hadn't yet been coined for this era), and various bearded boys and hairy girls have descended on us to help us Create Paradise. They tend to be either argumentative, predatory scroungers or plain parasites, especially the women. I try to stay clear of them after some initial contact; I don't trust them, and they give me the creeps.

After seeing an ad in the local paper I take a job in a Cairns timber yard. It is hard work, especially on the hands, stacking planks, carrying them in to be dressed. No gloves are available, and I am constantly getting splinters, breaking nails – no good for a guitarist. But it is out in the sun, and the August weather is still temperate enough to be enjoyable, and the money is good. I have been in the shack on my own since Brophy left, which is straining the finances a little. I would like to start saving for somewhere better to live, so Max and Beth kindly offer me their spare bed, now that it is empty, for which I pay a nominal amount, and try to make myself useful around the house. Looking through Max's little shelf of books, I notice one called *The Outsider*, by Albert Camus. 'What is this like?' I ask him. 'Camus? Read it.' is all he says. I am secretly grateful to hear him pronounce the name, as I was about to call him 'Kaymoos' or something. So I open it and begin reading:

Mother died today. Or, maybe, yesterday;
I can't be sure.

Immediately I am hooked – the doubting tone, the simple lucid dreaminess of the language, and I can't put it down. By the time I finish it I can feel that it has changed me in some small but important way. Mersault has in some sense entered my own personality; I believe I am more than a little like him. Not that I want to kill, of course, but there is in his apartness, his solitariness, something of my own. None of the books I had read for Miss Scholes' literature class speak so personally to me as this one does, except perhaps *Crime and Punishment*.

For some time Max had been talking of going after some mud crabs down along Yorkey's Creek, so one sunny afternoon the two of us take the VW down along the beach beyond where the road stops, park it on the sand, and head off over to the back beach where mangroves grow along the banks of the creek, and where Max has in the past caught fine large crabs. The weather is perfect and we take our time exploring the banks, looking for likely spots. Max drops in his baits and readies his net, though for some reason no crabs are in evidence. In no particular hurry, we chat away quietly, harbouring in the back of our minds that fisherman's hope that is always part of the exercise. We have been there for maybe an hour or so when Max says, 'You know, we should take a look at the car; I've just remembered that king tides are running at the moment, and when they come in they come in fast.' Again, not feeling any urgency, we amble back over the sand dunes to the front beach, see the little blue Beetle standing proud and alone on the sunny beach, and walk down to check. The water has come in a long way since we left it, and I notice that the sand has become darkened around the nearside wheels. 'Better move it,' says Max, so I get in, start her up, make to drive off. But the car doesn't move forward; the damp sand crumbles underneath the rear tyres and the car sinks down to its axles, wheels spinning, and will go no further. I get out, we try to push her, get back in with Max pushing and lifting, but she won't budge. She is stuck fast, and there is no way out. My father's old dictum of never stopping a car where it could get bogged flashed through my head, all too late to matter. And just to put the final touch of drama to our helplessness, we can see that in the short time we have been trying to move the car, the water has already come in far enough to begin lapping around the tyres. We have to move fast.

We are miles from a garage, and even the nearest house is a good twenty minutes away. We hurry along the beach to the road, make for the first house. The old fellow there has only a small car, and we all agree there is no way he could pull us out without himself getting bogged in the sand. He has a long heavy towrope, which he is happy to let us have, and we scurry back to see what use we can make of it. I know in my heart we will not be strong enough, the two of us, to pull her clear of that sand, but we will try anyway. By the time the little VW comes in sight, we can see she is already riding on the waves. We wade over to her, see that water is sloshing about the cabin floor, tie the rope to the front bumper and heave. She floats to the edge of the water, but then she is as heavy as a brick wall, and cannot be pulled up onto dry sand. It is hopeless. We can think of nothing better than to take our end of the rope and tie it around a palm tree at the top of the beach, so she won't actually float out to sea. Then we sit on the sloping sand, roll ourselves a cigarette each from Max's packet of 'Drum', and watch the doomed little car heaving like a boat on the growing swell. She looks so incongruous, so pathetic, floundering out of her element, that we suddenly see the absurdity of the whole event. This is mad, this is bizarre, this will be a story to tell our grandchildren, if they will believe it. We stretch back on the soft sand, look at the sky, look again at the car, look at each other knowing it is all over, and begin to laugh our heads off. We stay till the light begins to fade and the blue of the car merges with the blue of the sea, so we can barely see her, and it is time to leave her to her fate. We stump off back to the Knob in the dark and tell our tale to an incredulous Beth.

Next morning Max and I go to a garage and ask for help. A tractor is brought and we make our way to where we left the car the night before. The tide is out, a long, long way out, and there, still on her extensive tether, tipped up slightly on one side, is the little blue VW, high and dry as a beached whale. She is actually perched on a mound of sand, and when I prise open the driver's side door the cabin is full of damp sand, smooth and unmarked. There is no point attempting to start her. In fact, when we tie the rope to the tractor and begin pulling her up onto dry sand the wheels do not move round at all; they are seized fast, probably with sand or salt in the bearings. The dragging leaves deep furrows all along the beach until we get her up onto the asphalt road. Even then the tractor pulls the car half a mile before one or two of the wheels begin to turn. When we open the cover, the engine is full of sand, rust is already taking hold of some of the metal. That is it, we all agree; she is a write-off. And so endeth the life of my little blue VW; she has been a brave companion, has taken me far without a murmur of objection, and now her time has come. Vale.

For all its madness and ultimate unimportance, the event has a conclusive effect on my Queensland adventure. Because without the car, I am too hampered for any kind of life here – travelling to jobs, exploring different parts of the region, keeping my sense of freedom; all will be too difficult. I will have to leave, and go back home. Fortunately, being an old insurance employee, I had the wit to have comprehensive cover on the car, and when I phone them and tell them about the loss, they respond quite reasonably, indicate they would probably pay it, and send me a claim form. Within a fortnight I receive a cheque from them for £190, and a letter explaining that they were paying only 75% of the claim because of my negligent contribution to the accident. Still, I am delighted to have received this much, considering my negligence was more like 100%! I could, I ponder, buy another car with the money and so stay on in Cairns, but having already decided to leave, I am quite keen now to get back to Melbourne, start singing again. Besides, I've hit upon a novel idea: I can afford to fly home, and to thus embark upon my first ever experience of travelling in an aircraft. Why not?

I reflect; what has this whole Queensland venture meant to me? I have lived nine months now close to Nature, away from the city, the folk music scene, my friends and family. The exact timespan of a gestation, it occurs to me. Have I had a rebirth? Not quite, I think. In some respects, the experience did the same things for me as the time in the army – increased my self-reliance, weakened my family ties, made me in some ways stronger, certainly physically. Where the army imposed discipline, a pressure I am not unused to, Queensland threw me into the deep end of self-reliance, allowed me the freedom to sink or swim, take on the task of earning, feeding, housing myself, and of living alone finding some things out about myself. And if not a rebirth, certainly a significant change. I am not a light, scrawny youth any more, I am a man, brown and lean, strong in the body and hands – in fact my hands are a practical man's hands, not a clerk's. I have lived nine months with hardly a thought for women or sex, ambition, fame or worldly goods. Should I meet a Buddhist at this time I would be easily converted. And yet, the day has come for me to rekindle those familiar desires, to put all this self-containedness aside, and to go back to a society that will give me purpose and feed my ego. I only hope to have acquired enough good sense to know how to control this ego, how not to let it become the dreary, exploitative force that is all too evident in others, and has occasionally been in myself over these twenty-five years.

The September day arrives when I say goodbye to Max and Beth and their son, when like someone of means I take a taxi to the Cairns airport, board the plane – one of the new Viscount Turbo-Props – and get my first look at the world from the air. Receding below me is the beautiful sapphire and turquoise coast, the drama of jungle-green clumps of lush vegetation in between broad fields of already greening sugar cane, and the shining corrugated roofs of Cairns houses, their rectangular shapes making a neat abstract design from above, so different from the paint-faded, ramshackle, homely dwellings they are from the ground. That was Cairns. That was Queensland. I loved it, but before long my thoughts turn, with a degree of excitement, to Melbourne, to picking up where I had left off, and to what possibilities might lay ahead.

10

HOW QUICKLY ONE CAN FALL from paradise to hell. Of course that does not really describe the descent from Cairns to Melbourne, which are themselves at neither pole, but in personal terms it certainly happened that way. It began in the dingy inside room that passed for the Lounge at Tattersall's Pub in Russell Street, on the corner of Little Lonsdale Street. Tatt's, as everyone called it, was the chosen venue of The Push, a choice reciprocated by the proprietor, who welcomed the motley mix of artists, long haired scruffs, sluttish and gorgeous women, petty criminals and university professors who drank there. It was a mutually convenient arrangement: the proprietor took no trouble to keep the place clean or well appointed, and the clientele could dress, behave and talk more or less how it liked. Unlike other Melbourne hotels there was no separation of the sexes, no dress code and no food unless you brought it in. The building was run down and badly in need of painting, the toilets out the back were disgusting, the floors were always grimy. But it was the place to meet anyone in The Push, especially on a Friday night, when just about every one of them in the city packed into the place in the last hour before the six o'clock ejection and close.

The Lounge had an old sofa, where I was talking to someone through the wall of noise, when a shortish young woman came up to us from out of the murky background across the room. Her face was bright, eyes sparkling, her mouth smiling and sensual. She came over because she knew the person I was talking to, but almost immediately we, too, recognised each other. We had met at Max Beatty's Prahran loft on my first visit, over two years ago, before I had started singing, and I had noticed her clothes – black stockings, low-heeled black shoes with a kind of 17th century centre buckle, shapely, strong legs, a dark red woollen tunic over a black skivvy, dark brown hair wound into a tight baker's knot on her head. There was a crisp, style-smart charm in her manner, one that put out a beddable but choosy promise. Beverly. Beverly Charlton was her name.

'I remember you,' she was saying, and sat on the edge of the sofa, turned so that we were looking almost directly at each other. A few jokey familiarities passed between her and the friend, but she was directing her beam of attention mostly on me. In fact directly on me, sitting like a rabbit in a blinding spotlight. 'You've changed. I almost didn't recognise you. You're so *brown*.'

'I've been living up north, near Cairns.'

'Where Max and Beth are,' she nodded.

'I've spent nearly the whole time out in the sun.'

'You look like a gypsy,' she said, 'are you still playing the guitar? I saw you sing at Emerald Hill once; I love your voice.'

I explained I didn't have any work yet – I'd only been back a few days. It was obvious, I said, there were more singers around than when I left last January. She mentioned that Tom Lazar was starting a new place in the city, called Little Reata, but it was to be mostly for business lunches. 'He's a bit fed up with the folkies,' she'd heard. I made her laugh with the story of my drowned car, explaining that I had a little of the insurance money left, but I would have to start earning soon. Nominally, I told her, I was back living with my family at West Ivanhoe, but I wanted to get away from there as soon as possible. It was no longer home to me, and without a car it was too far to travel from there to inner city gigs. As closing time drew near and people were heading off to their various Friday night scenes, she asked me what I was doing that evening. I hadn't anything definite in mind – maybe look up Bob or Spike and June.

'Come to Arden Street with me,' she said. 'Do you know Bobby White? He was probably here earlier, but I don't see him now. We can get something to eat at Bobby's, and catch up with a few people.'

'Is he having a party?'

'Bobby is always having a party; if there isn't one planned he'll make one up. He's got a spare room he lets me use sometimes. C'mon, it'll be fun.'

And so I was lured into a new corner of The Push, into contact with a new crowd, some friendly and interesting, some obnoxious and dreary. White was himself an engaging, often crazy man, a northern Englishman in his forties, working all day at the Fishermen's Bend aircraft factory, drinking most nights at Tatt's, and partying on weekends whenever he could. He was at this time running a 'scrag house', i.e. a share arrangement, in a double-storied terrace in Arden Street, North Melbourne, not all that far from my own grandmother Nair's house. Funny to think Nair was barely a block away, and that the memory of my childhood was here, a ghost in these streets; Bob Campbell's old house was just around the corner. Bobby White had lots of acquaintances, mostly good-time ones, and they usually crowded into his house on weekend nights to indulge in the routine drunken talk-fests that passed in those days for a party.

Beverley behaved very strangely all evening – like a schoolgirl, dashing about from group to group, giggling, hugging different people, all in a hyperactive display of sexual success. She spent little time actually talking to me, except to introduce me to that friend, this acquaintance, a psychologist she knew, the pretty Push mistress of a young doctor, someone else who did something else. My head was spinning from the line-up of faces, none of whom I'd seen around the traps before. After the party we climbed into the single bed in Bobby's spare room. For all her up-beat libertarian talk, Beverly proved as sexually conventional as myself, perhaps even a little prim. She did not seem to like her own body much, which was inclined to be thick, a little lacking in shape about the middle, and she did not like to be seen naked. When in bed we began without preliminaries to fuck, she was impatient, eager to get it over with. Afterwards she laughed and claimed to be shy, afraid I would find her unattractive, and began talking at length about herself. She had been married, to someone who would not have fitted in to The Push, and they broke up a couple of years earlier, leaving her with a daughter who was now about four. Her aunt in Essendon looked after Meghan most of the time, though occasionally Beverly would have her for a day to show her off to her Push friends, and often took her to Tatt's. She received a support cheque every month from her husband, and lived mostly at her aunt's house rent free. Raving as she was in letting loose all this talk, I was utterly under her spell, flattered that such a hive of energy and, yes, sophistication, in Push terms anyway, had singled me out for her favours; I had seen during the evening how several other guys would have liked to be in my place. She was fun, attractive, judgemental, scattily intelligent, and I had fallen, not in love with her, but certainly romantically in lust. Wrapped round her in that narrow bed, I eventually drifted off to sleep, feeling as lucky and smug as a bridegroom.

Next day she insisted on taking me to her aunt's to see little Meghan, treating me already like a potential partner. I didn't mind – again, her view of me as a good catch, someone she could put her trust in, flattered me. I began to play up to the role, aware even while I was doing it that it was an extremely silly lapse. It was as if something about my nine months in Queensland had reborn me as an innocent gull, turned me naïve. We had spent the morning sleeping-in, fucking again, showering, feeding ourselves on eggs and toast from Bobby's fridge, then paying a visit to Tatt's mainly to see if any of her friends were there. A couple of the less interesting day drinkers stood in the bar, including a well-known burglar called Bill Collins, and we didn't stay long, soon leaving to catch the train out to Essendon. It was late afternoon when we arrived at her aunt's neat Californian Bungalow, prim with its roses and camellias and low brick fence. It quickly became evident that Beverly and her ageing aunt were locked in a constant war over just about every aspect of their lives, and the central feature in the battleground they were both trying to win was the child, Meghan. She was a cute little ginger nut who had grown quiet with confusion over who to love most, because she was unsure about who loved *her* the most – the one who cared for her every day, put her to bed, made her eat her supper, took her to kindergarten, or the one she saw once or twice a week, who smothered her with affection, spoiled her with presents, and abandoned her for days, sometimes weeks on end. No doubt, too, there was confusion over which of the men her mother introduced her to she should bank on seeing again. For this reason I presumed it was pointless trying to strike any close friendship with the little one, because it would only register as fake to both of us. Still she was a honey, and I made something of an effort to engage with her, at least.

Beverley's aunt was a silly and panicky woman, who would shrilly complain and then weakly give in to most of Beverly's demands. But on this occasion there was one matter on which she would not be moved: letting Beverly sleep with me in her bed. 'Not in my home,' was her mantra, 'What would the neighbours think when he leaves in the morning.' It didn't seem to occur to her that if I stayed the night on the *couch* the neighbours might jump to the same conclusion. The row went on while her aunt was cooking dinner, with me keeping tactfully mute while the two women stood their opposing ground. Finally, just as they sat down to the table Beverly exploded. 'I'll fuck who I *like!*' she screamed, picked up her plate of chops, peas and mashed potato and threw it with all her power right across the kitchen. Showing enough sense to keep out of it, I was at a loss to know what to do. As the mashed potato slid down the pale green wall I left my place, retrieved the chops and with absurd fastidiousness began to hunt down every pea that had scattered across the floor. By that time Meghan was crying hysterically, and Beverly had stormed off to her bedroom, leaving me to face a weeping, morally triumphant aunt. I wished I could get out of there, but I was trapped. And though Beverly lost the battle over where I slept that night, she nevertheless was so set on victory that in the early hours of the morning she crept in to my bed in the spare room and treated me to a tense, noiseless genital connection, after which she returned to her own bed wearing an exultant smile.

The next day was Sunday, and I needed to go home for a change of clothes, sort out one or two things, pick up my guitar to do some practice. Beverly insisted on coming with me, curious to meet my mother. And I was pleased to show her off; a son likes his mother to acknowledge his sexual triumphs. We took a taxi out to West Ivanhoe, stayed for an hour or so. While Beverly watched

TV in the lounge, I explained to my mother in the kitchen that she had a broken marriage, a little daughter, that we had slept together the two previous nights. But my mother annoyed me with her terse response. 'She's using you,' she said. I resented that; she didn't understand at all – we had genuine feelings for each other, she was vulnerable, insecure, admired my singing, wanted me to care for her and Meghan, too. What's wrong with that? I asked, rhetorically. I didn't continue to argue with her, and we left soon after, catching a bus to the city, with the intention of heading for Arden Street. But underneath my rationalisations, I knew she was right about Beverly. I just couldn't resist the flattery she was offering me.

Along the way we dropped in on a houseful of her friends in Carlton, all psychologists working in government institutions. The house was dim and badly decorated, a triumph of ugliness. The men wore grubby white shirts and dreary ties. Her particular friend Edith, who Beverly insisted on calling 'Teddy' and herself 'Sam' to imply that they had something going between them (this was mere talk, of course: they both had the most suburban sexual inhibitions), dressed in conventional twinsets and skirts, was, like me, too impressed by Beverly's relentless exuberance. In a way these people were on the fringe of the Push, partied and drank in it, but they also tenaciously hung on to their mainstream identities, claimed a kind of professional interest in 'alternative' behaviour, but strangely they were not detached from it enough, nor organised enough, to undertake any actual research on it. Obviously, I did not share Beverly's enthusiasm for them.

That night we stayed at Arden Street again, and Beverley was acting strangely, criticising me in oddly groundless ways. Why didn't I have a car? Why didn't I have some money? She had paid the taxi fare earlier in the day, and it rankled with her. Am I going to pay her back? Why haven't I started singing somewhere? We eventually resolved our differences under the spell of Bobby White's jokey, drink-fuelled powers of reconciliation, and went to bed for more sex, which was again tense and strained, far from satisfying. It took me a while to fall asleep, my head spinning with the events of the past few days and the conflicting emotions they had all stirred up. Things were moving somehow out of my control, and under their own headlong speed. After all, it was only days ago that I had basked in the peaceful retreat of Yorkey's Knob, no one to worry about but myself, no conflict, no churning emotions, only the comfortable simplicity of that sunny backwater. Now I was being drawn into some sort of emotional vortex, helpless and disoriented. Eventually I calmed down and drifted off, tucked in against Beverly's naked buttocks. But a couple of hours later something woke me, and I found myself alone in the bed. Rolling on my back, I waited, presuming she had gone for a pee. The house was silent, dark, no suggestion of movement. I looked at my watch: twenty past two. After ten minutes I realised she had not gone to the toilet, was not moving about. I got up and turned on the light; her clothes, bag, shoes were gone. In the morning I caught Bobby White as he was dashing off to work, asked if he had seen her. 'No,' he said, 'but I can guess where she's gone. Has she told you about David? They've had a thing going for some time; she used to bring him here until you showed up. She's probably gone to his place.'

I couldn't believe it. Another guy, just like that, without warning, without telling me anything about him. I was beginning to learn what troubles I had let myself in for with Beverley.

Over the ensuing several weeks – six or so – this became the pattern of our relationship. She dragged me into her chaos, and the pain she put me through took me by surprise. I never knew when she would be with me, or would go off somewhere else, and with someone else. She was not, I eventually concluded, promiscuous: there was only one other man she went to, an actor called David Mitchell. I saw them together in the pub a couple of days after that first defection, caught her eye and a few minutes later she came over to me. She made no explanation or apology, simply said that Mitchell and she had been lovers since before she met me, and that he 'needed her'.

'*I* need you,' I said.

'I know, and I'll come back, I promise; I don't want to stay with David, but I have to tell him gently; he's very sick, and I can't just run out on him like I did when I saw you that first night. Go to Arden Street tomorrow night, and I'll be there, truly.'

I swallowed this, just like I swallowed every one of her lies. Yes, she came back to me the following night, and yes we stayed at Arden Street again, and yes she talked as if we were now a settled item and I could depend on her. She persuaded me to go with her to the Punt Road house where Mitchell lived, to collect her things. 'David won't be there, he's gone to Sydney to audition for a part,' she explained. A typical Push house, it was a run-down, once gracious Edwardian bluestone with a rotting veranda and a garden let run to weed; inside it was derelict, unheated, almost devoid of furniture, stank of stale cigarettes and beer. It was apparently rented by the Coman brothers, Phil and 'Joe-Joe', who were notorious for their wild, alcohol-fuelled ways; 'Joe-Joe' was reputed to chew up beer glasses when drunk enough. Phil, who held a senior position in the Public Service, often got into fights. As Beverly collected clothes, shoes, knick-knacks from a murky bedroom with a double mattress on the floor and was stuffing them into plastic bags, a tall figure emerged from another room in an old torn dressing gown, scratching his unkempt hair and looking like something the cat dragged in. Beverly said curtly, 'Hello Phil.' He stood with an expression of distaste directed at us both, though hardly acknowledging my presence and keeping a bleary eye on what Beverly was doing.

'Don't take anything that isn't yours,' he warned.

'There's nothing here I'd want,' she snapped.

He took a few steps towards us. 'And who's this little prick? Your latest cuntsucker, eh Sam?' He came close enough to take the sleeve of my rust-brown jacket between his thumb and forefinger, and said contemptuously, 'Christ I hate people who wear fake suede coats,' and shuffled away toward the bathroom. It was true, my jacket was suedecloth, and considerably cheaper than the real thing. So? I was economising.

On the way to Arden Street in the taxi she said, 'Everyone in that place calls me Sam. David hates the name Beverly. So do I, actually. I think I'm going to officially change it to Samantha. So from now on, I want you to call me Sam.' She moved in close to me as if to signal I was the chosen one in her life now, as we drove to Arden Street. But the visit to Punt Road had begun to gnaw at my idea of her. What did she see in that lot? What was there that could possibly induce her to stay amongst them, in their stink and sleaze, the nihilistic tone of the place?

Hardly more than a week later, despite our having made the room at Arden Street comfortable, hung posters on the walls, bought a rug for the floor, and even talked of getting a place of our own, she had done it again – failed to turn up at a café in the city where we had arranged to meet. I went to Arden Street, but she hadn't been there. I went to Edith's and she said that Beverly had told her she was moving back in with Mitchell, and had taken Meghan with her.

'I wish she hadn't,' said Edith, 'Mitchell beats her. I wish she'd stay with you.'

Whether it was a reaction to the latest desertion or I was run down, or just bad luck, or a combination of all of these things, I immediately fell ill. For the want of anywhere else, I had gone back to Arden Street, hoping she might turn up. Sitting on the bed in the late afternoon, I felt tired, my throat was sore, I lay down and fell asleep. It was dark when I woke up, thirsty, shivering with cold, cursing myself for not getting under the blanket, went to the kitchen and drank two big glasses of water, then, fully clothed, climbed back into bed, this time under the covers. My whole body was now shaking violently, and my mind racing with crazy, disconnected thoughts jumping all over the place: she is betraying me she is laughing at me with Mitchell she is letting Mitchell hit her and hit Meghan as well there is a group of them at Punt Road pushing Beverly from one to the other striking her as they do with little Meghan helplessly screaming at them to stop stop stop I felt hot and dry and something had me around the throat trying to strangle me I tried to fight it away but couldn't make it stop couldn't make the pain go away and there was a sense of building building something getting larger and more and more threatening like a huge balloon inflating out of control.

Next thing I knew, Bobby White was leaning over me in the near-dark evening of the room, a firm hand rocking my shoulder, calling my name, softly asking, 'Are you okay? – you've been dreaming, yelling out in your sleep. I could hear you as I came in the front door …'

'I'm hot. Think I've got a bug or something …'

'I'll get you some aspirin.'

But my head got worse, and I stayed in bed for some timeless stretch, lost in some netherworld of fever. I kept sleeping and waking bathed in sweat, lost all sense of time, didn't know where I was or who the faces around me were, couldn't eat or drink, apart from sips of water from the glass beside the bed. At one stage a handsome, smiling young man stood over me taking my pulse, looked into my throat. 'Hi there; I'm Steve, Lee's bloke. I'm a doctor. You're having a rough time, might be pneumonia but probably just a bad dose of flu. I'm putting you on antibiotics, and we'll see what happens. But you'd better stay in bed for a couple more days.' He was joined by a slim, beautiful young woman, who smiled down at me. 'Hello,' she said cheerfully, and as if I should know her, 'I'm Lee, a big fan – seen you sing lots of times. We're going to make sure you get better.'

I had no idea who these people were or how they got there, and no idea how long I'd been in bed, but I was grateful for their presence, and eventually the antibiotics did their work, and I got better. By the time I was able to get up and eat and talk coherently again I learned it was Thursday. I had been ill since Friday, seven days, and Bobby White had looked after me, had found Steve through Lee, who it turned out was a friend of both Bobby and Beverly. But there was no sign of her, and no one had seen her all the time I had been ill.

The illness and my recovery marked the end of our brief, unhappy affair. We nodded to each other from time to time at the pub, or the occasional party, and I was tempted to ask for some kind of explanation for her final disappearance. Eventually, one evening at Arden Street she turned up by herself, looking smart and freshly scrubbed, in one of her saner moods, and we talked for a while. 'It was always David,' she said. 'He needs me. He's an alcoholic, he'll destroy himself if I'm not there for him.'

'He beats you,' I said.

'Not really, not in the way you imagine. He's never struck me with his fist or anything. His violence is only sexual; he fucks me very hard. You remember that time my period wouldn't come, and I thought I might be pregnant? Sex with David brought it on, he was so violent. That's how he is.'

'And you like him for it?'

'I don't mind it. He needs it, he needs me. *C'est la vie*. But you know what, he adores Meghan. She likes him, too. And he is a wonderful actor, would be famous if he didn't drink so much.'

I suddenly saw myself to be a gentle, ridiculous fool, with no idea of what women like, what they want from a man. I suppose I thought they were all alike, all a bit like my mother, wanting a nice, respectful, responsible husband type. Now it crossed my mind that maybe they prefer bastards, some of them, who carelessly do whatever they want with them. Maybe none of them like passivity in a man, which is what I've been doing, humiliating myself. There must be a way of being both strong and gentle, and really I should learn to be like that, I told myself. But all my behaviour with Beverley had been passive and weak. This was confirmed later that evening when Mitchell showed up to take her to the theatre. He walked into Bobby White's kitchen in an old gabardine coat, his thinning hair blond under the unshaded light bulb, and looked arrogantly around without saying a word. He could see immediately who his ex-rival was, standing in conversation with Beverly, but he did not condescend to speak to me. He just fixed me with a long, empty, blue-eyed stare, like someone confronted with an unknown species, a stare that said several things at once: 'I know who you are; you are a little piece of shit who presumed to sleep with my woman; I will not speak to you, will not give you the satisfaction of discomforting me, will certainly not give you the recognition you crave from me, and I am here simply to collect my property and leave this unimportant place.'

The power of Mitchell's contempt was almost aristocratic, and had the intended effect of making me feel inconsequential. But on the other hand it was also, I recall now, theatrical, illusory, and might easily have collapsed under threat of a serious challenge. I did not see this at the time, but accepted the contempt with respect, and was too impressed to even imagine it was an act. Just as well, really. There was nothing further to be gained from the whole business, assuming that I had already learned something about myself and women from the sad, mad affair. Something in me knew this instinctively, and knew that this had been a mere *cul de sac*, a distraction from the pursuit that really mattered to me, which was to get back to my music, to get out there and engage with the world, to do better what I had started to do, and to find out what was worth singing about.

11

THE FOLK MUSIC SCENE CHANGED in the course of 1963. Politics had
not been the initial force behind the 'folk revival' of the late 50s and early 60s.
There had of course been a political tradition in folk music in the U.S. that went
back to the 1930s in black musicians such as Robert Johnson, 'Leadbelly' and
Bill Broonzy, and also in Woody Guthrie, who was especially critical of capitalist
economics and class exploitation during the Depression. This continued in the
immediate post-War era in musicians like Pete Seeger and the Weavers, and
Sidney Carter and Ewan McColl in the U.K. They saw folk music as an
expression of the 'people's voice', and performed in alliance with workers' unions
and socialist organisations. A version of that tradition continued in Australia,
particularly in the Trade Union movement. So identified with the organised Left
did it become that folk music was at times banned from U.S. radio shows, and
Pete Seeger was jailed by the House Un-American Activities Committee at the
instigation of Senator Joe McCarthy, during his 1950s Communist witch hunts.
In the early 1960s this strain of the folk music tradition, while it had never
disappeared, still lay somewhat in the background of other popular music that
was being played to audiences.

The aspect of folk music that appeared in late 1950s popular music was
essentially nostalgic. There was among the young a growing taste for more
authentic values, increasingly sought in pre-modern ways of life – in the Past, in
lifestyles that eschewed technology, in indigenous cultures. The Kingston Trio
singing the old folk song 'Tom Dooley', and Harry Belafonte with calypso pieces
like 'Matilda' and 'Jamaica Farewell', which rose to the top of the charts, were
giving a hint of this interest. Then the simple, pre-modern acoustic guitar
received a new lease of life, and began to appear all over the place making a
statement of homespun musical values – portable, cheap, easy-to-play, and in the
right hands an extension of the performer's individuality. In 1960 and 1961 the
first albums of Joan Baez and Bob Dylan had little political content, relying
instead on reworked traditional ballads, hillbilly songs, negro spirituals and
blues. 'Folk', like 'Beat', stood for a retreat from the notion of Progress, and
from mainstream political engagement.

But in 1962 and 1963, the political attitudes that had been in general
ferment amongst the youth of Western societies broke through into the folk
music scene, and suddenly the songs that were taking over were regularly
protesting about one or another specific social problem. Pete Seeger was singing

against war and environmental pollution ('Little Boxes'), Dylan's second album *The Freewheelin' Bob Dylan*, contained the anti-war songs 'Blowin' in the Wind', 'the Masters of War' and 'Talkin' World War Three Blues'. His next album, *The Times They Are A-Changin'* broadened to address issues of race, class and nationalism in America, while trumpeting a new political enthusiasm amongst the young. Peter, Paul and Mary's popularisation of 'Blowing in the Wind' was the best-selling song in the world in 1963. Suddenly the protest song was born, and singers sprang from everywhere to join the party and get themselves politically engaged.

Into this stream of protest I leapt with the fervour of a born-again Christian. I saw in it a way of being more than just a performer of old songs, more than just a background attraction with a nice voice and a mellow guitar. It pushed me into a recognition of the political forces shaping the world, made me read the newspapers, listen to talks, opinions, take notice of the informed views of those around me, in the kind of detail I had ignored my whole life to this point. Of course it was not systematic or well-informed education in the way that a university course would have given me, but it did orient my mind to at least thinking about issues. I learned almost everything off the new Dylan albums, the Baez protest songs, began a search for more and more political material to sing along with the many traditional folk songs I still loved. By the end of that year my repertoire was somewhere over five hundred songs, and growing. I worked on ways of writing songs of my own, and of developing my guitar accompaniment to higher musical levels.

All this had begun to happen, in a sporadic way, in those six or so weeks when I had been distracted by Beverly, after my return from Queensland. Now that she had gone from my life, I could devote myself more seriously to music. Even so, I was finding it hard to get regular work. Occasional spots at *The Reata* and an Emerald Hill concert were not enough to keep me going, and my only solution was to get some sort of day job. Clerical work was my best option, nothing ambitious, just something easy and reasonably well paid. Answering an ad, I was hired by the Gas and Fuel Corporation of Victoria, and was sent to their Fitzroy maintenance and supply branch, in the shadow of the enormous gasholder in Alexandra Parade. My work was to keep sixteen plumbers supplied with jobs that came in by phone or on the teleprinter, and I ran into difficulty on the very first day. The little rectangular tickets describing the job – a gas leak, a meter change, etc. – were piling up on my desk, but when my plumbers phoned in they kept claiming to be too busy to take on any more jobs. Fifteen minutes before knock-off I still had a pile of tickets an inch thick on my desk when the office manager came down the aisle on his routine check. 'What are these?' he asked.

'The plumbers say they are too busy to take them,' I said.

The manager, a tall, heavier Randolph Scott type, leaned down close to my face, sending a whiff of halitosis up my nostrils.

'Listen: I want your desk completely clear of jobs by five o'clock every night. Get it?'

I said Yes, yet had no idea how I was going to achieve this. But as soon as the manager moved on, Neville, in the desk in front, turned and said, 'Want to know how to have your desk nice and clear every night?'

'Please,' I said.

He stood where the manager had been seconds before, picked up his pile of tickets, tamped them into a neat pack like playing cards, deftly ripped the pack in half and dropped it in the waste bin. 'Simple,' he laughed. I blush now to recall the irresponsibility I learned from Neville, especially in treating everything about the job, the place and its people, as a complete joke. Of course the poor paying customers had no idea half the time what was happening to their requests, or even if they'd called the right number. 'Fitzroy Fruit Palace,' Neville would often say when he answered the phone, or 'Joe's fish and chips', and they would hang up. In this way Neville would keep his workload to a minimum, earn the manager's praise for efficiency, and have himself a damn good time every day. He was the most anarchic, morally blind, happiest work mate you would ever come across.

When the affair with Beverly ended, I had not wanted to stay at Arden Street, so again, briefly, I went home to West Ivanhoe. My mother was preparing for the move to the new house she had built in Syndal. This was one of the great achievements in her life, the Australian Dream of home-ownership that she had always hoped and worked for. It was a cream brick veneer with design and features she had chosen, funded from a War Service Loan to which Richard was entitled, and a large enough block to enable her to finally create the garden she wanted. West Ivanhoe, being Housing Commission property, never seemed worth the trouble to her. But Syndal, this was hers, the reward for a lifetime of hard work and saving, and together with Richard, Ray and Susan (now eleven), she was eager to get her new life underway. I, preoccupied with my own interests, had never heard of Syndal; all I knew was that it was so far out in the eastern suburbs that I had no intention of moving there with them, even if I had wanted to go on living at home, which I did not. So I put the word around that I needed a place to live, and almost immediately someone at the pub – a guitarist friend of Karl Ogdon called Ian Deakin – offered me a room in his share house, in MacPherson Street, Carlton.

It was opposite the Carlton cemetery, a Victorian red-brick maisonette, solid, a little run-down, but comfortable enough. I had the middle of three bedrooms, and the others belonged to 'Deak' and a jazz musician whose name I forget. From a second-hand shop I bought myself a double bed and mattress, and a small chest of drawers, my only furniture. The bed sagged so badly in the middle that I tore a paling off the back fence and placed it across under the wire to support the mattress. Sitting unframed on the chest was a lovely large recent abstract painting by Bob, all sea-green and mysterious, which he had lent me. Unfortunately there was no atmosphere of communality in the place; we all had day jobs, and played music or went out in the evenings, would maybe run into each other at breakfast, but essentially it was just three blokes living separate lives at the same address.

One hot summer morning I was still half awake lying naked on the bed when I heard the front door slam. In my drowsy languor I vaguely registered that one of the others had gone out for something, so that when it seemed only seconds later that the doorbell rang, I assumed it was him returning to get his forgotten latchkey. Resentfully, I staggered out of bed, stark naked up the hallway blinded by the morning sunlight streaming through the entry window, opened the door and there, smiling blissfully and offering me the latest issue of a religious monthly, were two well turned-out ladies. Comprehension did not immediately come to me, so I simply stood baring all, with neither the wit nor the inclination to move my hands into a position of cover, and stared back at them. I will swear they never took their eyes off my face as they began to go through their well-rehearsed sales pitch. I did not speak. I simply closed the door on them in mid-sentence, and went back to bed.

Bob and Carol had a place in Carlton not far away, but things were going badly between them, and Carol had moved out to stay with friends. Whenever I had visited them in recent times there was a cold atmosphere in the house, and they spoke to each other only in a peculiar kind of baby-talk, delivered in the third person. 'Carol needs a sweetie right now, does Bob have a sweetie for her?' she would say.

'No sweeties for Carol,' he would reply, or 'Bob will go down the shop later and if she's good he'll buy her a sweetie.' It was hypnotically repellent to hear them. But now, apparently, they had stopped communicating completely, and their future together did not look rosy.

Around this time – early November – news of an important new performance venue began to circulate. Frank Traynor, the 'trad' jazz musician, who was in a relationship with Glen Tomasetti, was opening a folk and jazz club on the corner of Little Lonsdale and Exhibition Street in the city. On advice from Glen, Frank laid down that it was to be a club for serious folk performance and listening, not a coffee lounge or restaurant, seven nights a week, and Friday and Saturday nights after midnight would be given over to Frank's jazz musicians. It would be managed by the experienced Don Carless, who would also run it as a booking agency for the musicians, and keep tight control of audience behaviour. Don approached me in the pub, asking if I would like a regular weekly spot. As it happened, I was given two regular spots, Wednesdays sharing with David Lumsden and Fridays with Trevor Lucas. The creation of *Traynor's* gave a home to the Melbourne folk music scene, and totally transformed my personal approach and progress as a singer. I now had a regular income of ten pounds a week to supplement my Gas and Fuel wages, and enjoyed the convenience and security of a regular gig.

Within weeks I, like other singers, had built up a following, including of course a bevy of young women. While it wasn't quite the case that I took a different girl back to McPherson Street after every gig, I certainly had plenty of offers, and took plenty. Never had I dreamt of this kind of success, never realised the power of fame, modest though mine was. It was enough to be the centre of attention, in the spotlight, for some women to glower with desire for you, and to be seen with you. Oh yes, The Push had its own little celebrity industry.

I became close friends with my fellow performers David and Trevor, swapped songs and techniques, got to know their families. David's father had been in correspondence with Pete Seeger for some years, and they spent time together during Seeger's Australian tour. David had followed the great man in specialising in the five-string banjo, the only one on the Melbourne folk scene at that time. He also pioneered the 12-string guitar at Traynor's, though Trevor Lucas soon acquired one as well, and made it his signature instrument, playing it with the rhythmic force of a Leadbelly. During our Friday night sessions Trevor and I played separately, concentrating on protest songs, but David and I developed a 'bluegrass' blend of banjo with my guitar providing the bass support. We sang

American songs like 'Roll in My Sweet Baby's Arms', 'Banks of the Ohio', 'John Henry', and used the same approach on Australian songs like 'South Australia', 'Jim Jones', 'The Old Bark Hut' and so on, as well as protest songs from various sources, including contemporary ones. *Traynor's* became hugely popular with Melbourne audiences, and on Friday and Saturday nights in particular Don Carless regularly turned people away at the door, as the lucky ones crowded in, upstairs and down, to catch the latest acts by the growing band of performers.

After singing one Friday night in November I found myself with a friendly, freckle-faced girl with thick red-gold hair, frizzed-out to her shoulders. She invited me back to her flat close to the University, where she was a student. She was not my idea of a beauty, but she smiled radiantly and wanted me to stay the night, so I did. Two things made it a memorable event: as I moved in close to her under the sheets I ran my hand down her naked body in the usual way, when my fingers came upon thick hair growing on her inner thighs, and becoming coarser as it went lower, right down her calf nearly to her ankle. My arousal waned; there was something simian about all this ginger hair that put me right off, though I could hardly say this to her. Instead, I claimed that tiredness and the wine we'd drunk was the problem, and I turned over and went to sleep, without her suspecting the real reason for my lack of interest.

In the morning, the second memorable event occurred when she turned on the radio; while we had lain asleep a cataclysmic event had taken place in Dallas, Texas; Oswald had seized his moment of destiny, and the world was shaken. It has often been said that everyone knew where they were when President Kennedy was assassinated, and I certainly did. In the sunny warmth coming in the window of that little flat we sat over coffee and a slice of toast, unable to find anything to say or to imagine who or what lay behind the staggering news. For some reason I felt strangely sad that we had not made love the night before, that this happened to be the only occasion I had failed to respond to a girl's candid offer. Did I dream it, leaving the flat in the calm Saturday morning sunshine, passing under the plane trees along Swanston Street to the Carlton cemetery fence and around it to McPherson Street, the event seeming to have no reality on so pleasant and ordinary a morning, so far away? It affected my mood all day, indeed affected everyone I talked with that day. Different ones speculated that the murder was by a Right-Wing fascist, a Left-Wing protester, a lunatic, but no one had any answers or knew what it meant and what it could lead to. Suddenly the world seemed at once a drabber and more uncertain place, and in the days, weeks, months following the assassination, America seemed to be heating up to a point of explosion, especially on race issues.

The friendships among the musicians were in a sense the best thing about the folk scene. This may have been because the energy and purpose it gave us, and the inherent shareability of folk music, raised us above petty envy and cheap resentments. It was truly enjoyable to share the music, the recognition, the perks and performances with each other. Brian Mooney, who had adopted a Dublin persona out of sheer love of all things Irish, was one of the warmest, gentlest of men, with a fine natural tenor voice that he accompanied with simple arpeggios on a mellow old guitar. He painted a little, too – romantic landscapes with figures. Brian was one of the older singers on the scene, and had had his problems with booze and women, but he was enormously popular. At a noisy party one night in his Carlton loft, crowded with the usual throng of Push types and eager young women, there was a loud knock on the trapdoor in the floor, which was opened to reveal the cap and shining badge of a police officer. There had been complaints about the loud music. Two policemen, an older and a younger, rose up the ladder into the crowded room, and surveyed the scene with some distaste – beards, long hair, suggestively clad young girls drinking, the smell of joss-sticks. 'Okay, everybody listen,' came the command from the older officer, 'I want you to all quieten down or we'll put a stop to this. I'm a bit worried about the age of some of the girls here, so we'll be taking down names and addresses and checking with parents about some of you.' He cast a disapproving eye around the loft, the paintings, the oddball decor, and through the gloom spotted a print of a Modigliani nude on the wall amongst Brian's landscapes. Bodies parted as he approached the picture, at which he shook his head in dismay and said, 'Who did this?'

Brian spoke up, 'Modigliani,' he said.

'Right,' said the officer to his companion, 'get his address as well, and we'll pay him a visit.'

These were the days of Victoria's legendary Chief Secretary, Sir Arthur Rylah, who sent police into Melbourne bookshops to confiscate novels, and kept soft porn magazines in his drawer, all in the cause of protecting his teenage daughter, who, he freely admitted, did not exist. The very idea of public displays of sexuality produced paroxysms of unreason in Mr Rylah.

Day jobs were a hazard for tired musicians, as a favourite friend, the bass player Syd Clayton, discovered. Syd loved modern jazz and experimental music, and on more than one occasion when I dropped in on him we would end up playing 'accidental' music together, with bass, guitar, harmonica and anything else we could find that would make a noise. Syd had a quirky sense of humour. He liked to play with the names of songs: 'Do you know I can't get over a girl like you, so get up and answer the phone yourself,' he would quip. He had a little dog he was devoted to, and when anyone asked the dog's name he always gave them their own name. That is, if the visitor's name was Mike, Syd would say that the dog's name was Mike. It changed with every visitor. He had a day job as a postman for a while, and on his way to work one day he reached in his workclothes pocket to find, as he got on the bus, that he had left his wallet at home. 'Sorry mate,' said the driver, 'no credit possible; afraid you can't get on.' Syd shrugged helplessly, 'I have to get to work,' he said, and continued past the driver to sit in a seat. The driver refused to go until Syd had either paid or left the bus. A stalemate went on for some minutes, while the other passengers began protesting that they had to get to work too, and urged the driver to get the bus moving. Finally he gave in, and angrily took off. But as Syd passed him again to get off at his stop the driver demanded his name. Stepping off, Syd called back ,'Fred Splunge,' and hurried on to work. When he returned from his round later that morning there was a policeman waiting for him, insisting that Syd either make a full confession or be subject to an identification parade, and that charges would be laid. Syd confessed, and was charged, though the outcome has faded from anyone's memory. The fare was about ten pence.

A classical guitarist friend Don Lee worked for a very short time as a tram conductor, for which, being of somewhat timid and brittle disposition, he was ill-suited. Peak-hour trams were packed with seated and standing bodies, making it hard work for the conductor to push through to collect fares. On his very first day Don was finding it impossible to muster the necessary aggression to take on the crowd of passengers, let alone manage the work of issuing the tickets, collecting the money and giving change. Finally his patience snapped when people at the tram stop pressed up to board the already crowded tram against his explicit instruction. He took off the heavy leather bag, threw it forcefully to the floor, and stormed off the tram to the roadside, where he sat on the gutter edge with his head in his hands in despair. The tram driver, of course, could not move until his conductor rang the bell to give him the all-clear, so another stalemate ensued, with Don, driver and packed tram all in stasis. Then the passengers began calling Don back, sympathetically, pleading with him to remember the importance of his position, and offering to be better behaved from here on.

Several had crawled about on hands and knees, picking up the scattered coins and ticket-books and returning them to Don's bag. A man stood and offered Don his seat, and the conductor's bag was placed safely on his knees, ensuring that he could go the rest of the journey in peace and comfort, free from the terrible burden of squeezing himself through the crush. 'And don't worry,' said another kindly man, 'I'll pull the bell cord for you, so the driver knows when to go.' Don lasted till the end of the week, then reclaimed his freedom, and the dole.

I was clinging to my own day job by the skin of my teeth. Thursday mornings were a problem after working at Traynor's the night before, and I was often late, despite a hair-raising ride through the traffic on my bike down the slope from Carlton to Fitzroy, arriving sweaty and dishevelled at my desk under the disapproving gaze of the manager. During the course of the day I would tell my workmates, all married and mortgaged in the suburbs, stories about The Push, its characters and doings; they wanted to know more, and even persuaded me to take them to Tatt's one Friday night, to get a look at these weirdos for themselves. Instead of being intimidated, however, they took a remarkably short time to settle in, lean against the bar over a beer and engage in a pleasant if barely comprehensible discussion with a Bobby White or an Eltham painter down for some action. Because, arty though it was, Tatt's was also very Australian in generating a blokey sloppiness easily adopted by anyone regardless of class and education. So my workmates enjoyed it, finding the gap between themselves and The Push fraternity not as wide as they supposed. I reinforced this during our lunchtime games of tennis-ball cricket in the concrete yard of the Gas and Fuel Depot, where I disabused them of the idea that, just because I mixed with an arty crowd, I was no good at sport. They had a hard time with my fizzing chinamen, and great trouble getting me out while I smashed their bowling all over the yard.

At twenty-five, my life had settled into a pretty good routine: I had work, money, an amenable place to live, friends, an enviable sex life, and was building a reputation that was doing wonders for my self-esteem. If I had sat down and thought about it at all, I would have said there was nothing I wanted for right then, no dark spectres threatening my happiness and sense of self. Photographs show me to be clean-shaven and neat-haired – the unwashed look held no fascination for me – but not boyish in the face. The uncertainty of my teenage years were behind me, the traps of career-thinking, of subservience to dull men in corporate hierarchies, of the fall into a bad marriage, of clinging to the safety of family, were all now averted. I was free, my own man, pursuing the music that I liked best, on the path to some local, currently modest but potentially larger, success.

Yet, all was not perfection; there was a worm in the bud. Underneath the success was the unconfronted fact that I was taking a free ride on the train of fashion, and that I was not truly addressing my personal inadequacies with an eye for the long term. This feeling was conveniently suppressed while things were good, as they were right then, over that summer of 1963-4; nothing was happening that would force me to face these inadequacies. Yet within a short time, I would see the need to. Wonderfully, the change was not in the slightest to be a painful one. On the contrary, it was to come in the loveliest of guises, gentle and transcendent, for it would show me not only my shortcomings, but also how facing them could form the basis of a happy life for the long haul, regardless of fashion.

In later years, after decades of witnessing the parade of youth as a university teacher, I formed a theory about singing and what it means. Most of us, when we come to puberty and on into our twenties, experience a desire to sing or play music. We become like birds, driven by instinct to utter impassioned calls to the world, in the hope and trust that a sympathetic one of our kind will respond and become our mate. And so youth sings to the world in a plea for love, and when that love comes there is no further need to go on singing, which is why most people eventually cease and move on to dealing with the practicalities of life with their partner. They give up their rock band dreams, their *diva* ambitions, and settle into the important task of making a home. Of course, some don't; the theory applies to most people, not all. Some, a mere few, become professional singers and musicians, go on to make music for the rest of their lives. Are these perhaps ones that failed to find the right mate? The theory might not be as neat as that, but it is tempting to see, even in life-long professional singers, the sublimation of their instinctive love-calls, at least initially, into a practiced art that eventually takes over and becomes their emblem of natural passion. For the rest of us, we sing until our love-calls are answered.

12

BRIAN MOONEY HAD TOLD ME of a regular Friday evening *soiree* at the
Carlton home of the painter, Jim Meldrum. People would drop in casually,
maybe bring a friend, sit round in a circle on the floor with a glass of wine and
talk, read a poem, sing a song if they'd brought a guitar along, or even if they
hadn't, all under the friendly, faintly superior gaze of Meldrum, who would
punctuate the sessions with his gnomic Zen pronouncements. It was all a little
self-conscious, but harmless and very typically early sixties. Jim's wife would
make coffee and produce cake or biscuits, though in time she got noticeably fed
up listening to Jim's utterances, either from knowing they were something of a
performance specially for these occasions, or from having to live with them every
day, I couldn't tell which. But in a grim sort of way the sessions were fun, and a
good chance to keep in touch with friends every week. One particular night in
March – I have reason for remembering the month – I turned up with my guitar
and sang a song I had just learned, Bob Dylan's 'Don't Think Twice', for which
I had worked out a tricky accompaniment. Sitting in the circle around me on the
floor was a good-looking girl with short dark hair, who'd been brought along by
my housemate, Ian Deakin. I'd been so busy occupying the centre of attention
that I barely registered her, though it seemed to me that Deak, whose insecurities
tended to surface in a vague contempt for most people and events, was not
paying her any special attention either. Maybe this was because she was turned
out a little unfashionably – no long straight hair, no black stockings, no ethnic
smock. Later, when I enquired, Deak said with a certain pride that she had been
'one of the crowd who drank at the old Swanston Family Hotel in the city,
before Tatt's started,' as though this accidental piece of *avante garde* slumming
was sole justification for being seen with her, her one desirable attribute, which
somehow reflected well on him. And in any case, as I later learned, 'drank' is
hardly an accurate term for her behaviour in a pub, unless the odd gin and tonic
makes one an irredeemable lush. 'Laughed along with the drinkers' is more like
it.

I thought no more about her until one Thursday evening around eight
o'clock there was a knock on the door, and standing there was the dark-haired
girl asking for Deak, who was not at home. As she turned to go, I sensed she was
at a loss how to spend her evening, so I asked if she'd like to come to Traynor's
with me and Dave Lumsden, who at that moment was strolling up the hall
carrying his banjo case. 'We do a kind of bluegrass act,' I told her. I can't recall

how I knew her name was Jo Macrae, but Deak must have mentioned it. We bundled off to Traynor's in Dave's car, got her in free at the door, and she occupied herself for the evening in the background, occasionally sitting in the audience, while Dave and I had the usual busy time singing to the patrons, including a mooning group of young females who came regularly to hear us.

Back at McPherson Street around midnight, in the glare of the unshaded bulb of our scruffy sitting room, the three of us sipped coffee and chatted on the old brown vinyl sofa that constantly haemorrhaged grey stuffing from its bursting seams. After a while Dave went home, and I could give her my full attention. There was a lot to like about her looks; long trim legs in navy pedal pushers, a comfortably fleshed, not-fat body under her turquoise roll-neck sweater, bright eyes behind somewhat nerdy horn-rimmed glasses, a generous, laughing mouth in a clear-skinned face. Every few minutes a shock of wavy dark hair kept falling wonderfully over one eye. As we talked I realised she was easily the smartest woman I had ever been alone with – articulate, politically informed, more left-wing than I. She was a teacher of Secondary School humanities, shared a house in Carlton with a woman, had her own car. There was a nice mixture of capability and good humour about her.

Before I could move onto more intimate ground, however, the front door banged and shambling into the room came the tall, black-bearded figure of Deak, home from some party. He would have registered some surprise at seeing us together at this hour, perhaps was even a little miffed. In any case, he flopped down on the couch beside her, and as we explained how the evening had panned out, he reached a proprietorial arm up and around her shoulders, as in resuming control of a possession that had temporarily strayed but was now safely back where it belonged. I silently rankled, partly out of jealousy but also at his presumptuousness, when he had not even considered her important enough to take to his damn party. Soon after this she got up and went home, and Deak and I went to our rooms without saying another word to each other.

A few evenings later she dropped round, again enquiring whether Deak was at home. In fact he wasn't, but I thought I detected a distinct lack of regret about this, and when I suggested she might like to hear my latest Bob Dylan record, she was happy to stay. We actually went into Deak's room and used his record player because I didn't have one. After that we went into my room, talked, touched, kissed, and knew something was changing between us, a force drawing us closer; I noted the energy and sharp thought in her talk, liked the turns of phrase she chose, felt the fragrant, supple, dry warmth of her skin, inhaled the rich smell of her hair and body under her clothing, tasted the soft, salt-hint flavour of her mouth – oh yes, above all the smell and taste of her: she was always edible to me.

She stayed with me in my creaky double bed, with its fence-paling mattress-support in the middle, but we did not have full sex on that first night. I had mixed feelings about her unwillingness; on the one hand it made her seem conventional and immature. On the other, I was pleased to find she wasn't 'easy', that she expected more from a man than an erection and pitiful supplications. Perhaps this was because, like myself, she had grown up believing that sexual desire was inextricably bound up with other interests – trust, self-respect, worth, admiration, even political opinions – and that she needed, not security as such, but a firm idea that she was not being used for sport. But this makes her sound mistrustful and defensive, which she wasn't at all, not in any mean-spirited way. We had no contraceptives, and she may well have already sensed that I would not be much good at *coitus interruptus*; if she didn't have complete confidence in me, it was because I was not one to inspire complete confidence on the matter of sex. She was astute enough to see this, and yet still wanted to love me. At the time I was annoyed to have my ego thwarted, but I could also see that her refusal was not mistrustful so much as strategic; in future, I needed to be better prepared, and to learn that love best flourishes freely in the clear understanding of what we are doing. Strategy, I was to learn, was one of her great strengths.

The following afternoon, feeling chivalrous and triumphant at the same time, I broke it to Deak that I was interested in her, that, without going into details, she had come round to see him but had ended up in my room.

'Huh,' he scoffed, 'she's done that with me too. You won't get anywhere with her. Classic cock-teaser.'

He was sour, which was entirely typical of Deak, and I was pleased to hear it, and pleased to harbour my little secret, which was that I *was* getting somewhere, though not necessarily the same somewhere that Deak wanted to get to. Or maybe what was different was that instead of getting somewhere with her, I had the growing belief that I was *going* somewhere with her. That sense of a beginning, of the gathering momentum of an important journey, makes all the difference.

Yet we were not quite ready to fling ourselves wholeheartedly at each other, not yet. Without saying so, we both seemed to want to give our feelings a little test, to give them the chance to pass and fade should they want to. So it was another two weeks before I saw her. She had in the meantime come down with the flu, and had gone home to her parents in Castlemaine, taking with her a pile of essays to mark before end of term, which was coming up.

Then, when all that was over, she dropped in one Wednesday evening, straight from the end-of-term party at her school, Williamstown High. I opened the front door to her knock, and there she was smouldering amorously at me, somewhat drink-primed. Next moment we were all over each other in the hallway, and quickly, voraciously, like one of those scenes in a B grade Hollywood movie where the woman pulls the man's jacket down over his biceps and undoes his tie, we struggled out of our clothes while trying to stagger blindly in the direction of my bedroom. Shoes. It's the shoes that always destroy the moment, when you realise you are going to have to break rhythm, stop, sit down and undo the laces before you can even get your pants off. Fortunately, we were too eager, too aflame with desire to let it turn comic this first time, and if it felt a little stagey we just ignored that. Afterwards, we lay sweaty and happy among the detritus of underwear, socks, shirts, pillows and sheets wondering if it had really happened at last. Then, after a while, we took ourselves up to a Lygon Street café for a meal, talked non-stop about everything and nothing, before going back to McPherson Street for the night. By that time we had decided to move in together, to leave our current digs and establish a share-house of our own. And when, in her best matter-of-fact way, she said, 'I guess I'd better go on the pill, then', I confess my old Catholic upbringing that I'd thought was dead and buried was just for a tiny moment shocked by her strategic candour; I'd never met a girl who *organised* her sex life before. In fact I'd never met one who went on the pill before – that was then still a subject for newspaper sneering and girl's tattle. But when I reflected on her decision, I realised how reassuring it was and flattering to me because it signified the extent of her commitment, that she was free of doubt and totally with me for the long haul.

A real estate agent showed us a two-storey terrace at 250 Drummond Street, Carlton, four bedrooms for eight guineas a week. We looked at the pink and blue painted walls and asked him, 'Would the landlord pay for the paint if we freshened it up throughout?' He stroked his middle-aged chin and looked doubtful. 'Hmmm, he lives in Hong Kong. I could ask, but knowing the Chinese mind, they say No to everything.' The Cold War was still on, and China was in the throes of the cultural revolution, not to mention that for most Australians Chinese people remained Inscrutable and Mysterious, and more than slightly Untrustworthy. The agent's tiny racist whiff and silly drawling delivery somehow struck a chord in us, and 'knowing the Chinese mind' became one of those little private jokes between us, part of the mortar in the project of love we were steadily building together, and the small daily happiness we discovered in each other.

It took a little time, and a few terse misunderstandings, but eventually we found a style of humour we could share, one that might fairly be called ironic abuse. At first, when I said to her things like 'You have the ugliest feet I've ever seen, whereas mine are beautiful', she didn't get it, was even a little hurt. But in time she caught on and became quite adept at jokey insults herself. 'Running out on me again,' she would say if I went somewhere without her, 'off to your other woman. Just make sure you don't wake me when you get home.' In this way we managed to release small tensions, sustain each other's good temper, and keep our sense of proportion over matters that might easily descend into pointless seriousness. She would bluntly declare that I only wanted her for her record player and Beetle car, because I owned neither; my riposte was that she was after my money, of which I had none. Why we enjoyed such banter, I'm not sure. Like many of our generation, and especially our friends in The Push, we did not trust the conventional language of romance or the trappings of what we considered to be bourgeois culture. We eschewed clichés such as 'I love you' and 'darling', and other direct expressions of feeling; they seemed secondhand, used, not our own. Lovers should find their own language. Equally, the idea of any public announcement of an engagement would have been risible. We did, however, manage a small formality, when in Little Collins Street I proudly bought her a gold ring with a single centred garnet, which we both liked enormously, and which she wore on her third finger. It cost all of eight pounds. But it was our private moment, unshared with the world. We did not even *consider* the idea of marriage, did not raise it with each other, though we were openly living together, a decidedly precocious move in 1964, as her family was to affirm in a few weeks. There was in us a conviction that we were handling our lives in a new way, contrary to the way of our parents, and to a degree against their wishes.

Drummond Street proved the ideal launching pad in this first stage of our relationship. We put the word around that we had rooms to let, and soon had Bobby White, who had abandoned Arden Street, occupying the two small rooms at the back upstairs and an academic couple in the front downstairs bedroom. I say academic; Grant was a philosophy tutor and Kelly was his student, a situation for which his job would be in danger today. He was tall, blond and athletically good looking, but by temperament other-worldly and bookish; he could stand absorbed in a volume of poetry while a chaos of drunken argument or a party raged all around him. She, also blonde, was solidly pretty, mercurial and bumptious. They had a pact never to call each other names when they rowed, insisting that verbal wounding was too lasting, too bitter. So they threw things at each other, and punched. Kelly would emerge from their bedroom, blushing either from embarrassment or with the afterglow of their no doubt very physical reconciliation, and empty a newspaper sheet of broken crockery into the rubbish bin, the remnants of torrid battle. When they were not fighting they occupied the house in quiet, meditative bliss, or talked thoughtfully over her essays.

Bobby White had acquired a 16-year-old girlfriend, Caroline, who was still doing Leaving Certificate at the Presbyterian Ladies College. She would turn up at Drummond Street around four o'clock twice a week, usually with a classmate for company, and the two of them would sit at our dining table doing their homework, having told their parents they were going to the State Library after school to study. As soon as Bobby arrived home from work he and Caroline would go up to his room to shag for a half-hour, after which she would come down the stairs into the lounge looking punctilious and matter-of-fact in her spruce school uniform, collect her friend and homework, say a brief goodbye, and catch the tram home. Occasionally she and Bobby would see each other at weekends, but it was all strictly clandestine in respect to her parents.

The house became a drop-in centre for welcome and not-so-welcome acquaintances from the Push, and regularly buzzed with lively drink-fuelled talk of poetry or politics, musicians practicing and writing songs together, meals that burgeoned into communal dinners that somehow transmuted into virtual parties. Jo and I would walk over to Jimmy Watson's after we got home from work, catch up with friends, pick up some food and wine – three and sixpence a gallon flagon at King and Godfree – and make a communal meal for whoever was home. The ubiquitous Adrian Rawlins, who lived nearby, might show up conveniently as the food was being served, but while he was not explicitly welcomed, none of us would turn him away. He appeared one dinner time asking if we had a light in our outside toilet, which we did; his electricity had been turned off. He sat out there finishing an article for the *Jewish News*, and as he returned through the kitchen, sighted the leftover casserole on our dirty plates and asked for a piece of bread, which he used to greedily mop up the spoils while we looked on in amusement.

'Glass of red Adrian?' I offered.

'Thank you, dear boy,' he said in his suave baritone, licking his unwashed, post-lavatory fingers.

Around this time we had a fire in the gas oven, when the fat around a leg of roasting lamb caught alight. The problem became urgent when we realised it was too dangerous to open the oven door: the moment even a sliver of gap appeared, the air caused the flames to explode, threatening to leap out into the kitchen and onto us. We called the fire brigade, who pulled up in a massive red truck and delivered five large, uniformed, helmeted brigadiers, who marched thunderously down the narrow hallway, pressed into the kitchen and began an elaborate extinguishing procedure. Unfortunately many of the neighbours became intrigued by their presence, intrigued and somehow informally licenced to follow them into our house. Soon there was a crowd of total strangers, as well as the brigadiers, jammed into the kitchen giving advice, trying to help, or simply gawping around, taking the opportunity to check out how we inhabited the place. A fire seems to authorise all kinds of presumptuous behaviour, overriding decency, empathy and any right to privacy. Apparently in 1870s London the Prince of Wales liked to sit and watch burning buildings; he would have club chairs brought for his friend Christopher Sykes and himself, and hugely enjoy the spectacle in absolute indifference to the inconvenience, let alone suffering, of the recipients of the loss. Fortunately in our case the damage was minimal, apart from the roast leg of lamb, which sat in the pan beside the sink after everyone had gone, looking like the melted brake drum of a small car.

It seems to be the nature of happiness that it is unaware of itself at the time. The proof of my happiness lay in the productive busyness that characterised these months, the start of our new life together. There was so much going on that I had no time to reflect and tell myself that this was bliss. Jo was still teaching full-time, I still had the job at the Gas and Fuel Corporation, and was regularly singing at Traynor's two nights a week; suddenly we had more money than we could spend. Work, friends all around us, a good place to live, money, a sense of direction, all seemed the manifestation of the happiness that we found in each other, and took for granted.

For the first time in my life I began to be creative, though as I look back now I can see how inept these first attempts were. The new direction in folk singing, under the strong influence of Dylan of course, lay in song-writing. Increasingly, a singer's best path was to depart from the old folk songs and ballads and create new ones, ones that reflected the attitudes and events of the immediate present. Protest songs were in vogue in the mid-sixties, and though I sang them with great enthusiasm and commitment, dignifying them with the appellative 'political', it is no injustice that few have survived their immediate time, for they were crude concoctions on the whole, lacking poetry or musical distinction. They served a purpose, which was to raise consciousness of social issues, but had little value beyond that purpose. The main exception, again, was Dylan, who produced songs that transcended the genre; his bleak faux-Appalachian ballad 'Hollis Brown', for instance, with its minimalist tune and simple, hard-bitten flat-pick accompaniment the perfect vehicle for its bitter poetry, is to my mind a work of art as fine as anything in the total field of song writing, from Schubert to Cole Porter.

Along with pieces by Dylan, Phil Ochs and a few others, I began to include my own endeavours in performances, with some small success. A comic skit on a prison escape, 'Talkin' Pentridge Blues' went down very well with the audience at Traynor's , and I fashioned what feels now to be a piece of protest doggerel called 'The Voyager', about the recent submarine tragedy that cost eighty-two lives, which Trevor Lucas often sang, and in fact included on his first recorded album. I was doing just enough by way of writing to begin to appreciate how much I had to learn, and to experience once again that feeling that I was too raw and undeveloped, too ignorant not just of knowledge but of the skills that are needed in writing things that someone might want to read or hear. Being so close to Jo also made me aware of this; she possessed a clarity of thought, a skill with logic and argument, that was far superior to mine, which made me at once proud of her and my relation to her, and ashamed of my own ineptitude. I knew that the best way to learn song-writing was to write them, but I also knew I would have to do something about my general lack of education if I was going to get to grips with the peddling of words and ideas.

A couple of months into our relationship, Jo wrote to her parents in Castlemaine telling them of the new man in her life, and the change in her living circumstances. She wanted them to meet me, and of course to like me, to which end she proposed that we visit them for a weekend soon. It was so arranged – I must have taken the Saturday night off from singing – and we drove up after work on the Friday afternoon. On the way up she told me a little about them, including a sympathetic account of her stepfather's reluctant role as timetabler and disciplinarian in his position of Vice Principal of the local high school. By her own later admission Jo had broken the news of our relationship badly;

leaving the details till the actual meeting, she had simply written in her typically understated way that she had met this guy and had moved into a house with him. Inevitably, this had conveyed a particular image of a 'guy' they did not much like the sound of, and in the mind of her stepfather in particular it felt like a peremptory and unconsidered act, especially in not allowing them to meet me first. Their interest, therefore, was tinged with wary if not sceptical anticipation at what they were going to find.

Barbara, Jo's mother, greeted me in friendly tones and a warm smile. She had handsome, interesting, distinctive features quite different, at least on first meeting, from her daughter's. Where Jo was an enthusiastic, sparkling girl, Barbara was more patrician and considered, with a womanly intellectual style you might expect in a novelist or a violinist. Leaner-faced than Jo, brown-skinned and stringy, with a thick flourish of waved pepper and salt hair plaited and pinned high on her head, her youthful beauty had simply morphed into middle-aged beauty. One had to know mother and daughter some time before the similarity in their body structure became evident – the high, narrow hips, the long legs, the small, sexy pot belly, because you were misled by the contrast in facial breadth (has this a name?). I liked her immediately.

After the introductory formalities I cast around for signs of a second body, but found only the two empty lounge chairs beside the cheerily blazing open fire, a carved standard lamp with a craft-knit shade, a modest dining table with four solid high-backed chairs, and a busy but agreeable carpet underfoot. On the walls were smallish, intriguingly unfamiliar pictures, one of them, it turned out, an original Dorrit Black given to Barbara when they met as young women in Sydney in the 1940s. The whole house had a warm, unfussy blend of good taste and rusticity, the appeal of which struck me immediately its high-gabled, slate-roofed, decorated façade came into view at the end of the long driveway. We drove steeply up through a dense garden of giant trees and mixed shrubs, and not until the last moment did the sand-coloured Castlemaine slate cottage with the white painted trim reveal itself, and it was all colonial charm.

My curiosity to meet her stepfather was soon satisfied. 'Whit is waiting for you in the front room,' Barbara said, 'he'd like to have a word with you before dinner.'

The hint of measured seriousness in her voice, not to mention the Victorian archness of the very set-up of this arrangement – summoned like some errant schoolboy to the headmaster's office – filled me with foreboding as I made my way down the dim corridor into the front sitting room. This seemed an odd way to start a friendship, and I was already feeling a little nettled.

Taller than me, stretched to his full height standing on the hearthstone with his back to the fireplace, A.G. Whitley struck an intimidating pose that seemed calculated and more than a little theatrically silly. He wore grey slacks and a brown wool jumper over a white business shirt open at the collar, giving him the look of a vigorous, well-made man, busy, tanned, active. When he spoke your attention was drawn to a mouth wrought into severity by suppressed temper and other, less identifiable passions that, were they not clamped in a lifelong grip of self-discipline, might unravel into an ugly kind of self-indulgence. The enacted scowl felt practised at intimidating adversaries, but only at schoolboy level.

He shot out a hand and grasped mine in a predictably iron grip. 'Alf Whitley,' the deep voice said, 'you can call me Whit; everybody does.'

On the mantelpiece behind him, to which he gestured, was a familiar brown bottle and two glasses.

'Beer?' he said, and at my nod expertly filled the glasses, tipping them to one side as the golden liquid ran in, straightening them up just soon enough to produce the generally acceptable one-inch collar of white foam at the top of each glass. 'Here's health,' he offered, and silently we took our first sips, always the best moment of a cold beer, then he got straight to the point he had so clearly been rehearsing for some time.

'So what's this about you and Jo living together?'

The voice had gone even deeper. 'That's right,' I said, 'we've taken a house in Carlton.'

'*Why?*'

The question was so bald and unexpected that for a moment I was speechless. He leapt into the gap.

'I mean, why not get engaged and wait until you're married. *What's the big hurry?*'

I was ill-prepared for an inquisition on a subject that Jo and I had never thought twice about the rightness of doing. Because he was sternly awaiting an answer, I blurted out the first thing that came into my head. It also happened to be true, one of the practical matters on which Jo and I had agreed, which is probably why it leapt so readily to mind at that moment.

'Well, it's cheaper than keeping two places,' I said.

I thought he was going to strike me. 'Goddammit man,' he exploded, 'tell me you love the girl, tell me you can't keep your hands off her, *but don't tell me it's cheaper!*'

Memorable as his vehemence was, it wasn't the only display of feeling that took place in that room. It wasn't that he was not entitled to his anger, but that he had no right to demand a declaration of my most valued feelings on so little – practically no – familiarity with me, that prompted my own little display of pique. One of my many faults is an inability to take personal criticism phlegmatically: it always stings me, and I hit back. In my childhood I had suffered and defied no less an authoritarian juggernaut than the Christian Brothers, with their eight-inch coshes and torture chamber hallways and campaigns of hellfire and damnation. So I was not about to cave in to a High School bully who was taking advantage of my guest status in his home. I met his scowl with righteous silence, turned my back and walked out on him, carrying my beer, back into the dining room to the more amenable company of Jo and Barbara.

I sat through dinner hardly speaking, sulking of course, not wanting to acknowledge that they had anything in their lives to interest me. When asked by Barbara if I liked the Beethoven she was playing on the gramophone, I sullenly lied that I didn't. When asked about my own music, I shrugged a cryptic response. At a moment when both Whit and Barbara were not in the room, I put to Jo a selfish and brutal ultimatum: 'I'm going back to Melbourne straight after dinner,' I said, 'you choose what you want to do – either you come back with me or you stay here with them.'

It was a cruel choice to throw at her. She had planned that we would stay the whole weekend – sleeping separately of course – and hoped that the three people whom she most loved in different ways could all hit it off and become good friends by the time the weekend was over. Now it had crumbled to pieces all around her. And since it was her car we had driven up in, she felt a responsibility either to take me back to Melbourne or let me have the car, thus making it difficult for her to get back in time to teach on Monday morning. I'd cornered her, forcing upon her a choice she would rather not make. Of course, I knew what I was coldly staking out for myself: this was a test of her loyalty, of whether our relationship was going to survive this first, and probably most serious, obstacle. Them, or me. She undoubtedly felt the force of this, and it must have been causing her pain. To make matters worse she was already blaming her own ineptitude in telling them too much too soon. She dropped her head and wept a little. 'I'll come back with you,' she said. Settled, I thought. In my arrogance I might even have felt a shiver of smug triumph run through me.

We left after dinner in silence, unable to find much to say that would help me see things in a kinder light, and to understand Whit better. Had I been less defensive, less righteously pricked, I might have detected the fine principles in his outburst, principles with which I should have, and have long since agreed. Barbara was a different matter: I liked her instantly, and a bond grew between us that lasted the rest of our lives. But it took years and a wider experience of the world, during which time I had to get to the root of my oversensitive reaction to criticism – essentially the legacy of a pained childhood – before I could appreciate and feel a genuine fondness for Whit. And that is a later story, not for the telling here.

In these sanguine months at Drummond Street, as I have said, everything seemed to be falling into place. I had mentioned to Jo that I would love to own a Gibson J45 guitar, the kind Bob Dylan played at that time. I had already shifted from my old Tatay nylon-strung guitar that I'd started on under Karl Ogdon to a steel-strung Maton that Bill May custom built for me, strengthening the neck of a classical model with a steel rod. But it was not good for flat-picking, and lacked robustness. Browsing the classified ads one morning, Jo suddenly asked, 'What was that guitar you wanted?' Someone was selling one for thirty pounds. I rang and hurried out to the suburban house of a man trying to make a name as a multi-skilled entertainer for kids, for which he had bought himself an instrument to sing with on a recent visit to the U.S. But he couldn't play it, and had decided to try a different instrument. He took this brand new gleaming J45 out of its pristine case and passed it to me. Its strings were wrong and the neck was narrower than I was used to, but even so it had a fine, tough, singing quality that felt part of me the instant I held it. Thirty pounds was an absolute steal, and when I turned up at *Traynor's* with it, jaws dropped and Trevor Lucas grinned with envy. From then on, I flat-picked more and more, though it was fine for fancy finger-picking too. Trevor and I were becoming closer friends at this time; we were the only two using steel-strung guitars as our main instrument, and playing American and recently written music. He was producing quite magnificent blues now, and we often traded knowledge and ideas with each other; we both had a harmonica brace and blew riffs between verses. He looked wonderful when he played, with his tall angular frame and features, his bright red hair and beard, and a sonorous baritone voice all blending together in an expression of power.

We would meet frequently at Jimmy Watson's before going off to our separate gigs. On one of these occasions he made a surprise announcement: he and his pretty girlfriend Cheryl were getting married towards the end of the year, and going off overseas to explore the world. 'Why don't you come?' he casually laughed. Jo and I turned to each other. 'Why don't we?' we said. It was one of those moments when you both know it is the right things to do, like deciding to have a baby or buy a house. We wanted neither of those things, of course, but this – this was something else. It had never occurred to us that we could just do such a thing – just go off to this vague elsewhere called Overseas, as many young Australians seemed to be doing around this time. But now that Trevor had shown the way, we saw immediately that there was nothing to stop us. It would be an adventure, wherever it was and whatever we did there for however long, and that was all that seemed to matter to us; to do something spontaneous and extraordinary that would somehow cap off the happiness that we had found in each other. It would add a dimension of grandeur, an expansive gesture to augment the domestic scale of our joy so far. This was exactly what we needed, and we enthusiastically agreed right there and then to join Trevor and Cheryl on their ship when they left at the end of the year. We would see about tickets in the coming week or so. 'By the way,' he said before we parted that afternoon, 'we would like you to be Best Man at the wedding.' I wondered if my years-old charcoal suit would do an acceptable job, and even if it would, would it still fit me?

Jo and I have different memories of what followed on from this conversation in Watson's bar. She maintains that as soon as we agreed to go abroad, one of us turned to the other and, as casual as a comment on the weather, said 'Well, we might as well get married then.' My memory is that this was not said until a week or so later, at the city office of Chandris Shipping Lines. In the course of pricing the different cabin options, we were soberly advised by the female booking clerk that we would not be permitted to share a two-berth cabin unless we were officially married. It was at this point, in my recall, that I looked across at Jo and shrugged that consciously diffident, unromantic line, which was met with an equally diffident, casual grin: 'I guess we might,' she mused. I suspect Jo's version is right, but it has all become so confused in the telling and retelling over the years, that it is impossible to recall now the exact details of when and how the proposal took place. But it did, and within a short time, and quite without my participation, wedding plans were being discussed by the family females. Dresses, venues, food, invitations were all fussed over, as Jo's watchful cabal of relatives began to stir itself into preparation for the event it had ruminated on and anticipated for years; the passing into marital bliss of their favourite only child.

An unfamiliar figure from her family background appeared on the weekend of the wedding when we were visiting Castlemaine: her biological father, Ian Macrae. He was a handsome, morose man who had never really gotten over the failure of his wartime marriage to Barbara. Jo remained fond of him and saw him frequently throughout her childhood, but less so since then. Now he was down from Sydney for the wedding, at which he was to give Jo away. By the fire in the cramped sitting room at Castlemaine he quizzed me, out of a sense of fatherly duty I suppose, as to my future 'prospects', making deeply sceptical noises about the viability of singing for a living. 'You need some kind of steady job,' he insisted, to which I responded with some impudent flippancy to the effect that I would do only what pleased me. His remark, to my mind at the time, stank of everything about work, conformity, security and want of courage that I despised and had already so adamantly rejected. Now, however, it makes me blench to recall not just my arrogance, but my stupidity, for I was willfully blinding myself to certain important realities about myself and the world, and too imperceptive to see the important reality behind the tired cliché that Ian had uttered. Since the words of others would not succeed, it would have to be Life itself that would sheet home the essential lesson: know thyself.

Part of the spirit of general felicity that this year had brought was the growing reputation I enjoyed as a folk singer. As well as consolidating my regular spots at Traynor's, where my following was building steadily, I was receiving invitations to perform at one-off occasions, concerts, migrant hostels, public events. An invitation came from the organisers of the Ballarat Show asking me to 'name a fee'; I realised only too late that I could have asked for five times as much and they would have paid without a quibble. A friendly young reporter interviewed me at home for a piece in the *Sun News Pictorial*, and was so easy to talk to that I told him more than I should have about my job at the Gas and Fuel Corporation. 'I joke around when I answer the phone to the public,' I told him, naively thinking he would treat such things in confidence, and write only about my music. When I arrived at work Monday morning, I had hardly sat at my desk when the manager called me into his office. He pushed a copy of *The Sun* across his desk toward me, folded to show a single page bearing my photograph and an article boldly headlined 'Jester in the Fruit Palace.' He waited, clearly expecting an explanation. I shrugged, tried laughing it off. 'Just a joke,' I said, but I knew the game was up. 'A week's notice,' he said, 'I'll have what's owing made up and paid to you Friday night. Then clear out.'

I could've kicked myself, because we were set on saving as much money as we could for the trip, and it had been going so well. And Jo had gone onto part-time to manage the preparations for our wedding, which was only weeks away. So we would have to be satisfied with less in savings than we'd planned for, hoped for. But we didn't fret over it, took it in our stride. We seemed, back then, to have all the strength and resilience in the world; our happiness was not in the slightest bit fragile. On the contrary it gave us a feeling of invulnerability: nothing could beat us, nothing could put us off our stride. Not even when, the following Friday night, Bobby White held a party in the house, and someone in the crowd of mostly strangers he had invited dipped into the pocket of my jacket hanging in the stairwell and stole the eighty pounds paid to me that day by the Gas and Fuel paymaster, representing four weeks' salary and holiday pay. It was a hefty sum and a nasty thing to have happened, but again we managed to be unfazed by it. Angry, yes, but we got over it quickly.

Earlier in the year my family had moved to the new house in Syndal. My mother kept asking me out there, but I had been resisting. Then, when Jo and I became serious about each other, I took her with me and finally paid the place my first visit. It was a pleasant, well-built cream brick veneer, exactly what my mother had long wanted. Sensibly designed, on a large block, it was comfortable to move about in and had plenty of scope for a garden, which mum was keen to tackle. Ray, then just twenty-one, moved into it as well, along with twelve-year-old Susan and our dog Butch. I've forgotten about Butch. He was a Kelpie cross, smallish and excitable, and completely untrained. At Ivanhoe he was left on his own all day until his beloved family came home from work and school, at which point he would go literally barking mad, tearing around the perimeter of the big back yard, staying close to the fence, hurtling at full pelt round and round, over and over, leaping the waist-high pile of compost along the rear fence, until exhaustion pulled him up and he flopped, tongue dripping, on the back lawn. Later, when Richard had completely removed the compost pile, Butch was so habituated to making his leap at that spot that he couldn't help but gleefully do it anyway, sailing long and high over a completely imaginary compost pile. We laughed ourselves silly at the sight of him.

My mother and Jo got along well from the first. It was still a matter of tentative reachings-out, of exercising a polite warmth, but my mother was astute enough to recognise quality when she saw it, and was soon convinced that I had, finally, found the right girl. She asked if she could help with the wedding dress, a task her dressmaker's fingers were itching to do, though I think Jo's choice of a short plain dress, pill-box hat and cape with a fur collar, somewhat disappointed her; she would have loved to make an elaborate traditional gown, train and all, and to see her first daughter-in-law sail forth in full bridal splendour, but this was not Jo's way, nor mine for that matter.

Since neither of us believed in God, and practiced no religion, we really didn't care where we were married, and in any case we knew that weddings as such were really ceremonies for the family, to bring the tribes together in celebration, curiosity, or consolation, and beyond those important functions the event added very little to our feelings for each other. So we happily agreed to the choice of the Presbyterian Church in Castlemaine: it was a pleasant building, the service was uncomplicated, it had the virtue for everyone in both families of not being Catholic, and, Castlemaine being a small town, was conveniently near the reception venue and the home of Barbara and Whit.

For myself, I went through the ritual in a kind of cooperative daze, simply doing what I'd been told to do, dressing as required, shaking all the unfamiliar hands, saying all the customary things. Jo looked slim and elegant in her tight dress, her lovely legs on show, a dazzling smile so set it seemed only plastic surgery could remove it, though she still gazed upon the world from behind those nerdy glasses. Still, the effect was good, making her look intelligent as well as beautiful, and I was hugely proud. The August weather was kind, the wit and the champagne flowed at the reception, and went on until late into the evening. My brother Ray had momentarily teamed up with the gorgeously blonde Orme Lind, and drove us back to Melbourne in Jo's Beetle. We had foregone a honeymoon: the trip abroad would serve that purpose.

There was another party waiting for us at Drummond Street, organised, if that is the word, by Bobby White. Mostly scruffy friends from the Push, they revelled into the early hours of the morning, urging me to many bouts of celebratory skolling. Again, I cannot recollect who was there, but I do know that around one in the morning, exhausted after her long, taxing day, Jo made her excuses to take herself up to get some sleep. Naturally, since it was our wedding night, I felt it only right to accompany her to the epithalamial bed, and together we staggered up the stairs hand in hand, linked more in support than desire. She cleaned her teeth in the bathroom, then, while I stood unsteadily admiring while she undressed and slipped naked between the sheets, I had the sudden realisation that I was not going to be up to the task. 'If I lie down,' I mumbled weakly to her severed head on the pillow, 'I'll be sick.' This was the final anti-romantic climax to a day that in essence had been a kind of charade, for if you think about it, we had plighted troths before a God we didn't believe in, in a Church we never visited and was the denomination of no-one in either family, with a sheer pretence of celibacy before unknowing relatives, for reasons only of satisfying the moralistic shipping rules. This was the ultimate fraudulent ceremony. 'Go on then,' she laughed, 'go back to the party until you sober up.' I left her alone between the spotless sheets, giggling herself to sleep.

The final weeks before we left seemed to speed past in a blur. Trevor's wedding was a much grander affair than ours, held in Christ Church in Toorak Road, South Yarra, in full traditional regalia, with the copper-haired bride in billowing veil and train, the groom and his party in hired morning suits with top hats and white carnation buttonholes. Trevor tried to keep up the tone for the respectable relatives by holding the reception at Tom Lazar's chic Little Reata restaurant in the city and giving orders to Don Carless, guarding the door, not to admit any scruffy Push types, specifically Adrian Rawlins. But it took more than bouncers to keep Adrian out of a scene, and during the course of the afternoon there he mysteriously appeared mingling among the stylishly turned-out guests, beaming effulgently in tight leather pants, a matelot top and leather waistoat, with a red cravat at his throat, offering a bowl of strawberries and cream to a group of bemused aunts, who were convinced he was a major poet. God knows how he got in; there was something of an Ariel in him, I think, a spirit invoked by the occasion, as if any event connected to the Arts somehow magically conjured his presence out of the air, and Poof!, there he was, in full rotund spectre, the agent and master of ceremonies, his baritone laughter distinct through the hubbub, his insistence on protocol at once laughably baroque and yet irresistible. I was once eating with him in a St Kilda restaurant, when he suddenly broke away from our conversation and positively yelled across the room to a terrified woman, 'You put the potato *in* the soup madam! *IN* the soup!' He was a cultural snob, without a cent to his name, couldn't bear our Australian philistinism, but took it upon himself to put things right whenever he got the chance.

Someone, I'm not sure who, organised a farewell concert at the Emerald Hill Theatre in South Melbourne. Trevor, myself and a number of the regular folkies performed in what was a warm if ad hoc event. It must have been well attended, because the soft-drink supply ran out, and Jo had to drive around looking for an open milk bar to replenish it. Adrian seemed to get involved in the organising, too, and somehow managed to claim a percentage of the takings, much to our annoyance.

After this, it was for us only a question of getting ourselves ready to leave – selling the car, giving away books and records, and leaving valued items with our families. We bought a few clothes to take with us, though really we were travelling extraordinarily light, and I think managed to pack all our belongings into two modest sized suitcases. Clearly, we assumed we would be returning to Australia sometime, even if we had no idea when.

This story, as you see, is drawing to its close. Of course in my life it is as much a beginning of something as it is an end, though truly there is no end, at least not yet. It is a stage, with its distinct marking of an important transition from one set of necessary preoccupations to another, one vaguely coherent collation of acts, dreams, pursuits, emotions, relationships to another. Those relationships, my treatment of them, trouble me now. I note as I reflect how friendships came and went in my life, how particular people meant something important to me at one moment, only to be neglected, dropped and forgotten too soon in the next. I felt nothing about this at the time, but it is a cause of regret and guilt to me as I look back. Where were they now, those who were so significant to me once? So many I abandoned, like old clothing: as long as they fitted, pleased my sense of fashion, served my prevailing interest, I held them in close and frequent contact. But people are not clothes, they reciprocate and they grow as I do, and what I wish is that I could have somehow taken all my friends along with me for the ride. But that is not right either, for they are not my possessions, are not there solely for my benefit, have their own lives to lead. Yet I do regret losing touch with some of my old boyhood mates, Barry Roe, with Ron and Yvonne, with Arnold Winton, even with old girlfriends such as Margaret and Loretta, just as I regret the growing distance that took place between myself and my family. And my very good friend Bob Haberfield, a key figure in my maturation, though he remained on the fringes of my life in these years when I was busy singing to my mistress' eyebrow, I ignored him too often for too long. I am a lazy friend, too neglectful of the necessity of cultivation. Like a treasured garden, friendship needs attention and nourishment in order to survive. I wish I had learned that lesson in my youth. But these are things I did not think about as we prepared for the next big adventure ahead.

What do I find as I retrace the trajectory of my journey into adulthood? There is a pattern of mistakes and recovery, of enthusiasms and disillusion that dogged my efforts to negotiate the world of work. I cannot say that at this point I had come far, because I hadn't found a form of work that would expand me as a person, and a provider, on into the future. At the point that this leg of my journey stops, I thought I had found that work in singing and playing the guitar, but I hadn't in fact; I still had not addressed the question of my education, which of course I simply defected from when I left school at so young an age. I had not truly faced the fact that temperamentally I was not one of the world's manual workers, nor routine office workers, that I had a restless and creative intellect, and that it was in dire need of proper training. I wasn't going to get this merely by singing locally for weekly gig money, and I wasn't going to be able to get an education simply by staying put and hanging around the Push. Really I was becoming a kind of provincial autodidact. Sure, as a city Melbourne had been my stamping ground and had defined my limits, but it was a Melbourne of the old style, dull and bound by confining routines, like six o'clock closing, restricted dining regulations, paucity of night-life, the dominance of Anglo-Celtic culture and the entrenched racism and wowserism that went with it. In 1964 there was no sign that this was about to change, and up until this point I had reconciled myself to living and working within the confines that the city offered. The only way out, as others were finding, was to leave and look to a wider experience, to go out and explore the world. Take the risk, as I was going to yet again.

Sometimes, when you take the risk, you get lucky, as I did with Jo. You can never dismiss the element of luck in any of these moments that turn you in a new direction. Of course, I had the good judgement to catch her and hold onto her, because she, overwhelmingly, was to make the biggest and profoundest difference in my life. And where that would take me, where it would take *us*, was something we were about to discover in the course of moving away from all that made us secure – our families, her teaching career, my folk-singing future, our friendships. We often joked that the amount we'd saved to take with us on the trip – something over a thousand pounds – would have gone a long way to buying us a nice house in the suburbs, where we could settle down and raise a family. But that was the farthest thing from our minds. We didn't want security, we wanted adventure, risk, experience, we wanted to see and grasp the world. This was perfectly right, and I have no regrets about choosing the course we did. And yet I try to recall, now, whether I was hearing a little voice nagging away at the back of my mind, the voice perhaps of Ian Macrae delivering his unwelcome advice, and whether in suppressing this voice I was also suppressing my own suspicions that I had been living a delusion, that my singing 'career' was a kind of fraud, that my 'freedom' was a mindless drift, subject to whatever way the wind blew, and not being steered by me, because I really didn't know anything about navigating my life. If it was a suspicion, it would be some time before I would bring it into focus and start to do anything about it. The agent of this would be Jo, but that is all another story, and needs no introduction here.

The night we sailed for Greece, New Year's Eve, prompted a small epiphany in my regard for my mother. Jo and I were so caught up in the practicalities of boarding – checking tickets, passports, getting the luggage into the cabin, that we had no time for emotions. I still wonder at the insouciant way we went about the whole adventure, hardly allowing ourselves a moment's excitement through all the complications and talk of our itinerary. Our parents had also never travelled abroad, except in two cases to fulfil their wartime duties, but for them what we were doing was momentous and, they all instinctively knew, life-changing. They had the wisdom to see this. My mother looked into my face as we stood on the crowded deck, and her tears and long hug took me by surprise. There was a mixture of intense emotions in her eyes – envy, anxiety, pride, wonder and regret for me, for Jo, and a tangible fear that she might never see me again. I was more than surprised, I was shocked by this. I didn't think anything so drastic was at stake, but then I was young, and youth never takes finality, such as death, into consideration. Living is forever. The older generation can't think this way. They know only too well that everything is *en passant*.

At midnight the sudden horn of the *Ellenis* drowned our goodbyes and brought urgency to our hugs and kisses. For the first time I felt a current of excitement about what we were doing, and as we waved from the ship's balcony to our loved ones I put my arm around Jo and this time felt a pang of sadness intrude into the excitement; you move on to the promise of new experience, but you nevertheless have some sense of loss for the friends and places that gave you the old. Yet in some sense, I suppose, you take them with you, courtesy of that wonderful facility, Memory. We held on to each other as we searched hard for beloved faces in the crowd. Then, slowly, we became aware of a gap opening up between the wharf and us, and I stared down into the widening black water, far, far below. Finally, we were parting, the crowd of faces were growing less distinct, the darkness taking over and eventually all we could see across the black ripples were the little lights festooning the wharf. This was it. I wondered, of all things, if I would get seasick once we were out in the open sea.

Time of Arrival

WE WERE PASSING THROUGH THE TIMOR SEA on a warm and cloudless night. The three of us stood on a low ledge in the bows, peering into a black wind tearing at our hair and faces, snatching our voices from our lips. John, my friend of one week, stood free on my left, Jo my wife of four months holding my right arm. Directly beneath we could just hear the whisper of the cutwater slicing the sea. Nothing ahead was visible; for all we knew we were about to plunge over the edge of the world. Thrilling and frightening, the encounter drew into coherence the mixture of feelings that had been building over months around our larger action of risking the very journey at all. For it, too, was taking us blind into the unknown, believing only that it was north, it would become Europe, and it was necessary. We did not know why it was necessary, since it wasn't exactly a holiday (though it might have qualified as a honeymoon), it wasn't for the purpose of work—I had no folk-singing plans beyond hoping to pick up the odd gig here and there, and Jo had no thought of teaching. John likewise, he hoped, had given up teaching for good; he was determined to become a writer, and was putting all his faith in experience and solitude. We were simply *going*, open-minded, open-hearted, and would face whatever came along whenever and however it came. And this blind faith was somehow embodied in the progress of the *Ellinis* as she surged into the ocean ahead.

A week earlier, on New Year's Eve 1965, we had sailed away from the darkening wharf waving our farewells to friends and relatives in Melbourne. The next day was spent heading up the east coast towards Sydney, where we were to pick up more passengers. In Sydney we spent a couple of hours at the Elizabeth Bay apartment of Jo's maiden aunt Nan, along with her married sister Winsome. Very genteel it was, and I sat squirming in my tight jeans and trying not to slop my tea as the aunts sought to fathom if there was any substance to me, their newly acquired nephew-in-law. We also caught up with Jo's father, Ian, and back on board the ship were seen off by her cousin Bob Callander and his wife June. As we said our goodbyes, and the ship edged out of the harbour, her white flanks brilliant in the late afternoon sunlight, we had the sobering realisation that these were the last actual contacts we would have with Australia for quite some time, possibly years.

She was an elegant ship, the *Ellinis*, the latest in classic liner design when she was built in 1931. But she was ageing, and now that Chandris Lines was using her to carry assisted passage migrants from Greece and England to Australia, the years of hard work were beginning to show. Even during this first week of the journey a problem with the drive shaft showed up, and the captain had to radio ahead for a new part to be fitted in Port Moresby. Our dismal cabin, being the second cheapest on offer was relegated to a forgotten corner low in the bowels of the ship. It did have a single porthole, but the bunk beds were narrow, and the only cupboard had meagre hanging space and a couple of inadequate drawers. There was hardly width across the cabin for the two of us to stand side by side, and thankfully I was able to get my guitar under the lower bunk and out of the way. Along the corridor from us was a public bathroom and toilet, which we shared with several other passengers. A stink of engine oil and something sour, suggesting various kinds of badly managed waste, pervaded the whole area, including our room. So we spent as much time as we could on deck or in the bars and lounges.

The first days sailing were pleasant enough. Balmy breezes kept most people on deck, and we leaned on the railings in the sun and found much to enjoy about the sea, its vastness, its beauty, the way it separated us from the world we had known till then. A pod of porpoises raced boisterously beside the ship, distant islands rose into view and faded again, as if they were offering themselves to us but thought better of it. Sea birds circled above, squawking what could have been encouragement or mockery, depending on how one read their tone. But as life on board settled increasingly into routines, the only real variety of each day was found in the changing moods of the sea and weather around us.

The first time we walked into the bar lounge we found it occupied by noisy young males chanting at a mate who was in the throes of 'skolling' a can of beer:

> *Here's to Jonesy, he's true blue;*
> *He's a piker through and through.*
> *He won't go to heaven, he'll go the other way!*
> *Going down, down, down, down, down, down …*

'Jonesy' finished by brandishing the can to approving roars from the group. A harmless Aussie ritual, I thought, until it began to happen every day from about mid-afternoon to midnight for the entire journey. It was impossible to have a quiet drink in the bar when they were there. Nor was it just in the bar; they would turn up in all corners of the ship at any time of the day or night, on the sun deck, around the pool, on the promenade decks. But they were popular with many of the single women on board, who generally hung round them like flies, straw-sucking their Bacardi and Cokes, gin squashes, Black Tulips or Pimms, and posing decorously in skimpy bikinis, frolicking in the pool, or lying on the decks mercilessly scorching their bodies. No-one believed in skin cancer then.

Passengers were not as well-catered for as they are on cruise ships nowadays. There were no movies, the library contained a mere handful of books, mostly battered paperbacks of the Harold Robbins, Carter Brown type, or dreary travel books. No casino, no organised daytime games, though someone ran a Greek language class for beginners during the last week. In the concert lounge, where people could get up and perform, a man sang 'Moon River' on several occasions, and seemed to get worse every time. Sometimes a pretty teenage girl, who had learned all the slick moves of showbiz presentation, glided among the patrons in a flared skirt singing popular tunes already five years out of fashion, accompanied by her stocky father on a Hawaiian steel guitar. I performed a couple of recently written American songs, by Phil Ochs and Tom Paxton, but this was neither the place nor the audience for folk music of my kind, and it was met with polite indifference. Trevor Lucas fared better, singing more familiar gospel songs, and in any case he was better known than I amongst the eastern suburban crowd on board. These were patrons, some of them, of the Treble Clef restaurant in Prahran where The Seekers had a regular spot, and Trevor did the occasional gig. So compared with the cruise ships of today, the entertainment was ad hoc and ill-targeted. Occasional parties given by the captain were worth attending for the canapés and cocktails; it was at these we discovered the delights of daiquiris, in disbelief we'd never come across them before. In the main though, people had largely to create their own amusement, and for many that meant spending most of the time in the bar, or lolling in the chairs on deck, and trying to avoid the raucous youths.

One stroke of good fortune turned up at our dining table. A young man apparently travelling on his own responded to something I said about recently reading Henry Miller's *Colossus of Maroussi*.

'That mesmerising old fraud,' he said.

I thought the oxymoron clever, and absolutely right about Miller. We introduced ourselves; he was called John Samson, and he was headed for Greece, with no specific place in mind. What followed was the first of many lively discussions we had about literature and many other topics during the trip. We became friends, the three of us, from the moment of that first conversation, and it was a friendship that was to grow stronger and closer in the ensuing years.

Despite this welcome development, Jo and I didn't cope well with either the social life or the periods of boredom. Essentially we were out of our element, finding it hard to adjust. We had grown to like our friends in the Push, their politics, interest in the arts, their personal foibles, always a little marginal or bizarre. I had thought Trevor was like this, and one of 'us', and yet he and Cheryl seemed to prefer the company of the better-heeled, more mainstream types on board, and despite the fact that we had often performed together and I was Best Man at his wedding, we were not spending a great deal of time together. He was a more sociable being than I back then, was not especially interested in books or politics or the life of the mind: getting on in the music world was his thing, and I think he found my outsiderish introspection quite irritating to be around. Nor was he the only one. Jo, too, was at times disappointed in my failures of initiative, my reluctance to engage in social pleasures like dancing, learning Greek, my recoil from groups of harmless chat. Often I would simply choose to retreat into the cabin to play my guitar for hours on end. For the first time since we'd been together, we began having rows. I was feeling exposed, the protective cocoon of status I had received from singing to audiences was suddenly torn away, and in this vulnerable state I didn't quite know who or what I was, and how I should be regarded and regard myself. Worse, towards her I could be unpredictably short, or its opposite, show indifference, especially if she challenged an opinion or scrap of knowledge I came up with. Under these uncomfortable circumstances that pride in her educated mind I had when we first met began to turn defensive and querulous. Criticism or indifference, both would cause her hurt. She would weep quietly in her narrow bunk, and I would sulk in aggressive silence in the one above. Being unable to sleep together, unable to lock bodies in the comfort of a double bed, our fights lasted longer than they should have, our frustrations at being deprived of those moments when the physical presence takes over and closes the emotional distance, cruelly prolonged. Had we just been able to hold each other through the night, these petty defences might readily have broken down, especially since we were young and still getting to know each other. As it was, too often it took days of moody silence between us before our resentments passed.

I also began to pretend, and not just to myself, that I was a writing type, a literary man, and I borrowed some of John Samson's educated aura to pass off as my own. All this, I think, made it difficult for people to have confidence in me or my opinions, because the act wasn't especially convincing. And Jo had her own demons to cope with—a certain lack of confidence in herself, a sense in her that she, too, didn't really 'belong' amongst the eastern suburban social set that dominated the ship's culture, and that no-one found her interesting. I should have been able to reassure her that she lost nothing in comparison with any of the young women on the ship who actively sought attention. But in my head I was still in bachelor-land, didn't really know how to live with a woman in a spirit of companionship, how to consider her happiness. All that mattered to me were my own problems.

Sitting in the lounge one afternoon talking with John, I was struck by how much I liked listening to him, his deep voice, the blend of knowledge and slightly pressing opinion in one so young. There was a strength there, but also a vulnerability, an otherworld-liness that, oddly, brought out a measure of protectiveness in me. I could somehow see why he was on his own, why he had not found a niche in Australia that made him happy, why the term 'outsider' applied as much to him as to me. He spoke with close familiarity of the works of Homer and Sophocles, of Virgil and Dante, and of modern writers such as James Joyce, Conrad, and, with special passion, DH Lawrence. None of my friends in the Melbourne Push had this degree of erudition, and I doubted that even my old evening class tutor, Miss Scholes, had read as widely or with the kind of personal investment that John did. Such commitment, I thought, has in him come at the expense of that shell of defences, the many little compromises one makes with the stupid, the philistine, the brutal, the aggressive. I knew there were artists, writers, intellectuals, musicians—wasn't Bob Dylan one of them?—who had this degree of integrity, but the only one I had known personally up until then was my friend Bob Haberfield, and he had come to his convictions by way of experience and rejection of that philistine world, which he understood only too well. John, in contrast, was an innocent, and in his innocence was a kind of fragile beauty. I felt both privileged to be in his company and fearful that at any moment his seriousness could be mocked by an unsympathetic Australian eavesdropper, or a group of those rowdy drinkers, for he always spoke his opinions in a strong, sonorous voice, even in public. Happily, if he felt something similar about himself, he had the guts not to show it.

Port Moresby might have been an unscheduled stop—that broken propeller shaft could have been the cause—but everyone was pleased to have the break. The open lifeboats took us from the ship anchored half a mile off shore into the little harbour, but not without some drama on the way. A sudden storm blew up and over us, drenching us with heavy rain, and the Greek sailors in charge decided to turn back to the *Ellinis*. But as we turned in a shaft of sunlight, a huge wave struck us side-on, breaking over us and tipping the boat at such a pitch that we thought she would be swamped and we would all end up in the sea. The kind of laughter that can instantly turn to shrieks of alarm came from many of the passengers, but luck was with us and we made it to the ship, where we sheltered in her lee till the storm passed. After reaching the little harbour we spent a few hours strolling among ramshackle huts, on stilts and khaki-painted as though they still belonged to the army. The natives, sitting on the verges with small piles of fruit in front of them, ogled us with a suspicion edging on menace, while we registered mild alarm at their red mouths and teeth. 'Betel chewing,' a passenger said, 'it's a stimulant, like tobacco.'

The tropical feel of New Guinea reminded me of my nine months in Cairns only two years earlier. But whereas there was a happy, confident feel about the people on the streets of Cairns, even in the Aborigines I saw, Port Moresby felt sullen and poverty ridden. I had the eerie sense there was no purpose in the buildings being there, or at least conflicting purposes, depending on whether your perspective was native or white. The natives were meant to be learning and consuming what Australians were offering, which ranged from English teaching to selling them plastic buckets, the idea being that the administration was working towards a future handover. But in practice a kind of apathy ruled. There was a feeling that at any moment the jungle could reclaim everything, could overgrow the shacks, recapture the people, overwhelm the attempts to organise, drive out the white administrators, and leave the whole country to the fortunes of tribal law. And you felt that the people here at this moment, black or white, were not particularly bothered whether it went one way or the other.

For the next week or so we saw nothing from the ship but the Indian Ocean, in all its humors. A particularly rough passage south of Sumatra had us off our food for a day, and tossed us in our bunks, making sleeping difficult, but neither of us was actually sick. Then a few days later we passed through the most astonishing calm we ever imagined possible. The water on all sides was as still as a pond, the late afternoon sun and sky perfectly copied in the sea of glass stretching to the horizon. We could hear the droning engines and passengers talking thirty yards away, but no sound from the water. Other days, the waves moderated and were so dark that I believed I had grasped the origin of the colour navy blue.

At some stage during this time we crossed the Equator, and it was apparently an established custom that passengers hold a mock ceremony to mark the occasion. 'Crossing the Line' it is called, an old naval initiation rite for first-time sailors. The rowdy singles on board took the prime role in this, dressing one of them as King

Neptune, complete with cotton wool beard, cardboard crown, suitably weedy long robes and a broom-handled trident. He was assisted by a Queen Amphitrite, a strapping hairy-legged youth unconvincingly re-gendered by a grass skirt and a borrowed bra stuffed with tennis balls. Aided by several weirdly dressed assistants, they 'captured' numbers of squealing passengers, laid them on a makeshift table out on the pool deck, and watched by a cheering crowd, smeared the victims with what looked like shaving cream, tomato sauce, something pink and squashy from the kitchen, and a dusting of talcum powder, perfunctorily shaved it off with a table tennis paddle, and heaved them by hand and foot into the pool. The gods showed a preference for pretty bikini-clad girls as victims, but children, reticent dads and uniformed officers were not immune; all were smeared and shaved and sent screaming into the pool. It was an afternoon of knockabout fun that had the virtue of bringing some sections of the ship closer together for the remainder of the trip.

A second stop, again to replace that troublesome propeller shaft, was made at Colombo, capital of then Ceylon. We docked in the evening—it was already dark—and were told to be back by midnight, when the ship would depart, which would give us a tight couple of hours to see the city. Like bewildered sheep, John, Jo and I were helplessly bundled into a taxi and whisked around the town. The young driver was an enthusiastic guide, though his English was a little confusing at times, and he had an unsettling habit of turning his head around to smile at us in the back while the car was hurtling through the traffic.

'Ceylon is one hundred and ninety-nine percent Buddhist,' he told us, veering wildly onto the footpath, nearly demolishing a group of white-gowned citizens. The Buddhist festival of the Full Moon was taking place, and there were many people on the streets, in white or coloured robes, ducking out of the way as we raced among them. We had no idea where he was taking us, but within twenty minutes we found ourselves on the outskirts of the city at a rather grand colonial hotel standing in lofty isolation on a bluff above a beach. The driver said he would wait for us while we had a drink. The only other people about were a group sitting on the terrace looking out over the ocean, and when we made to sit at a nearby table, they loudly protested that we should come over and join them. It turned out they were three Russian engineers, spending time in Ceylon in an advisory role on local projects—the Soviet Union was keen to keep good relations with a country still finding its independent feet. Today they would be rich and fashionably dressed tourists from St Petersburg coolly throwing their weight about. But these men were warmly disposed, well-read, spoke good English, and were probably homesick. John soon got into a lively discussion with them on the merits of the poet Yevgeny Yevtushenko and several other writers, including I think a wild disagreement over Dostoyevsky, and in fact the whole event became so absorbing that we forgot about the time. My mind drifted away at one point, and looking out over the beach I thought to myself, 'What the hell are we doing here under a full moon out on some remote peninsula of Ceylon drinking beer and discussing literature with three crazy Russians?' And then I thought, 'This is what we came away for. This is the oddball, unlikely world that we'd hoped to find. Treasure it. Remember it. It won't happen again.'

The experience of getting back to the ship was just as weird. Not only were we desperately late—we'd left ourselves hardly enough time to reach the water-taxi—but when we did, and the rickety little craft with its handful of passengers chugged around with maddening tardiness, we couldn't find the *Ellinis*. She was anchored somewhere out in the blackness of the massive harbour amongst a scattered flotilla of passenger ships, freighters, tankers and other craft, their rigging lights a dazzling gallimaufry above the dark shapeless forms of their hulls. You couldn't make out one from another. And the harbour stretched endless, as we limped past ship after sleeping ship. The pilot of the water-taxi seemed as confused as we, and when he turned the boat around and headed back to a completely different part of the harbour, I began to fear that the *Ellinis* had weighed anchor and gone, left without us. 'Surely it wouldn't,' said Jo. 'I wouldn't put it past the Greeks to do anything,' said a terse John Samson. But when we finally found her, everything on board was calm and unconcerned, the crew sleepily unruffled as they helped us aboard. And contrary to the announcements that she would be departing at midnight, it was something like another hour before the ship got underway. We began to understand not to expect strict precision from Greeks on matters of time and place After two and a half weeks everyone was bored with ship life, which seemed to shrink down to dull routines and claustrophobic spaces. And every passing day worked to transform the boredom into actual irritation. The food had become predictable and unappetising; an oddly tasteless slab of dry roast turkey turned up on the plate every other meal, and the soup only slightly changed colour every day but not taste. We said that they probably added last night's leftover each day as a joke, but I suspect we had got it right. Within the ship there was a smell that, while not overwhelming, still pervaded every corner of life on board—the lounges, the dining room, our cabin. It was there in the food, in the sheets and blankets we slept in. No other smell was quite like it; an insidious slumgullion of rot, engine oil, the cancerous action of salt on iron, the souring of paint blistering with rust, waste emissions from below, all blended into the very air we breathed. Even in bad weather it was better gulping the breeze out on deck than putting up with that. It was one more reason for leaping at the opportunity to get off when the ship berthed at the remaining stops.

Temporary friendships formed between people with nothing in common, or who secretly disliked each other, but at least they broke the monotony for a few hours. We mixed occasionally in a group that included another pair of newlyweds, Bill and Ruth Morgan, whom Jo had known slightly at university, and David Keys, a lonely middle-aged teacher, who was inclined to morbid confidentialities about the break-up of his marriage. At least we had John to talk to, and each other of course. Despite our rows and the discomforts of the ship, we had no doubt about our love for each other, and the great joy we had in being together. I was enormously proud of her, felt I was the luckiest man on the ship, if not the planet.

One night when I was in the cabin feeling slightly unwell, Jo went for a walk around the decks by herself. When she got back she told me about something that had happened to her. Standing alone looking out over the sea at a brilliant full moon, a balmy breeze fanning her hair, she was thinking how it was the complete romantic Hollywood cliché, when, right on cue, a ship's officer, in full impressive uniform, quietly appeared beside her and began a friendly conversation. It was as if they were in some film set, following a script that, she was sensibly aware, was leading inevitably towards a proposition; by the time he had gotten to the point of inviting her to his cabin, she had already projected the whole scene and its outcome in her mind. The Greek officer was courteous enough, inoffensive in his way, but what took her interest was not the possibility for adventure he offered, but the sharp contrast in her mind between the romantic cliché of their situation and the certainty of the sordidness in the ending. It was a sort of epiphany for her, an awareness that she was no longer susceptible to the kind of dream that occupies girlish minds, that she now understood the deceptions of the sublime and how it erased its implications from consciousness. When she declined the officer's proposition and told him she was married, and was going back down to her husband, he accepted it politely, and they parted. But it was an experience vivid enough to shake her, to stick in her memory, as moments of heightened awareness in our lives are apt to do.

After she returned to the cabin and told me the story, it occurred to me to wonder whether it was not just the contrast between the ideal and the squalid that had come as a revelation to her, but the loss of freedom that her mature awareness inevitably entailed. I wondered if it slightly shocked, even pained, her that she suddenly felt closed, not to the particular proposition by that particular officer, but to the very idea of romance. She was no longer a girl, no longer single; she was a married woman and, however willingly and happily, had surrendered the freedom to be other. And that was perhaps another reason why it was memorable.

Standing at the port railing on a sunny morning, we suddenly saw a brilliant golden spit of land drift into view. Its sandy bank positively glowed, as if it had been lit from within.

'That,' said Jo, 'is Africa! The Golden Horn. Isn't it fabulous.'

There was indeed something special, something unlike any piece of land I'd seen before. You would never mistake it for Australia, or one of the tropical islands we'd been seeing every other day. Even in this small tip there was an unmistakeable majesty, and you felt like someone who'd been staring at a fingernail and only gradually realised that it was actually attached to the hand of Vladimir Ashkenazy.

Soon after this we berthed at the port of Aden, which was a well-known duty-free market town, built in the crater of an old volcano. Passengers eagerly scrambled onshore for some excitement, specifically the excitement of spending money and grabbing bargains. The narrow streets of the old market area were lined with motley shops and stalls selling clothing and knick-knacks, electrical goods, shoes, bags; there were food stalls and a hubbub of buyers, onlookers, noisy cryers. A man with stick legs deftly slipped though the throng with a massive pack on his back, a man with a donkey offered photo opportunities, a man played music on a lute-like instrument I'd never before seen, a man sitting on the ground was sharpening knives on an ancient stone grinder driven by a young boy energetically hand-powering the shuttle. Few women were in the streets. We pushed our way through crowds of Arabs wearing long robes and traditional headwear to bargain with the vendors for the cheapest prices. Jo and I became separated at one point when she went into a haberdashery stall and I wandered ahead, drawn by curiosity. When I went back to find her, she was fighting her way out of a crowded stall and visibly upset. 'I've just been really rudely felt up in there,' she said, 'it was horrible. I bought a sari, but I wish you hadn't left me. Let's get away from here.'

A man tried to sell me an impressive looking watch for two shillings, and as soon as I waved him away I regretted it; I'd lost the chance to say I'd once bought a genuine two-bob watch! I did get a Canon camera for less than half what it would have cost in Melbourne. We were approached by a huge smiling man dressed in a beige khameez, his skin the hue of matt ebony; he offered to drive us around in his taxi to see the sights, at a reasonable price, so together with John, we took him up and piled in. As he drove he told us he was from Somalia, where he had a family, and Aden was merely his workplace. He seemed more intelligent than a run of the mill driver, and totally trustworthy; I wish I could recall his name. We visited the Cisterns of Tawila, an ancient water-catchment of rock walls that tumbled down from a steep cliff top, with walkways that allowed a close examination of the cisterns. Then we motored around the bayside, where I took my first photographs with the new camera, a shot of local fishing boats, traditionally long-prowed and romantically Arabian, leaning over sadly stranded in the muddy shallows. This was on our way out to a desert oasis, where we strolled in the shade of date palms, and felt something of the lenitive effect that such places must have on desert travellers, anxious for relief from sun and hot winds. The treeless sands truly did stretch away to the inland horizon.

Afterwards we went to a local market place, not a tourist venue, and dawdled our way through canvas-covered stalls of produce—gleaming fish in boxes, live chickens hung up by the feet, hanging bunches of dark red dates, tables bearing small mountains also of dates, bags of unfamiliar cereals, bowls of bright spices, bunches of herbs, multi-coloured peppers. What we didn't notice as we pressed through the crowded walkways was that we were slowly being closed upon by a group behind us. Stopping to look at something, I turned to see that we were hemmed in by a group of decidedly surly looking Arab men. It occurred to us that we were probably being taken for British, and that we were, for that reason, courting a degree of danger. Yemen was still under British colonial rule at that time, and there were political forces gathering in different parts of the country pushing for independence. It was understandable that there was resentment among the local people towards anyone British, or seeming to be, and I was frankly scared as they began pushing up closer behind us. Suddenly our driver said, 'Come on, let's go,' and physically shepherded us away from the crowd and out beyond the stalls towards the street and his taxi. We sighed with relief in the car, and though the driver didn't want to talk about it other than to indicate that they were 'not good men', we realised he had gotten us out of a potentially disastrous situation quickly and neatly, before anything could actually happen. A memorable man, in more ways than one. And a memorable day, in more ways than one.

A couple of days later we reached the port of Suez, where the *Ellinis* would start to make her way through the Canal. Suez was not a large town, and we spent the evening exploring its quiet, well-lit streets and shops. A man with a horse and cart offered to drive us about, and we were just about to get underway when John said,

'Oh no, look at the poor horse.' A small, skinny, undernourished animal, it looked like it would struggle to haul the five of us plus the driver for any length of time, so we changed our minds and got back out of the cart. The man was furious. He pleaded that the horse was fine, was strong and healthy, could pull many times the weight of us. We refused to get back in, and he went off in disgust. We just hoped he didn't take his anger out on the poor horse.

In the morning passengers were permitted to disembark and take an excursion bus to Cairo, which then would take us north to Ismailia, ending up at the exit of the Canal at Port Said, where we would rejoin the ship. From the bus we had our first experience of the intimidating, impenetrable havoc of the city of Cairo. All we could grasp was that there were many poor and many rich, much ugliness and much beauty, a good deal that was shamelessly open to the gaze—sewers, the polluted Nile, beggars in the streets, hideous apartment blocks—and much that was majestic, historical and beautiful, with an occasional hint of opulence secreted behind high walls protecting huge mansions in manicured palm-treed grounds. This city, we could tell, would take a lifetime to know. We were taken on standard tourist visits to the pyramids, the great sphinx, suffered an uncomfortable ride on a camel, and afterwards were dropped at the Cairo Museum, where I tried in vain to take in the significance of ancient artefacts and culture, and where Jo and Ruth Morgan were pursued into the women's toilet by an attendant who insisted they accept from him their free single sheet of toilet paper.

Our bus was to pick us up at the international hotel mid-afternoon, but an hour after schedule it still hadn't arrived. The burning heat outside kept us inside in the air-conditioned lobby, where we sat sipping cool drinks in plush armchairs, bored and, in my case, a little anxious. I expected us any minute to be thrown out as cheapskates. I hadn't quite learned yet that this kind of space is regarded as a natural entitlement for westerners, whether paying guests or not. Luxury was our birthright, unavailable to Egyptians out in the streets. But I was keen to get out of there, wondering what the hell had happened to our bus, and hoping it didn't mean missing the ship at Port Said.

Around six o'clock it finally arrived, almost full with other passengers from the ship, and we were three hours behind schedule. Nevertheless, we kept to our itinerary, speeding through the twilight to Ismailia, though when we arrived it was too dark to see much of the town. We were whisked to a late dinner at a restaurant that seemed to be a favourite haunt of the local heavyweights, and we were served an unappetising-looking dried fish that we had seen hanging up in the markets. Ruth wouldn't touch it, nor would John I recall, but Jo and I were famished and got stuck in. It turned out to be delicious, amongst the best poached fish I've ever eaten. Then a small band in the far corner struck up with Arabic music, and a belly dancer came on. My first thought, being as interested in beautiful female bodies as any young man, was eager anticipation of a sexy, suggestive performance. And she certainly did that, and gave every impression of enjoying being the centre of attention. She made those fetching hip movements to the rhythms of the music, rolled her belly, snaked her shapely arms and spiked fingers sensuously, smiling demurely all the while. Yet after a while I began to feel uncomfortable. I looked around at the fat men dressed in *galabeyas* and business suits, fondling and clicking their *misbahas*, and dreamily leering at the girl, suddenly feeling that the whole situation was more than a touch squalid. And I was discomfited by the realisation that I was doing exactly the same thing. It wasn't the dancing as such that I disliked. Nor was it the ogling, or not just that. It was that the girl seemed so alone and vulnerable, just her and this roomful of mostly men, that there was an imbalance here. No other girl with her. This doesn't happen, I thought, in the old vaudeville chorus line, where you feel the girls to be having a good time as a troupe, which somehow gives the leg show a little edge of send-up. But here, in this night-club atmosphere, dominated by men with money and power, one lovely girl being ogled felt to me pervy, whereas twenty would have made it a joke. Safety in numbers.

The last days of the journey couldn't go fast enough for us. As we steamed north across the Mediterranean people began to organise themselves for the next phase of their travels, friendships began to dissipate, conversations to turn towards practical plans. Only now did we realize that Athens, which we were supposed to head for by our own transport, was some distance by bus from the port of Piraeus, where the ship was to dock. At least we had very little luggage—one small suitcase each, and my guitar in its case. There was one last, and best, captain's cocktail party, and the chefs made a special effort over the final night's dinner, though it proved to be still turkey, and still tasteless. Each table had been provided with a bottle of champagne, and we sipped and chummily toasted each others' fortunes.

When the *Ellinis* finally made its way into the spectacular, busy Piraeus harbour, past the dense jam of berthed ships, it suddenly dawned on us as we gazed from the upper deck that we were, finally, in Europe—crowded, civilised, industrialised, smoky, fascinating Europe. The impression was immediately qualified when we looked beyond the scattering of buildings and houses to the bare hills behind, but this only made it more intriguing, made us more eager to explore the place. No doubt we were quite scared of what might confront us when we disembarked, and how we would cope. We had no idea where we would go or what we were about to do. But wherever and whatever, we knew now that we were *there*, and that this was where the next and most important part of our adventure would begin.

People sought friends to hang onto and be with in the dispersal process, and we ended up travelling to Athens in a bus with John, Bill and Ruth, and Trevor and Cheryl. But there was also a phalanx of the rowdier drinking youths, singing their interminable 'chug-a-lug' song, and cheering idiotically at every female they saw through the window along the way to the city. When we alighted it was again a story of what to do next; a spruiker was handing out details of a hotel near the Acropolis, which a number of us took note of. Someone pointed us in the right direction, and the whole busload, including our rowdy fellow travellers, took off like sheep. With the 'chug-a-lug' song ringing through the cobbled streets, and watched from the windows and doorways of crumbling stone houses by wary women in black, we were like an invading horde out to appropriate anything we chose, violate anyone we fancied. We 'sensitive' folk, that is the seven of us, were embarrassed for, and by, the loutish behaviour of our compatriots, and we broke away from them to find the hotel on the card. When we did, it seemed clean and reasonably priced, so we booked in.

We then spent the afternoon exploring the area nearby. Our first call was, of course, the Acropolis, which was then completely open to unsupervised public access, and we posed for photographs next to the Parthenon columns, and surveyed the awesome beauty of the city in its setting. There is little to say about the Parthenon that has not already been said, except to register that its splendour had a powerful effect on me. We wandered the streets under the high south-eastern wall, which we discovered was called Plaka. This in 1965 was a ramshackle old area, full of run-down shops in narrow streets and walkways, with the occasional cheap-looking *kafeneon* or *taverna*, not especially crowded, the air pungent with smoke from the little braziers warming people as they sat on the steps of buildings, and the delicious aroma from the little cookers of the souvlaki-sellers in the streets. We couldn't resist a mini souvlaki, our very first, made in front of us from goat's meat and salad wrapped in a fresh, soft pitta, and garnished with locally made yoghourt. I've never had a better one since. We ambled into Syntagma Square, where in front of the American Express buildings backpackers and expatriates, spruikers for travel agencies, beggars, hippies and local office workers all gathered to pass the time or find a way through on their way to somewhere else. The pulse and meeting-point of the city.

By late in the evening we were ready to find somewhere to eat, and found a *taverna* off a square called Vironas, named in honour of Lord Byron. Inside was a bainmarie holding several dishes of lukewarm meat and vegetables floating in a pool of oil. The thought of eating it was almost too much for us, especially Bill and Ruth. But since there seemed nothing else available, and the owner was demanding that we sit down while he attended us, we gave in and agreed to try it. At face value, the owner was being nothing less than a bully, firmly signalling with his hands that we must sit, we must order, we must eat, and whatever objection we raised he would wave away as one he had an answer for.

'It's too cool, we like our food hot,' we complained.

'*Endaxi, endaxi,*' he replied, '*si kala*. Hot, hot okay.'

And we waited while he heated the food, and brought it to us in bowls with some dry brown bread. It was still not hot, despite his claims. What we hardly realised was that his bullying was basically a Greek's way of being hospitable, that his tradition required him to be insistent, not to take no for an answer, or he would appear to be uncaring. It was also, of course, good for business. Grudgingly, we struggled through the food, eating the meat and potatoes, nibbling at the bread, and leaving the golden pond of oil barely disturbed. Were I to admit it, it was more enjoyable the more I ate. It was the thought that was the obstacle; I was to learn later that Greeks rarely ate butter, and that the olive oil was not only better for you, it was in fact delicious with the absorbed flavours of the meat and vegetables it was baked in, soaked up with fresh brown bread. When in Greece, best to eat like Greeks, but at that stage we were still timidly clinging on to our fading Aussie identities.

Back at the hotel we were ready for a good sleep, and maybe even a cuddle-up (we were still in our twenties, I might remind you); was it a double bed for the first time in a month? At least it wasn't rolling about all night, as on the ship. But we were no sooner in our room than we heard yelling and loud screams of laughter, followed by heavy feet running down the passageways, and then the old familiar strains of the 'chug-a-lug' song coming from rooms nearby, and we knew we were back in the company of our Aussie shipmates, even drunker than usual by the sound of them. They'd found the place as well. The manager was either absent or indifferent to their racket, and we weren't able to get to sleep until well after midnight. To make matters worse, the bed turned out to be uncomfortable, and the room cold. Tomorrow we would look for another place.

We found the Hotel Phaedra, just off Adrianou, in the Plaka area. Their rates turned out to be more affordable if we were prepared to share rooms. Trevor and Cheryl were not, but when the manager offered us a decent sized room to share with Bill, Ruth and John, we took it. Three single beds, with little room left to move around in, so although sharing with two newlywed couples would place John like a bishop in a whorehouse, at least he would have the comfort of a bed to himself. The room would be even cheaper, the manager told us, if we were prepared to vacate it every morning by ten o'clock and not return until after five, so that the room could be used during the daytime. A little slowly, we grasped what 'used' meant in practice: commerce of the flesh. We didn't fancy that, so we paid the standard rate. Next morning we, along with Bill, Ruth and John, looked for a place to eat breakfast, and found a little café in Vironas. It was painted green and gave no sign on its shuttered front window that it sold anything at all, but Bill could see through the wire door little tables and chairs within. The place looked deserted as we pressed in and stood in front of a glass case containing tubs of yoghourt, but then a stout man with a heavy moustache appeared, and what followed was one of those conversations, very easy to have in Greece, where neither speaks the other's language, but somehow, through groping for words and trial and error in French, English, Greek, and the inevitable body language, both sides end up successfully conveying what they want. The man agreed to do yoghourt with honey, fried or boiled eggs or an omelette, toast and Greek coffee. Every morning that week the five of us turned up religiously to the green shop for our unmissable Greek breakfast. The yoghourt was sensational.

Trevor had a contact name and address, a young woman from the Melbourne Push who had been living in Athens for some time. The address turned out to be in the Plaka area, and when we found her she was keen to show us around, very much in the spirit of 'I'll show you how much I've become a virtual native here'. She took us to the fashionably outré flat of an Englishman, an artist of some kind, who was also part of the expatriate community, and who told us about a market nearby and how cheap it was to buy food and clothing. In its way this was the familiar Push culture all over again, and I was determined to avoid becoming part of it. Trevor and Cheryl, on the other hand, always impressed by arty types and anyone vaguely 'alternative', hung about with these expats for the next few days, until Trevor realised that their main disposition was torpor, and he made plans to move on to England as soon as possible.

Next day Jo and I wandered along to the far end of the Plaka area, found the market we'd been told about, and since it was January and much colder than I'd expected, I bought a warm Greek sailor's navy jacket and peaked cap, and a soft denim shirt, all for very little money. The cheapness of living in Greece came as a revelation, and we began to think about staying there for a time, if we could find somewhere we liked. But it wouldn't be Athens, on that Jo and I were agreed. Cities are not the place, we figured, to learn about how Greeks lived and their culture worked. Someone mentioned Hydra, where the Australian writers George Johnston and Charmian Clift had been living for a number of years. Again, I wasn't keen to join any established expatriate scene, and we dismissed that idea. Let's look for somewhere less known about, we thought. By the end of that week we had found a possibility. Vassilios, a Greek friend from the ship, dropped in on us a couple of times at the Phaedra. He had heard, he told us, of a lone Australian woman living in the town of Chania, on Crete. Apart from her, said Vassilios, he did not think there was an expat community there, at the quiet, non-tourist west end of the island. It sounded interesting to Jo and me, and to John, though he had already hatched plans to go to the small island of Kythera on his own. John had experienced a frustrating day down at Piraeus. He had arranged for a large trunk of his books to be sent separately on the *Ellinis,* but could not pick them up until all such luggage had been passed by customs. When he came back from Piraeus he told us a story: the customs officer had asked him what was in the trunk.

'Books,' said John.

The officer looked sceptical. 'Only books?' he asked. 'Everything in here, all books, nothin' else?'

'Nothing else,' said John, 'only books.'

The man shook his head in disbelief. 'Up,' he said, signalling for the lid to be opened. But John had not brought the key to the heavy padlock with him, thinking there would be no cause for it to be inspected, since Greece was completely free of book censorship—we had even seen Henry Miller's *Tropic of Cancer* on sale in an Athens book shop, though it was banned in England, America and Australia. The officer went and found a hammer and chisel, and took some time to forcibly break the padlock. He lifted the lid, shuffled around briefly in the contents, and ordered John to take everything out. After half an hour of unloading the books the trunk was emptied, and John was surrounded by many piles of his precious books, carefully packed back in Sydney to ensure they arrived undamaged. John exchanged looks with the officer.

'Hmm. *Biblio!*' the man uttered with disgust, and unceremoniously walked away, leaving John to repack a now unsecured trunk. 'Bloody Greeks,' he muttered as he finished the story. What he should have said, I learned many years later after some unhappy experiences, was 'Bloody customs officials.'

A few days later we were in Piraeus boarding the morning ferry for Crete. That was in itself an education into Greek habits. We had not realised that there were only a handful of bunks available for those wanting to snooze through the crossing, and those in the know were quick to grab them as soon as they arrived. The rest of us, including elderly women, had to find a seat and manage as best we could. Jo and I ended up cuddled together on an outside seat for the day. It was cold, but at least it was better than the public 'lounge', which was a windowless inside room that stank of stale cigarettes, vomit and shit, offering battered uncushioned seats. The smell of vomit and shit emanated from the nearby toilets, which had to be seen to be believed. There was vomit on the floor in several places, including the cubicles, and faeces all over the seats, on the floor, and in several places high on the walls. The imagination baulked at how it got there. Jo reported that though the ladies' lavatory was marginally cleaner, the women had to put up with men constantly coming in to use it in preference to their own. We were to learn that many Greeks, especially older villagers, begin vomiting the moment the engines start up, and they continue on until the journey is over, having somehow convinced themselves that this was the unavoidable price of travel. Only recently I saw a Greek woman do precisely this on a flight from Athens to Abu Dhabi, holding the sick bag to her face the whole way. But what possesses them to fling their ordure in every direction on a boat trip is beyond understanding.

It was evening when we arrived at the port of Heraklion, and walked along the 16th century Venetian wall to the town. As it grew dark we looked for a place to stay. It was a Sunday and there were few people about, and not much on offer as we traipsed around hoping to see a hotel. If this was the main tourist haunt of the city, we figured the rest of the island must have been like the far side of the moon. But in 1965 there was no tourist industry to speak of in Greece; it was still trying to get back on its feet after the War, and the people of Crete in particular were suffering from poverty and stress, getting through their days in a state of stunned preoccupation with the precious essentials of keeping warm, garnering food, and still trying to live with the loss of friends and family. Eventually we found a room in a side street not far from the harbour, in a house with 'pensione' on the wall, and a small group of people sitting on the landing at the top of the stairs inside huddled around a little glowing brazier. I can't recall whether we ate; maybe they fed us something, but for part of the evening we felt we should be sociable, so we joined the party around the brazier, smiling and nodding 'krio' at each other, and rubbing our hands to make the point; we were finding sign language increasingly essential in our common inability to cross the verbal divide.

In bed we told ourselves we were now on our own at last, and in Greece, where maybe our married life would properly begin. Not sharing, not in separate beds, not travelling, able at last to unpack our meagre belongings, and settle. And I might even get a chance to play some guitar again, who knows? Tomorrow we would catch the bus for Chania, full of expectation, and totally ignorant of what we would find. Again, this was the way we liked it: free to explore, prepared to make something good out of any situation life threw at us, and to do it together, loyal, loving, fixed only in our commitment to each other, but otherwise open to whatever change came our way.

In the morning, we took a walk about the old harbour, and visited the local museum, where we learned the extraordinary story of Knossos and the Minoan civilisation, remnants of which had been reconstructed on the outskirts of the city. We would learn more about the Minoans and their rituals over the coming months. In the museum shop we bought a little bronze replica of the Minoan snake goddess, which has lived with us ever since. She is always a delight to look at, with her Dolly Parton boobs and cat perched on her head, waving a snake in each hand as a symbol of her potency. Somehow she was to become a fitting companion to our time on Crete, and always has the capacity to trigger memories of our time there.

We caught the bus at 1 pm from the station in the centre of town. The journey was to take four hours. It was one we wouldn't forget.

2

THE ROAD FROM HERAKLEION TO CHANIA winds along the northern coast, dipping and climbing, sharply turning, through rocky plains, dropping into steep gorges, unstable-looking cliffs towering on one side, the blue sea over the edge on the other. We were seated in the very front of the bus, just behind the driver, so we had a stomach-churning view of every tilt and drop, every prospect ahead where the road disappeared into the vacant sky. The driver's approach to the narrow, gravel-edged sections of the route was to get through them as quickly as possible. Horn blaring, he recklessly threw the rattling old 1950s *Reo* around bends a mere couple of feet from the cliff edge, and if he was applying the brakes from time to time, they seemed to have no noticeable effect on our speed. Nor did we take any comfort from the prominent display of religious knick-knacks plastered all over the dashboard, or the Saint Christopher medal, patron saint of travellers, swinging crazily from its string attached to the rear vision mirror, or the outburst of song that the driver was occasionally given to; his driving technique relied on faith, faith that there was no-one coming round that blind corner, faith that the brakes wouldn't be needed, faith that a tyre would not blow, faith that the horn would deal with any obstruction that might lie in wait round the next bend. Despite all this, I was never seriously scared; there was something hilarious about it all, something abandoned and gay in this noisy, jumpy, crashing bus rampage, some sort of joy that the driver was experiencing that was infecting me, Jo perhaps less so. A quick look around at the concerned faces of the Greek men and women behind told us that no-one else shared my enjoyment, and I suppose that might have taken any smugness out of my humour. Nevertheless, the exhilaration of it all mattered more, and holding hands we went along for the ride like a couple of first-daters on the Big Dipper at Luna Park. After two hours of this, when the bus coasted into Rethymnon half way to our destination, I felt a tinge of regret as much as relief that it was all over. Chances were we'd never do it again.

Rethymnon is a town open to the sea, with long beaches stretching away on both east and west sides, and a little Venetian port, essentially for small craft, adjacent to the town proper. The people here had experienced a rough time during the war, were overrun with Nazi paratroopers in 1941, and, we were to discover to our advantage, had been bravely defended by Australian troops fighting beside the

Greek army and the local resistance until lack of equipment had forced a surrender. When they eyed you suspiciously and asked aggressively if you were 'Deutsch?' it was wonderful to see the smiles break out if you could reply 'Oxi, oxi: Australia'; the locals still thought of every Australian who came there as a hero, even mild mannered pacifists like us. They would have done anything for us then.

We got to Chania by early evening, and the bus dropped us on the fringe of the town, amongst modern, disappointingly dull bungalows, one of which turned out to be our *pensione*; we regretted accepting the recommendation of the tourist office in Herakleion, because we were sure we'd have found something better if we'd looked for ourselves. After dropping our stuff in the bedroom we headed off for the town centre with two aims in mind—to get some dinner, and ask about the Australian woman reported to be living somewhere in the town. The *pensione* landlady suggested we ask at a restaurant called the *Kavouri* on the old harbour front. That, she said, was where the resident foreigners usually ate. It was dark as we hiked along the road into town, with few streetlights to give any clear idea of what the place looked like. And even as the buildings grew older and taller, and narrow streets and alleyways came into view, there were few people about. It was winter, after all, and early evening, when only a few Cretans were just beginning to think about going out to socialise later in the evening.

A boy insisted on taking us personally to the *Kavouri* after we enquired of him in the street, and we had immediate success: the proprietor took us to a round table where a middle-aged, balding man in a grey tweed jacket was dining alone. We introduced ourselves, he got up, patting his mouth with his napkin and smiling warmly, and responded with almost elaborate politeness in an educated American accent and a sweeping arm gesture for us to join him. His name was Alan Bole, he was from New England, and he was a long-term resident of Chania. Yes, he knew the Australian woman very well, her name was Joan Healy, and in the morning he would phone her and tell her of our interest in meeting her. As a start to our time in the town, it couldn't have been better. We had dinner together, an enjoyable talk about what we were all doing in Greece, learned he was a writer, though not yet published, and learned also that he was very fond of the local red wine, or *krassi*, as it was called. But he was helpful, spoke fluent Greek, and when we told him where we were staying he insisted on enquiring about somewhere better for us, wondering aloud whether someone called Takis might have something. It got late and the restaurant gradually emptied, and when the proprietor started bringing in the chairs from outside, we knew it was time to leave. It was only as we walked home through the cold night that I realised I'd had too much to drink, and I just made it to the bathroom in our *pensione* in time to heave everything I'd eaten and drunk through the evening into the basin. Dear me, I was sick, retching until the early hours and with a head that felt like it had been split with an axe.

'We'd better be careful of the local wine then,' Jo laughed, snuggling up to me in bed, like spoons in a drawer.

We have been here a week now, making a start on our new way of life. I am so glad we came to Crete. Chania is a beautiful, ancient town, quiet, utterly without a tourist industry, no television, its buildings weathered and scarred with age, its people reserved, eyeing strangers with suspicion until the moment they are offered a greeting, and then they will burst into delighted smiles and say 'Herete, herete, kali mera, kali mera', and treat you like royalty. Few foreigners have been seen here since the war, and on one occasion when we walked along a narrow street that had become our habitual route to the beach a young girl ran up pleading with us to come to her house for a moment. Her father was ill and bedridden, and therefore unable to see the new foreigners everyone was talking about; would we come in and let him see us? So we stood at the end of his bed exchanging nods and smiles while his wife brought chairs and a little something for us to eat. There was nothing we could say to each other, but he was pleased we were Australians, remembered our war heroism, and was happy he had been able to meet us and see for himself what all the fuss was about at last.

Our apartment is in the old part of town, on the first floor overlooking the exquisite Venetian harbour. The days are slow, quiet, our activities mostly basic—eating, sleeping, walking, making love (it is, after all, the honeymoon we never had), reading our few books. I am enthusiastically and totally uncritically reading JD Salinger, Lawrence Durrell and Henry Miller; Jo is reading the Mary Renault books about the Minoans. I am still toying with the idea of writing (or perhaps more serious about it than the word 'toying' suggests), so I try to read with an eye for technique, though I am too ignorant to know what questions I should be asking, or even what technique in fact is. I have started making notes and observations on a foolscap writing pad we bought in Athens, in the hope this might be a useful tactic.

Apart from the occasional motor—a truck, a moped, the soft chug of a fishing boat—the sounds from the harbour walk just below our window are the sounds that have been heard here for hundreds of years: the occasional clang of dropped metal, a brief exchange of low male voices, a seabird screech, the repeated slap of octopus beaten against the wharf edge; they do it to soften them up for the table. The noise woke me about ten minutes ago, so I checked my watch—6.35, went for a pee, came back, scratched and yawned, and now I go to the window, open one of the shutters and gaze out upon a scene of dull grey light; the sun has not yet risen above the town buildings to our right, where the alleyways and shops lie still asleep in deep shadow. Jo slumbers on, hunched into the blankets and turned to the wall. Beneath our window fishermen are spreading their nets on the promenade to dry and repair after the night's catch. There is still plenty of passage through because the promenade is broad here, narrows in other places as it circles round two thirds of the little harbour, overlooked by modest double and triple-storied buildings, ancient stone faded and mottled by time; so like a stage-set, and you could walk all the way round in less than ten minutes. My gaze shifts out over the calm water to the harbour entrance, a narrow channel between the bluff of elevated land on the left and the elegant little Venetian light turret on the right, standing watch at the end of the long, low wall that leads back to the promenade. The wall was built as a breakwater in the 15th century by the Venetians during their occupation of the island. The beauty of this scene is scarcely believable. It is the first thing I want to see at the start of every day, puts us both in a happy mood. We are so lucky to be here, to feel this freedom.

We were lucky, too, to get this place, thanks to Alan Bole. The rent is, would you believe, five pounds—about ten dollars—a *month*; we calculate that the cost of everything here is cheap enough to enable us to live on our savings for six months or more. A consequence, unfortunately, of Greece's struggling post-war economy. Our landlord is a young man called Takis, whom Alan has known for some time. Takis and his widowed mother run a not very successful *kafeneon* downstairs, and live in the rooms upstairs, one of which they let to us, along with a sizeable adjoining lobby containing a makeshift corner kitchen—basically a two-burner *Portagas*—and a Turkish toilet leading off. The bedroom, with a double bed and a small table, is a decent size. Occasionally we see Takis or his mother, a small, attractive, grey-haired woman always in black, emerging from their quarters and passing through the lobby to go downstairs, and they will nod their respects; they are unusually formal and asocial, protective of their privacy. You feel if they didn't need the money, they would prefer not to let the room, and not have strangers living so close.

The toilet is taking some time to get used to. Basically it is a hole in the stone floor of a cubicle, with handles on the wall to hang onto and a bucket for depositing dirty wipes. Flushing is by water slopped from a nearby container. It is, we've been told, not only more hygienic than the modern seat toilet, but once you get used to it, a better way to clear the bowels. I'm not sure that the hygiene extends to the sewage system, however, since it seems to run a complicated course through ancient uncovered stone channels in the building down underground and probably out into the sea somewhere. I hope not the harbour.

There is a shower, but the water is cold only. We've bought a tin bath, which we fill with water heated on the stove, and take turns soaping up and rinsing each other off in the middle of the bedroom floor. Maybe when the weather warms up we will tackle the shower.

Takis speaks stilted, formal English, learned entirely from books. He sits for long hours either inside or out in front of his *kafeneon*, sleepily watching the world pass by, occasionally talking with a neighbour, though the conversation seems rarely to be an extended one or of much importance. It is strange that he is not married. He is passably good-looking, dresses well, is intelligent. His mother, you feel, takes priority in most things—his feelings, his finances, his range of interests. There is, however, one exception to this, and that is his occasional visits to the local bordellos. He told me, quite frankly one day when I was sitting at a table with him enjoying an ouzo, that there are three grades of bordello girl available—beautiful, medium and ugly.

'And which one do you take?' I of course asked him.

'I always have the medium,' he answered, with a self-satisfied smile.

This is typical of Takis' outlook on life; he would always take the medium. No sense wasting money on flights of passion, but on the other hand there are limits, and anyway someone of his standing—a property-owner—deserves something better than the worst. But he is gentle and friendly, and shyness I think is the main reason for his solitariness.

We have, of course, already met our Australian compatriot, Joan. She is also one of life's solitaries, but in a different way from Takis. She was a journalist in London after arriving from Melbourne in the late 1950s, but she has abandoned that and, like many of our generation, is looking for a more authentic—yes it was the cliché of the 60s but it was also the driving force of a robust and distinctive set of beliefs—a more authentic way of living. She rents a small, whitewashed stone cottage a mile or so west along the beach, away from the old part of town. Her life is dominated by her involvement with local Greeks, for whom she has become friend, marital advisor, child-minder, confidante and fight referee in the several years she has lived here. Small and feisty, dark hair a little ragged, Irish looks with freckles indistinct against her sun-browned skin, her whole presence is of ebullient, pocket-sized energy. There is one particular family she is engrossed in, the owners of a *taverna* on the beach just across the road from her house: Stelios and Marika Stavriolakis and their three children, Nikos, Elefthery and Anastasia. This family has been a gift to Joan, her source of endless stories, the personification of the very Greek spiritedness she came here to find. She is trying to work on a novel, though Stelios and his family are constant distractions, distractions one might suppose that claim her time and interest more than her writing does. Yet they are more trouble than she bargained for.

She is generous enough to drag herself away and help us with settling-in matters from time to time. Her Greek is fluent, her heart willing, and she has good contacts throughout the town. But she does not spend much time with the little expatriate group, who can be found most nights at the *Kavouri*. She has her own friends among the Greeks, and will only occasionally eat out; she lives on the very meagre earnings she scratches together giving English lessons to local children.

When Jo wakes we will go down to the shops and buy food for breakfast—a couple of small tubs of yoghourt, bread fresh from the baker's oven. Every little area of the town has its own bakery, where later in the day the women collect in groups gossiping or listening to the radio serial the baker has on, waiting for the bread to be ready or for their pans of roast meat and vegetables to be cooked; this is part of the community service provided by the bakery. We will eventually return to our apartment clutching our warm loaf, eat our yoghourt with honey, maybe make an omelette to share and a pot of coffee. I would go down now on my own to buy the yoghourt from the grocer just a dozen or so yards along the promenade from Takis' entrance, but I don't want to face him this early. He stands in front of his shop—an old boatshed opening onto the promenade, in which he stores a few boxes of vegetables, grains, olives, cold drinks in his fridge—looking proud and businesslike in his dark grey suit with dark shirt tieless but buttoned to the top, fondling his heavy black Cretan moustache. He is a kindly man, but this is precisely the point: whenever I go there he insists on my taking schnapps with him, and not just one. I'm lucky if I can get away from him after two. The first time was about 8.30 in the morning, and as I paid him for the yoghourt he took a bottle and two glass tumblers from a cupboard and had poured the schnapps and handed it to me before I had a chance to say no. 'Si ighia,' he prompted, and threw it down in one. I of course had to follow suit. The effect was of a fire running into my chest, and it certainly demolished the last vestiges of sleep. The second one hit just as hard; strangely it had no flavour, just shock to the system. But at—what is it, 6.45?—it would be too much, so I'll keep clear of him this morning, and when

Jo gets up we'll go to the little shop next to the baker, about five minutes walk away. Then we'll come back and eat, and plan something for the day.

Joan tells a story: Stelios Stavriolakis had been off work now for several months, and this made him very happy. It was true that his short, strong frame was growing portly, his black stubble beginning to blend grubbily in to his heavy moustache, but he didn't care. So what is a bit of fat, a degree of breathlessness? He could still please himself. For Stelios was a man of Zorba's philosophy, of his love of life, and indeed did he not teach Anthony Quinn to dance last year when they were making the film here in Chania? They all said he was the real Zorba, the man the story was modelled on. Labouring on the Souda Bay wharf depressed him, produced a kind of latent panic that life was running away from him, that his best years were going to waste in pointless moving about of crates and boxes, lengths of timber and steel, or in finding ways to skive behind sheds having a smoke with a mate. This was no way for a man to spend his time and energy. A man needs excitement, needs constant involvement with the important things in life, which are sex and adventure, and freedom. Without these, we shrivel and die. So it was a fortunate day when he got involved in an incident that resulted in his being placed on medical benefits, and complete rest, for the foreseeable future. Naturally he would forego the boredom of a rest, but not having to work! Ah, that would be an opportunity to live again! Anyway, the incident happened like this.

Marika, his wife of fourteen years and mother to his three children, had lost her interest in sex. Of course this was partly a consequence of her husband's philandering habits, his laziness around the house and his incompetence in running their *taverna*. The *taverna*, situated beautifully on the beach front, had long been in Marika's family and came as her dowry; run properly over the summer months, it might have made them a handy extra income, with Marika doing the cooking and Stelios waiting on tables and drumming up trade. But Stelios had no business sense at all. He would invite his friends around and let them eat and drink freely, steadfastly refusing to take their money. He would spend so much time chatting to pretty female tourists that other customers would walk away in frustration at being ignored. He would disappear for hours, sometimes days, leaving Marika to do all the work and wondering where he was, though she could make a pretty good guess: some woman. And so Marika was in a state of constant anger with Stelios, and relations between them had sunk to near unrecoverable depths. Thus his interest in other women grew only more intense.

There was a particular widow in her early thirties he had been seeing for some months, whose neighbours had long given up expecting her to remain faithful to the memory of her dead husband, more or less accepting that she made ends meet by entertaining men. She was not a prostitute in the way that the bordello girls were, but tried to keep her home and two children clean and fed and attending school. The neighbours regarded her matter-of-factly, and were quite friendly with her, providing she stayed clear of their own husbands. One afternoon Stelios quietly absconded from work, as he was wont to do when the mood took him, and cheerfully made his way to his girlfriend's house, looking forward to an hour or so of pleasure. But as he approached the front door, the woman from the next house came running along the footpath whispering urgently to him 'Oxi, Oxi Stelios'. Fear in her eyes, she implored Stelios, 'Don't go in there. She has another man with her, and he will cause trouble.'

'Who is he?' Stelios demanded.

'I don't know, but he is a big man, a strong man, maybe from Sfakia, and he is younger than you,' she told him.

Stelios hesitated, his eyes narrowing with suppressed anger. He knew about these Sfakians, from up in the mountains; they wore boots and carried knives, could be very dangerous. Suddenly he broke away from the entrance and began to run down the street, watched helplessly by the confused neighbour. It so happened that a good friend of Stelios, a sailor called Yanni, lived in a house not one hundred metres away from where they were, and in moments Stelios had disappeared through the doorway and just as suddenly emerged carrying a single barrel shotgun in his hands. Muttering angrily to himself, he broke open the gun as he hurried back, inserting a red cartridge into the breech. Passing the stunned neighbour, he opened the front door and charged in.

For a moment he waited, listening, and heard the rustling of linen and muted voices from somewhere within. With an urgent sense now of the role the situation demanded of him, he performed a sequence of noisy *balestras*, skipping down the hallway like a fencer, and turned at the bedroom doorway, holding the gun at his hip; on the bed were large amorphous shapes and movements under a white sheet, but no faces; the culprits were covered like children playing hide-and-seek, but left obscenely uncovered were two large feet protruding from the sheet, confronting Stelios like strange animals, bare, and dirty pink, their fleshy ugliness an affront to his dignity. The feet deserved his contempt, so he pulled the trigger and shot at them. Most of the shot peppered the wall just above the incumbents' heads, blowing away a large shard of plaster, but some had struck their target. All hell, as they say, broke loose—the blast of the shot, the woman's screams, the man's bull-like bellowing, and his own angry yelling all blended into a cacophony that brought the rest of the neighbours running to the front entrance to see what it was all about.

But the action was not yet finished. The man of the feet sat up and revealed himself, followed by the terrified woman, exposing strong shoulders and the beautiful purple areolae of her breasts as she hoisted herself upright. In the heat of the moment the man forgot about his bloodied, shredded feet, dived out of bed and felt for his trousers on an adjacent chair. From somewhere in his trousers he pulled a switchblade, and turned back to confront Stelios. By this time the woman had gotten out of bed too, and snatching from a chair her black dress and underwear and rolling it into a single parti-coloured bundle, she carried it around to the other side of the bed where her lover was standing in a pool of bright red, now enameling the stone floor. Stark naked on her knees she began trying to mop up the blood, her broad, bare backside moving rhythmically between the two men. For a long, covetous moment both lovers watched the action of that creamy curvature, and thought to stroke it. But the Sfakian, his efforts a hybrid of comic hop and tragic limp, was advancing on Stelios, knife in hand. Not having another cartridge, Stelios suddenly threw the gun at the man's head so violently he overbalanced and fell sideways against the corner of the bed. The gun missed its target, bouncing with a clatter against the wall, but Stelios had for a long moment become vulnerable as he tried to right himself. In that moment, the man saw an ample torso facing him, and with a wild thrust plunged the knife forward into the gut, making a ripping sound from his shirt as the flesh beneath received the blade.

At that point a fourth person entered the bedroom in the form of Yanni, who had tardily followed the gun-toting Stelios back to the house to see what would transpire, and, essentially to recover his shotgun, picked his way through the flailing bodies and bloody floor over to where his gun had fallen, and taking it up to examine it, he held it up to his shoulder and eyed the sights to see if they were damaged. All three—the widow, the man and Stelios—froze on the spot, instinctively assuming that anyone holding a weapon in that position was about to fire it at them. The woman sat back on her haunches, clutching the bloodied garments against her chest. The Sfakian, still holding the knife, actually put up his arms as if he were under sheriff's arrest in a Hollywood western. By this time Stelios was moaning pitifully and clutching his hands to his stomach. Suddenly realising the power he had unintentionally acquired, Yanni, who was by nature the mildest of men, barked at the tall man, 'Drop that knife!' (in Greek of course).

It clattered to the floor. No-one could think of what to do next. They stayed, the four of them, fixed to their positions, although Stelios continued to emit little groans, gingerly lifting his shirt to examine the damage. Yanni looked around in search of an idea, and was confronted by an astonished crowd of neighbours jammed into the doorway of the room, all waiting breathless to see what would happen. Someone said they should call the police. No, said someone else, they should call an ambulance. No, said a third, they should find someone with a vehicle to take both men to the hospital. Meanwhile, a woman charged forward and threw a towel around the widow's nakedness, and embracing her, ushered her sobbing pathetically from the room.

When the dust settled, the Sfakian turned out to be the widow's brother-in-law, a self-employed electrician who lived on the other side of town. He had never even been to Sfakia, and it was the first time he had been intimate with the woman, or so she claimed. Yanni was visited by the police, who confiscated his shotgun for evidence. Stelios was charged with causing an affray, and, when Marika found out about his activities, was thrown out of the house followed by his clothes—he had to sleep across the road at Joan's for the next few nights, until Marika realised that this was possibly going from frying pan to fire, and let him back in.

Joan related all this with great relish on the occasion of a recent visit to our flat. It was of course an embellished version of what was told to her by Stelios himself. How much truth was in it is anybody's guess, but some idea of its veracity may be gauged by Stelios' claims of the medical consequences of his stabbing: he'd had to have his liver removed, he said. And that was why he could never do labouring work again, and why he would have to subsist on medical benefits for the rest of his life. Whether the department of social services would see it that way would be a matter for the future, but for the time being he was enjoying the unemployment benefits. Needless to say, by the time Joan had finished the story we could hardly wait to meet this improbable individual, whose image in my head had already reached the proportions of a colossus.

Every foreigner here seems to be a writer. Charles Haldeman, an American friend of Alan Bole's, has just returned to Chania from a trip. He has two recently published novels, and is friendly, clever, boyishly good-looking in his mid-thirties, likes to socialise at the *Kavouri* a few nights a week. Then there is Fred, a small, gnomic figure in his late sixties who strolls about Chania behind his formidable Scottish wife Ann, like the couple in *Monsieur Hulot's Holiday*. Fred is Fred Perles, whose fame rests on his friendship with Henry Miller back in 1930s Paris, portrayed as 'Carl' in *Tropic of Cancer*. It is hard to reconcile this timid, henpecked husband with the sexual buccaneer of the novel, though you get the feeling that everything about him is role-play, even the pathetic husband. Eating together in the *Kavouri* one night there is a momentary glimpse of the old *roué* when he leans across to Jo sitting beside him and inserts his tongue in her ear, which prompts a loud giggle from her. Ann looks decidedly unamused, and within a short time slaps her hand on the table and in her broad brogue says, 'Well, c'mon Fred. It's ten o'clock, bedtime for us,' and they unceremoniously take their leave. How sad he looks, being dragged away like this, like an unruly child. His anarchic past is dead, though memorialised in his mentor's novel. Henry Miller is a ghostly presence among us all, even Joan, who once met him at a party. Miller remains a mentor for those who are disaffected with modern social conformity, even though they all know his books are mostly fantasies containing much bullshit, albeit very entertaining bullshit.

An exception to this is Richard Finch, who has recently arrived with his family and their nanny, Mrs Weekes, on holiday from England, where he writes for television as 'Arden Winch'. He objects that 'he doesn't believe a word' that Miller writes. Somehow this misses the point, in that it assumes we must read the books as truthful autobiographies. This is too literal and unimaginative. Miller is a scourge of guilt, a writer who entertainingly asks us to refresh our distinctions about sex, health, success. It is his questions that are true, not his imputed answers. Finch is a dogged type, a class climber, scornful of ideals. When I tell him I've begun to write he asks to read some of it. It turns out to be a mistake. He obviously thinks it is rubbish. He advises me to go to England and live somewhere like Cambridge, where I might meet people with good minds, people who know something. It doesn't seem a bad idea, although I can see the danger in my being a kind of autodidactic hanger-on, having my already outsiderish personality worsened by such a role. I mention Charles Haldeman to Richard, who wants to meet him. I take him and Fiona to the *Kavouri*, where he adopts a fraternal, co-writerly tone with Charles, says, 'You wrote *The Snowman*? Good work.' I don't say so, but I know Richard has never read *The Snowman*, simply by his reaction when I first mentioned Charles, asking me what he'd written. He and Charles go hugger-mugger into a discussion of royalties, lousy editors, greedy booksellers and so forth, the talk of professional writers. It turns out Fiona is the daughter of a big London literary agent; handy for Richard. Fiona Finch. I wonder if she thought of keeping her own surname?

Bill and Ruth Morgan arrive from Athens with a group of recent Australian arrivals, partly to look us up and partly to do a quick tour of Crete. Their friend, George Tibbits, one of Bill's university lecturers, comes with them up to our room. They stay for a while, talking art and music, specifically Mozart, whom Tibbits raves on about. He casts a doubtful eye at my pages of scrawl on the table, says sardonically, 'Your *magnum opus* is it?' I shrink in shame. How ignorant I feel, foolish in thinking of myself as a writer. I should just shut up and get on with learning a thing or two.

That night we all go to the *Kavouri*, including some Australians who accompanied Bill and Ruth over on the ferry. Alan and Charles are there, and at one point Charles gets into an argument with a persistently aggressive teacher amongst them. Alan has quoted a phrase in Charles' novel *The Sun's Attendant*, 'world-to-come is now', to which the teacher takes exception. The more Charles tries to defend it, the more literal-minded the teacher becomes. It's a contradiction, he says, you can't say something is 'to come' if it is already here. When I read the novel recently I puzzled over it as well, but came to the conclusion it was a paradoxical assertion not unlike the Zen Buddhist maxims that my old friend Jimmy Meldrum used to produce at his Friday night *soirees* in Carlton, where I first met Jo. Later, I would come to know 'world-to-come' as a central idea in religious eschatology— Christian, Hebrew, Hindu—for the next life, and Charles' twist on it is simply a call to live for the present rather than the future, the kind of thing that Henry Miller pleads for all the time. But this Aussie teacher has an agenda, a desire for victory over Charles, who will only defend the phrase by repeating it rather than by trying to explain it. 'It is self-explanatory,' he insists. When the argument stalls, the teacher suddenly shifts his attack onto Americans, specifically their current behaviour in Vietnam, and their attitudes to other nations. They are bullies and cultural imperialists, he says, trampling over everyone's rights, occupying other countries to the detriment of local cultures. It could almost be a thinly veiled reference to Charles and Alan being here in Crete. They are in a difficult position; neither has unqualified love for their country, and they are in Greece precisely because they prefer it to America, but the teacher's aggression has pricked their patriotic impulses. Alan, who is quite drunk, is stirred by the accusations, and in his subdued, New England manner, relates an anecdote about his sister-in-law's parents, who migrated from Germany after the First World War.

'They were sick and, and … crushed … from years of poverty and war in Europe, and they arrived after their journey defeated and tired of life itself. *Life itself!*' Alan asserts, as if it is scarcely believable that people could be brought so low.

'They'd hardly a rag to their back. They were only in their forties. But you know, when their ship approached New York harbour, and they saw that arm holding its torch appear on the horizon, they wept for *joy*, and the whole ship cheered, because *they knew what it stood for*; they knew it meant they could live like decent human beings again.'

After he finishes, Alan stares down mournfully into his tumbler of *krassi*, and when he looks up and confronts the table with a bravely defiant jaw, his large, blue, protruding eyes are brimming wetly. Everyone else at the table has gone silent, retreating into their own thoughts. My sympathies are with Charles and Alan, but I am probably just reacting against Australian rudeness.

Looking back now, I ought to have agreed with that teacher. After all, had I not been spending the last couple of years singing protest songs at Traynor's folk club and elsewhere that took the same line? Was I not anti-American too? Yet here I was, making friends precisely with Americans, and finding myself liking them. I suppose I was going through the process of learning the difference between a nation and its policies on the one hand, and particular people on the other. And the difference between living by ideology or by experience. Or, to put it simply, taking people as they come.

On the sand in front of Stelios' *taverna*, a group of us sits in a circle in the sun, the first day it has been warm enough to swim since we arrived. The distinctive tinniness of bouzoukis and the slightly Arabic violins of Hadjidakis and Thoedorakis resound along the beach. I hadn't realised the significance of this music until Charles explains that it is a new craze, part of a new spirit of Greek pride. It has been used in films like *Never on a Sunday* and *Zorba the Greek*, and so is becoming fashionable all around the world.

I am practicing the Zen art of how to succeed without trying, throwing small stones or shells at arbitrary targets.

'What are you doing?' asks Joan.

'The idea is to throw spontaneously, without taking deliberate aim. Deliberation is an inhibition. Zen believes you always succeed best when you act without prior thought.'

I'd bought some books in Athens, including some on Buddhism. I'd also bought Kant's *Critique of Pure Reason*, which as a philosophical method could hardly be more different. I don't understand either of them very well.

'So does it work?' says Joan.

'Sometimes.'

'Like everything else,' says Charles.

Jo lies delectably prone on her towel in a pink and blue striped bikini, which she made herself. It required very little material.

Stelios ambles down the sand in his white shirt, navy trousers and black shoes to join us. His thick body and broad smile stand above us, proudly; he loves foreigners, they represent glamour, heightened possibilities. But there is not much custom in his *taverna* this time of year, and the neatly spaced tables under the pergola are all empty. Alan notes aloud that Stelios has recently had the thick concrete pillars painted, alternate pink and green. A friend did it for him on the cheap, Joan says.

Charles quips, 'That is the pinkest green and the greenest pink I've ever come across'. Stelios grins with increased pride at what he takes to be a compliment.

Last year this *taverna* rang loud with music and shouting from the film crew of *Zorba*. Michael Caccoyannis spoke Stelios' praises, especially for his dancing and the tips he gave to Anthony Quinn. So *kefi* did Stelios become that he not only shattered plates on the concrete floor, but he did his rarely performed trick of lifting a table with his teeth and dancing with it. The guests went wild with delight, and threw money, which Marika carefully collected from around his feet.

Now he gazes along the stretch of beach with dog-like concentration, and it soon becomes obvious what he is looking at: two girls in bikinis walking along the water's edge. He watches them in silence as they pass us, chatting to each other. His look of dark longing is fierce, as he mutters in barely audible English, 'You fucken bastards …' I doubt he even knows what it means.

Somebody has a camera and begins taking snapshots. Stelios wants to be photographed with Jo in her skimpy swimsuit. He insists, and they stand arm in arm in front of the *taverna*, his grin one of unqualified lust as he eyes the profile of her face, then her breasts, then her face again. Soon after we are joined by his friend Fotis, also in a white shirt and trousers; it is standard for Greek men to dress in a relaxed formality whatever the weather or situation, a suggestion of small-businessmen on their day off. Fotis has a good-humoured, mischievous air about him, and talks enthusiastically in Greek to Joan, who laughs in mock-surprise at something he says. Then she shakes her head, muttering 'Oxi, oxi.'

Stelios produces one of those male conspiratorial laughs, from the back of the throat.

Joan says to me, 'Fotis says he will give you 70,000 drachma for one night with Jo.'

Jo protests, 'Why does he get the money? I'd be the one earning it!'

We all laugh, but apparently Fotis is serious. He is a nice man, Joan tells us. He's only recently been let out of prison for killing someone, but he's a good man. Looking at his pleasant, smiling face and cool manner, I can believe both statements.

The water is cold as I calmly sink my shoulders into it and sit on the sandy bottom. Little waves chill my flesh as the level moves up and down my back. On the sand, the group of friends talks happily in the sun, the *taverna* with its pink and green columns rising behind them. Above that, in the far distance, are the snow-covered peaks of the *Lefka Ori*, or White Mountains. Because they are chalk, they are white whether covered with snow or not. But at this time it is snow. I have never before swum in the sea while looking at snow-capped peaks; it is a strange and gratifying sensation.

Stelios came around the other night and called out to me from beneath our window. He wanted me to bring my guitar and go with him to the bordellos. Jo laughed, 'Why don't you go?—it might be interesting.' I wasn't enthusiastic, especially about the idea of playing Bob Dylan to an audience of Greek whores who couldn't understand English. But I went along, much to Stelios' pride and joy; he has adopted me as 'his foreigner', a showpiece to impress his friends. Some of those friends spent a good part of their time hanging out at the bordellos, not necessarily as customers, more as part of the social life there.

The area the women worked was actually quite pleasant—narrow streets, but clean and close-quartered, with doors and windows open to all and sundry, giving it a friendly, communal atmosphere. We sat at a little table outside one house, right next to a low open window looking into a sitting room, and ordered some bottles of beer. At the table was Stelios' good friend, Yanni, the sailor. They clearly have spent many a time drinking and whoring together, and their favourite running joke is focussed on Yanni's narrow-eyed, sea-weathered face, in which he has a deeply cleft chin. Every so often Stelios would lean across and squeeze the chin so as to deepen the cleft into a passable semblance of a vagina, which produces lascivious laughter and some obscene suggestions in Greek from both men. They were like young boys, preoccupied entirely with the naughty pleasures of the body.

One of the girls leaned out of the window, overlooking our little table. She had dark long hair and a hooked nose, and was wearing only a skirt and bra, so her pendulous boobs brazenly hung over the window ledge. Her eyes on me, she joked with Stelios and Yanni; I guessed it was at my expense, to the effect that I didn't look like much of a stud. But Stelios got a serious expression on his face; it was all said in Greek so I wasn't certain, but he seemed to be defending me on the basis that I have a beautiful wife. In the eyes of Greek men, a man with an attractive wife who can keep her happy has nothing to prove sexually, although there may be a certain suspicion until they actually produce children. In any case, sex was not the reason he had brought me to the bordellos: he wanted to show me off.

'Guitarra,' he said, pointing at my carry-case; I was to show them what an interesting and important friend he had. It was patently useless to protest that they wouldn't understand my songs, that they were in English and far removed from their own cultural interests. All they wanted was evidence that I could perform. So out came the Gibson, and I hooked up my harmonica, and played them a couple of American songs, complete with bluesy riffs, and they all laughed and applauded, and Stelios threw out his chest in pride and put a matey arm around my shoulders. It was all completely bizarre. No-one spoke English, so practically every word I sang or said was lost on them, and in any case irrelevant. I could have been spinning insults, calling their mothers every name under the sun, and they wouldn't have known or cared. I could only hope that Stelios and Yanni received the recognition they sought—possibly in free services from the girls—though there was no sign of that at the time. But we were in good spirits, the three of us, as they walked me home, and bid me a slightly drunken goodnight at the door to our building; there was no doubting, too, that my willingness to play along had allowed something to bond between me and Stelios, and that we would be good friends from that night on. He was a man's man, no doubt, and that unfortunately meant that, apart from wanting to impress them, he didn't have much respect for women. He would never have quite understood the need for any other attitude.

I try to see our life from Jo's point of view, imagine how she feels, about what we have done in coming on this adventure, about where we might be headed. Does she experience the same charges of the flesh as I do when we touch? What are the little irritants she has to endure? Is she afraid of the future, of where we might end up, or worse, of how painful the journey might turn out to be? But confidence is growing between us that any such matters can be spoken about, that we can declare our disappointments and annoyances without it threatening our happiness. We are still finding our way, still making little discoveries of our habits and manner of dealing with the unexpected, and so far we seem to be in accord. Yes, we have fights, misunderstandings mostly, little battles of the will, or disagreements about the meanings of things. I am still prickly on matters of knowledge, on those things that depend on a good education, and she picks me up on them, and won't usually suffer my foolishness. Yet she manages to extend to me understanding and unstinting love.

She likes her routines, has her favourite foods; salads, meat, fish, fruit, coffee. She isn't mad on tea, won't eat mushrooms, or even have them in the house. Doesn't take to beer, but she likes gin and tonic, and whiskey—I've known her put away a large tumblerfull. She won't wear jeans, prefers her handful of dresses, especially the pink one with the ruffled collar and sleeves, her long tight pants and roll-neck sweaters if it's cold. We had to get photographs taken to renew our visas. When they came back from the photographer we laughed over them, and still do, we look so young, so fresh-faced. She could indeed be sixteen, as the American serviceman said, and her dark hair, which she is, at my request, letting grow long, falls across her face, and her mouth is a little pouty with concentration, sultry and very kissable. Her eyes look straight out at the viewer, a clear, direct, open-souled gaze, utterly without guile, or defence, or apology: here I am. Me. Take it or leave it.

More often than not, the ideas for things we do together come from her— travel, shopping, a movie. I admire the way she thinks ahead. She won't say anything much for a while, won't give any indication of what is going on in her head until she is ready to present the whole plan, thought-through from start to finish. She will suddenly say, 'I've been thinking…', and what comes out will be a whole schedule of connected actions—a proposal to visit friends and thus get free accommodation (she loves economising), take in a place we've been interested in, buy something on the way we talked about months ago, and have it coincide with an event or local celebration that provides entertainment. Disorganised me, I just go by impulse depending on what I suddenly feel like doing, which as a consequence usually means I've just missed some significant event, have to pay to stay somewhere, and in any case choose a place that doesn't have anything we might be interested in buying. She constructs our lives so that we do things we get the most out of, and furthermore she does it without seeming pedantic or rigid.

I should remember that she is good at maths, geography, history, subjects that are fact-based, logical or require an understanding of sequence and order, and that she grasps the significance of this order—not just parrot understanding, but the meaning. That is my idea of a good mind, free from whim or romantic indulgence, capable of grasping ideas that are not necessarily personally affective. I can't do that at all; if I don't have some emotional investment in the subject, I don't learn it. So she complements my abilities, and without her I would never get to buses on time, never grasp the meaning of a historical building or region, never know where a country is in relation to another country without looking at a map. I would drift through life taking it as and when things eventuate, passively, not within my control, like a blind man with a stick.

And so we are learning to live together here, in this very basic, very uncomplicated way, largely detached from the Greek culture because it is not our own linguistically or by custom, and totally removed from our own culture, parents, social routines and friends. It is Us versus the World, though the World in this case is not an enemy, more a stranger who will befriend us if we want it to. There was something of the secret agent about the man, sitting in the shadow of the *kafeneon* verandah in sunglasses and stylish dark suit and tie, speaking excellent English in conspiratorial tones. And when he removed the sunglasses briefly to glance at the menu, the revelation of his half-closed, non-functional left eye only added to the image of mystery. But his manner was charming, well-educated, patrician; he had studied at Yale.

'You will find Mr Nikakis an agreeable enough man,' he was saying, 'a little dull unfortunately, but he runs the school efficiently, and will not interfere with the way you teach your classes.'

Soon after we had settled in, Jo had applied for and obtained a job teaching secondary school English classes at the Chania branch of the Brittanika Institute, a private school with its central office in Athens. This man, whose name I forget, was Director of Studies and had been visiting from Athens on the day she applied for the job, and might well have had the deciding hand in her appointment, as subsequent events suggested. After the interview, he took us both to a long lunch, where we addressed the problems of Greece, Australia, USA, the World. Charming as he was, there was something odd in his confidentiality, which was both intimate and formal at the same time. It was as if we were all old friends, but had never actually met before, a paradox that had the effect of turning us all into types rather than unique individuals. 'Oh yes, we are all of the same class of being,' it seemed to imply, 'we educated, politically savvy, worldly-wise people understand each other, just as we understand what goes on behind the scenes everywhere. We can dispense with mealy-mouthed niceties, we who grasp the *realpolitik*. Tiresias is our model and type, and we, like him, forgo sight in order to discern what is true.' His bung eye was half-closed, as if dropping to sleep with boredom, but the other eye was alert. He said surprising things, about political machinations in Athens, for instance.

'You must be careful, as foreigners you must be careful, if you are staying here for the next year or so. There are rumours.'

'What kind of rumours?' we asked.

'The Americans are worried about Mr Papandreou getting too close to the Russians.'

'We know nothing about Greek politics,' I said, and smiled, 'but we're aware of an American airforce base here in Chania.'

'A NATO arrangement,' he said, 'but not just that. Don't laugh. They talk with people, their chiefs talk with our military people. There is, I'm reliably informed, a secret dialogue going on at this very minute between the Americans and our generals. It is thought they are trying to push Mr Papandreou out. But we will see—the Americans cannot afford to be too blatant about it; any change will have to appear as though it came from within Greece itself. But in the meantime, there are many in the military who do not like much of what is happening in Greece at present, particularly the growing presence of the left, and of long-haired foreigners who take advantage of our poor economy, flout our morals.'

In two more years, 1967, his words proved prophetic, when the Colonels staged their infamous *coup*. We often wondered what happened to this man during those troubling times, and whether he even remained in Greece.

Jo discovered that the actual teaching was not easy. The students were undertaking the Cambridge Proficiency course for foreign language speakers, and local schools tended to teach it rigidly. The prescribed text was DH Lawrence's *Women in Love*, the language of which—mining terms for instance—they found difficult to follow. But she soldiered on, and not only was the money handy, but it opened up a couple of unexpected opportunities to get to know Crete a little better.

One such was an offer from Mr Nikakis to take Jo and me on a Sunday trip to Paleochora on the south coast, where student exams were to be held over the weekend. We sat in the back of a car driven by a young teacher from the school, Nikakis beside him, neither of whom said much the whole time, apart from pointing out little roadside shrines along the way, indicating places where Nazi troops had executed groups of men and boys in revenge for the activities of the local resistance movement. We arrived at Kandanos around 11 am, where the first exam was to take place. This town had to be completely rebuilt after the Nazis razed it in spiteful reprisal for its resistance, an atrocity committed well after Crete had formally surrendered in 1941. Receiving no explanation from Mr Nikakis as to how we were supposed to amuse ourselves, Jo and I hung about the village for some two hours, trying to stave off boredom by wandering among the little white painted stone houses and trying to imagine something of the lives that inhabited them. It was a scrubby region, with stony ground and stunted trees, and we were wondering what young people did in such a quiet, sleepy place, when a flimsy motorcycle bearing two laughing boys burst out of the silence with a deafening racket, and roared past us through the village. We stood and looked pop-eyed at each other.

Just as we were getting hungry and wondering where to buy something for lunch, Mr Nikakis summoned us to follow him. No explanation—we were simply to tag along and do as we were bid. Bewildered, we found ourselves among a group of local worthies ushered in to eat at the gracious home of the village doctor. This was held in a large cellar, with several women in black bringing in food from an adjoining kitchen. And what a feast it was! Dishes of baked goat's meat and okra, lamb and potatoes, a wonderful pork and rice cooked together, like a rich sloppy risotto, bowls of delicious savoury custard, all kept arriving and were passed around from guest to guest; we had been warned by Joan not to serve ourselves at such a feast, because the custom is that your companions heap piles of food onto your plate for you, and you would end up with more than you could eat. The repast was finished off with Greek coffee and fresh navel oranges the size of grapefruit, and sweet as ambrosia. When the Greeks put on a spread, there is no better food in the world.

Afterwards we drove on to Paleochora. This exquisite little village is positioned on a minute peninsula, with the sea close around eighty percent of it. Again Jo and I had to pass the time while Nikakis and his colleague administered the exam, but this time we enjoyed the services of one of the teachers, who was asked to show us the place. As she led us around, one sight stood out for us, another reminder of the grim events of the Nazi occupation: an execution wall, where local males were lined up and shot. The stone on one side of the building was pocked with hundreds of bullet marks, and was left unrepaired by the locals as a memorial to the events of those times. The young teacher described with feeling the hatred they still harboured for anyone and anything German, and the pride they had in Cretan heroism; there were many stories of resistance, such as the woman who ran a German paratrooper through with her scissors as he dangled helplessly in his harness outside her window. They did not surrender without a fight, these Cretans, whatever the odds. This trip taught us much, and gave us some insight into the hospitable but resolute character of the Cretan people.

Jo had developed a breathing difficulty, and was confined to bed. All week a cold mistral had howled outside our window, whipping the harbour into frothing waves that crashed across the promenade. I sat at our little table reading or trying to write, shivering next to the stinking old 'Aladdin' kerosene stove someone has lent us, listening to Jo's alarming wheeze. We think it was asthma, perhaps caused by the wind stirring up dust, or perhaps even the fumes from the kerosene stove, which is our only source of heating, so can't really be foregone. Whatever the cause, the result was persistent and frightening. More than once it brought back memories of my tubercular father as he battled with a similar desperation. We had tried aspirin and paracetamol, chest rubs and salves from the local pharmacy. I felt helpless and depressed to see her so down, so lacking in her usual energy and spritely humour. We had to find a doctor, that was clear, but since there was no house-calling service, we would have to wait until she was well enough to make her way to a clinic.

A knock on the door next afternoon was Takis timidly enquiring how the patient was faring, and then, unannounced, the black-clad figure of his mother stealthily advanced into the room carrying a tin basin of bottles and other things. All she said in her girlish voice was, 'Te kanate?'—how is she? We shrug and said, 'Not good.'

'My, ah mother, will make her healthy again with a Greek remedy, isn't it,' said Takis, gesturing to her equipment. It was a little puzzling that they hadn't actually asked if we wanted it, but I could see they just assumed it was time we submitted to some serious local wisdom.

'What do you think?' I asked Jo, as she worked herself upright in the bed.

'Might as well', she croaked, 'Nothing else has worked.'

Wordlessly Takis' mother moved forward, ripped back the blankets and gestured for Jo to remove her nightdress. She looked in Takis' direction. He took the hint and slowly left, saying he would wait outside should he be needed. His mother now signalled for Jo to roll onto her stomach, and the sheet was pulled up to cover her bum, but leaving her back bare. Then began a silent ritual of lighting a long taper and thrusting it briefly inside an upturned tumbler, which was then quickly clamped on Jo's back, with the rim firmly adhering to the skin; in seconds a dome of flesh was sucked by the vacuum up into the glass. It was weird to see the skin rising, like dough. She gave a soft yell as if she were being pinched. The procedure was repeated, quickly again and again, each time the gob of flesh lifting, and each time eliciting a surprised howl from Jo. This went on for a good five to ten minutes, until her back was covered in red welts and circular marks from the rims. The effect was of witnessing a kind of witchcraft in action, performed by someone who believes utterly in invisible demons, unhealthy spirits that can be sucked out through permeable skin. The very firmness of her technique, the speed and deftness of her movements, was a clear statement of this belief, this certainty that only the old ways, the knowledge from the past, can deal with such badness. Her own mother, and no doubt her grandmother, had practiced this too, had taught her how to rid the body of evil, and so it must be done firmly, with conviction, with no time given for the unwanted forces to resist or recover their powers.

When she decided that the cupping procedure has done its work, she removed the glasses, extinguished the taper, and suddenly took up a bottle of olive oil, poured and spread it over Jo's back. As if this were not enough, she then poured from a small tin jug a clear fluid on top of the oil, the smell from which immediately told that it was kerosene. For several minutes she then rubbed the oil and kerosene vigorously into Jo's back, which drew moans of pleasure, probably as much because the pain had stopped as from the relief provided by the mixture itself. The woman then replaced the covers over her patient, and uttering the single word 'Entaxi', she left the room; Takis met her outside. But before I closed the door he had smiled and said, 'She will now be healed; tomorrow, you will see that she is better.'

Unfortunately, she wasn't. Not the next day, nor the next. One way or the other, we would have to get her to a doctor. Joan helped out again here, and escorted her to the rooms of a GP she herself had used. It was a memorable visit. They were ushered into an ante room by a woman, who brought them coffee and a little serve of *glyka*, a cumquat in thick sweet syrup. The room was cosy and expensively furnished, more like a private home than a waiting room, and no other patients about. After being given adequate time to finish their coffee, the doctor appeared and invited them both into his surgery, where Joan was to translate.

He was a tall, lean, handsome man in his fifties, a sweep of long pepper-and-salt hair across his forehead, a slightly shaggy goatee a little blacker, a dark grey suit giving him a formal but warm suggestion of Edwardian elegance. Jo thought he was an absolute dish. He examined her and quickly recommended they go straight to cortisone injections, the latest wonder drug. She lay on the day-bed while he lifted her dress, lowered her tights and put the needle in her thigh just below her exposed buttock, which when he finished he gave a friendly slap as he said 'orea' (nice), and replaced her clothing.

In a couple of days her asthma had gone and she was up and about. She had to go back every day for ten days to complete the course of injections, which of course she did with no great reluctance. On each visit she had her little 'sweetener' in the ante room, and her friendly brush with her handsome healer. But though she could breathe better and had much of her old energy back, she could nevertheless strangely feel her lungs still bubbling silently underneath; the cortisone had dealt with most of the symptoms, but the underlying cause, whatever it was, was still there.

A dismal surprise awaited Jo when she returned to work after the illness: the good Mr Nikakis dismissed her and replaced her with another teacher. She'd been back a few days, not suspecting any problems, when she was summoned to the director's office and told 'finis', and to collect her wages at the end of the week. The sly little man had been negotiating with a Greek woman to take over, but of course had said nothing to Jo about it. As far as we could tell he was not dissatisfied with her teaching, but her illness had clearly annoyed him. It was a financial inconvenience, and Jo felt slighted. I was probably more outraged than she, so much so that I actually wrote off to that impressive, one-eyed man in Athens who had appointed her (over Nikakis' head it seems), complaining of her treatment. I received a prompt reply, saying he had rung Nikakis demanding an explanation, and was told that he (Nikakis) felt he was relieving Jo of the burden of the job, 'because she was chronically ill', and that he would be finding her a 'few other classes' to teach. But they never materialized, and we didn't pursue it any further. It's one thing to have support from Athens, but quite another to work directly under a man who is against your very presence every day. And in any case, Jo inherited some private pupils from Joan Healy, who was keen to cut her teaching and get on with her book. A better solution all round.

3

AS APRIL PASSED AND THE DAYS BECAME WARMER, we were visited by various friends. The Koops twins, Dalene and Frances, came to stay for a few days after I met them in Piraeus and brought them over on the ferry. Bill and Ruth Morgan dropped in with a friend, George Tibbets, who had been Bill's lecturer at Melbourne University. Tibbets raised my hackles when he peered at my writing notes beside the typewriter on my table, and sneered, 'This is your *magnum opus* is it?' I remember feeling small in the company of such superiority, and was glad when they left. Then a letter came from my old folksinging buddy Frank Capporino, saying he and his beautiful girlfriend Maisie Jones would be arriving soon. When we checked the date, we realised that they would actually be berthing in Piraeus in only a couple of days. I had a dose of the flu at the time, and didn't feel up to making the ferry trip across to the mainland, so Jo undertook to go on her own and meet them, then bring them back to stay with us.

The occasion gave her a memorable experience. Frank and Maisie had made a number of friends on the ship, including Aviva Leyton, wife of the Canadian poet Irving Leyton. It so happened that the Leytons were close friends of Leonard Cohen, the folksinger and poet, and Cohen, who was staying in Greece at the time, probably Hydra, turned up to meet the ship. They all had a party on board, and then, when paying passengers made their way to the dining room for their last onboard meal, Jo and Leonard Cohen were unable to join them, so they went off together to a *kafeneon* in Piraeus. She recalls little about it, and presumes he would be the same, given that he was pretty stoned as they chatted over the meal. Afterwards they returned to the others on the ship and eventually found a couple of vacant bunks for the night. Anything more happen between them? I've never pressed her on the point, and she probably wouldn't tell me if it did; we don't have an express agreement on 'confessions', which I think we both regard as unnecessarily dangerous. You can only hurt each other with that sort of information. Cohen was not famous then, was still known mainly by aficionados of folk music and Canadian poetry. Aviva told Maisie that Irving and Leonard were steadily writing letters to each other and selling them to a Canadian Library under a government-funded archiving project: a nice little perk for them both. The more letters they wrote, the more money they made.

Along with Frank and Maisie, Jo brought back two other travellers from the ship. They were the unlikeliest antipodean mates you could come across—a trim and swarthy young New Zealand dancer called Tom, shy and quiet, with his face buried in Kerouac's *The Dharma Bums* the whole time, and Ernie, part-owner with his brother of a Gippsland farm, now on his first venture out of Australia. Ernie was straight out of Steele Rudd—red-gold hair, blonde eyelashes, freckles everywhere, a bulbous nose forever blistering. He had come to see Europe carrying his snake-bite kit and fox whistle. Friday night in Sale Ernie and his brother would often stagger out of the local pub the worse for drink, drive back to the farm in their ute, and then engage in a fist fight for a bit of recreation before retiring to bed. But there was nothing mean-spirited about Ernie. He was an outgoing, likeable fellow, who readily made friends with everyone he met, especially the Greeks. He quickly discovered the benefit of greeting people in the streets with 'harete' and 'kali mera' to nodding, smiling householders and shopkeepers everywhere he went. At a *taverna* one night he became very 'kefi', and enthusiastically joined a group of local men dancing for the customers. So ecstatic with the wine and music did they all become, that it was not long before someone threw a plate on the floor, the customary gesture of approval. But Ernie did not know the custom; taking offence, and using all of his 14 stone strength, he hauled the chucker out of his seat and was about to teach him some manners, until restrained and pacified with an explanation. Once it was explained, Ernie could see the beauty of the gesture, and with the enthusiasm of the convert, proceeded to join in. I doubt the proprietor had many unbroken plates left by the time he closed the *taverna* that night.

Frank and Maisie found themselves a place to rent not far from us in Chania, and we spent most of the next couple of months in each other's company, along with John Sampson, who came over from Kythera to stay, and we all got along very well. We were now a tight little band of Aussies trying to pretend we were not tourists, although the locals didn't seem convinced. They still pointed at us as we walked past. We had meals together most nights, and began exploring the town and its surrounds a little more adventurously. Joan Healy more or less adopted us all, and we would regularly spend time at the beach in front of Stelios' *taverna*, listening to her stories of various doings among the local Greeks. With her talent for digging up interesting people, Maisie came upon a couple of American servicemen on the beach one day, who invited us all back to their Mess in the NATO base at Souda Bay, about 17 kilometres east of Chania. One of these was an African American called Brown: I never knew if it was his first name or his surname, but it was the only name anyone called him by. I had taken along my guitar. He and I had long conversations about folk music and Bob Dylan, I played one or two pieces, and I think he did the same. Jo and Maisie had fun dancing with various fellas, we ate hamburgers, drank beer. At one point we became separated from Brown and his friends, and found ourselves sitting with a bunch of Southern whites. From the first they seemed a sultry, isolated lot, and said little. When one of them asked how we came to be there, I said we'd been invited by Brown. He then asked me, in a deep Southern drawl, something I never believed I would ever be asked:

'Hey fella, you ain't a nigger lover are yuh?'

That word sent a current of shock up my spine. It was like we were rehearsing some script by William Faulkner. I'm pleased to recall that, despite the shock, I had the wherewithal to look him in the eye and say, 'Yes, as a matter of fact I am.' I don't think he said much after that, and we didn't stay at that table much longer. But a few days later, when we ran into Brown down at Stelios' *taverna*, we heard that we had been discussed at length by the group, who described us contemptuously as 'that long-haired Australian and his sixteen-year-old wife'; I have a photograph taken of me at that time, and I swear my haircut would've passed any army recruiting panel!

At Stelios' *taverna* John Sampson, Jo and I were planning to hitchhike south and east to the archaelogical sites of Phaestos and Knossos, when a lone American girl, tall, blonde and willowy, befriended us; her name was Carol. When she heard us discussing the trip she pleaded with us to take her along. Reluctantly, because she looked like trouble, we agreed, and the next day the four of us set out for the mountainous region of Sfakia, a remote and harsh place, proudly claiming never to have been occupied by foreign invaders—not the Venetians, nor the Turks, nor the Nazis, regardless of what might have been happening to the rest of the island.

On the outskirts of Chania a truck picked us up almost immediately and took us as far as a little village, where there was a turnoff to Sfakia. Just as we got there a bus arrived, and two Dutch girls got off; Carol knew them, and they told us they had just come from Sfakia, and not to bother because it was dreary and there was nothing much there. So we decided to take the road east to Rethymnon, and to make it easier to get a ride, we separated. Jo and I got there first, and had lunch— laughing at ourselves enjoying a bowl of roast meat, beans and potatoes literally floating in oil, a meal we wouldn't have contemplated a couple of months earlier. After the others joined us we set out in mounting heat to hitch to the mountain village of Spili, and stood for half an hour under a shady tree with not a car in sight the whole time. A woman in black took pity on us and came over to tell us that no cars came along here, but that there was a bus, which eventually did come. Slowly, painfully, this got us up into the mountains, from where we could look back at the spectacular sight of Rethymnon on the edge of a twinkling blue expanse of sea. So majestic. Eventually we arrived at Spili, its steep streets winding a narrow path through a lush array of vine-covered *kafeneons* and basic shops. Though the air in Spili was fresh and cool, it was sunny enough for us to enjoy coffee and a bite to eat out on a terrace high above the main street, and watch the locals quietly going about their daily business. Unsure how to continue, we enquired and learned that the bus in fact went on to a coastal village called Agia Galini, which was only twenty kilometres from Phaestos.

Now we found ourselves travelling over a high plateau of dry, dusty roads and rocky peaks. Mid-afternoon the bus stopped at another village, Akoumia Platela, which from the parking bay beside the road had spectacular views across the mountains and down the huge descending valleys. You really felt to be on the roof of Crete, and able to get a grasp of the rugged beauty of the whole island. Needing to pee, we asked the driver for directions to a toilet. He nodded towards a set of buildings below, which looked a bit uninviting, so I went behind a large rock. The girls were not so easily accommodated and made for the building; John and I could hear their giggles as we waited.

'You have to share with the chooks, rabbits and a donkey,' laughed Jo as she emerged. It was, she discovered, the general animal shelter and dunny, human or otherwise, and she'd had to watch where she stepped.

From there the bus turned directly south and arrived at Agia Galini around 6 pm. I don't know what we expected; it had such a mellifluous name that I probably had in mind a typical neat village of white-painted buildings so beloved of the tourist industry, but in fact it was nothing of the sort. It was scruffy and sad, with cheap holiday housing and a few decrepit fishing boats tied up at the wharf. A battered boat ramp ran down beside the stony, uninviting beach. There were few people in evidence, apart from a surly clan of French hippies hanging about the waterfront area. When we asked them if they knew of somewhere we might stay the night, they were rude and dismissive, and shrugged ignorance. We enquired in the town, and discovered that the local people were themselves unfriendly to foreigners, having for some time been besieged by various bands of hippy types. I suppose we were lucky to find a place to stay at all, only after we had convinced a hotelier that we were not one of 'them'. He turned out to be an interesting man, kindly and well-read, with an astute knowledge of philosophy. He had some very interesting things to say about Aristotle and Plato, whom he read in the original Greek, quoting occasionally in convincing and fine-sounding style. He also gave us a couple of tin mugs he had made with his own hands.

We left Agia Galini early the next morning, hoping to catch a bus at lunchtime in the next village, Kokkinos. We had been told by one of the more communicable French hippies that the walk to Kokkinos was twenty kilometres, unless you went via the beach, which was only a few kilometres. But after a short distance we came to a river, flowing into the sea and too wide and deep to cross. So we returned to the village and asked the hotelier what to do, and he showed us a little donkey path that enabled us to cross further inland, and then turn towards the beach again. The walk along the beach was a nighmare: hot and glary, not a grain of sand, just rocks, big mango-sized yonnies that shifted under your foot, wrenched your ankles at odd angles as you stepped on them, and after half a kilometre our legs were aching badly. It was such slow-going that we were in danger of missing the bus at Kokkinos, so we forced ourselves to hurry despite the discomfort. The heat was prodigious. After two hours sweltering, Jo and I stripped off and took a naked dip in the sea while the others went on ahead, too unfamiliar with each other to follow our example. In fact we took a couple of dips, so refreshing did we find it. Eventually we all made it to Kokkinos, had a nice cold 'lemonathe' only to find that the bus didn't leave from there, and we had a further walk to the village of Tymbaki to catch it. Fortunately, when we got there we learned that the bus wouldn't be leaving on schedule anyway, so we waited in the upstairs balcony of a *kafeneon* overlooking the dusty town square for well over an hour, eating lunch and ruefully nursing our aching feet.

Eventually we got to Phaestos, and as soon as we could take in its aspect, its age and what it represented, we knew it had been worth the trouble. High on the rim of a rise overlooking a huge fertile plain lay the clearly delineated outlines of a Bronze Age city, including a great palace. There were no buildings, just foundations, so one had to imagine what the city and palace might have looked like in its lifetime, which dated from about 4000BC, but what was left gave a strong indication of its grandeur. The city was destroyed by invaders in about 1400 BC, but now, standing on that hill one felt this glorious, wide vista of landscape to be exactly the same as to the eye of the beholder two thousand years ago. This is my favourite way to enjoy history—seeing the evidence and imagining what it was like in its heyday.

Carol had been bored by these ruins, and instead spent her time chatting up a couple with a car, managing to persuade them to take her with them to Herakleion. There was not enough room for all of us, so John went with her, and Jo and I took the bus. The four of us didn't meet up again until we got back to Chania. Jo and I stayed the night in Herakleion and the next morning took a bus to Knossos. This of course is Crete's prime tourist attraction, the brilliant partial reconstruction of the palace of King Minos of the Minoan civilisation, thousands of years before Christ. Here was the source of so many stories from Greek mythology, including its labyrinthine design by the famous Daedalus, who was said to have been kept a prisoner by the king so he could not reveal the plan of the labyrinth to anyone, and of how Daedalus and his son Ikarus built wings to enable them to fly away from the island. We walked through some of the corridors, with their beautiful dark red columns, and frescoed walls featuring the famous bull-leaping games, the charming snake-goddess (we still have the little metal replica we bought), beautifully painted dolphins and dancing girls, and were just as impressed by the palace's famous drainage system. The whole sense of the culture is one of civilised, clever, thoughtful people who lived a life of inventive amusement in an age when the rest of the world conquered, raped or ate each other. No wonder the best ideals of our history so often hark back to the ancient Greeks and their stories.

Rather than catch the bus back to Chania, we chose to chance hitchhiking the 140 kilometres. It took several lifts to make it, but two stand out in our memories, for similar reasons. The first was a farm truck that took us part of the way back to Rethymnon. There were two men already in the passenger seat, but they were quite keen to squeeze Jo in between them. It was my luck to be relegated to the back amongst boxes of vegetables, where I lay huddled against the cold wind, snoozing part of the time. When, after about an hour, they dropped us off Jo slid out of the cabin in a very peculiar way, sliding off the seat bum first, and looking hugely relieved to be on the ground. As the men got back in and the truck took off, she said, 'Thank god I'm out of there!'

'What was wrong?' I said, and she explained how they kept prodding and squeezing her thighs, and making leery propositions in their boorish way, the whole journey. She had been sure she would be goosed getting out of the cabin, which is why she got out the way she did.

'Well, first they asked if I was married. Then when I told them you were my husband, they asked if we had children.

'When I told them we didn't, the older one smirked, "Ah, he's no good; come home with me, I give you plenty children," and he made a fisted forearm the way they do.'

'Well,' I said, 'we can take consolation in getting a little revenge on them: when I moved off the bag I'd been lying on, I realised they were tomatoes, and many of them ended up as pulp.'

The second lift, again in a beat-up truck, had three men in the front this time, and again I was banished to ride on the tray at the back. By this time it was getting dark and very cold, and we were still more than an hour out of Chania, so I knew I was in for a rough time. But at least Jo was better off; the driver put her between himself and the door, kept his hands to himself, and concentrated on the road. After a time she fell asleep on his shoulder. Eventually we pulled into Chania, were dropped with pleasant goodbyes, and scurried home, cold and travel-weary, but so pleased with ourselves for having made the journey.

The trip had been only three days, but it felt like we had covered a month's tour, seeing so many different and memorable aspects of the island. It had been a glimpse into the heart of the Cretan mythos, a leap in our understanding of this ancient place, of its people, so toughened in the forge of a violent history and unforgiving landscape, of its contrasts of harsh beauty and dramatic vistas, its affinity with the sea, its fine tradition of hospitality, of its pride in defending its identity, and of its wonderful role as a generator of myth and culture. All this increased our understanding and deepened our feelings for this magnificent island.

Alan Bole saw me taking photographs along the promenade one day, and asked if I would bring my camera and take some of his house. I hadn't been there before, and was impressed by the old mansion, how beautifully furnished the rooms were, and how grand the view was from his workroom, across the harbour to the vivid blue of the Sea of Crete. A shaft of light entering through the open shutters of this generously proportioned room lit up a gorgeous Persian carpet, and cast into deep shadow the sofas and chairs, the small tables and fine paintings on the walls, giving the room a mysteriously reassuring feel, a conservative solidity, vaguely resembling a Velasquez painting.

Alan wanted all this caught in the pictures, and the spectacular view as well. I wondered to myself whether there was a specific purpose for the photographs; perhaps he was doing a bit of publicity for himself for a journal or publisher. But it became clear that this was not it. As he directed me to take several shots of him sitting at his typewriter, shirtless and concentrating, fingers at the keys, a cigarette burning in the ashtray beside him, I realised that the real subject was to be The Diligent Author At Work, and in a short time he frankly declared that it was all to impress his mother back in Boston. Her recent letters had indicated she was worried about him, so he wanted to reassure her. More pressing than this, however, was the fact that he relied on her to pay for his keep, and he knew her well enough to know she expected him to be making good use of her support. Any suggestion that he was wasting his time, not getting on with the novel he had promised to write, or worse, sliding back into his old drinking habits, could result in his mother refusing to send any more money. So the photographs were to be a kind of filial propaganda, the fiction of a son leading a sober, orderly life bringing his novel towards successful completion.

The truth was that he had hardly written a word for months. What he did with most of his days I did not know, because we had our own social life—friends, the beach, walking. But in the evenings there was no difficulty in locating where he was and what he was doing—at the *Kavouri*, or the bouzouki house next door, or one of the *tavernas*, either with friends or on his own until the small hours, leaving always with a skinful of krassi. He was a fragile, decent, intelligent and sensitive man, but he was lonely and he was an alcoholic. He was also gay, about which one had to be discreet in those days, especially in Greece. Charles Haldeman, his close friend and compatriot, and a successful writer, was also gay, but Alan seemed to draw little comfort from the friendship. I think they were not lovers, but neither were they rivals. I often noticed Charles take a protective attitude to Alan in arguments with others. Again, the mere presence of Charles might have hindered him in standing on his own feet, and might well have unintentionally contributed to a lack of confidence that was glaringly obvious to his friends.

I had the photographs printed and Alan sent them off; they must have succeeded in what they were meant to achieve, for he soon seemed to be happily re-established in his comfortable way of life, and we would see him at the *Kavouri* from time to time. We visited him at home again when we were included in a little ritual that he, Charles and Fred Perles conducted on a regular basis, when Ann Perles would make a batch of her 'famous' (according to her) hamburgers, which the little circle would consume before an almost offensively smug Ann, who would witter on with endless details of how she attained such gastronomic heights with such unpromising ingredients. It was during this meal that Ann, whose Glaswegian accent was all but impenetrable, had the front to refuse to pass on one of her English language pupils to Jo because she judged Jo's Australian accent too broad for the Greeks to understand. I could have rammed her hamburger down the chasm of her mountainous bosom.

By May there were clear signs of the arrival of summer; warmer days and nights, increased numbers in the *taverna*s every evening, more noise and activity around the town generally. We spent more time on the beach, or going for walks around Chania. I found it harder and harder to discipline myself to write, and indeed had no idea what I was attempting to do or how to go about finding out. Charles Haldeman made a few helpful suggestions, such as trying short stories or even just sketches of local people and places, and I did try a few of these, but when I look back on those efforts now (yes, I have kept stuff even from those days!), they are embarrassingly naïve and ill-written. When I think what sophisticated writing must have been coming from the typewriters of people years younger than I at the time, I blush to recall thinking what I was doing might have some value.

We were having a farewell lunch with the Finches at a beach front *kafeneon*, before they left to go back to England a few days later, when Richard, indulging his well-worked writing habits, told us this story about Mrs Weekes, the woman they'd hired as home help and nanny to the children for their Greek holiday.

It had started when Mrs Weekes was sitting on the harbour front on one of her afternoons off; the Finches had gone somewhere with the children, as they often did after lunch, leaving Mrs Weekes to her own devices until it was time for her to prepare dinner. On this occasion she had ventured round to the far side of the harbour, past the *kavouri* restaurant and connected buildings, to sit on a bench seat against the sea wall looking back to the town. She hardly noticed a man arriving and sitting next to her, until he spoke.

Now Mrs Weekes was in a particular way a handsome woman; she had a face of that English ovality in the mould of Brenda de Banzi and Jenny Agutter (Richard had met them both), straight light brown hair cut level with her ears, and a shortish stature, stocky but not fat. There was a northern vitality that showed in the ease with which she would break into toothy laughter. It was perfectly understandable that a middle-aged man would be prompted to make her acquaintance on a peaceful sunny day on a Greek island, even if he'd had something better to do.

'Excuse me, but you know you shouldn't be sitting here alone in this place.'

Completely misunderstanding him, Mrs Weekes moved to stand up. 'Oh really?' she said, 'am I not supposed to sit here?'

According to Richard, this was typical of the woman's naiveté.

'Of course you can sit here', said the Greek, 'you can sit anywhere you like. I only meant for you not to be alone.'

'O,' she said, 'that,' and settled back into her seat, 'Don't you worry yourself, I'm quite used to it thank you,' and no doubt she pulled her beige leather bag tighter into her lap, for security.

He was a pleasant-looking fellow, neatly dressed in a light suit and tie, his swept-back grey hair receding almost halfway on his sun-browned head. His eyes were bedded in deep sockets, like glints in two dark caves, giving nothing away (Richard enjoyed giving these little poetic touches).

At that point Mrs Weekes got up to leave. The Greek stood also, and with a little polite bow, offered his hand. 'Of course,' he said, 'I understand. But do you really have to go? Would you take some coffee with me perhaps? Have you tasted Greek coffee?'

'No, no, thank you all the same. Another time p'raps,' she said, and began to walk away. No doubt a little nettled that he'd been rebuffed, the Greek stood fingering his amber 'worry beads' and watched her go.

But she'd gone only about a hundred yards along the harbour edge, when she stopped. She stood, thinking Why am I running away like this? I haven't anything to do, anywhere to go, except back to the house where I'll be by myself. Haven't I been wanting someone to talk to? Well then. He seems polite enough, and at least he speaks English. And anyway, she told herself, it's not as if I've anything to lose.

So she turned about, and with a characteristic shrug, retraced her steps back to where the Greek had resumed his seat. Standing in front of him, she said, 'I think I will have that coffee after all, thank you. Where do we go?'

The Greek leapt to his feet, said he would take her to the *kafeneon* of a friend, and ushered her away back along the harbour front. He told her his name was Vassillios, he had been a merchant sailor, was retired and widowed. Two days later they met again in the same place, and this time he took her to the Chania market, the first of several excursions together. And so Mrs Weekes had started her little adventure, which would go—who knew where?

At the market Vassillios was attentive and eager to show off his knowledge of the local produce. He told her about the various olives and cheeses on the stalls, about the local fish and *malotira* tea—'Good for the stomach. No cancer,' he insisted.

It was at this point that Fiona joined in the narrative; she had clearly been bursting to put her oar in for some time, but had held back in deference to her husband's standing as the family *raconteur*. Now she couldn't hold back any longer.

'She came home with all this shopping—all this food that we didn't ask for, and which the children wouldn't eat ...'

'Well,' piped in Richard, 'they did actually like the fish.'

'But nothing else – not the fetta, and those disgusting wrinkled olives. And she did things like this a couple of times a week—brought something odd back from the shops, or said something cryptic, like when she came out with 'I tasted Greek coffee today', but wouldn't say where or with whom. When I asked her she simply said 'Oh, I have my places ...'

'Anyway, it was clear to us that she was up to something on her afternoons off, though at that stage we just thought she had grown a little more adventurous and had explored the town a bit more ...'

'But it was the change in her attitude that gave me cause for concern,' said Fiona, and without a hint of irony went on to remark on 'a kind of flippancy, a sense of enjoying herself all of a sudden. It was quite disconcerting, I can tell you, because she was being so *secretive* about it.'

Resuming control of the story, Richard conceded that strictly speaking it was none of their business what Mrs Weekes did with her spare time, though they were concerned for *her*, he insisted, because she was no woman of the world. It was only this morning that they had learned the whole story, in a way that took them completely by surprise. They were packing the luggage to send on ahead to Athens, when Mrs Weekes suddenly dropped the bombshell. Standing in the bedroom doorway, she said 'I'm sorry Mr Finch, but I'll not be going back home with you all on the ferry.'

Richard had asked her what on earth she meant, and how else she expected to get back to England.

'I don't know yet, but I'll not be going with you; I'm staying,' she replied.

Richard then went on to paraphrase Mrs Weekes' account of the situation. Apparently, he said, she'd met some Greek chap, and had been seeing him from time to time over the past few weeks, he had shown her around Chania, and eventually she'd fallen for him. Don't ask me what that means, he said; I didn't ask her myself. Anyway, she had gone far enough to make up her mind to dump us, stay on, rent herself a room somewhere off the harbour front. 'And she expected us to pay her her wages to date there on the spot, in drachmas, so she could pay the deposit on her room.'

'Quite, quite mad,' put in Fiona, 'and deceptive, giving us no warning like that.'

But it was not about to happen. With the wry tone of one who in knows in his heart his triumph is hollow, Richard explained how he had thwarted Mrs Weekes' plan. As she stood defiantly in the bedroom doorway, he calmly pointed out to her that she was not entitled to any wages because if she ended her agreement with them prematurely, they were entitled to charge her for the accommodation and meals they had provided while she was with them. There was no cash owing to her, he insisted.

Mrs Weekes stood frozen to the spot for a moment. Finally she said, 'What do you mean 'agreement'?'

She hadn't remembered, or if she had she'd neglected to read it properly before she signed it.

Richard had then launched into his clinching attack. First, he delivered a moralistic rebuke, insisting she had been derelict in her duty, had been deceptive, betrayed them, had set a bad example to the children by 'going off' in this selfish, and frankly indecent, way. He pointed out that if she'd wanted to strike up friendships of her own with the locals she could have invited them to the house, introduced them to him and his family, conducted such relations under their 'protective eye' (a term he had used only recently in one of his scripts). They would have been only too pleased to help her enjoy herself. But she had chosen to go behind their backs, and now she wanted to desert them in mid-journey. Well it was not on, he asserted. He explained the legal situation, that the agreement did not entitle her to any cash beyond what they'd already paid her (which was only twenty drachmas for occasional spending soon after they arrived). He pointed out that she would be foregoing a good reference from them; and finally he asked if she had really thought through the implications of what she was doing to herself. That her stupidity would ruin her life. By the time this diatribe had finished, Mrs Weekes was supporting herself against the door jamb. For some time she could not speak. She was searching for something to come back at him with. But nothing would occur to her. She had almost no money of her own, apart from a few drachmas and some English pounds. It would take ages to contact her bank in Cobham to send some of her savings. And there was no way she would ask Vassillios for money; that would not be right, even though he would probably not mind. And did she really want to burn her bridges to this extent, not being able to get a reference? Her mind was in confusion, she was not thinking clearly. The doubts began to weaken her resolve, make her doubt her own good sense. Had she gone too far, too impulsively?

She turned. Richard was anticipating defiance, and had his armory ready. But Mrs Weekes was not defiant. Her eyes were brimming with tears, and she could not look Richard in the face. Instead, her gaze dropped to the grey flagstones of the kitchen floor. Finally, dragging her eyes up to meet his infuriated face, she whispered in her broadest Yorkshire accent, 'Will you not give me t'wages I worked for, then?'

'Certainly not Mrs Weekes. The Agreement is quite clear on that; if you don't see out the three months, then you forgo the cash component of your entitlement. You've had free board and lodging with us, and that's all you get.'

She was keeping a brave face, would not let herself break down, but her face betrayed with pitiless eloquence the inner collapse of her hopes. Absentmindedly, she went across the kitchen table to pick up a tea-towel, which she silently shook and folded, then carefully positioned over the rail at the end of the bench. She could see it was hopeless. Why had she even imagined she could pull it off? Her, a lone woman in her fifties, presuming to go out on such a dangerous limb, taking a chance that some sort of beautiful life would magically emerge from this desperate action. And who was Vassillios really? She did not know much about him when it came to the point; he could be anything, she might have completely misread him. She suddenly saw herself as weak and self-deceptive. She had tried to be someone she was not, but reality will always catch up with you. That was it, that was what she was, and it was pointless and naïve and even self-aggrandising to think it could be any different. Feeling in her sleeve for her handkerchief, she finally let her gaze meet Richard's.

'I see. I understand Mr Finch. I don't know what I'm to do about the flat; the woman is waiting for me to turn up with the money.'

'There's nothing *to* do, Mrs Weekes; you haven't paid a deposit, have you?'

'No. But I've given them my word.'

'Well I wouldn't worry about that,' he said, turning to make his way from the room, 'I'm sure they'll find someone else to let the place to. So that's all settled then, eh?' He suddenly stopped and turned back, and said, 'Everything back to normal now?'

She nodded, blew her nose briefly and, in a husky tone uttered through lips bridged by a single unflattering strand of saliva, said, 'I suppose so,' and followed him out of the kitchen to check on the children's packing.

When he finished the story Richard stared at the unfinished *moussaka* on the plate in front of him, reached over and took one of Fiona's cigarettes from the packet. He lit up and stared into space somewhere overhead, blowing smoke from his nostrils. No one spoke, until; Fiona finally said, 'In any case, it's not as if we're ungenerous employers; we always insisted she have as many afternoons free as we possibly could. After all, we wanted her to enjoy herself.'

And so the Finches and their entourage ended their Greek holiday and went back to England. Their apartment, two rooms on a top floor opening onto a roof terrace, was bigger and had more socialising possibilities than our harbour-front place, and was only a little more expensive, so we decided to move. The landlady, Eleftheria, was a much more agreeable, generous-hearted person than Takis. She had fitted a shower and new flushable toilet for the Finches, even if it was under the stairs on the floor below, and in full view of anyone passing up and down. The new apartment was now the centre of our social life, which remained essentially lazy and directionless. With Frank and Maisie, and other friends who dropped in from time to time, we would regularly make a huge salad and fresh bread and cheese and get together on the terrace and talk for hours, sometimes about literature or music, often about politics, letting America have it for various reasons, damning recent Australian involvement in the Vietnam war. Pacifists all, yet here we were enjoying local admiration for deeds done by our countrymen in the last war. Even if we didn't like it, we ought to have been proud that the local people had rightly been deeply affected by Australian heroism. It was typical of the arrogance of youth that we held such attitudes in complete contempt.

Sometimes we would wander into town to eat at a little family *taverna*, which did wonderful char-grilled lamb chops, or pork or beef depending on what they happened to buy-in that day, with chips fried in olive oil, together with a simple, fresh salad of cos lettuce and spring onion dressed with only lemon juice and olive oil. Nothing fancy, nothing French—simply good olive oil and lemon juice. There was no menu as such, because there was no choice, but the food was sensational. And they would serve krassi in little metal jugs filled from the wine barrels marked 'his' and 'hers' positioned on a shelf high above the restaurant tables and chairs. And the chairs were locally made, wooden framed with brown woven wicker seats, handsome and very comfortable. Afterwards we would stroll back through the town in the summer twilight, the small group of us, bellies satisfied and tongues loosened by wine, full of friendly banter, privileged to be surrounded by the simple beauty and peace that Chania offered. It was a time like no other in our lives, different from anything we'd known before, or would experience again, a sort of pause in the progress of our lives, the sort of pause available only to the young and unemployed, at a time in their lives when, if they are lucky, they are unburdened by ambition, children, mortgages and money worries. That is the time for experiences that stay in the memory.

Of course it couldn't last. We knew, by the end of May that this life could not go on much longer. Part of it was the money: despite the low cost of living, our savings wouldn't last more than a few months longer and we would have to teach or do something for income. Did we want to teach? Jo didn't especially want to go back to it. I, lacking qualifications or experience, had never even considered it. I had a bigger challenge facing me: what was I going to do with my life? How was I going to find a working place in the world? Go back to music? But I was already out of touch with the folk music scene, and indeed out of love with it, or otherwise I would never have abandoned my success in Melbourne the way I did. I left it for the bigger world in order to expand my horizons, extend my experience, and now that this was happening I realised I could not go back. Greece had changed me, made me aware of a larger world. Now I had a greater sense of what was possible, what potential the world offered to those willing to plunge in. Plunging in was something I was only just beginning to grasp; I had tentatively put my toe in the water with folk music, and it had brought rewards, though of a limited kind. I had plunged into commitment with Jo, and it had rewarded me with a scarcely deserved happiness. Now, in this time of hiatus, of the still moment before the act, I was beginning to sense that my most frightening and unfathomable plunge lay ahead of me, the future beginning to issue its demand. Time to move, and not backwards—to Melbourne, for instance, which was possible because we still had our return tickets—but forwards, to a new place and a new challenge. I had no idea what it might be, or where I might find it, but we thought, Jo and I, that England would be as good a place to start as any. It wouldn't involve learning a new language, it would be fun to see, and we could probably get some kind of work there while we considered our options.

By June we had made a definite decision to journey by train across Europe to London. We gave Eleftheria a date for leaving the apartment, and began to weed through our acquisitions, aware of the need to travel light. One of the things to go was to be my black wool suit. In fact, when Eleftheria saw I was throwing it out, she offered us a month's rent for it, which prompted us to extend our stay by that much. When I went through the pockets before handing it to her, a few scraps of confetti fluttered to the floor; I hadn't worn it since our wedding!

One more recollection emerges from our decision to stay another month: thinking we were leaving, Eleftheria had promised the mattress on our double bed to one of her neighbours, a promise she felt bound to honour. So for the last month we had to sleep on the wire bed frame, which would have been bad enough, but was made worse by the huge valley on one side of the wire, in which we ended up hopelessly tangled together every morning.

Our friends were also making plans to pull up stakes, though Frank and Maisie stayed on for a little longer, and John Sampson was staying on in Kythera for a few more months. Joan Healy could see her time there coming to a close, and would return to Australia by the end of that year. So we began saying heartfelt goodbyes to our friends—Charles, Alan, Fred Perles, Stelios, Joan. We would be so sad to lose the quiet slowness of Chania, and indeed our magical island, its lovely climate, its harshly beautiful landscape.

What specifically had our time on Crete done for Jo and me, I now wonder? Well, all the things I have already mentioned—essentially, helping us to grow in new and unexpected ways. Our love of all things Greek, for instance. But more personally, in our relationship? This is harder to pin down. I have no doubt it brought us closer together, if that were possible. We had our strains, our arguments, made mistakes with each other. But we had only ourselves to get us through these times, no parents or any other resources to turn to; we failed or succeeded by our own efforts. I was not an easy person to live with much of the time. My uncertainties, a legacy of anger from my less-than-happy childhood, skin a little too thin to take criticism in the right spirit, set Jo a constant challenge, which she met with generosity. There was always our physical desire for each other to fall back on, and it was often very useful. But *liking* each other was just as important. I liked her smartness, her ability to think of practical solutions to problems. She, I think, liked my passionate energy, but how she grew to put up with my mood changes I will never quite know. Only she could give the answer.

It was a bright, early morning of what promised to be a burning hot day when we left. We were silent and contemplative leaving the town behind. As the bus passed along the shoulder of a hill on the way to the ferry, we gazed down upon a tranquil Souda Bay below us, surprised by the unusually green and lush quality of its setting. We had grown used to thinking of Crete as harsh, rocky undulating ground suitable only for goats and stunted olive trees. We hadn't seen much of this kind of picturesque softness, and it served as a reminder of the folly of narrow categorisations of Crete, and of any tendency to overlook its wonderful variety. Where else could you bathe in a warm sea and look at snow-capped mountains above you at the same time? And retreat to cool, vine-covered hilltop villages? And beautiful, old Chania, with its little Venetian harbour and its crumbling buildings, so far unspoilt by the modern world. Would we ever get to see it again? Could we ever get back there?

1983—eighteen years later

The first thing I looked for at Athens airport was a locker for my suitcase; overpacked for the trip, I had given myself an albatross to lug around the world for six weeks. A sign of my insecurity—travelling alone, unsure of what weather I would need to dress for, in fact generally unsure of what to expect in the course of research for a biography of the Australian writer George Johnston. There were many places to go—Greece, France, Italy, England, America—and many people to interview, and even though I had arranged times and contact details for all of them, the odds in favour of it all going to plan were pretty short.

Free of my albatross, I caught the bus into Athens and checked into the Astor Hotel. A peculiar smell of engine oil pervaded the building; my modest research grant imposed strict economies, so nothing above three-star hotels. The city had changed for the worse since I was last there—dirtier, political graffiti everywhere, a look of indifference in the people on the streets—none of that sanguine energy that greeted us in '65. There had of course been the dreadful Junta in the interim, and a great deal of social damage as a result. Settled in my room, I reflected on the work to be done. The first task was to ring Grace Edwards, with whom I had exchanged letters in recent months. She suggested she come to the hotel and we go somewhere for lunch.

Grace proved easy to interview—forthcoming and articulate, keen to register her admiration for George. We ate at the Delphi restaurant, sharing a carafe of local red, and the way she wanted to proceed was for me to put questions to her.

'Do you know who George's doctor was?'

'Yes, it was Doctor Nikos Anastosopoulos; I went with George to his surgery here in Athens several times.'

'Why did he stay on with you after the operation?'

'Because things were too bad back in Hydra. The doctor insisted that he change his way of living, and that meant not going back to the situation that had made him sick in the first place. He needed rest, good food, no alcohol or cigarettes. Most of all, he needed to get away from Charmian. So I offered him a room in my flat in the Metz.'

A thought came into my head, which I was sure was also in hers, though it was one I was reluctant to put to her, so it remained unspoken. I waited a second or two, and then said,

'How did you get along?'

Her eyes went down to the contents of her glass momentarily, and then came up to meet mine, 'Fine, fine. A quiet six weeks living with a man without sex, and we got along well together.'

That answered my unspoken thought. But did it? When eventually the topic got around to Charmian, there was a noticeable bite to her comments. 'She was only interested in men you know. Bored by women. The first time I met her, when I took George back to Hydra, she was quite aggressive towards me.'

I could see what might be going on here: had she been hoping to take George off Charmian, hoping that the offer of a quiet, peaceful life with a loyal and devoted woman would pull him away from this selfish, magnetic siren of a wife, who was, in Grace's view, destroying his ability to write? Maybe destroying his life? Simply, whatever the truth of her view of Charmian, she was jealous of her hold over George. Grace could well have been a handsome woman in those days—twenty-one years earlier—so she might have fancied her chances.

Our chat—it was hardly an interview—continued for over an hour, during which time I relied mostly on my mini-tape recorder, though I did take a few written notes. I told her I might want to talk again before leaving Greece, that my visit to Hydra the next day might produce some more questions she could answer. At some point I'd mentioned that I had some knowledge of Greece, that I'd spent six months on Crete in 1965.

'Oh,' she said, 'did you know Charles Haldeman?'

It turned out that he currently lived in Athens, and had become moderately successful, though was having problems with the authorities, something about proposed renovations to his house. She gave me his phone number before I left.

Back at the hotel I tried to replay the interview with Grace, only to find to my horror that I had forgotten to press the Record button as well as the Play button, and nothing of the interview had registered. I would have to ask if she would meet me again, go over it all a second time. Then I phoned the number she'd given me for Charles. A woman answered, and put him on.

'Hello Charles. This is a voice from the distant past.' I told him my name.

'Garry! How nice to hear you. What are you doing here?' I recognised those soft American tones, taking me back almost twenty years.

'I'm here for only a few days, researching a book. I was hoping we might meet up.'

'That would be wonderful. You must come here to dinner, though tonight is not good. Is Jo with you?'

'No, I'm alone this trip. Tell you what, I have to go to Hydra for a few days, and will be back Wednesday. Why don't I give you a call then?'

'That would be good, actually, because I'm not feeling too well today. But Wednesday, we'll have a nice dinner here for you and you can tell me all about what you're up to. OK?'

'Right, look forward to it. I'll call you Wednesday.'

'Till then. Bye Garry.'

'Bye Charles.'

Feeling cheered to have made contact with him, and tired from the flight, I slept well considering I was on my own. I'm so used to Jo beside me, I usually sleep badly without her. I was up early next morning to catch the hydrofoil to Hydra, which got in about 5 o'clock in the afternoon after a choppy journey.

The three days were moderately productive. I had to hang about a place called 'Jim's Bar' for over an hour waiting for the appearance of one of Charmian's old lovers, which didn't happen in the end, at least not that day. But happy chance produced another friend of Johnston's, a painter called Bill Pownall who had come to the island in George's last months there, in 1963. Bill walked into the bar with his wife, Francesca, and spotting me as a visitor he came over and we got talking. He was delighted about the biography, had admired George, and told me a touching little story. Charmian had organised a party to celebrate their return from six months living in England, and had asked people to bring along something to read aloud. Bill said,

'George got up and read some Conrad. Charmian read something from TS Eliot. Then an American poet called Bill—a nice chap, with a deep resonant voice—asked to read a passage of prose. It was a deeply felt, circumstantial passage from an unpublished novel describing the early years of a writer's life. After he finished no-one spoke, we were so carried away. I looked across at George and tears were streaming down his face. It was a passage from My Brother Jack.'

Bill also took me up to the ruins of Ghika's family house, where Sid and Cynthia Nolan had spent many days with the Johnstons. Ghika—his actual name was Nikos Hadjikiriakos-Ghikas—was a famous painter who had loaned the house to artists when he was away, and in 1955 Cynthia Nolan had snaffled it for eight months. A glorious 17th century mansion, it was some years later accidentally burned to the ground, and was now a mere tumble of stones situated high on the shoulder of a steep hill overlooking a tiny harbour west of Hydra village. I stood agape at the breathtaking 180 degree view north and west across the Aegean; the sun was going down, throwing *into dark relief a pattern of tiny islands resembling stepping stones leading away to the horizon. How often the Johnstons and the Nolans would have watched this sight, made comments on the spectacle present and past—and what a past, ancient and golden and seething with the actions of gods and heroes, ships and armies. I thrilled at the very thought of it all, hoping I might absorb some of its spirit.*

Next day I caught up with Charmian's ex-lover, the son of an English writer, and one of the many expatriate drifters who collect where the living is cheap and the demands are few. He talked at length about his affair, described the magical moment of first meeting her, how devastated he was when she left to join George back in Australia. I thought to myself, 'as if you would have ever been able to hang onto her', knowing that there had only ever been one man she took seriously. But the fellow was generous enough to take me to the old Johnston 'house by the well' in the town. He had to persuade the Greek owners to let me go in and look around, take a few snaps. But from old photographs back in Australia I knew that it no longer had the simple elegance that Charmian had created when they lived there—the new owners were antique dealers from Athens, and the rooms were cluttered with expensive stuff that distracted from the lovely proportions of the rooms.

A couple more people made valuable contributions to the story of the Johnstons' life on Hydra, which I taped or wrote out in note form, giving me what I considered would be a substantial and readable couple of chapters for the book. Then back to Athens; it was Wednesday, and I was looking forward to my evening with Charles Haldeman. When I rang, the same American female voice answered as before.

'This is Lee,' she said, then abruptly, 'who am I speaking to please?' I told her, reminding her that Charles had invited me to dinner that evening.

'Charles died last night.'

I couldn't think what to say. My first feeling was one of disappointment that I wouldn't be having dinner or seeing his house. How could he die just like that, without any preamble, no long illness, no dramatic warning. It wasn't right.

'What happened?' I blurted out.

'He had a perforated ulcer.' Detectable in the terseness of the voice was a slight catch, a betrayal of that moment before breaking. She must have been a close friend. There seemed no point in trying to explain to her who I was, how I knew Charles, or even how much I had been looking forward to tonight. All that had to be let go now.

'I'm terribly sorry Lee,' I heard myself say, and then absurdly I added, 'Thank you for telling me. It must be difficult for you …'

'Yes, it is, for all of his friends. There's nothing more I can say right now. Goodbye.'

'Goodbye.'

I sat stunned on the bed in the hotel for some time, recalling those days in Chania, when Charles seemed so strong and alive, and how I had looked up to him as the first real writer I'd met. A sudden neediness came over me. I desperately wanted Jo to be there with me, to hold her, talk to her about the past, about this awful news, about my own loneliness on this trip, living from hotel to hotel, going for days without a decent conversation with anyone, without intimacy. I resolved, and wrote in my diary, that when I get home I must spend more time with her, must take every opportunity to take her with me on my research trips, and that I wanted to do this whole journey again, go to every country, every place, every library and centre, revisit every person I've interviewed, only this time with her by my side, my confidante, my rock, my other self. I will do it all again, but with her, with her affirmation of love to temper the experience and then it will all mean something better, something less chaotic, than it can now. I will. I must. And I did—we did—the following year, 1984.

The nearest I could come to such at that moment was to ring Grace Edwards, and tell her the news. She was, of course, badly shocked. I remembered to say that my tape of our interview hadn't worked, and we'd have to do it again. But strangely, she declined. She said she couldn't do it that day because she was going to see friends on the Pelopponnis, but it had more than a whiff of evasion about it. And since I was flying out first thing the following morning, there would be no other chance. Unless I tried again next year, on that return trip with Jo I'd promised myself. Otherwise, I'd have to rely solely on the few notes I took, and of course memory, that unreliable witness. That liar.

We got to a blazingly hot Athens around midday, and made for the Phaedra Hotel, where we had stayed when we arrived six months earlier. The heat was a fierce reminder of the kind of high summer we were luckily about to avoid, with the eye-wounding glare off the white buildings, and the waves of heat rippling the air above the city. Scanned from the hotel roof Athens seemed to flatten itself down around the skirts of the Acropolis into its urban valley in defensive retreat from the sun. The hotel had no air conditioning, and the room was so hot that we took our bedding up on the roof terrace and slept the night there. Early next morning we made our way to Piraeus station, where we were to board the famous Orient Express, the train that would take us north the length of Greece, through Macedonia to what was then Jugoslavia, then to Italy and on to Paris. The carriages were waiting for us at the station in the cool morning stillness, empty and silent, giving us absolute choice of where to sit. In our ignorance of European travel we presumed this would last the whole journey, and spread ourselves out, put our feet up and laughed happily at our luck. We would soon enough be roundly disabused of that particular fantasy.

Yet it was a truly wonderful train journey. The countryside was mostly rich farmlands and quiet rural villages, reminding us that change is slow in this part of the world, and occurs mainly in the cities; rural life goes on as it has for hundreds of years, essentially peasant-based regardless of the change from horse to combustion engine. By midday we'd arrived at Skopje, where we drank the best railway coffee we've had before or since. Heading west through Nils towards Belgrade the neatly laid out farms looked communal and well run; like most outsiders, we'd thought that Tito's Jugoslavia was a particularly successful form of socialism, and that he had managed to keep the country happily unified in its postwar reconstruction after the especially savage treatment they'd received from the Nazis. No-one spoke of Croatia or Serbia in those days, though sadly it was to prove that national and ethnic hatreds were simmering beneath the surface, had been for a long time, and that eventually it would all erupt and the nation would tear itself to pieces in hardly more than a generation.

We hadn't planned on seeing much of the city of Belgrade. In fact we thought we would only be changing trains there and travelling on immediately that night. Though mildly irritated by the inconvenience at least we could carry our modest belongings with us in one move, so we got off the train to look for the next one. What followed was a bewildering sequence of misunderstandings and miscommunications between ourselves and the railway staff. The station platforms and foyer were crowded with people hurrying in all directions, many carrying luggage and massive bags, clutching chickens and dragging children. The sense was of people eager to get out of the country, though for the life of us we could not understand why. In all the chaos we could not get a clear idea of what was happening with the carriages, which were being shuffled into two sections—one to go north to Munich, the other south through Italy to Paris. The upshot was that we failed to board our carriage, and the train left without us. We were stuck in Belgrade for the night. An information clerk told us that we could use our tickets to catch the train the next day, and in the meantime she booked us into a *pension* and gave us the directions.

Starving by this time—there had been no food on the train—we found a little café not far from the station where we ate something agreeable—can't remember what—and then caught a very lovely little old electric tram that took us to the other side of the city. It was quiet, almost deserted, with few cars about and few shops open, and not what one would call a gaily lit metropolis. There was a tangible feel of the aftermath of the War, with vacant allotments, sombre buildings, the signs of economic stringency, the shabby remnants of a sick Europe hanging over everything. And yet there was a human-scaled peace and dignity that stubbornly lived on, despite the appalling events of twenty years earlier. It seemed not so long.

The area around the *pension* was dark and deserted, the building itself plain red brick like an old factory or warehouse, ugly and possibly bomb-damaged at one end. We pushed at an uninviting corner door, and found ourselves stepping in to a large, bare corridor, cold and unlit apart from a weak glow at the far end. Following the glow, we came to a spiral staircase, again in darkness, except that we could see the source of the glow a couple of levels up. The light wasn't from the first level, which was a circular landing with doors facing into it all the way round, all in darkness. The whole place was alienating and mystifying, like something out of a Kafka story. Climbing up to the next level, we stepped into an identical circular landing with identical doors, but lit by a single bare globe. There was a white button on the wall, which I pressed. Suddenly one of the doors burst open and from a brightly lit room a well-dressed man in his forties emerged with a warm and energetic greeting.

'Bonsoir madame, monsieur; vous desirez?'

Jo had enough school French to get us by; he was in fact expecting us, and introduced us to a group of other residents sitting in a circle in his room. Chairs were drawn up, and we sat making a farcical attempt to converse with people who spoke French, Serbian, Greek, Russian and a smattering of English all in fragments that conveyed much less than our faces and body language, which indicated polite tolerance more than interest. By this time we were desperately tired, stressed from the alarm of missing the train, still trying to adjust and get some degree of purpose out of the whole unexpected turn of events. The manager finally showed us to our room, taking us through one of those forbidding doors into a surprisingly comfortable space with two single beds, a draped window and a few pieces of serviceable furniture. After a wash in a communal bathroom—another of those doors off the landing—we got into our sleepwear and were about to flop when something made Jo go over to the window and draw back the curtain. Moonlight flooded across the room.

'Come and look at this, love.'

I joined her; a huge full moon floated over the shadowed houses and fields, perfectly reflected in a dark river passing below and bending on to disappear behind the silhouetted townscape. It could have been a stage set for a production of *Rusalka*.

'That,' she said, moving in close to me, 'is the Danube.'

Of course the buzz of all those romantic associations instantly gripped us. In that lump-in-throat, tear-in-eye moment we thought 'Us—here—looking at the famous inspiration for so many beautiful creations, raw mates all the way from bland Melbourne, taking in this real thing.' Though of course we were not taking in simply the 'real' thing—we were in thrall of a romantic legend that was only indirectly, symbolically, connected with the physical presence before our eyes; our feelings had been conditioned for us since childhood by tales in books, in films, in music, a whole history of European culture. Yet this did not make the experience less vivid, less true or moving for us; in fact they made it more so. The world comes to us enriched with all its associations, and we take them all, the complex within the simple, as a complete package. The real and the dreamt belong together, in constant equilibrium, ultimately inseparable; the particular and the general find meaning in each other. If lovers are in one sense all the same, they are in another sense all unique.

We were so happy in that moment, gazing over what was an absurdly theatrical scene, arm in arm on a quest to consume the world, or as much of it as we could wolf down. What with her brains and my passion, no inconvenience could throw us off the track, no challenge was too great. We kissed, and needless to say, went to bed and made love—gentle, generous and grateful love.

Next morning, happy for the opportunity to explore the mysteries of a little-known socialist city, we went out to walk the streets. The city itself, even in the daytime, was unusually quiet, still with few cars and no great numbers of people out and about. Shops were sparse and small scale—no great chain or department stores, though there were many official-looking buildings of several stories, surprisingly intact considering the bombing. A bookshop we stopped at seemed to have a good range of works in different languages, including English, with DH Lawrence well represented. To our tastes, the city had an agreeable, unhurried feel about it, and its emptiness not at all depressing.

We sat in a tidy public park, very open and treeless, where city office workers and small family groups gathered on the grass and basked in the cool sunshine. Someone at the *pension* had recommended a restaurant, so at lunchtime we went looking for it, again catching that dinky little tram; it felt hardly bigger than an extended dining table. You entered at the front, moved along as you progressed towards your stop, and alighted at the back, like food through a caterpillar. Everyone happily cooperated. I have no doubt some Melbournians could benefit from lessons here.

The restaurant we were looking for eluded us, but we saw one in a main street that took our fancy, given the very reasonable prices on the menu posted outside. Inside, the place was well appointed, with heavy dark furniture, white linen tablecloths and formally dressed staff, though permitted smoking put Jo off—she has never smoked, and can't stand the smell. I, in those days, rolled my own, but I tried always to keep it clear of her. Luckily, there was an outside eating area, and this proved delightful. There was just a single row of tables under a canopy in the street outside, with a decorative iron fence between the tables and the footpath, so you had fresh air and privacy both. And the food was wonderful—I had an authentic beef goulash with potatoes and cabbage cooked in a spicy stock; can't recall Jo's meal. There was a deeply middle European feel to it all—the flavours of the food, the atmosphere of the restaurant, the situation of our table, the courtesy of the waiter—a blend of Austria, Hungary, Russia, Czechoslovakia; we imagined ourselves in Vienna before the First War, or Prague in the 1920s.

Late that afternoon we returned to the station to catch the Paris leg of the Orient Express. Again, the platforms were crowded with people anxiously pushing their way to the carriages, and squeezing into every available space. After we identified our carriage we looked for a seat, but though it was still some time before the train left, every seat was occupied and every available space for luggage was full. Before long people were hanging out of the windows, it was so crowded. We went back to the ticket office and pleaded for help, pointing out that we had useable tickets. But it was no good—seats were not reservable and it was everyone for himself. We supposed we might have found single seats somewhere in separate carriages, but we weren't prepared to do that, even if we could find such. What to do? The booking clerk said we could maybe take a different train to Trieste, and from there we could find one that went to Paris. That sounded fine, except that there wasn't one now until the following morning. So it was one more night in the *pension*. Given that we found Belgrade to be a pleasant enough city, it didn't bother us, and so that's what we did.

The morning journey to Trieste was comfortable, and made more so by the company of some friendly Jugoslavs. Though we had to rely only on gestures and monosyllables, they were helpful folk, and happily shared their food with us. On the Italian side of the border the countryside changed, and where there had been ordered fields of rich crops right up to the railway line, there was now wild grass and unfenced terrain. Gradually the train did a wide circle in order to enter Trieste from the north, and then, careening down a long incline with the breaking sea curving round the shore on the right and mountains overlooking us on the left, we had a spectacular view of the city ahead, surely one of the world's finest approaches to any city.

It was early evening as we left the station, and headed for the tourist office to book accommodation. The manager was the most helpful and agreeable man imaginable, and since he was just closing up the office as we left, he offered to take us to a restaurant he frequented himself, and we had a spaghetti meal together. But the *piece de resistance* was yet to come: our *pensione* was in a classy commercial area, with cobblestone streets and Italian fashions behind tall plate glass windows. The entry to the building was through an unprepossessing door, after we had buzzed the concierge and she told us to come to the first floor. Once inside, we found ourselves in a grand foyer, surrounded by glamorous shops, all of course closed at this time of evening. The staircase was a huge cream marble edifice with a magnificent polished balustrade curving up to a high first floor. As we reached the top, a stumpy woman with black-dyed bouffon hair greeted us in Italian and took us to our room. The door into it was through a partition wall that felt unpromising, but once inside our fears evaporated. The room was grand in proportions, softly lit and expensively furnished, with authentic looking Italian Renaissance pictures in heavy frames round the walls, and the centerpiece—a handsomely carved and polished queen bed raised on a platform—might have been designed for royalty. This was the most opulent bed we'd ever encountered, a gold guarantee of a good night's sleep, and when we thought that only five nights earlier we had been tortured in Eleftheria's bare wire ravine, we marveled at the extremes of travel. This bed, like Trieste itself, made us feel lucky, and grateful for the civilised touch that Italians brought to their way of life, something we had not been aware of before this night.

The final section of our journey, Trieste to Paris and across the channel on the ferry, was unremarkable. We saw little of Paris, as we had to catch a train to Calais almost immediately we arrived. The crossing to Dover was straightforward, though the white cliffs did carry a certain resonance for us, and made a distinctive announcement that we were finally coming to a familiar culture—a second home, so to speak, with our own language, our virtues, our vices. It was time now to look for decent work, to earn a little money, to find out about this country of cricketers and famous writers, of filmmakers and musicians we admired, of its famed level of civic responsibility, and a newly-elected Labour Party, of challenges to its class system. Perhaps it could offer us something, perhaps not. But we were looking forward to finding out. And the obvious place to start was London.

4

FIVE WEEKS WE HAVE BEEN HERE NOW. We haven't found an apartment we like. Our money is going fast, and soon we will have to decide what to do with the return boat fares; either cash them in, or go back home to Australia. We have another year to decide, but need could force it upon us much sooner.

At the moment we are in a flat at the top of a three-story building in Powys Square, Notting Hill Gate. The building has seen better days, is dark and gloomy, has no lift, and we share a bathroom and toilet on the mezzanine below with tenants on the second floor. One is a friendly Indian man, Gupta, who chats to me while we wait on the landing for the toilet to be free. So far I haven't spoken with any other tenants.

We were cheerful when we first arrived. That week we were in a bed and breakfast in Earl's Court—'Kangaroo Valley'—notorious for Australian backpackers. We were given a voucher on board the *Ellinis* for a week's accommodation in London, and it proved useful. Nobody was particularly friendly there, especially the woman who ran the place, who might have been miffed that we didn't have to pay her direct, but the English breakfasts were good enough to allow us to skip lunch. Every day we went round the agencies looking for an apartment, a dispiriting process that gradually became frenetic; London was teeming with visitors seeking accommodation, and we kept missing out. We thought we'd found one at Manor House where two girls were moving out, and when we enquired, the downstairs tenant, a middle-aged man, said the landlord was away and couldn't be contacted, but that we could use a spare room of his until the landlord was available, which we did. It was a comfortable arrangement, eating together, watching television in the evenings. He was a film buff, a fan of the new British social realism, which was also influencing popular TV shows like 'Z Cars' and 'Cathy Come Home'. One night WH Auden came on the screen, being interviewed on the BBC. I couldn't believe my eyes. I was watching one of the world's great poets, as if I was watching Shakespeare or Dickens chatting in front of me. Anyway, after two weeks the landlord came back, and he seemed annoyed that we were there without his permission. He refused to let us have the girls' flat, demanded that we leave, mean bugger. So we've found Powys Square, for the time being anyway, but it's dismal.

Our life couldn't be more different than it was in Chania. Gone is all that raw beauty, the sun and sea, the warmth, the friendliness of the people. Here, if you are not established or wealthy, this city will take your money and grind you down. The other night we were walking home from the station, gazing in a shop window, when suddenly a man ran up behind Jo and punched her hard in the middle of her back. She staggered against the shop front doubled-up in pain; I chased after him, but he was being shepherded away by a mate, and then they both ran off. I had to go back and see to Jo. Fortunately she was all right once the shock had passed, and seemed to have suffered nothing worse than a bruising.

Through Trevor Lucas we are meeting a few people, going to the occasional party. There was a session in his flat with a very fine guitarist called John Renbourn, who suggested some places I might find work. A few days later Trevor and I went to The Troubador, London's prime folksinging venue, but the manager said there was a queue a mile long to get a gig, and anyway since Trevor was already doing the occasional appearance there, he said 'one Australian is enough'. There is a depressing view of Australians as colonial inferiors in England, even amongst people who affect egalitarianism. How different this is from the attitude of Greeks. So, the possibility of my doing any paid singing is remote. This does not upset me much, because I've really lost my passion for performing, and can't be bothered to go through the whole process of building a name again. There are larger problems for me to consider, but which I am not yet ready to face. Like what I'm going to do with myself for the rest of my life.

Jo has already found work, what is called 'Temp Typing', where she gets paid by the hour to type up dreary accounts lists. Tomorrow I have an interview for a job in the accounts department of a wholesale grocery firm in Holborn. It will at least get me out of the flat every day.

My nerves have been on edge lately. I am re-reading Kafka's *The Trial*, which strikes me as appropriate for the life we lead: depressed, claustrophobic, purposeless. In fact I'm not just reading it, I've been trying to turn it into a script in the hope it might make a television drama, beavering away during the mornings for the past two weeks on the little Adler typewriter we bought in Aden. That seems a lifetime ago now. I haven't any idea what I'm doing with the script, but it occupies the time. An incident happened the other night which I'm sure would have delighted Kafka. Every time we make a noise on our creaky floor the people below us bang on their ceiling in complaint. I think it must be Gupta, or at least his wife, though strangely he never raises the matter with me when we meet at the toilet on the landing. He just smiles and wags his head from side to side in that

Indian way. Anyway, one night they must have been unusually sensitive, because when I merely walked across the room the banging started. I tried tiptoeing, but the floorboards still creaked and the banging still ensued. Jo and I got to the point where we wouldn't move, just sat imprisoned in our chairs watching television in silence, the sound barely audible. The constraint was becoming tortuous. A moment came when I needed to change the channel, so I got down on my hands and knees and stealthily crawled, one limb delicately placed after the other, towards the television set. Just as I was reaching up for the control knob, the floor gave a creak, actually a comparatively soft creak, but that was enough: the response was immediate, the bangs even louder than before. I couldn't help it, but I snapped, and still on all fours, screamed down at them as if they were living under the floorboards, 'Bastards! Bastards! Shuddup!' I've no idea if they heard me, but there was no further banging that evening. I didn't feel victorious, though. I suddenly saw myself as paranoid, a Joseph K. or Gregor Samsa, the man who turned into a cockroach. I really can't go on in this state, nor can we go on living in this place.

A young man we befriended at a party given by one of Trevor's acquaintances invited us to an Anarchist's Ball, which sounded such a bizarre idea that we simply had to go. Somehow it seemed just right for the absurd life we were living. It was at this same party that we came across an old boyfriend of Jo's, the actor John Joyce. In fact I recall feeling a momentary pang of jealousy when I came across them in one corner of a crowded room actually in each other's arms doing a little snogging. But he seemed a genuinely nice fellow, and I couldn't begrudge her a little nostalgia for a relationship that had once meant something, though I was trusting it didn't mean too much. Jealousy has never been a serious issue in our relationship. Possibly because we have always felt right together, and have never found anyone else we'd be tempted to take up with. If we had, I dare say we'd be as susceptible to the green-eyed monster as anyone else. But Jo especially is not the jealous type, and has always taken any little flirtations of mine in good humour, probably because she never felt them as a threat, though she has been known to deliver an acid comment in passing. I, on the other hand, could easily react badly to such in her if I thought her involvement was serious. But simply the fact that it has never happened in a long and rich social life is testament to the security we feel in each other; or have we just had good luck?

Anyway, the Anarchist's Ball proved an all too rare moment of delight. It was held in the Fulham Town Hall, where people came dressed in anything and everything, wildly hurling themselves around the Grand Hall to a live band on stage. They were a friendly, mad lot, mostly art students, writers, musicians, philosophers. The women were basically two types—ones who came in outrageously bizarre variations of dress and undress, and ones who turned up in frumpy tweed suits and sensible shoes, occupying themselves in the kitchen preparing the food, and were probably paid-up members of the Anarchist Federation of Britain. In one corner of the Hall I stood amongst a group listening to a reading by the poet Adrian Mitchell. I liked one of his poems so much that after he'd finished I went up and told him so. He thrust his script into my hand. 'Here, have it,' he happily said. It was unevenly typed in red ink on a crumpled scrap of foolscap, but I treasured it as if it were first prize in a lottery, and I still have it to this day.

With our meagre savings and pathetic income, we continue to watch our spending. But some things are essential to keep our sanity. Such as music, especially for Jo; I can play my guitar, but she depends on the radio or recordings. We recently bought a cheap record player, and thanks to her new job at Imhofs Record Shop in the city, we have been able to afford four LPs—the Mozart *Symphonie Concertante*, Bartok's *Concerto for Orchestra*, and two Janos Starker recordings of the Bach cello suites. In these cold winter days, when the sun disappears into a grey half-light by four o'clock in the afternoon, we hunker down and listen to them over and over in the gloom of our flat, as a kind of refuge from an alien and depressive London. And these sublime works become the accompaniment to our dependence on each other, our resistance to the harsh world outside. Us against them. It was years later that I learned this to be a frequent theme of the poetry of John Donne, who remains one of my literary heroes.

> *For love, all love of other sights controules,*
> *And makes one little room, an everywhere.*

A letter from John Sampson informs us that he is coming to London to stay for a time—maybe a year or two. Like us, he needs to earn some money. We think when he arrives we'll suggest the three of us go into shared accommodation, which will enable us to get a bigger and better apartment and live more economically.

My job at the wholesale grocery is another story from Kafka. I sit at a desk in a room full of clerks looking at pages of figures that I am supposed to do something with. The 'something' was explained to me by the Manager, Miss Bowler, but I didn't really grasp it, although I kept nodding that I did, mainly out of boredom. Instead, I read my library copy of Kafka stories, which is in my centre drawer; I can open it just enough to see in, and since I am looking down it can appear that I am reading the pages of figures; to be more convincing, I make movements with a pencil in my hand. Every now and then Miss Bowler comes and checks on me, and finally notices me reading the novel. 'Get on with your work,' she says coldly, 'and read in your own time.' She is a focal point for everything I hate about this job—its dour, pointless encroachment on my time, on my thoughts, its frustration of my need for something enjoyable, something that matters. I can't imagine Miss Bowler mattering to anyone on earth, or for that matter anyone on earth mattering to Miss Bowler. She has a metallic face, a mask of denial over all feeling except suspicion. She looks at the world as if convinced it is up to something illicit, or worse, something pleasureable.

There are some friendly staff I have lunch with, in particular a nice old gentleman, Mr Walsh, well past retirement age, who works at a reduced salary, and a young cockney girl from the typing pool. She asks me about books, of which she says she knows very little.

'Could you recommend a good novel I should read?'

I think about what she might like. She has a chirpy disposition and a Cockney sense of humour. I suggest *Catch-22.*

'What's it about?'

'It's very funny. It's about the army in World War Two. I think you'd like it; it takes the piss.'

She laughs, takes a pen out of her bag and writes the details on a scrap of paper. Mr Walsh is prompted by the mention of war to relate an anecdote. 'We did more than take the piss, in the First War,' he says, 'I've known blokes shoot their own officers in the back for ordering them out of the trenches. I couldn't take it, on the Front. I got out of it, and you'll never guess how.'

'How?'

'Shot me own toe off.'

The girl shrieked, 'Oh my gawd! Why did you do that?'

'I had to be careful, like; if it was sussed that you'd done it yourself, you could be executed for cowardice. I told them I'd been wounded in an exchange of fire. They didn't like it, and had their suspicions, but they couldn't prove it was deliberate.'

He is a lovely old fellow, Mr Walsh. I admire him for what he did—choosing life over probable death. I feel exactly the same about the Vietnam War, which is taking place at this very moment; there is no way they would ever get me involved in that disgusting event, which must be a journey through hell for those involved. And for what? What business of ours is it if the country turns Communist? 'The thin edge of the wedge,' my mother calls it in a letter from home, in which she also makes the astonishing point that 'we should be helping the Americans there, because they helped us fight the Japanese in WW2.' So what are we doing, taking turns at favours, right or wrong, regardless of the reasons, and the cost in lives?

A parcel came from the BBC today, returning my typescript of *The Trial*, and politely turning me down. I'm embarrassed I even sent it. As a vote of confidence in my writing efforts, Jo has bought me *The Concise Oxford Dictionary* as a Christmas present.

On the landing one evening I asked Gupta about cooking curry. 'I'll tell you,' he said with surprising firmness, 'very few people know how to make a good curry; the secret is onions. You must use at least six of those large Spanish onions (they were as big as navel oranges), and lots of lard.'

The following night under his instructions I made a curry that was heavy on turmeric, coriander and cumin, packed with onions and gleaming with boiling lard, with whatever meat and vegetables we could fit in the pot after that. It tasted essentially of cumin, we ate very little of it, and I'll never forget the sight next morning of a congealed yellow cake of lard in which pieces of meat were stranded like dead animals in a mudflat. Clearly, Indian men were no more reliable culinary advisors than Australian men, especially me in those days; I had no idea how to cook.

Being so close to Portobello Road, we would wander down there on Saturdays, when all the market stalls—clothing, furniture, bric-a-brac—were out in full array, and there were many fascinating things on show. We cheered ourselves up by buying a couple of bargains—four beautiful large soup bowls with a blue Victorian pattern, and a lovely cedar desk, which we got for eight pounds. Notting Hill was just becoming an area popular with West Indian and African migrants, who often roamed the streets in unhappy or resentful groups; they were not having a great time of it in those days of entrenched racism.

Desperate for social contact, and probably because they at least gave us a reminder of Greece, we took the train to Cobham, Surrey to visit Richard and Fiona Finch. We got a somewhat mixed reception. They did give us lunch, and we talked about Greece, including the fact that Mrs Weekes had astonished them by returning to

Crete. 'Apparently,' said Fiona, 'she only came home to settle her affairs, end the lease on her flat, sell her furniture and so on—walked out on us of course, though after our little contretemps on the day she left we were happy to see the end of her. She'd gone within the week. Met some man in Chania, and I suppose she's shacked up with him. We were amazed she could get up to anything like that, although I did often wonder what she'd been doing with her time. So there you go—we never know, do we? Anyway, we did get a card from her, about a month after we got back, saying she was enjoying Chania much more this time, and that her daughter was going to be joining her. I guess she is planning to stay on indefinitely ...'

Naturally, we thought 'good for you Mrs Weekes', because no-one in their right mind would want to work for the Finches, and because it felt exactly right, proof of Greece's fatal charm for anyone open to it. We stayed for the afternoon, sitting in their dingy old living room disagreeing with just about everything they said, except that when I told him of an idea I'd come up with for a television play, he said it was so good that if I didn't write it soon, he would do it himself. So much for friendship. My idea was in fact pretty ordinary, and I very quickly lost interest in it. The event confirmed for me, however, the impoverished tenor of Richard's creative imagination.

We also contacted Robin Douet, the filmmaker, and his wife at the suggestion of Joan Healy, who had worked in journalism with them. They had another guest for dinner, Charles somebody, who when he learned I was a folksinger suddenly grew interested, telling me that he knew a lot of people in the music industry and that maybe he could be my manager. He hadn't even heard me sing, but I could see that what he had in mind was a possible easy investment, especially one that would cost him nothing. He invited us down to his country retreat in Bosham, West Sussex, for the weekend, where he wanted to hear me sing and meet his friends and neighbours. It was a disaster. I loathed his philistinism, and class pretensions, and I suspect he wasn't impressed with my singing. We were sitting in the garden when a nice old gentleman, working as his gardener, came up and asked about some planting issue, removing his cap and calling Charles 'sir'. I, in my bumptious Aussie way, said, 'Do you let him call you that? Do you want him to?'

'Oh, of course,' said Charles, 'he enjoys it. It makes him feel secure.'

Whether or not that was true, I could tell that it certainly made Charles feel important.

The rest of the weekend was just as bad. Neither he nor his wife really wanted to hear me sing, and we ended up spending most of Saturday in the house next door, where the people were much more interesting and their teenage children were delighted when I played them a few songs. At breakfast on the Sunday morning, Charles' wife said in her best county accent, 'What time church service would you like to go to?'

"Oh, I'm sorry,' I said, 'I'm not religious; I don't go to church.'

'But we're not *religious*,' she replied, 'it's just what everybody does. It's the blessing of the boats today. It's a lovely local custom, a *social* occasion.'

I resisted her pleas, and she turned her back on me and disappeared; I heard their car as they drove off to the service.

This was my first real taste of Anglicanism, and it struck me that it was even more of a social institution than Catholicism, which at least affected a degree of religious mysticism. Not that I cared about that.

The upshot was that we were frozen out of the household for the rest of our time there. They came home from their service and said nothing to us about lunch or any plans for the day. We drifted around the house for a while looking for something to do, and ended up back in the neighbours' house, until we decided to slip off and get the train back to London. It was the last we saw of any of them, including the Douets. To them we were now socially untouchable. Of course, we were partly at fault, but I still remain proud that we didn't accommodate ourselves to those smug types, who I came to realise represented a particular kind of Englishness that you have to get past in order to find the good qualities the country and its people have to offer.

Eventually Jo managed to find a job that was at least amusing and which brought us a couple of decent friendships. The Television Maintenance Company of Kensington was the grandiose name for a two-man outfit just in the next street from us, owned by Peter Moorhouse, assisted by a twenty-something gay part-time playwright and actor, Jack Harvey. Years later I saw Jack performing in a BBC television production of *Timon of Athens*. After war service Peter had lived a somewhat confused life, wavering between a bohemian and a good husband and father. He had a stammer which he could use to good effect in telling a story, was widely read and perceptive, had done oddball things, like live on a barge in the Liverpool docks for many years, had strange nomadic girlfriends, one of whom he claimed could stand on the edge of his barge and pee into the water like a man. He was a member of the Communist Party, and regularly took part in anti-nuclear rallies. On the other side of his personality, he had married the eminently sensible

Beryl, with whom he had four delightful children, all living on his beautiful Cumbrian property in the remote hills of Broughton-in-Furness. He motored between here and his London 'business' life every week or so, a hell of a distance, and the strain was beginning to show on both him and Beryl. Peter was no businessman, and it was becoming clear to everyone, including Beryl, who had put up the money for the business, that Peter's main interest in London was in seeking out writers, artists and women to spice up his life. As soon as he saw Jo his eyes lit up, and I believe he imagined all kinds of possibilities with her in his employ, and even better, she would be able to run his office with ease and efficiency. The office work was mainly organising maintenance visits, mostly replacing the cathode tubes that had such a limited life in those early TVs. She had some hilarious times with customers, who were local pensioners, flat-renters, Council tenants and hookers. She would come home full of stories relayed by Jack and Peter, or of things that had happened to her during the day. She answered the phone to a man once who said in a lilt she had trouble recognising: 'My portable teevee is not working. My name is O'Mear—Tubby O'Mear.'

'Can you bring it in for us to have a look at, Mr O'Mear?'

'Good, I'll be around in a while.'

Expecting a portly Irishman, she was surprised when a large black man turned up with his TV, spelling out to her that his name was Tubi Omer, and he was African.

In a short time we all became friends—dinners and picnics with Jack and his partner, actor Donald Pelmear, and Peter ate regularly at our flat. Once we stayed at Broughton-in-Furness where the bored and frequently nettled Beryl did her best to be hospitable, and we went with the children exploring the bare hills of that ruggedly beautiful landscape. Sweet on Jo as these three men were, and occasionally critical of some of my behaviour, I never felt threatened by them. I suspect Jack might well have been bisexual enough to fancy her, but with me and Donald in the way there was no chance. There were in fact demons that were harming our relationship at this time, but they were not caused by, or solvable by, this friendly little crew of outsiders.

Summer was coming to an end, the days were getting colder and dark earlier. London was dirty, ugly, crowded and expensive. My interest as a performer in the music scene all but disappeared at the end of 1965. But engagement with the music going on all around was still important to me, though changes were taking place that I found disorienting. The two forms of music that had for some years been at odds—the folk revival and the 'pop' phenomenon—polarised the youth of the 60s into thinkers and non-thinkers, idealists and idolaters, politicos and sleepwalkers. The two groups disliked each other, each resisting the other's values in language, dress, behaviour and cultural tastes. It may be difficult to believe, but I think much of this general polarisation revolved around the choice of instruments, specifically the guitar. The folk revival had been built on acoustic instruments— harmonicas, squeezeboxes, recorders, flutes, mandolins, banjos, and centrally, the Spanish guitar, and its American steel-strung derivatives. Pop music, in contrast, was driven by electrified instruments, either by means of microphone pick-up or amplifiers, and the electric guitar was the centerpiece of its identity. The differences were not just a matter of taste. Acoustic instruments were portable, which meant they could be played anywhere to anybody, freely and spontaneously if desired. They did not need to be plugged into an electrical system provided by a corporation (an electricity company, a radio or TV station, a commercial venue), which would be ineluctably connected to the broader economy. This, along with its strategic targeting of mass audiences, made it difficult for pop music in those days to conduct sustained criticism of establishment politics, and generally it served rather than resisted capitalist interests. Folk music, on the other hand, was relatively free, in so far as it chose to be, of financial and political constraints, and it built a tradition going back through early Dylan, Joan Baez, Pete Seeger to Woody Guthrie, Leadbelly, and black blues singers like Bill Broonzy and Lightnin' Hopkins. All of these folk/blues musicians sang against the interests of big-business, political corruption and social injustice. The establishment sought to silence them, either by banning or even jailing them, but in so far as they could stay on the move, in the streets, or in trade union protected venues, folk singers could not easily be silenced. And that freedom, that tradition of left-wing resistance, was made possible largely by the nature of acoustic instruments.

One might object to this argument on the grounds that much jazz, which uses electric instruments (though its traditions are built on acoustics), also participates in political protest and 'alternative' values to the mainstream. This is true, but the political effectiveness of jazz is constrained precisely by its prioritising of artistic creativity over all else, and this limits both its mass appeal and its polemical power. Somehow the essential ambivalence of jazz is summed up in its characteristic adherence to songs of popular romantic agony (i.e. 'blues') mixed in with its modernist devotion to avant garde experiment; the two modes should be at odds, and yet in what must surely be the most unacknowledged version of the politically unconscious, they get away with the reputation of a single cultural identity: 'jazz'. But it works as a form, probably for the very reasons I've touched on.

It was essentially political bias that lay behind my shock and disappointment when Bob Dylan turned to electric instruments and a rock-band backing in 1965. I, like many others, believed he had sold out to the forces of the music industry, and thus to capitalism. I have since modified my view, and recognise that his determination as an artist was to get above and beyond economics and politics, to write songs out of his personal experience and interests, more than a political commitment that he no longer felt. He has probably succeeded in this, though I would maintain that the values in his early political music, as in Woody Guthrie's and Pete Seeger's, are vigorous and important, and offer something more than, and better than, artistic individualism. I think that in many cases political art is better and more influential than actual politics, and that politicised artists are more valuable than politicians themselves. The fact that songs like 'Blowing in the Wind', 'The Times They Are A'Changin', 'This Land is Your Land' and 'If I had a Hammer' have been sung by generations of political activists take these songs out of the confines of individual expression and into the realm of historical change: they are social, not merely individual, musical achievements, and in that respect are more important. Very little that Dylan has written since he 'went electric' is memorable in the larger sense, or could serve a wider purpose than self-expression. No-one else, except for occasional other professional artists, sings them, and the various twists his 'career' has taken him through have made him certainly an artist, but in the eyes of those people whose taste is decided by the media, merely a celebrity. It is Dylan the figure, the survivor, the grand old man of Pop, who they go to see, not the teller of tales that can change people's minds and behaviour. I don't judge him too harshly for this; it simply makes him exactly like the rest of us who have had to accommodate our lives to the inescapable fact that we live in a capitalist world, and the best we can hope for is to resist practicing its worst calumnies. Dylan is no saint, nor even a hero, but then he has made it clear that he never wanted to be, and I think we are better off without either.

The noticeable lack of idealism, accompanied by the move into an increasingly bizarre drug culture during the following years, was the final nail in the coffin of my desire to continue in the music scene. The drug culture took me by surprise, and for a time I didn't know what to make of it. At first I could see no harm in it, and took the view that it was a matter of personal choice and not a moral issue. I smoked a little dope, though it never seemed to have the effects on me that others claimed for it. But as LSD hit the market, and people began building their lives, their relationships, their artistic activities, around the hyper-real experiences it gave them, I backed away from it. I was still getting to terms with normal artistic experience, let alone the intensified and heightened kind that drugs apparently provided. I guess I was a little scared of them, having always been reluctant to put chemicals into my body—my bathroom cabinets have always been littered with prescribed drugs that I've failed to take. And then there was the commonsense view—probably a rationalisation—that when you returned from the heightened world that drugs took you to, you still had to live in the everyday world and face its problems, so they did nothing to enable you to handle the realities of life. Jo was of much the same mind, except that she didn't even smoke, so we kept clear of those scenes, and no doubt saved ourselves a lot of money in the process. Wowsers? Not in any other respect.

Of course, the classical music scene was largely removed from all this social upheaval; it lay in a world that seemed above it all, and about which I knew nothing, except for an increasing interest in and regard for classical guitarists. I had always liked listening to Segovia, and had heard the criticisms of him from fledgling players anxious to Kill off the Father: his playing was too idiosyncratic they said, he did not respect the composer's wishes and so forth, but such objections were trivial beside the great beauty of his pieces, and I would have done anything to be able to play like him. I was also becoming more aware of the gifts of John Williams and Julian Bream, his devoted followers. I even went along to John's father Len Williams' school in London with the intention of starting seriously, but after talking to one of the teachers I could see that the road would be long and hard, and that my situation did not provide for another long period of poverty while I practiced eight hours a day to become listenable-to in five years time, at best. But I knew enough about the instrument to teach myself on a hobby basis, and to this end I bought myself an inexpensive but serviceable classical guitar. My old Gibson didn't get much of an airing after that.

John Sampson arrived and we found a better apartment, the ground floor and basement of a Victorian house in Ladbroke Grove, with two spacious bedrooms, a good country-style kitchen, and central heating, which was essential now that winter was properly upon us.

As we moved into 1966 our social life began to pick up. Jo's friends from work often dropped in, especially Peter, who was grateful to get away from the dismal, half-renovated flat on his business premises. In March Frank Capporino and Maisie Jones arrived from Europe, where they'd been touring after they left

Greece. They slept on our bedroom floor until they could find a place of their own. Other Aussie expats would drop in from time to time, and we soon found ourselves having a regular get-together on Saturday nights. The talk about politics, art, literature, philosophy, or just everyday practicalities would be lively amongst our new-found English friends, together with old mates from home. All this was enjoyable enough for us to begin feeling less depressed about London, and less tempted to go back to Oz.

But there were some moments of strain amongst all the conviviality. One of John's Sydney friends, Ian Harrison, turned up one day with a young woman asking if we could put her up for a while. Ian, it turned out, was a habitual Good Samaritan, and the young woman, Alice, a Sydney actress who had been in London's Maudsley Psychiatric Hospital after a nervous breakdown, could be released only into a stable home, and in the absence of her parents, Ian thought Jo and I would provide that stability. For the first few days she slept on a couch in our bedroom, but after she began stealing Jo's knickers and flirting with me, she was banished to the couch in John's room. Alice proved to be constant trouble. She never lifted a finger to help with the housework or cooking, and expected everybody to drop everything to please her. She was certainly emotionally unstable, but it was more selfishness than madness, possibly the result of overindulgent parents. Before long she was in John's bed, and naively he thought he was in love with her. Then her fiancé arrived on the scene, and she began seeing both him and John. When she flashed an engagement ring, John immediately ran out and bought her one himself, insisting it was he she was going to marry. She then claimed she was pregnant, but nobody knew to whom. Her parents arrived from Sydney and promptly married her off to her fiancé; John was devastated. Except that it was never at any stage funny, the whole event was farcical. The last we heard of her was that she had gone north to Manchester to have her baby and live with her husband.

One significant outcome to it all was that Maisie Jones, who had been expressing what I thought an unusual degree of fury towards Alice (given that it was not she who had to live with her) came around one night to sympathise with John, and voilà, she ended up in his bed. More than this, she immediately told Frank that after years together she was leaving him, and that she and John were going to move into a place of their own. It is with some embarrassment that I say I did not take this news well. I am somewhat conservative, I've discovered, when it comes to my friends' relationships: if I have always known them as a couple, I like them to stay that way. When they start swapping partners, inexplicably it is I who feel betrayed, and I who get righteously angry. Frank was the nicest bloke you could meet—warm, generous, idealistic, with handsome northern Italian good looks, like a big puppy in some ways. Maisie, on the other hand, I had always found slightly irritating. A beautiful and certainly intelligent woman, there was nevertheless an element of bluff to her intellectual pretensions, an overcompensation for an insecurity somewhere. So far, this had always been mitigated by being Frank's girl; you felt that if she loved this man, she must be pretty decent and pretty genuine. But her switch to John seemed to my biased, and certainly unreconstructed, male mind in those days, a tactical more than an emotional decision; John had the better prospects, so she moves onto to him. Ah me! I am a harsh and too often wrong judge of character. It happened to be Maisie who would become famous; John never achieved the writing success he promised, and their relationship to last the next forty-seven years! So I am hardly in a position to criticise their choice.

Despite the intensified social life at Ladbroke Grove, Jo and I were going through a bad patch in our marriage. I had become very hard to live with. There she was, working full time at the Television Maintenance Company of Kensington, which meant she was living regular hours, getting up early, shopping on the way home, cooking the meals, and doing most of the housework, while I stayed in bed. Having been sacked from the job at the wholesale grocery, I began trying to use my time to 'write', which I was doing increasingly into the small hours of the morning, turning in at 4 am, sleeping till lunchtime, and playing my guitar or talking to whoever was in the flat during the afternoons. I was still smoking, including in the flat, which Jo hated, and I was bringing in no money. I would go out at one o'clock in the morning to buy cigarettes at a machine, and walk the streets of Notting Hill in a kind of brooding reverie, deluding myself that my self-absorption was some sort of affirmation of my genius. In fact my writing was self-indulgent rubbish, because I knew almost nothing, and had no idea how to go about expressing or changing that fact. I had somehow convinced myself that the mere desire to be a writer was enough to make me one, regardless of the fact that I had no training, no education of the kind necessary to know what writing entails, and insufficient humility to go out and seek those skills. No wonder Jo was deeply unhappy, as indeed I was myself. We were living in different time zones, in different social spheres, in different psychological realities. My night-time walks enabled me to construct a fantasy, in which I imagined myself alone against an uncaring world, feeling that Jo was being increasingly drawn towards that world, joining the enemy; I came back to the flat one night and wrote a piece about how I would have to leave her if I was to become the writer I believed I could be. So much was out of kilter between us, we seemed headed for an inevitable split-up. She would confide in her friends at work, especially Jack, who was protective and sympathetic to her, and increasingly critical of me. I was being framed as the bad guy, and I was making sure I lived up to the image.

Yet she stuck by me. She would complain, or she would make helpful suggestions that I would usually reject, she would write home to her mother about her feelings of gloom and frustration, and some of the responses from home questioned my worthiness of her, but she never ceased to give me her unstinting love and loyalty. It was this, as well as a strong instinct for survival in us both, that got us through and eventually out of the hole we were in. We had been talking of getting out of London. One desperate thought was to migrate to Canada, where we might make a new start—she would teach, I would maybe write or go back to music, or something else might turn up. The Canadian authorities looked doubtful about me, but she was acceptable, providing she was willing to take a teaching job in the middle of Prince Edward Island, out in the wilderness. The sudden thought of the remoteness and all that snow turned us off, and we junked the idea.

At least I was getting a good amount of reading done. I read hungrily, in the belief that I was finding things of deep importance to my life. I was on the look out for pearls of wisdom, little keys to the secrets of life, which I was sure must exist somewhere. This is what someone with an inadequate education, such as I had, is inclined to think—that there is knowledge locked away just out of reach, and that if I read the right people I will gain access to it. And so there is, of course, though the mistake I was making was in thinking that it could be obtained passively, in a short space of time, like a birthday present. It would take many years for me to see that it doesn't work like that, and that knowledge, wisdom, all that clichéd bundling, are not things you can possess or assume. All there is is learning from experience, and that is not a possession but a journey; and if you do learn things there is no guarantee you can hold on to them. 'There is only what is lost and found and lost again and again', said the poet. Finding is an experience, and losing is an experience, and you might, if you put in the work over a lifetime, learn something from both. At least this is what one hopes for one's old age.

But I read Kafka, and Nietzsche, and Reinhold Neibuhr, and Sartre and Zen Buddhism, and all I can say now, looking back, is that I am glad I did, and I am glad I read them with such inquisitive passion, because I did learn things from them, even if they were not the things I was hoping for. What did I learn? I didn't know it at the time, but I was learning significant, small steps in the history of ideas. Only later, when I undertook to repair my fragmented education, did I acquire the context that enabled me to see that these ideas were not 'the' key, or 'the' truth, but interesting ideas that took their place in the larger picture of history. They were not necessarily new, and they were not necessarily wise or even good ideas, but they lived in the flow of human thought over many generations and in disparate cultures, and once I began to see them in that context I realised that what was necessary was to *understand* them, not necessarily believe them. And this was a liberation, but it was a liberation I did not, at that moment in London in 1965 at the age of twenty-seven, enjoy. I was still trapped in the darkened cell of not-knowing, groping for the answer to a riddle I could not even put words to.

I sought the words among people who claimed to have them, or at least claimed to know where they could be found. This was a group I was introduced to by a friend of Jo's Aunt Nan, who gave us her contact details. We visited her and she asked us, 'Are you only interested in material things, or are you looking for something beyond this, something spiritual?' The question made me recoil a little. I am always suspicious when people want to foist their 'spiritual' notions upon me, which is, I know, unnecessarily defensive and narrow-minded of me, but I think I'm an inveterate sceptic; I imagine the Catholic Church brought me to that. Anyway, this group met every week in Don's house—a large house—in Hampstead. How is it, I've often wondered, that people who are into 'spirituality' often seem to have so much money? Something ironic seems to have happened to them, and they are burdened with the very material benefits they say they are determined to reject. Anyway, the people in this group were pretty well-off, and they were, I must admit, extremely pleasant folk. We had some good conversations in a circle in Don's ample sitting room pursuing philosophical interpretations of personal experiences—anecdotes really. Jo went only the once; she is a political animal, and these people had no interest in politics. I stuck it out for some months, and became good friends with them. When they learned I could play the guitar, they asked me to visit a centre for 'gifted children'—I think it might have been run by followers of Rudolph Steiner—and play songs for them, and teach them a little music. I did, and enjoyed it, and I could see that this was the sort of thing that passed for social service for them—attending to the care of 'special' people whose needs might be ignored by the usual instrumentalities. Yet somehow, implicit in their view, children without such 'gifts' were not important, or could be safely left to others to bother about. The politics of this troubled me.

I gave up going to the group after a time, feeling that somehow the discussions were not robust enough, too polite and constrained, but not before I had enjoyed a slice of luck courtesy of two of them. He was a famous jazz musician who had given up playing—Cy Laurie—and his partner Suzannah had inherited a small cottage in the village of Toot Hill in Essex, where her father had lived and died. It was now standing unused. I had mentioned to them our desire to get out of London and get to know something about the England outside of it, and they suggested we consider their cottage. We did, the rent was cheap—£5 per week—and though it needed some renovations, it promised to serve our purpose, and in a matter of weeks we had made the move. So that weekly group proved to be of material use after all; as for its spiritual value, I'm afraid it didn't have much effect. I remained essentially a materialist.

Just around the time we moved to Toot Hill, a new fashion began to develop in London, and by extension in Britain everywhere. New styles of clothes, hairstyle, behaviour, music and graphic art were emerging to give a markedly different, upbeat feel to Britain, one intent on leaving behind the dour old Post-war image of struggle and poverty. It was the start of what came to have various names—Swinging London, the Swingin' Sixties, the Psychedelic Era, the Sexual Revolution, and its more serious and radically political wing, the Student Movement. A great deal has been written about these changes, much of it exaggerated or just wrong, but while Jo and I were witnesses to it all at relatively close hand, we were really only fringe participants more engaged on the trajectory of our personal lives than in joining the social revolution. We were of course affected by it. Jo loved the colourful new clothes, the miniskirt—she had the legs for it—the swirling, brilliant dress patterns, the shiny plastics, and I happily took to flower shirts and tight, bright woollen jumpers to go with my flared hipster jeans and lengthening hair. I recall that though we could barely afford it we bought her a glamorous white fur coat, which had come into vogue, and in which she looked gorgeous. We were quite aware of the Drug and Pop culture raging all around us, led of course by the Beatles and the Rolling Stones. We listened to them occasionally, watched performances on television by them, or The Kinks, The Who, Sonny and Cher and others, but never with the mad devotion that was sweeping the youth of Britain. Now in our late twenties, we were from an earlier generation, and already being left behind by a much more confident, somewhat narcissistic youth eager to push every boundary of experience.

In the months before we made the move to Toot Hill, Jo had left the Television Maintenance Company to take a teaching job, something she'd been avoiding since we arrived in London. We simply had not been able to manage on her salary, and teaching paid so much more. She spent one term at the Edith Neville Primary School behind St Pancras Station, looking after a class of Council Estate kids who had all failed the notorious 'Eleven Plus' exam, and then before we actually left London, during the school summer holidays, she took another 'temp' typing job in the office of a plastics firm. Her job was to act as secretary to a clerical officer who had lost most of his staff in an office reshuffle, an unprepossessing man in his fifties who dictated letters as if to demonstrate a mastery of every cliché in the business lexicon: 'yours of the 15th ult.' and 'at your earliest convenience', 'at this point in time' and that kind of thing. She would sit in front of him on a very low chair in a miniskirt, notepad on her lap, her long legs tucked up virtually under his chin, and he would do his best to look businesslike and devoted to the task in hand. He wasn't so much pervy about her presence, more taken by his renewed sense of importance in having his own secretary to dictate to.

By undertaking the move to Toot Hill, we were making a decision about our immediate future, one that was at that stage open-ended; we had no specific plan to go back to Australia or anywhere else. We were signalling our willingness to give life in England a decent try, and to see what we could make of ourselves, particularly me, so I suppose it could be said that there was a stronger element of commitment in this decision than any other since we were married. This is reflected in the fact that we finally cashed in our return boat fare and bought a car, a little green minivan, for which we paid £80 to an American academic in Holland Park, who stunned me when we chatted about Camus' *The Outsider* by telling me that the 'outsider' character in the novel is the Arab who is killed by Mersault; I couldn't believe how anyone could get it so wrong. But his car was in good condition and, we thought, very reasonably priced, and would open up new possibilities for us in getting to know the English. And so it did.

5

OUR LITTLE COTTAGE IS VERY BASIC, needs a bathroom, which Cy, the landlord, is going to do himself, with my help, and there is no heating or furniture. The rooms are small with heavy oak lintels over the doors and bumpy, hand-rendered plaster between exposed beams stained black, Tudor style. These are all authentic, not modern fakery. The ceilings are low, giving the place a cosy, cave-like feel, and proved easy to heat. Upstairs, the second bedroom has a lintel over the doorway that is so low it strikes me in the chest if I don't bend almost double. I love the door to the stairwell, which is made of heavy vertical planks, and also the latch, an ancient iron thumb-lever you press down to raise a bar. There are old iron catches and horizontal stays on the casement windows too. Surrounding the house, the garden is wild grass and shrubs gone to riot, and we plan to keep it that way; no fussy English country garden ambitions here. Though we want to make it comfortable, we also know it won't be our permanent home; our plans are too open for that just yet.

Cy told us of a furniture auction at Brentwood, a few miles away. There we bought ourselves a couple of decent chairs, a better bed and a very nice used rug for the sitting room. What with the Victorian desk from Portobello Road, the chairs, my new guitar hanging on the wall, a long white paper lampshade hanging in one corner, and the paraffin heater in the centre, the room feels civilised already. A bit of Old England.

An important event has been the acquisition of two ginger tomcats. A friend at Jo's place of work had a cat that had just littered, and unable to choose between them, we took both, and very cute fellows they are; somehow they seemed to be asking for Russian names, so they have become Nicolai and Alexi, and they form the other half of our little Toot Hill family. We know we should get them neutered, but it is so remote out here there might not be many other cats they could mate with, so we'll wait a while to see if this becomes a problem. We would be reluctant, however, because neutered cats can have far less personality, and tend to become furry blobs eating and sleeping all the time.

Jo has found a job teaching at the Epping Secondary Modern School. She drives in every day in the minivan, a journey of maybe fifteen miles. The kids are hard work, because having failed the eleven-plus exam, which means they have already been marked by the system as failures, they have little motivation to learn. But the pay is reasonable, and we can get by on it.

I stay home, play some guitar, am still trying to 'write', and have begun some stories about Greece, and plans for a novel about my Queensland experience three years ago. But frankly I'm getting bored; I don't at present have the inner contentment to spend hours at a desk. I need to engage with people, to be out learning about the English. I must find a direction to my life. I must find a job— no, I must find a profession. I never thought I'd hear myself say that again. What I need, and never had of course, is a profession that satisfies me.

Today we had a letter from Jo's mother, Barbara, who writes long, informative reports from her side of the family. She says she is missing Jo, and wonders how long we intend to stay, and, more pertinently, what we think our purpose is in being here. Would we not be better off at home, where I might be able to work towards some kind of career? Alas, neither of us has an answer to these questions; in being here we are simply following our instincts, doing what feels interesting. We are not homesick, still feel we are on our adventure 'abroad', still looking for experience to teach us about life, chancing that something will happen to transform our vision, give us an answer to this question of purpose. What would be the purpose of being home in Australia at present? I would be no nearer to knowing what I want to do with myself. At least I can say I am still open to whatever England may have to offer. But we can't say anything as vague as this in our letters back, so we simply say I am 'writing a book' and leave it at that. My family doesn't communicate much. I get the occasional brief letter from my mother, but she is no writer. Nor is my brother. Sometimes I find a brief note from my sister Sue in the envelope from my mother. They think of us as being on holiday, indulging in a kind of leisure in the English countryside, and that we'll be home soon. Anyway, one item in Barbara's letter particularly caught our eye: she has floated the idea of coming to stay with us for three months next summer. Jo is thrilled at the prospect, and I too will be pleased for the opportunity of getting to know her better; I already like what I've seen of her, but that has been all too brief and superficial so far. She is resigned to travelling on her own, since apparently there is 'no way' she could get Whit to venture out of Australia. He seems to regard going abroad as a kind of betrayal, for him anyway, and is of the firm conviction that everything he wants is right there in his own country, so why bother to look elsewhere? We'll have to make the spare room habitable by the time Barbara arrives, though that is many months away yet.

The other day, Jo asked, 'What about journalism?' But I have no idea how to go about it, how to qualify, where to train. I should look into it.

We are getting to know the local area pretty well. Last weekend we had a visit from Jo's cousin Margot—a lively, lovely girl, who arrived in London a few weeks back and is sharing a house in Willesden with a girlfriend. She arrived for the weekend, and we all went exploring in Epping Forest, which at the moment is spectacularly autumnal. It is a fabulous place, quiet and densely treed, such that you feel completely cut off from the busy world nearby. You can get the same feeling in the Australian bush sometimes, especially in remote rainforests, but the visual experience in Epping Forest is quite different. When we were larking about, dangling from tree-limbs, hiding from each other, kicking through deep layers of yellowing oak and elm leaves, the place seemed timeless; it might have been exactly like this in Shakespeare's day—nothing but the natural world. Except of course that in our case we were taking photographs—that makes a difference. We tried to take fashionably 'different' photographs from the norm, a la Beatles, posing idiotically up trees or looking for oddball objects. In one case we found an old rotting tree stump that looked like some weird animal, and we attached a cord to it and photographed Jo looking like she was 'leading' it through the forest. That sea of leaves indicates, of course, the coming of winter, and we have already noticed how much more clearly the seasons here are marked off from each other than in Australia. Summer was full of sun and colour, with the daylight lasting until well after ten in the evening, and the trees and shrubs glowing with a green so luminous you would swear it was electrically charged. Never have I seen this green in Australia, this vivid signal of English nature:

> *No white nor red was ever seen*
> *So am'rous as this lovely green ...*

wrote the poet, capturing the passion of what that more recent poet called 'the force that through the green fuse drives the flower'. I really am beginning to love this country. Now, towards the end of autumn, the twilight moves in sooner, the nights grow colder, and the trees reveal their skeletal branches through tattered bits of leaf against the clouding sky. It is all a drama, and a reminder of how much the whole history of these parts, of England, of Europe, revolves around the clearly defined quartet of seasons. Our thoughts are already turning to what the reality of a winter out here might mean.

Over the ensuing months we made friends, settled into country life, got the cottage into a presentable and comfortable state after Cy and I finished the bathroom, and hunkered ourselves down against the cold, relying more than we liked on the performance of our stinky paraffin heater, placed in the middle of the room with both of us sitting close beside it reading or watching TV. An unpleasant surprise arrived one cold dark night when a knock on the door proved to be a man from the television hire company, there to repossess our set. Apparently we should not have taken it with us when we moved to another county, even though we were happy to continue the payments. He was a pleasant enough man, and was actually quite embarrassed to deprive us of the set in the middle of a program, but he did have to take it away with him. Next day we went into Epping and bought ourselves a little black and white portable, which we soon adapted to and which served us admirably.

Then, against the odds, I found a job. The Science department at Jo's school needed a laboratory assistant; Jo remembered my experience as a trainee chemist in my early twenties and thought I might be interested. She was right, and the school was happy to appoint me. Moreover, they offered me a half-day weekly leave if I wanted to pursue some relevant study, so I enrolled in 'A' Level Biology at a Ware Polytech in Hertfordshire, about an hour's drive from Epping. The head of the school Science department, Tony Curnock, proved a communicative, sociable chap, very 'county', very Tory, and I was to have many lively conversations with him in my time there, from politics to literature, sport and science. If the menial laboratory work was mostly tedious and potentially demeaning in that class-ridden society, nevertheless I was treated with respect and generosity by my workmates. The job at least connected me to English life in certain ways that I found interesting. Part of this came from my position. Not being a teacher, I could form a relatively disinterested view of how the school ran. There were many problems, mostly to do with the low status of Secondary Modern schools generally, and these showed in poor relations between staff and pupils. Discipline was a problem, and I worried for Jo's wellbeing in such an atmosphere.

Now that we were working in the same place we drove there and back together every day in our little minivan, and left the cats to their own devices (which included a little cat hole beside the back door, where we placed their food, and which was occasionally raided by a hedgehog, and a few voles and shrews, living in the back garden). Those trips in together have stayed in my mind, driving along the Epping Road through beautiful English countryside, dipping and winding around tight, shaded bends, scaring up the odd pheasant from neighbouring farms, getting stuck behind a tractor with a drayload of hay. One time we were driving home, chatting away, and as we crossed a plateau where the road is fairly straight for a couple of miles, I thought something whitish blew under the car on the left as we speeded past. Then it occurred to me that I had felt a small bump as well, so I stopped to check. Back behind us, on the side of the road, was a young rabbit stretched out on the grassy verge. I picked it up. It was warm, floppy, and dead, though there was not a mark on it anywhere. Its neck must have been broken when it ran into the rear wheel. We took it home, cleaned and skinned it in the kitchen while the cats went out of their minds from the gamey smell. They wolfed down the lights and liver we threw them, and then we made a wonderful rabbit casserole, with a rasher of bacon, onion, carrots and some herbs, slowly cooked in a white wine gravy. One of the best rabbit casseroles we've eaten, and all from the unlikeliest of accidents.

In the midwinter cold and wet we had trouble getting the car started, a consequence of the poor positioning of the Mini's distributor, just behind the front grille, where it was open to water and frost and the rapid perishing of the rubber electrical leads. I quickly learned how to solve the problem: as soon as we got up in the morning I would take off the distributor cap and leads and dry them in the oven while we had breakfast. It worked beautifully every time. On frosty mornings the road was so iced up that the front wheels, which are the driving wheels, would simply spin and fail to take us up the steep slope to the Epping Road turnoff, so I would have to drive half a mile downhill to where the road was flat enough to gain sufficient run-up to propel us up the hill. There was no car heater, and on more than one occasion it was so cold that our breath froze on the inside of the windscreen, and refroze as fast as Jo could wipe it off with a cloth as I drove, trying desperately to see where I was going.

At the school we began to make a few friends. Mike Gibson drove us down to his home town of Southampton during the holiday break; we all stayed at his parents' house, and he generously took us sightseeing around the region and over to the Isle of Wight. Then we befriended a vocational guidance officer called Liz Willson, who lived with her husband Pete in a flat on a working farm over towards Brentwood. They were a handsome pair—he a dark-haired pleasant young man, she a tall, blonde English rose, who wore miniskirts and long white boots. And at lunch times I often went over to the art department to chat with Lew Davies, an art teacher with a great sense of humour, who loved to give burlesque summaries of the various cock-ups committed by the school administration, staff and pupils; his favourite phrase was 'the mind boggles'. Lew lived in Ilford with his wife and child, and painted large, urban realist streetscapes. These friendships were helping us to settle into life in Essex, which I must say I was coming to like more and more. On the whole the people were gentler, more socially engaged than the kinds of Australians I had grown up with. This was most noticeable on the road, where English drivers are generally courteous and unaggressive, and rules are strictly followed.

Friendships notwithstanding, life was no bed of roses for us during these months. Despite having two incomes, which were in any case not high by English standards, we were struggling to stay out of debt. There would always be something—repairs to the car, gas and electricity bills, clothes, and just our food bills—all seemed to swallow our money, leaving us next to nothing for any holiday travelling or pleasures beyond an occasional movie or concert. We began once again to question what we were doing in England, and letters from home were asking the same thing. Both our jobs were stop-gap and less than satisfying, were taking us nowhere, and we still had no exit plan. These things, and the strain of teaching uninterested children, began to affect Jo's health. She developed a strange jaw pain, for which the doctor's had no answer, and she was dogged by sinus and throat infections. Nor did she like the gloom and cold of the English winter. Her usual ebullient self would show only in social situations where she could relax, but for the rest of the time she was down in spirits, and was taking days off work with increasing frequency. This was making her unpopular with the other staff. One morning I went in without her and reported her sickness to the office. Fifteen minutes later the vice-principal came storming into the science lab and assailed me for what he considered were Jo's derelictions of duty. My only recourse was a counterattack for his aggressive language, and I responded in kind with some carefully chosen words; it pulled him up short and he stalked away and never spoke to me like that again, despite there being other days when Jo could not get to school. In my heart I knew that we couldn't go on like this. She was ailing for something. Could she be wanting to go home, but for my sake not admitting it? Did she need to stop teaching? Her real interests and abilities are intellectual and academic, and she was neither trained nor equipped for minding unruly and bored children.

Letters of support and some money from our parents back home eased our minds a little, and we went through Xmas and the winter break with brave faces and hope for a better 1967. We certainly felt we were learning about English winters: when we left the front casement window half open for the cats to use, we woke up to a virtual ski-run of snow sloping down from the window to the sitting room floor, with little padded footmarks up and down it where Nico and Alexi had made their morning excursions. No wonder we'd shivered through the night in our upstairs bedroom, with no heating and the house covered in a foot-deep blanket of snow. When we got up we looked at the back garden, it was a field of white. Jo put on her Wellington boots and plodded through it, leaving a trail of deep footprints, followed by one of the cats hopping from hole to hole behind her. These two little charmers were our surrogate children, more affectionate and engaging than any cats we'd had before. They were quite different in personality. Alexi was very neat and fussy, a slightly smaller head and body than his brother, a little aloof at times, though he liked to play with me when I was sitting at my desk, determined to distract me from whatever I was doing. He would curl up in a tidy little ball at the foot of our bed every night, and always try to organise himself to look his best smooth-coated, dapper self. Nico was the opposite. You could anthropomorphise Nico into a large, untidy fisherman type, who would lay his shaggy body down any which way anywhere, a little stupid and babyish, and who insisted on climbing under the blankets between us when we slept. Both would go out to attend to necessities early in the mornings, and would return bounding up the stairs making little chirping noises, and resume their cosy places with us; happy families—mum, dad and the twins. We were expecting them to start talking within the next few months.

Epping Secondary Modern was depressing us both. The staff themselves were fighting against their own lowly status in the education system, and many of them were little better than time-servers. I was amazed at the views of some of them, ranging from cynical mockery of children to ignorant fundamentalist Christian dogma. One man, no teaching qualifications, hired to take rowing and sailing, was often asked to stand-in for a science class, and preached to the students on the wrongness of the theory of evolution. Somehow it came as little surprise to me one day when I saw him through the internal classroom window strangling a boy over a desk, he had to be dragged off the boy by the vice-principal and another teacher.

Another man, the senior English teacher no less, practised relentless mockery on his students. 'Sorry about your affliction,' he would say to a child who had not performed well, 'blame your parents for having you.' The atmosphere was one of constant warfare between the staff and large groups of students, and it is doubtful that much learning, or taste for it, took place in most classrooms. Jo decided she would look about for another teaching job in the area when the academic year ended.

The most important event we looked forward to at the end of winter was Barbara's arrival from Australia. She had been hoping to get leave from her position as librarian at Castlemaine High School, where Whit was vice-principal, but in April we learned they had turned her down. By that time she was so excited at the prospect of coming over that she decided to do it anyway, and resign from the job. She was arriving in June. We planned to take her on a driving tour through the West country to south Wales. For the purpose, we had side windows and a decent back seat fitted to the Minivan.

For some reason the modest library in Epping had purchased a complete set of the works of the American novelist William Faulkner published by Gollancz, and I began borrowing them, steadily reading my way through the whole set. My interest had been sparked by a talk on the radio by an American professor, who had delivered a brilliant exegesis on *The Sound and the Fury*. So clear and engaging was he that when I spotted them in the library, I was primed to tackle them, and pounced. Most of them had never been borrowed. Over several months I became a Faulkner addict, and remain so to this day. It was my first serious engagement with difficult literary texts, notwithstanding my love affair with Kafka the previous year in London. But I had read Kafka naively, having no historical or critical context in which to understand him. Now, for the first time, I was beginning to grasp the value of listening to critical scholarship. I began to look at writing, especially fiction, in a new way.

Winter finally gave way to spring, and once again we were struck by that powerful feeling of marked seasonal change that is so different from Australia. The green budding of the trees, the appearance of flowers, the colouring of the fields as we drove between Toot Hill and Epping every day, the lengthening of the daylight hours, the warmer sunshine, all combined to cheer us up, and make life seem more hopeful. We developed a real love for the English countryside, especially around Epping Forest, and the little drives to Theydon Bois, or through Greensted village to Ongar. There is a wonderful little church at Greensted, the oldest wooden church in the world, and we often took friends there for a meditative poke about. With all this peaceful beauty surrounding us, our depressions began to seem temporary, our problems solvable.

The school year finally wound up at the start of summer, much to Jo's relief, and, in June, right on schedule, Barbara arrived. We drove to Heathrow to pick her up and take her back to Toot Hill. Her lean, handsome face looked tired and aged, as people do at the end of such a long flight, but clearly happy and excited about seeing Jo again. And it would be a good chance for me to get to know her at last, since we had seen little of each other to this point. She was pleased with her little room upstairs, opposite our bedroom, and amused at the ridiculously low doorway. It was just the kind of old-world oddity she had come all this way to experience. After a few days settling in we readied ourselves for our tour, satisfied that she would be comfortably snug travelling in the new back seat and able to take in the views through the new windows. Unfortunately the prospect from a Minivan on English country roads, with all those high hedgerows, is not ideal, a drawback we hadn't foreseen. But we would have needed a four-wheel-drive to improve on it, and they were few and far between in those days, and way outside our budget.

It so happened that Barbara had been given the address of some people in Gloucestershire by one of her work colleagues, who insisted we should look them up. She wrote to them, and received a friendly reply inviting us to stay a night with them on our way through. Since it was more or less on the way to Wales, it suited us well. How unsuspecting we were of the ramifications that this little digression would bring to our lives! But I mustn't get ahead of myself. We drove into the rich hilly Cotswold countryside around Stow-on-the-Wold, across vast gently sloping landscapes, passing through ancient villages of local ochre-coloured stone. We came to their village—Alderton—but got lost looking for the house. Finally we found what we calculated had to be the shared driveway of 9 Church Road, the left fork disappearing behind a thicket of shrubs and trees. Hesitantly taking the car up the curving drive, we suddenly were confronted with an imposing Georgian mansion standing in a broad acreage of lovely garden. The lawns were neatly cut, the trees healthy and graceful, the building a warm pale stone with an apron of crushed quartz around it and a white-painted glassed conservatory gleaming on the far side. The two storeys developed into three storeys at the rear, and its many rooms promised generous proportions and high ceilings. It was the perfect English country house, large and elegant, and worth a fortune.

'We must have the wrong address,' gasped Barbara, 'these can't be our sort of people.'

'Well, it's 9 Church Road,' said Jo, 'we'd better knock and find out.'

In their reply to Barbara's letter all they had said was that they had 'enough room' to put us up; we had no idea what 'enough room' would turn out to mean. As we pulled up at the front entrance a couple emerged, smiling and eagerly approaching. It was impossible not to like them instantly—he tall and lean, tightly curled hair receding from his high forehead, sleeves rolled up, a man of practical bent from head to toe, yet sharp and sensitive, she a lovely pale-complexioned redhead with brilliant laughing teeth and sparkling eyes that devoured you in friendship. Ian and Elizabeth Parkin, and scooting about the place were their three young children, Kate (8), Alison (6) and Matthew (3). Despite their stately pile they were neither rich nor aristocratic. In fact they weren't even English. Both came from Melbourne, were teachers until the children came along, and now Ian taught economics at Prince Henry's Grammar School in Evesham. How they came to own such a house is some sort of a story.

After being demobbed from the Australian navy in 1946, Ian married Elizabeth, whom he'd met while he was completing a degree at Melbourne University. Soon after, they travelled to England, and Ian enrolled for a degree in Philosophy, Politics and Economics at the University of Oxford, where he coached the college crew at St Catherine's. After a brief return to Australia, during which time Ian taught rowing at Newington College in Sydney, they decided they loved England so much they wanted to go back and live there. When the job at Evesham came up they began to look long and hard for a suitable house, something they could make interesting for themselves. The Rectory at Alderton came to their notice, but they were sceptical; it was badly run down and the grounds—over an acre—had become overrun with blackberries and weeds. There was no heating apart from open fireplaces. It would cost a fortune to restore, let alone maintain, which on a teacher's salary, even two teacher's salaries, would have discouraged most buyers. But the Parkins were not most buyers. The selling price of £3500 was not in itself beyond possibility, with a mortgage to their limit. It would be the upkeep that could keep them struggling. They wrestled with the problem through one sleepless night, and then they made a promise, an undertaking to each other: they would take it on only if they did everything themselves—the garden, the maintenance, everything. It had to cost them no more to run than an ordinary home, and they had little to spend on doing the place up fit enough to move in; most of that would also have to be done by them.

They proved to be geniuses at it. For those blackberries, Ian answered an advertisement giving away an old defunct tractor. Being a car buff from his youth, he set about doing the repairs to the engine and making it serviceable, and ploughed and leveled the whole garden. They then shaped it, grassed it, planted an orchard in one area, a vegetable patch in another, kept a few of the larger trees. A weekly furniture auction at Evesham knocked down large items such as Victorian dressers and bookcases, extension tables and sofas, mostly too big for ordinary English houses, at ridiculously cheap prices. Gradually they furnished every room—chests of drawers for five shillings, a massive kitchen dresser for ten shillings, a beautiful glass-fronted bookcase for a pound. The first winter that they froze through, with a child on the way, convinced them that they must find a way of heating the fifteen or so rooms economically. Central heating would be too expensive to buy and run, so Ian began looking for secondhand gas fires. He ran the gas pipes himself and placed an appropriately sized heater in every room, thanks to a wonderful invention called Yorkshire fittings, which made pipe-joining simple. All these were the kinds of skills they became adept at, and by the time we arrived the place was a beautifully kept, warm but grand family home with busy parents and children running happily around all over the place. If ever there was an example of the philosophy of self-help, the Parkins were it. Samuel Smiles, you would have laughed in pleasure.

But there were more surprises in store. Ian himself held political opinions quite out of keeping with his place in the village. Having the grandest house might have given him high status in some villages, but Alderton was not like that and the Parkin family found it easy to fit in. They were radical in some respects, certainly in economic and social policy terms, on which Ian was well informed and up-to-date. Yet they were universally liked, and Ian would jump at the chance to help anyone in need. He held a monthly discussion group in the house, to which anyone in the village could come and debate the current state of affairs in the country, or anything else that took their interest. There was no hidden agenda to his politics—he would willingly and openly put his views to all, and being so well informed he was infuriatingly difficult to defeat in an argument.

So into this enchanting family we suddenly found ourselves unexpectedly thrown. Our admiration was happily reciprocated when, after dinner, I brought out my guitar and sang a few songs. The response was warm. In fact, the whole family seemed to take the songs personally, as if something had been awakened in them. This was particularly true of an old Dutch folk song called 'When First I Came to This Land', which I had learned in Melbourne from Martyn Wyndham-Read.

When first I came to this land,
I was not a wealthy man.
So I got myself a shack, and I did what I could.
And I called my shack, 'break-my-back',
For the land was sweet and good,
and I did what I could.

As I ran through the verses, which told of a man reflecting on his success in making a home and family from humble beginnings, I could see in it Ian's and Elizabeth's own story. They also liked my renditions of the comic Irish 'Johnny McEldoo' and 'Finnegans's Wake', and some fine Australian songs, including 'Jim Jones' and 'South Australia'. Whatever else the effect of this evening had on the family, and more of that can later be told, it certainly ensured that our visit was popular. We had a grand time, Jo, Barbara and I, enjoying the Parkin generosity, and the particular blend of laughter and seriousness that they generated around them. It was to be a friendship that had many more episodes to come.

Next day we embarked on our camping trip, heading off to Wales via a spectacular route suggested by Ian. We drove through Hereford across remote mountainous countryside, treeless and rock-spattered, down to the coast at Aberaeron and along narrow twisting roads that took us through grey Welsh villages, where we found places to pitch our tent while Barbara stayed in B&Bs. At the extreme tip at St David's we camped on a grassy verge near the beach only to be washed out by heavy rain during the night, and so had to sleep in the car. We drove north to Aberystwyth and visited the astonishing Harlech castle, where you could stand on the parapets and survey the oceanic plain below for approaching enemies, feeling like an unassailable medieval lord. Then to Barmouth and along to Bontddu, where we stayed a freezing night in the tent. At one stage we got lost on a remote rocky road and Barbara asked an old fellow wheeling a bike if he could give us directions. She could understand not a word of his reply, except the word 'boneshaker', referring to his bike. We had certainly chosen to see Wales the hard way, but we wouldn't have changed a minute of it. We got back to Alderton after about a week, proud of our adventurousness but also quite pleased to be back in our cosy beds at the Parkins', who had insisted on us returning to them for another night before we went home to Essex.

Over the remainder of her stay, Barbara managed to use her time profitably. We would all go down to London from time to time to see Margot or a show or perhaps other contacts she had on her list. She stayed a week with an acquaintance at Lowestoft in East Anglia. She also made very good friends with a local Toot Hill woman, Jenny Jones and her family. Jenny was a stunningly beautiful and lively young woman with two small children, and a husband who was a distinguished lithographer at the Slade School of Fine Art in London. Stanley commuted every day, catching the train from Chipping Ongar. We, too, became good friends with the Joneses, and over the rest of our time there spent many an enjoyable hour chatting and eating with them. By the time Barbara was leaving she and Jenny had become firm mates, and continued to write to each other for years afterwards.

It was a sad day when we took her to the airport and saw her off, especially for Jo. They really did miss each other, mother and only child. Within a couple of weeks of her departure we got one of her vivid, articulate letters, telling of her difficulty with settling back to the old routines: *It's funny, even after only three months, the way I feel; as though I have changed, and just a bit my values, and all here are just exactly the same and expect me to be. It will be better for you and Garry, for instance, when you come back after a long time—you will expect—and be expected—to be different.*

It seemed that her visit and the time she spent with us, even though she said later in the letter that she wished she'd got 'closer to us', managed to convince her that there was some sense in our staying on in England while we worked out our future. Even so, I could sense that Jo was asking herself much more pressingly what exactly we were doing about it. But she tried to keep this to herself. Perhaps, too, she thought that things might start to improve, now that we had new friends in the Parkins and the Joneses, and that she had a new job to go to when the teaching year began—she had been successful in applying to Loughton Secondary Modern, about half an hour's run from Toot Hill, and was hoping against hope it would be an improvement on Epping. In the meantime, I would stay at the school, and get on with my 'A' Level Biology class at Ware College. It was beginning to really catch my interest.

6

THE BALL CLIMBS AS HIGH IN THE AIR as I can throw it with a cricketer's arm, the left arm. Leaning back to the point where the spine aches, so to catapult with maximum power, I can make a tennis ball almost disappear from sight. Shielded eyes following its flight, Matthew gets more and more excited, especially as I catch it every time. We face each other, father and small son and I, a trio of clowns on the green sward, where you happily fall down, inhale the cool aroma of grass. Oh, those summer evenings at the Parkins', the house and its garden a vision like something by Gainsborough, happiness in our hearts. It was a world apart, a better, more practical, more justified, more generous, more secure and for that reason more unreal world. How I would go back to it.

'Again, do it again,' he shrieks. Ian laughs his encouragement.

'Keep your eye on it, Matthew, don't lose it.'

A dragonfly drifts between us, hovering as if in thought before circling and moving off. Time to pull a trick. Grunting, I fling upwards again, but when they look to see how high it goes, I slip the ball unnoticed into my pocket while continuing to stare up at the sky. The Keith Miller trick.

'Where is it?' Matthew calls.

'Still up there. Keep watching, it'll come down in a minute.'

He waits, breathless, searching the space above. He looks at me, and I shrug, show him my empty hands. Yes, I am a magician. Ian has seen the joke, but only says, 'Keep watching Matthew. Don't lose it.'

The boy is totally mystified. It doesn't occur to him that he is being tricked. These are his gods, after all.

The late afternoon air is abuzz with insect and birdcalls, all around us a heady mixture of scents—flowers, garden compost, new-mown grass. In the far corner Jo and Elizabeth are in conference over beds of flowers—roses and hollyhocks, azalias and foxgloves. We have never yet grown such things, indeed are dismally ignorant of gardening, and long to learn about it. Up until now our domestic skills have been confined to cooking, washing dishes, making beds and cleaning the floors. It impresses us how much the Parkins know, how they have full command of everything to do with running a home—the kitchen, the garden, the laundry, car maintenance, building repairs—Ian's workshop is a wonderland, and he will master any job from welding to bricklaying. Their world is a mixture of the beautiful and the practical—richly coloured and well-weeded flowerbeds, healthy fruit trees, beds of foot-long runner beans and juicy tomatoes, full lettuces and fat zucchini. How raw and undomesticated, what totally urbanised beings, Jo and I are when we come to this sort of world.

This is only our second visit, and so far it has been a love affair on both sides. I have spent part of the afternoon singing to them all, digging up old songs from my repertoire I haven't thought about for ages. The kids couldn't get enough. In fact, since our first visit both the girls have decided to learn instruments, Kate the violin and Alison the cello. Jo says it has been my influence that decided them; I hope it's true.

After a dinner of roast chicken and potatoes, beans from the garden and a pleasant white wine, we talk while the children busy themselves in their rooms. Ian and Elizabeth love to chat in the evenings. They treat television as an antisocial activity, banished to a small room upstairs at the rear of the house, with an uncomfortable old sofa and a couple of chairs. If you want to watch a program, you have to actually take the trouble to go off on your own to do it. So chatting in the evening, about every topic under the sun, from personal to political, from music to where to buy cheap furniture, is their form of entertainment. In fact, I had been reading a little philosophy, a subject Ian studied in his PPE at Oxford. For some reason I've long forgotten, our talk comes around to Hume and Kant of all things, and something I say about Hume's influence on Kant prompts Ian to demur: it could not have happened, he says, because Kant was earlier than Hume. I say that he is wrong, that the Englishman came first, and Kant took issue with some of Hume's ideas. There is no heat in our discussion, but we both stand our ground, until a serendipitous interruption by the children running into the room forces us to break off. Kate is pressing me to sing 'Johnny McEldoo'—the third time today—before they go off to bed. I take up my guitar and go through it, three intensely delighted faces mouthing every mad Irish word along with me as I sing. They know it better than I do now. Then they bubble off to bed, and Elizabeth brings in coffee and the adults settle down to more talk.

We still don't know a great deal about each other, and especially my background history has begun to puzzle Ian—why is it that I am doing such a menial job? He probes: what is my background—my family, my schooling, my working life, how did I come to play folk music?

And so, with Jo adding the odd detail I am inclined to overlook, I give a sketchy account of my growing up, the death of my father, the decision to send me to a Catholic School, my hating it and leaving to go out to work at the age of fourteen, the saga of my varied and unsatisfying jobs, national service, singing, meeting Jo and coming abroad, and now hibernating dreamily in a kind of cozy cul-de-sac in Essex.

Ian is appalled. He deplores the decision to send me to a Catholic School, and sympathises with my decision to leave, though what offends him most is that the adults around me—specifically my mother and stepfather—had let a child with my ability give up school at fourteen to go and work in a factory. Ian's outrage is something of a shock to me, especially in that it obviously springs from deep convictions about raising children. It brings on the sudden realisation of what has gone wrong with me, the waste that has been allowed to go on, and of my ignorance of much that a decently educated person takes for granted. He does not show any pleasure in doing this—on the contrary, his anger is driven by a warm concern for my welfare. He begins talking about university. I should be doing a degree, he says.

'I couldn't afford it,' I reply.

But Ian doesn't accept this. The English system might well allow me to do it, he says. If I can get a place in a course, I might well be eligible for financial support. And I could be accepted under the Mature Student scheme, without having passed 'A' Level or 'O' Level subjects.

'You've got the ability,' he says confidently, 'and you'd enjoy it enormously.'

No-one before has taken me this seriously; I simply have to treat what he says with the utmost respect. When, around midnight we finally go up to bed, I am unable to sleep. My head is full of unsettling questions, realisations, plans about how I might begin to embark upon a direction. Ian has brought me to some kind of crisis point, and I know that it is now time for me to act.

In the morning I stand in my pyjamas in our huge and comfortable bedroom with its plush pink carpet, looking out across the green sunlit Gloucestershire countryside to the distant Cotswolds. Jo lies in bed asleep, while I think on how to engage her in my personal anguish when she wakes. I know she will support me in whatever I choose to do, know that whatever sacrifices she might have to make, she will make them. I am also confident in her practical know-how, that she will always come up with good sensible proposals to get the most out of our circumstances, our meagre savings and income, and to find manageable places to live in. She is my anchor, no doubt; without her, who knows what kind of life I might drift into.

When she wakes up it is clear this is not the time to foist my turmoil upon her. It will keep till we have time to talk it through; she is keen to get down and join the others for breakfast. As we descend the stairs to the big family kitchen, the smell of percolating coffee and freshly made toast wafts through the hallway. Ian is already there, sitting in the slatted armchair in the box window reading a book. He looks up and says, 'You were right about Kant; I remembered it wrongly, which shows how little I took in of my PPE.' He hands me a book showing the dates of the two philosophers, and some information on them both. Joined by the ever-happy Elizabeth, we settle down to talk over breakfast, and they make practical suggestions of how I might enquire about university courses, where I should begin finding out about grants, eligibility and so on. And he affirms that he would be pleased to write a reference on my behalf when it came to the application process. It all begins to look, if not rosy, certainly a distinct possibility.

Jo was not much happier at Loughton Secondary Modern School than she had been at Epping. Coming in as a new teacher often meant you were handed the classes that nobody else wanted, and in the system then operating this inevitably landed you with the difficult students. She battled on, driving herself to school in the mini after dropping me off at Epping each day, still struggling with health issues which by now I was convinced were caused by low morale. I was not much happier in my pointless job in the school laboratory, though at least my Biology studies at Hertford College were proving to be enjoyable. The feedback I was getting from the excellent woman taking the class cheered me enormously, and my confidence grew. I dissected frogs and rats, examined life-forms under the miscroscope, drew cellular organisation from slide models, wrote essays about evolution, plant and animal differences, and varieties of reproduction, working from excellent textbooks. It was all very absorbing, giving me a reawakened taste for learning, and respect for scientific method.

If our jobs were not bringing us much joy, at least our friends were. Sometime in autumn I heard from my old mate Bob Haberfield, who had got himself married in Melbourne and had arrived in London with his Melanie. They quickly went on to Birmingham, where they stayed a few days with Bob's brother Brian and his wife, and then they headed for Paris, but on their way they stopped a couple of nights with us. It was good to see him again—looking very smart in a dark grey suit, and Melanie very pretty and very young. Another transformation; gone was the drifting and unkempt Beat, he had given up playing flamenco guitar, and was back working hard at freelance artwork. In Paris he had jobs awaiting him creating record covers for Pathe-Marconi, so they planned to get a flat and live there for the foreseeable future. When they were settled, we would pay them a visit.

Our solid body of good English friends made life interesting and sustained our desire to stay in the country. Gradually, without realising it, we were becoming expatriates, surrogate English, with changing accents. Our friends no longer quite thought of us as Australian, just socialised with us as part of the local social fabric. The most recent was a couple, Bernard and Celia, both child welfare officers, who lived at Harlow and were great film buffs. Together we joined the Epping Film Society, and would regularly have dinner somewhere followed by a film in a local community hall, where we would have to wait in the dark while they changed the reels on the 16mm projector; it took me back to the films of my childhood in the Mount Macedon Church Hall, where we would also wait impatiently in the dark, whistling and cat-calling while the reel was changed or mended. We saw some interesting films in that Epping group, including *Battleship Potemkin* and a number of British neo-realist works, such as *Saturday Night and Sunday Morning* and *Billy Liar*, all in black and white. If I add friends Lew and Hilary Davies, Liz and Pete Willson, Jack and Donald from London, Stan and Jenny Jones and the Parkins, we had a rich social pool to draw on. Also, friends and relatives from Australia—Joy Bear in Birmingham and Helen Calf in London, her cousin Margot and her fiancé Geoffrey from London, Jo's Aunt Nan—would drop in on us from time to time. Margot had brought Geoff to meet us after he arrived from living for some time in Greece, where he had got into some bother with the family of a woman he had become involved with. An odd man, a chemist by training, he liked to show off his encyclopedic knowledge of just about everything under the sun. When they arrived at Toot Hill for a weekend, Jo had cooked a fancy roast dinner, but the large-girthed Geoffrey, not being satisfied with our substantial fare, went to the pantry afterward and requested a can of baked beans as a chaser. Moreover, and much to my annoyance, he helped himself to my only three bottles of wine, drinking two of them entirely by himself—we'd had enough after one bottle. When Jo relayed this event in a letter to her mother, she reported that Whit had been shocked beyond belief at Geoff's behaviour: the most insulting act possible, he said, is drinking the last of a man's grog, especially if he was not drinking it with you.

I recall a party we went to near Xmas of that year, 1967, during a very cold spell that brought deep snow all over Essex, especially Toot Hill. The party was at the home of Judy, a leggy art teacher colleague of Lew Davies; Judy's partner George was an obsessive Tolkien fan, and could recite the whole of the first paragraph of *The Hobbit* from memory. On the way home, with Liz and Pete Willson in the car, the snow and ice were rapidly thawing, and I tried to drive the mini through a deep channel of water flooding across the road. Once again the mini's poor design let us down, and the distributor cables got soaked and the car stalled, right in the middle of the flood. We all had to get out in our best clothes and shoes—Liz and Jo were in their fur coats—and push the car out while the freezing water streamed around our ankles. It was a memorable night for another reason, too: Liz and Pete were vocational guidance consultants, and during the evening they were encouraging me about the idea I mentioned of going to university. In fact Liz took us to meet her parents in Norwich over the following weekend, so that I could talk with her father, who worked in administration at the University of East Anglia, and could advise me about making an application. Mr Barnard proved very useful, telling me all about the University Central Council on Admissions (UCCA) and different application strategies.

By this time Jo and I had had a long serious discussion about it all, and had come to the decision to pull out all stops in getting me into a university course. The first thing I had to do, we worked out, was establish my UK residential status. During her mum's stay Jo had taken her to Paris, along with Margot and a couple of her girlfriends, and they had a great time. By way of checking on her ability to get back into the country on an Australian passport, Jo had rung the Home Office and asked about our residential status.

'What was stamped on your passport when you first entered the country?' the officer asked.

'Nothing. Just the date.'

'Well then you can come and go freely, you're a resident.'

'How long can we stay?'

'As long as you like.'

This was to prove a crucial anomaly, for anomaly it was; usually Australian citizens came on a 6-month work permit, and either had to renew it or leave the country. But, by mistake, no such condition had been stamped on our passports, so we were regarded officially as residents. Among other things, this meant that I might well qualify for a County Council Grant to attend university.

I now seriously began the process of applying. After more talking with Ian Parkin and Mr Barnard I decided on two strategies—one to apply to Exeter Teacher's College to do a teaching degree in Biology, for which my performance in 'A' level Biology plus my two Victorian matriculation subjects, English Expression and Literature, would be taken into account. And second, after studying the information provided by UCCA, I would apply to six universities for admission to their particular literature courses, placing the University of Warwick as my first choice; they offered an honours degree in English and American Literature. I was hoping to get in under the Mature Entry scheme, which made anyone over twenty-three eligible to apply without the normal 'A' level subjects, but could be considered on the strength of their experience with the support of a referee after a satisfactory interview by the university. I saw that Ian Parkin's offer to act as my referee could prove crucial.

Just the fact of making the decision suddenly made a huge difference to our lives; succeed or fail, it was giving us both a direction and me something specific to aim at. My writing had come to nothing so far; I had sent off a couple of chapters and a synopsis of the novel I had been working on to Richard Simon at Curtis Brown. This was through Stanley Jones, who knew Simon, so I anticipated getting a sympathetic reading. But still no dice—they 'didn't think it was right for their list at this stage', and Stanley was apologetic in relaying the decision to me. So now I threw myself wholeheartedly into the Biology study, and continued determinedly reading through the collection of Faulkner novels in the local library. The response from Exeter Teacher's College was surprisingly fast in coming. They were keen to have me, probably because of the shortage of teachers, particularly in Science, and wrote that a pass in my 'A' Level Biology along with my two Matriculation English subjects from Melbourne would be perfectly acceptable to them. I could start at the beginning of the academic year, next October. We would not know about the County Council grant for some time yet, but at least this was a real breakthrough, and I began trying to think positively about the idea of becoming a Biology teacher. And yet my preference, and my continuing hope, was that I would get a place in a proper university to study literature, in particular the one at Warwick.

There was something more happening that would shape our future: in March of the new year Jo found she was pregnant. This was no accident: now that we knew what course of action I wanted to pursue, and that we would be staying on in England for the next three years at least, with the chance of financial support, she had decided it was time. 'Besides,' she told me, 'I'd like to have a baby before I get much older,' and I could see that it had been on her mind for some while. In fact, I was sure now that the spate of mysterious illnesses she had been suffering was not just because she was depressed about the teaching, but also frustration at wanting to start a family. Anyway, she stopped taking the pill and immediately got a result. 'Success first time,' she wrote happily to her mother on April 1st, 'Garry really thinks he's clever … It looks like it's due at the end of November.' It was wonderful news for us all. Even so, given our circumstances, it would be a risk if I didn't succeed in my applications, because Jo would have to give up teaching and I would have to take on some sort of work to keep us all. Chances were we would have to return to Australia with our tails between our legs, although Jo very quietly, and her mother likewise, was becoming increasingly happy at the idea of giving birth back in Oz. Indeed, the letters from home, especially Barbara's, told of the growing anxiety amongst our families, not knowing what my university plans might mean for their chances of seeing us in the near future, though of course they were full of high hopes for the outcome to Jo's condition. Barbara was now regretting she'd spent all her spare money on coming to England when she did— she would have felt far more useful being there to help Jo when the baby arrived.

For the Easter holidays we went to Paris to visit Bob and Melanie. There was no room for us to sleep in their little flat in Rue de Faubourg Saint Denis (though its prodigiously high ceilings made it seem spacious) so we took a room just around the corner, and spent day times with them. Bob was busy doing record sleeves for Pathe-Marconi—his own painting had been shelved for the time being—and was very into the current Dylan albums, especially *Highway 61 Revisited* and *Blonde on Blonde* for its originality and surrealistic imagery. He enthused over a number of pieces that excited him, as in the image in 'Memphis Blues Again':

Gran'pa died last week …
I knew he'd lost control
when he built a fire on Main Street
and shot it full of holes.

I could see what he liked about this stuff, being such a devotee of Salvador Dali and René Magritte, but I was never more than lukewarm towards it. I still preferred the political Dylan, still considered the political message of 'Hollis Brown' superior to the drug-inspired aesthetics of 'Desolation Row', impressive-sounding as this was. Music historians now defend Dylan for abandoning 'simplistic' political messages, but as I have already said, in my view his political songs were one of the great things about the 1960s.

As it happened Melanie was pregnant too, at exactly the same stage as Jo, so they had some common ground to meet on. Bob had acquired a kitten called 'Oiseau', totally crazy, would claw its way up the tall curtains in the living room and run hell-for-leather around the plaster shelf at the top of the wall. He also took us to some of his favourite places in Paris, including a wonderful 'Working Man's' restaurant, where you could get good food and wine cheap, and of course we chased up many beautiful art nouveau buildings, including the Metro stations. It has always been wonderful for me to look at the world through Bob's acute eye for the beautiful, the marvellous, the strange; he, more than anyone, taught me how to approach the visual world in a way that I'm sure I would otherwise have missed. We went to the Louvre and the Orangerie, and to the cinema where we saw *Some Like it Hot*. At the Vincennes Zoo, Melanie, in her struggling French, rounded on the animal keepers for their treatment of the monkeys, prodding and goading them with long poles for no reason. Somehow, I can't think why, but we all felt we were important, strutting around Paris, passing judgment, defenders of the good, scourges of life's bastards. Maybe Paris made us feel that way, but alas our stay was all too brief. Before we left Bob told us they would be moving to London, where Melanie would prefer to have her baby, and where she could be closer to her family and the living expenses might be lower.

Back in Toot Hill I learned that I'd been granted an interview by the University of Warwick. I drove alone to Coventry, where the lecturer in charge of American Literature, a young and boyish Dr Clive Bush, was friendly and welcoming. After chatting for a while about my background, he asked me about my reading, so I was able to rattle on about Faulkner; he asked me to spend half an hour writing out my views on Faulkner's South. Straight off the top of my head, not knowing exactly what was required, I plunged in with observations, names of characters—ghosts of the Civil War—the way Faulkner's South was haunted by that defeat, the family legacies, hoping it all made some kind of sense. He took it away to read, and came back smiling: he would be supporting my application and I could expect to get a formal offer in due course through the UCCA system. I drove home to Essex happy and full of pride. We could now begin to make detailed plans for both expectations—baby and uni—both major turning points in our lives.

Through this time, the spring and summer of 1968, life grew busier, which helped us to put the waiting for news from UCCA out of our minds. We had numerous visitors at Toot Hill, including Jo's Aunt Nan, about whom I'd heard so much from Barbara and Jo, but had met only once, briefly, when our ship docked in Sydney for a day. Barbara's letters often mentioned her sister Nan, who was currently on a tour to the US and England, and being a strong believer in the importance of family, and particularly fond of Jo, there was no chance of her passing up the opportunity to come and see us. I was aware of a certain amount of family trepidation about this meeting between Nan and me, mainly because of her zealous Christianity and my atheism, quiescent though it mostly was; surely, they thought, we would detest each other. But nothing could have been farther from the truth. Nan certainly was religious—she was a member of the Moral Rearmament movement and her beliefs coloured every aspect of her life, but I found her possessed of a wonderful idealism and generosity of spirit, a love of art and music and ideas. We did, however, try to keep clear of the uncomfortable subject of religion. She was a stately virgin in her late 60s, with a large head capped in short white hair, a somewhat manly face, and behind her rimless glasses gleamed faintly shadowed eyes of falcon-like alertness. We talked at length during her stay, about England, about our lives, about all kinds of high-falutin subjects—she was not one for small talk—and at all times she was interesting, open-minded and a fine listener. I came to know, as did Jo, that in Nan I had a friend for life.

In April I heard from UCCA that I'd been given, not a definite offer from Warwick, but a 'Waiting List' place. I was of course deeply disappointed, as was Jo. She had already written back home telling everyone of my successful interview, but now she had to write again with the news that it was not actually certain that I would be going to university. She told her mother that my family had always thought that university 'was not for people like us', and that my big fear was that my background was always going to be against me. This was true enough, and certainly I had moments of self-doubt when I read the UCCA letter, and my feelings of pride gave way to despondency. But I didn't give up hope. I quickly wrote to Clive Bush at Warwick asking if something had gone wrong, and what my chances of eventual success were. A prompt letter came back telling me not to worry, that I was first on the waiting list, and would certainly be offered a place, but wouldn't hear this formally until August. We still had the agony of waiting, but I managed to breathe easier, though we still didn't quite feel able to make definite plans to move away from Essex, my job and our house. Tony Curnock, my tweed-wearing, Sunbeam-driving boss at the school, was annoyed at this situation, as he had a right to be, given that he needed to start looking for a replacement laboratory technician before the school year started. He saw no reason why Warwick couldn't make their decision straight away, since it did not depend on my 'A' Level results. Impatiently, Tony picked up the phone and rang the university, asking in his best County accent to speak directly to the Registrar.

'You have an applicant Kinnane on your waiting list; I'm his employer. Why can't a decision be made immediately?'

A period of silence followed while the Registrar checked the applications, and I stood breathless with my eyes fixed on Tony holding the phone. Then, clearly, the Registrar said he would relay the call through to the Head of English. So Tony put the same question again, and, after a few minutes more of silence, he was being told something.

'Well, he's a married man with a child on the way,' Tony replied in crisp, no-nonsense tones, 'and they need to get their accommodation sorted as soon as possible. So what's the hold up?'

A few more anxious seconds of silence while Tony listened, until finally he said, 'Thank you very much, I'll let him know.'

After putting down the phone, Tony paused while he looked directly at me— the most ham-acted, self-important, patrician-eyed, smug-mouthed and calculated pause humanly possible—and simply said:

'You're in.'

He then donned his grouse hat and walked, in somewhat stately silence, from the room, but not before pausing at the door and turning back to say to me:

'Make us a cuppa, there's a good chap. Back soon.'

Late in April news came from Trevor Lucas of a reunion of Melbourne 'Folkies' in London. As well as Trevor there was Martyn Wyndham-Reid and Brian Mooney. Brian had graduated from being an imaginary Irishman to an actual one, having married an Irish girl and taken up residence in Galway, where he was to stay for many years and raise a family, continuing to sing and paint. Much as I enjoyed seeing my old friends again, I knew in my heart I was heading now in a different direction from when I was one of them, and would probably see little of them again. This is an aspect of my personality that has frequently surfaced, and which I am not proud of whenever I look back on it. The cavalier way I have let friendships lapse, or have not taken the trouble to keep in touch, must have often seemed arrogant to people over the years. I have no excuses to offer, and my one explanation is to put it down to a kind of laziness, but I suspect it runs deeper than this. I suspect that my periodic dissatisfaction with myself and the life I am leading at different times has created in me a fear of being 'fixed' by my friendships, and a fear that I am trapped in the way that friends regard me. I presume they will not understand me correctly if I change from the person they know and like to one who is different from that, so I avoid the discomfort by avoiding them. This is a very reductive and unfair assessment of their capacity to be flexible, and in itself ascribes to them the very 'fixity' that I fear they will exercise on me. It is part of a desire to keep my life orderly, manageable, and it makes me somewhat narrow and less generous than I would like, shrinking my life down to a limited demand on time, interests and sympathies. I often wish I were one of those expansive, generous-hearted, welcome-all types who let people into my life regardless of their views of me—a sort of skinnier Brian Blessed; but I know I have neither the confidence nor the heartiness to live like that. In my defence, I can say that I hang loyally on to the handful of close friends I have kept, and care deeply about what happens to them and their loved ones; it is just a pity that I have not extended this loyalty to the many more good people I have been lucky to call my friends at one time or another, and have thereby wasted enriching opportunities. Ah, Life. Like so many things in this world, I'd have made a better fist of it if I were doing it for the second time.

In June Jo finished at Loughton, hoping of course that this was the last teaching job she would have to do for some time. It had become a slog for her, the constant battle with uncooperative students in poorly run schools; like most teachers, she got great enjoyment from it when the students wanted to learn, but that was becoming less and less the case. Now, with the move north ahead of us, including packing up and finding accommodation, there was plenty to do over the summer break. Bob and Melanie came to stay for a few days just before they moved into their London flat, so they had to bring their cat Oiseau with them. As it happened, she was on heat, a condition that won her unstinting attention from Nico and Alexi, both toms you'll recall. Oiseau played the coy mistress for much of time, backing herself into an open cardboard box, with just enough room either side of her to roll about seductively, but denying access from the rear. Our two went bananas trying to find their way in, though Alexi, typically superior, eventually gave it up as too much trouble. Nico, on the other hand, fell completely in lust, and sat on the rug facing her for hours on end, looking lovesick and sorry for himself. 'Please', he was thinking, 'please have pity and let me in'. At some point when we weren't looking we figured that he finally got his wicked way, because in London a few months later Oiseau produced a litter of kittens with ginger markings; of course, for all we knew it had been the suave Alexi who had coolly beaten his brother to it, moving in to suit himself at the opportune moment.

Later that month we went to London for Margot's Registry wedding to Geoffrey, which went off well, with them both looking happy to have sorted out their various reservations. Then we visited the Parkins, who had become our surrogate parents by this time, and always ready with practical advice and help.

When we arrived Ian said, with that engaging mock-seriousness that was more serious than mock and always took me unawares:

'Matthew is still waiting for that ball to come down.'

Apparently he kept nicking out into the garden and peering up expectantly, still brooding over the mystery.

We talked about the move now that Warwick was settled, and they suggested Coventry as our best bet.

'In fact,' said Ian, 'why don't you think about buying a place? It'd probably be cheaper than renting if you could get a mortgage, and you'd make something on it when you left.'

Such a possibility had never occurred to us; we'd never bought any property, hardly knew what a mortgage was, and certainly didn't realise how affordable it could be. We said we'd look into it. Meanwhile I told Ian about problems we were having with the Mini. It had already cost us money to repair a leaking fuel tank, and the mechanic had informed us that the frame underneath had nearly rusted through—a common problem in England, where the salt laid on the roads to thaw the snow in winter plays havoc with car bodies. A bad time to have to replace the car, with money tight and a few years of economic stringency ahead of us. Ian suggested trying an auction place he knew at nearby Tewkesbury, so next morning we went along to see what was on offer. Customers were allowed to inspect the cars in the yard waiting to be sold, and to start them up, but not drive them out of the yard. We saw a handsome little red and white 1956 Vauxhall Velox, which was very clean and sounded fine when we ran the engine. Impulsively, I decided to bid for it, and when the hammer fell I'd got it for £100. Driving it back to Alderton, however, I discovered a problem: it wouldn't shift from second into top gear. Ian had a look and concluded it had been a botched gear-box job, and would probably cost as much to repair as I'd paid for the car. We decided to leave it with Ian to rerun it through the auction the following week. He phoned me when he had done this and said, 'I put it back in the auction, and it slowly got up to £80, which I thought was looking good, until the auctioneer turned to me with a helpless look and said, "I haven't had a bid yet."' All the 'bids' had so far been fictions. It didn't sell that day, or the week after. Finally, on the third attempt, someone paid £80 for it, and Ian, feeling guilty because it was all his idea, made my refund up to £100 out of his own pocket.

Nor were our car trials over, though I gave up on the auction idea. A week or so later I traded the Mini in on a nice-looking white VW Beetle for about £300 from a car yard in Ongar. On our trip up to look for accommodation in Coventry the engine blew up, and we had to limp home in abject misery. It cost over £100 for the parts to repair it, with the labour covered under warranty. Such are the joys of used cars. Our finances were continually coming under strain, but Barbara back in Australia was managing to send us a little money from time to time, often rescuing us from dire straits when there were bills we were unable to pay.

When we finally got to look around Coventry for somewhere to live, it was clear there was not much on offer, and rents more expensive than we'd hoped. Buying a house looked a better prospect, and Jo enquired with the local Council. The problem was the County Council Grant—we didn't know for certain that we would get it, and even then we would need to find around £500 of our own money to get a mortgage. Jo asked her mother if she could spare a loan, and we contemplated selling the car, but it was beginning to look too tight and chancy to subject everything else to the delayed advantages of ownership, when it was *now*—the next three years—that we needed money. So we kept looking for rental prospects, and the only one possible was an offer in response to an advertisement we placed in the local paper. We looked it over without enthusiasm, because although it was reasonably priced at £6 per week including rates, it had a totally inadequate kitchen with a 2-burner stove and no bench space, and the ugliest carpet in the world—green and orange roses two feet in diameter. When we went back a week later to settle the rent, we decided it was too awful, and pulled out. Luckily, Clive Bush and his wife Rachel offered us a room for a few days in the empty university digs in Kenilworth, where they were wardens, so we had some time to look around. While we were there they arranged a dinner, inviting a friend they particularly wanted us to meet—another mature student who was in his third year studying literature, but doing the English and European stream rather than American. It proved an auspicious occasion. He arrived with the obligatory bottle of wine, a dark-haired, good-looking Irishman about my age and size—a little heavier—with a softly resonant Dublin accent and the manners of a prince. Vincent Mahon, he was called, and by the end of the evening I was hoping we would get to see more of him, much, much more.

One idea we had was a Council House, and our enquiry looked hopeful, though it would mean settling for an 'unpopular' area—meaning Asian and West Indian immigrants. That didn't necessarily worry us, but we nevertheless had to wait for a flat to come vacant, which could take months. The university Housing Office had nothing for people in our situation, and the few ads we could find were for expensive houses—the likes of £10 pw. By this time we had learned that the Grant from Essex County Council was approved. With allowances for a wife and child we would get around £12 pw, so it was going to be lean living indeed, and I would probably need to do some sort of paid work in the summer vacations. But it was manageable. After several more unsatisfactory inspections we still had not found a place, and by mid-July we were getting desperate. But then an ad appeared in the local paper offering a 'large house needing redecorating' for a mere £3.10 pw, giving an address to write to. No, we thought, let's front up right away and try to see it. Luckily, the landlord, old Mr Gurney, seemed to like us or else be in a particularly good mood, for he happily agreed to show us the place. It was just what we were after—3 large bedrooms and two sitting rooms, plus a small dining room leading onto a scullery kitchen. Admittedly there was no heating of any kind, no water to the bath and no hot water system at all, the lavatory was down at the end of the good-sized yard, and there was no furniture or floor covering. There was a large crack in the lintel over the front door, though it didn't look dangerous. The place was going to need work, but it would be worth it. Would Mr Gurney pay for materials if we put in the redecorating work?

He was a nice old gentleman, not in the slightest a mean landlord. Tall and lean, with a long nose and pendulous ears and lips, prodigious hands and feet, he animated his deep lined face with a generous, gap-toothed mouth. While we stood in the dining room talking things over, I rolled myself a cigarette, using the sweetly aromatic 'Old Holborn' tobacco I so liked at that time.

'Oh,' said Mr Gurney, 'Old Holborn eh? I used to smoke that years ago. Is it still tenpence ha'penny a packet?'

Dear old Mr Gurney—he'd not been keeping up with the way of the world, which was probably one reason he wanted such a low rent for the house.

'No Mr Gurney; it's three and six now.'

'Don't tell me!' he said, 'Here, give us a sniff.'

'Would you like to roll one?'

'Oow, I couldn't could I? Do you mind?'

I handed him the small yellow and brown tin and the packet of papers. He was happy to pay for redecorating materials, he said, if we did the work, 'And, lucky for you, I've already made a start on the woodwork upstairs.' When we looked at the balustrading it was the most repellant shit-brown imaginable, but we bit our tongues and said nothing, and made it clear we loved the place.

We returned the following week to finalise the details. 'Just as well you came to see it last week,' he said, 'I've had forty letters this week asking to rent the place.'

We concluded we were destined to have it. And over a cup of tea in his sitting room, along with Mrs Gurney, he told us an extraordinary tale.

'You know that crack in the lintel over the front door?' he said. 'Well that happened on the night of the bombing, November 1940; we were living there then. It was the most incredible night of our lives. It started about harpast nine, we heard the planes come over and didn't think nothink of it at first, thought they was ours. But then the bombs started to fall, on and on—mostly over towards the city and away from us, but even so it was loud and—oh relentless it was. Crash, crash, crash. You know Coventry wasn't all that well defended, none of us dreamed we would be targeted—it was London, always London that was copping it. Anyway, I said to her (nodding at Mrs Gurney) we'd best clear out of here, we don't wanna be inside if the house gets hit. So we got in the car and drove out to Kenilworth. Well, when we got to Kenilworth we got out of the car, and you know it's a bit of a hill and you can see Coventry quite clearly from there. It was a clear night—a big full moon that night—which is unusual for Coventry at that time of year—nearly Christmas it was—usually there's fog. Well we looked back, and the whole city was burning—fires everywhere, flames leaping high up into the sky, which I worked out later was the Cathedral going up, and the bombers were still givin' it to 'em, still pounding the place on and on. And then she turned to me and she said, 'But our house and all our things are still there. Everything we own. We have to go back.' I realised she was right, there was no sense in staying out there, so we got in the car to drive back. Well. I've never seen nothink like it. When we got close-in there were buildings burning everywhere. It was hard to find a way through, rubble and stuff everywhere, fires in front of us. We turned down one street, just north of the city, and the whole street was on fire, road and all—gas pipes I suppose, but you couldn't drive down it, it was just one whole big burning street, and bodies lying in the road. Oh, it was awful. Then we went another way, and turned down where the road goes under the railway line—thought we might get through there. But you couldn't get through the underpass because the train had been hit and a carriage was dangling—just dangling—over the side and blocking the way. God knows if there was anyone in it, I s'pose there would have been. Anyway, I don't know how but we got home to Gulson Road, and the house was still standing, hadn't been hit, though plenty nearby had, and that's probably how the lintel got cracked from the shock. Inside there was nothing to do but go to bed, there was no electricity, no gas or water or anything. Even though the bombs were still going on in the city and industrial areas. So we went to bed and tried to sleep through it, which we eventually did. When we woke up I looked at me watch and it said nine o'clock, but I thought it must have been wrong for it were still dark, there were no lights or anything, and it was dead quiet so we knew the raids must have finished. I went out in the street to see if anyone was about but I couldn't see a thing. And then we grasped that it wasn't quite black dark but a kind of dark grey, and you couldn't see the sky or anything else much and we realised, didn't we love, that it was ash, that the sky and the air all around and over everything was just full of ash. It was actually nine o'clock in the morning, and the sun was shining up there somewhere, but no-one in the town could see it because everything was just covered in this thick blanket of dark grey ash. God it was awful. And the smell, and the air toxic, and the quiet with everyone in shock, or dead, or who knows. We'll never forget it, will we love? But we were one of the lucky ones. There were hundreds killed, and most of the city was destroyed.'

There was now only the winding-up of Toot Hill, the transporting of our moderate haul of belongings, including of course Nico and Alexi, about whose travel capabilities we were decidedly anxious. In the last couple of weeks in the cottage we did have a couple of visitors, John McClelland, a good friend of Jo's parents, who was attending a conference of hospital managers in London, and a much more difficult guest, Ian Harrison, the 'Good Samaritan' who had been responsible for introducing the mad Alice into our lives when we lived in the flat in Ladbroke Grove. Now it was Ian who needed help—he was depressed and broke, and worse, had no qualifications to get him into the kind of work he wanted, which was social work. He had been brilliant running an Adventure Playground in London, but when that finished he was at a loss to know what to do. We talked long hours into the night about the possibility of him applying for some sort of course—university or similar—but I could see that his lack of confidence and a quite paranoid belief that The System would always defeat his plans was a huge stumbling block. He left us with a little more hope than he'd arrived I think, but I was anxious for him and insisted that he keep in touch with us when we moved. But he never did, and I don't know what ultimately became of him.

There had been much talk between us and the family over names for the baby. Lots of suggestions for a girl came up—Melissa and Melanie and Camilla and Clara—but we always liked Anna best, and felt it went well with Kinnane. Boy's names were more of a problem. Jeremy and Benjamin—god knows why we considered Biblical names—were possibles but posed certain problems, not least that there was already a Jeremy in Barbara's family whose reputation didn't altogether make the name attractive to us—very right wing. I don't recall that we ever did decide on a name for a boy.

So now there was just the move into 173 Gulson Road, Coventry. It occasioned the first real setback we experienced since we left London. About a week after we arrived, and still living in the chaos of arranging furniture, decorating, and beginning the plumbing I had planned, Nico and Alexi disappeared. We had kept them inside all week, knowing they would be unfamiliar with the urban environment of Coventry if they got out, and planned to train them gradually to explore outside. Eager to find their way home, they tried climbing up the chimney, scratched at the windows, cried pitifully. But the first night we allowed one to go—it was Alexi—he simply didn't come back. That made Nico all the more anxious, and he got out when we opened the back door the following night, and he, too, didn't return. We waited all next day in hope, and roamed the streets calling them and asking if anyone had seen them, but to no avail. We felt terrible, and both of us went into a deep depression for a week. I remember we listened over and over to one of our favourite recordings—the Mozart Piano Concerto No. 21—for solace, and to this day I can't hear the slow movement without tearing up, so vividly does it rekindle the sadness we felt. But we had to pull ourselves out of it, there was work to be done, and much that mattered to look forward to.

With the sage advice of Ian Parkin and the brilliant simplicity of Yorkshire fittings, I managed to fit a secondhand gas fire in every room, install an instant hot water system and, with the help of an actual plumber, fit an inside toilet in the scullery cupboard. Pete and Liz Willson, our friends from Essex, came to help us get stuck into the decorating. Using a mixture of paint and wallpaper we brightened up the rooms, painted the front door vivid yellow, and the hideous mottled glitter wall tiles around the dining room fireplace a nice flat dark blue. On the floor in the big room upstairs we put our lovely old rug we'd bought in Brentwood, and through the dining room and kitchen laid linoleum fetchingly patterned in black and white diamonds. We must have picked up some more carpeting for the bedrooms somewhere, but I can't recall where.

By the time I was ready to start at university the place was ship-shape, warm and comfortable, more than adequate for the small family we were about to become. In fact, we decided to let the spare bedroom, and a few days before classes began a post-graduate student from Cambridge answered our ad in the Student Union. Tall, blond, bespectacled and dogged with nasty acne, Hugo Radice appeared at our front door, eager and willing to join us. He proved to be a gentle, thoughtful housemate, notwithstanding a fiercely active socialist. But more of that later.

One other discovery at Gulson Road: the back corner of the yard was overgrown with blackberries, which the locals called brambles, and in this late summer were dotted with juicy black fruit fatter than I'd ever seen. It wasn't so much the fruit that was the discovery—it was that I found I could make jam. Numerous pots of lovely, rich, blackberry jam. It was something to cheer us up in the wake of the terrible loss of our little ginger mates.

7

THAT FIRST WEEK AT WARWICK was like trying to make sense of a stirred-up ants nest: hurrying bodies—young, fashionably dressed, eager-faced—looking for this lecturer, that room, the other building. I knew no-one except Vincent Mahon, who, being a third-year veteran, was keeping himself well clear of this first-week chaos. The Department of English and Comparative Literature was temporarily housed in one wing of a white-tiled building. I passed along its brightly lit corridors reading the names on the gallery of doors, wondering who they were and what they looked like, all unknown to me then. Even the fame of one Dr Greer was confined at that time to the second and third year students, and those who had seen her doing oddball street interviews on TV.

The university itself was a mere three years old and still mostly a building site, with piles of materials strewn about, trucks, safety fencing propped in pockets of vast fields of grass scarred with mud-tracks between buildings. The exception was a single white concrete path that snaked across from the faculty buildings to the Student Union, a path every lunch hour crowded with pilgrims heading for the mecca of the refectory, the bar and the pervasive broadcast music; it was all Rock, of course, exclusively high fashion bands like Cream, The Band, The Who and such. 'Wheels on Fire' burnt into my brain as the soundtrack to my radically altered life. 'The Weight' beat a daily accompaniment to meals of gluggy pasta or congealing stew in the Union refectory, or sucked-up mouthfuls of Coke as I squatted among fellow students holding shouted conversations over the deafening PA. I was a generation older than them, and they all seemed frighteningly beautiful and deeply learned in the current fashions, from choice of clothes to the producers of the best marijuana. 'Lebanese Red' was all the go, cheap and plentiful. Personally, I never touched the stuff. Well, rarely.

Once past the confusions of orientation week, I worked out the protocols of the tutorial and how to make the most of the lectures, and began to find the whole experience inexpressibly wonderful. It was a privilege to be immersed in that world of ideas, of language used well, of argument and opinion, of learned minds and civilised rivalries. It was shaping up to be the happiest, most intellectually stimulating time of my life. First year consisted of four subjects in each semester—in my case Italian language and literature; the Epic Tradition (reading Homer,

Virgil, the Bible as literature, Milton); Medieval literature; Modern literature. There were long hours of reading into the night, writing essays that sorely tested my powers of argument, clarity of expression, ability to work to deadlines.

The lectures could be stimulating or boring, depending on the lecturer. The tutorials, consisting of no more than ten students, provided a blend of directed discussion and intimacy in which my talkative tendencies were often exposed as rhubarb and uninformed. Considering the laziness of many students, the academic staff was on the whole friendly and 'soft' on us. There was one exception to this, though I would not experience his tutorial methods until third year: Professor George Kirkpatrick Hunter, the head of department and controlling architect of the whole course. I did get an inkling of his intellectual rigor from his lectures in the Epic course, which were closely argued expositions on the historical and philosophical nature of Epic, including a treatment of the Bible that put some of my pre-university reading into a new perspective. On one occasion early in the semester I was foolish enough to raise my hand and ask a question during a lecture, something undergraduates rarely did. I suppose being that much older made me a little less intimidated, and I admit to a partial desire to show off my esoteric reading in front of the younger students. He had been talking about the meaning of the Abraham and Isaac section of Genesis. It so happened that I had a couple of years earlier read Søren Kierkegaard's discussion of the issue in *Fear and Trembling*, and it had occurred to me at the time that the assertion of faith in Abraham's willingness to sacrifice his son is somewhat undermined four chapters earlier in Genesis, when the Lord tells Abraham that his wife Sarah will bear him a son, to be called Isaac, and that He will place the future of his religion with Isaac 'and with his seed after him'. In other words, Abraham *knows* that Isaac will live to become a man, a father and leader of his people, so for this to happen the child-sacrifice on the mountain will have to be in some way voided. The test of Abraham's unquestioning faith in the Lord is therefore no test at all.

I put this to Professor Hunter in my question. After a moment's hesitation he gave me a humourless Caledonian grin, and asked me my name. 'Well Misterrr Kinnane,' he replied in his broad Glaswegian brogue, 'ye mus' note rread the Baibul as thawe it wearr a *knowvel*.' Of course, I said to myself, that is a perfect answer. I was suitably corrected, but it did not, it emerged later, harm my standing in his eyes, though I daresay some of my fellow students thought I was either mad or up myself.

I won't get bogged down in the details of my studies, which would have little meaning for most people. But I will take the opportunity here to discuss the whole issue of the teaching of literary studies as I found it at Warwick back then, compared with how it has been eroded and trivialised in the past two decades in most universities around the world, especially, but not exclusively, the second-rate ones. George Hunter had designed the undergraduate course to take advantage of the British Honours degree system, which specialised in a selected major discipline right from the start, and took only three years to complete. You spent little time on disciplines other than your chosen field, which in my case was literature. It was designed to give a solid foundation to the study of literature as a historical body of knowledge, from medieval to modern, encompassing the intermediate four centuries of important literary achievements. Critical reading was eclectic, unformulated and of secondary importance to knowledge of the works themselves, and biographical approaches were discouraged. Theory, as such, was largely technical and insignificant. There was no important genre or writer left out, and the Epic course gave a background and a reference point in the Classics for much of the later literature in English. It was a comprehensive program designed to serve the student going on to teach or conduct postgraduate research in literary studies in English, and it is the kind of course that has now largely disappeared.

In this day of total student choice, where no subjects are mandatory, graduates might emerge having studied nothing earlier than the 20th century, instead filling their time doing 'creative' writing exercises that are mostly unreadable and certainly unpublishable, exchanging jargon-filled gossip on Hollywood 'icons' (was there ever a term more misused?) or reading theoretical or politically correct demolitions of classic works they haven't read nor are ever likely to. Their idea of the 'historical' is largely limited to works belonging to the fashion before the current one. Norman Mailer and Samuel Beckett, for instance, are 'historical'.

The natural distractions affecting the young lead them to favour the familiar over the non-familiar, so if you don't require them to learn something outside their immediate comfort zone, they usually won't. We are raising a generation of 'literature' graduates who've never studied Shakespeare, can't read Middle English, let alone Old English, have never heard of Pope or Fielding, have no idea how to read Milton, are too impatient to finish 19th century novels, and seriously entertain the notion that white, male, heterosexual writers should be banned from university syllabuses altogether. I am, therefore, forever grateful to GK Hunter and the belief in literary history that shaped the course at Warwick, and the legacy that has been such a central and enjoyable element in my life. Today's students don't know what they're missing. Am I simply curmudgeonly? I don't believe so. It is not just a question of the young student's healthy right to choose the Present over the Past;

the problem is they aren't taught that it is only when the Present becomes the Past that you can get it into proper perspective, and undergraduates need to study the Past in order to weigh the value of the Present. Enough, I'm done.

As I drove off to a daily university life that was hugely enjoyable for me, my heavily pregnant Jo was having a less-than-enjoyable, indeed lonely time of it in the house at Gulson Road. But she kept herself busy and as cheerful as she could, attending a clinic on natural childbirth methods and breast-feeding; she gathered that there was some resistance to it in hospitals, so was steeling herself to take on the establishment if necessary. She was also insisting that I be present at the birth, which might be putting us in line for another battle with the conservative medicos, though I must say I was more scared of the actual birthing than the doctors. Jo was reading Spock and other writers on raising children, and exploring the consumer world of nappy-liners and wet-strength tissues, and the homey economies of knitting rather than buying expensive baby clothes. Her body was growing increasingly uncomfortable, giving her sleeping and indigestion problems, and she came down with a tummy bug, for which the doctor was absolutely useless. About as useless as I was, though I at least offered moral support.

We did try to keep life as normal as possible, visiting Jo's friend Joy and her ill-mannered husband Andy in Birmingham; it was his birthday and I gave him a box of mini-cigars, which he proceeded to smoke in front of me all evening without a hint of offering me one. Or we would go over to the Parkins for a weekend, which always gave us a great fillip, as did the magical drive through the Cotswolds along the way. And Kate Parkin delighted us with a puppet show, including a dog-puppet who sang 'Please give my bone to my master when I'm gone', a send-up of country and western sentimentality that had us rolling about in laughter.

One afternoon quite suddenly Jo's aunt Irene and uncle George dropped in on us on a motoring tour they were doing through England. The house was in its usual chaos, but we managed to feed them before settling into a long and animated discussion, heated at times, on the politics of the age. Hugo, our radical boarder was there, and in typical fashion didn't hold back. George and Irene were lively, conservative, well-heeled folk who took a right-wing line on just about every aspect of life. He was a successful self-made man—owned a small engineering firm—and aunt Irene once proudly announced that she could not live in any suburb other than Melbourne's Toorak. At one point Hugo was arguing against elitist salaries, insisting, with some very cogent reasoning, that all incomes should be the same. Uncle George found this preposterous. 'What if,' said Hugo, 'I could find a formula for organising the country's economy so that every person, whatever job they did, was paid the same salary as everyone else, and that it was a salary that gave them a comfortable lifestyle—better than most have now. Would you agree that would be a good thing?'

'No,' said uncle George, 'because as the owner of the factory, or the manager, I deserve more.'

'So that whatever they got, you believe you deserve more than them. It's a comparative, and competitive thing: they don't deserve the same as you, even if it were possible?'

'Absolutely,' said uncle George. He wasn't being perverse; he was serious. And of course he had the vast majority of people in the developed world on his side, and no doubt still does. But even now, in the 21st century, I'm still with Hugo, in principle; in practice, of course it could never happen. That, in my view, is further evidence of our tragic propensity to failure.

We argued long into the night, though it never became unpleasant, never turned nasty. Hugo was too nice a chap, and uncle George and aunt Irene were cognisant of their visitor status, both in our house and in the heartland of class distinction, good old monarchist England; they didn't want to seem to be red-neck colonials. So we agreed to differ, the night came to a close, and they went on their way. Looking back, I suppose it was a case of student idealism versus older generation 'realism', but even after all these years I'm still not inclined to accept self-interest as a satisfactory economic philosophy; it might provide jobs, but if that were the main aim of industrial capitalism it does it neither efficiently nor with any security for anyone, especially in unregulated markets. If profits come first, satisfying work will in most cases come second, and the rich and powerful will always exploit the poor and vulnerable.

I so enjoyed making friends among my fellow students. They were, in keeping with the times, eager to be radicalised, open-hearted, always respectful to me as an older colleague. Indeed, they flattered me much of the time, listening intently as I ran off at the mouth and threw my opinions about in class and out. I can't match faces with their names now, but there were Sarahs and Janes, and Judiths and Sallys, and there were Martins and Steves and Alans and Richards. No first-name Madisons or Addisons, Kennedys or Rileys, no Jasons or Jaxsons or Bradens or Kaydens; celebrity had not yet become the sole measure of worth or interest among the young, and communication was still largely face-to-face, not text-to-text.

The new young editor of the university paper, *Campus*, asked me to be Arts editor, and this gave me the very pleasant privilege of free tickets to most of the theatrical and musical events at the university and in Coventry. Every week we would produce an edition, and I would stay back in the Union office till late at night writing copy and helping with the layout. Both in class and in-between I got involved in the life of the university as much and as deeply as it was possible for me to do, given of course the circumstances of my life as a married man about to become a father for the first time, and needing to get home to see my poor abandoned wife occasionally.

It was too easy to forget that other dimension to my life, with Jo on her own much of the day. At least we had made the house comfortable, our meagre income supplemented by Hugo sharing the house, and we had a reliable car. But there is no denying the fact that she was lonely much of the time, with few friends around her, and our Australian families too far away to help her through these last months of pregnancy. The Parkins, with their welcoming warmth and common sense, especially Elizabeth's, were the nearest thing we had to a family at that time in 1968. And the drive through the Cotswolds to visit them in Alderton was always hauntingly beautiful, and recurs in my dreams even to this day. The first time we did it was in summer, when the lush, hilly countryside was steeped in that luminous green that is unique to England. The sloping fields, the oaks and elms forming darkening tunnels over the roads, the silent farms and ochre-stone village houses betraying not a sign of their residents behind lace curtains, play in my mind like an old film. And even more vividly, the memories of the region in wintertime, when the green has gone, and in its place snow sits on leafless boughs and spreads across fields and fringes the rooftops like whipped cream. Patches of black ice made driving hazardous, and the villages seemed even more deserted than before; it was as if the whole world had gone into hibernation. One time, driving across an open section just past Stow-on-the-Wold, the car suddenly broke down and wouldn't re-start. I stood on the roadside clawed by a freezing wind, trying to figure out what had gone wrong. In the end we had to walk to a farmhouse and ring the Parkins, who came to rescue us. The car had to undergo major electrical repairs, which kept us happily ensconced in the Parkin home for days.

Despite all our preparations, the Great Moment caught us napping—literally—on November 11th when Jo's contractions came and her waters broke at five in the morning. My first task, as we'd agreed, was to ring the hospital and tell them we were coming. Our budget did not run to owning a phone, so I had to go out and find a public one. One thing I hadn't done was to ascertain where the phone boxes were situated. I drove the Beetle down Gulson Road towards the city hoping to see one any minute, but with no luck. Frantically I circled the deserted city centre until I spotted one not far from the cathedral, so I pulled over, got my money ready, only to find it had been vandalised—the coins wouldn't go in. I drove some more, and found another. Same thing, with the receiver detached from the body and dangling by its cord from the door handle. God I cursed those vandals. Eventually I found one in working order, actually only one street behind our house, an area I hadn't thought of searching first. By that time it was 5.45 am. The coins went in and the hospital emergency answered; I never thought a calm voice could sound so irritating. 'Just put a towel under her and bring her in,' she said, as if Jo was a radio or a toaster to be repaired.

I can't recall all the steps in the process, but Jo's insistence that I be present at the birth was respected by the hospital staff, and I stood beside the bed holding her hand while she struggled through the labour pains, bravely smiling at me in between efforts. The tiny dark-haired crown appeared, but it took a long period of pushing and puffing before the little one finally emerged, at 11.20 am. Jo described it soon afterwards in a letter to her mother:

… I was never frightened or panicky, and earned a few compliments from the midwives because I was so relaxed. I certainly wouldn't say it was painless; I had a bad backache most of the time, but it wasn't unbearable and I'm sure a dentist could hurt worse. It was marvellous to have Garry there, not just for his presence, but he could help by holding my back, or putting a wet flannel on my forehead. Poor thing got a bit worried at the end, because she slowed down just as her head should have come out, and when she came she was bright blue—she had the cord around her neck, which probably accounts for the slow birth.

Unexpectedly I was ordered to stand away from the bed. The big African nurse, after announcing 'It is a little girl', whipped the baby away over to the other side of the room, under the opalescent light of a line of windows. Things went suddenly a little tense as I realised that not a sound had yet come from the baby, and for what seemed an eternity the nurse silently worked at something over her (clearing gunk from her mouth and throat, as it turned out). As the other midwife went over and assisted her I thought to myself, 'Oh no, not a disaster, please, after all this waiting and hoping; we couldn't bear it.' But eventually it came, the little cry, and Jo looked across at me and gave a tired but beatific smile. The unwashed baby was brought to her and placed in her arms, a real madonna-and-child moment, and we whispered to the squirming bundle, 'Hello little Anna Louise'. I remember having the astonishing thought that there was suddenly another person in the room, and she hadn't come in through the door! Another realisation was that she had arrived at the eleventh hour of the eleventh day of the eleventh month—Armistice day; surely an auspicious beginning for our first-born!

Jo stayed in hospital all that week, so of course I had to fend for myself. When I told some of my student friends about the situation, two of the girls suddenly decided to turn all domestic, and insisted on coming round to cook and clean for me; I think they got a kick out of playing housewife for a few days. Since I had two essays to get in by the end of that week, I was quite happy to let them have their fun. When Jo and Anna came home we had a head-wetting party, consisting mainly, once again, of my student friends, who had become a great lot of mates. Vincent was among them, and we enjoyed ourselves far into the night. Little Anna's features had acquired definition by now, and everyone was besotted by her—a healthy sturdiness, very even facial structure, and the widest, happiest grin imaginable. And we were the proudest parents on the planet.

Letters of congratulation came from back home, and Jo's mother Barbara especially was feeling her maternal instincts suffering constant frustration. How painfully she wanted to help Jo, how terribly she wanted to hold her granddaughter and begin to form a connection. She sent us a poem she penned, just before the birth, expressing her joy:

> *So blow all the bugles and sound all the trumpets*
> *And clash all the cymbals, and dance and rejoice*
> *With me as a grandma, a joyful old grandma—*
> *Sing heigh and sing ho at the top of your voice!*

Even Whit, Jo's stepfather, was moved to write a rare missive of good wishes, including some tongue-in-cheek patriotic sentiments about teaching her 'The Man From Snowy River', and the magic names 'Bradman, Phar Lap, Barassi and Laver'. 'You will not, please,' he wrote, 'deny her her heritage.' My mother too, wrote her warm regards, and undertook to send some classy baby clothes from the company where she was now the forelady on the factory floor.

And so 1968—the most momentous year in my life—drew to a close. I turned thirty in December, just as my first term of academic studies ended. Everything we had hoped for at the beginning of that year had successfully come about—my university entrance, a comfortable house, a beautiful daughter, a loving wife, who gave me every ounce of support she had to give. I was a lucky man, though I doubt

I ever stopped to think so: I was too happy, too busy, too immersed in all this multifarious activity, intellectual, emotional, practical, to pause and appreciate fully the wonderful things that were happening. As I've said before, you rarely reflect on your happiness at the time; you simply live it.

To round off the year, we spent Christmas with the Parkins. They met us as we emerged from the car, fussing over little Anna, and ushering us protectively into the house. As we brought up the rear, Ian said to me, with his characteristically gentle irony, that young Matthew 'was still waiting for that tennis ball you threw to come down.'

It happened, too, that this visit resulted in Ian causing another decisive change in me, and in Jo as well. As I'd found when we first met, he was easy to talk with about serious matters, such as philosophy and education, and of course he had played a seminal role in my decision to go to university. Probably his central interest apart from his home and family was politics, which he taught along with economics at Prince Henry's Grammar School. He even ran an informal conversation group for the Alderton village, which would meet in the sitting room every month to discuss politics and current affairs. His views on most things were definite and fearlessly argued, even though he knew, as a socialist, they could make him unpopular with his neighbours. On this Christmas visit I had mentioned something about Israel and the PLO, which were still very much in the news in the aftermath of the 1967 War. The views I had to this point subscribed to were, like most of the armchair Left and others who had been influenced over the years by mainstream articles in the Press, decidedly pro-Israel. This was a largely uninformed and unexamined view, based on a vague sentimental attachment to the idea that the Jews deserved a country of their own after the Holocaust and the generally shabby deal history had delivered them. I said something to Ian critical of Yasser Arafat, and he quickly and firmly put me in my place. I was surprised. I thought sympathy for Israel was a good socialist attitude. Not in my view, said Ian. After some brief and confused resistance, I saw that he knew what he was talking about. It was, he insisted, a brutally unfair decision on the part of the world powers—essentially Stalin, Churchill and Truman—to simply hand over Palestine to the Jews, resulting in a stateless, homeless diaspora of innocent Palestinians. It was not they who had perpetrated the Holocaust, and yet they were being made to pay for it. And how would we feel, he argued, if the powers had decided to give, say, Victoria, or Tasmania, to the Jews or anyone else, simply because they wanted it? Wouldn't we try to get it back, by whatever means we could? He had no time for the scriptural arguments claiming the region as a god-endowed Jewish

Homeland, when it meant that in real terms innocent Palestinian people would be simply driven out of their homes at gunpoint just to placate Zionist demands.

I couldn't deny the veracity and strength of his case. I suddenly saw the whole situation—the War, the PLO, all those news articles over the years of my youth extolling the virtues of the kibbutzim, and depicting a proud military defence, the sentimental fashion amongst Western youth to spend time working on a kibbutz, the demonisation of Arafat—in a new light. I had, I realised, swallowed all that rhetoric whole and without question. Ian said it was the same in Britain, except for a handful of astute observers of Middle Eastern politics, such as the Labour politician Christopher Mayhew, and Jonathan Dimbleby in his book *The Palestinians*. It was not Israel that was being starved of our sympathy, but the Palestinians; it was not the prospect of the destruction of Israel we should be concerned about, but the reality of the already accomplished destruction of Palestine.

Of course I have come to realise that the situation has developed and grown more complicated since, and that the behaviour of El Fatah and the PLO during the 1970s and 80s, and of Hamas currently, have not always helped the Palestinian cause. They do seem at times to work against the prospect of a separate Palestinian state, which now I think is the only realistic solution possible. But from its inception the American-backed-funded-and-armed Israel has used unnecessarily brutal, racist and inhumane force on the Palestinian people, running them off their land to build illegal settlements for Israelis, and persistently disregarding UN calls for them to cease and take the Palestinian case for a settlement seriously. Always they attempt to justify their actions with the claim that they are simply defending their right to exist against a terrorist organisation that wants to wipe Israel off the map. What they will not face is that their own security can only come, in the long run, with a fair settlement of the territorial issue and the creation of a viable Palestinian state. They pay lip service to these aims, while at the same time ensuring that they can't occur, treating the Palestinian people as if they are low-life, and in practice giving them nothing but the constant impression that they want to wipe them out. What is so short-sighted about this is that it is not just the Palestinians who hate them, but pretty-well the whole Arab world; it's about the only thing that unites Arabs. The fact is Israel is surrounded by bigger, wealthier and more populated countries that would be quite happy to see its demise, and will, if and when they ever sort out their own political problems, sometime in the future likely seek to overrun Israel, either culturally, politically or militarily. No matter how heavily armed, when besieged a small military state can last only so long against a tide of enemies who have the future on their side, because weapons can't nourish a people and a culture. Only peace and productive relationships can do that. Nor can Israel rely forever on US support, which in turn relies on the size of the Jewish vote and finance. The demographic is changing, and the Muslim vote and Arab oil power will inevitably exert as much or even more power over US administrations than is currently the case. And the more cruel and immoral Israel's behaviour is, the more it will lose support, as world disapproval strengthens. The radical Left and the more astute liberals in Israel know this and are working to change it, but for the moment the nationalist Right is in power—as it seems to be everywhere else—and there is nothing to stop them pursuing their murderous and self-defeating aggression.

8

FROM THIS TIME ON OUR LIFE took on a new set of interests and routines, which pretty much set the pattern for the foreseeable future: raising children, managing a house, engaging in politics so far as time would allow; Jo went round at election times 'knocking up' for the local Labour Party, which meant knocking on doors and offering lifts to those who couldn't get to a booth on their own. We discussed literary, historical and political ideas, in addition to keeping up a social life, and of course the all-important business of finding enough money to live on while I was a full-time student. It was a busy way of life, and suited us fine, so long as we could keep the family ship afloat and maintain an optimistic hope that it would all eventually resolve into a financially secure and interesting kind of work, preferably for both of us, and certainly for me. Up until this point I had been the problem, the passenger really, to Jo's role as the driver. She could ultimately go back to teaching or build a further career on that base if she chose, but I had to find a direction that would both satisfy me and bring in an income to support us. So making a success of my literature studies was imperative, and this meant performing well in my university exams and essays. Fortunately, I enjoyed the daily work so much that it was no hardship at all to become totally immersed.

But while academic success was important, there were many other aspects to life that could easily have been distractions; thankfully they didn't prove to be so. We were lucky in that our past experiences prepared us to fit in with the emerging political *zeitgeist* around us. Now we were being radicalised even further by the experiences we were going through—Jo by being a mother trying to involve herself in the local community at a time when second wave feminism was beginning, plus she was contemplating applying to Warwick to resume her History studies, and I by my involvement with the Student Movement that was emerging in 1968. We had both long been left-wing, I had sung protest songs in Melbourne, we had participated in anti-nuclear and anti-Vietnam war marches, were interested in the prospect of communal living and alternative cultural movements, without ever being totally committed to these. What we were about to go through in the next four or five years crystallised our thinking on such issues, in so far as our thoughts were able to be detached from those uncontrollable forces that shaped our lives regardless of what we thought.

First was the question of house sharing. We had never been enthusiastic about the standard nuclear-family-in-a-suburban-home-with-a-huge-mortgage, and like many of our generation we were open to the idea of house sharing, and even that of a commune, with certain provisos, which there always must be. Our ideal would have been to jointly own with compatible others a large house with a garden and multiple rooms, enough to balance individual privacy with communal activities, and rearing of children. That obviously was not likely in the present circumstances, but we hoped it might come about some day. We had shared happily back in Melbourne, and were glad, now that we had a place big enough, to have students living with us preferably sharing meals and chores rather than as just room-renters. At least we could go that far in living communally.

When Hugo Radice joined us in Gulson Road, the plan was for this sort of arrangement. But unfortunately it was not to last long. Clive Bush, the lecturer who had been so helpful in admitting me and had extended his hospitality while we were house-hunting, asked a return favour of us: could we accommodate the son of a friend of his family who had been accepted into the Coventry Polytech? The problem was, he had gotten his girlfriend pregnant (while they were both still at school) and, at their families' insistence, they had married, and the only way her mother would agree to them living together was if they were being 'cared for' by an older family as they waited for the baby to come. Clive believed we would fit the bill admirably. Reluctantly, we felt obliged to agree to it, and so asked Hugo if he wouldn't mind finding another place. We felt bad about it, but being Hugo he gracefully agreed to vacate, and the newlyweds, David and Jill, moved in.

It didn't work. From the start, Jill never made an effort to fit in; her mother had 'inspected' us beforehand, and clearly didn't approve, and had pleaded with Jill to remain at home. Having chosen to come, she stayed in her bedroom all day while David was at the Polytech, and went home to her parents at weekends and every other opportunity, leaving David alone with us. He was pleasant and did his best to include himself, but eventually the strain told, and after their baby was born he dropped out of his course and joined Jill back in Kent (or wherever it was). Unfortunately, they had caused us to lose Hugo.

Our next guest was an older student, John Wheway, a few years younger than me, studying philosophy. His main interest was writing, he had already had a novel published, and I found him enjoyable and helpful to talk to over a coffee at the university. He also played a mean game of snooker, which we usually did in the basement of the Union building. We began to spend perhaps too much time together, joined the university literary society, and when Faber accepted three of his stories for their 'New Writing' series, he offered to put in a word for me if I wanted to submit something similar for their next volume. I did, and was ultimately unsuccessful, despite their enthusiasm about one of the stories. John didn't have a grant, couldn't afford to keep up his room on Campus, and asked if we could put him up until the summer break, which we did. But he was a burden and a sponger, too selfish to wash a dish or sweep a floor, despite getting his board and lodging for free. Jo found him an irritating presence, and was relieved when he finally went.

At the end of that summer we acquired yet another housemate, a postgraduate student of Politics called Cathy. She was quiet and no trouble, but neither was she much of a contributor, apart from paying in a small sum for running costs. She preferred to have separate eating arrangements, which in her case were haphazard and very little, and she lived to a different time schedule, sleeping till late in the mornings, staying up half the night in her room. The main problem with Cathy was her boyfriend, David Lazar. David was Jewish and South African, a very savvy aficionado of left-wing politics, and a postgraduate student at the Polytech. He was also an irritating housemate, immature and petty-minded. He came out for breakfast one morning after Cathy had already eaten, picked up their packet of grapenuts, only to find it empty. He then launched a relentless tirade. I've never heard anyone so abusive over a matter as trivial as breakfast cereal.

'You know I particularly like grapenuts, and you've left me none!' he said in his whiney, victim voice. It could have been an Oscar Wilde play, except it wasn't funny.

'There were only a couple of mouthfuls left,' said Cathy, 'someone had to be the last.'

'You are so *greedy* Cathy. You always do this. So greedy, so inconsiderate. You knew I would want them, and you ate the lot. I hate to say this, Cathy, but you are a very selfish person; you really need to take stock of yourself, maybe get some help or something. People who are as selfish as you can never live successfully with other people. I can say this because my own brother was like that, and everybody hated him because he was so selfish. You know you really ought to see someone about your priorities, Cathy, because you're going to end up a lonely old woman if you live like this …'

On and on he went for a full ten minutes, stalking about the house flailing his arms, retreating to his bedroom but emerging instantly to resume the attack, until Cathy was sobbing pathetically at the table, her head in her hands and the grapenuts pushed away, uneaten and soggy in their bowl of milk.

There was another occasion when I could have cheerfully throttled him. As their relationship stuttered along, one of them, probably David because there was a girl at the Polytech he had taken a shine to, suggested that they should have an 'open' relationship; these were very fashionable in the 60s and 70s, though I never knew one that worked. David had already had an affair with this or some other girl, and, conforming to their 'honesty' agreement, confessed it to Cathy. She was hurt, but accepted it without rancour or bringing matters to a head. Then, during the summer break of that year, Cathy went to Wales with a group of students, but David wanted to stay home and get on with his PhD. She rang one day and, adhering to their policy, told him she was sleeping with one of the guys in the group. The effect on David was incendiary, although predictable. He stomped around the house all day raving and whining, driving us mad going over and over the same pointless, hypocritical complaints. 'How could she do this to me? Who is this guy? I mean what does she know about him? He could be anybody. What are his politics? I mean there are some very reactionary people among those Politics students. She could be creating a lot of trouble for herself; she's already got chronic cystitis, how's that going to get better?' And the oh-so-predictable, 'It's not so much that she did it, it's the *way* she did it—sneaking off to Wales like that, pretending it was about her research ...' By the end of the day he had made himself so distraught that he went to bed without any dinner, saying he was 'too ill' to stay up and watch television, which I had planned to do. There was a famous film about India showing that I was eager to see—*Shakespeare-Wallah*. I had never seen it. I'd sat down—I think Jo was putting Anna to bed—just as the film was about to start, when David emerged from his room. His hang-dog features told he was mired in self pity.

'Garry,' he said, 'I know this is an awful thing to ask. I know how much you want to see the film, but I'm really distressed. I mean I really feel quite suicidal, and just need you to sit with me while I talk it through. I can't cope with what she's done to me, and I really need you to sit with me please. I know it's a big thing to ask, but I've no-one else to turn to. Please, please come into my room and sit with me.'

Weakly, I protested that this was my only chance to see *Shakespeare-Wallah*, but he wouldn't take no for an answer. So I turned the TV off and sat with him, barely able to suppress my anger, as he whined on and on about his distress, until the time came that the film was over. He said a contrite thankyou, that he thought he'd be able to get to sleep now, and I could go back to watching TV. Too late of course. Why *didn't* I throttle him?

My point about all this failed sharing was that it taught us something about our communal ideals: they could never work unless the particular people liked, respected and cooperated with each other on a daily basis. Essentially, they have to like each other a lot. And there are very few people who do so and want to live together. So the practical matters, the house, the financial and ownership arrangements, the management of chores and so on, important though they are, are always secondary to the personalities and characters of the people, and the feelings they have for each other. Unless these are right, no communal lifestyle will work. And never having found such people, we eventually ended up, Jo and I, living the standard life of a nuclear family. As it turned out it was not, all things considered, such a bad thing.

The second matter of my politicisation was another lesson in self-discovery. The late 60s were politically heady times. During 1968 the media had been full of the growing unrest in France and America, and the May protests in Paris involving a mix of students and workers had almost succeeded in overthrowing the government. In the US widespread student revolt grew out of the Civil Rights movement and anti-Vietnam war and anti-nuclear marches in various cities across the country. There were protest incidents, involving violent police reaction, on several university campuses, notably Chicago. Inevitably this had spread to Britain, and at Warwick the various left-wing student groups—Marxists, International Socialists, the British Communist Party and others—became more or less united in their attacks on British support for the Vietnam war and on some of the more egregious sins of capitalist politics. There was a lot of hot debate in the Student Union about university complicity in such doings, and groups of workers such as the Socialist Workers in Coventry were invited onto the campus by students wanting to join forces with them. Many students became less interested in their studies, and more in political activism, and some staff also were notably engaged in the debates, specifically Germaine Greer and the social historian EP Thompson.

Unsurprisingly, given my background, I got caught up in these activities. Although not a member of any one of the radical groups—I was never a joiner, and in any case wouldn't have been able to decide which group I preferred—I was sympathetic to the general mood of protest, and in my own way committed to the ideals that lay behind it. To me the students seemed to be demanding a fairer, more honest, more open set of values generally than the capitalist system offered, despite its claims to democratic principles. I wanted change, and I went along with the notion that it could only happen if some form of force or coercion was used. I went on marches, attended protest meetings, and when the students took the dramatic step of forcing their way into the university administration to search files for any skullduggery, I joined the hangers-on without actually entering the building or opening any drawers or files. I read only what was photocopied afterwards and widely disseminated around the campus.

The gist of the 'break-in' was that the students did find evidence of disturbing secretive activities by the administration, including the Vice Chancellor John Butterworth. The most worrying of these at the time was evidence of 'deals' being done between the university and commercial interests, in particular Lord Rootes, the motor industry baron, to favour teaching and research fields that would benefit local industries, especially his company, by the university's School of Engineering. The student objection to this was that it interfered with academic freedom, which insists that staff and students should be free to follow whatever lines of enquiry interest them, without fear of favour to the commercial or ideological interests of the world outside. A fine ideal, which was clearly still alive in 1968, but which, unfortunately, was to be steadily eroded in a few short years, so that now, in the 21st century, there is probably not a university in the world that would see anything wrong in a company paying a university to conduct research on its behalf. Indeed, I'm sure some universities positively spruik for such a deal. I can just imagine the offer made over lunch in some posh Club. 'You want to endow a MacDonald's Centre of Health Science? No worries, here's the form—just make an appropriate donation, give us your nomination for the inaugural professor and we'll do the rest.'

Someone must have identified me as I joined the crowd outside the university administration building, because later that week a courier knocked on the front door at Gulson Road and issued me and others with an injunction that prevented us from re-entering the university administration building and from publishing any unauthorised university document. Since I was not involved in doing either, the order eventually lapsed without further development. Of more significance, within a few weeks EP Thompson had resigned from the university in protest, and had written a hastily put-together book, published in amazingly quick time by Penguin, called *Warwick University Limited*, exposing and attacking the university's ugly complicity with the business world. Both the resignation and the book were a major blow to the university's credibility, especially since it exposed what few people knew at the time, which was that the university had been planned right from its inception as an institute that would serve Midland business interests, and that 50% of its teaching and research resources was to be directed to

Engineering and Business schools. Only the university's failure to attract sufficient student numbers in those areas prevented the plan from being carried out.

All this took place in the spring of 1970, while the mood of defiance and unrest bubbled along on campus, although police intervention and the passing of time helped the university administration to hold out and eventually quieten things down. They were clearly looking to the summer break and the student vacation dispersal to bring matters to a close, and in the end this is what happened. There was also some disquiet amongst many basically sympathetic supporters, like myself, about the motives and tactics of the more vociferous and bloody-minded of the radical students. The Left has always been dogged, not only by disunity, which is an understandable consequence of impassioned debate, but also by its own critical negativity. Unity, I have found over many years of observing the way things get done or don't, is best achieved when people are actually creating something together—building, playing music, or constructing a definite program of some kind. When you are stuck in opposition mode, concentrating your efforts on dismantling or destroying or simply rebelling, it is easy to lose sight of constructive goals, such as 'what do you want to put in its place?' The radical Left has historically been so entrenched in the negative task of obliterating capitalism that it has failed to construct a vision of governable social justice that is sufficiently appealing to the majority to capture their support. And by 'construct' I mean also finding a way to defend that vision against powerful but ultimately undemocratic vested interests that influence voter choice, such as the business/media alliances.

My disillusion, then, with the student activists at Warwick was based on what I perceived as their entrenched negativity and untrustworthy motives; there was a sense with some of the leaders that their aggression was personal and opportunistic, rather than properly political. And this, I discovered, could be dangerous. I went with a group of fellow Leftists to a meeting in Coventry with some Socialist Worker unionists from local factories. There were, maybe, ten of us in all, sitting around a table in a local Council hall. The workers were older, fierce-looking men with restless countenances, barely tolerant of us privileged, glib-toned youths who'd had the temerity to come and curry favour with them. I understood something of this difference from each side, being older and having started my working life in factories at the age of fourteen. The only memory I have of what was said at this meeting was a statement by one of the men that suddenly made me realise how out of place I was, how out of my depth, and that these were people I could never stand alongside either to support or judge, because they inhabited a different mental and social world than I did. 'What we want,' said one of the men, directly, 'is for you students to get in there and help us smash these Coventry factories so that they can't function; this is the only way to defeat capitalism: destroy its means of production.'

I was stunned by the raw simplicity, the unquestioning violence, and the repulsive defeatism of this. I knew in that instant I was not a revolutionary. I had no list of objections I could respond with, though afterwards, some time afterwards in fact, I could of course articulate them to myself—that destroying factories is also destroying workers' jobs, that it would fail because the companies would rebuild them, that the police would intervene and jail us etc. The best objection I came upon, however, was a couple of years later, when I said, somewhat apologetically, to a lovely Leftist Italian female student, 'I've come to the realisation that I am not a revolutionary I'm afraid.' She smiled and gave a very Italian shrug, 'What is the use of being a revolutionary when there is no revolution?' she said. A simple, obvious, but nevertheless often overlooked fact.

This brings me to the point that others have made about the 'failure' of the 1968 radical movement, and its aftermath, especially its implication for the Left. As in my personal case, generally our hearts were not in it, not truly. There was nowhere for it to go, except in two directions: one, politically into further rebellion and destruction, which was unsustainable socially and individually: no economy can be built on a state of revolution, and no full individual life can be lived within it. It simply cannot be sustained. Time, given uncontrollable social dynamics and the protean desires of young people, will wear it down.

The other exception is not political but cultural. In the 1970s the Left began to divert its energies into a *cultural* radicalism. Clothing, hairstyles, 'hippy' cults, experiments with communes, the drug culture, rock (instead of folk) festivals, all dignified by the term Counter Culture, signified a retreat from practical politics. At first it was all an attempt to maintain the illusion that the young were creating an 'alternative' society to the mainstream, but the unexamined holes in this finally got so numerous that it quickly fell apart. Or, more accurately, 'alternative' gradually became absorbed into the mainstream, where it was commercialised and watered down into new fashions for the marketplace. By the 1980s a new generation of young were so sick of the stinking corpse of the Counter Culture and its hypocrisies that they instead put their faith in Money, which was at least more brutally honest even if it was more dishonestly brutal than the dreams of the Love-in generation. On the intellectual level, the new Left in the universities began to reconstruct the world through theoretical remodelling, in what became the rhetorical foundation for postmodernism. Deconstruction was the unbeautiful flower of this philosophy, and 'theorising' became a surrogate for action. By these means the Left has steadily moved into a state of superficially, sometimes even happily, expressed despair over the possibility of creating a just, or even simply a better, world. Where their heroes were once Marx and Engels, they were now Derrida, Foucault and Frederick Jameson. Where youth once wanted to change the world, it now wanted to identify with its celebrities. Naturally, in these circumstances, the way was now open to the Right to flood in and take over. Which is exactly what has been happening world-wide in the past two decades.

I did not give up my interest in politics, but attempted to see the study of literature as often as possible from a broadly political, though basically humanist, perspective. This was not, in my undergraduate days, a sophisticated approach, and tended to show itself in my choice of authors and critics, though it was not exclusively sympathetic to Leftists. In fact, I came to the view that politically almost every important author in the English and American canons could be seen to contribute in some degree to the cause of decency and freedom from forces that would lock us into moral and intellectual, and therefore political, darkness. Most great writers, from Chaucer and Shakespeare to Faulkner and Mailer, I concluded wrote with assumptions that were not just compatible with ideals of decency and human progress (even if that progress was only linguistic or experiential), but actually worked to promote new conceptions of those ideals. Fundamentally, I have come to believe that good literature is good for our humanity and our capacity to know right from wrong, and this extends to our political principles. It is not a question of whether a work promotes democracy or not: Shakespeare's 'good' royals are admirable because they take their political responsibilities to their whole society seriously, and try to answer the needs of all their subjects from the lowest serf upwards. On the other hand, modern novelists are constantly showing us the failures of democracy to even care for those same classes of people in our own world. Good quality writing is rarely on the side of the cruel and the wicked, though it may make use of cruelty and wickedness in the construction of its argument. I still hold to this belief, even while coming to see that many of the writers I admire have weaknesses of omission, and in some cases commission, in this or that aspect of social attitudes. Women and 'otherness', for instance often do not fare well in many great works written before the 21st century (though I would not find Shakespeare guilty of either). But to a large extent, from this point on my interest in politics found expression through cultural and literary activities, rather than in political action, which I suppose puts me in exactly the same position as what Richard Rorty calls the 'cultural Left' that has become so entrenched in theory since the failure of 1968. And yet while I would agree that studying literature is not the same as being politically active, this is not to say that I think that 'poetry makes nothing happen', as WH Auden claimed. In its widest meaning, poetry can alter consciousness, and an altered consciousness can make you behave differently. But I suspect such altered consciousness can take one no further than humanist biases and socialist sentiments, and one ends up being, not a revolutionary activist, but a good liberal democrat, having to plump for the purely cultural, that is, theoretical, revolutions of postmodernism and its attendants, confining my political action merely to the polling booth.

I hugely enjoyed my activities at the university, including my work for the student newspaper, *Campus*, placing poetry and reviews, interviews with staff and visiting notables, and doing much of the typing and layout myself. A particular perk was free tickets to opening nights at the Belgrade Theatre in Coventry. This was a fine theatre, often used for trial-runs of edgy productions before the risks of London theatre-goers and critics, and they had a policy of open forums after the show when the audience could stay behind and engage with the director and actors about different aspects of the play. As a reviewer I found this a useful and stimulating opportunity to get my ideas straight before taking Jo home and then rushing back to the university at midnight to write my review and position it in the layout for printing. We witnessed a number of seminal moments at the Belgrade, including first productions of John Arden's *Live Like Pigs*, Peter Shaffer's *Equus*, a reworking of *Loot* by Joe Orton and a young, gorgeous Timothy Dalton as Atahuelpa in *The Royal Hunt of the Sun*. It was a good chance for us to get out together, and for me to do a bit of non-academic writing for a change.

In fact, I kept my interest in creative writing alive for much of the first two years at Warwick. I completed a draft of a novel (never published) over the summer break of 1971, wrote short prose pieces for various student publications, and was elected president of the university Literary Society, which was well supported by a grant from the Student Union and by the interest of a number of English department staff. This kept me mixing among the creative types, and gave me the task of attracting established writers to come and give talks. I wrote to a number of such, including Tom Stoppard, Jon Silkin, John Stallworthy, Ivy Compton Burnett and William Empson. Courteous declines came from Stoppard and from Compton Burnett, who sent me the most alarming card which said that she 'was sorry that (she was) too disabled by an accident. ICB', in a hand so shaky it looked as if she had actually suffered the fall in the act of writing it! No accident is recorded by her biographer, Hilary Spurling, so Ivy might have been fobbing me off with an excuse, but I sensed otherwise, and that she would really have liked to come. I was disappointed; she's always been a favourite writer of mine. But Stallworthy came and gave an interesting talk on poetry, as did Empson, whose visit gave me some of the most memorable few hours of my life. I have to give a brief account of this.

William Empson was one of the most brilliant literary critics of his time, who extended the close-reading methods of IA Richards to new and broader dimensions. He was also precocious and eccentric in the classic English mould, had begun the first part of his ground-breaking work *Seven Types of Ambiguity* while still an undergraduate, and had been deprived of his Cambridge Fellowship in 1929 for keeping condoms in his room. So, now unemployable in British universities, he took posts in Japan and China during the hectic years of the 30s and 40s, when he produced two seminal books—*Seven Types of Ambiguity* and *Some Versions of Pastoral*, plus a volume of collected verse. Apart from a stint at the BBC during the War, he did not return to Britain until he was appointed to a Chair at Sheffield in 1953, by which time he had won a reputation as literary lion, but with a private life as bizarre, alcohol-fuelled and sexually complicated as any Parisian bohemian. I was excited at the prospect of meeting him, which was to be at Coventry station, after which I was to take him to his room in student digs. From photographs I'd seen, it was no trouble to recognise that stocky body and strange beard, flourishing from beneath the chin like a snowy cravat below a clean-shaven face, save for a white Colonel Blimp moustache. After a cursory handshake he put down his bag in the middle of the station walkway and began to remove his pullover, saying, 'Now what we must do is find a chemist.' He wanted to buy some Neutradonna to 'settle his nerves' for the talk he was soon to give. This was an antacid powder with a Belladonna component that acted similarly to cannabis. In the chemist's we were waiting to be served behind two old ladies, when Empson said loudly, 'What kind of drugs do you like? Is there anything I can stand you? I suppose you rather like the sort that Harold Wilson can't tax, ha ha.' The ladies moved quickly away from our vicinity.

I took him to dinner at the staff club, along with Claude Rawson and several student literary society members, and afterwards to a lecture room. His talk was well-attended by students and staff. George Hunter was there, Bill Righter, Germaine, Bernard Bergonzi, Claude Rawson and others. It was in two parts—a disquisition on Coleridge, who he said had written *The Ancient Mariner* on opium, and went on into some barely comprehensible cloudland of his own, followed by a reading of a number of his poems, which was the highlight—powerful, visceral but at the same time linguistically playful pieces in mostly traditional forms, such as the villanelles 'Missing Dates', and 'This Last Pain'. Bill Righter quipped to me that both were about Empson's alcoholism, but it was a woefully inadequate view.

Afterwards, I walked a tired, cadaver-faced Empson to his room in the Residence halls. As I left he asked if I could show him around Coventry the next morning, before he caught the train to London. It proved a delightful little adventure through the Empson sensibility, sprightly and on form after a good night's sleep. At our first stop I thought he was going to be killed when he got out of the car and without looking stumped straight across the road, chin jutting, into the path of a fast approaching truck. The truck didn't alter speed or course, and neither did Empson, who seemed oblivious of the danger. The two bodies, the hard and the soft, missed each other by feet as I stood horrified; part of my fear was selfish, not relishing the prospect of losing a famous poet on my first excursion as president of the Literary Society. I saw then where he was headed: a pub. It being 11 o'clock, the place was just opening, so there was no-one inside but the landlord. 'What would you like—join me in a brandy?' he said, and cavalierly I agreed. He then asked for the following items: a glass of peppermint, a glass of water, a glass of gin, and an empty glass. Like a mad stage professor, he mixed a cocktail, adding a generous helping from his tin of Neutradonna, and drank it in one gulp. Then he swallowed his brandy. 'Right,' he said with a brisk rub of his hands, 'let's go.' The potion had done its work, the new man had risen, and the shaft from his eye aimed straight at the art gallery.

Safely inside the gallery, which was provincial enough to hang any old incompetent painting of Lady Godiva, he charged around impatiently looking for something to take his interest. A largish streetscape by the Lancashire painter LS Lowry, clearly a pride of the collection, had a uniformed guard standing beside it. Empson pitched towards it in what could have been construed as an assault, causing the guard to make a protective move across with his arm extended, but the assailant stopped with his nose about eighteen inches from the picture, as everyone froze. 'Hmf,' said Empson, scrutinising the painting with disgust, 'That's a bit *friendly*, isn't it.' Then we left and made for the new cathedral, standing beside the bombed ruins of the old one.

The huge Graham Sutherland tapestry of a seated Christ looking down the central aisle from above the altar takes your eye as you enter, and so it was the first thing that Empson commented on: 'He looks like a member of some committee!'

he sourly muttered, clearly hoping for something better. The work he hadn't seemed to notice was the grand glass entrance with its lovely etchings of angels and saints. Inside, he shuffled around the side aisles, still unimpressed. The chapel of Gethsemane he dubbed 'a cheap piece of pantomime'. Looking back now, I'm not sure what he expected to find in the place, but since he was a consistent critic of Christianity throughout his life, his contempt was hardly surprising.

More to his taste was the Chinese restaurant where we went for lunch, and he chatted happily with the waiters in Cantonese as he skilfully plied his chopsticks. It was then that he told me that he had lost the manuscript of a book on a train in China, a book he was never able to rewrite. I had this sudden image of a priceless script lying in an empty train circuiting the backblocks of western China, until eventually the crowds push in and the script is trampled to oblivion by countless worker's boots, and finally picked up and dumped in the rubbish by a scrupulous cleaner. No doubt this was unlikely to have happened, but I've often wondered how true the story was, since it hasn't been mentioned in Empson's letters, nor in the comprehensive biography written by John Haffenden. He might have dreamt it up, or misremembered, but he certainly said it to me. And wouldn't the world like to know if there was indeed another book.

Two more whiskies at another pub, and we drove merrily to Coventry station. He put down his bag in the walkway precisely as he had done the day before, and while I held his coat he once again removed his pullover and stuffed it into his bag. We said a matey and, certainly on my part, heartfelt goodbye and he disappeared through the gate. The mad, wonderfully English professor. It was about two o'clock on a sunny Saturday afternoon as I walked into the street, my head spinning with a fine blend of whisky and euphoria. And relief I hadn't lost him to that bloody truck.

At the end of my first year Jo's mother, Barbara, wrote a letter in which she added a postscript that rubbed me up the wrong way. 'If Garry doesn't get a job this vac.,' she wrote, 'I will feel very strongly like writing him a straight letter about hopping in and doing some work to keep his wife and family, and writing his best-seller later on once he knows his dependents will eat.'

I was stung by what I considered was an unfair accusation of some kind of self-indulgence on my part in wanting to write. She would be singing a different tune, I thought to myself, if I did manage to sell some work and make some money, even though I was doing everything I could—including giving guitar lessons at a music school behind our house—to supplement the grant that kept us going. Of course money was a constant problem with Jo unable to work, and her parents made several generous donations to our coffers, but it wasn't as if I was living it up while my family was starving. Still, I felt chastised, and tended to blame Jo for having written home in such a way as to draw this kind of opprobrium upon me. It was only many years later, reading through family letters and coming across her response to her mother's criticism, that I realised the full extent of her loyalty and defence of my efforts. 'You seem to have got it wrong,' she wrote, and in a tone rarely used to her mother, 'he fully realises the need to support his dependents. He's registered at the Employment Exchange asking for work as a laboratory technician, and in the meantime we'll get National Assistance, which is more than some jobs would pay him.'

It took some spirit on her part to back me in this way, and it gave me an inkling of why my path had, even in the most difficult days of our domestic struggle, been so relatively smooth for me to give my studies and interests the necessary concentration: she was always giving me her loyalty and support, though I'm sure there were times I didn't deserve it. No wonder I have always felt unconditionally loved by her.

Teachers and critics played an important role in forming my literary tastes and opinions. I was fortunate in having Germaine Greer as one of these, for whatever else one says of her—and I don't deny she has a big appetite for celebrity attention and sometimes produces scatty arguments that feel to have a fair amount of bluff in them—she was a superb lecturer (less so a tutor, but I was in her class when *The Female Eunuch* came out, and the distractions it caused her were uncontrollable). Germaine could be acid-tongued and dismissive, but she was also funny and precocious, and always deeply, professionally, communicative; she gave eighteen lectures on 18th century poetry in my 2nd year that ranged from Pope to Lady Winchelsea and other little-known women poets, bringing in metrical and poetics issues, pop-cultural comparisons, breaking into song, rescuing Swift from the conservatives, in what was a mesmerisingly dynamic weekly performance. She brought poetry alive, made it feel urgent and relevant, and fired my enjoyment of 18th century culture where others had made it feel only dull.

She also mothered female students in a very touching way. In my first-year Italian class, two girls stopped coming after a few weeks. I noticed this because they were both good-looking, and their absence made the class just a tad less interesting to me. Then one day I came across Germaine in the corridor of the English department, and she swooped on me; did I have a car? Was I doing anything for the rest of that morning? Could I give her a lift to Leamington Spa, the hospital? She explained along the way: she had for a few weeks been visiting two first-year girls in the hospital after they'd been hit by a car while hitch-hiking home from university. She was buying them little things—tissues, cosmetics, fruit—to make them more comfortable until they recovered. I had no idea. More importantly, no other member of staff knew about them. And they were not even Germaine's students. She was simply alert to such things, and once she was she felt compelled to act. I knew of a number of similar instances of Germaine's genuine concern for others during the time I knew her, and grew to really like her. She could be shocking at times, and those with more delicate sensibilities could find her hard to take. I was sitting in the Union bar with her and a number of other students one time when a young man, probably not a student, walked into the bar dressed completely in black leather. Germaine looked across at him and said, quite audibly in her Aussie voice, 'Oh, I could fuck that!' I wondered what some of the other staff would have made of it; I can think of one who'd have wanted her arrested.

One of the great extra-curricula treats were lunchtime open lectures given by Edward Thompson, growing out of his interest in early 19th century social history. He talked on Romantic writers of the period, specifically Wordsworth and William Blake. The lectures were hugely popular, with students from any and every discipline crowded into every available space in the room, sitting in aisles and lining the walls. Thompson would come into the room with an armful of books a foot high, balance them in front of him on the lectern and, without referring to notes, proceed to talk directly to the audience, and as he talked he would absent-mindedly pick up each book with its marker protruding and quote the relevant passage as he came to it, all in a smooth operation that looked, but wasn't, rehearsed. Every now and then he would pause, remove his spectacles and rub the lenses down a grubby pullover, while peering majestically over the throng with narrowed eyes, the heavy bags of flesh under them suggesting a fearful rate of working through nights. Then a faint grimace would break from that generous mouth framed by its strong, furrowed jaw, in turn framed by a head of thick, shaggy hair, and he would return to his task. He seemed a figure of kindness and leonine nobility, and everyone hung on every word, as he explored the relation between rural and urban working classes and their effects on the language and vision of the poets. And what I gained from listening to him was the sense that there was a politically interesting and valuable connection between literature and the struggles of history, between writers and the wider population, even those who were not sophisticated readers. Not just the novel, which is of course an intrinsically demotic form, but also poetry, which historically made politically useful contributions to everyday language, or what Wordsworth called 'the very language of men'. So, this too, this experience of the great EP Thompson, helped me form my literary tastes.

The strongest influence on my studies, however, was not really political at all, but methodological. And that was exercised by George Hunter, with whom I took the Shakespeare option in 3rd year. George (and I can call him that now because I am an old man) was an extremely hard taskmaster, a brilliant escapee from the Glasgow working class who would not tolerate slackness or wooliness of thought in the slightest degree, which occasionally drew from weaker vessels the unfair cliché 'fascist'. He was no fascist, but he did have all the unforgiving stringency of the secular Calvinist. He demanded of his Shakespeare class a full-sized essay every week on a topic he would set that was relevant to the play, and there was a new play every week. He would stand at the door of his room at 9 am each Monday, handing back the essay he had marked on the weekend, and if you had submitted no essay, you were not admitted to the tutorial—you would be flicked away with a forefinger. The tutorial was tightly managed by him—no free-for-all discussion. He would say to a student, 'Er, Miss Jones, what do you think of the proposition that *King Lear* is a play about redemption?' You suspected a trap lurking in the question, but had no choice but to risk it. After Miss Jones had given her answer, he would turn to one of the others and say, 'Mr Kinnane, what do *you* think of Miss Jones' comments? Do you think it's *adequate?*' He was not trying to stir up dissent between us students so much as ensure that everyone was a participant, even if they didn't especially want to be at that moment: no slackers, everyone involved. And of course it was good for us, forced us to think even at that time of the morning (his was the only class that began before ten o'clock), and taught us a great deal about finding *arguments* within and about the plays.

Stories about George were legion. Even if they disapproved of his methods, students admired his style and reputation. He wore checked flannelette (not quite hair) shirts and jeans or work-trousers, heavy 'bovver' boots and sometimes a cloth cap over his greying crew-cut, and usually rode a bicycle to work, though he liked cars. Where the usual academic taste ran to solid English Rovers or sensible Austin 1100's, George liked huge American gas-guzzlers. It was rumoured that when he applied for the inaugural Chair at Warwick, the interview went something like this:

Scene: a generous and well-furnished university room, lined with books and business-like filing cabinets; a panel of professionals sits around a solid oak table grilling an oddly dressed candidate who looks like he is wearing a too-small demob suit over a tieless flannel shirt. The chairman of the panel, a distinguished Shakespeare scholar, addresses the candidate in a slightly patronising tone:

'Well, Doctor Hunter, we see your impressive list of publications here. I don't think all of us have had the chance to read them, so perhaps you could take the opportunity here to tell us something about them …'

Momentary silence. The candidate shifts impatiently in his chair, then speaks firmly and humourlessly in a Scottish accent.

'I beg your pardon. Do you mean to tell me that you have not all read my publications in preparation for this interview?'

The chairman looks about him, giving his colleagues a nervously empty but good-humoured smile, then answers in solemn sotto voce:

'Ah, that's right I'm afraid. Haven't all had the chance yet. Could you be so good …?'

'No. I will not. If you haven't read them I'm sorry, but I'll not tell you about them now.'

Embarrassed silence, before the interview proceeds to administrative matters. Two weeks later, George Hunter receives a letter appointing him to the job.

I once sat at the refectory table in the Student Union with him and several other undergraduates—he never ate in the staff club if he could help it—discussing a Russian production of *Hamlet* that had been on TV the night before (I think Germaine was there as well). After various opinions had been expressed, I asked George what he thought. 'I liked it,' he said, 'but I did find that they used some very strange idioms in the translation.'

It took a moment to sink in, but then it dawned on me: where we had been reading the English subtitles, he had been listening to the Russian lines. And he knew the language well enough to spot the oddities in the translation. I later learned that during the War he had worked as a translator of Japanese dispatches intercepted by Intelligence. This linguistic precocity was, of course, in addition to the standard old-school British educated man's knowledge of Latin and Greek, and maybe French, German and Italian, and his professional familiarity with Old and Middle English. I wouldn't have been surprised, in the end, to learn he'd had a bit of Old Norse, Chinese, or even Inuit! So in George Hunter I had met, and had the privilege to be taught by, one of the finest scholarly minds of the post-War era.

As far as my taste in literary critics went, I was generally eclectic, though I responded especially to the IA Richards/William Empson approach. The close readings of texts, learning to be alert to the wonderfully suggestive ways in which the language is used by great writers, was never to my mind a dull pursuit. On the contrary, it seemed to me to be a form of reading that places one closest to the mindset of the writer, and often beyond it. Especially beyond it, because from the little occasions of ambiguity, shifts in emphasis, loaded word-choices and so forth a reader could extrapolate and expand the meaning of the work in a number of directions—psychological, historical, political. In this way you read literature from inside outwards, so to speak, from the page to its relation to the world outside, which satisfied in me both a need for precision and for the drama of the history of ideas. Most of the critics I have admired—Richards, Empson, Kermode, Raymond Williams, Northrop Frye, Sartre, Eagleton and even, at times, the irritating old FR Leavis—have helped in my modest development of this approach. Further, I have always found it a valuable aid in teaching.

And to end this little deviation, a word on the 'death of the author' notion ushered in during the postmodern era. As we know, this idea is really about denying the author's sole responsibility for the meaning of a text, which Roland Barthes wanted transferred across to the reader. It has some good effects going for it. Might I say, though, that English criticism has always known that the reader has an interpretative role; how else could they give different students top marks for different arguments about the meaning? There was never one sole meaning available, whether the interpretation aimed at the work itself or the author's supposed intentions. But the new paradigm of 'reader-response' criticism is not the final answer either, because something dictates that a reader cannot simply invent a view about what a text means. If I try to argue that *Anna Karenina* is 'conceivably' a novel about American slavery, everyone is going to think I am mad, mischievous or illiterate. Some element, or elements, of control are operating, probably a mixture of common sense and authorial rhetorical skill. You cannot overlook the fact that a text does not write itself, but is purposefully written by an author who designed and executed it to have certain effects, and that our arrival at 'meaning' is significantly influenced by that execution. To ignore that design and execution is not only to risk arriving at a meaning that is totally incomprehensible to others and therefore serves no social purpose, but it is barking-mad ego-tripping. Okay, have your own private interpretation that you can cling to in the attic of your imagination, but don't expect others to value it. The discussion of literature is a social matter, as indeed is language itself. If I existed in isolation I wouldn't need language at all, let alone literature.

We made some new friends around the time the political kerfuffle at the university was coming to a head. I had noticed a tall, interesting-looking young Indian man, lean and handsome, with a fetching way of smiling and frowning at the same time, around the English department corridors and in the Library, and eventually got to talking with him. When he told me he lived with his wife in Coventry, not far from us, I was able to give him the occasional lift in my Beetle to and from the university. His name was Rajiva Verma, he was from Delhi, and he was, lucky man, studying under George Hunter for a PhD on Shakespeare, after which he had a lectureship waiting for him at the University of Delhi. From our first meeting we got along extremely well, and so did Jo with his wife Meera. In fact, we became a close foursome for the rest of our time in Coventry, and our friendship has continued up until this day, I am happy to say. Meera, a lovely young woman with a broad smile and a treacle-toned voice, sweet and dark, was completing an MA in Politics. We went with them to Stratford to see *The Tempest*, and Rajiva pointed out to me that the production had modeled Ariel on the ash-covered appearance of an Indian Saddu, or holy man who renounces all material attachments. This was only one among many interesting observations Rajiva has made about literature over the years, and he is always particularly good on Indian myth and culture. When we got back to the car park on that occasion, Meera's handbag had been stolen from the back seat of the car, so we all had a miserable drive back to Coventry. She did get back her small purse, minus the cash of course, but the handbag—a valuable one—and some notes belonging to her supervisor, unhappily were never recovered.

We often ate at each other's houses. Meera was amazing in the way she could produce a delicious Indian repast from the hopelessly inadequate kitchen in their small first-floor flat, and she would give me good tips about how to improve my curry-making, including introducing us to basmati rice, long before it was ever available in the supermarkets; in 1969 it could be bought only in Asian groceries. Later, when we had the two children, they would babysit for us while we went to a movie or a play, and one time we took them to the Parkins for a weekend, giving them a taste of Cotswold countryside and English village life that they absolutely loved. And when Meera was not at the university she would spend time with Jo, which was a gratifying counter to the loneliness of being stuck so much in the house with the children. By the time we left Coventry Rajiva and Meera had become our best friends.

It isn't easy to account for the tenor of our lives during these three Coventry years, simply because so much was happening to us. Today I am able to read through the many letters—over 250 of them—between us and our families back home, most of them between Jo and Barbara, who was an especially good correspondent. What these letters do is remind me of our general busyness and fundamental happiness. The busyness should be understandable, given my studies and attempts to keep writing, guitar-playing and Jo's tasks as a wife and mother and both our contributions to running the house. But as I read through Jo's account of our week-to-week existence I am struck by the range of other activities we were able to sustain. There were our regular opening night attendances at the Belgrade Theatre, which I reviewed. As well, we went often to Stratford, where we saw the famous Peter Brook production of *A Midsummer Night's Dream* and *The Tempest, Richard III, Measure For Measure, Twelfth Night* and Judi Dench's Portia in *The Merchant of Venice*. And we got to many memorable movies—*Midnight Cowboy, Women in Love, Oh What a Lovely War, If, Easy Rider, Le Bonheur*, among lots of others. Jo sometimes travelled to Oxford and London to conferences on feminist politics. And then there was the constant stream of visitors—our English chums such as Liz and Pete, Lew and Hilary Davies, Peter Moorhouse, Jack and Donald, not to mention student friends—and Australians passing through, usually family connections, and also Bob Haberfield, who was now living in a Buddhist commune in Wales, but would occasionally drop in. The house was regularly abuzz with visitors, so not just a domestic nursery and study. We also managed to get away for holidays from time to time—usually to the Parkins, but once for an extended stay in Devon, where I took movie pictures of a little naked Anna running on the beach and playing in the sand. I'd picked up a secondhand Standard Eight camera and projector in a local shop in Coventry, and made a number of inept movies of our activities. The shots of Jo on the beach reveal a modest but growing bump under her blue swimsuit frock, which in a few months would become our second daughter. We also went to occasional student parties, including one in which everyone indulged in the late 60s fashion of taking off their clothes and standing around awkwardly naked while holding a drink, or, more entertainingly, or alarmingly depending on the body, dancing; Jo and I were both struck by how different the human body can look when the everyday harnesses and coverings are removed. We also went to an end-of-year gathering of the staff and students of the English department, at which Germaine insisted on enviously stroking Jo's pregnant belly, and as a reward made us a gift of a large, pleasant-looking green two-lidded chest which she said we could use to store toys. In fact we put blankets in it, because its slam-down lids made it highly unsuitable for children. All of these doings, vividly described in Jo's letters home, remind me of the richness of our lives in those Coventry days. I say 'rich', though this includes days of outright chaos and confusion, especially when I had essays to get written or there was simply too much to be done.

But 'happiness' is a less demonstrable matter. I know that despite our busyness Jo went through periods of loneliness, frustration and depression. This was especially true after our second child, Lucy, was born on the 8th of December, 1970. After a long and frustrating day of labour, the baby came relatively easily and settled in to a manageable feeding routine—Jo breast-fed them both, and Lucy was easier than Anna. But she did develop '3 month colic' and cried a great deal at night. With me busy on my studies, and Anna now two and a daily handful, Jo struggled to keep up her spirits over what was a long and very cold winter. I recall seeing the traffic along Gulson Road stalled for half a day on the frozen road in a snowstorm, everything covered in a sheet of impenetrable white. We all came down with frequent colds. I contracted a virus that was difficult to shake, and then Anna got very sick with bronchial pneumonia and had to be hospitalised; at one point she passed into unconsciousness, turned grey-blue, and we thought in abject terror that we might lose her. Through all this Jo grew deadly tired. Never did the days seem so short and dark; never did Coventry seem so bleak, nor the lack of Aussie sunshine so debilitating. She wanted her mum, as any girl would, trying to cope with two small children on her own much of the time. She worried about our lack of money. She felt bereft of close friends, despite the warmth and help that she got from Meera and other friends. As her letters testify, she wanted nothing more than to go back to Australia, back to some sort of comfort, and away from this constant struggle with the weather, poverty and isolation. When I began talking about possibly pursuing post-graduate study, she wrote to her mother that she was hoping I would choose to do it in Australia, and she could escape this dreary English way of life.

Her concerns were real, and of course I shared them. I knew she was unhappy, that our future was uncertain, our income meagre and savings non-existent, and I did give her less help than I should have. I suppose I too often made light of the problems, not wanting to give in to depression myself, which could only have made matters worse. I kept saying to her, and to myself, that things would get better as soon as I knew what prospects for the future I had, which depended on how well I did in my exams. It was just a question of holding out until that time, which was, in that winter, still eighteen months away. In the meantime, couldn't we count our blessings? And of course she did this, and she never showed the worst of her anxieties to me or others around her. But she did unburden some of them onto her mum back home, and it was a good thing she did.

In this, my final year, emerging from that bleak winter, and still somewhat below par from that long bout of 'flu, I was trying to put everything into my studies. My essays got consistently good marks, but I was not getting many clear-cut Alphas. I had the nagging sense that my teachers had decided I was not up in the first class category, which should never have surprised me given the huge gap in my secondary schooling—practically non-existent—depriving me of the knowledge-base that standard-intake students enjoyed. Once people have decided at what level you belong, it is fearfully difficult to change their minds. Everything would depend on a stellar performance in the 50% exam component of the degree, to be conducted in June.

In the meantime, we acquired a couple of new friends in Andy and Sue Winterburn, from Yorkshire. Andy, who had been a bricklayer, was admitted under the same mature student scheme as I, and was just starting his degree. He wrote poetry, and when he found I'd been president of the staff–student Literary Society he sought me out, and we became mates. Equally important, with Meera often busy in the daytime with her MA studies, Jo found in Sue a wonderfully supportive sister-in-arms. The Winterburns had two small boys, Aidan and Tom, and lived within easy walking distance of Gulson Road, and so Sue and Jo became regular companions, sharing not just their motherhood interests, but politics, literature and general gossip to a degree that made a real difference to them both. Finally, her loneliness might abate.

That Easter the Winterburns and we went together to holiday in Yorkshire, where Andy had a friend who gave us his cottage on the moors for a week. It was a lovely time, we all got along well, including the children; Anna and their little boy Aidan, both three, were inseparable. Our walks and drives gave us a real sense of that harshly beautiful northern landscape, particularly around Harrogate. I was taken by the characteristic sight of tall redbrick chimneys rising out of green valleys, a mix of 19th century industry and Nature that instead of symbolising the cultural conflict of that era, had now mellowed with time into an aesthetic harmony that had no relation to modern life except as nostalgic remnants.

We paid a visit to Haworth to see the Bronte house. I shivered at its bone-chilling cold—at least this gave a true sense of what that afflicted family lived with—and imagined I could feel something of the spirit of tuberculosis, if not the actual bacilli, in every room. On the way back we passed through small towns that had once been hives of industrial activity but were now reverting to decrepit villages, their mills silent and steadily becoming overgrown with grass and weeds.

I realised when we got back to Coventry, and having spent long hours talking with Andy about writing, that a gradual and unnoticed change had come about in my outlook and in what I wanted for myself. Not unnoticed by Jo, I must add— she was aware of it, but said nothing. It was in my attitude to academic work and university life generally. When I began the degree my purpose was little more than to get a qualification that would enable me to find a bearable job—such as teaching—while I pursued the main goal of becoming a writer. And I had at first kept writing and sending off stories and a novel, all written in the breaks between terms, and having them rejected by publishers. I wasn't particularly disheartened, and believed I was learning and gaining valuable experience, and would eventually crack it. But as I moved into second and third years and the workload became heavier, and my enjoyment became more intense, creative writing gave way to essays, and I spent as much time on critical reading as on the literature itself. I liked the complex of ideas, the sense of history, the intensive focus on language and argument that literary studies entailed. Without fully realising it, I was gradually becoming an academic.

And so I was thinking more and more about how to stay in the field, and saw that I would have to undertake post-graduate studies somewhere. My friend Vincent Mahon had already graduated with a First and was a year into a Bachelor of Letters degree at Linacre College, Oxford. I began exploring the possibilities, and by March, 1970 had decided to make approaches to Linacre and to the Australian National University for a PhD scholarship. Success in either of these would be pretty-well contingent on getting a First, so I was putting all my hopes for the future into that possibility.

The offer of a place at Linacre came remarkably quickly. I have no doubt that Vincent's influence came into play in this, not because they would have consulted him, but because he was making such a success of his place in the college and in his studies. His Irish charm and air of integrity and perception always impressed academia (not to mention everyone else), and there was a general assumption, certainly amongst the Warwick faculty, that he was headed for a university career. He had therefore set a precedent that worked in my favour in the eyes of the Linacre Principal, John Bamborough, who organised an interview for me with both his Board and the Oxford Faculty of English Language and Literature. I had to come up with a research topic, since I'd worked out that my best option was the BLitt, which was based on an 80,000 word thesis and took only three years, whereas the DPhil (Oxford doesn't use the abbreviation PhD) took another two, and the reputation of the BLitt was as high as a doctorate from many other universities.

After hastily scrabbling about, boning up on William Empson's *Some Versions of Pastoral* and talking with a few of the faculty staff, in particular Bernard Bergonzi, who had become a strong supporter of me in several respects, I decided on an exploration of the treatment of the 'Child in Victorian Fiction', especially in George Eliot and Dickens. This seemed to impress the Linacre interview panel, only two of whom were in the literature field, and John Bamborough had arranged for me to go straight round to St Hilda's college afterwards to 'have a chat' with my prospective supervisor, Catherine Ing. An elderly and vaguely frail lady, she was also gracious and benign, indeed enthusiastic about my topic, and so I felt that my visit to Oxford had gone well. In a short time I received a letter from Bamborough offering me a place, but advising me that it was dependent upon my getting a State scholarship from the Department of Education and Science. And that was almost certainly dependent on my getting a First. No money, no admission.

The exams were for me a form of terror. Jo had told me how she had developed a technique for succeeding in exams, which served her well in her Matriculation results back when she was a schoolgirl. But such skills are a legacy of a good secondary education, and I had practically none, and so no exam technique. As I scrutinised the print on the green paper before me, constantly aware of time running away; every question seemed impenetrable, not what I had prepared for, and I grew rushed and panicky. I forced myself to at least keep writing for the full three hours of each paper—nine of them—but I had little sense that I was answering the questions properly, and little time to ponder over rewrites and canny arguments. To this day I have nightmares about sitting exams and not being able to perform. I went home afterwards in abject certainty that all my hopes were about to crash. It would be months before the results were posted, so we would have an anxious summer, with no idea what to tell friends or family back home what our next move would be. At least I had the Oxford offer, and I began exploring ways of getting funding—scholarships, grants, even a loan of some kind, if I failed to get a State scholarship.

When the results finally came out in August I was disappointed, though not surprised, to find I had missed a First. The list placed me in 2.1—the next level down. I drove home from the university almost weeping with despair and self-pity, with a pit of fear in my gut, knowing I had to tell Jo. What it would mean for us, I dreaded to think. Home to Australia with our tails between our legs, I feared in my depressed state, and under our own steam, travelling on what would have to be borrowed money. A life as a school-teacher, with probably little time or energy to write. Oh, what a difference it would have made, I kept telling myself, if I'd been able to get into that elite top category. Jo, of course, was sympathetic and heaped praise on me for doing so well, determined to take only positives out of the situation.

But as it turned out, it made no difference in effect, and I need not have been so cast down. For a start, it was a very high 2.1, and I'd missed a First by a mere whisker. Let me explain in detail what this means. The system of Humanities marking back then, at least at Warwick, was no system at all, but a vague belief in the idea of an objective standard. Either a work did or did not meet this objective standard, even though such a standard was never formulated, described, made the subject of training or even discussion by the faculty claiming to use it. It was assumed everybody 'just knew'. This meant that a First class mark could be given to any number of candidates. If it was a 'good year', there might be six or seven Firsts handed out. If it was a 'poor year' there might be only one, or indeed none. The 'objective' standard was of course never objectively arrived at, but was always the subjective opinion, albeit an experienced one, on the part of the examiner/s. The notion of an objective standard therefore meant nothing more than an intuitive sense that this piece of work or this candidate fell into an essentially mystical level of 'quality' called First Class. I don't say that this is an entirely wrong way to judge students' work; it's worth noting that it produces surprisingly little disagreement between examiners who double mark the same work, so there is at least a set of common values that operate within a discipline, even if its only source is baton-passing. That is, each generation learns from the last. But in the late 80s and 90s the unsystematic nature of this method of marking came under scrutiny by the new rationalists in university administration armed with business studies degrees, and they moved quickly and ruthlessly to wipe it out.

The system used today, at least by the University of Melbourne and no doubt most others, is all about ranking, not preserving some notion of an objective standard. The examiners, using their judgment which, though experienced, is of course still subjective, rank the candidates in qualitative order, and then an agreed percentage of categories is formulated—commonly 10% or 15% of Firsts, about 40% of Seconds, maybe 30% of Thirds, and 15% of Fails. The percentages can vary, but this is determined in advance in accordance with university or departmental policy, and scrupulously applied. Under this system departments will never give less than 10% of the candidates a First Class ranking. Their primary consideration is the interests of the candidates, not the department's own reputations, nor some illusory notion of maintaining an objective standard. They know that their students are competing for postgraduate awards and so on, so they give as many Firsts as the system provides for them to do. If Warwick had used this system, and given out six Firsts instead of three, thus meeting a 10% requirement, I would have been one of the six. I was close enough for this, Bernard Bergonzi told me in the corridor of the department soon after I saw the results. 'Don't let it bother you,' he said matter-of-factly, 'it needn't hold you back. In fact, you might be interested to know I also missed a First—got about the same mark as you.' This cheered me up no end, when I considered how successful and respected he was. And in fact his words proved to be right; I never was held back by missing that First.

While we waited for news of the scholarship, we took the kids to Swanage in Dorset for a summer holiday. A friend of a friend let a cottage to us cheaply, and we spent ten days exploring the lovely country and the seaside. Anna, now getting on for three, took one look at the beach and headed straight out to sea, fully clothed. I had to wade in to the very cold water in my trousers to rescue her. Lucy, a naturally happy child, was good-humoured despite cutting two new teeth, and loved being taken around in her pusher on the many walks we took in the area. The weather was quite warm in the last days, and we actually got some sunburn on the beach, something we'd hardly imagined possible.

Back in Coventry, news finally came in early August that I had been awarded a State scholarship, which would pay all fees to Oxford and provide us with an annual income of about £1100—not much for a family of four to live on, but manageable if I could do some part-time teaching, and better than we'd been receiving so far. Our families back in Australia were disappointed to learn we wouldn't be back soon, but of course they were pleased for me, and sent their congratulations. Now we had to face all the difficulties of moving out, finding accommodation in Oxford, and, not least, finding out how one goes about writing a thesis, and whether or not 'The child in 19th century fiction' was a viable topic. But I confess I was relieved and excited that I had achieved what I was after—to move into the next level of academic study. By way of celebration, Bernard Bergonzi generously took me to dinner at a favourite restaurant in Warwick. 'So,' he said as we touched our wineglasses together, 'you have an academic career ahead of you. Is it what you wanted?'

I thought he might be presuming more than was warranted so far, but his comment did take me a little by surprise. Is that how it happens? I thought, and realised immediately that yes, in England, once you've made it to Oxford you pretty much have the ticket to where you want to go next. So, I'm 'in', I said to myself, wherever that proves to be. But then, I don't imagine I'll be looking to England in the long run. Does the class system apply as much to Australia? Will an Oxford degree get me a university job back home? Flushed with my success, I confidently answered to myself that of course it would. Oxford has international clout, surely? I would walk into a university job anywhere, wouldn't I? So I simply assumed that all would be well, and that in the meantime the four of us were going to live the scholarly life amongst clever folk like ourselves in one of the loveliest towns in England. What more could we ask for?

9

FROM MY FIRST EXPERIENCE of university life I was attracted by its idealism, its incitements to wring the best out of oneself, and its respect for difference. And it was capable, from time to time, of wearing its learning lightly, with wit and humour, making it an ideal workplace. Oh, I know there are many defectors from these principles among both staff and students, but I am thinking less about actual behaviour than about an idea that inhabits the lecture rooms, the seminars and debates and sports fields and libraries, even the refectories. There is a kind of *expectation* of decency within oneself and one's dealings with others that I had never felt in any previous walk of life. It came from doing something you really loved, and the closest I had previously come to it was among the musicians in the Melbourne folk music scene, but that was on a small and limited scale compared with the many opportunities university offers. In all my previous working life in factories and offices the prevailing tone was obedience to authority, competitive self-interest, adaptation to dullness and orthodoxy, and almost nothing of that sense of freedom that comes from making your own important choices and failing or succeeding according to your ability to act upon them.

In a factory the expectation is that you will shut up and perform the routines, as if you are an extension of the machines you operate. If you enjoyed the work this was simply a lucky spin-off. And in an office the expectations are that you will do exactly the same except that your thinking and talking will be in the interests of the Company, and you will behave only in accordance with your status and position. Both, like the army, discourage difference and independent thought; all claim to be imparting discipline, when they are really only enforcing obedience. At university I learned that the only discipline that matters is self-discipline, which requires much more than the willingness to follow orders.

So this is what academia was coming to mean to me—a kind of retreat from the outside world of unadmitted compromise and bad faith. I knew this was what was meant by the ivory tower, though the implication that universities don't know much about that 'real' world outside is of course quite wrong—they know plenty about it, and usually know very well why they don't want to be controlled by it. The thought of spending the rest of my life working in a university was almost too good to be possible. I wanted that life, though I had little idea then that it might not, after all, be so different from that other world I keenly wanted to reject.

Oxford gave me a number of pleasant surprises. I knew the place was beautiful from the couple of visits we had paid there—with Jack and Donald, and once to visit Vincent in his flat, when he took me to a favourite pub and showed me around some of the haunts. And I'd seen a few of the colleges when I went up for the interview at Linacre. But what I hadn't counted on was its social temper, in the 1970s anyway, its essentially open-minded treatment of 'otherness', and this includes race, colour, religion and class. I had assumed it was an even more elitist environment than the rest of England, and so it is, but in a special and less offensive (to me at any rate) kind of way. Being working, middle or upper class cuts little ice within the Oxford college and faculty systems. The 'class' division is not so much between students, fellows and tutors, but between Oxford and the world outside. Once you are admitted into the system, you are not greatly better or worse than anyone else, even if you happen to prove stupid. Oxford will fail you, of course, but it won't degrade or insult you—on the contrary, it will be as sympathetic as the rules will allow.

I never heard a foreigner—an African or Indian or Australian or American—complain of prejudice on the basis of their race, nationality or religion in Oxford. On the contrary, the college system is designed to give them an adequate substitute for family, a warm base from which they can pursue their studies and extend their social life without fear of rejection. Its aim is a community of scholars, a democracy of the elite, in which the greatest insult to oneself is to fall into the crudities of the world outside. This is not quite true of the treatment of wives and children, however; there was still a vestige of the monastic tradition, which in the early days had no truck with marriage, and so wives can often feel excluded—as they in fact are from many of the Oxford rituals—and colleges made no provision for small children, push-chairs, changing-rooms and the like. At least they didn't back in the early 70s.

So I, at least, as an Australian and from the working class, felt unexpectedly welcome. Everyone assumed I was clever like most everyone else, even though I had my own desperate insecurities about that, and so it was never a subject of conversation. What they most asked about was *what you were doing*, and less about your problems or what your background was.

And then there was the fact that the university doesn't have a separate campus, but is intermingled with the town itself. This helps prevent too much of an ivory tower mentality amongst the academics. For instance, being able to drop in straight from the Bodleian Library to the Oxford market for fresh meat and vegetables or shop in Marks and Spencer for reasonably priced clothes, helped you to move out of the rarefied world of ideas into the practicalities of everyday life with a certain ease and pleasure. I loved it that you could see normal old ladies with their shopping trolleys stumping along High Street beside smug undergraduates with upper-class accents. Again this only emphasised that Oxford is self-contained; everyone within the city is part of it, an insider, and it is the world outside that is Other.

Linacre College was an especially agreeable social base. Its inaugural principal, John Bamborough, was a living embodiment of the Oxford style. Urbane, witty, a lover of amusing stories, he also maintained his scholarly interests, including the odd supervision—he was a Renaissance scholar, had written a readable study of Ben Jonson and was for decades engaged in an edition of Robert Burton's *The Anatomy of Melancholy*. He not only created Linacre College, in 1964, but established its particular mission, which was to house postgraduate students whose first degree was from outside Oxford, and so to bring together successful scholars from all parts of the world. He fought hard against conservative resistance to establish this identity, which was something of a reflection of his own personality and interests. On top of it all he was a diligent administrator, communicative and fair. Personally, I was entranced by him, though I was perhaps more inclined to appreciate his jokes than his critical acumen.

Accommodation has always been a big problem in Oxford, especially for those with families. On a visit to the Parkins, we mulled over the options. The typical student flat was going to be inadequate, and renting a whole house would be expensive and difficult to find; few Oxford landlords did that on a medium-term basis. Ian Parkin, in his typical off-the-square way of thinking, suggested we might look at buying ourselves a house. The idea seemed preposterous—us, with no money, on a student scholarship, *buying* a house in Oxford? But Jo could see the possibility, once Ian had pointed out that a house mortgage was the cheapest money to borrow and so you aimed as large as you could stand. It was also possible to obtain a deposit-free mortgage from the County Council, with a discount in lieu of tax-deductions for those with incomes too low to pay tax on, and the likelihood of a further grant to install a bathroom. We reckoned we could afford about £3000. We talked to the Council, and it all seemed possible, if we could find anything so cheap. And we did; we looked over a place in St Clement's, a tiny, tiny two-up two-downer, with no bathroom and needing lots of renovation. Could we tackle it? They wanted a little more than our maximum, so we would have to talk them down a bit, but yes, we were giving it serious thought.

And then a letter arrived from Linacre College, offering us one of their flats in Bradmore Road. It was comfortable, though not spacious, in a lovely old house in a leafy part of Oxford, near the public gardens. The prospect of not living through renovations, which I would have to undertake myself, when I was trying to get my BLitt done as soon as possible, was too attractive to resist, and so we took up the Linacre offer, and dropped the buy plan. We've often regretted it, especially since we discovered only after we'd moved in that Linacre rentals were strictly for the first year only, after which you were on your own. We hoped to revisit the buy plan, but by the end of that year—1972—the inflation monster of the decade had already awoken, and Oxford prices had moved decidedly out of our range. We've always fantasised over how we might have profited had we gone ahead with the buy plan, and seen its value steeple in the space of three years. How many such stories do all of us have of the ones that got away, of the opportunities lost or not taken, had we had the foresight to look into the future at the time? But we haven't and we didn't, and the chances went begging. Then again, we should weigh these against the ones that we *did* take, the luck that we *did* have—all too easy to forget when indulging in the might-have-been—and keep our perspective on a life subject to the uncontrollable forces of luck, for both good and ill, in this beautifully unpredictable world.

The flat was barely big enough for us, and was on the top—the fourth—floor with no lift; it was a huge job moving our stuff down from Coventry and into the flat, even after we had culled our largish household of furniture. The girl taking over the house at Gulson Road brought her gigantic father down from Leeds to help with the move, and we spent all morning loading and unloading the vans while his daughter did some shopping. When lunchtime came around and he said he was hungry, I suggested we get some fish and chips. He paused, aimed a sceptical eye at me, and asked in his broad Yorkshire:

'Are you shooer? Can you get good fish and chips this far south?'

I assured him you could.

'Well then, I'll have cod and chips twice if that's all right.'

I bought them at the local shop and we sat on the stairs in our near-empty house with a cup of tea and parcels on our laps, chatting about this and that. He was a fine old chap, very northern working-class, had rarely travelled out of Yorkshire, and was clearly proud that his daughter had become the first member of the family to have gained a university place. The eating over, we scrunched up our paper and as we washed our cups in the kitchen he said to me in tones of true wonder:

'By 'eck; who'd a thought you could get fish and chips that good this far south; it's amazing.'

He made me feel like a weary world traveller, knowledgeable in all forms of international cuisine.

In Oxford, Andy Winterburn and Rajiva had come down to give us a hand moving in, and I vividly recall the three of us manoeuvring the washing machine up those four flights of narrow stairs. It took all of an hour to get just that job done. And all that year Jo and I uttered many a curse as we lugged Lucy's pushchair or carried a weary Anna up those dreadful stairs. But the flat was in a convenient and pleasant position—6 Bradmore Road, only two doors from where the writer Walter Pater had lived in the 1890s.

Once again Jo was left mostly on her own during the day as I attended the initiation rituals that Oxford required, and she wrote home to her mother briefly reporting on the flat and the progress of the children:

Anna won't be able to go into the large overgrown garden without one of us, so she'll be cooped up in the flat while I get on with the work. I pray that I'll get her into a play school or some such soon. The only two days she has been really good in the last few months has been when we've visited the Parkins, and I suspect the space has something to do with it. She is still mostly possessed by the devil, but when he leaves her she is a sweet child, loves singing and drawing, wants to help and do as we do (we've had to promise her a 'grazor' for when she has whiskers on her face!). She practically gave up eating for a couple of weeks, so we tried having our tea with her, which helped, although it is a nuisance as we have to eat to suit her ... Lucy is no trouble, so is in danger of being forgotten. She crawls around happily eating everything she can get. She's had trouble this week with her centre top teeth, which are now through. We suspect she is going to be a redhead—I found it extraordinary enough to have a blonde daughter!

To be fair to Linacre Jo was made welcome whenever she came in for lunch, wheeling the kids in front of her in their brand new red double-seater pram—a veritable Maserati of child transport (but significantly cheaper).

The Oxford rituals are what make the place different from other universities, and were part of the reason the new universities eschewed them. Matriculating in Latin in the Sheldonian was one academic occasion Jo *could* attend, which she did along with the glamorous pram containing a sleeping Lucy and a hyperactive Anna. In the solemn hush of the proceedings, as we shuffled forward in our absurd academic attire losing the struggle to look dignified, I heard from the upper gallery a familiar little voice sing out over the hush, 'There's daddy!!' and I felt a little blush of sentimental pride. All the hoops to be jumped through—the dressing up in caps and gowns for the College photograph to identify our Year, the wearing of 'sub-fusc' to official dinners and other events, undergoing the mandatory probationary courses—Elizabethan Handwriting, Bibliography, Prolegomena to 19th century studies—before getting down to proper research seemed at the time mere nuisance rituals. What I hadn't realised was how these activities were part of the Oxford conditioning, working to turn me into a certain kind of scholar for the rest of my life. Almost unwittingly I learned to value a great library, the fundamental significance of primary materials, a respect for the practice of protecting and using sources. In later years these were useful tools for the writing of biography. Without intending it, I was becoming a literary historicist, and something of an empiricist when it came to constructing arguments for publication. If, for instance, I had gone to Cambridge instead, there is every chance that my critical skills, my focus on ideology and argument, would have been greatly enhanced. The Cambridge tradition in literary studies is strong in criticism and theory, an emphasis that goes back through Terry Eagleton and Raymond Williams to FR Leavis, William Empson and IA Richards. The Oxford emphasis, on the other hand, has been historical, producing the editors, bibliographers, historicist scholars like George Hunter, Claude Rawson, AL Rowse, Christopher Ricks, Richard Ellmann, figures less known to the public (and to undergraduates), but who are important in keeping the 'body of knowledge' of literary studies evaluated and available. Of course, there is much whimsical and mindless grubbing around in forgettable literary products of the past in Oxford, but then not everyone who came out of Cambridge was a Raymond Williams. Put simply, Oxford at its best provides the material foundations on which Cambridge enacts the drama of interpretation and value judgment. This is an oversimplification of course, and both schools practice both modes at a respectable level of professionalism, but nevertheless the contrast in their traditions is real, and in the field of literary studies Cambridge remains the glamorous sister to Oxford's dogged achiever.

There was a setback soon after I started on my research topic when it became apparent that the topic of 'The Child in Victorian Fiction' had already been well covered in a book by Peter Coveney. Somehow, I had failed to consider that this might have been a possibility, mainly because I had come to the topic by way of my reading of William Empson's *Some Versions of Pastoral*, which was essentially a psycho-social argument for the continuing relevance of pastoral in people's way of thinking, and so not especially historical, which the Coveney book is (which happens to contradict my generalisation about Cambridge in the above paragraph, for Coveney was a Leavisite). Looking back now I should have persisted with the topic, because Coveney had not addressed it in the way I, under Empson's influence, could have, if I'd thought harder and more creatively about it. But the mere fact of the book shook my confidence, and I couldn't at that early stage see a way forward apart from picking amongst trivial leftovers of Empson's and Coveney's arguments. So I panicked, and told Catherine Ing that my topic had evaporated on me. She was calm and patient, and said just to keep reading and thinking, and that something was sure to emerge. And indeed it did.

David Foxon, the distinguished bibliographer, hearing of my dilemma from Catherine Ing, sent me a note at Linacre, and when I saw him suggested a field of possible research. He had come across some interesting popular Victorian satirical publications that deserved to be better known—I could do a socio-historical exegesis, which might lead to publications as well as satisfying the BLitt requirements. I tackled them circumspectly, not knowing their literary worth, but was soon hooked and happily absorbed in Victorian popular writing and ephemera, and in the history and theory of satire. Foxon, with my supervisor's help, had rescued me. Now I had the pleasant duty of sitting in the Bodleian Reading Room pawing over journals that had not been read for over a hundred years, trying to make sense of satirical poems, prose pieces, popular novels and sketches; as with most topical or political satire, it is necessary to understand the people and issues being targeted, and this of course required my reading up on the social and political history of the period. It proved to be enjoyable work, though the nagging sense of its marginality to the literary canon, and therefore it's unlikely usefulness in teaching, at least at undergraduate level, never quite went away. This was to become a factor in my eventual difficulty in getting an academic job, as we shall see.

For Jo, Oxford offered her a much happier life than she'd had in Coventry. The children were no longer babies, which meant that while they were no less work, they were more interesting and allowed her to get out of the house more often. I took Anna on the back of my bicycle to her play school in South Oxford several mornings a week, and Jo was regularly able to take 2-year-old Lucy to the park and shops. More important, through Vincent and his now partner Deborah, we became good friends with a group of fellow post-graduates who had a strong commitment to feminist politics. The young women of the group held regular consciousness-raising meetings, and their male partners began doing the same. Our argument was that it made little point for women to change their attitudes and circumstances if men didn't change theirs, since they had to occupy the same social, and in some cases, emotional world. The women's group was a great help to Jo, not just in giving her someone to talk to about issues that mattered to her, but they gave her practical support. It surprised her to find them idolising her because she was a mother; they listened respectfully to her views, and offered to take care of the children when she needed their help.

In the flat immediately below us in Bradmore Road was an American couple called Chris and Sharon. They hadn't been married long—in fact they married on the news of Chris's admission to Oxford, and the Linacre flat was their first home together. Chris was doing a history thesis, and I think Sharon might have trained as a primary teacher, but she wasn't a student, and I think she felt a little intimidated by the academic *hauteur* of Oxford. She was friendly and pretty, the epitome of American innocence, and she lived on an emotional knife-edge, ebullient one moment, distraught the next, usually over the smallest thing. We tried to play Bridge one evening, and when she at one point made a bad play, Chris, who was as mild a man as you'd find anywhere, gently pointed out to her that she was meant to play in cooperation with him as her partner, not against him; she collapsed in tears. The game had to be abandoned.

She came up one evening to ask Jo, 'What do you do with green beans? I saw them in the market, but I'm only used to them frozen or canned. How do you cook them?'

They bought a turkey for Xmas and invited us down to dinner. When Sharon took it out of the oven, only the outside to a depth of a couple of centimetres was cooked, but there was enough edible meat in the surface slices and the wings to feed the four of us. The following day Sharon put the turkey back in the oven and roasted it enough to give herself and Chris another meal, but it was still not cooked through. So the next day, and the rest of the week, Sharon kept heating the bird and slicing meat off, until the weekend came and she thought they'd leave the last remains for a cold Sunday dinner. Chris took it out of the oven to carve it, turned it over and was confronted by a seething body of white maggots. How long had it been like that?

In the basement of our building, which was much more spacious than the flats above it, a secretive young man and his female partner had moved in just before us. I would see his name on the notice board at Linacre from time to time, and note the profusion of mail in his college pigeonhole and front letterbox, and I met him once or twice coming in and out of his flat. He was very reluctant to talk. He was studying some religious or philosophical topic, but didn't socialise in the Common Room and didn't seem to participate in any College activities. Eventually I learned that he and the woman were part of some religious sect that was trying to establish itself in Oxford. They were the 'advanced guard' of the organisation and he wasn't especially interested in academic life at all. Towards the end of that first year when, like the rest of us, they were meant to be moving out, we learned a surprising thing. An enormous corner house just along from us on the opposite side of the road, a real North Oxford mansion, went up for sale. It was going for what would now be the equivalent of millions of pounds. The sale was over very quickly—less than two weeks—and we learned it had been bought by the couple in the basement on behalf of their religious sect, the money provided by a rich woman. Mission accomplished, no doubt, and I don't think he had anything further to do with the College, or his academic studies. One thing you can say about religion, in those days as much as in these, is that there's money in it.

While I was settling in to my academic work, Jo was preoccupied with the possibility of making a trip back to Australia with the two girls. Barbara had been missing Jo terribly, and had become so anxious to see the kids that it prompted Whit, who had just retired and was cashed-up with his superannuation benefit, to offer to pay their fares for a Christmas visit. Jo was torn; much as she would have enjoyed it, she could see that it would make more sense for Barbara and Whit to make a trip to England and spend some time in Oxford near us. Trouble with that was that Whit would never agree to get on a plane and leave the country; the very idea horrified him. But for Jo to drag the kids across the world would not only cost more than Whit probably realised—about $1000—but it could be upsetting for them and make life a little less enjoyable for me, who would have to stay behind and work. The tone in Jo's letters was equivocal, leaving the decision to Barbara, but her subtext signified a lack of enthusiasm, so that in the end Barbara chose to come to Oxford without Whit. She planned to stay six months.

That first Christmas in Oxford went off well, despite power cuts. There was Chris and Sharon's turkey, and the Winterburns came down from Coventry for Boxing Day. Anna was thrilled to see young Aidan again. The girls were growing fast, with Anna at playgroup and Lucy taking her first steps.

Soon after the start of Hilary Term Jo and I started teaching classes for the Workers' Educational Association, the modest stipend helping with our strained finances. The WEA was a philanthropic organisation set up in 1903 to give the

British working class access to some basic learning. Eventually it expanded into serving middle-class interests, especially women with time on their hands, and some retirees. Jo ran a literature class out at Thame, and I taught a 'Literature and Film' group in the Oxford Prison.

That was in itself an educational moment for me. Every week I had to wait with the other visitors in a tiny room reeking of stale cigarettes before being admitted through clanging old iron gates into dark and suffocating rooms. Then I would be ushered into a windowless basement cell full of bored males, attending classes only because it got them off dreary duties, to undertake pathetic efforts at discussing books. When I told the class our first topic would be DH Lawrence's *Women in Love*, some of them nudged each other and grinned salaciously, obviously reckoning they were going to see some hot lesbian action on screen, with maybe a bit of games *a trois* thrown in. But the films never happened. The one moment the class enjoyed was when we flouted the rules and snuck into the chapel, where the men knew a TV was kept behind the altar, and we all sat in the pews and watched 'Top of the Pops', starring the delectable Pan's People. I had told the governor, at our first meeting, of my plan to study a novel and a film version of it together, and he had enthusiastically promised to have the films sent from the County library. But they somehow never turned up, and since this was the part the inmates were most looking forward to, they grew frustrated and eventually lost interest in the class altogether. Seeing out the term was a dispiriting exercise, and the classes degenerated into pointless chatter. What they really wanted was to talk about their cases, and to encourage me to take them up with the authorities, as if I had any influence. Of course they were all innocent, if you asked them. As men, they were a peculiar mixture of the slick and the stupid, led by one smart-mouthed individual who clearly had the rest under his thumb. His attitude was either mock-serious or serious mockery of everything and everyone, including a cyclist he threw off a bridge because he was carrying onions and therefore 'looked French', and a dumber inmate who, he proclaimed, had 'walked into a pub and started openly handing out forged five-pound notes'; the poor inmate simply blushed and gave an embarrassed grin as everyone in the room looked at him. I met this fast-talking 'leader' walking along the High Street about a year later, after he had been released. 'Hey teach!' he called to me, crossed the road to buttonhole me and shake my hand. 'I want you to know we really appreciated those classes you gave us while we were inside; you know, it's people like you who make prison bearable. Well done.' My attitude to him was just about to soften, when he added, 'By the way, you couldn't lend me a quid could you? I'm skint.'

I looked at him, mesmerised by his truculent mouth, and my heart turned cold. 'No, I couldn't,' I said, and went on my way.

Over the next couple of years Jo and I both taught further classes in small villages around Oxford. It was a rewarding, though not lucrative, way of gaining some adult teaching experience, and gave us insight into Home County life amongst the middle classes, especially non-working women. They were generally thoughtful, well-read, distinctly able but bored folk often whiling away the hours at home with little to do but tend their husbands and gardens, and grateful for the chance to use their minds.

One pleasant feature of undertaking research was spending quiet hours in some of the best Libraries in England. The Bodleian, of course, was my routine place of work for the three years of my tenure. The main reading room was always a delight, with its high leaded windows, the sweet camphoric smell emanating from desks and tables. And the Duke Humfrey's section, a dark medieval chamber in ancient oak with creaky floors, and though I rarely had occasion to go there, I envied the medievalists who worked in such an otherworldly place. The Radcliffe Camera has an elegant 18th century interior, though I found it a cold, somewhat deserted place to work in, with nothing of the busy warmth of the reading room.

A special pleasure were the few days I spent on several occasions in the British Library reading room in London. A circular space with beautiful pale timberwork and sky-blue leather upholstery bathed in the natural light from the vast dome high overhead, this has been the workplace of many an important thinker and writer, and generator of many an odd story over the years. There was a woman, it is said, who during one period made sure she was first in the door when it opened every morning, so that she could sit in the seat that had been regularly occupied by Karl Marx. She wanted no-one else to have it. And Catherine Ing, my supervisor, loved to tell of the time she found herself sitting next to a man who put the book he was reading aside while he reached in his bag, took out and noisily unwrapped a parcel, and proceeded to eat a smoked herring.

Libraries, especially the grand, historic libraries, are the true memories of the world, treasure troves of what has been salvaged from the past, and a civilising influence over all who spend time in them. It is no accident that library staff are invariably helpful, efficient, calmly persistent in their duties, and do not seek (nor are generally given) the recognition they deserve for their part in the intellectual life of the literate world. All this I only discovered by being given the opportunity to pursue postgraduate research.

In March of 1972, with much eager anticipation on both sides, Barbara arrived for her six month stay. After various efforts on our part to find her a college flat came to nothing, she had to do a hasty search and settle for a small room on the top floor of a north Oxford house. She soon settled in and went about forming a very important relationship with her two granddaughters—it was love all round, and Barbara's patience and intelligence proved to be a great help to us. Until she got herself a part-time job typing manuscripts for a professor, Barbara saw them daily, took them for walks in the park, shopping, ate with us, went for drives with us into the country. I had started playing cricket for my college team, and they all—Jo, Barbara and the girls—came out to a village match and hung about all day on the green while I did my stuff (including, I might add, one of the best slips catches I've ever taken). Doubtless they were bored out of their minds, but I look at a few photos of that day now with fond memories. It was certainly a time when Barbara cemented the affection between her and the girls, and affection they cherished for many years to follow. The same can be said for her relations with me: for while she had reservations—I think she would have liked her only daughter to have married someone altogether better formed, in looks and accomplishment—she only ever wished me well, and eventually came to respect my own efforts to improve and provide for my family, satisfied that I truly did love her beautiful Josephine. So we became friends, and never crossed words.

The months of her stay seemed to fly, especially for Jo, who depended on her in numerous ways, especially with the girls, who talked of her constantly when she wasn't around. All the more painful for Barbara, then, when she was the cause of a frightening accident with Lucy. Knowing we had to move from Bradmore Road, Jo took Barbara and the kids to inspect a house in Chilswell Road, South Oxford, and while they were there Lucy ran around a corner straight into the lighted cigarette Barbara was holding in her fingers. Screaming in pain, going in and out of consciousness, Lucy was held in a frantic grip of love and remorse by Barbara in the back seat of the car while an anxious Jo drove through the peak-hour traffic to the Radcliffe Infirmary. Poor Barbara swore she would never smoke again, though it was several years before she could finally quit. The damage was temporary: a blister on the cornea that doctors said would heal in 24 hours—the eye has faster regenerative powers than any other body organ—and Lucy was given a local anaesthetic, an eye protector and taken home. All was soon well again, and Barbara and Lucy brought, if possible, even closer together.

When in September of that year Barbara had finally to go back to Australia, her absence was temporarily compensated for by the arrival, the unlikely but welcome arrival, of my mother, Thelma, for several weeks to stay with us. It was her first venture out of Australia, and since her husband Richard, just like Barbara's husband Whit, could not be persuaded out of his Aussie male comfort zone of the pub, mates and sport, she was forced to take the bit between her teeth and go it alone. I met her at Heathrow, and was a little shocked to find her pale and aged, probable indications that the flight had been a tense and wretched experience for her. After a few days with us she picked up again and was back to her lively and healthy self. She arrived just as we were moving out of the Bradmore Road flat into a house in Chilswell Road, South Oxford. But before we made the onerous move, we had arranged to spend a couple of weeks in a rented cottage at Swanage, on the Dorset coast. It was a delightful time, and gave Thelma a chance to get to know her granddaughters, and to see something of England, which she had always longed to do. Despite the cool weather, we spent whatever time we could on the sandy beach, where Anna with typical bravado plunged naked into the cold sea, and Lucy, now almost two, played in the sand or watched her sister from the safety of her pram. One rainy day we drove to Lyme Regis, which my mother loved. The novel *The French Lieutenant's Woman* had not long been out, and we all braved the sea-wind to walk out on the Cobb to re-imagine the scenes of Fowles' reworking of Jane Austen's *Persuasion*. Thelma bought one of the huge sea urchin shells from a stall, and we had lunch in a cosy café while the rain pelted and the wind howled outside. It was a memorable day, and one my mother would long remember.

The move into Chilswell Road saw us settle into a particularly happy period in our life, though underneath the happiness Jo was still longing for Australia and her family. The children were growing into lively minded, lovely little characters who were constantly demanding attention but repaying it in ladles full. We acquired a kitten, called Tom, who showed remarkable forbearance at being mauled from pillar to post by the girls; Lucy would carry it round by the throat, like a bottle. Also, we seemed to be managing on our modest income much better now, to the point that Jo was able to take Thelma to Paris for a few days. They enjoyed themselves, two girls together, getting to know each other better, visiting Versailles and Notre Dame, trudging up the Champ Elysees, where some man tried to pick up Thelma (not Jo!), all while the harried husband coped with the girls at home, though I admit to having quite a bit of help from friends—my fellow literature student Charlotte Boydell, Vincent and Deborah, and our neighbour Cheryl, who fed me a couple of times.

We were sad to see Thelma leave in October; she had been a great help, and it had occurred to us how brave she was to make the long journey on her own. A few years later I learned something more of the emotional price she had paid for her adventurous spirit. She had been determined to see Rome on the way back, changed her ticket to do it, and found herself on her own in a strange and busy Eternal City, unable to manage the language, unable to fathom how to get to the sights she had come for. In her small and shabby hotel room, tired, bewildered, afraid and desperately lonely, she burst into tears like a teenage girl, and wished she hadn't come. But the next morning she mustered her courage again, and found her way to the Trevi fountain, a sight she had longed for since she had seen the movie *Three Coins in the Fountain*, back in 1954. Unfortunately, the fountain was being cleaned and was not working that day, but at least she could take in its magnificent sculptures and grand conception. She managed to find a tour that took her to St Peter's, The Colosseum and other famous places, so she was able to fly home satisfied with her decision to make the journey, and indeed satisfied with the whole adventure she had undertaken—to England, to Paris, to Rome—one that had been important for us all.

The visits of Barbara and Thelma during 1972 had been important in two ways: they had given us much needed help and support with the kids, and they had served us with a reminder of what lay in store for us when we returned to Australia—as if Jo needed reminding of that—where whole tribes of relatives and friends were eager to see us and welcome us back into the fold. Even I, much as I loved England now and part of me wanted to stay and continue reaping the benefits of its literary climate, even I was beginning to feel the wisdom, the necessity, even the attraction, of going home. And it *was* home, whatever reservations we had nursed about it over the years. I have very little of the nationalistic spirit in me, in fact recoil from expressions of patriotic fervour, don't at all mind finding fault with my country on the smallest pretext. But it is my country, I grew up there, Melbourne city and Victorian bush were the educators of my eyes, my ears, the mode of thinking and feeling it gave me, my sense of the meaning of colours, of places and people, of who was to be loved, who hated, and why. It is not because it is Australia; it is because this is where *I* became who I am, just as it would be for anyone in any place.

And now, with all the reports of the transformations being wrought by the new Whitlam government, it may even be that most of my fault finding would no longer be applicable. There could be many changes for the better to return to.

10

VINCENT'S GIRLFRIEND DEBORAH RETURNED from a family Xmas in the States in the New Year, just in time to coincide with Anna's contracting chicken pox. Actually it was Vincent we were concerned about, since he had not had it, and was the one most at risk. In the end he managed to avoid it. Deborah took up residence in our spare room, and she was a lovely acquisition to the household. Not only was she a friend, but an important member of the women's group Jo had joined, bringing a wider circle of visitors to the house, which was good for the children as well as us. She was a philosophy student, and we had some stimulating conversations on matters from politics to aesthetics. On one occasion she was preparing a duck for dinner, when Anna, now four, spotted the naked duck on the table prior to going in the oven. She was puzzled, remembering that her only experience of ducks was of feeding the live ones in the Oxford gardens.

'What is that?' she asked.

'It's a duck,' said Deborah.

After some hesitation, Anna said,

'Is the duck dead?'

'Yes, it sure is,' said American Deborah. A few moments' more hesitation, and Anna said,

'Debbie, does the duck *know* it's dead?'

Deborah, the philosophy PhD, was bowled over. 'Wow Anna, you sure know how to raise interesting issues; that would keep a seminar going for a whole morning.'

In January I had the benefit of a piece of literary luck, a more or less personal meeting with WH Auden. As well as admiring his poetry, I was always fascinated by Auden's face. Lined and deeply furrowed in all directions, it was, he himself had said, 'Like a wedding-cake left out in the rain'. The first time I saw him speaking had been on a small black and white television screen soon after we arrived in England in 1965, and I could hardly believe I was looking at so great a man in such an ordinary situation, like coming across Shakespeare on a bus. And the voice, the first time you heard it, had a surprising, soft, duck-like tone that didn't seem compatible with the Oxford accent.

It happened that Linacre was situated in those days (it has since moved) right next to Christ Church in St Aldates, and I would sometimes see him puffing his way down or up the hill along the Christ Church wall. He looked to be, as he was, struggling with emphysema, fighting for breath in the notoriously damp Oxford air. A postgraduate mate with a reversible name I never seem to get right, like Martin Stewart, was doing studies in American History, and casually asked, 'Interested in coming to a seminar with WH Auden? My supervisor at Christ Church is running a series on modern American culture and history, and Auden has agreed to take part. There's only six of us, so it should be quite interesting.'

Interesting was hardly the word. We got there a little early, sat ourselves at a battered round table in the middle of the ancient and rickety room. Eventually Auden appeared, ushered in by a grey-haired professor of American History, dressed suavely in a neat suit and gown. Auden wore a shabby dark blue suit and crumpled grey shirt with a loose multi-coloured wool tie. He stood unsmiling and breathing hard while one of the students fetched him a chair. He carried this to a position some eight feet away from the table, and sitting in it, half-turned away from the company so that his direct, straight-ahead gaze would have been out of the window at the blue sky. From this position he could, if he chose, occasionally turn his face to the table almost as though he were delivering an aside. Everything about his body language suggested he would rather have been anywhere but here.

The seminar got underway briskly, led by the professor, who moved into his stride with obvious relish. The topic was The American City, with special reference to New York, and recent developments in its 'multicultural identities', to use the professor's jargon. I can't recall his argument in detail, or any of the responses from the students. I think Martin (or Stewart) and one other student put in their modest sixpenneth, but the rest of us stayed quiet, hanging back to watch the big guns fire. The professor, clearly conscious of his performance before the great man, kept a tight rein on the flow of talk, most of which he did himself.

The discussion had been going some twenty minutes and Auden had still not said a word. In fact, he hardly seemed to be paying attention at all. He lit a cigarette—which I think was against the rules, but no-one said anything—and sat turned aside from us, gazing out the window as if he were not of our party at all, but just happened to be sitting nearby. Nevertheless, because of the position of my chair, I was close enough to observe at length the ancient lizard's face, the barrel chest and a portion of varicose-veined, pale stick leg—the sad leg of an aged smoker—exposed between trouser cuff and sock; and to note his boredom. The topic had come around to that of violence in urban centres, with the professor's talk continuing freely and at times glibly on a matter that is fundamentally remote from academic life. He was becoming noticeably uneasy about Auden's lack of participation, and kept flicking looks across in the hope that a little eye contact might draw a response to some of his assertions. 'What we have, of course,' the professor was saying, 'is not so much a problem of law and order or moral failure, as someone like Saul Bellow has recently tried to argue, but a new kind of class struggle. In the ghettoes of Los Angeles and New York, unemployment, poverty, lack of education all conspire to give racial and ethnic minorities no chance of using the system to their benefit. "A riot," Martin Luther King once said, "is the language of the unheard." So for young urban blacks, with no other means of self-expression, violence is a kind of poetry.'

He paused here and directed a question across to Auden. This was his chance to play his ace, and to put an end to Auden's recalcitrance. I, for my part, was silently irritated about that too-easy connection between poetry and violence, a crude sociological metaphor.

'Wystan,' he said expansively, 'you've been living in New York recently, and we've all seen the reports of muggings in the subways, attacks on innocent people in the streets, thugs roaming the city at night. What's your view on all this? Is it worse than a decade ago, are the reasons different now, does violence always come down to a matter of chance or are the explanations glaringly obvious?'

There was a moment of silence as we all waited. The suddenness of the question, not to mention the huge, sociological canvas on which the problem had been painted, had perhaps confounded him. He stammered a little before he lisped, in his softest, limpest duck voice:

'Well ... it's terribly nice where I lived.'

And he said not another word for the rest of the seminar.

I have very little memory of what was said after this because I lost interest. All I could think of was how sad, how out of touch, how old-dufferish Auden's comment was. Disillusioned, I walked with Martin (or Stewart) in silence till we got to Christ Church gate, where he finally said, 'Well, that was a load of old bollocks then, wasn't it?'

But as I reflected afterwards, perhaps it wasn't so silly a comment after all. Perhaps it wasn't a sign of his inattention, or lack of interest in the subject. It might have been right on the money. What if it was the only way he could participate, which was to speak only for himself, from his own experience, in the simplest, ungeneralised language? It would put a different slant on it. It would be the only way he could say anything true—to himself, to the seminar, to language.

A little solipsistic perhaps, but this is the direction in which age takes us. No, maybe I'd learned something from the seminar after all.

They were busy times in the Chilswell Road house with friends staying over—Margaret, Leslie, Deborah, Charlotte, friends such as John Sampson and Maisie Jones up from London (we had gotten over our quarrel), relatives visiting England; we sang Irish folk songs with Vincent and Bob Connon in the little sitting room, cooked a curry dinner for Rick Gekowski and his wife Barbara. And this is not to mention getting on with the research, taking the kids to nursery school, feeding them and putting them to bed, Jo teaching a 'Women and Literature' course for the WEA, taking my mum to Paris, and all of us somehow finding the time to talk about politics, sex, literature and god knows what else, usually at the table, which seemed to be always able to accommodate unexpected arrivals. And there was so much good will going round between us all. It was a wonderful experience and entertainment for the kids, as well as for us of course, and was, as Vincent later wrote to me, 'a golden period' in our lives. And how we took those good times for granted, hardly thinking they might never come again; you do, when you're young, you think in the present, assume you will live forever.

But, as always, there were darker moments. A lecturer friend from Warwick University, Gloria Cigman, had a house in Oxford, so we saw her from time to time. She had an old school chum, Virginia, who had married the novelist BS Johnson, and since they were visiting Gloria in Oxford she asked us—me, Jo and the kids—to join them for a picnic on the riverbank at North Oxford. I had met Bryan Johnson before—briefly at Warwick, when I had invited him to talk to the Literary Society about his experimental approach to writing. He was helpful and forthcoming with his views, which, for an *avant garde* writer, were oddly closed-minded; he believed that inventing stories was telling lies, that descriptive writing was obsolescent Victorianism, views which he had repeated in various forums for years. I didn't altogether agree with them, but I could see that in a world where there was plenty to discourage a struggling writer, he drew much-needed conviction from them; but there was a hint of personal fragility in the dogmatic way he clung to them.

On this pleasant summer day in 1973, things went quietly but smoothly while we sat on a blanket and ate our lunch, the children—theirs and ours, all small—playing about us, the conversation flagging a little, despite Gloria's and Virginia's efforts to keep it rolling. Bryan was quiet. Then he got up and removed himself from our company and sat on the grass about 100 yards away, staring morosely at the water. He stayed there for the rest of the picnic—over an hour—and uttered not another word. No-one had said anything obvious to upset him, no opinions had clashed. He was simply in the darkest of moods.

About four weeks later I had a phone call from Gloria, who had heard from Virginia. Bryan had killed himself—got drunk, sat in a warm bath, cut his wrists and bled out into oblivion. Days before he had been talking strangely, dangerously, had struck Virginia, such that she felt the need to get herself and the children safely out of his way, and had taken them to stay with friends. When she returned with a friend, they found a silent house with all the lights on and Bryan dead in the bath. A note simply said, in the manner of his friend Samuel Beckett, 'this is my last word'. It was a sad end for a novelist of courage and integrity, dogged by an inability to live with his disgust at an imperfect world.

Gerald, a friend from Ruskin College, invited us for dinner, where he and his wife Marina introduced us to their friends Stan and Rosie from Dundee, where Stan lectured in the university English department. Out of this meeting came an invitation from Stan and Rosie to visit them in Dundee, and in May we did just that. I had a little research to do in the Dundee Library on John Edward Jenkins, local MP and author of *Jinx's Baby* and other satirical novels of the 1870s, so it was a serendipitous invitation. Dundee, on the 'silvery Tay', bathetically praised by its celebrated bard, William McGonagall, the 'Dundee Rhymer' and 'best bad verse writer of his age', proved to be windy, cold and too provincial for our tastes. I filmed us with the kids on a pleasant afternoon's visit to St Andrews (of golfing fame), which is a lovely old university town on the sea front, where the ruins of the old cathedral offered an ideal fun park for us and the kids, hiding and seeking between grave stones and fallen pillars. We still have the film.

A lectureship in English was currently available, for which Stan offered to recommend me, but the remoteness, the weather, and the constant disagreements between me and an aggressive Stan put me off, so I politely declined to apply. Perhaps it was foolish to have done so, perhaps it might have been a launching pad for an Australian job, who knows? But then again we might have found ourselves stuck there for years, and I doubt our marriage would have survived it; Jo would have left me and taken the girls home to Oz, I'm sure, rather than become a permanent fixture of Dundee.

More and more now my thoughts were turning to job-hunting, mostly Australian, but I also kept an eye on English possibilities; Jo had her heart set on going home, so the former was our agreed priority, but secretly I would have preferred the latter. I would have loved, at least for a few years, a job in a good English university, which would undoubtedly have been a good platform for a senior post back home. I began sending off applications, though it was premature; I would have been foolish not to finish the thesis before I left Oxford, but I don't think I fully grasped how difficult it would have been to do it while holding down a full-time lectureship.

During the late winter an event occurred that produced a response in me that even to this day I do not understand, nor know quite what it was I was feeling or why. Jo and I, along with Vincent and, I think, Deborah, had been to an evening of traditional English dancing at one of the older colleges, where they played Elizabethan music and taught you Galliards, Pavanes, the Roger de Coverley and so on. I quite enjoyed it, but not as much as Jo, who has always loved dancing. When the college held another evening a few weeks later, Jo was keen to go but I wasn't, and so was happy to stay home with the kids. Deborah must have been away somewhere, so Jo went along with Vincent. I thought nothing of it until it got to around midnight and they still had not come home, so I gave them up and went to bed. At around two o'clock something woke me, and Jo was still not home, not in the bed beside me. I began to get concerned, first over their safety, but then this gave way to darker thoughts. Soon I was sitting in the bedroom with the light off waiting for them in a full-blown paroxysm of idiotic jealousy. This took me by surprise, because as I've already said, neither of us had shown any signs of this corrosive emotion before, and I didn't imagine I ever would. But I kept thinking that Vincent was so damned attractive, and they liked each other so much, why would they not? When they finally arrived home at 4 am, Vincent went straight to bed, and as Jo entered the room I confronted her, quietly but with righteous self-justification.

I won't try to recreate the scene; I can't remember what I said anyway, but I was hurling accusations. Her response came down to the only one she felt able to make: she threw the question of doubt straight back at me. She would not respond with a denial, because that would imply that I had a right to ask if she was faithful; I had no basis for such a question, and therefore no reason for putting it. What she said was, How could I claim to love her if I didn't trust her?

Was I being melodramatic? Yes. The problem was, I didn't *really* believe in my own feelings; I was in a panic, irrational and fear-driven. It had little to do with Jo, and much to do with my own self-confidence, which was built somewhat precariously on the need for her commitment to me. It is a short step from need to demand, but it is a step that shifts the balance from love to possession, and possession is the killer, the stifler of freedom, and freedom is the oxygen of love. What prompts a man to take that ill-considered step? I wish I knew. What I suspected but wouldn't admit was that my jealousy was self-induced, was founded on nothing but fear and suspicion, on something that was not there; and so there was no conviction in it. But it soured things for a couple of days, with a black intensity not usual between us, until I came to my senses. The whole event, and my behaviour, took me unawares, gave me a glimpse into psychic shadows I hadn't seen before, and that I would certainly be better-off without.

Events at Linacre turned political in the months leading up to the summer break. I had been elected to the Common Room committee just at a point when a group of the new intake discovered that the college was buying South African sherry for sale at the bar. This was at a time when the anti-apartheid movement was getting into full swing under Peter Hain, and had already managed to stop tours by South African cricket and rugby teams to Britain. There were some students at Linacre who felt strongly that academic boycotts of South Africa should be upheld in every possible way, and so they began to press for the college to change its buying policy. The Fellows were outraged, and stubbornly opposed the move. I spoke and voted for change at the committee meeting, but it was overwhelmingly lost. I remember Paul Turner, a Fellow in English Literature, coming to me afterwards and deploring my action. 'I thought you were more civilised than that,' he said. If it hadn't been for my personal view that College sherry was hardly an issue that South African blacks gave a damn about, I might have served him a mouthful in reply. Civilised! As if defending a thoughtless and unnecessary piece of cheap economising by the College made you civilised. But then Oxford doesn't really value politics, doesn't like to get its hands dirty.

By this time I had settled into the task of writing up my thesis, having done most of the research in the Bodleian and other external libraries, and so I worked almost every day in the small library at Linacre. These were the days before computers, so all notes were taken by hand, all 'writing up' done on a typewriter. It was convenient for me to take on the role of Library Secretary while I was doing this, so I oversaw some book purchasing and re-shelving, and generally acted as caretaker, which enabled me to come and go as I pleased, even till late at night. I took to working alone in the silence, my little green desk lamp my cheerful companion in the dark, with two brandies at my right hand bought from the bar downstairs, and replenished occasionally as I felt the need. It was a very nice way of working, though after three slugs probably not conducive to the degree of grammatical and bibliographical precision that Oxford requires. That would come back to bite me.

One of the ways of relieving the discomforts of long hours at my desk was table tennis in the room next to the library. There was usually a willing opponent somewhere around, especially approaching lunch time, and so I began to play every day. As with many sports, I can quickly develop an aptitude if I put in the practice. I soon regularly beat all comers, including those tricky Italian and French amateurs who resort to all kinds of illegal spin and surprise tricks. My Canadian-Irish friend Bob Connon was an equally good player, and when the College tournament was held we played off for the championship. This was another one of those character-revealing events. In the first two sets I absolutely creamed him, playing an aggressive game that saw all my smashes going in and Bob on the back foot unable to gain any momentum. But then the fatal change happened; I went on the defensive, saying to myself 'I only have to win one of the next three sets and the championship's mine'. Big mistake. It allowed him to make the running, his confidence came back and he beat me 3-2. Typical of me, I thought: I always start well, then I can't keep it up and end up running second-best. It's always been the same; initial brilliance, then the descent into the ordinary. *C'est la vie.*

We had been given notice at the start of our tenancy by our landlord, Mr Belcher, that we might have to move out of Chilswell Road at the end of the academic year, because he was planning to sell the house, but not having heard any more about it since, we thought maybe it wouldn't happen. But it did; we knew in May that we would have to be out by the end of June. Our annoyance over the move was considerably mollified when we quickly found a bigger, much better house at 4 Princes Street, East Oxford, which had no time limit on our rental. The landlord proved much nicer, and lowered the rent on the agreement that we would look after the garden. Deborah moved with us, as did Tom, the cat. In fact, Tom gave us a pleasant surprise when he produced a litter of kittens, prompting an immediate change of name to Thomasina. This was very exciting for the girls, and on more than one occasion one of us caught two-year-old Lucy descending the stairs doing her old trick of carrying a mewling kitten in each hand by the throat, offering them to us as presents.

In Princes Street our lives were more comfortable than at any other time in England. The house had good sized rooms, and interesting little areas, such as the 'outside' kitchen/dining space, situated under a transparent cover. It had once been a paved yard, and kept the feel of openness to the light, while being perfectly protected from the elements. This led onto the garden, which had a splendid prepared-turf lawn paid for by the landlord and laid by me; the garden had raspberries and blackberries growing along the fence, and two healthy apple trees that during that summer bore immense crops, so much so that I took a barrow-load of Bramleys up to the local fruit shop and got £3 for them. Which reminds me of another piece of consumer luck that Jo experienced at the Oxford open market, where a particular butcher would hold a weekly 'performance/auction' of meat, joshing and flirting with the women shoppers as he theatrically knocked down chops and steak at bargain prices. She saw him hold up a sizable lump of frozen beef for something like 70 pence, so she called out 'yes'. It turned out to be beautifully tender, and from which she was able to get two excellent grills, a roast, a casserole and enough mince for a bolognaise sauce. When she went back the following week to buy some more at that price, the butcher threw his eyes to the heavens. 'Lady,' he said good-humouredly, 'that was the biggest mistake of my life; what you bought last week was a whole beef fillet. I don't know what got into me!'

I should say a word about Catherine Ing, my thesis supervisor. Supervisors for Oxford postgraduates are the key to your enjoyment, if not the whole academic success, of your thesis work. An indifferent or unsympathetic supervisor can destroy the whole enterprise, and even cost you your career. I knew a Linacre student in philosophy who fell out with his supervisor so badly that he never completed his degree, and so never obtained a university post; he was forced to do something else with his life, and was never happy. When I lost faith in my initial research topic, Catherine Ing kept up my spirits with commonsense advice, and unstinting support. She believed I would find another, and when I did she insisted on keeping me as her student, and generously adapted her interests to accommodate my new subject. Fortunately she was so knowledgeable in 19th century literature already that it was no great trouble for her to do so.

She was a Fellow of St Hilda's College, had written a very elegant study of Elizabethan Lyrics early in her career, and then moved into 19th century literature, where her publications were mostly historical and biographical articles. Not a 'high flyer', but like many of the women Fellows, conscientious and sympathetic, she could be almost maternal in her efforts to keep up your morale, knowing full well that postgraduate research can be an isolating, lonely and uncertain pursuit. A lean, tense woman, a cat-lover, with the hoarse voice of the life-long smoker, she was not in these years in the best of health. Linacre held frequent dinners to which one could bring one's supervisor, and Catherine loved to come along; after a few glasses of red she would become a wonderfully lively, ebullient centre of attention, retelling all the old Oxford jokes and 'blue' stories about various dons, stories that had been handed down over the generations. The classicist and poet, CM (Maurice) Bowra, Fellow of Wadham, former Vice-Chancellor and oft-quoted wit, was one of the favourite topics. With a great twinkle in her eye, Catherine would tell the story of Bowra in conversation with one of his more proper colleagues. Bowra had suggested that sometimes it's better to tell a lie than to offend people. The colleague looked deeply shocked, sat back in his chair and solemnly proclaimed 'Do you know, I'd sooner commit *adultery*!' Bowra laughed, 'Well wouldn't we all, old chap, wouldn't we all!'

And then of course she would tell the story about Bowra bathing nude with male friends on the little secluded area down on the Isis known as 'Parson's Pleasure', when some undergraduates came punting past. The others hastily covered their genitals, and hissed at Bowra to do the same. But Bowra put his hands up to cover his face, much to their alarm. 'What were you thinking?' they asked him afterwards.

'Well I don't know about you, but my students recognise me by my *face*,' he replied.

Ah, the Oxford stories. Will they ever fade away?

An email from Vincent came the night before last. At least I thought it was from Vincent—it had his address on it. I had written him a week or so earlier, a long newsy email about the family and about my doings in recent weeks. We don't write as often as we used to. I suppose this is inevitable when you don't see someone for years at a time, and Vincent doesn't seem to have mastered Skype. He prefers the written word, and certainly my drawer is full of handwritten letters from him over the years, good, full letters containing his thoughts and plans, as well as the day-to-day doings that, for a writer, are the essential glue of a well-constructed letter. He writes thoughtfully, economically, the virtues of the playwright he became. Academia didn't really suit him—all that jockeying for power, the petty jealousies; he's above all that. Since we've resorted to emailing in recent years the letters have grown shorter—more like messages than letters, just giving a quick report on the latest. On both sides, that is. We are running out of mental energy, no doubt, and there's something about email that discourages the long narrative.

Anyway, as I say, I thought it was from Vincent, but when I opened it the first sentence was actually about *Vincent. 'I am terribly sorry to say that Vincent has been in hospital for a week with sepsis.' I quickly dragged the cursor to the end of the email and saw that it was from Penny, Molly and Emily—his partner and their two daughters. As I read on, the seriousness of his situation became obvious; the doctors hadn't yet diagnosed the problem, but he had been in and out of intensive care, had eaten little for three weeks, was on a nasal drip and antibiotics. At his age (76), and with a replacement aortic valve done over ten years ago, he might not have great reserves of strength for an attack of this kind. Of course I sent off a quick reply to the girls saying all I could say in the circumstances—that we sympathise etc, keep us informed etc, that we 'pray' it will turn out ok. Why did I say that—'pray' it will be ok, when I do nothing of the kind? The big problems draw out the clichés. I never pray, which for me would be a less-than-honest expression of impotence. 'Hope' is not much better, but at least it is honest. So I hope it will be ok.*

That night I began to reflect on our friendship over the years. What is it that creates a bond between two men? The feeling is as mysterious as any love between a man and a woman. Hetero relationships are notoriously unpredictable, and no-one seems to know, even on the day of marriage, whether or not they will stay happily together for the rest of their lives. Male friendship, made of completely asexual respect and interest in each other that may last a lifetime, is just as unpredictable and in a way more mysterious, because physical attraction is not a factor. And yet appearance does play a role. I always liked Vincent's features—the clearly defined jaw, those strong wonderfully shaped forearms, the deep, sonorous Irish voice, and kind, intelligent eyes—I could see exactly why women found him attractive. Modesty, absence of male aggression, is another aspect of his attractiveness; he is never on the make, has never, for instance, elbowed me in the ribs on a train and said 'get a load of that', or 'boy you don't get many of those to the pound' about the breasts of some girl sitting opposite. He takes women too seriously for that, probably more seriously than some of them take themselves.

I fear the worst. Some extension of my life is about to disappear. Let's hope it doesn't come to that, and that I'll see him when we go to England in August back to normal again. Hope. What else can I do?

I had a happy encounter with the distinguished biographer, Richard Ellman. I knew by a recent lecture he had given that he had a continuing research interest in the late 19th century, especially in anything that might have interested James Joyce. Somewhere in *Ulysses* Joyce mentions the dissolute activities of Edward, Prince of Wales. In my reading of anti-monarchist satires I had come across a reference to a little *frisson* enjoyed by Edward and his chum Christopher Sykes. Apparently the Prince had instructed the London Fire Brigade to advise him of any large fires they were attending, so that he and Sykes could be there. Armchairs would be placed in good view of the burning building, and the Prince and Christopher would sit back in comfort with a port and a good cigar to enjoy the entertainment. Sometimes they would ask to put on a fireman's helmet, and take a turn at holding the hose. All the kind of deliberately provocative public school behaviour that the Prince and his upper-class cronies habitually enjoyed, offering, as it were, two fingers to the *hoi polloi.*

So I called Ellman saying I had an anecdote I should like to pass on to him, and he invited me round to his rooms in New College. 'New' of course is misleading: it was founded in the 14th century, and has some of the loveliest old buildings in Oxford. Just walking across the cloistered quadrangle was to be transported to a late medieval otherworld. Ellman's room was not so engaging, however: bizarrely cluttered with a hotch-potch of higgledy-positioned armchairs, it looked like the dusty unlit storeroom of some old men's club. The shelves seemed to be packed full with nothing but editions of *Ulysses* in all sorts of languages. The place had an unused feel about it, as if he chose to spend most of his time elsewhere—a comfortable home somewhere in North Oxford, maybe.

I told him about the prince's pyrophiliac ventures with Sykes, at which he shook his head in disbelief, all the time smiling with that cherubic face that must have disarmed so many reluctant interviewees over the years (one of the best tools in a biographer's, or any interviewer's, kit is a friendly smile). Ellman took down some notes, asked a couple of questions, and thanked me for the story. I doubt he ever made use of it, at least I never read any mention of it by him. From my point of view it was simply a chance to meet the great man. I'm glad I did, because in a few short years he would be dead from motor neurone disease. His study of Joyce is in my view a wonderful model for literary biographers, and one that, a few years later, served as an inspiration to my own efforts in the genre.

How we loved those summer walks along the river in Oxford, Jo and I, with friends or just with the kids; we would take them in their red double-seated pram—one behind the other—along the gravel paths between the dense shrubbery and colourful beds of the botanical gardens to the pond, where the girls would shriek with delight as they threw pieces of bread to the ducks to make them dive and squabble, and we would sit on a bench seat and watch them with pride; it was difficult to imagine our life without them now, at a loss to recall those few years of childlessness. Emboldened by our attention, they would run ahead of us along the footpath that wound among the tall trees and undergrowth along the riverbank, beneath a canopy of lush, English green, moving in and out of sunlight and shadow, bright then dark, bright then dark, with the river flowing gently beside us. Then they would rush back, laughing and breathless, to report to us on what lay ahead round the next bend. Or we would cross the river at a little footbridge with iron balustrading, and pause in the middle to stare down into the black water, reflecting the doubles of every tree and shrub along the banks. On other days we would stroll through Christchurch Meadows, which was equally green and lovely, the four of us dwarfed by the huge elms and oaks, drawn along its winding paths into a world that had hardly changed for hundreds of years, feeling small, but privileged, to be part of something larger and older than ourselves. These are days that melt into one overarching memory, into one timeless vision that stays always the same, always idyllic, always summer, always happy, an illusion confirmed and fixed by a photograph of those times that in later life we occasionally take out and study. A golden time in all our lives, as Vincent said. So lucky we were, to have had it.

Now that she was approaching five, it was time for Anna to start school. She was a lively, active child. I choose my adjectives carefully here, because she was not easy to raise. Of course, the problem was her high energy and appetite for experience, not naughtiness. In fact, she tended to be obedient once it was clear in her mind what was required. But Jo and I were often so busy that we let her fend for herself rather than keep a tight rein on her development, and naturally she explored everything that came within reach. She was adventurous, inquisitive, talkative, loved singing, drawing, making new friends. So in September she started at Primary School, in the junior section, and immediately loved it. All those opportunities to make friends, *do* things! So attentive was she that she would come home and repeat, virtually word for word, lessons that had particularly impressed her. One day she reported that the vicar had come and given them a talk on Jesus.

'Did you know,' she said to us, 'that Jesus is the staff of life?' and she delivered to us pretty well the whole sermon about our need for Christ to feed us, without of course having the faintest idea who Christ was, what the word 'staff' meant, and how it all related to what we ate for dinner.

She told us she had a boyfriend at school, and would mention him often by name (which I've forgotten), what he did that day, what his likes and dislikes were. It was only when she had her birthday party in November that we got to meet the boyfriend, and discovered something about him that she'd completely neglected to tell us: he was absolutely black. It seems she didn't notice, or didn't think it worth mentioning. There was also the 'magic' front door to the school, which she told us in great earnestness had to be walked through on 'tippy-toes', and of course she obeyed the requirement to the letter. Lucy, still only three, was forming her own little sense of self as well, currently going through a phase of endless self-referential questions: 'I've got two shoes on now, haven't I mummy? I'm a lucky girl, aren't I?' Jo was looking forward to getting her off to play school.

At the end of that summer we borrowed some equipment and went on a camping trip to South Wales. It rained the whole time, practically washed us out of our tent, and after two days we gave up and came home.

After an uncountable number of job applications, I finally struck it lucky. One or two had come close to succeeding: through Jo's uncle Jim Bingham in Wagga, where he was Regional Director of Education and deeply involved in the creation of the Riverina College of Advanced Education, I was virtually guaranteed a lectureship in Humanities if I chose to apply. I declined though, not feeling the need at that stage to take anything but a proper university job, where I could expect to be allowed time to do research; CAEs didn't provide that. Then I was interviewed in London at the Commonwealth Universities' Office for a job at the University of Auckland. The other interviewee sitting outside the interview room was a tall, odd-looking woman who, when I tried to engage her in friendly chat, cut me off with an abrupt 'I don't think we should talk to each other at all!', which shut me up very promptly. She got the job, though I heard later that she lasted three months at Auckland, and unceremoniously walked out on them.

Finally I received a reply to an application to Monash University for what was called a Senior Teaching Fellowship, saying that I should contact Professor Arthur Brown, who was on sabbatical leave in London, and giving me a number to ring. I mentioned this to a couple of people at Linacre, including Gloria Cigman, who raised an eyebrow. 'Oh dear,' she said, 'Arthur *Brown*; anybody who's been to University College London can tell stories about him; the last time I saw him he had passed out in the corridor in a pool of his own vomit.' Grounds for apprehension for some, perhaps, but not me, not if I was in with a chance of a job at Monash, which would take us directly back to Melbourne. So, early evening, I called the number, and a woman's voice answered. 'Hang on a minute,' she said, her voice terse, unfriendly. I waited what seemed an age—probably six or seven minutes—before a faint, slightly slurred male voice at the other end muttered, 'Who's this?'

I told him.

'Come to the Carpenter's Arms twelve o'clock Friday,' he mumbled, and hung up. Hmm. I could see that I was heading for an unconventional interview.

This is how it went: The Carpenter's Arms is a little London pub near UCL, which I learned had been Arthur Brown's university for many years, until Monash appointed him, only a year before, to a Chair in the English Department, to oversee, of all things, studies in Bibliography. Why an Australian university should want a Bibliographer was unfathomable, since our meagre libraries have few books of any value in them, and our universities conduct practically no teaching or research in bookmaking, printing, bibliographical history or theory. What would he do at Monash? Well, I was to discover that eventually, and the answer was— very little. His appointment had been largely to secure a Chair to which the department had become administratively entitled, but which the current Head of Department, David Bradley, did not particularly want filled by anyone who might challenge his power in the department. Bradley was a competent administrator, but an academic underachiever, who feared a 'high flyer' might make his life difficult. At least this was to be my reading of the situation, based on my subsequent experience.

So, I turned up at The Carpenter's Arms on the Friday, naïve and ignorant of all the political chicaneries of academia, and entered the dim lounge looking for Professor Brown. He came over to me, a smallish, wiry RAF type (he had indeed served in a bomber squadron in the War), clipped moustache, smartly turned out in a navy reefer jacket and white shirt open at the throat, proffered an unnecessarily strong and bony handshake, courteously smiling and totally unprofessorial. He took me to a round table in the corner, and introduced me to three men in grubby dark suits, all obvious drinking buddies from way back. Asked, I agreed to have what they were having, which turned out to be pints of Guinness, a drink I had little experience of to that point. Over the next hour or so we sat holding a *jejune* conversation while relentlessly putting away several more pints of Guinness, until I was becoming aware of losing my grip on any kind of purposeful thought. 'Eat something, must eat something,' I told myself, accustomed to a good regular intake of food at midday. So I ordered a salad from the bar, along with another round of Guinness (because, as I had been summarily advised, it was my turn) and when the food came, my four companions stared at it as if it were a plate of *ordure*; one of them, with only a trace of irony, said, 'You're going to eat that, are you?' 'Certainly,' I answered, as one intent on self-preservation at any cost, and proceeded to eat. 'Tell us an Australian joke,' said one of them, who I think was the Chief Librarian. For some reason, probably the level of my inebriation, one sprang immediately to mind, which in my over-eager state I thought would be appropriate. It involved my saying the word 'fuck' many times, and ended up with the punch line, 'What do you think we did? We had sexual intercourse, naturally!' Nobody laughed, but then nobody disapproved either; it seemed I had struck exactly the right level of scatological pointlessness. When yet another pint of Guinness turned up, I clung to a flickering awareness that nothing had yet been said about the job I was supposed to be applying for, so I made a brave decision to raise it before it became utterly too late for anyone to say anything coherent about anything.

'So, what about this job? I said. 'Am I going to get it?'

Brown sat back with a mischievous air, looked around the table at his companions, and said heartily, 'What do you say, gentlemen? Does he get the job?'

'Of course, of course,' they all answered, 'seems a good enough chap. Give him the job.'

'It's only a Teaching Fellowship at this stage,' said Brown, 'but you'll get the next lectureship that comes up.'

I've no recollection of leaving the pub, of how I got to the station, or home, nor for that matter how I avoided being sick everywhere on the way, but I wasn't and I made it back to give the news to a delighted and hugely relieved wife. I had a job, and one, finally after half a lifetime in search of it, I really wanted. We were going home, and right to Melbourne, where we wanted to be. As Ian Parkin said when we told him the news, 'The lawd will provide!' I just wished the lawd had gone about providing in a less chaotic, and more sober manner.

It has come, the email from Penny. Simple, straightforward: 'We are writing with sad news that Vincent passed away last night. For those of you who weren't already aware, he has been in hospital for the past 5 weeks or so with sepsis and endocarditis. There have been times when he seemed to be on the mend and we hoped to bring him home again. However, after 4 weeks of battling it became clear that a full recovery would be unlikely and the doctors decided to stop treatment—to give him peace from interventions and make him comfortable.

'Although sad, we take great comfort in the fact that he was completely rested in his last moments, with his two daughters holding his hands and music playing softly in the background. He had been in his own room for a couple of weeks, away from the buzz of patients and hospital activity, with a big window and walls that were covered in pictures of the people he loved (including, of course, Beckett and Joyce.)

'All of us who have been lucky enough to have known Vincent will remember that he had an extraordinary life. His insatiable passion for art and literature was infectious and we are pleased to say that this didn't wane even when he was admitted to hospital. Once, his close friend Zoe sat with us, reading from Seamus Heaney's 'The Haw Lantern' to his approving nods and smiles. On the topic of Irish poetry, we inevitably found ourselves talking about Yeats, one of his favourites. Zoe was reciting 'The Song of Wandering Aengus' by heart, and was struggling to recall a detail from one of the lines, which involves the protagonist pulling a fish from the water. What kind of fish was it? Vincent, who we thought was sleeping, pulled his oxygen mask slowly away from his face, paused and told us—'trout.' It was one of many lovely moments we shared with him in his final weeks, where his character filled the room and made us all smile.

'Vincent has close friends all over the world, and we understand that many of you will be unable to join us for his funeral. However, we would like you to know you will all be very welcome if you do choose to come. It will be a humanist service and burial on Friday 12th June in Clayton Woods—a beautiful spot overlooking the South Downs.'

This has hit me hard. This is a friend I cannot afford to lose. But I suppose I must accept it. Vale Vincent, my very good friend, you will often be in my thoughts.

It was late on a morning when people were coming for lunch that Jo broke the news to me. The visitors were friends—Leslie, and Margaret perhaps—and I don't recall interruptions from the kids, so Anna was probably at school and Lucy playing happily with the guests. She indicated for me to come into the sitting room, she shut the door and stood facing me in what seemed to be a manner braced for confrontation, or some exchange of a serious kind. There was certainly tension there, and I held my breath.

'Love, I've got something to tell you, and I don't know how you'll react.'

Naturally, a current of fear ran through me.

'What?'

'I'm pregnant.'

We had decided two children were enough, and had been diligently practicing different forms of contraception for the past three years, with Jo finally having a wire 'loop' IUD fitted. They were supposed to be foolproof. She had become disenchanted with the Pill, which always made her gain weight.

'Pregnant? But what about the loop?

She still looked worried, but for myself I felt a huge wave of relief. God knows what I thought she'd been about to confess to—an affair, wanting a divorce, cancer. But this, this was fine.

'As far as I know it's still in there. But it hasn't worked, I'm definitely pregnant. So what do you want to do?'

'Well what do *you* want to do?'

'I'd like to have it. But how do you feel about another one?'

The apprehension in her voice was palpable. She was afraid I would not want it. How could she think that? I wondered. How could she not know me better than that? Did she really believe I would order her to get rid of it, that I would not want a child we had made together? I had the sudden realisation that I must, at times, have become intolerant, and it was true. I did have too many moments of anger, too many selfish habits that came cruelly through as a sort of dictatorship in how we would live our lives, and that it was *my* developing career that took priority over where and when we would do this or that, including returning home to Australia or staying on in England. She had long been terrified I would want the latter, and her letters to her mother were full of expressions of longing to go home, longings she would never use to put pressure on me, because it was *my* need that she put first. She had become so used to putting her own need second that she was afraid to come straight out and tell me what she wanted. I put my arms around her.

'I'm delighted,' I said, 'I think we should have it; it's wonderful.'

We kissed, and our relief flooded into laughter. It was a moment I would never forget. I couldn't stop myself bursting into mock boasts.

'Haha!' I proclaimed to her, and soon after to everyone else in the house, holding up my arms in triumph like an Olympic champion, 'Haha! My seed is stronger than any bloody old IUD, or any other challenges that science puts in its way! Garry's sperm will have its way!'

And as we went out to the kitchen where our friends were preparing lunch, I continued the bombast, advising Leslie, our scholarly and highly political feminist friend, 'You wanna get pregnant? I'm your man. See me any time, 'cos mine are the genes you need!'

Sometimes it's fun to play the fool.

I happened to be working in the Bodleian one morning when I spotted George Hunter at one of the desks. He was down from Warwick engaged in some particular research, so, a little warily because he always seemed unapproachably busy, I said a quiet hello on my way past him. I was surprised by the warmth of his response and enquiry after my progress, so much so that I took the bold step of inviting him to lunch with me at Linacre. I was never reluctant to ask friends to eat at Linacre, because by Oxford standards the food was excellent. I remember John Dawson, a fellow postgraduate from Jesus College, asking me there one lunch time, which gave me an insight into what most of the colleges that fed undergraduates served up: some Oxo-flavoured sludge that purported to be curried meat, and stodgy rice under a prodigious heap of diced carrots, followed by unset jelly and lumpy custard; typical English school fare. Linacre was not at all like that.

George accepted graciously, and arranged to meet me outside the Reading room. We made our way down St Aldate's, chatting more easily than I could have imagined; I'd been told, by Germaine and others, that he could be a charmer in the right circumstances but until then I'd always seen him through undergraduate eyes, was a bit scared of him. I can't recall what we talked about—probably not about academic matters much, more likely about family, children, Warwick staff I had been closest to—Bernard, Gloria, Germaine, Vincent, who had been given some part-time teaching there. He was pleased about my Monash job, had assumed I would always go back to Oz. At the lunch table we were joined by John Bamborough, who I had to introduce, and they ended up either side of me in a longish chat about Renaissance issues—a Shakespeare man and a Ben Jonson man, together over coffee in the Common Room; what could be more civilised? I felt smugly useful, not to mention privileged, to be included among the mandarins, maybe not as an insider but plausibly as someone finally visible, someone coming into view. It was the first time I experienced a sense of being within the *profession* of literary studies, and that maybe I *belonged* in the university community after all. An auspicious moment.

Just before Xmas I received a visit from the Monash Head of English, David Bradley. He'd written briefly that he would be in Oxford over the break, and could he drop in and introduce himself. It was a lightning visit, I don't think he even sat down, and we barely had time to get beyond the handshake before he left. A largish man with an affable smile and a pleasant voice, Bradley had personally run English at Monash for many years, the sole Professor in a big department. His charming manner gave little away, I was to learn, of the wily tactician he had always been. I still don't know why he paid me that visit in Oxford, unless it was to check that I was 'all right' in some vague sense. At least the house was tidy, my wife and kids were good looking, bright and white (you never knew with older Australians then), and there were no signs of my being a drug addict or an axe-murderer; I don't know what else he was checking on in such a brief exchange, certainly not my academic interests or abilities, which he seemed to regard as of no importance.

I had to rush now to get the thesis written up and submitted before we could leave for Australia. Then early in January Anna got tonsillitis; she had developed quite a history of throat problems, so with the latest bout the doctors recommended she have them removed. Just as she had two years earlier, our little mite went into the Radcliffe Infirmary, where she had a pretty rough time. In fact the bleeding was so persistent that she had to go back in for a second stitching. Through it all she was brave, excited when we visited, but keen to come home. This and other distractions were making it difficult for me to get the last parts of the thesis finished and submitted.

Finally I got it off, hastily typed by the wife of our College barman, and within a week or so had heard that my aural examination, called in Oxford a *viva voce*, was to be heard by Dr James Maxwell, Fellow of Balliol and the editor of *Notes and Queries* and Jacqueline Bratton of University College London. I was relieved because I had already had some contact with Maxwell—he had accepted my first academic publication, a note on Popular Victorian Satire in *Notes and Queries*— and I assumed he would be at least familiar with my work, and hopefully in sympathy. And Jacqueline Bratton had been a student of Catherine Ing's, so she might be interested too.

We got down to packing things into a large crate—clothes, books, items of furniture and other bits and pieces that had become dear to us—and shipping it back to Australia by sea, leaving us with just the basics to get us through the remaining weeks. As part of the job conditions, Monash was paying our air fares back to Melbourne, including an allowance for removal expenses, all arranged through the Victorian Agent-General in London, who were quite efficient in ensuring that we would get back in time for the start of the academic year, in late February. But then a complication arose that really put the cat amongst our pigeons. Seeing her doctor for a check-up, Jo discovered she would have to return separately from us; being three months pregnant, she could not have the required smallpox vaccination, so either she had to be placed in quarantine for two weeks, or reside in a smallpox-free country for that length of time, before she could enter Australia. Her friend Margaret Cerullo was back in Boston by then, so, the US being smallpox free, Jo arranged to stay with Margaret for the two weeks before I would arrive in Melbourne with the girls, so that she could be there to greet us.

That meant that inside those two weeks I would have to take my *viva* exam, look after the kids and the household, then pack everything up, get on the plane and fly home with them, all on my own! Was ever a pregnancy less opportune?

Before Jo flew out, Vincent and Deborah took us for a farewell dinner at Oxford's poshest restaurant, *The Elizabeth*, in St Aldate's. Jo and I both had very superior pepper steaks, and experienced for the first time the vacuum-method of making coffee, mesmerised by the alchemic mystery in the glass bowl on the table. It was a grand feed, a glittering evening with us all dressed in our best clothes, yet the whole time tinged with the sad realisation that it marked the end of our time together in Oxford, and that though we would stay friends, our lives would never again be as close, as intimate, as they had been these past few years. We sat at our little table, uttering mostly small talk, unable to broach the melancholy truth that lay heavy on our hearts that night.

With Jo gone, and only two weeks to get everything done, my life became a frenzy of closures. Of course, I had much help from friends, especially Vincent, Deborah and Leslie. They did babysitting while I got rid of stuff, arranged to sell the car, saw to all the bills—phone, electricity, gas, rent—the cat (a nice young woman in the neighborhood took her in) and paperwork for the journey. In the midst of all this my *viva* went disastrously. The examiners liked the material and arguments of the thesis, but the number of typographical and quotation errors was so high that they could not, in all conscience, pass the thesis until I had corrected all those mistakes. This had been, of course, a consequence of the enormous rush of those last weeks, not to mention my brandy-fuelled evenings writing up the thesis in the Linacre Library. But now, what was just as bad as the 'referral', as the exam result was called, was that I had nowhere near enough time to get the corrections done before our departure date, which was in only a few days time. What the hell was I going to do?

My luck was in. Or was it a case of chickens, in the form of a good deed, coming home to roost? Two friends at Linacre, my Canadian-Irish rebel-singing, Jameson's-drinking, table-tennis combatant Bob Connon and Romira Worvill, prettiest girl in the Common Room, had recently become a couple, thanks (they claimed) to me. They had been eyeing each other off for some time, circling warily each for their own reasons—Romira wondered if Bob was serious or just flirting, Bob wondered if Romira was too conventionally 'nice' for him. When they separately consulted me for an opinion I encouraged them both to plunge in, on the theory that they would never know until they tried. They did, and it worked, they were both immediately besotted, and I got the credit. Now, when they heard my cries of woe over coffee in the Common Room, they were eager to help.

'Don't worry,' said Bob, 'give us the thesis with the corrections marked to be done, and Romira and I will sit in the Reading Room and do them. No problem.'

I had until September to resubmit the thesis, so there was plenty of time for that part of it. I couldn't thank them enough, and to this day am deeply grateful to them both for their generosity and kindness. It all worked out well, except for their relationship, which in a few years sadly failed. But that is another story; for mine, I got my BLitt (Oxon), and was on my way to some sort of university career.

On the day we left, I drove to the airport in our Morris 1100, with Vincent beside me and the girls in the back seat covered in luggage. The arrangement was that Vincent would drive the car back to Oxford and hand it over to the guy who bought and paid for it, having generously agreed to let us make this last use of it. I recall very little about the process of getting off, except that it was more like an uproar than a process. Somehow I got through the boarding routines, which were a lot simpler in those pre-terrorist days, the girls in tow and juggling the luggage and all our various travel-aids—colouring books, story books, pencils, cardigans, soft toys for cuddling, cabin-luggage with clean knickers, pyjamas (we were stopping overnight in Singapore), summer clothes because it would be hot in Melbourne, the camera and, for some crazy reason, our transistor radio—to go into the cabin with us. I was too busy keeping tabs on all this to have any feelings other than those needed for survival, so I had no time for sad reflection, long goodbyes or finding the right words of farewell to my dear friend. I turned and looked at him as we passed through the entrance to the Boarding Gates, and saw him quickly disappear behind bodies coming along behind me, but it was a panicked, frustrated look and wave that could express nothing of what lay in my heart. That would have to come later, when I might, god save me, have time to attend to my more human feelings.

But Vincent had time. He stood watching me and the girls as we passed out of sight to the Boarding Gates, and he had those hours it took him to drive on his own back to Offchurch, to his flat near Warwick University, where he by now had been appointed to a lectureship. He wrote to me only a couple of days later about that return from dropping us at the airport:

Sunday night.

I felt very saddened on the way back to Offchurch. After your plane took off, I stood for I don't know how long looking after you at the sky, wondering if I'd ever see you again, feeling that hollowness that comes at the end of something. I shall miss you a lot.

The only way not to feel the loss too much is to be assured that we shall meet again after some years, as you say, here, America or Australia. In a sense things are never over and I shall still feel strong links with you and Jo all those thousands of miles away. But it is a situation in which we could both neglect correspondence, feeling it unnecessary. We ought to keep up our friendship by sharing what we can, in letters. This is very easy when dramatic things happen (when, two or three plays hence, I become 'the most exciting <u>young</u> playwright working in these islands at the moment', I'll <u>telephone</u> you!), but one has to make an effort at other times. That's it, then. If you need anything here at any time do draw on the many obligations I feel to you. I want to thank you for all sorts of things. You are a generous friend. A safe and interesting but not too interesting journey,

Love, Vincent

The flight home was nothing short of a nightmare. The aircraft was an early Boeing 707, narrow-bodied, a single aisle between two rows of three seats, and we were in economy class, well towards the rear, which meant all service was slow reaching us. The children had their own seats, but 3-year-old Lucy, missing her mum terribly, and bewildered by all this radical change in her life, clung to me like a limpet, whimpering in my lap for most of the journey. She wouldn't eat anything, would take only occasional sips of lemonade. The Singapore Airline stewardesses, chosen for their looks more than their intelligence, were not used to catering for children in those days, and the 'cuisine' was completely unsuitable. At one stage they brought round a snack, consisting of a rollmop and pickled onions, which of course neither of the kids could bear. When Lucy asked for an orange juice, she was brought a tall spectacular concoction embellished with umbrellas and swizzle sticks; she took one look at it and burst into tears. Anna, thank god, was her usual chirpy self most of the time, and when drawing and colouring books grew boring, she wandered up and down the aisle chatting to the passengers in her best charming manner.

It was the stopover in Bahrain that was the killer. It had been scheduled to be an hour at most, which would have taken us to Singapore by 6 pm, in time to get to the hotel and settle the girls down for the night. But for reasons never explained, the plane stood on the Bahrain runway for six hours with its engines, and therefore its air-conditioning, switched off. We were permitted to disembark for an hour at one point, and traipsed across the baking concrete apron to a primitive shed packed with Arabs also waiting for some flight action that would move them on.

At least that place was air-conditioned, but in seemingly no time at all we were ushered back to the plane where we sat for another two hours in the stifling heat, with not a word from the crew to set our minds at rest. Passengers began to speculate about bombs, hijackers, engine failure or just sheer incompetence, and were growing increasingly ill-tempered. We finally took off and eventually landed in Singapore, but well after midnight. By this time the passengers were so desperate to get off the plane that they rushed to get to every exit point before anyone else, which meant that a lone father, loaded with bags and kids' paraphernalia, not to mention carrying one child and towing the other, was last every time. There being no boarding bridge, we had to make our way across the busy, unlit tarmac, between aircraft and vehicles and baggage carts, with invisible planes roaring over our heads in the black sky, and the passenger terminal ahead lit up as for a party. It was a bizarre experience, and a fearful one for the girls.

At customs we were, again, last in the queue, and missed the hotel bus outside. The next one was an hour later; we were all tired to a frazzle, and when we finally reached the hotel it was after 2 am. I was so overwrought by the whole chaotic experience, bitter at the selfishness of the other passengers, angry with airport staff for their indifference, that I was sure I'd never be able to relax and get some sleep. I'll never forget walking into that incredibly glamorous hotel that night: the gleaming foyer was empty apart from the clerk, the huge building seemed asleep, the lift whisper-quiet as it took us up to some astronomical level. When we entered our suite I looked around in absolute awe. It was massive, with indirect 'atmospheric' lighting, two huge double bedrooms, a tall-windowed lounge that would hold a conference, Asian carved screens, expensive artwork and pottery in little feature-lit nooks, a gourmet kitchen, plush furniture and rugs, and every surface oozing quality and money. We felt dwarfed and humiliated by the incongruency of it all. The girls froze, I burst into tears. We probably should have eaten something—it had been hours since we'd been given a snack on the plane, which the girls hardly touched. But we were too exhausted, too undermined. I changed them and myself into our pajamas, we all got into the gigantic king-size bed, turned on the television, and snuggled together in the ritzy sheets and blanket, the three of us like exiles in some foreign paradise. We were missing terribly the one person who could've made it all right. Then, adding to our emotions, what should appear on the screen across the room but the serial 'Black Beauty'—probably the girls' favourite show—with its heroic girls and horses, and its romantic theme music. Again, in a sort of melancholy despair, I helplessly teared up, and eventually, after some time, along with my clinging little bundles, lay in a superficial and unsatisfying sleep.

In the morning we were all chipper again, went down and had a sumptuous breakfast. Once she spotted the swimming pool, Anna was adamant about what she was doing the rest of the morning. Not having her swimsuit in the overnight bag, I let her go in in her knickers, which no-one seemed fazed about. Our flight to Melbourne didn't leave till the afternoon, so we lazed beside the pool in the warm Singapore sunshine, doing our best to recover from the previous day's ordeal. The final leg of the journey was relatively comfortable—it was overnight and we were all still tired after our reduced sleep in the hotel, so we got some shuteye on the plane, ready for an early arrival in Melbourne.

In the morning the windows were uncovered and the cabin was flooded with golden light from a spectacular dawn sky. I peered out, marvelling at the blueness of the air, and the fluffy white clouds drifting below. And soon the breaks between them, which had been revealing a shining expanse of sea, showed that familiar landscape that every Australian knows so well, that dry, wide brown land, 'home'. Our excitement mounted, and I wondered what kind of place I was returning to, what changes might have occurred.

Disembarking, hearts-in-mouth, we followed the throng along corridors, again stuck at the end of the long queues through immigration and customs. But a nice official gave us a truly humane welcome when he took the girls off me and out to where their mum and a tribe of family were waiting. Lucy, weightless and trembling, felt like a little bird in Jo's arms. And Anna gave everyone a full description of the journey, including our Singapore delirium. Weeks later she drew a menacing picture indicating how haunted she still was by the experience, a picture of black and red aircraft entangled in a hostile black sky above a terminal building of remote modernity. Lucy, for her part was waking at night screaming in terror for months after we'd settled in to the house. She wasn't the only one; I had a recurring nightmare that I'd got it all wrong, and had to go back to England and make the trip all over again!

But we were at last home, and when I emerged out into the meeting area, greeted by my smiling Jo, the family crowding together kissing, hugging, everyone talking at once, and all saying that everyone looked fine though we all actually looked older and changed, I thought I'd never seen such a beautiful bunch of people in my life. We eventually made our way to various cars and somehow were transported to my mother's home in Syndal, where a big family reunion lunch was waiting for us—my little sister Susan and her new husband Peter, Ray and his new wife Jenny, my lovely old Ninny with a bewildered smile, too old and deaf to know what was going on, Jo's mother Barbara and her step-father Whit, her cousin Margot and husband Geoff, and others I've forgotten. Melbourne was in a searing February heatwave, and coming from an English winter we all felt overwhelmed. On the drive, which seemed to take forever, the city looked changed and alien—massive freeways everywhere, huge conveyer belts of streaming cars, all bigger, slicker, faster than the cars we were used to in England. Everything felt impersonal, roaring, speeded-up—no pedestrians (no footpaths for that matter)—frighteningly ugly, hot and polluted compared to our dear old green England, and our lovely peaceful, bicycle-friendly Oxford. My brother Ray drove us in his racy yellow Torana, and he too looked changed—older, heavier, ageing lines at the back of his neck, chin doubling—as I'm sure I was to him. We were not the young men we left ten years earlier, and the changes slightly shocked us both. But the reception was warm and happy for us all, though I'm sure Anna and Lucy were bewildered and disoriented, already missing their Oxford friends, still anxious that they might lose sight of Jo again, wondering when they were going to see something familiar to give them their bearings. My mother had organised beds for us all at Syndal, and despite the oppressive heat the girls insisted on being tucked in with a blanket in their usual English way. Sometime in the next few days we would take stock and work out how and where we were going to start making a new home for ourselves, a new life, a new job, new schools—new everything. And in a few months there would be another arrival to augment the family, when Jo's mystery bundle would reveal itself to the world. And reveal itself it did, the following July, to be a very handsome, healthy boy, Corley Macrae Kinnane. Despite assurances that I could be present I was at the last moment excluded from the birth by a bossy nurse, who also insisted on giving Jo pain-killers against her wishes and shifting her across to another bed in the middle of a contraction. But the baby came quickly, albeit with considerable intensity for Jo, and he was soon on the breast and brought home, where he was doted on not just by proud parents, but by two adoring sisters. And so, with this final arrival, now we were five.

So that was it. That was our overseas adventure, almost ten years and it had come full circle. Back now to where we started, but the fundamentals had changed; it was not the same we, and the place was not the place we had left, and the people were not the ones we had known. Pasty-skinned and posh-sounding, more like immigrants than homecomers, Jo and I were not quite Australian again, not yet, and not quite English either.

Something her mother had said in a letter after her 1967 visit resonates, that she felt she had changed, but that everything else had stayed the same. 'It will be better for you and Garry,' she wrote, 'when you come back after a long time, you will expect—and be expected—to be different'. Well, those expectations had been met, and we were different. How? I can't do better than say it was a feeling of having grown up, of the world having become a little smaller and more within our grasp, giving us more self-confidence, than when we left. Emerson and Chesterton notwithstanding, travel does not narrow the mind; perhaps tourism narrows the mind, in the sense they meant it. Living amongst different peoples for a length of time is a wonderful way to grow, and ten radiant years in Greece and England expanded us, in several important respects, to which it has been the whole purpose of this account to testify. I don't need to reiterate it. How could we not have changed, or not improved?

And so, too, this volume marks the end of my longer journey, the story of the first 36 years of my life, from the first awakenings of consciousness, through the uncertainties of childhood and youth, to a state, not of manhood, for I reached that merely by getting to 21 years of age, but to maturity, a state in which I was now a husband, a father, and a man with a direction in his life. I will not take the story any further, simply because it grows too complex, too connected with many living family and friends, and is no longer possible to tell from a single point of view. The lives of my children, for instance, belong to them not to me, and can only be told authentically by them.

The story has not been one of triumph, for obviously I can claim no importance as a subject, I am neither rich nor famous, nor have I had to overcome great adversity. It is simply the story of a human progress, of one who lived through interesting times with a degree of awareness, perspicacity and more than his share of good luck. I tell it in the assumption that an ordinary life like mine can in its own way remind people that we are, each of us, unique and important simply for who we are and what we have lived through, and that we can find affirmation in sharing our experiences. If life is essentially about experience and what we make of it, then it is not only the grander lives that deserve to be written, but anyone's and everyone's. That is perhaps not just an opinion: it might even hope to be a philosophy and, I trust, a decent one.

Lightning Source UK Ltd.
Milton Keynes UK
UKHW040813251022
411061UK00002B/350